A NOTE TO READERS

The Buying Guide has been an important consumer resource since 1931. Most of its pages are devoted to giving you the best buying advice we can on expensive purchases such as cars, appliances, home-entertainment gear, and computers and home-office equipment.

The Buying Guide also includes:

- **Repair Histories to help you gauge how reliable a product is likely to be.**
- **Product recalls gathered from the last 12 issues of CONSUMER REPORTS, to help you avoid unsafe products.**
- **An alphabetical listing of manufacturers' telephone numbers, most of them toll-free.**
- **A directory of the last time CONSUMER REPORTS published articles on various subjects and products.**

I wish you another year of sensible and satisfying shopping.

Rhoda H. Karpatkin
President

ABOUT THE BUYING GUIDE

The CONSUMER REPORTS Buying Guide, the 13th issue of CONSUMER REPORTS magazine, contains the latest buying advice distilled from all our testing of the major consumer products. The reports in the Buying Guide outline the basic information you need to consider—the pros and cons of the choices, what's new in the marketplace, likely places to find the product, what you can expect to pay, and an explanation of the features.

The Buying Guide is a reference work, with the information presented in a succinct and concise manner for quick and easy use all year long. The information and

models in the Ratings have been reviewed and updated, with the latest information on model availability and the latest prices.

The Buying Guide covers the major purchases of kitchen, living room, and home office. Through our extensive reader surveys, we can tell you about the reliability of refrigerators, washing machines, TV sets, and more. See the Reliability Chapter, page 7.

The Buying Guide also covers cars, with profiles and Ratings as well as advice about buying or leasing new or used cars. We also present an easy-to-use reference to the reliability of more than 200 models of cars, sport-utility vehicles, minivans, and pickup trucks.

For easy reference to past issues of CONSUMER REPORTS, you'll find an index of the last full report in the monthly magazine at the back of this book. The original CONSUMER REPORTS publication date is also given at the top of each report and each Ratings table. Back issues of CONSUMER REPORTS are available in most libraries. Some reports are also available by fax from CONSUMER REPORTS by Request; see page 346.

The Buying Guide also collects a years' worth of product recalls, based on notices issued by governmental agencies, as published in the monthly issues of CONSUMER REPORTS.

ABOUT CONSUMER REPORTS

CONSUMER REPORTS is published monthly by Consumers Union, a nonprofit independent testing organization serving consumers. We are a comprehensive source for unbiased advice about products and services. Since 1936, our mission has been to test products, inform the public, and protect consumers.

We buy all the products we test off store shelves, just as you do. We receive no special treatment. We accept no free samples; if a manufacturer sends us a free product, we return it.

We test products in 50 state-of-the art laboratories at our National Testing and Research Center in Yonkers, N.Y.

Our Ratings are based on lab tests, controlled-use tests, and expert judgments by our technical and research staff. If a product is high in overall quality and relatively low in price, we deem it A CR Best Buy™. A Rating refers only to the brand and model listed.

We survey our millions of readers to bring you information on the reliability of hundreds of auto models and of major products like appliances and electronics gear. Reader-survey data also help us rate insurance and other consumer services.

We report on current issues of concern to consumers. Our staff of researchers and editors brings you in-depth information on matters that affect your health, money, and well-being.

We accept no ads from companies. We do advertise our own services, which provide impartial information and advice to consumers. We don't let any company use our reports or Ratings for commercial purposes. If that happens, we insist that the company stop, and we take whatever additional steps are open to us.

Readers' letters. We welcome reader comment. Write: CONSUMER REPORTS, P. O. Box 2015, Yonkers, N.Y. 10703-9015. We regret we are unable to respond to individual letters.

Subscriptions. U.S.: $24 for 1 year, $39 for 2 years, $54 for 3 years, $69 for 4 years, $84 for 5 years. All other countries, add $6 per year. (Canadian rate is C$35. Goods & Services Tax included. GST #127047702.) School Order Program: 62¢ per copy, minimum 20 copies per issue (September through May). See inside back cover for more information.

OTHER INFORMATION SERVICES

In addition to CONSUMER REPORTS magazine and the Buying Guide, CONSUMER REPORTS provides other services to give you unbiased advice to help you make important choices and decisions:

Consumer Reports Special Publications. We publish a series of specialty buying guides, sold on newsstands and in book stores.

Consumer Reports New Car Price Service. Our reports compare sticker price to dealer's invoice. Call 800 269-1139. Details on the back cover.

CONSUMER REPORTS (ISSN 0010-7174) is published 13 times a year by Consumers Union of U.S., Inc., 101 Truman Avenue, Yonkers, N.Y. 10703-1057. Second-class postage paid at Yonkers, N.Y., and at additional mailing offices. Canadian postage paid at Mississauga, Ontario, Canada. Canadian publications registration no. 2665247-98. Title CONSUMER REPORTS registered in U.S. Patent Office.

Consumer Reports Used Car Price ;ervice. Find the market value in your ırea for a wide variety of used cars. See ›age 357.

Consumer Reports Auto Insurance ›rice Service. Compare the cost of auto nsurance for the coverage you need; find he best price and receive our money-aving, how-to-buy insurance guide. See ›age 359.

Consumer Reports Cars: The Essential Guide. This CD-ROM covers ıew and used cars, minivans, pickups, and SUVs. $17.95 postpaid. Call 800 331-1369, ext. 171. See page 359.

Consumer Reports Online. Our Web ite *(www.ConsumerReports.org)* covers ıutos, appliances, electronics gear, and nore. Free areas provide useful listings, ecalls, and shopping guidance. Members ›ay $2.95 per month for unlimited use, ncluding searchable access to test re-›orts and product Ratings. For more nformation, see page 360.

Consumer Reports on Health. Monthly newsletter on nutrition, fitness, and a range of medical matters. To subscribe (12 issues, $24 a year), write to us at P. O. Box 56356, Boulder, Colo. 80322-6356.

Consumer Reports Travel Letter. Monthly newsletter with travel values. To subscribe (12 issues, $39 a year), write to us at P. O. Box 53629, Boulder, Colo. 80322-3629.

Zillions. Bimonthly magazine for kids 8 and up. $16 a year (6 issues), $26 for 2 years. Write Subscription Dept., P. O. Box 54861, Boulder, Colo. 80322-4861.

Consumer Reports by Request. Specially edited reports available by fax or mail (U.S. only). See index, page 346.

Consumer Reports Television. Produces specials, videos for home and school, and a nationally syndicated consumer news service, Consumer Reports TV News, shown on more than 90 stations weekly. For more information, call 800 729-7495.

CU is a member of the Consumers International. Mailing lists: CU occasionally exchanges its subscriber lists with hose of selected publications and nonprofit organizations. If you wish your name deleted from such exchanges, send your address label with a request for deletion to CONSUMER REPORTS, P.O. Box 53029, Boulder, Colo. 80322-3029. Postmaster: Send address changes to the same address. Back issues: Single copies of 12 preceding issues, $5 each; Buying Guide, $10 each. Write Back Issues, CONSUMER REPORTS, P.O. Box 53016, Boulder, Colo. 80322-3016. For back issues in microform, write UMI, 300 N. Zeeb Rd., Ann Arbor, Mich. 48106.

Consumer Reports BUYING GUIDE

Consumers Union
President: **Rhoda H. Karpatkin**
Executive Vice President: **Joel Gurin**

The Buying Guide
Editor: Andrea Scott
Managing Editor: Linda Coyner
Special Editor: Mary Weber
Special Publications Staff: Michael Quincy, Pauline Piekarz, Michael Rivera; Joyce Childs
Designer: Larry Buster
Production: Eric W. Norlander, *Project Manager;* Peter Cusak, Jennifer Dixon, Reed Fox
Copy Editor: Dave Cook
Manufacturing/Distribution: William Schaefer

Consumer Reports
Editorial Director: Jacquline Leo
Editor: Julia Kagan
Executive Editor: Eileen Denver
Design Director: George Arthur
Assistant Design Director: Timothy LaPalme
Production Manager: Maggie Brenner
Consumer Reports TV Joyce Newman, *Director*
New Media Nancy Macagno, *Director*
Zillions/Education Charlotte Baecher, *Director;* Karen McNulty, *Managing Editor*

Technical Division
Technical Director: R. David Pittle; **Senior Director, Technical Operations:** Jeffrey A. Asher; **Director, Technical Policy & Public Service:** Edward Groth III; **Assistant Director, Technical Operations:** Thomas Deutsch **Appliances and Home Environmental Products** Mark Connelly, *Testing Director;* Geoffrey Martin, *Manager, Home Environment;* Tara Casaregola, Bernard Deitrick, Frank Iacopelli, Angelo Mannino, James Nanni, *Senior Project Leaders;* Emilio Gonzalez, Tim Mooney, Carol Sherwin, Mary Tobias, *Project Leaders;* Ginny Lui, Jack Toback, Bessie Wong, *Assistant Project Leaders;* Candido Baetiong, Ruth Greenberg, Martin Spiegel, David Trezza, Michael Visconti **Automation & Instrumentation** Robert Karpel, *Program Leader;* Karl Hoedl **Auto Test** David Champion, *Testing Director;* Alan Hanks, *Facilities Manager;* Eugene Peterson, Kevin Sheehan, Gabriel Shenhar, Richard Small, *Engineers;* Anita Lam, *Data Management Administrator;* Joseph Nappi, *Technician Supervisor* **Chemical & Textiles** Bert Papenburg, *Testing Director;* Edward Kippel, *Program Leader;* Peter Heinlein, Edward Miller, *Senior Project Leader;* Joan Muratore, Pat Slaven, *Project Leaders;* E.A. Lopez, Charles Spatola, *Assistant Project Leaders;* Susan Cronin, John McAloon, Li Wang **Electronics** Alan Lefkow, *Testing Director;* Evon Beckford, *Manager, Video & Opt* James Boyd, Dean Gallea, *Program Leaders;* G DiSalvo, *Senior Project Leader;* Christopher Bucsl Gerard Catapano, Carolyn Clifford, Robert Dur Larry Picciano, Harvey Reiver, *Project Leaders;* Sus Daino, Robert Lew, *Assistant Project Leaders;* Ker Allen, George Irizarry, William South **Mark Information** John Lowe, *Director;* George Bates, Rob Geissensetter, Julie Levine, *Planning Specialists;* Elinc Kochis, Michael Rosato, Joyce Ward, Karin Weisburg *Senior Analysts;* Jerry Greene, *Market Information Liais* Tom Ferrara, *Analyst;* Michael DiLauro, Mari Gladman, Kelly Moomey **Public Service** Cynth Langlois, Deborah Wallace, *Project Leaders* **Recreati & Home Improvement** Donald Mays, *Testing Direct* Michael Mitariten, *Manager, Power Equipment;* Dav Tallman, *Program Leader;* John Galeotafiore, Mauri Wynn, *Senior Project Leaders;* Werner Freitag, E Saperstein, Gary Vickers, *Project Leaders;* Marc McEnt Thomas Mutchler, Ralph Petrucelli, Robert Solomc *Assistant Project Leaders;* Alex Beauchamp **Statisti** David Burn, *Director;* M. Edna Derderian, Kei Newsom-Stewart, Martin Romm, Jed Schneid *Statisticians* **Information Management** Don Farl *Manager* **Test Sample** Celeste Monte, *Director;* Lar Greene, Annette Lowman, Corrin Wong **Admini tration** Carol Johnstone, Lida Anderson, Elai Blackburn, Marie Miller, Olga Vassall, Paulette Wat Paula Welch, Maria Zarrilli

Information Services/Research Norman Leonarczy *Director* **Information Center** Saralyn Ingram, *Associ Director* **Survey Research** Charles Daviet, *Associa Director* **Circulation** Simon Aronin, *Director;* Ile Malina, *Associate Director;* Allen Williams, *Promoti Manager;* Will Michalopoulos, *Manager, Retail Sa and Marketing* **Customer Relations** Micha D'Alessandro, *Director* **Auto Price Services** Pai Amidon, *Manager* **Consumer Policy Institute** *Je Halloran, Director* **CR on Health** *Ronald Buchhei Managing Editing* **CR Travel Letter** *W. B. Leonar Managing Editor* **Fundraising** *Paula Bernett, Direct* **Public Information** David Berliner, *Senior Consulta* Linda Wagner, *Manager* **Media Liaison** Rana Aro **Consumer Reports Radio & Special Progran** Edwin Partikian, *Director*

RELIABILITY

Getting things fixed

If a product breaks during its warranty, the repair is usually covered. Arranging for the repair can be another matter. It sometimes means taking a day off from work to wait for the service technician or driving to a distant repair center. With some products, you can ship the broken item to a repair center or retailer. Then, of course, you're out the item for however long the repair takes.

With some products, there's another problem: You can't get them fixed. The very designs and manufacturing methods that have given us better, cheaper, and more durable goods—solid-state circuitry, molded-plastic construction—also make some of them difficult or impossible to repair. When such products break, you have little choice but to get rid of them.

For products that can be repaired, here are some strategies:

Fix it yourself

People are most likely to fix products with mechanical innards: cars, clothes dryers, mowers, vacuum cleaners, and such. Many electronics manufacturers advise against do-it-yourself repairs because of the products' complexity and potential shock hazard.

Major-appliance manufacturers offer the most help to do-it-yourselfers, through toll-free telephone numbers and service manuals. Many books offer general fix-it-yourself advice. When you're ordering parts, make sure they're for the right model. Jot down the model and serial

How long things last

A product's useful life depends not only on its actual durability but also on such intangibles as your own desire for some attribute or convenience available only on a new model. These estimates are from manufacturers and trade associations.

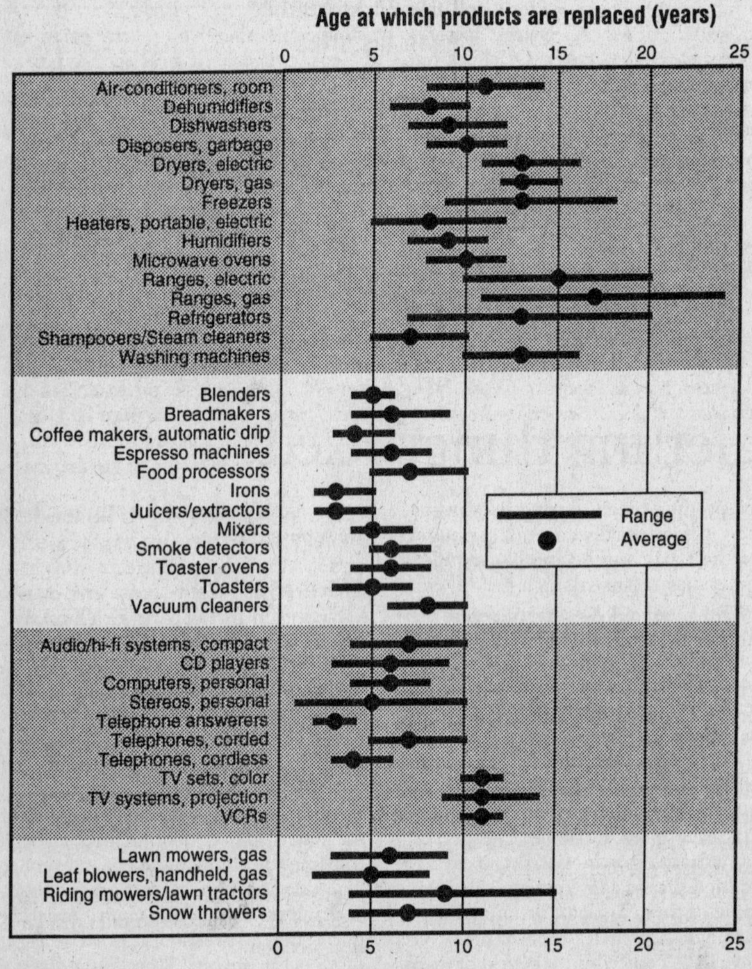

Source: APPLIANCE magazine, a Dana Chase publication.

numbers from the appliance itself, not the packaging or the owner's manual.

Have it fixed

Manufacturers typically require factory-authorized service for warranty work during the warranty period. The owner's manual usually provides a toll-free number to call for the nearest factory-authorized service center. Or check our listing of manufacturer phone numbers on page 342.

Authorized repairers, accredited by a company to fix its brand, sometimes earn a commission for parts, an arrangement that can lead to unnecessary replacement. Shipping time and cost may make a local shop more appealing than a factory center.

Independent centers can be a good choice for products that are out of warranty. If possible, get a referral.

Get rid of it

Sometimes there's no repair option, or the cost of repairs is so high that fixing the product makes no sense, or the product is near the end of its useful life. If the product can't be sold or donated to charity, try recycling it. Look under "Recycling" in the yellow pages.

Extended warranties

Most products covered in this book come with a manufacturer's warranty that covers parts for a specified period and labor for a sometimes shorter period. Anywhere from 90 days to one year is a typical warranty duration.

For many products, you'll get a vigorous sales pitch to buy an extended warranty or service contract. The retailer or manufacturer makes a lot of money by selling such warranties.

With an extended warranty, you're betting that the appliance will break down after the manufacturer's warranty expires but before the service contract does, and that the cost of repairs will exceed the cost of the contract. That's possible, but it's a long shot. Not only are products more reliable today, but they are often made in such a way that any defects tend to appear early—within the first 90 days or so, when the original warranty is in effect.

However, there may be instances when a service contract might be worth considering:

- If the likelihood of the product breaking is relatively high, as it is for some brands or types of product. (See the brand repair histories on page 10.)
- If an item will cost a lot to repair.
- If the replacement cost for the product is high.
- If an item is going to be knocked around, like a laptop computer or a camcorder. But read the contract's fine print about use that might be considered abuse. A warranty might not cover such breakage.

Some extended warranties entitle you to special benefits, such as a loaner during the repair; some warranties grant a partial refund if no claim is ever made.

If the idea of extra protection is appealing, consider using a credit card. Items bought with Amercian Express and certain "gold" or "platinum" Visa and MasterCards are covered for an extended period beyond the manufacturer's warranty, up to as much as one year. Some standard Visa and MasterCards also offer that kind of protection.

Repair histories

Microchips and integrated-circuit boards have greatly improved the reliability of home-entertainment equipment. TV sets of yore had tubes that would burn out and mechanical tuners that would wear out. Modern sets have few moving parts to slip or break. The same is true of stereo equipment: Receivers and speakers, and even CD players with their various changing mechanisms, need relatively few repairs. Tape transports are a trickier mechanism, so repair rates for camcorders and VCRs tend to be higher.

Appliances, often with motors and plenty of moving parts, can still break down quite a lot. Lawn mowers and vacuum cleaners are fairly troublesome products. Refrigerators are another good example. Without an ice-maker or water dispenser, their brand repair rates are 10 percent or less. With those additional mechanisms, they're 15 to 20 percent.

We know about product reliability from our testing experience but also from an extensive, regular survey program that asks readers of CONSUMER REPORTS magazine to report their real-life experiences with various products. Every year, CONSUMER REPORTS asks readers to share their experiences by filling out our Annual Questionnaire. New this year: repair histories for vacuum cleaners and computers.

Repair histories apply to brands, not to

specific models of these products. They only suggest future trends, not predict them. The reliability of a company's products can change for many reasons—company ownership changes, its products are designed or manufactured in a new plant, its quality-control procedures improve. Still, what readers report over the years has been consistent, enough for us to be confident that using these repair histories can improve your chances of buying a trouble-free product.

The graphs represent the percentage of each brand's products purchased new that have ever been repaired, according to our most recent surveys. Products covered by a service contract are excluded, since the repair rates for those products are much higher than for products without one. Histories for different product types are not directly comparable, since the histories cover products of different ages, and older products tend to break more often.

Some of the repair histories have already appeared in the monthly issues of CONSUMER REPORTS; some appear here for the first time.

Compact-disc players

Based on more than 103,000 responses to our 1996 Annual Questionnaire. Readers were asked about any repairs to single-play and changer tabletop models bought new between 1992 and 1996. Data have been standardized to eliminate differences among brands due to age and usage. Differences of less than 3 points aren't meaningful.

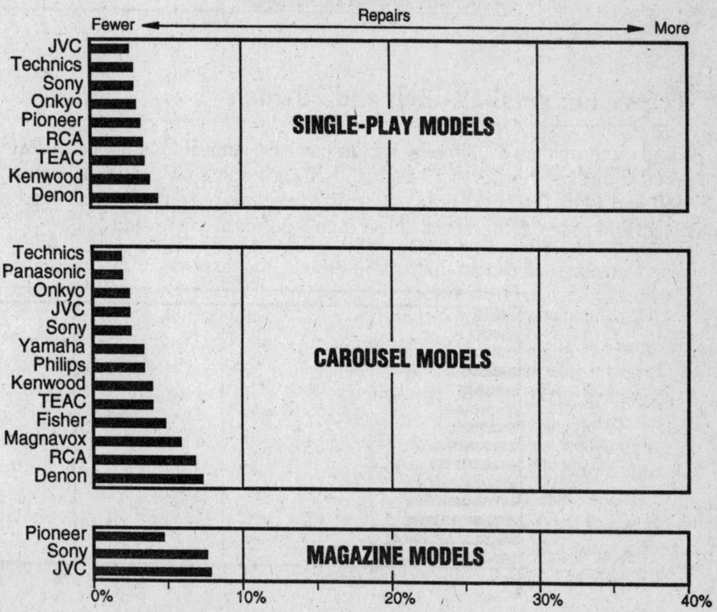

VCRs

Based on more than 200,000 responses to our 1996 Annual Questionnaire. Readers were asked about any repairs to VHS VCRs bought new between 1991 and 1996. Data have been standardized to eliminate differences among brands due to age and usage. Differences of less than 3 points aren't meaningful.

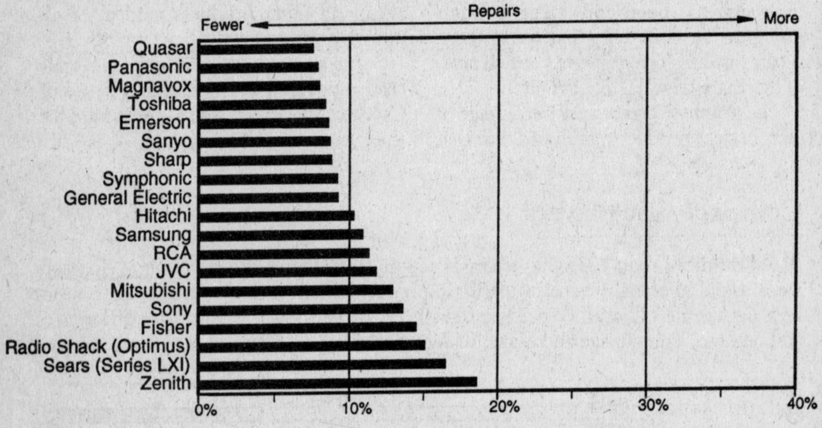

Television sets: 19-inch and 20-inch

Based on more than 67,000 responses to our 1996 Annual Questionnaire. Readers were asked about any repairs to 19-inch and 20-inch color TV sets bought new between 1991 and 1996. Data have been standardized to eliminate differences among brands due to age and usage. Differences of less than 3 points aren't meaningful.

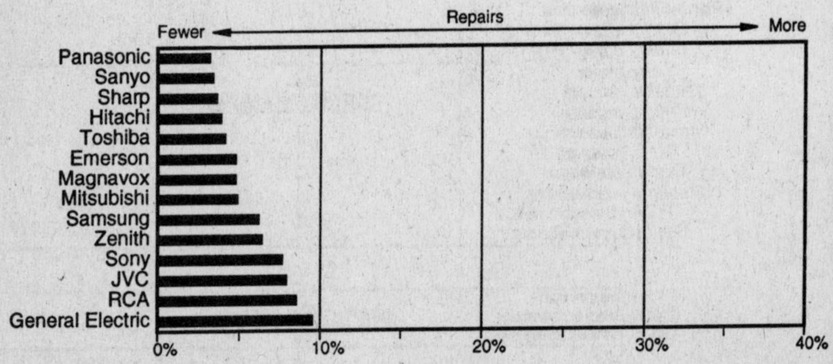

Television sets: 25- to 27-inch

Based on more than 95,000 responses to our 1996 Annual Questionnaire. Readers were asked about any repairs to 25- to 27-inch stereo color TV sets bought new between 1991 and 1996. Data have been standardized to eliminate differences among brands due to age and usage. Differences of less than 3 points aren't meaningful.

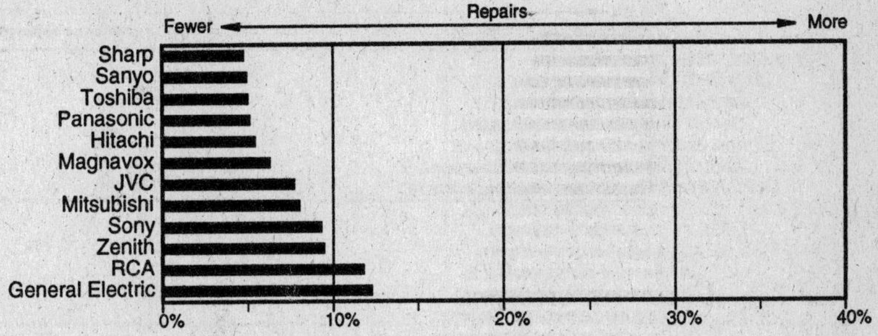

Television sets: 31- to 35-inch

Based on more than 23,000 responses to our 1996 Annual Questionnaire. Readers were asked about any repairs to 31- to 35-inch stereo color TV sets bought new between 1992 and 1996. Data have been standardized to eliminate differences among brands due to age and usage. Differences of less than 3 points aren't meaningful.

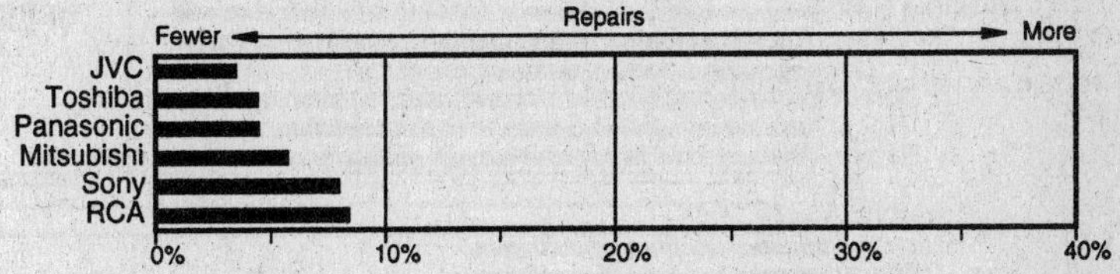

Compact camcorders

Based on more than 49,000 responses to our 1996 Annual Questionnaire. Readers were asked about any repairs to compact (8mm, Hi8, and VHS-C) camcorders bought new between 1991 and 1996. Data have been standardized to eliminate differences among brands due to age and usage. Differences of less than 3 points aren't meaningful.

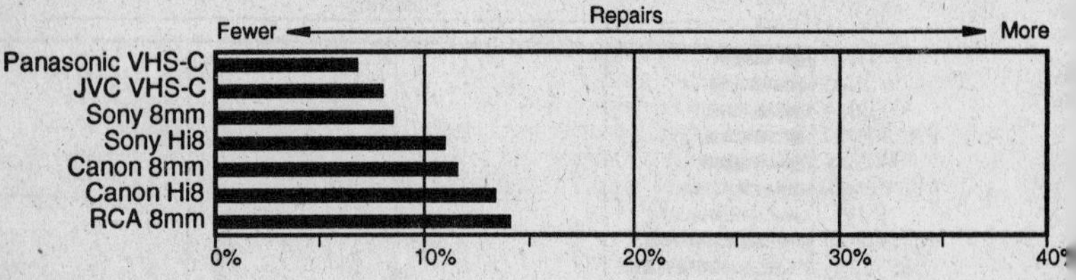

Full-sized vacuum cleaners

Based on more than 157,000 responses to our 1996 Annual Questionnaire. Readers were asked about any repairs to full-sized vacuum cleaners bought new between 1991 and 1996. Data have been standardized to eliminate differences among brands due to age and usage. Differences of less than 3 points aren't meaningful.

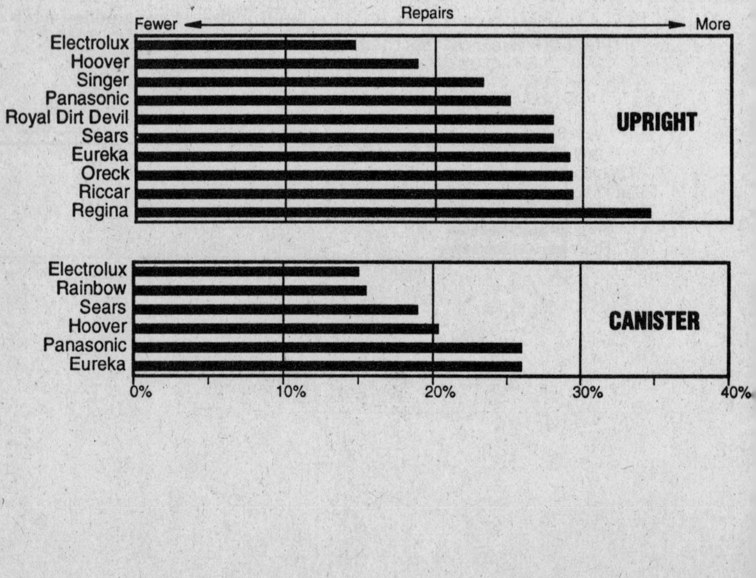

Gas ranges

Based on more than 19,000 responses to our 1996 Annual Questionnaire. Readers were asked about any repairs to freestanding, single-oven, self-cleaning gas ranges bought new between 1990 and 1996. Data have been standardized to eliminate differences among brands due to age. Differences of less than 3 points aren't meaningful.

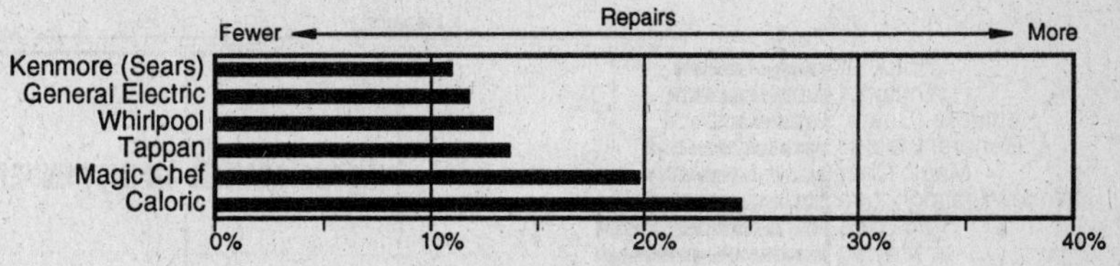

Electric ranges

Based on more than 38,000 responses to our 1996 Annual Questionnaire. Readers were asked about any repairs to freestanding, single-oven, self-cleaning electric ranges with a smooth top or conventional coil burners bought new between 1990 and 1996. Data have been standardized to eliminate differences among brands due to age. Differences of less than 3 points aren't meaningful.

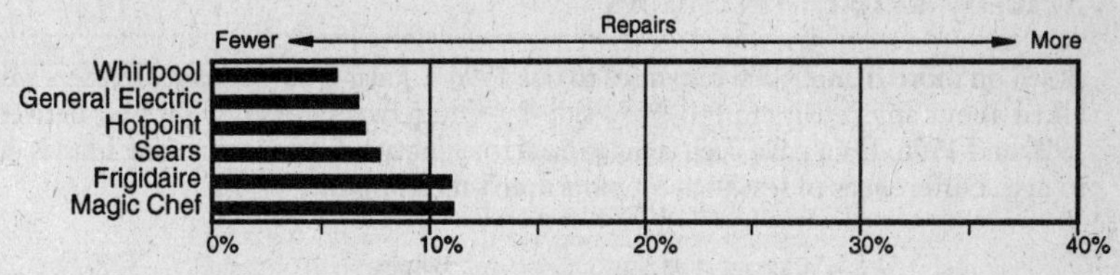

Top-freezer refrigerators

Based on more than 49,000 responses to our 1996 Annual Questionnaire. Readers were asked about any repairs to full-sized, top-freezer, two-door, no-frost refrigerators bought new between 1990 and 1996. Data have been standardized to eliminate differences among brands due to age. Differences of less than 3 points aren't meaningful.

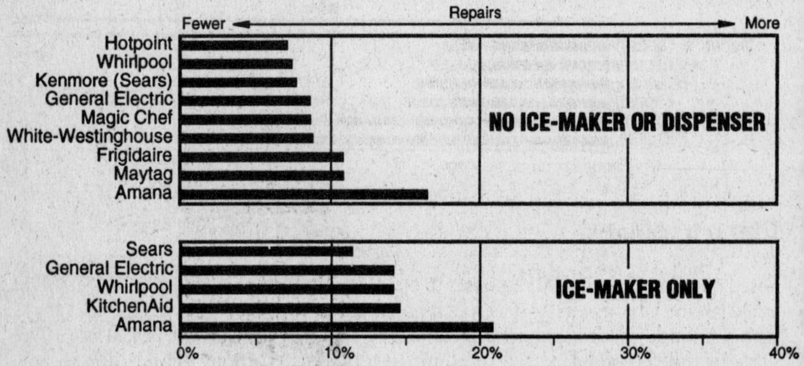

Side-by-side refrigerators

Based on more than 27,000 responses to our 1996 Annual Questionnaire. Readers were asked about any repairs to full-sized side-by-side refrigerators bought new between 1990 and 1996. Data have been standardized to eliminate differences among brands due to age. Differences of less than 3 points aren't meaningful.

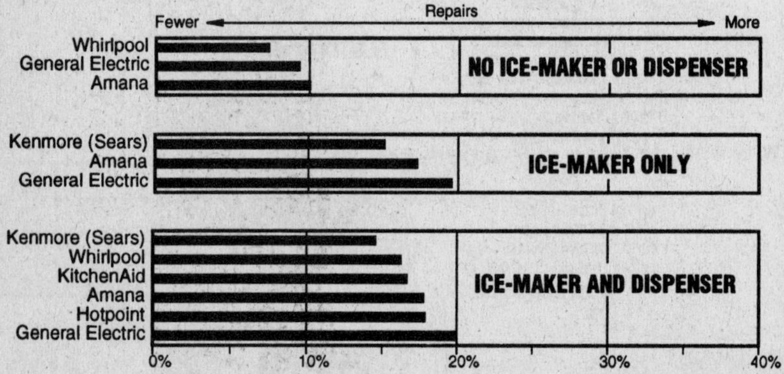

Washing machines

Based on more than 141,000 responses to our 1996 Annual Questionnaire. Readers were asked about any repairs to full-sized washers bought new between 1990 and 1996. Data have been standardized to eliminate differences among brands due to age and usage. Differences of less than 3 points aren't meaningful.

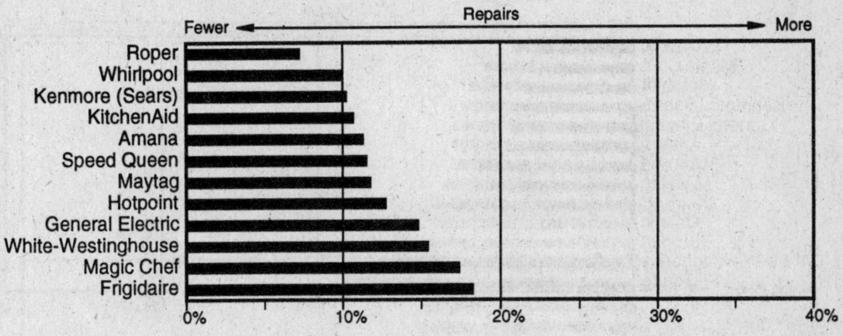

Clothes dryers

Based on more than 101,000 responses to our 1996 Annual Questionnaire. Readers were asked about any repairs to full-sized electric and gas clothes dryers bought new between 1990 and 1996. Data have been standardized to eliminate differences among brands due to age and usage. Differences of less than 4 points aren't meaningful.

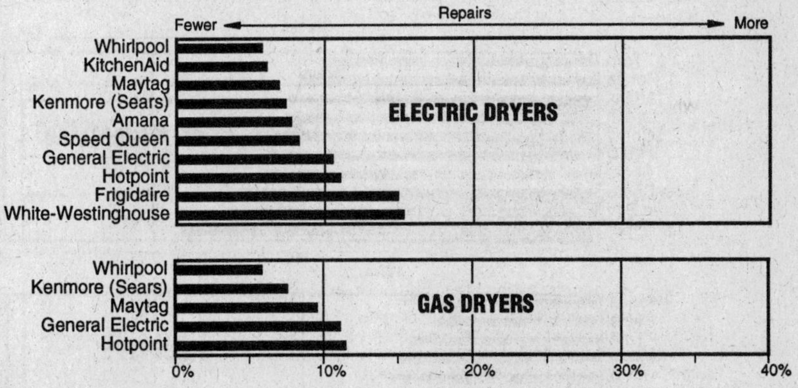

Dishwashers

Based on more than 129,000 responses to our 1996 Annual Questionnaire. Readers were asked about any repairs to installed dishwashers bought new between 1990 and 1996. Data have been standardized to eliminate differences among brands due to age and usage. Differences of less than 4 points aren't meaningful.

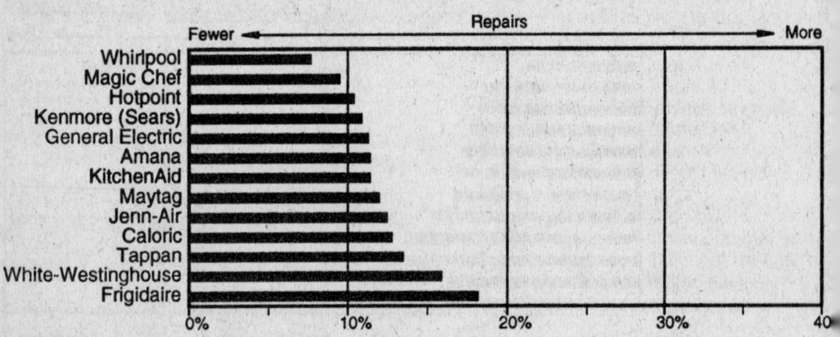

Self-propelled and push-type gasoline mowers

Based on more than 54,000 responses to our 1996 Annual Questionnaire. Readers were asked about any repairs to self-propelled and push-type gasoline mowers, with a cutting swath less than 25 inches, bought new between 1991 and 1996. Data have been standardized to eliminate differences among brands due to age and usage. Differences of less than 4 points aren't meaningful.

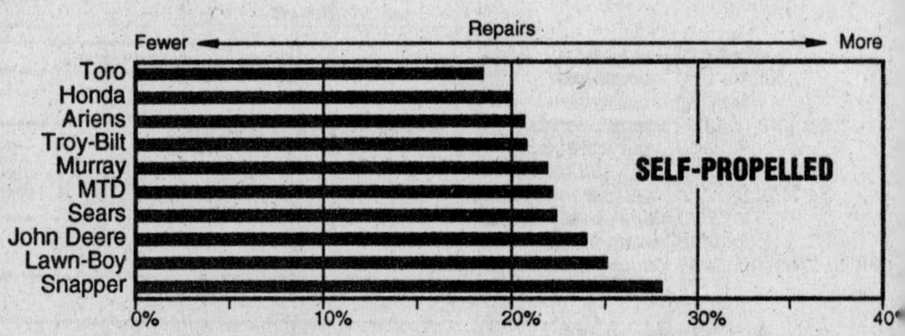

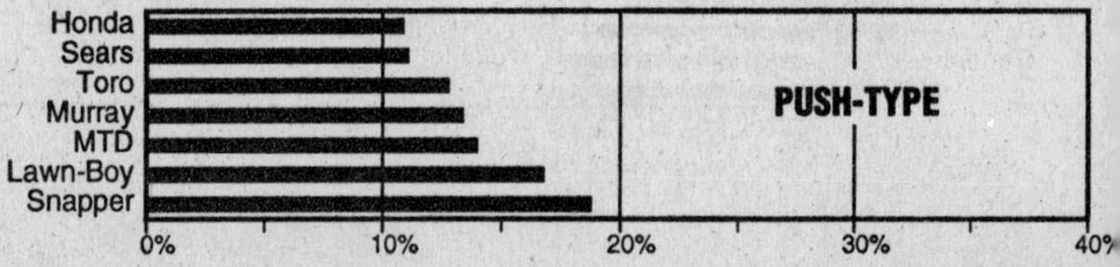

Types of lawn mowers

Repair rates for lawn mowers vary according to the type of mower. Apart from the manual and electric mowers, all are gasoline-powered. Based on more than 143,000 responses to our 1996 Annual Questionnaire. Readers were asked about any repairs to manual, electric, and gasoline walk-behind mowers, riding mowers, and lawn tractors bought new between 1991 and 1996. Data have been standardized to eliminate differences among types due to age and usage. Differences of less than 3 points aren't meaningful.

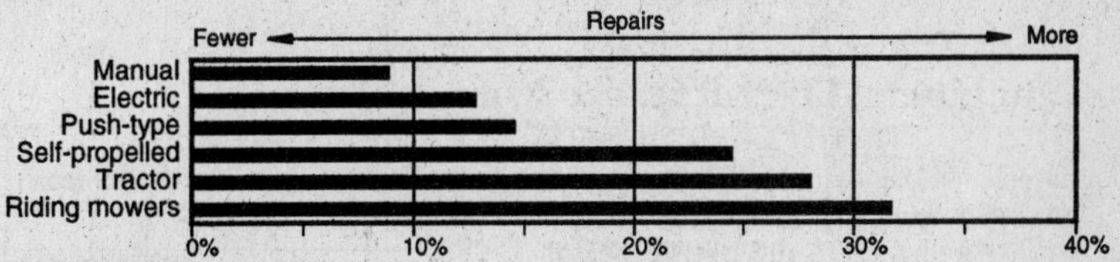

Tractors and riding mowers

Based on more than 17,000 responses to our 1996 Annual Questionnaire. Readers were asked about any repairs to tractors and riding mowers, with a cutting swath of 25 inches or more, bought new between 1991 and 1996. Data have been standardized to eliminate differences among brands due to age and usage. Differences of less than 5 points aren't meaningful.

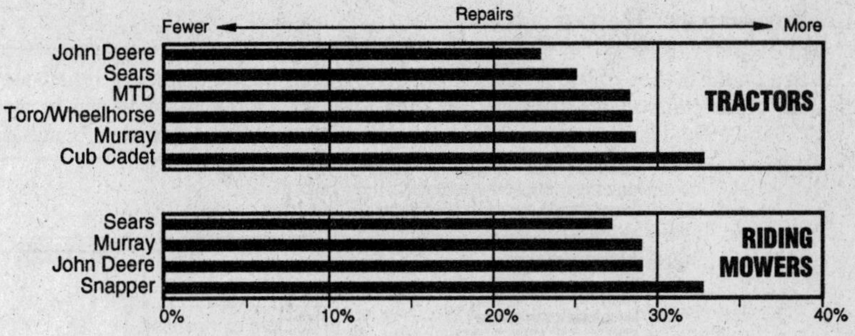

Desktop computers: Overall reader score & repair rates

Our 1996 survey included questions about computers. As befits this complex product, our questions were more probing than those we ask about TV sets or washing machines. Readers' overall ratings were closely tied to satisfaction with the manufacturer's servicing (see page 221). When telling us whether any part of their computer needed repair, readers distinguished among core components—the processor, memory, hard drive, floppy drive, system board, power supply—and peripheral components like the monitor, fax/modem, and keyboard.

Computers: Overall reader score

Based on more than 26,000 responses to our 1996 Annual Questionnaire. Readers were asked to rate the overall performance and reliability of Pentium, 486, and Mac OS desktop computers bought new between 1993 and 1996 without an extra-cost service contract. A score of 100 would mean all consumers rated their PCs excellent; 80, very good. Differences of less than 3 points aren't meaningful.

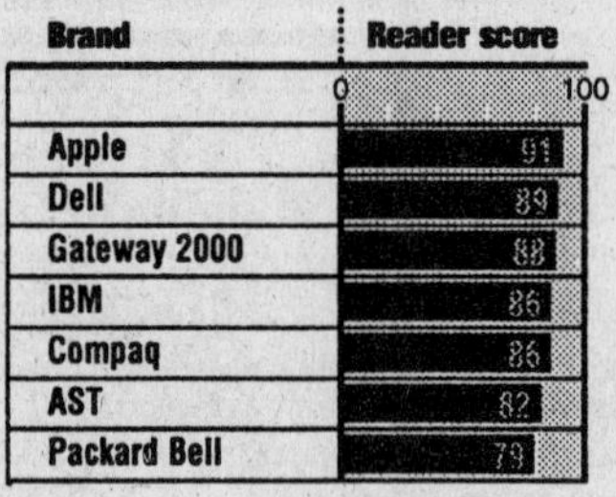
Brand
Reader score
0
100
Apple
91
Dell
89
Gateway 2000
88
IBM
86
Compaq
86
AST
82
Packard Bell
79

Computers: Repair rates

Based on more than 26,000 responses to our 1996 Annual Questionnaire. Readers were asked about components that were part of the original computer bought new between 1993 and 1996. Data have been standardized to eliminate differences among brands due to age and usage. Differences of less than 3 points aren't meaningful.

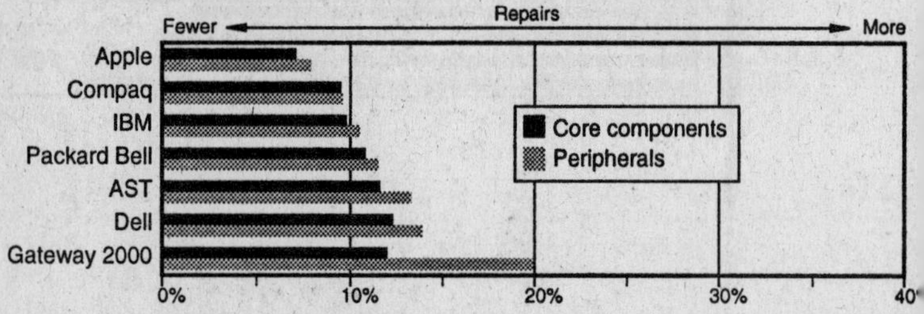

HOME ENTERTAINMENT

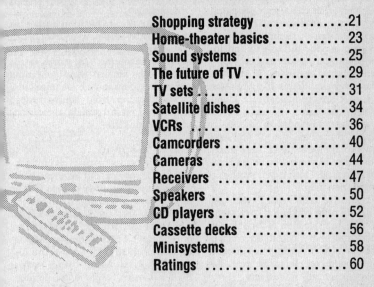

Shopping strategy

The marketplace for electronic gear is complicated and highly competitive. Here are four things to think about before you buy a TV set, VCR, receiver, or other video or audio components.

Where to buy

Specialty stores and boutiques usually boast soundproof listening rooms and good service. Expect to find gear from high-end brands and prices close to suggested retail. Installation is usually available.

Electronics/appliance superstores are hectic, high-volume selling machines. Among the best known are Best Buy, Circuit City, and Nobody Beats the Wiz. Superstores account for much of the gear sold. Expect lots of models from big, fast-selling brands—Sony, Pioneer, JVC, RCA, and the like. They may have listening rooms and installation services. But the environment can be crowded and the sales pressure strong.

Superstores don't always have the lowest prices. Some items may be marked way down, while others may be close to suggested retail. Sale-priced models may be "out of stock" and have no definite arrival date.

Department stores that sell gear offer competitive prices during sales, but selection may be limited. Manufacturers may supply each chain with goods that carry unique model numbers, which makes comparison-shopping difficult. Sales help may be difficult to find and knowledgeable assistance in short supply. Installation may or may not be available.

Mass merchandisers like Wal-Mart and Kmart feature mainstream brands like Sharp, Magnavox, GE, and Sanyo, as well as low-end brands like Soundesign and Yorx. You probably won't find separate audio components at these stores; one-piece minisystems or boom boxes are more typical. Don't expect much sales or installation help.

Warehouse clubs like Costco and Sam's Club offer good prices, not ambience. Product selection is variable and limited, and brand availability changes all the time. On occasion, you'll discover great bargains on electronic gear. But service is practically nonexistent.

Mail-order operations like Crutchfield and Sound City advertise in stereo and video magazines and publish their own catalogs. Before you buy mail-order, check for complaints with the consumer-protection agency in the seller's state or municipality. Ask the seller about shipping fees, and "restocking fees," (that is, a charge if you return something). Check if the product comes with a U.S. warranty from the manufacturer, which makes repairs easier. And keep a record of all telephone transactions and correspondence.

When to buy

Manufacturers of home-entertainment products commonly introduce new models once a year to stimulate sales and keep up with or stay ahead of competition. Dealer inventories can't always keep pace, which means older models are carried over long after newer ones have arrived and years after they've been officially "discontinued."

Sales are usually plentiful during the winter holiday season, when most home-entertainment gear is sold. You're also likely to encounter sale prices in the spring, when retailers want to clear out old models. New models are introduced by manufacturers from January through August and reach retailers' shelves one or two months later.

What to spend

Speakers, power, and features are the variables that most often push models up in price. Brands such as Proton and Pro Scan video gear and Denon and NAD audio gear are "prestige" brands and are priced higher. Specialty dealers and boutiques sell them with little or no discounting. Mass-market brands such as RCA, Panasonic, Sony, Pioneer, Technics, and JVC are widely available in stores and by mail, usually at substantial discount. Many companies, including Sony and Panasonic, manufacture separate lines of entertainment gear to reach both the popular and the prestige markets.

Our tests through the years have shown that prestige brands hold no substantive performance advantage over mass-market brands with similar features. Indeed, we've found that many prestige brands tend to give you fewer features for the money.

Extended warranty?

Extended warranties are offered for just about any electronic component. Indeed, shoppers can expect a vigorus sales pitch. Selling exteneded warranties has gone from a sideline business to a multibillion-dollar industry. By some estimates, retailers can make more money selling service contracts than they can from the sale of the merchandise.

Home-entertainment equipment tends to be reliable and long-lived. If solid-state circuitry is going to fail, it usually fails early, well within the manufacturer's warranty. Entertainment gear, especially components with few or no moving parts, often lasts for 10 years or more, problem-free. Machine parts that are more likely to wear out from heavy use — or accidental breakage—are usually excluded from coverage.

Many extended warranties don't extend the manufacturer's warranty significantly. They run concurrently, duplicating existing coverage. A better way to get extra protection is to buy with a credit card that doubles the manufacturer's warranty.

Still, there may be instances when an extended warranty might be worth considering. For more information see "Extended Warranties" on page 8.

If electronic equipment breaks, repairs can be costly. You can improve your chances of buying a trouble-free product by consulting the reliability section of our reports and the brand repair histories that start on page 10. The brand histories are based on reader experiences with actual products. •

Home-theater basics

A home-theater system makes watching TV more like going to the movies by surrounding you with sound.

Home-theater systems have shifted from pricey equipment for videophiles and film buffs to simple setups for any TV watcher. The equipment is easy to come by. Speakers are sold specifically to augment the viewing experience. Nearly all receivers have circuitry built in to decode special "surround" soundtracks. Large-screen TV sets often have surround-sound circuitry built in, too.

To make movies seem more real, theaters surround audiences with speakers that make you feel as if you're in the middle of the action. Movie-makers use various techniques—Dolby Surround, Lucasfilm THX, Dolby AC-3—to shift the sound according to the action. Those effects are what home-theater systems re-create. The most common means is through a Dolby Surround soundtrack, found on videotapes, laser discs, and even TV programming, played through a Dolby Pro Logic decoder.The newer Dolby AC-3 system provides more independent channels of sound, but it has yet to gain widespread use.

In a full-fledged home-theater system, connecting in the receiver, TV set, or stand-alone decoder processes the soundtrack and plays it through five or six speakers. Three speakers in front carry most of the action, and two at the sides or rear carry ambient background sound. Some systems add a subwoofer, placed anywhere, to carry the deep bass rumbles.

Building a home-theater system with separate components—receiver, VCR, speakers, TV set—can easily cost upward of $1500. The system will take up plenty of real estate in your living room, and it can be a chore to wire together, although you can often arrange for professional installation.

While generally less powerful and less

flexible than component systems, packaged audio systems promise to make home theater simpler and more compact. For $400 or so and up, you can buy "home theater in a box"—usually five speakers and a receiver or processor that you connect to your TV set and VCR.

You can also get big sound without installing a full-fledged system, as described in "Other home-theater options," below.

The gear

Receiver. Most home-theater systems use a Dolby Pro Logic–equipped receiver, available for $200 to $500 or more, depending on its power. Look for a receiver with at least 80 watts for each of the three front channels. Another option: a TV set with Dolby Pro Logic circuitry.

Speakers. For a full setup, you'll need at least five—two front, two rear, and one center. The front speakers produce most of the sound and should be the best quality you can afford. The left and right speakers should sit to either side of your TV set, far enough apart to produce a noticeable stereo effect. Ideally, those two speakers and the listener should form an equilateral triangle. If you already own a decent set of stereo speakers, they will probably suffice.

The center speaker carries most of the dialogue and sounds that move across the screen. If your receiver's center channel has more than 65 watts of power, be prepared to buy a speaker that's up to the challenge; many of the cheapest models are not. Since more and more sound effects depend on a smooth transition of sound from one side to the other, the center speaker should come close to matching the sound quality of the left and right speakers. A center speaker should be placed above or below the set; many are designed to lie across the top of a 19-inch or larger TV set. Because it's close to the TV set, the center speaker must be magnetically shielded so it won't interfere with the picture.

In a Dolby Pro Logic system, the rear speakers handle only ambient sounds—applause, the din of traffic, the rumble of distant helicopters. As a result, they can be smaller and lower in quality than the front pair. Also called surround speakers, the rear pair should go behind you, high on the wall, and facing away from your viewing position, since reflected sound will enhance the surround effect. Almost any set of serviceable speakers will do, including a set from an older sound system. You can also use additional satellite speakers available with some three-piece systems.

Some home-theater systems use a subwoofer for the bass. With frequencies that low, you can't tell where the sound is coming from, so subwoofers can be hidden beneath or behind furniture.

TV set. Your present set may do just fine. It doesn't need fancy sound, provided the set has audio output jacks. The set need not be huge, although a big-screen TV set is a popular choice. If you opt for a set with a screen 31 inches or larger or for a rear-projection set, you'll need to sit far enough away so you don't see the scan lines. A rule of thumb: The closest viewing distance should be four times the screen height.

VCR. A VCR with stereo hi-fi capability costs as little as $200—only $30 or so more than mono VCR. Other video sources, including laser-disc players and the new digital video disc (DVD) players, provide high-quality sound, too, along with far better pictures than videotape. Laser discs never caught on, except with film buffs. DVD is likely to replace them, and perhaps videotape, eventually. To see the benefits of DVD, you need a fairly modern TV set. To hear the benefits, you need a Dolby Pro Logic receiver and a multispeaker home theater. DVD players cost between $400 and $1400. See "Movies on disc," page 38.

Other home-theater options

You can get some of the feeling of home theater without setting up a whole system. Here are two strategies:

Use fewer speakers. A home-theater system can have fewer than five speakers and still create a semblance of surround sound by using a receiver's Dolby Pro Logic settings to electronically fill in some of the missing sound.

The "phantom" mode on the receiver allows you to eliminate the center speaker. It distributes the center signal equally to the main left and right channels. You can use the TV set's internal speakers as the center channel—if the quality of those speakers is acceptable to you.

A receiver's Dolby 3 mode uses only the three front speakers; the rear surround speakers are not used. Instead, delayed surround signals are sent to the front left and right channels, creating a slight echo effect.

Skip the Pro Logic. You can improve the stereo effect from a TV set simply by connecting a pair of external speakers. A plain stereo receiver can amplify the sound of any TV set, as long as the set has audio output jacks. If your TV set doesn't have those jacks, you can use a hi-fi VCR as the TV tuner. Some TV sets have ambience modes, such as SRS or SEq, that can create pleasing surround effects.

Deluxe home theater

Dolby Pro Logic receivers send the same signal to both rear surround speakers. Dolby AC-3 receivers, their upscale digital relatives, produce separate left and right surround channels, so you can hear sound circling around behind your head as well as in front of it. AC-3 models also produce a sixth, optional channel that directs low-frequency special effects to a separate, powered subwoofer.

AC-3 equipment is still quite expensive compared with regular home-theater gear. AC-3 receivers cost at least $700, and you'll need to buy a DVD player or AC-3-compatible laser-disc player ($400 and up). Titles with AC-3 soundtracks are limited but growing in number.

Yet another enhancement to Dolby Pro Logic is THX, a sound reproduction format similar to those used in the best movie theaters. A complete home THX system, including special speakers, costs about $4000 and up.

Sound systems

You don't have to pay a lot to get superb sound, and you can often find it in one easy-to-use package.

Until recently, if you bought a simple, all-in-one sound system, you sacrificed a lot in sound quality. Manufacturers offered packaged systems as an option for people who couldn't afford separate components or didn't care enough to pick each one.

That's no longer true. Today, packaged systems—rack systems, minisystems, even some boom boxes—can play music decently, even admirably. Speaker quality, amplifier power, and convenience features are the main items that push models up in price.

To help determine the type of gear you'll need, think about these questions:

• How do you listen to music? If you often listen to music for its own sake, your best bet is a system built of individual components. It's the surest road to highest fidelity, mostly because it lets you choose the best speakers. When you buy separate components, you can choose a cassette deck with Dolby C or Dolby S noise reduction, a CD player that's the same brand as the cassette deck to simplify the recording process, and a receiver with plenty of power. Overall, a component system that costs $1000 to $1500 should satisfy most people who listen seriously, though it's possible to spend a lot more.

People who use music as an accompaniment to another activity may deem sound quality important enough to pick out individual components. But an inexpensive rack system or a minisystem might also do nicely.

For listening on the go, a good portable CD player costs less than $100, a radio/tape player less than $50. Or consider a good quality boom box—the best of them sound nearly as good as a decent minisystem.

• How much can you spend? If you're on a limited budget and starting from scratch, consider a minisystem (about $300). Or start with a basic component system: a low-priced receiver ($250), an inexpensive CD changer ($200 or less), and the best speakers you can afford. Shop around—discounts of 20 or 30 percent are common.

Another option is to upgrade an existing system. The simplest way to do that is to improve the speakers. If your receiver is more than 15 years old, it probably lacks digital tuning, a remote control, home-theater electronics, and other useful features found on current models. Unlike older cassette decks, some modern decks can make tapes with just a smidgen less fidelity than you'd find on a CD.

• Where will you be listening? Room size and "liveness"—whether there are a lot of hard surfaces to reflect sound or soft, upholstered ones to absorb it—affect the quality of the sound. You'll need more receiver power to fill a room that's large or plush.

• What kind of music do you listen to? If you like to listen to loud, deep bass—be it classical organ or Nine Inch Nails—you'll need a more powerful receiver and bigger speakers than if your tastes run to quieter music.

Sound-system options

Minisystem. A small system in an all-in-one package, a minisystem offers reasonably good overall performance. Compared with a system of separate components, it's cheaper, more compact, and simpler to hook up. Just attach a simple connector or two, plug in the system, and play.

Unlike component systems, minisystems usually can't be upgraded with bigger speakers or other components, nor can you add a second pair of speakers to send music to another room. Minisystems also usually lack adjustable bass and treble controls, features that help overcome speaker defects. The lower-priced models have limited power and anemic bass—good enough for a bedroom, but not a living room.

Price range: $200 to more than $1500.

A **boom box** combines an AM/FM stereo radio with built-in antennas, one or two cassette decks and, quite often, a CD player in a portable package that runs on household current or batteries. Models weigh anywhere from less than 10 to more than 20 pounds.

Small boxes usually have nondetachable speakers that lack the wherewithal to reproduce sound faithfully. Larger ones often come with good-sized speakers that can be detached and moved for a better stereo effect. Overall sound quality can be quite pleasing in the bigger boxes, though not on a par with a decent rack or component system. Nor can boom boxes play as loudly or deeply into the bass range as minisystems can. Except to pay more for a boom box with a remote control or with speakers that have a better reach into treble and bass.

Price range: about $50 to $150 for a small box; $150 to $250 or more for a bigger one. Price correlates with size and whether there's a CD player.

Rack system. Like their smaller minisystem cousins, rack systems are a package deal, but with full-sized components dressed in furniture-style cabinetry. Unlike minisystems, rack systems require assembly (the cabinet) and some wiring. They come with floor-standing speakers and with plenty to power them—at least 80 watts per channel. A dual cassette deck, CD player, and remote control are standard. Higher-priced models include home-theater capabilities.

The size of the speakers allows good bass reproduction, which makes rack systems a notch higher in quality than minisystems. Overall, the best rack systems match the performance and versatility of a decent component system, but at a lower cost. Some manufacturers cut costs by cheapening the cabinets, which are typically constructed of plastic-covered particleboard with thin back panels.

Price range: $500 to more than $1200. You should be able to get a good rack system for $800.

Component system. This type of system is the most flexible and capable of the highest sound quality. You can choose the best of what each manufacturer offers, upgrade individual components, or add new ones. The downside: A component system costs more than simpler systems and takes some effort to set up. A typical system includes a receiver, a CD player, one or two pairs of speakers, maybe a cassette deck, and even your old turntable. Most receivers also allow you to hook up video equipment—a TV set, a VCR, and a DVD or a laser-disc player. If you'll be making tapes from CDs, consider getting a cassette deck and CD player of the same brand. That way, tape-making features such as synchronized starting are more likely to be available.

A receiver itself incorporates several components—an amplifier, a preamplifier, and a digital AM/FM tuner. Purists have long maintained that separate devices for each of those functions provide the best possible sound. While sensitive lab instruments might be able to tell the difference between separate components and a top-notch receiver, we have found that human ears cannot.

Price range: $800 for a good basic system, $1000 to $1500 for a full-featured one. Spending more than $1500 buys more features, not better sound quality—nice-looking speakers, a subwoofer for deep bass, a jukebox CD player, an ultra-powerful receiver. Once you enter audiophile land, the sky's the limit.

System setup

Boom boxes are the simplest of all systems to use: If you run them on batteries, you don't even need to plug them in. Minisystems come next in simplicity; just connect the speakers and antenna and you're set. The manufacturer includes speakers that match the minisystem's receiver, eliminating some of the decisions needed to put together a component system. Rack systems also come with speakers that are right for the system, but they require some assembly.

Component systems require more decisions, including determining the power of the receiver and its compatibility with speakers. Once you've figured out your component choices, shop for the best price. If you can't install the system yourself, you can hire someone to do it. Many stores, especially specialty stores and boutiques, offer this service.

Power decisions. Generally, the more power a receiver can deliver, the louder you can play music. Each doubling of loudness uses about 10 times as much power. To fill a good-sized living room with loud, undistorted sound, you usually need 65 to 100 watts per channel (each channel corresponds to one speaker). If you play recordings at high volume with strong, deep bass or a wide dynamic range, or if your speakers require extra power, stay close to 100 watts per channel. For a small room—a bedroom or dorm room—you need about 35 or 40 watts per channel to play music loud. With less than 20 watts per channel, as found on some minisystems and boom boxes, don't expect loud bass.

Power claims tend to be lower for Dolby Pro Logic modes than for stereo mode. Look for Pro Logic power that's even across the front channels—80/80/80, say. To meet federal guidelines, manufacturers are conservative in how they rate receivers' power. Our own measurements are often a bit higher than the manufacturers'.

Don't skimp on power. When a receiver runs short on power—while playing peaks in the music, say—it produces a harsh distortion called clipping that can damage speakers. Keeping the volume control turned down won't help; the effect can occur even when the volume is only halfway up. Fortunately, even low-priced receivers usually have plenty of power these days.

Speaker/receiver compatibility. As a receiver runs, its power supply and amplifier heat up. The heat is due to the power the amplifier puts out; the amount of heat also depends on the resistance of the speakers—the impedance—measured in ohms. At a given power level, the lower the impedance, the higher the current draw and the hotter things get. Thus, a pair of four-ohm speakers heat up the receiver more than a pair of eight-ohm speakers. Therein lies a problem in mating speakers with receivers.

Although a speaker's impedance has nothing to do with its quality, you'll find more four-ohm models among the more expensive speakers. Mass-market brands such as Sony, Pioneer, and Radio Shack generally include a mix of speakers rated at eight and six ohms. Companies like Bose and Cerwin-Vega market different lines for different retail venues, some with eight-ohm ratings, some with six, some with four. You'll find many of the high-end "salon" speaker lines are made up entirely of four-ohm models.

The labels on many receivers say they shouldn't be used with four-ohm speakers. (That restriction is necessary for a receiver to earn a seal from Underwriters Laboratories.) What happens if you ignore the label? Probably not much. But monitor the temperature of the receiver. If its cabinet gets uncomfortably hot to the touch after a half-hour's play of bass-heavy music, you're probably overheating internal parts. Turn the volume down to cool things off and think about getting a new receiver.

Positioning speakers. The ideal placement for two speakers in a sound system makes an equilateral triangle at least six feet on each side, with you as the third point. With a satellite system that has two small speakers and a bass module, you can place the large bass unit practically anywhere—the ear can't tell what direction deep bass sounds come from—in the same triangle you would use for a pair with the small satellites. For a five- or six-speaker system, maintain that triangle with the front right and left speakers; put the center front speaker above or below the TV; angle the two rear surround speakers away from you, and just behind you; and put the bass module wherever it fits.

These positions, of course, are the ideal. In most homes, you must put the speakers on the bookshelf or next to the couch. Experiment if possible—speaker placement can greatly affect the sound of your system. The closer a speaker is to the corner of a room, the stronger the bass. That can give a boost to a small bass-light speaker. But putting a big bass-rich speaker right in the corner can make the bass sound muddy or boomy.

Adding a second pair. Most receivers provide outputs—labeled main and remote or A and B—for two pairs of speakers in stereo mode, so you can listen away from the receiver, in a different room. If you want to play two pairs loudly, you need a receiver with 100 watts or more per channel, since two pairs of speakers need more power than one.

In addition, some receivers are better suited than others for adding a second pair of speakers. If the remote speakers are on a separate circuit from the main speakers—"in parallel"—all four speakers should sound as they were designed to. But if the extra pair are on the same circuit as the main speakers—"in series"—the sound will be altered and often degraded.

The arrangement of the circuitry also affects impedance. Two pairs of speakers in parallel produce the equivalent of lower impedance, which can cause the same problems for a receiver that four-ohm speakers do.

A receiver has the preferred parallel design if its switches and output jacks have labels that refer to three modes—A, B, and A+B—with a higher impedance noted for the A+B mode. Otherwise, you can't easily tell how the receiver is wired. A knowledgeable salesperson might be able to tell from the manual. Or you can call the manufacturer (see page 342).

The future of TV

Technology and standards are changing fast. Here's what you need to know to buy today.

The state of TV service

Up to now, there's been more talk than action when it comes to innovations in TV service. For years, cable operators, phone companies (who can send out TV signals over special lines), and others have been promising a flood of new and improved services. But they've generally been slow to deliver on their promises, unsure whether they can recoup the huge investments such new services require.

The stall in improved TV service can be traced to 1995, when Congress deregulated cable rates for cable companies that faced a certain level of competition. At the time, cable's chief competitor was thought to be "wireless cable," a challenge to cable that never truly materialized. Despite the number of companies that have invested in wireless cable, service is limited to a small percentage of homes in selected cities.

Now, the leading challenge comes from satellite-TV services. But dish systems don't fully compete with cable either; they don't provide local stations. Dish systems require a location with an unobstructed "view" of the satellite. And dish systems are typically more expensive than cable.

Trends in TV

In the meantime, TV sets continue to evolve as they accommodate new needs and technologies. These changes include the merging of TV/video functions with those of the computer to produce new multimedia products like WebTV.

Introduced by Philips and Sony, WebTV consists of an Internet terminal (a box the size of a small VCR) that you connect to a TV. While you're surfing the Net, however, you tie up the phone line. Web pages can also be harder to read on a TV set than on a computer screen. But WebTV does allow you to splash around in cyberspace without investing in a computer, and will soon introduce an upgraded box that simultaneously displays live TV and Internet information.

Most people, however, will probably continue to use their TVs for viewing regular broadcasts, with a significant number trading up to larger sets. In 1996, TV sets 25 inches or larger accounted for 49 percent of all sets sold. Prices of sets continue to drop. Five years ago, the average price of a 31- or 32-inch TV set was $1200. Today, you can buy a similarly sized set with plenty of features for as little as $650. A top-of-the-line model will cost closer to $1600.

With high-definition television (HDTV) expected to be available in 1998, the trend toward bigger and bigger screens will continue, since the superior visual resolution of HDTV will allow viewers to sit closer to the set without being distracted by scan lines. The first big-screen sets using the new technology, however, are likely to cost much more than today sets of comparable size—between $6000 and $10,000, by current estimate.

Only people looking for a TV costing more than $2000 should consider delaying their plans waiting for HDTV. Here's why:

• **Programming plans are fuzzy.** It's unclear how many HDTV signals will be available when the first sets hit the market. The federal government lent each television station, without charge, a second channel for digital television (DTV) broadcasts, of which HDTV is the highest-quality format. Broadcasters have been slow to commit to using these channels for HDTV; instead, they want to use them for other digital broadcasts whose resolution may not be significantly better than today's broadcasts. Cable stations are also vague about HDTV programming plans.

• **Converter boxes are coming.** These devices, which manufacturers say will cost $200 to $800, will turn HDTV broadcasts into signals your conventional TV can use. Converted HDTV signals are expected to be freer of static than current analog signals. But the boxes won't offer the high resolution of an DTV set. Don't be fooled into buying a costly regular TV by promises that a converter will transform it into a DTV.

What should you buy in this pre-DTV era? A set that costs no more than $2000, which includes models from 27 to 35 inches and some projection TVs. Many such sets have good picture quality and an S-video input, which supports a higher resolution and will make the most of those better signals.

Satellite systems already use a digital format, which may let them adapt more easily to DTV. The digital-video-disc (DVD) format, which offers full-length movies on discs that resemble CDs, also offers digital signals. (Current DVD players and discs can't produce HDTV-quality images.)

TV sets

Big-screen TV sets have come way down in price, but the best values can be found among sets now considered "mid-sized"—those 25 and 27 inches on the diagonal.

Last CR reports:
27-inch sets, March 1996;
25-inch sets, February 1997;
31- and 32-inch sets, March 1997
Brand repair histories: pages 12 to 13
Expect to pay: $100 to $5500

What's available

Small sets. Sets with a 13-inch screen are often regarded as "second" sets, so manufacturers tend to make them plain. Expect monophonic sound and sparse features. Price range: $150 to $400.

Sets with a 19- or 20-inch screen are also seen as second sets; 19-inch sets cost less and have fewer features. Most 19-inch models lack high-end picture refinements such as a comb filter and stereo audio. Models with stereo sound usually have extra inputs for plugging in a VCR or a laser-disc player. At best, the built-in sound is equivalent to a mediocre boom box. Price range: $200 to $500.

Mid-sized sets. Sets with a 27-inch screen used to be considered large but are now considered standard size by many manufacturers. TV sets with a 25-inch screen (a size difference difficult to discern, according to our panel tests) are their economy-minded cousins. Sets with a 27-inch screen are usually priced higher and frequently offer more features, including picture-in-picture, special sound systems, and a universal remote control. Comb filters, which allow a set to render greater detail, are commonplace on 27-inch sets but are missing from most 25-inchers. Price range: $240 to $1500.

Large sets. Sets with 31- or 32-inch screens represent the entry level for big-screen TV. For proper viewing, you'll need about 10 feet from the screen to the seating. The largest direct-view sets (40-inch sets) weigh hundreds of pounds and are too big for conventional component shelving. Price range: $550 to $3000.

Projection sets. These offer still more picture area—40 to 80 diagonal inches—but typically picture quality won't match that of a set with a conventional picture tube. You'll want a viewing distance of more than 15 feet for a 50-inch set, even more for larger ones. Brightness and, to some extent, color vary as you move off to the sides of the screen. Large sets and rear-projection sets come with plenty of features, such as ambient sound and custom settings. Price range: $1500 to $8500.

What's new

Lower prices for large-screen sets. Now that the larger sets have been on the market for a few years, their prices are dropping, especially for 31- and 32-inch sets. Once averaging about $1200, they now start as low as $550.

Features trickle down. Comb filter, picture-in-picture, on-screen menus, MTS stereo—features once found only on top-of-the-line models—are commonplace on smaller and less expensive sets.

Reliability

Readers report that among 31- to 35-inch sets purchased new from 1992 to 1996, JVC, Toshiba, and Panasonic were among the more reliable brands. Sets from Sony and RCA were among the less reliable brands.

Among 25- to 27-inch sets, the more reliable brands included Sharp, Sanyo, Toshiba, Panasonic, and Hitachi; General Electric and RCA were among the less reliable. For more information on those sizes and 19- and 20-inch sets, see the brand repair histories, page 12.

Shopping strategy

Choose a TV set primarily by picture quality, price, and its brand's repair history. Most sets today have a picture that's close to the best quality possible under current broadcast standards. (For advice regarding the future of TV sets, see "The future of TV," on page 29.) Features such as comb filters and dark screens help a set render greater detail and produce sharper pictures. Don't put too much stock in the differences in picture quality you see in the store. Those sets may not be getting a uniform picture signal, or they may not be uniformly adjusted.

Sound quality is variable. In general, TV sound gets better as sets get bigger. Sets that are 19 and 20 inches generally deliver sound no better than a mediocre boom box. But TV sound is easy to improve by playing it through external speakers. Audio outputs are common on sets 20 inches and up. Some high-end sets have an amplifier to power external speakers. For more about boosting TV sound, see the report on home theater, page 23.

Before you buy a big-screen TV, make sure to measure the space you've allotted for TV watching. For best viewing, you'll need to sit far enough away—about four times the screen size—so you don't see the scan lines. If you must sit closer, consider a smaller set.

Regardless of the size TV you buy, it's important to try out the remote control. Make sure you like the layout of the controls, the legibility of its labels, and the structure of the on-screen menus.

If you don't like the remote that comes with the set, you can buy an aftermarket universal remote control for $15 or so.

Decide what to spend. The best value in mid-sized TV sets are 25-inch models, which sell for as little as $200 (mono) or $250 (stereo). Such sets are relatively inexpensive, in part, because they often lack many features common on 27-inch models.

You can find a 31- or 32-inch set for less than $600. By spending more, you get a set with picture-in-picture (PIP) and sound-enhancing features. Sets that cost $1000 and up may add such features as a second tuner for PIP (so a VCR need not be used) and a high-grade picture tube.

What's in the stores. Some brands, including Sony, Hitachi, and Toshiba, do not offer 25-inch sets, only the 27-inch size. The biggest-selling 25-inch brands are RCA, Magnavox, and Zenith. For big-screen brands, RCA, Toshiba, and Sony account for about half the sales. All the major brands currently offer at least one 31- or 32-inch model.

For all TV sets, models are available for about a year after they're introduced—not long enough for us to include Ratings in this guide. New models are introduced in the summer when the old models begin to disappear from store shelves.

Key features

• *Recommended, if available:*

Automatic volume control. This compensates for the annoying jump in volume that often comes with commercials or channel changes.

Beeping remote. On some Magnavox sets, helps you find a misplaced remote.

Comb filter. A picture-enhancing feature. It increases visual detail and cleans up image outlines by reducing extraneous colors. Most 27-inch and larger sets have it.

Flesh-tone correction. This automatically adjusts skin tones that are too green or red.

Remote control. TV remotes for the larger sets (20-inch and up) are the universal type: They work a VCR and a cable box, with buttons that feature channel selection and volume, with less emphasis on tape controls. An auto code-entry remote makes setup easier: Instead of punching in a code for each device you want the universal remote to operate, the remote searches for the device's code.

Stereo capability. Superior to mono sound, the stereo effect is subtle unless the signal is piped to external speakers.

Video jacks. Better than the standard antenna jack for plugging in a VCR or other video gear. For video games or a camcorder, a set with additional jacks on the front makes hooking up easy.

Video noise-reduction filter. This smooths out "noisy" images. Useful if you have reception problems.

• *Useful for particular needs:*

Active-channel scan. This lets the tuner run through the channels, pausing at each for a few seconds.

Alarm and sleep timer. They use a built-in clock that turns the set on or off at a predetermined time.

Audio-output jacks. These let you run the set's sound through a hi-fi system.

Ambience modes. These go by names like Sound Retrieval System (SRS) and Spatial Equalization (SEq). They're electronically enhanced stereo effects that attempt to envelop the listener in sound.

Built-in-speaker amplifier. This allows the set to drive a pair of external speakers directly, which improves both the sound quality and the stereo effect.

Channel block-out. Renders certain channels unavailable—usually, to limit a child's viewing.

Channel labeling (or captioning). Helpful if you have lots of channels, this lets you program channel names—ABC, MTV, CNN, ESPN—to appear on screen with the channel number.

Closed captioning when muted. This automatically displays captions when you mute the sound.

Commercial-skip timer. This changes channels when a commercial comes on, then automatically returns to the original channel after a time period you've selected.

Multilingual menus. They often come in English, Spanish, or French.

Picture-in-picture (PIP). This lets you watch two channels at once, usually with one shown as a small picture superimposed over a corner of the full-screen picture. The best PIP design has its own tuner. Most TVs don't: You must hook the tuner up to a VCR or a cable box that has a video output.

Programmable audio/video. This lets you customize picture and sound settings. On some sets, each input retains its own settings to compensate for signal differences from VCRs and camcorders.

S-video jack. Lets you make the most of high-band sources such as an S-VHS VCR, Hi8 camcorder, laser-disc or DVD player, or a satellite-TV system.

Separate audio program (SAP). Lets a viewer switch to another soundtrack, say, in Spanish, with certain broadcasts.

White-balance controls. To tint background whites toward red or blue.

• *Not worth paying extra for:*

Flat screen. It's supposed to reduce distortion at the picture's edges, but we have seen little effect in our tests.

Small-dish satellite systems

Picture and sound quality is uniformly excellent. Systems differ mostly in convenience and programming.

Last CR report: December 1996
Expect to pay: $200 to $800

More than seven million small satellite dishes have been sold since 1994, making dishes the most successful electronic product ever introduced. Today's dishes, more compact and less costly than their sports-bar-sized relatives, use digital technology to provide TV features beyond what cable and phone companies can deliver. Dishes provide a number of long-awaited TV features: They use digital technology, the signals from which are all but immune to the noise, interference, and static that plague the analog signals from regular antennas and cable systems. As a result, satellite-dish systems have a large channel capacity that allows dishes to offer a vast choice of movies, including pay-per-view selections at video-store prices.

Each system has its own programming packages, which are available only with that system—so you can't, say, watch DSS programming with EchoStar equipment, though nearly all the channels familiar to cable viewers are included in each system. Unlike cable, satellite programmers cannot provide you with local channels—their programming is intended for a national audience. (For local channels you'll have to use an antenna or a cable service.)

A dish usually requires an investment in equipment, and as with cable, there's a monthly fee for programming. A setup, including professional installation and a receiver, costs as little as $400. Basic programming packages are as low as $20 a month. Sometimes a package deal or rebate lowers the price further.

What's available

Each system has its own satellite with a distinct location in the sky. Whether you can receive a particular service depends on your ability to install a dish with an unobstructed line of sight to the satellite, its signal unblocked by hills, buildings, or trees. A local satellite-TV installer can tell you which systems can be accessed from your location.

The major systems are Digital Satellite System (DSS), EchoStar/Dish Network, and Primestar. Each offers a similar array of programming choices and the same basic setup: A dish to receive the satellite signals, a receiver linked to the dish for decoding them, and a remote control. Equipment for the best-selling system, DSS, is made by a number of manufacturers.

What's new

The price of small-dish satellite systems has dropped as the number of programming choices and satellite systems has grown.

Such growth benefits not only satellite subscribers but cable subscribers, who can expect to see improvements in their service as cable companies are forced to compete with satellite systems.

At present, cable companies cannot match the seasonal sports packages, the pay-per-view selections, and the high-quality picture and sound offered by satellite systems.

In the near future, condominium owners and apartment dwellers may also have easy access to satellite service. Mandated by Congress to provide equal access to cable and satellite service, the Federal Communications Commission is looking into creating rules that would allow urban dwellers access to satellite service without having to hang a dish off their building walls. Manufacturers are working on systems where a single dish could feed hundreds or even thousands of apartments at a time.

On the horizon: Digital satellite transmission of modem signals, that'll speed up Internet access.

Shopping strategy

Satellite systems offer high-quality picture and sound and a wide choice of channels, but cost more to set up than cable and don't carry local channels. You might decide it's worthwhile to get basic cable service and use the satellite system for premium channels and sports packages.

When choosing among satellite systems, look at price, convenience, and programming. Note that the number of channels a system claims it offers is often misleading, since some of the channels are devoted to pay-per-view offerings and to duplicate or variant versions.

Decide what to spend. Small-dish satellite equipment costs between $200 and $750. Prices vary mostly by whether the system can service two TV sets independently. For $80 or so, you can purchase a kit to install the dish yourself. To pay a professional to do the work will cost about $200.

Programming costs range from $20 to $90 per month, depending on the programming packages you choose.

What's in the stores. DSS receivers are sold by a number of manufacturers, including RCA, Sony, Panasonic, and Toshiba. You'll find DDS and EchoStar systems in warehouse clubs, electronic stores, retailers such as Sears, and through specialty satellite-system dealers. Primestar is sold at Radio Shack and directly by the company.

Key considerations

Channel block-out. Most systems have the same channel block-out capability as many new TVs to limit the programming children can access. Blocked-out channels appear only after you enter a personal code number on the remote.

Dish size. Dishes vary in diameter from 18 inches for DSS and EchoStar to 39 inches for Primestar. You may need a larger, more expensive dish if you live outside the continental U.S. But you shouldn't encounter any zoning problems erecting a small dish, since the government has voided almost all laws that prohibit their installation on a home. Although you can install DSS and EchoStar dishes yourself, we recommend professional installation.

Program guides. With a DSS system, you typically have an on-screen grid that allows you to browse program listings up to three days in advance. You can access information about a specific program with one button-press of the remote and call up the program with a second press. EchoStar makes you step through several menus to access program information. Primestar's new Primefinder remote has color-coded buttons that let you "hypersurf" to any of 10 programming categories.

Programming packages. Basic programming packages usually include at least 40 video channels and as many as 30 audio channels. As with cable, premium channels are included in the more expensive packages. But satellite systems give you more choices—up to five selections of each premium channel, music channel, and pay-per-view movies are available simultaneously. Pay-per-view events can be ordered using the remote control and on-screen menus; the charges are added automatically to your monthly programming bill.

Remote control. All systems come with an infrared remote to operate the receiver. Aftermarket remotes that can operate satellite equipment are available as well. A radio-frequency remote, which can operate the receiver from another room, costs $75 or so.

Two TV sets. A dish system can serve many TV sets, but they will all get the same program. To view separate programs on two TV sets, you need to purchase a dish with a dual low-noise block converter (LBN). Dual-LNB dishes typically cost $50 to $200 more than the single-LNB dishes supplied with low-priced setups; single-LNB dishes usually can't be upgraded for dual-LNB use. To view channels independently, a second TV set also requires its own receiver, at a cost of $150 or more. A two-TV setup also incurs an additional programming fee.

VCRs

New features make VCRs easier to use. Worth getting: hi-fi sound and a programming aid such as VCR Plus+.

Last CR report: October 1997
Ratings: page 79
Brand repair histories: page 12
Expect to pay: $125 to $925

What's available

Format. Almost all VCRs sold are VHS models. Other formats—8mm, S-VHS, Hi8—are scarce (only Sony currently offers Hi8 VCRs). High-band VCRs offer excellent picture quality, special effects, and tend to have editing features, but require expensive tapes that can be hard to find.

Sound. A monophonic VCR records sound decently; it typically costs $150 to $250. But some hi-fi models can be a much better value. For little more—$170 to $450—it records near-CD-quality sound and can play surround-sound movies.

Programming aids. Since programming a VCR remains a technological bugaboo to many, manufacturers keep trying to make this task easier. VCR Plus+, once a separate product, is now an integral feature built into many models, costing $20 to $50 extra. You use the remote to enter a program code found in the TV listings of newspapers. VCR Plus+ uses that code to automatically switch to the appropriate channel at the appropriate time.

If you use a cable box and want to program your VCR to record shows on more than one channel, you'll need a cable box controller. If you want this feature, look for a VCR with what's called "VCR Plus with C^3".

A new breed of programming tool is even more intuitive. StarSight is built into a few TV sets and VCRs and is also sold as an optional feature. Like the tabular listings provided by cable channels or in the newspaper, StarSight lays out programs by time a week in advance and is updated daily. It lets you view the listings using on-screen tables sorted by type of program (sports, science/nature, and so forth). You simply choose a program and set your VCR to record a show with a few button-presses. The guide costs $15 to start up and about $4 a month thereafter.

What's new

Features once available only on high-end VCRs are now showing up on some lower-priced models. VCRs with four video heads, which allow cleaner-looking freeze-frames, are now the norm. Features like auto clock set, which updates the VCR time automatically, are now common.

Programming aids like VCR Plus+ continue to offer refinements. With VCR Plus Gold, you enter your zip code, and the VCR downloads the data overnight from a broadcast station. Index Plus+ generates an index of recorded programs at the beginning of a tape and lets you fast-forward to a selected program.

Due to the rapid spread of the DSS small-dish satellite system, a growing number of VCR brands allow programmed recording of DSS channels.

Even as the VCR becomes easier to use and more capable, a new technology threatens to replace it: the DVD (digital video disc) player. See page 38.

Reliability

According to our 1996 Annual Questionnaire, roughly 1 in 10 of the VHS VCRs our readers bought from 1991 to 1996 have needed repair. A number of brands ranked among the more reliable ones, but no brand stood out as the best. Zenith, Series LXi (sold at Sears), Optimus (sold at Radio Shack), and Fisher were among the less reliable brands. See the brand repair histories on page 12.

Shopping strategy

VCR picture quality varies, according to our tests, and price is not a reliable guide to the best picture. Spending more generally gets you more features, such as programming aids like VCR Plus+.

A basic two-head VCR is all you need for taping TV programs for viewing later with or without special effects.

For watching stereo movies, choose a hi-fi model for more theaterlike effects. (See the report on home theater, page 23.) If the retailer's display models are hooked up, see how easily you can follow a VCR's on-screen operating and programming instructions.

Decide what to spend. Spending an extra $10 to $40 will get you a hi-fi VCR. To fully appreciate a hi-fi model's CD-quality sound, you must connect it to a good sound system.

More features aren't always better. Buy only the features you know you'll need. Don't pay extra for the ones you won't use. If you have trouble programming, consider buying a model with VCR Plus+, $20 to $50 extra.

What's in the stores. RCA and Magnavox are the biggest-selling brands. Emerson is now a Wal-Mart brand. Magnavox, the best-selling low-end brand, is likely to be available from mass merchandisers and price clubs. Sony tends to price its electronic gear on the high side, as do some smaller brands such as Mitsubishi. Lower-priced brands—notably Samsung—may offer good value and are worth considering.

Using the Ratings. The models in the Ratings represent the best value in VCRs—hi-fi models that are low- or mid-priced. The tested models were scored primarily for picture quality. As is typical of electronic gear, those models stay on store shelves for about a year until new models are introduced in the winter and spring. Models listed as similar to those tested should perform much the same as the tested models; features may vary. If you

Movies on disc

The digital video disc, or DVD, has the potential to do for prerecorded movies what the CD did for music. A DVD can contain enough digitally encoded data for four full-length feature films and high-quality soundtracks. For now, you can only play back DVDs; recordable discs are still in the future.

Based on a test of three of the first DVD players on the market, we found picture quality to be excellent—about the best of any format currently available on the consumer market. We found picture flaws nearly impossible to detect, aside from the usual limitations of the current TV format. Picture resolution was far superior to conventional VHS videotape, although still well below what high-definition TV will offer.

The DVD format is designed to make excellent use of a home-theater setup. The discs have a Dolby AC-3 soundtrack, which splits sound into five full-range discrete channels plus a deep-bass channel. To get the full benefit of movie sound effects, you need an AC-3 receiver and six speakers.

We used some of the first DVD movie releases in our tests. The sound effects of the movies we watched varied considerably from movie to movie in their ability to give us a sense of being "in" the movie. Sound quality, however, is top-notch—what you'd expect from digital recording.

Standard features on DVD players include:

• Quick searching. Discs typically have about 40 "chapters," listed on the dust jacket, that allow you to skip forward or back rapidly.

• Multiple screen formats. Most discs store a movie in both "standard" (an aspect ratio—picture width to height—of 4:3) and "widescreen" (16:9) formats. The widescreen version, which appears letterboxed on a regular TV set, more closely matches the proportions of movie screens and future high-definition TV sets.

• Parental control codes. These prevent movies with certain ratings from being played back unless a code is entered from the remote control.

Despite the potential benefits, there are still good reasons to wait before buying. DVD players now cost about twice as much as a good hi-fi VCR. You'll also have to spend over $1500 for a new Dolby Digital receiver or AC-3 receiver with an outboard decoder to take full advantage of DVD soundtracks. Prices will almost surely tumble as more manufacturers introduce players and more AC-3 receivers. And there aren't yet many movies on DVD, although that's expected to change, too. Discs are priced at $20 to $25.

can't find a model, call the manufacturer; see page 342.

Key features

• *Recommended, if available:*

Auto channel set. This automatically programs the channel lineup to skip empty channels. Standard on most models.

Auto clock set. By using information in the broadcast signal to set the VCR's clock, it eliminates the flashing "12:00." Some models have an automatic daylight savings control; others have a control that adds or subtracts one hour at the press of a button.

Auto tracking. Standard on most models, it eliminates the need to adjust the tracking control for each tape viewed.

Auto speed-switching. Slows recording from SP to EP if too little tape is left to complete a programmed recording.

Auto rewind. When the tape reaches its end, the VCR automatically rewinds it.

Cable-channel capacity of 125 channels. Plenty for most cable users, and a standard feature.

Commercial advance. Currently on a few General Electric, Hitachi, ProScan, RCA, Sony, and Samsung models, this lets the VCR bypass all commercials during playback by locating fades-to-black, changes in sound level, and other clues, and then fast-forwarding past them. The feature worked well in our tests.

Go-to. Searches the tape by time to find the passage you want to watch.

Index search. Similar to go-to, but more helpful. It places an electronic "bookmark" on the tape each time you begin to record, so the VCR can quickly skip to that segment on playback.

Plug and play. Automatically sets the channels and time as soon as you plug in the VCR and attach it to cable service or an antenna.

Power backup. This lets the VCR retain clock and program settings during brief power outages.

Programming via menus. Found on virtually all VCRs, even those with more advanced programming. A menu on the TV screen prompts you through the programming routines as you set time and channel with the remote or with controls on the console.

Quick-start transport. Cuts the time needed to shift from stop to play, play to rewind, or play to fast forward. Standard on most VCRs.

Remote control. Standard even with low-end models. A universal remote—one that works TV sets, VCRs, and cable boxes of various brands—is now common. A VCR universal remote features tape controls; channel selection is secondary. A well-designed remote is comfortable to hold and has clearly labeled buttons grouped by function and differentiated by size, shape, or color. Look for a model that makes often-used buttons stand out.

• *Useful for particular needs:*

Dimming display. For bedroom VCRs, this turns down the console's brightness.

Extra heads. Most current VCRs have four heads. Only some of the cheapest models have two; these can't produce special effects such as clean-looking freeze-frames.

Front-mounted audio and video jacks. They allow quick-and-easy hookup of a camcorder or a second VCR.

LP speed. A medium speed between SP and EP in length and picture quality.

Multilingual menus. These come in English, Spanish, or French.

One-button skip. Lets you fast-forward 30 seconds or a minute with each press of the button.

Quasi S-VHS playback. Lets you play higher-resolution S-VHS tapes, but without improved S-VHS picture quality.

• *Useful for people who edit tapes:*

Audio dub. Lets you add music or narration to existing recordings.

Flying erase head. Lets you insert segments without noticeable video glitches.

Jog-shuttle. Located on the remote or the console, this is a two-part control—one part to let you shuttle quickly, the other to slowly jog frame by frame. It's especially helpful for editing tapes. On many models, tape-motion controls are made to look like a shuttle wheel.

Title generator. Lets you superimpose printed titles and captions.

• *Not worth paying extra for:*

Auto head-cleaning. This consists of a tiny felt-tipped arm that gently rubs the video heads whenever a tape is inserted. Machines without this feature have worked fine for thousands of hours.

Picture enhancements. Features such as Mitsubishi's Tape Optimization and Sony's Automatic Picture Control are supposed to improve signal quality and thus enhance picture quality.

Camcorders

Even inexpensive models produce fine video these days.

Last CR report: October 1997
Ratings: page 81
Brand repair histories: page 14
Expect to pay: $400 to $2100

What's available

8mm. Compact and light, 8mm camcorders use cassettes about the size of an audiocassette. Most cassettes hold two hours. The tapes won't play in a standard VHS VCR; copy the tape onto a VHS cassette or connect the camcorder to a TV set and use it for playback. (8mm VCRs exist, but aren't commonly available.) The pictures produced by 8mm camcorders are of similar quality to those from VHS-C, but 8mm produces better sound than non-hi-fi VHS-C models. Price range: $400 to $1000.

Compact VHS (VHS-C). Another compact format, these models use cassettes about the size of a cigarette pack. Tapes typically hold 30 minutes on fast speed, 90 minutes on slow. VHS-C uses an adapter to play tapes in any VHS VCR. Price range: $450 to $1000.

Full-sized VHS. They use the same cassettes as a VHS VCR. Most tapes hold two hours at the recording speed typically used (SP). These camcorders are bulky and heavy—more than five pounds. Camcorders in this format, once the dominant type, are now fading away. Price range: $400 to $1000.

'High band.' Hi8 and S-VHS-C, premium variants of compact camcorders, deliver a sharper picture than 8mm or VHS-C models. But you'll get the full benefit of that enhanced video resolution only if you watch the tape on a TV set that has an S-video input and use Hi8 or S-VHS-C tape. Price range: $850 to $2100.

Digital video cassette (DVC). Digital models use the newly standardized DVC format, which can record very high quality images. Some digital models have the ability to transfer digital video and sound directly to a suitably equipped PC for editing or viewing. Prices are high for now, as is typical of new technology, but have already started to come down substantially. DVC models have been introduced by Sony, Panasonic, JVC, RCA, and Sharp. Price range: $2000 to $3500.

What's new

In addition to the new DVC digital format, manufacturers continue to make improvements within the limitations of the existing formats. As a result, camcorders sold today are apt to be smaller, lighter, and easier to use. Features that used to be found only on high-end models—color LCD viewfinders, image stabilization, built-in video lights, a wide-range zoom lens, and stereo audio—continue to migrate to lower-priced models.

Other features. Sony's 8mm long-play option provides twice the recording time of SP, but with a degraded image quality in the models we tested in 1996. Colors tended to flicker in hue and saturation.

Canon's FlexiZone focusing feature lets you direct the focus by positioning a small rectangle in the viewfinder image. Wherever you move the rectangle, that's where the camcorder focuses. FlexiZone can also lock the exposure setting to the lighting in that rectangle. In our tests, the feature worked as described and can be helpful in problem situations, although the manual focus and exposure overrides can also handle problem situations well.

Reliability

According to reader surveys, about 1 in 10 compact camcorders bought from 1991 to 1996 has needed repair. Among compact formats, Panasonic VHS-C and JVC VHS-C, and Sony 8mm models have been among the more reliable; RCA 8mm and Canon Hi8 models have been among the less reliable. See the brand repair histories on page 14.

Shopping strategy

Any camcorder can do a decent job of recording family gatherings or baby's first steps. While overall picture quality and color vary, picture quality is only loosely

Battery basics

In a recent reader survey, insufficient battery life was the number one complaint readers had about their camcorders. Most units, including those in our most recent test, come with a nickel-cadmium battery pack that lasts up to about an hour. If you tape longer, consider buying a larger-capacity battery. They cost about $60 and can typically double battery life.

Manufacturers recommend that you discharge the battery after every fifth charge to avoid a "memory" effect, which prevents batteries from charging to their full capacity. Pushing a refresh button, a feature available on most models, will drain the battery completely in about four hours. You can instead leave the camcorder on for a couple of hours, but the discharge will be less complete. Recharging takes about an hour.

Some models can also run on alkaline batteries for about an hour. That's handy when there's no electrical outlet nearby or when you don't have time to recharge the battery.

connected to price. In our most recent tests, we found some models priced at $400 or so that could produce pictures as good as those costing $600.

The choice of format determines the size of the camcorder and the running time of the tape. The compact formats—8mm and VHS-C—are the biggest sellers. Stepping up to a high-band version—Hi8 or S-VHS-C—used to cost extra, but now Hi8 prices overlap with those of standard models. High-band models produce slightly sharper images.

Sound quality also separates the formats; 8mm is inherently superior to non-hi-fi VHS-C. The built-in microphone on most camcorders, however, would not do justice to a performance of Beethoven's "Fifth." All are adequate for speech, and the best are likely to be fine for a school musical or recital.

Decide what to spend. A basic 8mm or VHS-C camcorder starts at about $400. Spending between $500 and $850 gets you extra features that may make shooting fun or more convenient, but have little effect on basic performance. Spending more than $850 can buy a Hi8 or S-VHS-C model.

What's in the stores. The biggest sellers are Sony, Panasonic, RCA, JVC, and Sharp. Sony is the major maker of 8mm camcorders, while Matsushita (maker of Panasonic) and JVC dominate the VHS world.

Using the Ratings. For our most recent tests, we took a quick look at four basic models. Thxe models were evaluated primarily for picture quality. A panel of trained experts looked at footage shot at each models' available speeds, in sunshine and under controlled stuidio lightly, to rate the quality of the images. Those noted as similar should perform much the same as the tested model, although less features may vary. New models are introduced starting in January and February. If you can't find a model, call the manufacturer; see page 342.

Key features

• ***Features you'll usually find:***

Fade. Lets you add professional-looking fade-in and fade-out effects—but most effective when used sparingly.

Speed control. Every camcorder includes an SP (standard-play) speed. A few 8mm models have a slower LP speed, which doubles recording time. All VHS-C camcorders have an even slower EP (extended-play) speed, which triples recording time. The slower speeds almost always mean some loss of picture quality.

Zoom. Typically a rocker switch—you press one end to zoom in, the other to widen the view. On most camcorders, the zoom ratio ranges from 8:1 to 16:1. Some offer a digital zoom that extends the range to about 200:1, but with some fall-off in picture quality. Some models let you vary the zoom speed by how hard you press the switch.

• ***Extras you'll sometimes find:***

Audio/video input. This lets you record material from another camcorder or from a VCR—useful in copying part of someone else's video onto your own.

Battery options. Most models let you install a bigger battery than the original. Extra-capacity batteries typically run about twice as long as the one supplied. For more information, see "Battery Basics," page 41.

Color viewfinder. Nice to have if you must watch an event from behind the camcorder, or if color aids your narration, say, when you're taping a tour of your flower garden. A color viewfinder isn't any better than a black-and-white one for composing and focusing.

Editing features. An edited tape can

be more fun to watch, but editing can be a chore: Only one in three readers had used their editing features in the past year. You hook up the camcorder to a VCR and edit while looking at the TV screen, at a fold-out LCD screen, or through the viewfinder. Features that help a camcorder interact with a VCR can make editing easier (for our report on VCRs, see page 36). For example, an optional editing remote control can be synchronized with a VCR or a VCR jack that lets you use the camcorder to control tape maneuvers in a similarly equipped VCR. "Random-assemble edit" is a feature that remembers the start and end of scenes you select and then copies them automatically to a tape in the VCR. It also has a jack for an optional editing remote control that works with a same brand VCR, as well as audio dubbing, which lets you add background music to a scene you've taped. Standard on camcorders is a flying-erase head, which provides clean transitions—no rainbows or glitches—when you record one scene over another.

Electronic image stabilization. This increasingly common feature aims to iron the jitters out of handheld shots. Effectiveness varies somewhat from brand to brand, according to our tests. Some versions of this feature can slightly mar picture clarity. At best, image stabilizers provide only a moderate improvement in steadiness. A video tripod is still the best tool for steady shots.

Fast shutter speeds. Speeds faster than the "normal" 1/60th of a second can be useful to study, say, a golf swing in slow motion or frame by frame but don't enhance picture quality at normal speed. The fastest speeds require bright daylight.

Focus selection. Autofocus adjusts for maximum contrast; manual-focus override is sometimes needed for problem situations, such as in low light. With motorized manual focus, you may have to tap buttons repeatedly to focus just right.

Fold-out LCD screen. Higher-priced camcorders often have a small LCD screen that lets you monitor the taping from a foot or so away from the camcorder. In some models, the screen replaces the viewfinder. A screen makes it easy to watch replays of a tape on the camcorder, but its image washes out in bright light, and it cuts battery life significantly unless it is turned off.

Manual controls. In many high-end camcorders, these let you control exposure, shutter speed, white balance, and focus at your option.

Microphone jack. Unlike the built-in microphone, an external microphone doesn't pick up noises from the camcorder itself, and typically improves audio performance.

Remote control. This is handy when using the camcorder as a playback device. Remotes are not dependable at large distances or in sunlight. Some remotes are as small as a business card.

Title generator. Lets you use a built-in character generator to superimpose printed titles and captions.

Compact cameras

The APS format has some benefits, but the established 35mm format continues to dominate. Both types have performed well in our tests.

Last CR report: November 1997
Ratings: page 74
Expect to pay: $100 to $400

Compact cameras, with or without zoom, outsell 35mm single-lens relfex cameras. In return for the compactness and convenience of these small cameras, you give up the ability to see exactly what the lens sees.

APS and 35mm

The APS (for Advanced Photo System) format attempts to redesign the entire business of film handling, processing, and filing.

Here's how APS differs from 35mm:

Price and availability. Prices of APS film and processing remain high, but both are generally available. As of spring of 1997, some one-hour chains were offering on-site processing, but only in about 1 out of 10 of their outlets. Most one-hour labs still farm out APS film, which means a longer wait.

Print quality. APS film has a transparent magnetic coating that some APS cameras make use of to record data, such as date and time of each shot, and exposure-related information for the film processor. Our most recent tests comparing prints from 35mm and APS cameras revealed no significant differences in overall print quality.

Film-handling. APS makes film loading slightly simpler and more foolproof. It's perhaps APS's biggest advantage so far over 35mm. You simply drop in a film cartridge. The camera does the rest. APS gives you a choice of three print shapes: regular (4x6 inches), wide (4x7), and panoramic (4x12). Some 35mm cameras allow regular and panoramic shots. Only with APS can you change the shape of your pictures when you order reprints.

Storage of negatives. APS negatives are stored inside the original cartridge, safer than loose negatives. An index print, with thumbnail photos of all exposures, is standard with APS and available at some labs with 35mm.

Date stamp. An APS camera can record the time and date on the film's magnetic coating so the processor can print the date of the shot on the back or front of the print. Some 35mm cameras can imprint the date in the picture.

What's available

In both formats, there are basic choices:

Cameras with a long-range zoom lens. A zoom range of around 3 or 4x offers a lot of flexibility in composition. Cameras with a zoom like this also have autoexposure and autofocus. Price range: $180 to $500.

Cameras with a medium-range zoom lens. These cameras also have autoexposure and autofocus. With a zoom range of around 2x, they can adjust the framing of a shot only moderately. Generally, the less powerful the telephoto end of the zoom, the more compact the camera. Price range: $150 to $200.

Cameras with a fixed lens and autoexposure. A fixed-focal length lens often rules out intimate close-ups but is adequate for travel scenes and group shots. This type of camera is good enough for snapshots. Such cameras can be smaller and lighter. Price range: $50 to $150.

Basic and single-use cameras. These are for people who want to aim and shoot and who aren't fussy about results. Such cameras have no adjustment for exposure or focus. Those without a flash restrict you to shooting outdoors in bright light. Price range: $5 to $50.

Shopping strategy

Most compacts deliver acceptable photos. Some even match the quality of a single-lens reflex camera under some conditions. Zoom models can handle distant subjects and wide-angle group shots. Medium-range zoom models offer a good compromise between flexibility and "pocketability." Specialized features that might draw you to a certain model include a panoramic option, weatherproofing or an infinity focus lock.

Whichever camera you're interested in, hold it to your eye and check its viewfinder, controls, grip, and balance.

Before buying a camera, consider its

Another type of camera: Single-lens reflex

If your interest in photography is casual, you'll probably be satisfied with an inexpensive compact camera or even a single-use camera. But if you have the interest and the time to invest in photography as a hobby, consider a single-lens reflex (SLR) camera, which accepts interchangeable lenses and special accessories that can adapt to all photo situations. SLRs are now available in APS format.

One advantage of an SLR is that what you see is exactly what the camera sees—the view is through the camera's lens. Our tests through the years have shown the optical quality of all the major brands of SLRs to be consistently high. Look for the features you want, then shop for price. These days, SLRs are generally sold without a lens, or are bundled with a zoom lens—a good, versatile choice. But watch out for packages that include a name-brand camera and an inferior off-brand lens.

Here are the types you'll come across:

- **Auto-focus SLRs. Price: body only, $230 to more than $1200. Expect to add another $100 to $150 for a moderate-range zoom lens.**
- **Manual-focus SLRs. These are still available in some brand lines. Price: body only, starting at less than $200 to more than $500. Manual lenses are priced similarly to autofocus ones, but the selection may be more limited.**
- **SLRs with non interchangeable lenses. These highly automated hybrids offer less versatility than an SLR but more than a compact. This type, promoted mainly by Olympus, has an SLR viewfinder and a built-in zoom lens. The zoom ranges go from about 28 to 35 mm at the wide angle end to 110 to 180 mm at the telephoto end.**

weight; lugging extra ounces around your neck or in your pocket or handbag quickly takes a toll. Also, a heavy camera is harder to use.

If you like to shoot close-ups, consider a zoom model, which will allow you to compose for a tighter shot.

Nearly all cameras these days run on batteries—either alkaline AA cells or expensive but long-lasting lithium cells. Battery life depends on the size and type, on the camera, and on the flash's range.

Decide what to spend. The more you spend, generally, the more features you get: zoom, autofocusing, and autoexposure. Expect to pay extra for a model with a zoom lens.

Few people pay list price for a camera. The discount you get depends on the local competition. Check ads in magazines and newspapers, and ask local camera stores whether they'll match competing discount-store prices.

What's in the stores. Discounters like Caldor, Lechmere, Nobody Beats the Wiz, the GoodGuys, and Fedco are where most compact cameras are sold.

The top-selling brands include Kodak, Canon, Minolta, and Olympus.

Using the Ratings. Almost any of the models tested would be a fine choice. The Ratings are based on performance and convenience, including tests that reveal image quality—lens sharpness and freedom from flare, from distortion, and from chromatic aberration. Don't disregard models lower in the Ratings. Some have special features you may want. If you can't find a model, call the manufacturer; see page 342.

Key features

Autoexposure. This regulates the shutter speed and lens opening. In our tests, all such cameras have given nicely exposed pictures in most lighting conditions when using appropriate speed film.

Autofocus. This frees you from having to focus the camera manually and ensures crisp pictures almost every time. Some models aim an infrared beam at the subject to measure its distance from the lens; some analyze detail in the image to determine the correct focus.

Built-in flash. This automatically activates whenever it's needed.

Motorized film-handling. Automatic film loading, film advance, and rewind ensure that the camera is properly loaded and ready for the next shot. With APS cameras, you simply pop open the film compartment and drop in the film cartridge. With 35mm cameras, you open the camera's back, insert the cartridge, and pull out the film leader a few inches just before closing the back—still a simple job.

Weatherproofing. Some models are sealed for protection from sand and spray, although not from immersion in water.

Receivers

Modestly priced models now offer full video switching, surround-sound capabilities, and lots of power.

Last CR report: February 1996
Price range: $150 to $1100

What's available

Basic **stereo-only** receivers make up the low end of the market. They're fine for a conventional component-audio system. A power output of 60 to 100 watts or so per channel is the norm. Expect to spend $175 to $250. Some high-end brands offer basic models with more power, for a lot more money.

More than three-quarters of receivers on the market are **A/V surround-sound** receivers. These have connections for hooking up video gear and audio-switching capability, and they can drive extra surround-sound speakers.

Dolby Pro Logic is a form of sound processing that converts special coding, found on most movie soundtracks and some network TV programs, and directs it to three front speakers, for main movie sound, and to two rear speakers, for "ambience" sound. Entry-level Dolby Pro Logic models can be had for about $250.

Spending more—$400 or so—buys a receiver with more connections, more power, and features such as other surround modes. Models priced at more than $500 typically deliver lots of power and switching abilities.

THX receivers are another type of surround-sound receiver. They use a patented design to simulate the acoustics heard in theaters. A THX receiver typically has a Dolby Digital AC-3 decoder, six amplifiers to handle the six channels of sound including a subwoofer (for deep bass rumbles), and controller components. An entry-level THX receiver costs $1400 to $2000; a complete setup, $4000.

Dolby Digital AC-3 receivers split the sound into five full-range discrete channels, plus a deep-bass channel. The format is sometimes referred to as "5.1 format" for the five main speakers plus the subwoofer. (Dolby Pro Logic is a four-channel format even though it uses five speakers.) To take advantage of the format, special software and an AC-3-compatible video source are needed. (See "Movies on disc," page 38.) Price: $700 and up.

What's new

Now that Dolby AC-3 is about to supersede it, the price of Dolby Pro Logic has fallen so low that all but the cheapest component receivers come with it.

Manufacturers have beefed up the power output to the center channel to equal that of the left and right main channels. That gives home theater a more dramatic impact and prevents the center channel from being "outshouted" at loud volume.

Receivers with front-channel power of 80/80/80 watts or more are common. Surround-channel power remains considerably lower, since those speakers aren't expected to reproduce power-hungry deep-bass frequencies. The typical power—20 to 50 watts per speaker—is more than adequate.

Reliability

Component receivers have been around for so long that few bugs are left in their design; they also have few moving parts, which adds to their reliability. As a result, receivers are generally quite reliable products.

Shopping strategy

For some years now, very good and excellent performance has been the norm in our tests. Receivers typically deliver an accurate frequency response, essential for faithful reproduction of music. Radio reception is less of a problem, too, though the ability to capture a station in rural areas does vary. Even the lowest-powered models these days have ample power to fill an average-sized living room with sound.

For information on setting up a home-theater system, loudspeaker compatibility, and power requirements, see pages 23 through 28.

Decide on what to spend. Stereo-only models are inexpensive but limited.

Decide on the features. A no-frills model is worth considering only if you

How much power do you need?

Even inexpensive receivers have plenty of power. But if you want to figure out how much power your sound system actually needs, here's how:

Determine the sound "liveness" of your listening room. A space with hard floors, scatter rugs, and plain wood furniture will be acoustically "live"; one with thick carpeting, heavy curtains, and upholstered furniture, relatively "dead."

Locate the room size (in cubic feet) and liveness type in the chart and note the multiplier. Look up the speaker's minimum power requirement, as determined by the manufacturer, in the speakers' owner's manual. To determine the watts per channel needed, multiply that figure by the multiplier.

For a 4000-cubic-foot room with average acoustics, the multiplier is 1.5. With speakers that require 12 watts of power, the minimum amplification you'd need to drive the speakers at moderately high volume is 18 watts of power per channel (1.5 times 12). To do justice to bass-heavy music, however, you'd need to double or triple that figure.

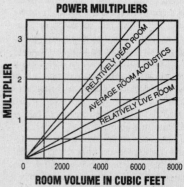

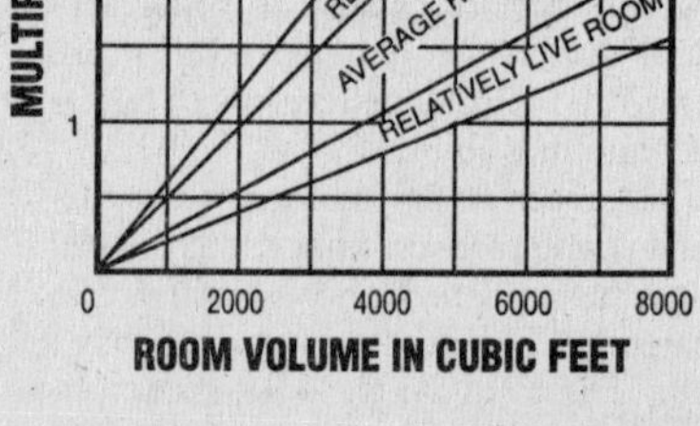

don't think you'll ever incorporate video components in your system. For about $100 in most brand lines, you can step up to a Dolby Pro Logic model. Dolby Pro-Logic is currently the dominant form of surround sound on prerecorded movies. At the high end are models with THX or Dolby Digital AC-3, enhanced home-theater systems. Spending more buys power and features like a learning remote control, a graphical user interface, or more surround-sound modes.

What's in the stores. Receivers sell under more than 30 brand names. But five companies—Sony, Pioneer, Kenwood, Technics, and JVC—sell more than 80 percent of the models.

Key features

• *Recommended:*

Bass boost is helpful for making small speakers sound fuller.

Digital radio-tuning is now standard, along with features such as seek (automatic searching for the next listenable station), direct-tuning buttons (to key in a station's numeric frequency), and 20 to 40 presets to call up your favorite station at the touch of a button. To catch stations too weak to pick up in the seek mode, most receivers also have a knob or buttons to let you step up and down manually. Manual stepping is convenient in one-channel increments. But most models creep in half- or quarter-steps, forcing a lot of unnecessary button tapping.

Direct frequency radio-tuning lets you enter a station's frequency on a keypad.

Digital signal processing is becoming common. DSP alters the sound signal by adding delays or reverb to simulate the acoustics of a nightclub, concert hall, or arena—a "soundfield," as it's called.

Tone controls let you adjust bass and treble. Easiest to use are knobs—one for bass and one for treble. A graphic equalizer breaks the sound spectrum into more sections, a design that confers either greater control or greater confusion, depending on the design of the receiver and your mechanical aptitude. It's not much more effective than bass and treble controls unless it has at least seven frequency bands. Instead of tone controls, some receivers come with "tone styles" such as jazz, classical, or rock, each accentuating a different frequency pattern; often you can craft your own styles, too. Since tone controls are most useful in correcting for room acoustics and listening preferences, not musical genre, the tone-style approach seems needlessly indirect.

Tone-control bypass temporarily defeats any tone-control settings.

Remote control generally works only with the same brand of equipment and only if those components aren't too old. The design of audio remotes lags way behind that of video remotes. It's hard to find a receiver remote that feels comfortable in the hand, has easy-to-find primary-command keys, and buttons grouped and differentiated by size, shape, and color. More often, you'll see rows of small, crowded look-alike buttons.

Speakers

Speakers are the key to good sound. Buy the best you can afford.

Last CR report:
Budget speakers, February 1996;
Speakers for home theater, March 1997
Ratings: page 60 (budget models); 63 (home theater)
Expect to pay: $30 to $600 or more

What's available

Mini. Smaller than a shoe box, these speakers are useful as extension speakers in the kitchen or workshop, as rear speakers in a home-theater system, or for transforming a personal tape player or portable CD player into a more substantial sound system. Don't expect great bass. Price range: $100 or less per pair.

Bookshelf. These are sized to fit on a bookshelf and are suitable for a medium-sized room. Most lack the size to produce a rich, loud bass, but can do a very good job over the rest of the sound spectrum. They're also good as the surround speakers in a Dolby Pro Logic system. Price range: $100 to $300 per pair.

Floor-standing. Speakers this large have a woofer of sufficient size to push the volume of air needed for full, loud bass. You'll find the best value—and sound to satisfy most listeners—among the less expensive models of this type. Floor-standing speakers can fill an average-sized living room with loud sound and a large living room with fairly loud sound. This size is also suitable for use near the TV set. Price range: $300 or more for a decent pair. More expensive speakers are built like furniture, with wood cabinetry. They're often designed in unusual configurations and with exotic-sounding materials or technology., but speakers can produce superb frequency response without resorting to titanium, beryllium, or "oxygen-free copper wiring." Speakers at this level are intended for large rooms or serious listening. A drawback to this type is its size.

Satellite/subwoofer systems. Whether purchased separately or in sets of three to six speakers, satellite/subwoofer systems consist of a bass module and two to five small, easy-to-place satellite speakers for mid-range and treble tones. The small satellites fit easily on shelves or above a TV set; they're also easy to mount on the wall. The bass module can be put anywhere—behind the sofa, under the bed—since the ear cannot tell which direction bass frequencies come from. As such, these speaker sets can be an excellent solution to the problem of getting good sound without overwhelming the room with large floor-standing boxes. Volume controls are often found on satellite systems that use a powered bass module; they adjust the match between the bass module and the satellites. Price range: $300 and up for a three-piece system.

Powered speakers. These have built-in amplifiers, so you can hook them up to a computer or a portable CD player and have a sound system without the need for a receiver. Some are quite small and provide low fidelity; others are potentially on a par with bookshelf speakers. Price range: $20 and up per pair.

What's new

With the rise of home theater, speakers are now marketed in two ways: as pairs or sets of "audio" speakers, for traditional stereophonic listening, and singly or in sets of three or more "video" speakers for equipping a home theater. Video speakers designed for the "center" channel typically have magnetic shielding so they can be close to a TV set without distorting its picture.

Reliability

Speakers are likely to last for years without problems, although playing music too loud can damage them. So can a bad match between speakers and receiver, as the section on page 28 explains.

Shopping strategy

Investing in speakers will do more to improve your system's sound quality than money spent on any other component. Our tests show that, except for the bass part of the sound spectrum, even cheaper speakers usually reproduce sound accurately. But speakers of equal accuracy are likely to sound different, so it's a good idea to listen before you buy. At the least, make sure you can return or exchange the speakers if they don't sound as good at home as in the showroom. If you can audition speakers in a listening room at the store, compare only two pairs at a time, and make sure they're equally loud; each time, judge the pair you prefer against the next pair. Take along a recording you know well that gives both the bass and treble ranges a good workout.

Check the speakers' impedance. Higher-impedance models (six or eight ohms) allow more freedom in choosing a receiver (see "System Setup" on page 27).

You don't have to spend a lot of money to create a home theater, nor do you usually have to buy a new set of speakers. By using an existing stereo pair for front and a second, smaller pair for surround sound, you need only buy a center-channel speaker to complete a Dolby Pro Logic system.

Decide what to spend. For a budget system, you may not want to spend more than $200 per pair or set, especially if your music isn't bass-heavy. Spending $300 to $600 buys speakers that should satisfy most listeners, even in the bass. Spending even more buys better bass, the ability to play louder, and a nicer cabinet.

For home-theater speakers, a center-channel speaker or pair of surround speakers costs $80 to $250; three-piece packages range from $100 to $300. In general, price correlates with accurate sound reproduction.

What's in the stores. There are more than 300 brands of speakers, many made by small American companies. Bose is the biggest-selling brand.

Using the Ratings. In our most recent tests, we looked at center-channel and surround speakers, measuring accuracy based on their frequency response. We also list budget-priced conventional speakers that are still available from our February 1996 report. Expect speaker models to be on store shelves for two to three years before being phased out. If you can't find a model, call the manufacturer; see page 342.

CD players

Superb sound capability is the norm. Base your decision on disc capacity, price, and features.

Last CR report: February 1997
Ratings: page 67 (full-sized); 71 (portable)
Brand repair histories: page 11
Expect to pay: $75 to $800

What's available

Single-disc players. This is the least expensive type and, compared with other component-sized models, the most compact. It usually has a lot of features to make taping from disc to cassette more convenient. Price range: $100 to $200.

Carousel and magazine changers. Multiple-disc changers, which hold 5 to 10 discs, can play hours of music nonstop, and come in two varieties.

A magazine changer uses a slide-in cartridge the size of a small, thick book. Capable of holding 6 to 10 discs, each cartridge doubles as a convenient disc-storage box. A carousel changer, which holds 5 or 6 discs around a platter, is easier to load and unload than the magazine type; most let you change discs that aren't playing without interrupting the music. Carousel players that use a slide-out drawer can fit in a stack of components; those that load from the top must be on top. Price range: $200 to $300.

CD jukeboxes. Also known as megachangers, jukeboxes can store 25 to 200 discs. They're marketed as a way to manage and store an entire music collection. Most models let you segment your collection by musical genre, composer, artist, and so forth. Inputting all this data can be tedious. Models that allow connection to a computer keyboard make the task easier. You can set a jukebox to shuffle and play random selections all night or play discs only from your choice of genre.

To enjoy these conveniences, you have to tolerate some drawbacks: CD jukeboxes can be bulky, inconvenient to load, or noisy and slow in selecting CDs. Price range: $200 to $800.

Portables. The current crop of players averages several hours more playing time on a pair of AA batteries than did the players we tested just two years ago. And new models are also generally equipped with better headphones, the most important determinant of overall sound quality in a portable (see "Headphones for portables," page 54). But appreciable differences abound in battery life, headphone sound, and resistance to sudden jolts.

Portable CD players can be plugged into a wall outlet using an AC adapter. Most take two AA cells, but some require four. Battery use can be prodigious and varies considerably from model to model, according to our tests. Over the long run, rechargeable batteries are the cheapest way to power these units, although rechargeables last only about half as long as alkalines between charges. Most CD portables come with a built-in charger, and many throw in a set of rechargeable batteries, usually of the nickel-cadmium type. Price range: $80 to $200.

What's new

Component CDs are now a mature product, with little real innovation and change. Jukeboxes and portables are another story. For as little as $350, hundreds of dollars less than even a year ago, you can buy a CD jukebox that holds 100 to 200 discs. Prices for portables are dropping, too. According to our most recent tests, portables are using batteries more efficiently than they used to, and they are better at resisting the bumps of walking or a car ride. "Buffers," a memory feature that continuously stores music the machine can draw on when jolted, are becoming more common and much more lengthy—up to 40 seconds, in some models. (They still can't withstand the jolts of jogging.)

Reliability

CD players are very reliable devices. On our 1996 Annual Questionnaire, readers reported their experiences with CD players bought new between 1992 and 1996. Overall, single-disc machines and carousel models were extremely reliable, magazine changers slightly less so. We had insufficient data to evaluate the repair histories of CD jukeboxes. For more information, see the brand repair histories on page 11.

Shopping strategy

Virtually every CD player can produce superb hi-fi sound. The differences in sound reproduction we've uncovered in our tests are apparent only to a trained listener or a laboratory instrument. More significant are the differences in how well the players handle adverse conditions, like being bumped or playing a damaged disc. Spending more buys more features, not performance.

Multi-disc models are now priced only a little higher than single-play units. We think the carousel design is easier to use than the magazine type. (If you have a CD system in your car, however, you might want a compatible magazine changer at home; many auto systems are based on magazine changers.) If uninterrupted play isn't crucial, consider a single-play model. You're likely to get more features for the money than you would with a changer. Consider a jukebox if you're willing to spend the time organizing your discs.

Decide what to spend. Prices also track with disc capacity, with single-play models the cheapest and jukeboxes the most expensive. (Magazine changers tend to be costlier than carousel changers.) Expect to spend less than $100 for a basic portable. Portables that come with a car kit—the cigarette lighter and cassette adapters for power and sound—typically cost $20 or $25 more than equivalent models without the kit. But those models won't necessarily have other features or attributes that are useful in the car. Models with long memory buffers generally cost more than those with shorter buffers or none at all, though that additional memory may not increase bump resistance.

What's in the stores. Look for closeouts of discontinued models in late summer and early fall and for sales during the heaviest buying periods—December and June. Component CD players are marketed under more than 40 brand names. Five brands account for most sales: Sony, Pioneer, JVC, Technics, and Kenwood. Sony's Discman line makes the largest number of portable CD players. Other major brands include Panasonic, Magnavox, and Aiwa.

Using the Ratings. Most recently, we tested portables, although some of the componet-sized models are still available from our Febuary 1997 report. In our most recent test, all the portables proved capable of delivering excellent sound. Pick the model with the level of bump resistance and features you need for the ways you'll most often use it. For an earlier report, we tested component models. If you're interested in a model that excels at playing scratched or fingerprint-smudged discs, choose a model that scored well at handling problem discs. Similar models should perform much the same as the tested model; features may vary. If you can't find a model, call the manufacturer; see page 342.

Key features

• *Recommended for full-sized models:*

Calendar display. This shows a block of numbers representing the tracks on the active disc and highlights the track that's playing. As the disc plays, numbers for previous tracks disappear—and you can see at a glance how many selections are left.

Numeric keypad. On the remote and the console, this lets you punch in the numbers of the tracks you want to listen to. It's faster than holding down Up and Down buttons to get to a particular track.

Remote control. It's still not standard equipment, so make sure the model you're considering has one. Buttons on the remote should be grouped by function or color-coded and be visible in dim light. CD remotes are typically fairly simple and work only the player.

• *Useful for particular needs:*

Delete track. Allows you to skip over music you don't like, then play the rest of the disc from start to finish.

Favorite-track selection. You select favorite tracks from your discs; the unit then "remembers" your selections when

Headphones for portables

Headphones are the weak link in personal stereos. Most give you much lower sound quality than the walkabout or CD player is capable of. These small headphones are especially poor at handling low bass. Replacing them can markedly improve the sound you hear. In our tests, we've found that replacement headphones have reproduced sound more accurately than most of the headphones that came with the personal stereos.

The top performer, the Sennheiser HD 580 Precision, was indeed very precise—as it should be, given its $300 price. Other models tested were much less expensive—the Koss Porta-Pro Jr., $40; the Sennheiser HD 36, $25; the Sennheiser HD 445, $70 (formerly HD 440 II); the Optimus (formerly Realistic) Pro-60, $50; and the Aiwa HP-A081, $10. The Aiwa and the Sennheiser HD 36 are by far the best values of that bunch. The Aiwa headphones come as original equipment with some Aiwa personal stereos.

Headphones come in different styles. The ones that are likely to give you the best sound are the muff style, which sit on or over the ear, or the ball style, which pivot to better contact the ear. Bud headphones, which sit inside the ear, can be better at insulating you from outside noises.

discs are reinserted.

Music sampling. Scans a disc and plays a few seconds of each selection—like scanning up and down on a car radio.

Shuffle play. Mixes the playing order in a random sequence. Look for nonrepeat shuffle.

Single-play drawer or slot. Found on some magazine changers and jukeboxes, this lets you play a single disc without disturbing the ones already loaded.

• *Useful for taping:*

Auto edit. You enter the cassette's recording time, and the CD player lays out the disc's tracks, usually in sequence, to fill both sides of your tape.

Comprehensive time display. Lets you flip among four figures: time elapsed or time remaining, for the current track or the entire disc.

Digital output. A jack used for a digital conduit—either a fiber-optic or coaxial cable—to a digital recording device such as a minidisc recorder or a digital tape deck.

Fade out/fade in. Performs the audio equivalent of a movie fade for less abrupt starts and endings on tapes you make.

Music-peak finder. Scans for the loudest passage in a track you're going to record, so you can adjust the tape deck's recording level correctly and quickly.

Running-time total. Lets you total the time of tracks you're recording so you can fit the maximum on a tape.

Synchronizing jack. Lets you connect a cable to a tape deck of the same brand so you can start and stop both machines simultaneously.

• *Recommended for portables:*

AC adapter. Standard with nearly every portable. Besides running the player on house current, typically the adapter can also charge rechargeable cells.

Battery-level indicator. Virtually all players have some sort of indicator, usually a light that flashes, giving you little warning that your batteries are about to run out. The best show a scale that gets shorter, to reflect power remaining.

Hold/lock. Almost all players now have this important feature, which disables the controls so you don't inadvertently activate the player, turn it off, or change tracks. Some models lock controls electronically; others physically shield vulnerable controls under a moveable cover.

Rechargeable batteries. Supplied with a few players, otherwise rechargeable AA cells cost $5 to $30 per pair.

Track displays. All players have an LCD display that shows which track is playing. Many models also provide the elapsed time. The best displays add the time remaining on track and disc.

Cassette decks

Unlike receivers or CD players, decks vary a lot in performance. To some extent, you get what you pay for.

Last CR report: February 1996
Expect to pay: $100 to $1000

What's available

Dual-deck models. These decks are the most common. Also called "dubbing" decks, they lend themselves to copying tapes and playing cassettes in sequence for long stretches of uninterrupted music.

Dual decks come in two varieties: single-record models that allow playback from both cassette wells but can record from only one; and dual-record models that allow playback and recording from both wells. Dual-deck models usually give up a little in audio performance compared with single-deck machines. They tend to suffer slightly more from flutter (a wavy, watery sound defect), and their frequency response is slightly less accurate. Price range: $100 to $500.

Single-deck models. The tape drive in a single-tape deck used to be a cut above that in a comparably priced dual-deck machine, but dual-decks are catching up. Price range: $100 to $1000 or more.

What's new

Although cassette tape is, in many ways, a moribund medium, this analog technology still serves a need that digital competition such as the minidisc has yet to meet. One reason: price. Minidisc recorders run $350 and up; portable minidisc players start at $200. And it's still not clear whether the medium, invented and propelled by Sony, will ever catch on—not that many people are eager to rebuild their entire music collection from scratch.

In the meantime, other types of digital recorders and players have either disappeared or just haven't caught on. Digital compact cassette (DCC) is dead. Digital audio tape (DAT) has yet to move out of the professional realm. And CD-R, recordable CD, is still very expensive, generally more than $1000.

On the horizon is DVD-audio, a CD-sized disc that can hold much more music than a CD, and can display song titles and lyrics on the player.

Shopping strategy

Cassette decks have probably gotten as good as they are going to get. They are still the medium of choice for recording and playing music at home. The best decks can satisfy all but the most critical ear, despite tape's inherent limitations—slow access to individual tracks, background hiss, and a limited ability to capture the whole audible spectrum. A deck that has Dolby S, the most advanced noise-reduction circuitry, sounds nearly as clean as a CD player.

Decide what to spend. All but the cheapest decks should be capable of producing good or very good sound. Expect to pay from $200 to $500 for one that performs well. More money buys more convenience but may not improve the sound quality.

You can spend less by opting for a portable deck. Portables include boom boxes and walkabouts, most of which are playback devices only. You can hook up most walkabouts to a stereo system and get decent playing performance, although the small controls may not be convenient. Boom boxes sell for about $40 and up; walkabouts, $20 and up.

What's in the stores. Sony, JVC, and Pioneer are the leading brands.

Key features

• *Recommended:*

Adjustable bias control. This helps adjust the deck to the brand of tape you're using. Automatic bias control sets itself.

Autoplay. Will start playing the tape when it's fully rewound.

Autoreturn (memory rewind). Lets you cancel a recording and return to the tape's starting point.

Autoreverse. Automatically plays the flip side of the tape when you reach the end of side one.

CD sync. Links the deck to a CD player of the same brand to simplify recording.

Dolby noise suppression. Standard these days on most components. Dolby S, a step up from Dolby B and C, enhances the ability to reproduce noiseless loud and soft passages (dynamic range).

Intro scan. Plays the first few seconds of a track to help you choose which selections you want to hear.

Music search. Lets you move the tape directly to a particular track.

Real-time tape counter. Especially useful if it shows elapsed time in minutes and seconds and the tape time that remains.

Record mute. Inserts momentary silence between cuts when you record continuously; the silences can act as markers for search and scan features.

• *Features for tape monitoring:*

Three-head design. Found on many single-deck machines, this lets you monitor the music off the tape as you record.

Two-button recording and dubbing. Helps avoid inadvertent taping by requiring you to press two buttons instead of one.

Turntables: Going but not gone

Mindful of all the people who still treasure their collections of vinyl platters, major home-electronics manufacturers including Sony, Technics, Kenwood, and Onkyo make single-play turntables. Many models we've seen are priced at less than $200; a few sell for under $100. That's not too different from what they cost when we last tested turntables, in the early 1980s.

Many modern turntables come with the cartridge—the part that holds the needle, or stylus—already installed. The units work the same way they did years ago, rotating the turntable by direct drive or belt drive. Neither design holds an advantage, in our experience.

The once-ubiquitous "phono" input on the back of a receiver is now missing on some component receivers and on almost all minisystems. To compensate, many turntables are now designed with their own preamplifier. That allows you to connect them to the receiver via the "aux" line input, the same way you would an extra CD player or cassette deck. Be sure you get the right type for your system.

Minisystems

These instant sound systems are small and easy to set up. Watch out for confusing controls.

Last CR report: February 1996
Expect to pay: $200 to $1500

A minisystem offers reasonably good overall performance without the cost, clutter, and wiring headaches of a component system. These bookshelf-sized stereo systems typically come with a remote control and the following components: a digital AM/FM tuner powered by an amplifier, which can vary from less than 20 watts per channel to more than 100; a CD changer that holds 3, 6, or even 50 discs; a dual-well cassette deck; and small detachable speakers.

Components that are specifically designed to work only with each other make for easy use but are also a limitation. You can't upgrade most minisystems with bigger speakers or other components, nor can you add a second pair of speakers to send music to another room.

In our tests, we've found that minisystems, even good ones, are apt to be a notch below low- to midpriced component systems in quality because of limited speakers and unimpressive cassette decks. Adjustable bass and treble controls help overcome speaker defects, but many minisystems lack them.

What's available

Minisystems vary in size. Most have cabinets that measure about 11 inches wide and 14 inches high, with a molded facade that looks like many individual components in a stack, though most are one unit. (Standard-sized components are 17 inches wide.) A few minisystems are truly separate components; others can be divided in two and placed side by side on a shelf. More compact "microsystem" models, some as narrow as 6½ inches, are also available. Just about any minisytem can be used to enhance the sound from a TV set or VCR, but you'll need a separate remote to control the video. Price range of minisystems: $200 to $1500.

What's new

While minisystems mimic the functions of a rack system or a component system, they add some capabilities of their own. The controls are more integrated than on a component system, but sometimes confusingly so. Displays are often vivid, even hyperactive. Karaoke, which lets you sing along to special recordings using a microphone, has become quite common.

Shopping strategy

First, look for features you need. Also consider amplifier power. For a large living room (15 by 25 feet or more), you'll need 80 to 100 watts per channel. An average living room (10 by 25 feet) requires 40 to 80 watts per channel; a bedroom or dorm room (12 by 14 feet), 20 to 40 watts per channel.

Decide what to spend. Don't expect much from minisystems costing less than $300—they're not much more than glorified boom boxes. Systems in the $350-to-$500 price range begin to look and feel more like hi-fi separates. They generally have a CD changer instead of a single-disc player, a receiver with more power (20 to 50 watts per channel), and a good complement of features. Even in this price category, speakers and cassette decks can be problematic, our tests show.

What's in the stores. Sony, Aiwa, and JVC are the biggest-selling brands of minisystems. As with most electronic products, shelf life is short, with new models being introduced frequently.

Key features

Minisystems have many of the same features found in full-sized components; see the reports on receivers, CD players, and cassette decks. Some features are specific to minisystems:

Built-in clock. A clock lets you program the system to turn on at a predetermined time. You can also set the system's cassette deck to record from the radio, just as you time-shift with a VCR.

Karaoke. A feature that lets you sing along to background music and vocals. Some models come with a microphone.

Remote control. A minisytem's remote operates components that are designed to work together, which allows for a more simply designed remote than that for a component system of mixed brands. The downside: Buttons often perform two or more functions. And there are typically no buttons to work video components, such as those on the remote for a component receiver.

How to use the Ratings in the Buying Guide

- **Read the Recommendations for information on specific models and general buying advice.**
- **Note how the rated products are listed—in order of performance and convenience, price, or alphabetically.**
- **The overall score graph gives the big picture in performance. Notes on features and performance for individual models are listed in the Comments column or "Model details."**
- **Use the handy key numbers to find out the details on each model.**
- **Before going to press, we verify model availability for most products with manufacturers. Some tested models listed in the Ratings may no longer be available. Discontinued models are noted in Model details or Comments. Such models may actually still be available in some stores for part of 1998. Models indicated as successors should perform similarly to the tested models, according to the manufacturer. Features may vary.**
- **Models similar to the tested models, when they exist, are indicated in Comments or Model details.**
- **To find our last full report on a subject, check the reference above the Ratings chart or the eight-year index, page 346.**

Ratings Budget loudspeakers

& Recommendations

The tests behind the Ratings

We measure speaker performance in an echo-free chamber and then use a computer to simulate the effects of a room's walls and a receiver's tone controls. **Accuracy**, measured for tones ranging from deep bass to those a bit higher than most adults can hear, is given greatest weight in the **overall score.** For **bass handling**, we test bass to see how loudly you can play without much distortion (important for bass-heavy music). We measure **impedance** in ohms, a figure that affects the amount of current a speaker requires of a receiver. **Suggested minimum power** is what the receiver needs per channel to produce fairly loud sound in an average-sized room. **Price** is approximate retail.

Typical features for these models

• Sold in pairs. • Eight-ohm rating by the manufacturer. • Sound best if placed about 3½ feet from the side wall and 1 foot from the back wall.

Recommendations

Our tests show that, except for bass, even cheap speakers can accurately reproduce sound. Still, equally accurate speakers are likely to sound different. Listen before you buy. One model—the Yamaha NS-A636 ($120)—offers a low price and very good performance. We judged it a CR Best Buy.

See Buying Guide report, page 50. Last time rated in CONSUMER REPORTS: February 1996.

Overall Ratings

E ⊜ VG ⊖ G ○ F ◒ P ●

Listed in order of performance

Key no.	Brand and model	Price	Overall score (0–100; P F G VG E)	Accuracy	Bass handling	Impedance	Suggested min. power
1	**Altec Lansing** 85	$200		93/92	○	6 ohms	10 watts
2	**B.I.C.** Venturi 62si	265		92/92	⊖	7	10
3	**DCM** CX-07	190		94/87	⊖	6	6
4	**Phase Technology** 3T	260		92/89	⊜	6	13
5	**RA Labs** Mini Reference	224		91/91	○	4	11
6	**Pinnacle** AC 650	300		91/88	○	4	14
7	**Advent** Baby III	170		91/84	⊖	5	22

Key no.	Brand and model	Price	Overall score (0–100; P F G VG E)	Accuracy	Bass handling	Impedance	Suggested min. power
8	Yamaha NS-A636, A CR Best Buy	$120		91/85	⊖	7 ohms	6 watts
9	Optimus Pro LX5	300		88/88	●	6	16
10	Paradigm Titan	210		87/84	⊖	5	23

Model details

1 Altec Lansing 85 $200

• 17x9¾x9¼ in. • 15 lb.

The best accuracy makes this the top-rated model. Black cabinet. Tone correction for best accuracy: Set the bass to -1, the treble to -2. **Recommendation**: Excellent performance and a relatively low price make these a good value.

2 B.I.C. Venturi 62si $265

• 14½x9x8½ in. • 13 lb.

Compact size, very good bass handling, and magnetic shielding make this a good choice for home theater. Black cabinet. Tone correction: None. **Recommendation**: Excellent performance and a relatively low price make these a good value.

3 DCM CX-07 $190

• 15x8½x8¾ in. • 12 lb.

Magnetic shielding, very good bass handling, and built-in overload protection circuit to prevent speaker damage. Needs relatively little amp power. Black cabinet. Tone correction: Set the bass to +1, the treble to +3. **Model availability:** Discontinued. **Recommendation:** Excellent performance and a relatively low price make these a good value.

4 Phase Technology 3T $260

• 15½x8x8½ in. • 11 lb.

The best model for handling loud bass. These speakers are also sold singly at half the price per pair. Black cabinet. Tone correction: Set the bass to +1, the treble to +2. **Model availability:** Discontinued. **Recommendation**: Excellent performance, but on the expensive side.

5 RA Labs Mini Reference $224

• 14x8½x8¼ in. • 10 lb.

If you play loud music for long periods, use these only with a receiver that can handle Four-ohm speakers. Black cabinet. Tone correction: None. **Model availability:** Discontinued. **Recommendation**: Excellent performance and a relatively low price make these a good value.

6 Pinnacle AC 650 $300

• 16½x10x8¾ in. • 13 lb.

Only inaccuracy is a dip in the upper mid-range. For best sound, try these speakers farther than the usual 3½ feet from the side wall. If you play loud music for long periods, use these speakers only with a receiver that can handle 4-ohm speakers. Dark wood-finish cabinet. Tone correction: Set the treble to +2. **Recommendation**: Excellent performance, but on the expensive side.

7 Advent Baby III $170

• 16¼x10x6¾ in. • 13 lb.

The drop in treble makes for a muted sound (largely correctable). Black cabinet. Tone correction: Set the bass to +2, the treble to +5. **Recommendation**: Very good performer.

8 Yamaha NS-A636 $120

• 16¼x10½x11½ in. • 14 lb.

Big for this class, these speakers may not fit on a bookshelf. Magnetic shielding allows positioning near TV set. For better sound, try these speakers against the back wall. Black cabinet. Tone correction: Set the bass to +2, the treble to +5. **Recommendation**: Unusually low price and very good performance make these **A CR Best Buy**.

Can't find a model? Call the manufacturer. See page 342.

Ratings continued ▶

Ratings, continued

9 Optimus Pro LX5 $300

• $10\frac{1}{2}$x$6\frac{1}{2}$x6 in. • 7 lb.
A large spike in mid-bass creates a boomy sound quality. Since these speakers are not magnetically shielded, putting them close to a TV set can cause distortion. Black cabinet with unusual dipole tweeters mounted on top. Tone correction: None. **Recommendation:** There are better choices.

10 Paradigm Titan $210

• 13x$7\frac{3}{4}$x$9\frac{1}{2}$ in. • 10 lb.
Spike in mid-bass creates a boomy quality that may sound disturbing. Black cabinet. Tone correction: Set the bass to -1, the treble to +1. **Recommendation**: OK.

Some of the best mid-priced models from the March 1995 report are still available. All of these were judged good or better.

Ratings of mid-priced loudspeakers

Listed alphabetically

Brand and model	Price	Type	Recommendation
Allison AL 120 [1]	$400	Conventional	Good performer, good value.
Bose Acoustimass 5 Series II	725	3-piece	Very good performer with excellent bass.
Cambridge Soundworks New Ensemble [1]	600	3-piece	Good performer.
NHT Super Zero/SW1P	650	3-piece	Good performer.
Paradigm 7seMk3 [1]	575	Conventional	Good performer.
Phase Technology 7T	600	Conventional	Very good performer with excellent bass.
Signet SL-280 B/U	700	Conventional	Very good performer.
Yamaha NS-A325	500	3-piece	Very good performer, good value.

[1] *Needs receiver that can handle four-ohm speakers.*

For the most recent product Ratings

Ratings *Speakers for home theater*

& Recommendations

The tests behind the Ratings

Overall score mainly covers performance in tests in our anechoic chamber, where we measure how smoothly and uniformly speakers reproduce sounds. The center-channel speakers were scored for performance in Dolby Pro Logic normal mode, which reduces the bass; surround speakers were scored for use in a Dolby Pro Logic surround channel, which limits both the bass and treble. Closely ranked models aren't significantly different in overall quality. The **impedance** and **minimum power** measurements help match speakers to receiver; some impedances we measured were lower than the manufacturer's claim. Your receiver should deliver at least this amount of power per channel for the speakers to work properly. **Price** is approximate retail. Surround-sound speakers are typically sold in pairs, while center-channel speakers are sold singly.

Typical features for these models

• Spring-loaded wire connectors that accept dual-banana plugs or bare wires. • One or more woofers and a tweeter. • Removable black grille.

Recommendations

Most of these models would make fine home-theater speakers. If you're looking for a home-theater center-channel speaker, consider the B.I.C. V-52si ($80). Modestly priced, this all-around speaker was an excellent performer and a CR Best Buy. The more expensive Polk Audio CS200 ($200) was another excellent performer, but may require a receiver to handle speakers with a fairly low impedance rating. For surround speakers, the Cambridge Soundworks The Surround II ($250) has an effective design for producing greater sound diffusion.

See Buying Guide report, page 50. Last time rated in CONSUMER REPORTS: March 1997.

Overall Ratings

Within types, listed in order of overall score

Key no.	Brand and model	Price: Center channel	Price: Surround (pair)	Price: 3-piece package	Overall score (0–100; P F G VG E)	Impedance CR/mfr.	Minimum power
	CENTER-CHANNEL SPEAKERS						
1	**B.I.C.** V-52si [1] **A CR Best Buy**	$80	—	—		6/8 ohms	10 watts
2	**Polk Audio** CS200	200	—	—		4/8	20

[1] *Tested as a center-channel speaker.*

Ratings continued

Ratings, continued

Key no.	Brand and model	Price: CENTER CHANNEL	Price: SURROUND (PAIR)	Price: 3-PIECE PACKAGE	Overall score (0–100; P F G VG E)	Impedance CR/mfr.	Minimum power
	CENTER-CHANNEL SPEAKERS *continued*						
3	**Boston Acoustics** CR2	$200	—	—		6/8 ohms	5 watts
4	**Bose** V-300 [2]	130	—	$250		6/6	20
5	**Allison** MS-202	180	—	—		4/8	7
6	**NHT** 1.1C	175	—	—		6/8	23
7	**B.I.C.** V-52CLR	180	—	—		5/8	27
8	**Phase Technology** T-Center	200	—	—		7/8	17
9	**Infinity** Minuette Center Channel [2]	150	—	290		9/8	4
10	**Sony** SS-CR600 [2]	180	—	280		6/8	6
11	**Cambridge Soundworks** Center Channel II	160	—	—		6/8	20
12	**Radio Shack** Optimus Pro CS-3	130	—	—		6/8	12
13	**Technics** SB-CSS90 [2]	95	—	170		9/8	5
	SURROUND SPEAKERS						
14	**Cambridge Soundworks** The Surround II	—	$250	—		8/8	4
15	**Pinnacle** AC400	—	140	—		6/8	5
1	**B.I.C** V-52si [3]	—	160	—		6/8	7
9	**Infinity** Minuette Surround Pac [4]	—	160	290		6/8	4
16	**Altec Lansing** 120	—	200	—		5/8	4
4	**Bose** V-300 [4]	—	—	250		6/6	13
17	**Boston Acoustics** CRX	—	200	—		5/8	4
18	**Radio Shack** Optimus XTS-10	—	80	—		8/8	5
10	**Sony** SS-CR600 [4]	—	—	280		6/8	6
13	**Technics** SB-CSS90 [4]	—	—	170		10/8	7
19	**DCM** CX-007	—	160	—		10/8	8

[2] Center-channel speaker of three-piece package. [3] Tested as surround speakers. [4] Surround speakers of three-piece package.

Model details

Notes on the details: Dimensions are in order of height, width, and depth.

Center-channel speakers

(Prices are per speaker)

1 B.I.C. V-52si $80

• 11 ¾x7x7½ in., 8 lb. • Magnetically shielded • Black cabinet • 7-yr. warranty

An all-around speaker, which we tested for both center-channel and surround use. **Recommendation:** Excellent performance at a very low price makes this A CR Best Buy.

2 Polk Audio CS200 $200

• 6¼x18x6 in., 9 lb. • Magnetically shielded • Black cabinet • 5-yr. warranty.

May require receiver that can handle 4-ohm speakers. **Model availability:** Discontinued. **Recommendation:** Excellent but expensive.

3 Boston Acoustics CR2 $200

• 5½x15¼x5½ in., 6 lb. • Magnetically shielded • Uses binding posts instead of spring-loaded connectors • Nonremovable grille • Black cabinet • 5-yr. warranty

Recommendation: Excellent but expensive.

5 Allison MS-202 $180

• 5x19x11 in., 12 lb. • Magnetically shielded • Uses binding posts instead of spring-loaded connectors • Black cabinet • 5-yr. warranty.

May require receiver that can handle 4-ohm speakers. Produces directional treble, causing a change of sound if you aren't seated directly in front of the TV set. Has a built-in overload protection circuit designed to prevent speaker damage. **Recommendation:** Very good but expensive.

6 NHT 1.1C $175

• 12x7½x9¼ in., 12 lb. • Magnetically shielded • Uses binding posts instead of spring-loaded connectors • Black cabinet • 5-yr. warranty

Model availabilily: Discontinued. **Recommendation:** Very good.

7 B.I.C. V-52CLR $180

• 6½x20¼x10¼ in., 15 lb. • Magnetically shielded • Black cabinet • 7-yr. warranty

The only tested speaker judged suitable for Dolby Pro Logic "wide" mode, which reproduces the full bass range in the center channel. **Recommendation:** Very good performance.

8 Phase Technology T-Center $200

• 6¼x20x7¾ in., 15 lb. • Magnetically shielded • Black cabinet • 5-yr. warranty

Produces directional treble, causing a change of sound if you aren't seated directly in front of the TV set. **Recommendation:** Very good.

11 Cambridge Soundworks Center Channel II $160

• 4¼x14x7¾ in., 8 lb. • Magnetically shielded • Uses binding posts instead of spring-loaded connectors • Black cabinet • 7-yr. warranty

Recommendation: Good but expensive.

12 Radio Shack Optimus Pro CS-3 $130

• 5x14¼x9¼ in., 8 lb. • Magnetically shielded • Dark gray cabinet • 5-yr. warranty.

Recommendation: Good.

Surround speakers

(Prices are per pair)

14 Cambridge Soundworks The Surround II $250

• 6¾x5¾x4½ in., 4 lb. • Nonremovable grille • Black cabinet • 7-yr. warranty

Each speaker designed for left or right position only, and has effective design for greater surround-sound diffusion. Optional wall-mounting brackets available. **Recommendation:** Excellent.

15 Pinnacle AC400 $140

• 9¼x6x6¾ in., 6 lb. • Black cabinet • 7-yr. warranty

Recommendation: Very good performance at a relatively low price.

Can't find a model? Call the manufacturer. See page 342.

Ratings continued

Ratings, continued

1 B.I.C. V-52si $160

• 11¾x7x7½ in., 8 lb. • Magnetically shielded • Black cabinet • 7-yr. warranty

An all-around speaker, which we tested for both surround and center-channel use. Can also be bought as single speaker. **Recommendation:** Very good and inexpensive.

16 Altec Lansing 120 $200

• 11½x7¾x6 in., 10 lb. • Includes wall-mounting brackets • Black cabinet • 5-yr. warranty

Speakers have effective design for greater surround-sound diffusion. **Recommendation:** Very good but expensive.

17 Boston Acoustics CRX $200

• 8½x4½x5 in., 4 lb. • Includes wall-mounting brackets • White cabinet • 5-yr. warranty

Each speaker designed for left or right position only; has effective design for greater surround-sound diffusion. **Model availability:** Discontinued. **Recommendation:** Very good.

18 Radio Shack Optimus XTS-10 $80

• 8¾x4¼x6 in., 3 lb. • Nonremovable grille • Black cabinet • 5-yr. warranty

Wall-mounting brackets available. **Recommendation:** Very good performance at a low price.

19 DCM CX-007 $160

• 8¼x5½x5 in., 3 lb. • Nonremovable grille • Black cabinet • 5-yr. warranty

Has built-in overload-protection circuit designed to prevent speaker damage. **Recommendation:** Good overall.

Three-piece systems

(Prices are per system; center-channel speakers are magnetically shielded.)

4 Bose V-300 $250

• 6x11x7 in., 4 lb. (surround speakers weigh 3 lb. each) • Comes with speaker wire and wall-mounting brackets • Nonremovable grille • Dark gray cabinet • 5-yr. warranty

Center-channel speaker sold separately as V-100, $130. **Recommendation:** Very good overall. The best choice among the three-piece systems.

9 Infinity Minuette Surround Pac $290

• Center: 4¾x10½x4 in., 4 lb. Surround: 7x4¾x3¾ in., 2 lb. • Comes with wall-mounting brackets • Black cabinet • 5-yr. warranty

Speakers also sold individually: $160 for surround pair, $150 for center channel. Center-channel speaker produces directional treble, causing a change of sound if you aren't seated directly in front of the TV set. **Recommendation:** Very good.

10 Sony SS-CR600 $280

• Center: 6¾x17x7½ in., 13 lb. Surround: 8¼x6¼x6¼ in., 4 lb. • Comes with speaker wire • Black cabinet • 3-yr. warranty

Center-channel speaker also sold individually as SS-CN200AV, $180. **Model availability:** Discontinued. **Recommendation:** Very good for surround; good for center channel.

13 Technics SB-CSS90 $170

• Center: 5½x16¾x 5¾ in., 7 lb. Surround: 8¼x5½x5 in., 3 lb. • Includes wall-mounting brackets • Black cabinet • 3-yr. warranty

Each surround speaker designed for left or right position only, and has effective design for greater surround-sound diffusion. Center-channel speaker also sold individually as SB-AFC32A, $95. Center-channel speaker produces directional treble, causing a change of sound if you aren't seated directly in front of the TV set. **Recommendation:** Good in surround; poor in center channel.

Ratings *CD players*
& Recommendations

The tests behind the Ratings

Our tests show that all models deliver first-rate audio. **Overall score** is based on ability to handle problem discs, bumping during play, and convenience. **Problem discs** reflects the player's ability to cope with scratched or dirty discs without halting. **Locate speed** reflects the time to start a track, jump from track to track on a single disc, and for multi disc changers, to jump from one disc to another. **Taping ease** incorporates features that simplify copying discs to cassette. **Price** is approximate retail. Models similar to those we tested are noted in the Model details; features may vary.

Typical features for the models

• Remote control. • One-year parts and labor warranty. **Single-disc models:** • Measure about 17x4x12 in. (WxHxD). **Carousel models:** • Measure about 17½x4½x16 in. (WxHxD).

Recommendations

You won't go wrong with the sound quality of any of the tested models. For the best combination of overall performance and price, consider the Technics SL-PD987 ($225) and Kenwood DP-R4080 ($200), both carousel players.

See Buying Guide report, page 52. Last time rated in CONSUMER REPORTS: February 1997.

Overall Ratings

E ⊜ VG ⊖ G ○ F ◒ P ●

Within types, listed in order of overall score

Key no.	Brand and model	Discs	Price	Overall score (0–100; P F G VG E)	Performance: PROBLEM DISCS	Performance: LOCATE SPEED	Performance: TAPING EASE	Convenience
	SINGLE-DISC MODELS							
1	**Onkyo** DX-7210	1	$180		⊜	⊖	⊜	⊖
2	**Technics** SL-PG450	1	150		⊖	⊜	⊜	⊖
3	**Yamaha** CDX-490	1	240		⊖	⊜	⊜	⊖
4	**JVC** XL-V282BK	1	170		⊖	⊜	⊜	○
5	**Sony** CDP-XE500	1	160		⊖	⊜	⊜	○

Ratings continued ▶

Ratings, continued

Key no.	Brand and model	Discs	Price	Overall score (0–100; P F G VG E)	Performance: Problem discs	Performance: Locate speed	Performance: Taping ease	Convenience
	CAROUSEL MODELS *continued*							
6	**Technics** SL-PD987	5	$225		⊜	⊜	○	⊖
7	**Kenwood** DP-R4080	5	200		⊖	⊖	⊖	○
8	**Yamaha** CDC-655	5	280		⊖	⊖	⊜	○
9	**Sony** CDP-CE405	5	190		○	⊖	⊜	⊖
10	**Onkyo** DX-C330	6	275		⊖	⊖	◒	○
11	**Denon** DCM-260	5	270		⊖	⊖	◒	○
12	**RCA** RP-8055	5	105		○	○	◒	◒
	MAGAZINE MODELS							
13	**Optimus** (Radio Shack) CD-7300	6	240		○	⊖	○	○
14	**JVC** XL-M318BK	6+1	225		⊜	○	◒	○

Model details

Single-disc models

1 Onkyo DX-7210 $180

• 36-track program memory
Calendar display. Has delete-track program. Displays running total of program time. Can be operated by an Onkyo receiver remote. Headphone jack. But: A bit slower to locate tracks than other single-disc models. Small buttons on remote. **Model availability:** Discontinued. **Recommendation:** Excellent, and the fullest-featured player we tested.

2 Technics SL-PG450 $150

• 21-track program memory
Excellent at resisting bumping during play. Calendar display. Displays running total of program time. Has jack to automatically start a Technics cassette deck. Headphone jack. **Model availability:** Discontinued. **Recommendation:** Excellent; very good value.

3 Yamaha CDX-490 $240

• 25-track program memory
Calendar display. Displays running total of program time. Has jack to automatically start a Yamaha cassette deck. Two-year parts and labor warranty. Has output for minidisc, DAT, or DCC player. Headphone jack. **Model availability:** Discontinued. **Recommendation:** Excellent, but expensive.

4 JVC XL-V282BK $170

• 32-track program memory
Calendar display. Displays running total of program time. Has jack to automatically start a JVC cassette deck. Can be operated by a JVC receiver remote. But: Remote's numeric keypad lacks "telephone" configuration. Similar: XL-V182BK, $150; lacks remote. **Recommendation:** Very good.

5 Sony CDP-XE500 $160

• 24-track program memory
Calendar display. Displays running total of program time. Has music-sampling program; hookup for minidisc, DAT, or DCC player; headphone jack. But: Can't display time remaining on disc and the play mode isn't clearly displayed. **Recommendation:** Very good.

Carousel models

6 Technics SL-PD987 $225
• 5-disc changer • 32-track program memory
Has music-sampling, delete-track programs. **Recommendation:** Excellent; among the best choices if you often play scratched discs.

7 Kenwood DP-R4080 $200
• 5-disc changer • 32-track program memory
Calendar display. Displays running total of program time. Has jack to automatically start a Kenwood cassette deck. Can be operated by a Kenwood receiver remote. Has headphone jack. But: Small buttons on remote. **Model availability:** Discontinued. **Recommendation:** Excellent; very good value.

8 Yamaha CDC-655 $280
• 5-disc changer • 40-track program memory
Calendar display. Displays running total of program time. Has jack to automatically start a Yamaha cassette deck; output for minidisc, DAT, or DCC player; headphone jack. Two-year parts and labor warranty. But: Small buttons on remote. **Model availability:** Discontinued; successor: CDC- 665. **Recommendation:** Very good, and among the most convenient carousels for making tapes, but expensive.

9 Sony CDP-CE405 $190
• 5-disc changer • 32-track program memory
Calendar display. Displays running total of program time. Has music-sampling program. **Model availability:** Discontinued. **Recommendation:** Very good, though there are better choices if you often play scratched discs. Among the most convenient carousels for making tapes.

10 Onkyo DX-C330 $275
• 6-disc changer • 40-track program memory
Carousel tray moves bi directionally, which makes it easier and faster to select discs. Displays running total of program time for one disc at a time. **But:** Play modes not clearly indicated. **Recommendation:** Very good, though among the least convenient models for taping.

11 Denon DCM-260 $270
• 5-disc changer • 20-track program memory
Displays running total of program time for one disc at a time. Has headphone jack. But: Remote numeric keypad lacks "telephone" configuration; buttons are poorly labeled. **Recommendation:** Very good, though among the least convenient models for taping. Also, Denon has been among the less reliable brands for carousel models.

12 RCA RP-8055 $105
• 5-disc changer • 32-track program memory
Carousel models come no cheaper than this. But: Can't show time remaining on disc or track, or display track number and time simultaneously. Remote keypad small; buttons small, poorly labeled and organized. **Model availability:** Discontinued. **Recommendation:** Good, though RCA has been among the less reliable brands for carousel models.

Magazine models

13 Optimus (Radio Shack) CD-7300 $240
• 6-disc changer • 32-track program memory
• WxHxD:16⅝x4⅛x11½ in.
Has delete-track and music-sampling programs, jack to automatically start an Optimus cassette deck. Can be operated by an Optimus receiver remote. Has headphone jack. **Model availability:** Discontinued. **Recommendation:** Very good, though not for those who play a lot of scratched discs.

14 JVC XL-M318BK $225
• 6-disc changer plus single-disc slot • 32-track program memory • WxHxD: 17⅛x5x14 in.
Calendar display. Has music sampling program, jack to automatically start a JVC cassette deck. Can be operated by JVC receiver remote. Headphone jack. But: Lacks display of time remaining on disc. Small buttons on remote. **Model availability:** Discontinued. **Recommendation:** Very good, and among the best choices if you often play scratched discs. But among the least convenient players for taping, and most other changers have been more reliable than JVC's magazine models.

Can't find a model? Call the manufacturer. See page 342.

Ratings *Portable CD players*

& Recommendations

The tests behind the Ratings

The **overall score** is based mostly on the sound as delivered through a player's headphones, the ability to handle problem discs, and resistance to sudden bumps. Features, ease of use, and battery life were also considered. **Headphones** reflects how accurately the supplied headphones can reproduce sound. **Problem discs** scores the ability to play discs that have scratches, smudges, or other defects. **Bumps** reflects skip-free playback during a range of shocks and jolts. **Ease of use** combines our judgment of a player's controls, features, and other conveniences. **Price** is a rounded national average.

Typical features for these models

• Headphones, typically on-the-ear type. • Bass-boost control. • AC adapter. • Low-battery indicator. • Auto power off, when the player is idle for a time. • Repeat-track switch, "resume" feature, shuffle play, and programming. • Display showing elapsed track time. • Hold lock. • One-year warranty covering parts and labor for player (typically 3 months for headphones).

Recommendations

Although the two excellent Panasonic models that top the Ratings—the SL-S651C and similar SL-S650 ($200 and $180, respectively)—are pricey, you don't have to spend a lot to get a very good portable CD player. Two other much cheaper Panasonics—the SL-S221C ($100), which comes with a car kit, and the similar SL-S220 ($80) which lacks the kit—scored nearly as high and are CR Best Buys.

See Buying Guide report, page 52. Last time rated in CONSUMER REPORTS: November 1997.

Overall Ratings

E VG G F P

Listed in order of overall score

Key no.	Brand and model	Price	Overall score (0–100: P F G VG E)	Headphones	Problem discs	Bumps: Buffer on	Bumps: Buffer off	Ease of use	Car kit
1	Panasonic SL-S651C	$200		VG	E	F	F	E	✔
2	Panasonic SL-S650	180		VG	VG	VG	G	VG	—
3	Panasonic SL-S221C, A CR Best Buy	100		G	E	VG	VG	VG	✔
4	Panasonic SL-SW415	180		F	E	E	E	VG	—
5	Sony D-465	200		VG	F	E	VG	E	—

Key no.	Brand and model	Price	Overall score (0–100; P F G VG E)	Headphones	Problem discs	Bumps: Buffer on	Bumps: Buffer off	Ease of use	Car kit
6	**Panasonic** SL-S220, **A CR Best Buy**	80		○	⊜	⊖	⊖	⊖	—
7	**Sony** D-E307CK	125		⊖	○	⊜	⊜	⊜	✔
8	**Sony** D-E301	110		⊖	○	⊜	⊜	⊜	—
9	**Magnavox** AZ7566	150		⊖	⊖	⊜	⊖	⊜	✔
10	**Aiwa** XP-529	120		⊖	○	⊜	⊖	⊖	✔
11	**JVC** XL-P33	100		⊖	○	⊜	⊜	◒	—
12	**Aiwa** XP-760	100		○	○	⊖	⊖	⊜	—
13	**Aiwa** XP-769	120		○	○	⊖	⊖	⊜	✔
14	**Magnavox** AZ7261	70		⊖	○	—	⊖	⊖	—
15	**Panasonic** SL-S125	70		○	⊖	—	○	⊖	—
16	**Magnavox** AZ7356	100		⊖	◒	⊜	⊖	○	✔
17	**Craig** JC6151K	100		⊖	⊖	⊖	◒	○	✔
18	**RCA** RP-7927	110		○	⊖	⊜	⊖	◒	✔
19	**Sony** D-153C	90		⊖	◒	—	○	○	—
20	**Optimus** (Radio Shack) CD-3530	100		[1]	○	—	◒	○	—
21	**Sony** D-162CKC	90		⊖	◒	—	◒	○	✔
22	**Craig** JC6131K	80		◒	○	○	◒	◒	✔

[1] *No headphones supplied. Overall score calculated using Radio Shack NOVA-42 headphones, $15, judged very good.*

Model details

Notes on the details: Car use, scored only for models that include a car kit, considers the most important factors when driving: bump resistance, car-kit adapters, lighted display and controls, a line-out jack; the score downplays battery life and headphone sound. **Battery life** is estimated with alkaline cells and is rounded to the nearest hour.

1 Panasonic SL-S651C $200
2 Panasonic SL-S650 $180

• Car use: ⊜ [(1) only] • 10-sec. buffer • Battery life: 14 hr., buffer on; 19 hr., buffer off

Relatively small and slim, these essentially similar players offer the longest battery life of all models. They have a remote control [wireless with (1), wired to the headset cord with (2)], a lighted display, digital-signal processing (DSP) and a line-out jack. (1), adds a car kit and illuminated controls. (2) is a bit less adept than (1) at handling problem discs but adds an external snap-on case that holds two additional AA cells, roughly doubling play time. But: Have in-ear headphones, a type some people find to be uncomfortable. **Recommendation:** Excellent players, if rather pricey. (1) is among the best for car use.

3 Panasonic SL-S221C $100
6 Panasonic SL-S220 $80

• Car use: ⊖ [(3) only] • 3-sec. buffer • Battery life: 12 hr., buffer on; 14 hr., buffer off

Ratings continued ▶

Ratings, continued

These players—essentially similar except that (3) adds a car kit—are relatively small and slim and have a line-out jack. (3) adds a lighted display. Similar model: SL-S225, $90, lacks car kit but includes rechargeable batteries. **Recommendation:** Very good players and excellent values. (3) is well-suited to car use. Each is a **CR Best Buy.**

4 Panasonic SL-SW415 $180

• 10-sec. buffer • Battery life: 13 hr., buffer on; 15 hr., buffer off

Orange plastic case has gasket and clamps to help keep out moisture, sand, and the like. Line-out jack. But: Headphones—which vibrate (rather annoyingly, we found) when set to a VMSS, or "virtual motion sound system" setting, are only fair. Similar models: SL-SW-S405, $150; has regular, rather than VMSS, headphones. **Recommendation:** A very good player, if on the pricey side—and you may want to invest in better headphones.

5 Sony D-465 $200

• 20-sec. buffer • Battery life: 15 hr., buffer on; 18 hr., buffer off

Features backlit display in a stylish, relatively small, slim player. Rechargeable batteries, included, provide 10 to 12 hours of play—twice as long as other models with their rechargeables. Has music sampling, optical digital output, line-out jack, volume-limiting switch, and mini-to-RCA plug cable. But: Labor warranty only three months. **Recommendation:** A very good player, but among the most expensive, and a poor choice if you own very scratched discs.

7 Sony D-E307CK $125

8 Sony D-E301 $110

• Car use: ⊖ [(7) only] • 10-sec. buffer • Battery life: 12 hr. , buffer on; 14 hr., buffer off

These two models are essentially similar, except that (7) has a car kit. They have music sampling, line-out jack, volume-limiting switch, and mini-to-RCA plug cable. But: Labor warranty only three months. Similar model: D-E305, $120; lacks car kit but adds rechargeable batteries. **Recommendation:** Very good players. (7) is a very good choice for car use.

9 Magnavox AZ7566 $150

• Car use: ⊜ • 20-sec. buffer • Battery life: 4 hr., buffer on; 6 hr., buffer off

Has backlit display, illuminated controls, music sampling, and digital-signal processing (DSP). But: Lacks bass-boost switch. Battery life was among the poorest, and does not charge rechargeable cells. **Recommendation:** A very good player and among the best for use in a car, but relatively expensive.

10 Aiwa XP-529 $120

• Car use: ⊖ • 5-sec. buffer • Battery life 6 hr., buffer on; 8 hr., buffer off

Somewhat bulkier than most. Display shows time remaining on track and disc. But: Cassette adapter for car degrades frequency response. Labor warranty only three months. **Model Availability:** Discontinued, but may still be in stores. **Recommendation:** A very good player.

11 JVC XL-P33 $100

• 10-sec. buffer • Battery life: 5 hr. , buffer on; 7 hr., buffer off

Has music sampling. But: Some may find its in-ear headphones to be uncomfortable. Significant treble loss when buffer circuitry is on. Battery life was among the poorest. **Recommendation:** A very good player.

12 Aiwa XP-760 $100

13 Aiwa XP-769 $120

• Car use: ○ [(13) only] • 10-sec. buffer • Battery life: 9 hr., buffer on; 11 hr., buffer off

These two models are essentially similar, except that (13) has a car kit. Display shows time remaining on track and disc. But: Labor warranty only three months. Cassette adapter increases background noise slightly. **Recommendation:** Very good players, though (13) is no better than OK for car use.

14 Magnavox AZ7261 $70

• Battery life: 8 hr. • No buffer

Has music sampling. Similar models: AZ7265, $80; adds a car kit; AZ7268, $90; adds a car kit and amplified speakers. **Recommendation:** A very good player.

15 **Panasonic SL-S125** $70

• Battery life: 13 hr. • No buffer
A relatively small, slim player. Has line-out jack. Includes rechargeable batteries, though these provide only four to five hours of play. Similar model: SL-S120, $60; lacks rechargeable batteries. **Recommendation:** A very good player.

16 **Magnavox AZ7356** $100

• Car use: ⊖ • 3-sec. buffer • Battery life: 11 hr., buffer on; 12 hr., buffer off
An expensive model if you use batteries, since it takes four AA batteries, not two. Lacks programmability, ability to charge rechargeable batteries, repeat-track switch. Cassette adapter increases background noise slightly. Similar model: AZ7351, $80, lacks car kit. **Recommendation:** A very good player; a fine choice for car use.

17 **Craig JC6151K** $100

• Car use: ○ • 10-sec. buffer • Battery life: 4 hr., buffer on; 7 hr., buffer off
Has music sampling, line-out jack, carrying bag. But: Battery life was among the poorest. Labor warranty only three months. **Recommendation:** A very good player, though no better than OK for car use.

18 **RCA RP-7927** $110

• Car use: ⊖ • 3-sec. buffer • Battery life: 5 hr., buffer on; 6 hr., buffer off
Has lighted display, wireless remote. But: Battery life was among the poorest, and it cannot charge rechargeable batteries. Lacks hold lock. Does not show elapsed track time. **Recommendation:** A good player.

19 **Sony D-153C** $90

• Battery life: 12 hr. • No buffer
Includes rechargeable batteries, though these provide only four to five hours of play. Has music sampling, line-out jack, volume-limiting switch, and mini-to-RCA plug cable. But: Labor warranty only three months. Similar model: D-151C, $75; lacks rechargeable batteries. **Recommendation:** A good player.

20 **Optimus (Radio Shack) CD-3530** $100

• Battery life: 4 hr. • No buffer
Has music sampling, line-out jack, and mini-to-RCA plug cable. But: Battery life was among the poorest, and lacks low-battery indicator. No headphones or AC adapter included. **Recommendation:** A good player.

21 **Sony D-162CKC** $90

• Car use: ◒ • Battery life: 10 hr. • No buffer
Includes plastic car-mount platform, with Velcro strips to attach player. Has music sampling, line-out jack, and volume-limiting switch. But: Labor warranty only three months. **Recommendation:** A good player, though a poor choice for car use.

22 **Craig JC6131K** $80

• Car use: ◒ • 3-sec. buffer • Battery life: 4 hr., buffer on; 5 hr., buffer off
Has music sampling, line-out jack. But: Cassette adapter degrades frequency response in car use. Battery life was among the poorest. Does not show elapsed track time. Labor warranty only three months. **Recommendation:** A good player, though a poor choice for car use.

Ratings *Compact cameras*
& Recommendations

The tests behind the Ratings

The **overall score** is based on performance and convenience. Differences of less than 15 points were judged not significant. **Weight** includes batteries and film. **Focal length:** A 30-60-mm APS zoom gives coverage similar to that of a 40-to-80-mm 35mm zoom. **Image quality** is based on image sharpness and freedom from flare, from distortion, and from chromatic aberration. **Film handling** is the ease of loading and unloading the cameras. **Flash range** is the maximum distance at which the camera will take acceptable flash pictures with ISO 100 print film. **Pocketability** indicates compactness. **Price** is an estimated average based on a national survey.

Typical features for these models

For 35mm and APS models: • Automatic fim loading and handling. • Autofocus • Autoexposure. • Auomatic film-speed setting. • Focus hold. • Exposure lock. • Built-in flash with fill-flash capability and red-eye reduction. Self-timer. **Except as noted, all have:** • A slowest shutter speed of ¼ second or longer. • Built-in lends cover. **For all 35mm models:** • Warning if subject is too close. • Window on the back that shows the type of film being used. **For all APS models:** • Easy, foolproof automatic film loading • A choice of three print shapes, which can be switched in mid-roll. • Date and time recording on film. **All models lack:** • A window for checking film type.

Recommendations

Among 35mm models, the Olumpus LT Zoom 105 ($335) is an excellent but expensive choice. The other 35mm zooms in this group and among those listed from a previous report (see chart on page 78) are all less expensive. And some have special features you might want. Among nonzoom 35mm models, the Yashica T4 Super Weatherproof ($180) from a previous report is still the top choice. Among nonzoom APS models, the Kodak Advantix 3700ix ($155) and Konica Super Big Mini BM-S100 ($110) are excellent choices. The Canon Elph 490Z ($390) is an excellent but expensive zoom. A less expensive alternative is the pocketable Vivitar Z360ix ($140).

See Buying Guide report, page 44. Last time rated in CONSUMER REPORTS: November 1997.

Overall Ratings

Legend: E = Excellent, VG = Very good, G = Good, F = Fair, P = Poor

Within types, listed in order of overall score

Key no.	Brand and model	Price	Weight	Focal length(s)	Image quality	Film handling	Flash range	Pocketability
	COMPACT 35MM MODELS							
1	**Olympus** LT Zoom 105	$335	10 oz.	38-105 mm	E	VG	14 ft.	VG
2	**Canon** Sure Shot 105 Zoom	200	10	38-105	E	VG	16	VG
3	**Leica** Mini 3	250	7	32	E	G	11	E
4	**Fujifilm** Discovery 290 Zoom	165	10	38-90	VG	VG	12	G
5	**Pentax** IQZoom 90MC	195	8	38-90	VG	VG	12	VG
6	**Samsung** Maxima Evoca 115 (zoom)	240	11	38-115	VG	VG	16	VG
7	**Yashica** Microtec Zoom 90	180	11	38-90	VG	VG	15	VG
	COMPACT APS MODELS							
8	**Kodak** Advantix 3700ix	155	7	24	VG	E	10	E
9	**Canon** Elph 490Z (zoom)	390	11	22.5-90	VG	E	11	VG
10	**Konica** Super Big Mini BM-S100	110	6	28	VG	VG	11	E
11	**Nikon** Nuvis 125 i (zoom)	290	10	30-100	VG	E	11	VG
12	**Vivitar** Z360ix (zoom)	140	7	30-60	VG	VG	13	E
13	**Fujifilm** Endeavor 400ix Zoom	360	9	25-100	VG	E	9	VG
14	**Minolta** Vectis 40 (zoom)	400	12	30-120	VG	VG	18	F
15	**Minox** CD 25 [1]	180	6	25	VG	VG	8	E
16	**Yashica** Acclaim 100	120	6	25	VG	VG	8	E
17	**Fujifilm** Endeavor 100	120	6	25	VG	VG	8	E
18	**Nikon** Nuvis Mini i	120	6	25	VG	VG	8	E
19	**Olympus** Newpic AF200	90	7	27	VG	VG	5	E

[1] *Similar to (16), (17), and (18).*

Ratings continued ▶

Ratings, continued

Model details

Notes on the details: Framing accuracy is the percentage of the actual picture area you see in the viewfinder. Above 80 percent is reasonably accurate. **Smallest field** is the width of the smallest subject that fills the frame at the closest regular (not macro) focus; the smaller the better for tight close-ups.

35mm models

1 Olympus LT Zoom 105 $335
• Framing accuracy: 82% • Smallest field: 5 in. A fine zoom model, light and compact. **Features:** Choice of panoramic or regular format pictures. Optional wireless shutter release. Spot-metering mode. Weatherproof. Has date/time imprinting. **Recommendation:** An excellent but expensive choice in a zoom model.

2 Canon Sure Shot 105 Zoom $200
• Framing accuracy: 86% • Smallest field: 7 in. A fine zoom model, light and compact. **Features:** Versatile multiarea autofocus. But: Flash illuminates less uniformly than most. Self-timer doesn't cancel automatically. **Recommendation:** An excellent choice in a zoom model.

3 Leica Mini 3 $249
• Framing accuracy: 83% • Smallest field: 25 in. Very compact and light. **Features:** Infinity focus lock. Backlight compensation. But: Lacks lens cover. Less convenient than most for eyeglass wearers. Has continuous-advance mode only; may waste a shot now and then. **Recommendation:** An excellent but expensive nonzoom camera.

4 Fujifilm Discovery 290 Zoom $165
• Framing accuracy: 80% • Smallest field: 9 in. **Features:** Prewinds film to end, advances back into cartridge. Optional wireless shutter release. But: Lacks low-battery warning. **Recommendation:** Excellent but relatively bulky.

5 Pentax IQ Zoom 90MC $195
• Framing accuracy: 68% • Smallest field: 9 in. **Features:** Choice of panoramic or regular format. Versatile multiarea autofocus. Optional wireless shutter release. But: Self-timer doesn't cancel automatically. **Recommendation:** Excellent except for framing inaccuracy.

6 Samsung Maxima Evoca 115 $240
• Framing accuracy: 79% • Smallest field: 5 in. A wide zoom range. **Features:** Choice of panoramic or regular-format pictures. Infinity focus lock. Exposure-compensation. Automatic zoom modes. Self-timer can take more than one picture. Can make multiple exposures. Switch for continuous-advance mode. Optional wireless shutter release. Has date/time imprinting. But: May leak light in bright sun. **Recommendation:** Very good; has many features.

7 Yashica Microtec Zoom 90 $180
• Framing accuracy: 82% • Smallest field: 6 in. **Features:** Flash zooms to maintain range on telephoto shots. Versatile multiarea autofocus. Infinity focus lock. Self-timer can take more than one picture. Backlight compensation. Automatic zoom mode. Switch for continuous-advance mode. But: May leak light in bright sun, fogging fast film. **Recommendation:** Very good.

APS models

8 Kodak Advantix 3700ix $155
• Framing accuracy: 84% • Smallest field: 21 in. Very compact and light. **Features:** Warns when subject exceeds flash range. Large lens/flash separation helps reduce red-eye. Infinity focus lock. Film-compartment interlock prevents accidental opening. But: Flash illuminates less uniformly than most. **Recommendation:** An excellent choice in a nonzoom APS camera.

9 Canon Elph 490Z $390
• Framing accuracy: 75% • Smallest field: 7 in. A pricey model with a 4x zoom. **Features:** Has separate "macro" setting for close-ups. Versatile multiarea autofocus. Large lens/flash separation helps reduce red-eye. Warns when subject is too close. Spot-metering mode. Optional wireless shutter release. Exposure-compensation. Automatic

zoom modes. Switch for continuous-advance mode. Film-compartment interlock prevents accidental opening. But: Self-timer doesn't cancel automatically. **Recommendation:** Excellent but pricey.

10 Konica Super Big Mini BM-S100 $110

• Framing accuracy: 79% • Smallest field: 11 in. One of the lightest, most compact models tested. **Features:** TV mode for shots of TV screen. Warns when subject is too close. Infinity focus lock. Backlight compensation. But: Short lens/ flash separation worsens red-eye. Rewinds film in midroll when you change battery. **Recommendation:** An excellent nonzoom model.

11 Nikon Nuvis 125 i $290

• Framing accuracy: 69% • Smallest field: 7 in. **Features:** Warns when subject is too close. Infinity focus lock. Optional wireless shutter release. Film-compartment interlock prevents accidental opening. **Recommendation:** An excellent nonzoom model except for framing inaccuracy.

12 Vivitar Z360ix $140

• Framing accuracy: 74% • Smallest field: 7 in. The lightest, most compact zoom model tested. **Features:** Warns when subject is too close. Infinity focus lock. But: Rewinds slowly. **Recommendation:** Excellent and very portable.

13 Fujifilm Endeavor 400ix Zoom $360

• Framing accuracy: 71% • Smallest field: 5 in. Wide zoom range. **Features:** Warns when subject is too close. Flash zooms to maintain range for telephoto shots. Infinity focus lock. Self-timer can take more than one picture. Optional wireless shutter release. Film-compartment interlock prevents accidental opening. But: Rewinds slowly. **Recommendation:** Pricey, but excellent.

14 Minolta Vectis 40 $400

• Framing accuracy: 73% • Smallest field: 12 in. A feature-laden camera with 4x zoom. **Features:** Has separate "macro" setting for close-ups. Can reload partially used film. Weatherproof. Flash zooms to maintain range for telephoto shots. Infinity focus lock. Rewinds quickly. Auto zoom mode. Switch for continuous-advance mode. Optional wireless shutter release. But: Lacks built-in lens cover. **Recommendation:** Very good, with lots of features, but pricey and bulky.

15 Minox CD 25 $180

• Framing accuracy: 75% • Smallest field: 13 in. A no-frills, nonzoom camera. **Features:** Short lens/flash distance worsens red-eye. Rewinds slowly. **Recommendation:** Very good but basic.

16 Yashica Acclaim 100 $120

• Framing accuracy: 75% • Smallest field: 15 in. Similar to (15).

17 Fujifilm Endeavor 100 $120

• Framing accuracy: 76% • Smallest field: 11 in. Similar to (15).

18 Nikon Nuvis Mini i $120

Framing accuracy: 75% • Smallest field: 11 in. Similar to (15).

19 Olympus Newpic AF200 $90

• Framing accuracy: 77% •Smallest field: 33 in. A no-frills nonzoom camera. **Features:** Bare-bones viewfinder makes accurate framing difficult, especially for eyeglass wearers. Rewinds slowly. Slowest shutter speed is 1/30 sec. Flash range only 5 feet. **Recommendation:** Very good except for viewfinder. There are better choices.

Can't find a model? Call the manufacturer. See page 342.

Ratings continued

Ratings, continued

Other camera models to consider

The following models, reported on in December 1995 and 1996, are still available. Within types, listed in Ratings order with updated prices.

Product	Price	Weight	Focal points	Flash range
35MM MODELS				
Yashica T4 Super Weatherproof	$180	8 oz.	35 mm	10 ft.
Yashica Microtec Zoom 70	170	9	35-70	11
Ricoh R1	190	6	24 and 30	7
Pentax IQZoom 80-E	140	10	38-80	11
Canon Sure Shot 70 Zoom	140	10	35-70	11
Kodak Cameo Motor EX	55	7	34	9
APS MODELS				
Minolta Vectis 25 (zoom)	265	9	30-75	15
Canon Elph (zoom)	310	7	24-48	7
Fujifilm Endeavor 250 (zoom)	230	8	24-55	8
Nikon Nuvis 75I (zoom)	185	8	30-60	11

Ratings *Hi-fi VCRs*

& Recommendations

The tests behind the Ratings

In the **overall score, picture quality** is given the greatest weight. Trained panelists compared identical side-by-side images, recorded at both standard-play (SP) and extended-play (EP) speed and played back on the same machine. We give SP greater weight than EP. **Tuner selectivity** is how well a VCR filters unwanted signals from channels next to the one being watched or recorded. **Auto clock set** and **cable channel-changer** are key features; see the report on page 36 for details. **Price** is the estimated average.

Typical features for these models

• At least 125 cable channels. • Four video heads. • VCR Plus. • Universal remote. • Programmable 365 days in advance. • Programmable for eight events at a time. • Index search. • Warning if two shows are programmed for the same time. • Audio/video jacks on the front for easy camcorder hookup. • Childproof lock. • No power backup. • One-year warranty on heads and parts, three-month warranty on labor.

Recommendations

Most of these models would make a fine choice. The three top-rated models are worth considering first. The Sony SLV-775HF ($300) has standout picture performance in both SP and EP, but Sony has been one of the less reliable VCR brands. The Panasonic PV-7662 ($290) produces equally good pictures, and the brand has been one of the more reliable ones. The Samsung VR8807 produces very good pictures in SP and EP mode, and at $220 is a good value. For basic tape-viewing and recording, consider the Quasar VHQ760 ($170).

See Buying Guide report, page 36. Last time rated in CONSUMER REPORTS: October 1997.

Overall Ratings

Listed in order of overall score

Key no.	Brand and model	Price	Overall score (0–100; P F G VG E)	Picture quality SP	Picture quality EP	Ease of use	Tuner selectivity	Auto clock set	Cable channel-changer
1	**Sony** SLV-775HF	$300		⊜	⊖	○	⊜	✔	✔ [1]
2	**Panasonic** PV-7662	290		⊜	⊖	○	○	✔	✔
3	**Samsung** VR8807	220		⊖	⊖	○	⊜	✔	✔ [1]
4	**Toshiba** M-683	250		⊖	○	○	⊜	✔	✔
5	**Hitachi** VT-FX624A	270		⊖	○	○	⊜	✔	✔
6	**Sharp** VC-H978U	230		○	○	⊖	⊜	✔	✔
7	**RCA** VR626HF	290		○	⊖	○	⊜	—	✔
8	**JVC** HR-VP644U	260		⊖	○	○	⊖	✔ [2]	✔ [1]
9	**RCA** VR631HF	230		⊖	◒	⊖	⊜	—	—
10	**Mitsubishi** HS-U580	380		⊖	◒	○	⊜	✔	✔
11	**Quasar** VHQ760	170		⊖	○	○	○	—	—
12	**GE** VG4261	180		⊖	○	◒	⊜	—	—

[1] Cable mouse. [2] Plug and play.

Model details

1 Sony SLV-775HF $300

Performance in SP mode is about as good as it gets. It automatically switches from SP to EP to fit long recordings, and has power backup. But: It lacks index search, and doesn't alert you if you've manually programmed two shows for the same time. You can't program more than a month in advance. **Recommendation:** Excellent overall, but Sony has been one of the less reliable brands.

Ratings continued ▶

Ratings, continued

2 Panasonic PV-7662 $290
Picture quality is comparable to (1). You can program from the console or the remote. There's some on-screen help for using the menus. The remote has a shuttle control. But: You can't program more than a month in advance. **Model availability:** Discontinued. **Recommendation:** Very good overall, and one of the more reliable brands.

3 Samsung VR8807 $220
Picture quality is very good in both modes. The console and remote have a shuttle control. It automatically switches from SP to EP to fit long recordings, and has power backup. But: It lacks index search. You can't program more than a month in advance. **Recommendation:** Very good overall, and a good value.

4 Toshiba M-683 $250
It automatically switches from SP to EP to fit long recordings. But: It lacks index search and a childproof lock. It can be programmed to record only six programs (though for a year in advance). You need the remote to select the video input. **Recommendation:** Very good overall, and one of the more reliable brands.

5 Hitachi VT-FX624A $270
It has power backup. There's some on-screen help for using the menus. The console and remote have a shuttle control. The one-year labor warranty is better than most. But: It lacks a childproof lock, and doesn't alert you if you've manually programmed two shows for the same time. **Recommendation:** Very good overall.

6 Sharp VC-H978U $230
You can program from the console or the remote. The console has a shuttle control. But: It lacks index search, and doesn't alert you if you've manually programmed two shows for the same time. **Recommendation:** Very good overall.

7 RCA VR626HF $290
Has a "go to" search feature. But: It lacks audio/video jacks on the front and a childproof lock. **Recommendation:** Very good, especially if you record TV shows in EP and want to program the VCR a year in advance.

8 JVC HR-VP644U $260
You can program from the console or the remote. The remote has a shuttle control. It has power backup. There's some on-screen help for using the menus. But: It lacks a childproof lock, and doesn't alert you if you've manually programmed two shows for the same time. **Recommendation:** Very good overall.

9 RCA VR631HF $230
There's some on-screen help for using the menus. But: EP picture quality is worse than most. The remote, though well-designed, isn't universal. It lacks audio/video jacks on the front. **Recommendation:** Very good overall, but not the best choice if you do a lot of recording in EP.

10 Mitsubishi HS-U580 $380
It has VCR Plus Gold, jog-shuttle controls, and can be programmed from the console and remote. It switches from SP to EP to fit long recordings, and has power backup. The six-month labor warranty is better than most. But: EP picture quality is worse than most. It doesn't alert you if you've manually programmed two shows for the same time. It can't be programmed more than a month in advance.You need the remote to select the video input. **Recommendation:** Very good overall; full-featured, but expensive.

11 Quasar VHQ760 $170
You can program from the console or remote. There's some on-screen help for using the menus. But: It lacks audio/video jacks on the front, and doesn't alert you if you've manually programmed two shows for the same time. You can't program more than a month in advance. **Model availability:** Discontinued. **Recommendation:** Good; a basic, inexpensive model from one of the more reliable brands.

12 GE VG4261 $180
It's not as easy to use as other tested VCRs. The remote isn't universal. It lacks audio/video jacks on the front. **Recommendation:** Good overall.

Can't find a model? Call the manufacturer. See page 342.

Ratings *Camcorders*
& Recommendations

The tests behind the Ratings

Picture quality is based on judgments made by a panel of trained viewers. They looked at footage shot at each model's available speeds, in sunshine and under controlled studio lighting, to rate the quality of the images. "Very good" images, by our standards, are fairly stable and sharp but may have a hint of noise—snow or flickering—especially in saturated colors, and some details may be blurred. **Price** is the estimated average, based on a national survey.

Typical features for these models

• Color viewfinder. • Automatic and manual focus. • Power zoom lens. • Tripod socket that fits on a video tripod. • Flying-erase head for clean transitions between scenes. • Rechargeable nickel-cadmium battery pack that provides 30 to 60 minutes of operation. • Battery charger and AC adapter.• Clock and calendar with lithium "button" backup battery. • Indicator to warn of condensation on the recording drum (leave the unit in a warm, dry spot for a while). • Built-in microphone. • One-year warranty on parts; 90 days on labor.

Recommendations

Even inexpensive camcorders can make good tapes these days. Of the basic models we tested, the 8mm Hitachi VME230A ($400) offers the best value. It combines very good picture quality at standard-play speed with the good sound quality of 8mm. According to the manufacturer, that model will be discontinued in early 1998. The VHS-C Panasonic PV-A207 and the 8mm Sony CCD-TR86 performed about as well but cost more. If you want a built-in light for shooting in dim places, choose the Panasonic or Sony. If you plan to do a lot of editing, choose the Hitachi or Sony.

See Buying Guide report, page 40. Last time rated in CONSUMER REPORTS: October 1997.

Ratings continued ▶

Ratings, continued

Overall Ratings

E ⊜ VG ⊖ G ○ F ◒ P ●

Within types, listed in order of overall performance

8 mm

Hitachi VME230A $400

Picture quality: ⊖ at SP; LP is not provided.
It has 12x optical zoom, extended to 24x with digital zoom; battery refresh; a remote control; and an optional editing remote control. It can use six AA alkaline batteries instead of a rechargeable battery. Opening the battery compartment is tricky; it's easy to drop the camcorder if you're not careful. **Model availability:** Discontinued, but may still be available in some stores.

Sony CCD-TR86 $570

Picture quality: ⊖ at SP; ○ at LP.
It has 15x variable-speed power optical zoom, extended to 30x with digital zoom; a built-in light for recording in dim settings; a built-in lens cover; a remote control; and a jack for tape editing with Sony VCRs. It can use six AA alkaline batteries instead of a rechargeable battery. **Model availability:** Discontinued, but may still be available in some stores.

VHS-C

Panasonic PV-A207 $490

Picture quality: ⊖ at SP; ○ at EP.
It has 14x variable-speed power optical zoom, a built-in light for recording in dim settings, a built-in lens cover, and battery refresh. It "knows" when special occasions occur, and it can be set to display messages such as "Happy Valentine's Day" on February 14. **Model availability:** Discontinued, but may still be available in some stores.

JVC GR-AX720U $530

Picture quality: ○ at SP; ◒ at EP.
It has 18x variable-speed power optical zoom, a built-in light for recording in dim settings, a built-in lens cover, battery refresh, a remote control, and audio-dubbing capability. Random-assemble edit, to mark the start and end of scenes, makes it especially easy to edit tapes. Similar: JVC GR-AX220U, $400, has a black-and-white viewfinder and no remote control or built-in light; JVC GR-AX420U, $480, has no built-in light.

For the most recent product Ratings

See the monthly issues of CONSUMER REPORTS magazine. Or check out Consumer Reports Online. Our Web site *(www.ConsumerReports.org)* covers autos, appliances, electronics gear, more. Free areas provide useful listings, recalls, shopping guidance. Members pay $2.95 per month for unlimited use, including searchable access to test reports and product Ratings.

MAJOR APPLIANCES

Washing machines

Washers these days all get clothes clean. Differences are in capacity and energy efficiency.

Last CR report: July 1997
Ratings: page 104
Brand repair histories: page 17
Expect to pay: \$350 to \$600 (top-loader); \$800 to \$1000 (front-loader)

What's available

Washers differ mainly in how they agitate the clothes.

Top-loaders. Most people buy a top-loader because that's mainly what's available. Top-loaders have some advantages over front-loaders: They're easier to load, and you can add items mid-cycle. They're usually designed to handle larger loads, and their wash-cycle time is faster. They're also \$300 to \$400 cheaper than front-loaders. Their tub capacity is approximately 2.5 to 3.2 cubic feet. Price range: \$350 to \$600.

Front-loaders. Rather than using an agitator, front-loaders alternately tumble clothing clockwise and counterclockwise. Clothes-washing performance proved comparable to that of top-loaders in our test.

While a front-loader costs more to buy, it uses less energy and less water (especially hot water) than a top-loader. In a regular-wash cycle, a front-loader uses about 16 to 25 gallons; a top-loader, 37 to 46 gallons. Front-loaders also handle unbalanced loads better. Some can be stacked with a dryer. The design, long popular in Europe, is being adopted by U.S. manufacturers. Tub capacity of old front-loading designs used to be smaller than that of top-loaders, but new designs are competitive. Price range: $800 to $1000.

Compact models. In this size, there are not a lot of models to choose from, and they tend to be expensive. Their tub capacity is about two cubic feet. Some compacts are portable. They can be stored in a closet, rolled out, and hooked up to the kitchen sink for use.

What's new

Manufacturers have become increasingly motivated to sell more efficient models, not because of consumer demand, but due to the federal energy-efficiency standards enacted in 1994, with more stringent measures expected in the years to come. With the exception of a White-Westinghouse model that was recently discontinued, most front-loaders in the U.S. have been supplied by specialty manufacturers or imported from Europe, like the Swedish-made Asko models. This year, Frigidaire introduced a new front-loading washer. Amana is expected to introduce a model also. Other manufacturers say they will stick with the top-loaders, planning to achieve the mandated energy savings with the familiar top-loading design.

Reliability

Washing machines are fairly troublesome machines. In our 1996 annual survey, readers reported on their experiences with top-loading washing machines bought new between 1990 and 1996. Roper was among the more reliable brands; Frigidaire and Magic Chef, among the less reliable. We lack sufficient reliability information on front-loaders. For more information, see the brand repair histories on page 17.

Shopping strategy

For now, because of price and availability, a top-loading machine still makes more sense than a front-loader, unless your water and energy rates are very high. Beyond that basic choice, differences among washers are ones of capacity, energy efficiency, and features. You can get a rough idea of energy use and operating costs for any washer by checking its yellow "energy guide" label, which makes comparing models fairly easy. Our recommendations on features are noted below.

Decide what to spend. You'll find the best value in a mid-priced model with few features. For such a model, you should pay less than $500, sometimes a lot less. Features like extra wash/spin options, a porcelain top and lid, or an automatic detergent dispenser add a little to convenience but don't significantly improve washing performance.

What's in the stores. You'll find the biggest selection in top-loaders. Four brands—Kenmore (Sears), Whirlpool, Maytag, and General Electric—account for most of the washers sold in the U.S.

Using the Ratings. We tested 18 full-sized machines. Two were front-loaders; the rest, top-loaders. All did a very good or excellent job in about the same time—45 to 50 minutes. The tests turned up bigger differences in capacity and in water and energy efficiency.

Basic components and performance may be very similar among certain washers within a brand or a "brand family" (a collection of brands made by the same manufacturer). Comparable models are listed together (the higher-rated model first) in "Model details." In addition, models similar to those we tested are indicated. If you can't find a model, call the manufacturer; see page 342.

Key features

Controls. Look for dials and buttons that are clearly labeled, logically arranged, and easy to push and turn. Also desirable: an illuminated control panel, a cycle-indicator light, and a buzzer to signal the end of a cycle.

Cycles. Regular, permanent-press, and delicate are all you really need. The cycle you choose may also determine the speed and water temperature, though on many models those choices are up to you. Extra speeds let you tailor the washer's actions to the load, if you want to bother.

Dispensers. Some machines have dispensers that release bleach and fabric softener at the appropriate time. Avoid small dispensers whose shallow design may allow undiluted bleach to splatter onto laundry. A proper dispenser should filter bleach to the bottom of the tub, where it can mix with water before contacting your clothes.

Drain height. A washer must drain into the sewer line, which may be higher than the top of the machine if the laundry room is in the basement.

Fill level. The most economical way to wash is with a full load. When that's not practical, adjustable fill levels let you save water, detergent, and energy. On most large-tub models, the minimum fill requires roughly half as much water as the maximum. A selection of three fill levels is usually enough to meet most needs.

Finish of the top and lid. Porcelain-coated steel, though prone to chip, withstands scraping and scratching better than a painted finish.

Lid/door opening. Top-loaders have a lid hinged at the back or at one side. Make sure the direction fits your installation. The door on front-loading washers opens to the side.

Noise. Models vary greatly in the noise they generate. Some claims for quietness didn't always correlate with our sound measurements.

Service-accessible design. Accessibility is an important feature in the event a part fails. GE models are the most service-friendly; removing the front panel provides easy access to almost every major component.

Temperature settings. You generally need only three wash temperatures: hot, warm, and cold, followed by a cold rinse. Warm water doesn't rinse any better than cold water, so a warm rinse wastes energy. Automatic temperature control, a feature found in Kenmore models, helps adjust the temperature of incoming water, possibly useful if you have unusually cold water piped to your house. It worked in our tests, although not perfectly.

Tubs. Many, including those in Maytag, Kenmore, and Whirlpool models, are porcelain-coated steel. If the porcelain chips, the steel underneath is apt to rust. That won't happen with a tub made of stainless steel (in Amana and Speed Queen models) or one made of plastic (available in GE, Frigidaire, Magic Chef, Admiral, and White-Westinghouse).

Clothes dryers

Virtually any dryer will dry clothes adequately. You'll pay extra for convenience features.

Last CR report: March 1997
Ratings: page 108 (full-sized); 112 (compacts)
Brand repair histories: page 17
Expect to pay: $250 to $500

What's available

Full-sized models. They vary only slightly in width, the critical dimension for fitting into cabinetry and closets—27 to 29 inches. Full-sized models vary in drum capacity from 5½ to 7 cubic feet. The larger the drum, the more easily a dryer can handle bulky items and the less likely big loads will come out wrinkled. Gas models, which contain more hardware, cost somewhat more than electric models. Price range: $250 to $500.

Compact models. These models, typically 24 inches wide, have a drum capacity roughly half that of full-sized models—about 3½ cubic feet. Compacts can be stacked, using additional hardware, atop a companion washer. Compacts take longer to dry clothes than full-sized models—they don't gauge dryness as well, and they operate on half the voltage. Typically, the lint filter is inconveniently located in the rear of the drum. Compact dryers are usually fairly simple, with few convenience features available. Most are electric. Price range: $300 to $350.

What's new

More mid-priced dryers now come with a moisture sensor, a feature previously limited to top-of-the-line models. Dryers with a moisture sensor use metal contacts inside the drum to measure moisture on the surface of the clothes. Such sensors gauge dryness more accurately than thermostats, which measure the moisture of the vented air. On automatic settings, a dryer with a moisture sensor will complete its cycles in less time than a dryer without a moisture sensor, which means it overdries less and, therefore, is more energy efficient.

Some Whirlpool models have an Easy Clean 100 lint filter that can go up to 100 loads before cleaning, without affecting dryer performance. It makes the dryer noisier, however.

Safety

Dryers vent their exhaust through a duct that you or an installer must attach. Of the four types of duct available, two may be dangerous. Flexible-plastic and flexible-foil ducts can sag over time and allow lint to build up inside them, creating a fire hazard. Flexible-metal and rigid-metal ducts are much safer choices.

Don't mistake flexible foil for flexible metal. Flexible foil looks like wrinkled tin foil wrapped around a loose wire frame. Flexible metal looks smoother and holds its shape when bent. A plastic duct looks like an oversized vacuum-cleaner hose. In a recent survey of our readers, we found that half used a flexible-plastic duct.

Reliability

Data from our 1996 Annual Questionnaire show that Whirlpool (gas and electric models) and KitchenAid electric dryers have been among the more reliable brands of dryers among models purchased between 1990 and 1996. White-Westinghouse and Frigidaire were among the less reliable brands. For more information, see the brand repair histories on page 17.

Shopping strategy

Nearly all the dryers we've tested in the past six years have dried ordinary laundry loads well. If you have gas service, opt for a gas dryer. Although gas dryers are priced about $50 more than electric dryers, they are cheaper to run. The money you save should offset the price difference within your first year of ownership. Models with a moisture sensor don't overdry as much as models controlled by a thermostat, saving a little energy.

Decide what to spend. Prices range from about $250 to $500. Cheaper models should dry clothes fine. Spending more buys a model with a moisture sensor and convenience features such as a drying rack or a lighted drum.

What's in the stores. Kenmore (Sears), Whirlpool, General Electric, and Maytag are the major brands you'll find.

Using the Ratings. All the tested models performed well. Differences in overall score stem mainly from minor differences in drying tests using four types of loads (a 12-pound mixed load, a 6-pound mixed load, a 6-pound load of all-cotton men's dress shirts, and a 3-pound load of delicates). If you can't find a model, call the manufacturer; see page 342.

Key features

Antiwrinkling. Most dryers allow you to extend cool tumbling from 15 minutes to a couple of hours. This useful feature, called Wrinkle Guard or Press Guard, among other names, helps prevent wrinkling when you can't get to the dryer right away. Some models with that feature continue to tumble the finished load without heat; others cycle the drum on and off intermittently.

Controls. Electronic controls, available on high-end models, may be slightly more convenient to use than dials—once you've mastered them. Our tests show that electronic controls tend to work more precisely. But dials generally work well enough and are easy to use as long as too many choices aren't squeezed onto them. Another type of control, mechanical touchpad buttons, lets you start the machine, select the temperature, and activate other options.

Cycles. Basic dryers offer at least one automatic drying cycle. Pricier ones typically offer two or three—regular, permanent press, and knit/delicate, for instance—plus unheated settings. More dry and less dry options on the automatic settings allow you to fine-tune drying needs according to the load.

Door. A large opening makes loading and unloading easier. Doors open down or to the right. Some are reversible and can be made to open either to the right or to the left.

Drum light. A drum light makes it easy to spot stray socks or debris from pants pockets.

Drying rack. This rack remains stationary while the drum rotates around it. You can use it to dry items that you don't want to tumble, such as sweaters or slippers.

End-of-cycle signal. Most models have a buzzer or other warning sound that signals the end of the drying cycle. You can adjust loudness in some models, or turn it off entirely.

Lint filter. A top-mounted filter is generally easier to clean than a filter that fits inside the drum. Some models have a signal to warn you when the lint filter is blocked.

Dishwashers

Our tests still turn up significant differences in how well this appliance cleans dishes. Avoid budget-priced models that lack a filtration system.

Last CR report: January 1997
Ratings: page 100
Brand repair histories: page 18
Expect to pay: $250 to $1000

What's available

Built-in models. Most dishwashers by far are attached permanently to a hot-water pipe, a drain, and an electrical line. Most models also fit into a 24-inch-wide space under the kitchen countertop, between two base cabinets. Compact models require less width.

Price range: $250 to $1000 for domestic models. European models are priced higher, anywhere from $600 to $2000.

Portable models. For kitchens that aren't big enough to accommodate a built-in dishwasher, these models are functionally similar to built-ins. They come in a finished cabinet on rollers so they can be rolled over to the sink and hooked up to the faucet. Price range: $400 to $500.

What's new

A new dishwasher is likely to be quieter and more energy efficient than the one you now own, especially if yours is more than a few years old. A couple of decades ago, a typical model used about 14 gallons of water during a normal wash cycle. The new KitchenAid and Kenmore models used only 6½ gallons in our most recent tests, with no sacrifice in cleaning performance. That's probably a lot less than you'd use washing dishes by hand.

Reliability

In our annual survey, readers reported that for built-in dishwashers bought new between 1990 and 1996, Whirlpool and Magic Chef were among the more reliable brands. White-Westinghouse and Frigidaire were among the less reliable. See the brand repair histories on page 18.

Shopping strategy

Consider a dishwasher's water consumption and noisiness as well as its washing ability and features. You needn't pay more for a water-efficient model, but the quietest machines can be fairly expensive—$600 and up. Noisiness, of course, isn't an issue if the machine operates when you're out of earshot. Many models can be set for a delayed start—when you're asleep, say, or at work.

Our tests have found no good correlation between washing performance and price, except for low-priced models with simpler wash systems or no filtering systems. Those models tend to redeposit, not dispose of, tiny bits of food.

Some of the highest-priced models are equipped with "smart" controls that adjust water consumption—and thus energy consumption—according to the dirtiness of the load. Energy efficiency is linked to a machine's water consumption, since most of the energy a dishwasher uses goes to heat the hot water. In our most recent tests, water use in the normal cycle ranged from 6½ to 10 gallons.

Decide what to spend. Spending

more for a dishwasher usually gets you a quieter machine with more features and, sometimes, higher efficiency. High-end models with electronic controls range in price from $400 to more than $800. Models that use mechanical controls usually cost from $300 to $500 and may perform just as well. European-made models such as Bosch, Miele, Asko, and GE's Monogram line are substantially more expensive than domestic models.

What's in the stores. The best-selling brands are Kenmore (sold by Sears), Maytag, General Electric, Whirlpool, and KitchenAid.

Using the Ratings. We tested dishwashers for how clean each left china, glassware, flatware, and serving pieces that had been smeared with various foods, scraped, and left standing overnight. We also measured electricity and water consumption and evaluated ease of use.

Models noted as similar to the tested ones should perform much the same as the tested models, but usually have different cycles and loading niceties. If you can't find a model, call the manufacturer; see page 342.

Key features

Basket with a cover. The force of the water spray can knock small items into the bottom of the machine, where they can be damaged. A covered section of the flatware basket can hold small items in place.

Controls. Mechanical controls—simple push buttons and a dial—let you reset cycles quickly. They do the job fine and cost less than electronic controls. Electronic controls use touchpads with displays that show the time for, say, counting down the time remaining in a cycle or flash warnings about malfunctions. Some displays spell out the problem; others show codes you decipher using the owner's manual.

Cycles. Most dishwashers offer a choice of at least three cycles—light, normal, and heavy. Dishwashers clean best on their heaviest cycle, but that uses the most water. The normal cycle is usually a compromise between wash quality and water usage. A rinse-and-hold cycle helps you wait until you have enough for a full load. Other cycles—"pot scrubber," "soak and scrub," "china and crystal"—aren't worth the extra expense. All dishwashers let you choose a heated dry cycle or an electricity-saving, no-heat dry.

Filter. Our tests have shown that machines with filters clean much better than those without them, usually bottom-of-the-line models. Look for self-cleaning filters, which require no attention.

Noise. Quiet operation is a major selling point, but claims and labels are a poor guide, according to our tests. The quietest models fill with water almost silently and make little racket during washing and draining, the noisiest part of the cycle. European-made models have been the quietest in our tests.

Racks and shelves. Most designs put cups and glasses on top and plates on the bottom. Rack variations include folding shelves that let you add extra cups and glasses; adjustable or fold-down tines, which better accommodate larger items; and racks that adjust to let you add space above or below far taller items.

'Smart' operation. The highest-priced GE and Maytag models offer this feature, which adjusts the wash and rinse cycles for each load according to the level of soil detected on the dishes.

Tub. A porcelain-coated steel tub resists stains better than a plastic tub, but porcelain is vulnerable to chipping. Stainless steel is probably the most durable tub material, but may cost extra.

Ranges, cooktops, & ovens

Basic performance varies very little. Watch out for inconveniences that are hard to live with. Freestanding ranges offer the best value.

Last CR report: Gas ranges, May 1997; Electric ranges, October 1996
Ratings: page 113 (gas ranges)
Brand repair histories: page 15
Expect to pay: $150 to $2000 or more

What's available

Cabinetry and floor plan will probably dictate the width and position of the range. Here are the common choices:

Freestanding ranges. These can fit in the middle of a kitchen counter or at the end. Widths range from 20 to 40 inches, but most are 30 inches. Price range: $200 to $1500.

Built-in ranges. They come in two variations: slide-ins, which fit into a space between cabinets, and drop-ins, which fit into cabinets connected below the oven. Drop-ins lack a storage drawer. Both types look built in. Price range: $450 to $1600.

Dual-oven ranges. With two ovens, the second oven—or sometimes a microwave—is usually above the cooktop. Price: about $1000.

Cooktops and wall ovens. A cooktop paired with a wall oven allows the most flexibility in layout. Most cooktops are 30 inches wide and are made of porcelain-coated steel or ceramic glass, with four elements or burners. Some are 36 inches wide, with space for an extra burner. Modular cooktops may have a pop-in grill, a rotisserie, or other options.

Wall ovens come in 24-, 27-, and 30-inch widths. You can install an oven at eye level, nest the oven under a cooktop, or stack two ovens. Together, a cooktop and wall oven typically cost considerably more than an all-in-one range. Price range: $150 to $800 for the cooktop; $375 to $2000 for the oven.

Cooktop types

Gas. Gas cooktops can be glass, porcelain-coated steel, or stainless steel. Gas burners are easy to adjust and shut off instantly. But even so-called high-speed burners tend to heat more slowly than electric elements. Burners that are sealed, with no space for spills to seep below the cooktop, are a bit easier to clean than conventional, unsealed burners. Most sealed-burner ranges have several burner sizes, often one or two medium ones (9000 British thermal units per hour), a small one (5000 Btu/hr.) for simmering, and one or two large ones (up to 12,500 Btu/hr.) for fast heating. Standard, unsealed burners typically produce 9000 Btu/hr.

Electric. These elements offer quick heating and the ability to maintain low heat levels. Coil elements are the most common and least expensive type. A second type, solid discs, have all but disappeared. Coils are fairly forgiving of warped and dented pots, and if they break, they're easy and inexpensive to replace. Spills burn off the coils and drip into bowls that are easily cleaned; heavy spills may go into wells under the prop-up cooktop.

Electric cooktops usually have a porcelain surface. A smoothtop uses a sheet of ceramic glass—black or patterned gray—under which the elements are located. A patterned surface shows smudges and fingerprints less than a shiny black surface. Spills are easy to clean, but sugary foods, which can pit the glass, should be wiped up promptly. Burnt-on spills have to be scraped away (most smoothtops come with a razor scraper). Maintenance also entails the regular use of a special cleaner.

On both types of cooktop, indicator lights signal when the surface is hot, even if the elements are off. Some glass models have a temperature limiter to guard against overheating.

Smoothtop elements may be:

Radiant. Essentially, these are very thin coil elements. For efficient heating, radiant elements require flat-bottomed pots about the same diameter as the element.

Halogen. These are tungsten-halogen bulbs. Halogen burners heat up slightly faster than radiant ones with the same wattage, but radiant elements come in higher wattages. These elements work best with flat-bottomed pots sized to match the elements.

Induction. "Magnetic induction" from a high-frequency electrical coil heats the pot without heating the glass surface. Removing the pot from the surface turns off the heat. Pots must be magnetic metal—iron or steel. Induction elements are the most expensive type of heating element.

What's new

The "commercial" or "professional" look—burnished chrome or stainless-steel panels set off by brawny black grates and knobs—is making its way from high-end lines like Viking into more traditional lines like General Electric, Kenmore (Sears), and Frigidaire. Models with chrome styling cost more than similar, conventionally styled models.

Smooth cooktops and sealed burners make ranges easier to clean. Controls are becoming smooth, too, as electronic touchpads replace traditional dial controls.

Manufacturers are still trying to push ranges with a built-in convection oven, which uses a fan to blow hot air around the oven to speed baking. The feature hasn't caught on. We don't think it's worth the $200 or so it adds to the price.

Reliability

According to our reader surveys, electric ranges have proved more reliable than gas models. Models with conventional dial controls have been slightly more reliable than those with electronic oven controls.

In our 1996 annual survey (involving ranges bought from 1990 to 1996), Magic Chef and Frigidaire electric ranges were less reliable than most. Caloric and Magic Chef were the least reliable gas ranges. See the brand repair histories on page 15.

Shopping strategy

For years, almost every range we've tested—gas or electric—has cooked, baked, and broiled just fine. Differences center on cooktop cleaning and other aspects of use.

Gas or electric. Gas burner flames respond instantly to changes in setting. Electric burners are slower to respond, but not as slow as they once were, especially for glass smoothtops. Historically, electric ovens have had the edge in roominess and evenness of heating, but the ovens in today's gas ranges are catching up in both respects. On average, a gas range costs about $100 more than a comparable electric one.

Decide on the configuration. The freestanding electric range with coil elements is the most widely sold type. It's dependable, comes in a wide selection of models, and is relatively inexpensive. You'll pay a premium for stylish, specialized, built-in modular units.

Decide what to spend. You can buy a basic electric or gas range for less than $300. For $150 to $200 more, you get a self-cleaning oven. Sealed burners add another $50 to $100 to the price of a gas range. We recommend both labor-saving features. You'll probably also get electronic controls instead of dials. Spending more than $1000 buys lots of extras, including electronic controls and "professional" styling.

What's in the stores. General Electric, Whirlpool, and Kenmore (Sears) account for more than half the electric ranges sold. General Electric and Kenmore are the top-selling brands in gas ranges, with Tappan, Magic Chef, and Caloric clustered in the second tier.

Using the Ratings. We tested 30-inch freestanding models, checking for speed and evenness of cooking as well as for ease of cleaning and other convenience factors. Models can usually be found in stores for a year or so before being discontinued. New models start to appear in the spring. You'll often find the best selection and best prices in late summer. Those listed as similar models should perform much the same as the tested models; features may vary. If you can't find a model, call the manufacturer; see page 342.

Key features

Broiler location. In electric ovens and in self-cleaning gas models, the broiler is easy to reach, at the top of the oven. In manual-clean gas ranges, the broiler is in a drawer beneath the oven.

Cooktop cleaning. Sealed burners on gas cooktops make cleaning easier. Electric smoothtops can be easy to clean but require special cleaners. Other features that ease cleaning: porcelain drip pans; a glass or porcelain backguard instead of a painted one; seamless corners and edges, especially where the cooktop joins the backguard; a raised edge around the cooktop to contain spills; and non-chrome edges. On a conventional cooktop, look for deep wells to contain spills, minimal clutter under the cooktop, and a top that props up for cleaning.

Cooktop controls. Dials are still the norm. Freestanding electric ranges have the controls on the backguard; freestanding gas ranges, in front of the cooktop. On electric ranges, controls may be divided left and right, with the oven controls in between, giving you a quick sense of which control works which element. Controls clustered in the center of the backguard stay visible when tall pots sit on back elements.

Downdraft vents. These eliminate the need for a range hood by venting the range from underneath. Such an installation is useful for a cooktop in an island or peninsula.

Oven capacity. Models with similar exterior dimensions may differ in capacity because of shelf supports and other protrusions. Some ovens are so small that you can't cook casseroles on two racks at the same time. Ovens that double as convection ovens typically sacrifice space to the fan.

Oven cleaning. We strongly recommend a self-cleaning oven that uses a high-heat cycle (as high as 1000°F) to turn accumulated spills and splatters into ash. When the cycle is complete, you wipe away the residue with a damp sponge. The option typically costs $150 to $200 extra. Many ovens are lined with porcelain enamel that's cleaned with an oven cleaner.

Oven controls. Models with dial controls and an analog clock/timer are generally less expensive than electronic controls, which have tended to break down slightly more often.

Electronic controls—digital timers with touchpads and light-emitting diode (LED) displays—may be easier to clean. They're more precise, too. The designs easiest to use have prompts and a phone-style keypad for entering time directly.

Microwave ovens

Mid-sized models offer the best combination of price, cooking speed, and capacity.

Last CR report: August 1996
Expect to pay: $100 to $275

What's available

Most microwave ovens are designed to sit on a countertop. Some medium-sized models are specifically designed to be mounted over the range. Size aside, the main difference between large and small ovens is the power produced by the magnetron, which generates the high-energy microwaves that do the cooking. The higher the wattage, the more powerful the oven and the more quickly it heats food—a difference that's especially noticeable when you cook large quantities.

Manufacturers define size according to their measurement of the cooking cavity. Our own assessment is often smaller, since we measure usable space. How size translates into three dimensions depends on the design of the cabinet.

Large-sized ovens (1.4 cubic feet or more) hold lots of food, but they take up lots of space. Most generate 1000 watts or more. Large models aren't big sellers. Prices range from $200 to $300.

Medium-sized ovens (0.8 to 1.39 cubic feet). These also can hold lots of food, but are much less bulky and sacrifice little in capacity, versatility, or power. These models typically generate 800 to 1000 watts. Price range: $150 to $275.

Compact and subcompact ovens (less than 0.80 cubic feet). These are somewhat larger than toaster ovens, but may be too small for some dishes or frozen dinners. For basic chores like popping corn and warming beverages and leftovers, a small oven may be fine. They're the best-selling size. Their power is typically 600 to 700 watts. Price range: $100 to $150.

What's new

Prices and exterior sizes of microwave ovens continue to drop—so much that they are becoming more a small appliance than a major one. Today, you can buy a medium-sized oven for as little as $150. The last batch of ovens we tested are about two inches shorter and as much as four inches shallower than older models. All-black, all-white, gray, almond, and faux-stone cabinets are replacing the wood-grain look.

Reliability

The 1996 Annual Questionnaire did not provide brand reliability for microwave ovens.

Shopping strategy

Most of the ovens we've tested recently proved easy to use and quite capable of handling typical microwaving tasks.

Decide what to spend. Large-sized models have the largest capacity, the greatest power, and the most features. They're also the most expensive type and take up the most space. A medium-sized oven offers the most value. This size usually costs less than larger models yet has many of the same features. Consider a compact only if you're pressed for space or have modest needs.

What's in the stores. People buy microwave ovens most often at discount stores like Wal-Mart, appliance/TV stores, and Sears. Sharp dominates the microwave-oven market. Other major brands include General Electric, Kenmore (Sears), and Panasonic.

Manufacturers revise their model line practically every year. Changes may be trivial, but the model number is changed nonetheless. New introductions typically occur in spring and summer.

Key features

• *Recommended, if available:*

Direct cooking-time entry. Most ovens have 10 numbered electronic touchpads plus 2 or more special touchpads for reheating, popping popcorn, defrosting, and other tasks. Ordinarily, to set a heating time, you enter it directly: for example, 2, 3, 8 for 2 minutes and 38 seconds. A less convenient design requires you to enter that time by tapping a minute pad twice, a 10-second pad three times, and a second pad eight times.

Instant-on. This feature cuts down on button-pressing: Just enter the cooking time, and the oven starts. There's no need to touch "time" or "start" to get things going.

Moisture sensor. This useful feature figures out when to shut off the oven by measuring the moisture that has escaped from a dish of food. In our tests, ovens with a moisture sensor reheated food especially well. The sensor is also helpful for other tasks, such as cooking vegetables.

Shortcut touchpads. Some ovens let you tap in extra minutes or half-minutes to extend the time of an active setting.

Turntable. This improves cooking uniformity, but it also reduces usable space. A turntable with a lip around the edge helps contain spills.

• *Useful for particular needs:*

Child lockout. Nearly standard on mid-sized and full-sized models, this lets you punch in a code to disable the unit.

Food programs. Many ovens have settings for cooking specific foods, such as potatoes or muffins. Typically, these settings time the cooking automatically.

Refrigerators

Except for some small models, modern refrigerators do a good job of keeping things cold. Energy efficiency and convenience vary.

Last CR report: February 1997
Brand repair histories: pages 16
Expect to pay: $450 to $2000 or more

What's available

Refrigerators come in all sizes, from inexpensive cubes suitable for offices or dorm rooms to enormous built-ins that approach restaurant proportions.

Top-freezer models. The most common type, these are generally less expensive to buy and run than comparably sized side-by-side models. They offer the widest choice of sizes, styles, and features. Width, the critical measurement, ranges from about 24 to 36 inches.

The eye-level freezer offers easy access. Fairly wide shelves in the refrigerator compartment make it easy to reach things at the back, but force you to bend or crouch to reach the bottom shelves. Nominal capacity ranges from about 10 to almost 26 cubic feet, but we find that usable capacity is about 25 percent less. Recent tests have shown that the smallest sizes, those suitable for apartments, are noisier than larger models. Most are available with ice-makers.

Price range: 23-cubic-foot and larger models, $1000 or more; 20- to 22-cubic-foot models, $750 to $1300; 18- to 19-cubic foot models, $500 to $800; 14- to 16-cubic-foot models, $450 to $700.

Side-by-side models. These tend to be large—about 19 to 30 cubic feet of nominal capacity, 30 to 36 inches in width—and the most expensive to buy and run. Advantages offset the costs for many: You can store food at eye level in both freezer and refrigerator compartments. The high, narrow compartments make it easy to find stray items (but hard to get at items in the back). The narrow doors require minimal clearance to open. The freezer is large (but space is often sacrificed for the ice-maker). Ice and water dispensers are a common feature. Price range: 24- to 30-cubic foot models, $1050 to $2150; 20- to 22-cubic foot models, $800 to $1300.

Bottom-freezer models. This type represents tiny part of the market. Fairly wide eye-level shelves in the refrigerator compartment allow easy access to frequently used items. The freezer is low; a pull-out basket typically aids access. In-door ice and water dispensers are unavailable. Price: 20- to 22-cubic-foot models, $850 to $1100.

Built-in models. Built-ins, sized from 20 to 33 cubic feet, are only 24 inches deep, a half-foot shallower than conventional models, so they fit flush with surrounding cabinets. This type may be configured with the freezer on top or as a side-by-side. They're also taller and wider. You can furnish them with custom door panels to match the cabinetry. Price range: $2000 to $6000, plus installation.

Built-in-style models. These can accept door panels to match cabinetry but aren't quite as shallow or wide as true built-ins. This type may be configured with the freezer on the bottom or as a side-by-side. Nominal capacities range from 20 to 24 cubic feet. Price range: $1700 and up.

Compact models. With no more than six cubic feet of nominal capacity, these cubes are rudimentary devices. The freezer section is typically within the refrigerator compartment and gets no colder than 15° or 20° F. At those temperatures, ice cream turns soupy after only a few hours. If you adjust the control to make the freezer colder, items in the refrigerator compartment might freeze. Nor do compacts defrost automatically. Price range: $150 to $400.

What's new

The U.S. has banned manufacture of ozone-depleting chlorofluorocarbons (CFCs), including the chemical commonly known as Freon, used for decades as a refrigerant. Instead, refrigerators now use hydrofluorocarbons (HFCs) as their coolant and hydrochlorofluorocarbons (HCFC) in their insulation. The latter can also affect the ozone layer, but to a far lesser extent than CFCs.

Despite this major change, our tests show that new models appear to be as competent and efficient as older designs, and they cost no more.

Reliability

For years, our reader surveys have shown that refrigerators with ice-makers and water dispensers have been more likely to need repair than refrigerators without these features. In our 1996 survey, readers reported that among top-freezer models without ice-makers or dispensers bought between 1990 and 1996, Hotpoint, Whirlpool, and Kenmore were among the more reliable brands. Top-freezer models from Amana were the least reliable.

Among side-by-side refrigerators bought during the same period, General Electric and Amana tended to be less reliable than other brands, especially when equipped with ice-makers and dispensers. For more information, see the brand repair histories on page 16.

Shopping strategy

Even with improvements in energy efficiency, a refrigerator uses a lot of electricity over its life, typically 15 years. Operating costs depend largely on how big the refrigerator is and whether it's a top-freezer, side-by-side, or bottom-freezer model. But design matters, too. Over the years, our tests have regularly shown that some manufacturers make more efficient models than others. The bright yellow Energy Guide label on models in the store can let you make comparisons.

Before you shop, measure your space carefully, including space to open the doors. Note that some models can be flush against a side wall, and others need space for the doors to swing open. Top- and bottom-freezer models have doors that can hinge either on the right or left, depending on the kitchen workspace.

Decide what to spend. A top-freezer model gives you the most refrigerator for the money. But kitchen layout or personal preferences may send you to another type. In general, the larger the refrigerator, the more feature-laden it will be. An in-door ice-maker and dispenser, for example, may add $200 or so to the price. An automatic ice-maker is standard on some models or can be added on; kits cost between $70 and $100.

What's in the stores. The easiest brands to find are the top sellers: General Electric, Kenmore (Sears), Amana, and Whirlpool. Kenmore models are made by General Electric and Whirlpool. General Electric also makes Hotpoint models, and Whirlpool makes Kitchen-

Aid. Such family ties often result in strong similarities between refrigerators that bear different brand names.

Key features

Automatic ice-maker. These devices typically produce three or four pounds of ice a day and use about a cubic foot of freezer space. Today's ice-makers appear to be sturdier than the trouble-prone devices of old, but models with an ice-maker still have a higher repair rate than those without.

Door bins. These help contain items and can be removed for cleaning. Some have covers to guard against spills and to protect smaller items.

Door-shelf adjustments. These help prevent items from tumbling or sliding when the door is opened. Shelf-height extenders support tall bottles. "Snuggers" hold articles tight; some double as bottle holders.

Freezer light. Handy for locating items if unit isn't packed to the top.

Humidity-controlled crispers. Some refrigerators have controls that allow you to adjust humidity in their crisper drawers. The controls work, we found, but aren't worth the extra cost. Our tests show that crispers without controls can retain moisture just as well.

In-door ice and water dispenser. Allows you to get a few ice cubes or a cup of ice water without having to open the refrigerator door. For the convenience, you must sacrifice a couple of cubic feet in freezer space.

No-frost operation. This is practically a given these days, except on the smallest, cheapest models. Most self-defrosting models defrost about once a day, after their compressor has run for a certain number of hours. State-of-the-art systems modify the defrost cycle as needed.

See-through compartments. Transparent crispers, dairy compartments, and meat drawers let you tell at a glance what's inside.

Separate temperature controls. A single control that governs the main compartment and freezer (usually found on small, apartment-sized models) works fine, but separate controls make it easier to keep ice cream soft while maintaining a cold refrigerator.

Spill-proof glass shelves. These are much easier than wire shelves to clean and to adjust in height. Sealed, raised edges help contain spills. Some shelves slide out for better access, or fold or slide sideways to make room for tall items below.

Temperature-controlled meat drawer. Most refrigerators have a separate drawer for storing meat and fish. Some can send chilled air directly into the drawer, allowing it to be kept colder than the main compartment, which optimally should remain at 37° F. For storing fresh meat and fish, the meat drawer should be kept at 30° to 32°.

Utility bins. These are useful for storing odds and ends on shelves. Some have covers. Some are made to hold eggs, but we think it's better to keep eggs in their original carton.

Wine-bottle rack. Prevents bottles of all types from cluttering the door or rolling about on shelves.

Freezers

Chest freezers are tops in performance and efficiency, but self-defrosting uprights are more convenient.

Last CR report: October 1997
Ratings: page 117
Expect to pay: $300 to $700

What's available

Three types of freezers are sold, each in a range of sizes. Only two manufacturers produce the brands you're likely to see in stores. For more on "What's in the stores," see page 99.

Chest freezers. These are best if you buy a lot of food in bulk and store it over long periods. They are also good for large, bulky items. Because of their design, chests excel in almost every aspect of cold storage, and they run very efficiently. Their walls encase cooling coils that surround the frozen food stacked in the storage compartment (there are no shelves). Since the door opens from the top, only the warmest air escapes when it's opened. When the door is closed, its weight helps seal the unit. Our tests show that chests do better than uprights when the power goes off.

But chests take up more floor area than uprights, and they fall short on convenience. Except for some hanging baskets, the space is undifferentiated, making it hard to organize food. Defrosting has to be done manually; automatic defrost is not available. Price range: $300 to $600.

Manual-defrost uprights. Similar in size and shape to refrigerators, these provide eye-level storage and have a door that opens outward. This type comes with four or five shelves, nonadjustable because they contain cooling coils. The shelves make it easy to organize and rotate food, but may be hard to fit bulky items. Ice forms on the wire-covered cooling coils, which makes defrosting a real chore. Price range: $300 to $550.

Self-defrost uprights. The most convenient type, these freezers are very similar to refrigerators. Shelves are adjustable or removable, and many spaces are further apportioned by wire racks, bins, and baskets. A fan circulates chilled air throughout, keeping the temperature fairly uniform despite cold-air losses inherent in a design with a vertically opening door. The automatic-defrost feature cycles on periodically, adding somewhat to the energy used. Price range: $500 to $650.

What's new

Self-defrost upright freezers have now taken over as the fastest-selling type of freezer, despite the premium you pay for that feature and the energy costs involved.

A new feature is supposed to help make manual-defrost uprights more competitive by making them more convenient to defrost. "Flash defrost," a power-assisted feature, circulates hot refrigerant through the coils to speed up defrosting. But you still have to empty the freezer, store the food, and drain the water.

Shopping strategy

To make the investment worthwhile, you'd have to save $50 to $125 on food a year over, say, a 12-year period. Pick a freezer type and size, then buy by price and features.

Decide what to spend. The smallest,

cheapest freezers—chest or manual-defrost models—cost about $300. Expect to pay extra for the greater capacity and the convenience of an upright. Automatic defrost can add $200 extra to the price of a similarly-sized manual-defrost upright.

What's in the stores. Nearly all freezers sold in the U.S. are made by two companies: Frigidaire and W.C. Woods, a Canadian manufacturer.

Frigidaire sells under its name as well as Gibson, Kelvinator, Kenmore (Sears), Tappan, and White-Westinghouse. Woods makes Admiral, Amana, Magic Chef, Maytag, Roper, and Whirlpool models.

Using the Ratings. For our most recent report, we tested 19 models ranging in capacity from 7 to more than 21 cubic feet that represent the three types. We ranked them primarily for cold-storage performance—tests for temperature uniformity and stability. Energy efficiency and convenience were also considered. Within brands made by Frigidaire, models of the same capacity should perform similarly. The same is true for brands made by Woods. If you can't find a model, call the manufacturer; see page 342.

How to use the Ratings in the Buying Guide

- **Read the Recommendations for information on specific models and general buying advice.**
- **Note how the rated products are listed—in order of performance and convenience, price, or alphabetically.**
- **The overall score graph gives the big picture in performance. Notes on features and performance for individual models are listed in the Comments column or "Model details."**
- **Use the handy key numbers to find out the details on each model.**
- **Before going to press, we verify model availability for most products with manufacturers. Some tested models listed in the Ratings may no longer be available. Discontinued models are noted in Model details or Comments. Such models may actually still be available in some stores for part of 1998. Models indicated as successors should perform similarly to the tested models, according to the manufacturer. Features may vary.**
- **Models similar to the tested models, when they exist, are indicated in Comments or Model details.**
- **To find our last full report on a subject, check the reference above the Ratings chart or the eight-year index, page 346.**

Ratings *Dishwashers*

& Recommendations

The tests behind the Ratings

Overall score is based primarily on washing performance. **Washing** performance is based on treatment of china, glasses, and flatware, plus serving bowls and a platter, that had been smeared with various foods or filled with various beverages and drained. After scraping, soiled items sat overnight before being washed. Even the best models left a few water spots, soil particles, and grit on our very dirty test load. To assess **noise,** two staffers listened to each machine. **Price** is approximate retail. Models similar to those we tested are noted in the Model details; features may vary.

Typical features for these models

• At least three wash cycles plus a rinse-and-hold cycle. • Center wash tower with enough space above lower rack to hold at least an 11½-inch platter upright and above upper rack to hold tall (7½-inch) glasses upright. • Plastic tub and door liner. • Programmable for a delayed start.

Recommendations

Most of these models did a fine job of washing even our dirty test load. If a quiet dishwasher isn't a priority, the Kenmore (Sears) 1676 ($430) is a fine choice and a CR Best Buy. It has mechanical controls; its brandmate, the 1582 ($490) performs similarly and has electronic controls. The KitchenAid KUDS24SE ($680) and its similar brandmate, the KitchenAid KUDR24SE ($610), combine excellent cleaning with low water consumption and low noise levels.

See Buying Guide report, page 88. Last time rated in CONSUMER REPORTS: January and July 1997.

Overall Ratings

E ⊜ VG ⊖ G ○ F ◒ P ●

Listed in order of overall score

Key no.	Brand and model	Price	Overall score (0–100; P F G VG E)	Washing	Noise
1	**Maytag** IntelliSense DWU9962AA	$700		⊜	○
2	**Frigidaire** Gallery FDB636GF	380		⊜	⊖
3	**KitchenAid** KUDS24SE	680		⊜	⊖
4	**KitchenAid** KUDR24SE	610		⊜	⊖

Key no.	Brand and model	Price	Overall score (0–100; P F G VG E)	Washing	Noise
5	**Kenmore** (Sears) 1582	$490		⊜	○
6	**Kenmore** (Sears) 1676 **A CR Best Buy**	430		⊜	○
7	**KitchenAid** KUDI24SE	520		⊜	○
8	**Maytag** DWU9902AA	525		⊖	○
9	**GE Profile** CleanSensor GSD4930X	550		⊖	⊖
10	**White-Westinghouse** MDB631RF	375		⊖	⊖
11	**Kenmore** (Sears) 1562	365		⊖	◒
12	**GE Profile** GSD4030Y	380		⊖	○
13	**Whirlpool** DU980QPD	480		⊖	○
14	**Whirlpool** DU930QWD	430		⊖	○
15	**Maytag** DWU7402AA	400		⊖	◒
16	**Whirlpool** DU900PCD	360		⊖	◒
17	**Hotpoint** HDA900X	295		○	◒
18	**Amana** ADU6000C	385		○	◒
19	**Magic Chef** DU4500	340		○	◒

Model details

Notes on the details: Energy cost/yr. is based on use of each machine's normal cycle at national average energy rates: 8.31 cents per kilowatt-hour of electricity, and 61 cents per therm of gas. Gallons per cycle and cycle length also apply to use of normal cycle, including heated wash water and heated drying.

1 Maytag IntelliSense DWU9962AA $700

• Energy cost/yr.: $67 electricity, $37 gas • Normal cycle: 8 to 10 gal., 95 min. • Electronic controls

A digital display gives remaining time in cycle, alerts you (in words) to any problems. Automatically adjusts water used to dirtiness of load. Also offers regular cycles. But: Front panel not reversible. Loading features: Upper rack: terraced; long "snugger" (to secure light plastic items); fold-down shelf; stemware holders. Lower rack: adjustable and fold-down tines; fold-down shelf; can hold 14-inch platter upright. Covered section in silverware basket. Warranty: 3 yr., parts and labor; 5 yr., controls and wash system; lifetime, tub/door liner. **Recommendation:** Excellent, but expensive and less frugal with water than most.

2 KitchenAid KUDS24SE $680
4 KitchenAid KUDR24SE $610
7 KitchenAid KUDI24SE $520

• Energy cost/yr.: $61 electricity, $42 gas • Normal cycle: 6.5 gal., 110 min. • Electronic controls

These three models are similar, except (7) is a bit noisier than its siblings, and all three have different numbers of cycles. None has a center spray tower to hamper loading, but all have a center spray arm, which limits vertical loading space. Front panels not reversible. Loading features: Upper rack: terraced, with stemware holders, (3) and (4) only; spring clips for lightweight items, (3)

Can't find a model? Call the manufacturer. See page 342.

Ratings continued ▸

Ratings, continued

and (4) only; fold-down shelf, (3) and (4) only; adjustable tines, (3) only. Lower rack: fold-down tines, (3) only; fold-down shelf, (3) and (4) only. Silverware basket can be split into two parts, each with a covered section, on (3) only; (4) has covered section in silverware basket. Warranty: 1 yr., parts and labor; 5 yr., controls, heating element, and motor; lifetime, tub/door liner. **Recommendation:** Excellent (3, 4); very good (7).

3 Frigidaire Gallery FDB636GF $380

• Energy cost/yr.: $55 electricity, $36 gas • Normal cycle: 6.5 gal., 100 min. • Mechanical controls

Center spray arm; limits vertical loading space in lower rack. Front panel not reversible. Warranty: 2 yr., parts and labor. 20 yr., tub/door liner (parts only). **Recommendation:** Excellent and quiet, but from one of the least reliable brands.

5 Kenmore (Sears) 1582 $490

6 Kenmore (Sears) 1676 $430

• Energy cost/yr.: $60 electricity, $41 gas • Normal cycle: 6.5 gal., 100 min. • Electronic controls (5), mechanical controls (6)

These two, which differ only in their controls, are among the best at washing silverware. The digital display on (5) gives remaining time in cycle. But: Center spray arm; limits vertical loading space. Not as good as most at washing glasses. Loading features: Upper rack: adjusts in height; fold-down tines; fold-down shelves; utensil basket. Silverware basket has covered section. Warranty: 1 yr., parts and labor; 2 yr., parts only; lifetime, tub/door liner. **Model availability:** Discontinued. **Recommendation:** Excellent (5); very good (6)—a CR Best Buy.

8 Maytag DWU9902AA $525

• Energy cost/yr.: $64 electricity, $35 gas • Normal cycle: 10 gal., 95 min. • Electronic controls

A digital display gives remaining time in cycle. But: Front panel not reversible. Loading features: Upper rack: terraced; long "snugger" (to secure light plastic items), fold-down shelf, stemware holders. Lower rack: adjustable and fold-down tines; fold-down shelf; can hold 14-inch platter upright; covered section in silverware basket. Warranty: 1 yr., parts and labor; 2 yr., parts only; 5 yr., controls and wash system; 20 yr., tub/door liner. **Model availability:** Discontinued. **Recommendation:** Very good, but less frugal with water than most.

9 GE Profile CleanSensor GSD4930X $550

• Energy cost/yr.: $64 electricity, $34 gas • Normal cycle: 6 to 10 gal., 110 min. • Electronic controls

A digital display gives remaining time in cycle, alerts you (in codes) to any problems. Automatically adjusts water used to dirtiness of load. Also offers regular cycles. But: Front panel not reversible. Loading features: Upper rack: terraced; spring-loaded holders (for lightweight items); adjustable, fold-down shelf; stemware holders. Lower rack: fold-down tines; can hold 13-inch platter upright; silverware basket can be split into two parts, each with covered section. Warranty: 1 yr., parts and labor; 2 yr., parts only; 20 yr., tub/door liner. **Model availability:** Discontinued. **Recommendation:** Very good.

10 White-Westinghouse MDB631RF $340

• Energy cost/yr.: $52 electricity, $33 gas. Normal cycle: 6.5 gal., 85 min. • Mechanical controls

Center spray arm; limits vertical loading space in lower rack. Front panel not reversible. Warranty: 2 yr., water-distribution system (parts only); 2nd to 10th year, tub/door liner (parts only). **Recommendation:** Very good and quiet, but from one of the least reliable brands.

11 Kenmore (Sears) 1562 $365

• Energy cost/yr.: $60 electricity, $41 gas • Normal cycle: 6.5 gal., 100 min. • Mechanical controls

Upper rack has less vertical room than most others; it cannot hold tall (7½-in.) glasses upright. Center spray arm; limits vertical loading space in lower rack. Cannot be programmed to run at later time. Loading feature: Upper rack has utensil basket. Warranty: 1 yr., parts and labor; 2 yr., parts only; lifetime, tub and door liner. **Model availability:** Discontinued. **Recommendation:** Very good, but noisy.

12 GE Profile GSD4030Y $380

• Energy cost/yr.: $55 electricity, $30 gas • Normal cycle: 8.5 gal., 95 min. • Mechanical/ electronic controls

The most energy-efficient model tested. Loading features: Upper rack: terraced. Lower rack: can hold 13-inch platter upright; silverware basket can be split into two parts. Warranty: 1 yr., parts and labor; 2 yr., parts only; 20 yr., tub/door liner. **Model availability:** Discontinued. **Recommendation:** Very good.

13 Whirlpool DU980QPD $480

14 Whirlpool DU930QWD $430

• Energy cost/yr.: $63 electricity, $42 gas • Normal cycle: 7 gal., 100 min. • Electronic controls

Model (14) has fewer cycles and fewer loading features. Center spray arm; limits vertical loading space in lower rack. Loading features: Upper rack: adjusts in height; (13) also has fold-down shelves. Utensil basket, on (13) only, and silverware basket are on door. Warranty: 1 yr., parts and labor; 2 yr., parts only; 5 yr., electronics and power board; 20 yr., tub/door liner. Similar: DU940QWD, $450. **Recommendation:** Very good, and from one of the most reliable brands.

15 Maytag DWU7402AA $400

• Energy cost/yr.: $68 electricity, $38 gas • Normal cycle: 10 gal., 95 min. • Mechanical controls

Cannot be set to run at a later time. Front panel not reversible. Loading features: Upper rack: terraced; fold-down shelf. Lower rack: adjustable tines; can hold 14-inch platter upright; silverware basket has covered section. Warranty: 1 yr., parts and labor; 2 yr., parts only; 5 yr., wash system; 20 yr., tub and door liner. **Model availability:** Discontinued. **Recommendation:** Very good, but noisy and less frugal with water than most.

16 Whirlpool DU900PCD $360

• Energy cost/yr.: $63 electricity, $42 gas • Normal cycle: 7 gal., 100 min. • Mechanical controls

Upper rack has less vertical room than most others; it cannot hold tall (7½-in.) glasses. Cannot be set to run at a later time. Loading feature: Silverware basket is on door. Warranty: 1 yr., parts and labor; 2 yr., parts only; 20 yr., tub and door liner. Similar: DU915QWD, $380. **Recommendation:** Very good, and from one of the most reliable brands, but noisy.

17 Hotpoint HDA900X $295

18 Amana ADU6000C $385

• Energy cost/yr.: $60 electricity, $36 gas • Normal cycle: 9 gal., 100 min. • Mechanical controls

Model (18) adds extra cycles and extra warranty coverage. Loading features: Upper rack: terraced; fold-down shelves. Lower rack: can hold 13-inch platter upright; silverware basket has covered section. Warranty: 1 yr., parts and labor; 2 yr., parts only, on (18) only; 10 yr., tub/door liner (20 yr. for 18). **Model availability:** (17) discontinued. **Recommendation:** Good, but noisy and less frugal with water than most.

19 Magic Chef DU4500 $310

Energy cost/yr.: $62 electricity, $35 gas • Normal cycle: 9 gal., 40 min. • Mechanical controls

Upper rack is terraced; lower rack can hold a 13–in. platter upright. Warranty: 20 yr., tub and door liner. **Recommendation:** Good, but noisy and less frugal with water than most.

Ratings *Washing machines*

& Recommendations

The tests behind the Ratings

Overall score is based primarily on washing performance. **Washing** measures how well a machine cleaned soiled and stained swatches in a standard load. **Capacity** reflects how large a load the washer could effectively circulate. **Water efficiency** assesses how much water the washer used per pound of laundry washed. **Energy efficiency** considers the machine's electrical consumption and the energy required to heat water for a warm wash, averaging the costs for electric and gas water heating. **Price** is approximate retail. Models similar to those we tested are noted in the Model details; features may vary.

Typical features for these models

• Continuously variable water-level control. • Water hoses for attachment to water-supply lines. • Lid that opens back. • At least two agitation and spin speeds, and at least three speed combinations. • Agitation and spin speeds that automatically match the cycle selected. • Lip on top to contain minor spills. • One-year parts-and-labor warranty (many models also have longer parts-only warranties for the drivetrain or tub).

Recommendations

Any of these machines can do a fine job of washing clothes.The excellent front-loader Frigidaire FWT445GE ($800) is the washer to choose if energy conservation is a priority for you. Otherwise, look to a less expensive top-loader. Two fine GE models included in an earlier report (July 1996) remain in stores: the WPSQ4160T ($500) and WJSR2080T ($400). Brands at the bottom of the Ratings—White-Westinghouse, Magic Chef, Speed Queen, and Frigidaire—have been among the least reliable over the years. See brand repair histories, page 17.

See Buying Guide report, page 83. Last time rated in CONSUMER REPORTS: July 1997.

Overall Ratings

E = Excellent, VG = Very good, G = Good, F = Fair, P = Poor

Within types, listed in order of overall score

Key no.	Brand and model	Price	Overall score (0–100: P F G VG E)	Washing	Capacity	Efficiency: WATER	Efficiency: ENERGY
	FRONT-LOADING MODELS						
1	**Frigidaire** FWT445GE	$800		E	E	E	E
2	**Asko** 8005 (compact)	900		VG	F	E	E
	TOP-LOADING MODELS						
3	**Kenmore (Sears)** 2693	600		E	E	VG	F
4	**GE** WPSQ3120T6	510		E	E	VG	G
5	**Kenmore (Sears)** 2683	500		E	E	VG	F
6	**GE** WWSR3090T6	480		E	E	VG	F
7	**Whirlpool** LSL9345E	510		E	E	G	F
8	**Maytag** LAT9706AA	590		VG	VG	G	G
9	**Amana** LW8203	480		E	E	VG	F
10	**KitchenAid** KAWS677E	500		VG	E	VG	G
11	**Maytag** LAT9406AA	540		VG	VG	G	G
12	**Whirlpool** LSR5233E	440		E	E	G	F
13	**Admiral** LATA300AA	440		E	VG	G	F
14	**Hotpoint** VWXR4100T5	410		E	G	F	F
15	**White-Westinghouse** MWX645RE	430		VG	G	F	F
16	**Magic Chef** W227L	460		E	VG	G	F
17	**Speed Queen** AWM472	480		VG	VG	G	F
18	**Frigidaire** FWS645RB	470		VG	G	F	F

Model details

Notes on the details: Comparable models are listed together, the higher-rated model first. Dimensions are HxWxD, rounded up to the nearest inch. Water used is for the machines' maximum load at the maximum water setting.

Front-loading models

1 Frigidaire FWT445GE $800
• 36x27x28 in. • Water used: 34 gal. Among the quietest models tested. Handles unbalanced loads better than others. Has automatic detergent dispenser, extra-rinse setting option, adjustable end-of-cycle signal, and stainless-steel inner tub. Door locks during use, but can be easily opened if cycle is interrupted. No water-level selector; machine determines amount of water to use. 2-yr. parts-and-labor warranty. But: For best results, must use special detergent that's fairly expensive. We lack sufficient data to report on reliability. Has timed bleach dispenser that, if over-

Ratings continued ▶

Ratings, continued

filled, can overflow onto a dry load. Lacks self-leveling rear legs. Similar: Gibson GWT445RFS, $900. **Recommendation:** An excellent machine, but expensive—unless you can expect a utility rebate or a substantial saving in operating cost because you pay above-average water and energy rates.

2 Asko 8005 $900

• 32x24x25 in. • Water used: 21 gal.
Compact design; much shorter and much smaller in capacity than the other models tested. Has automatic detergent dispenser, "on" light, and stainless-steel inner tub. Heats water when hot wash is selected. Handles unbalanced loads better than others and extracts the most water from clothes at end of cycle. No water-level selector; machine determines amount of water to use. Door locks during use; can be opened if cycle is interrupted, but a screwdriver is required. But: For best results, must use special detergent that's fairly expensive. We lack sufficient data to report on reliability. Lacks lip on top to help contain spills; has no liquid bleach dispenser. Lacks self-leveling rear legs. Warm rinse not available with warm wash. Requires 20-amp receptacle (not regular 15-amp receptacle of other models). Space between outer housing and inner cabinet can trap fingers; the danger increases when machine is operating. **Recommendations:** A very good machine, but worth considering only if space is at a premium.

Top-loading models

3 Kenmore (Sears) 2693 $600
5 Kenmore (Sears) 2683 $500

• 43x27x27 in. • Water used: 42 gal. (3), 41 gal. (5)
These models are similar, except (3) is among the quietest models tested. (3) also has 5 selectable wash/spin speed combinations and continuously variable water levels, while (5) has 4 combinations and 5 levels respectively. (3) also has an automatic detergent dispenser. Both have the most logical and legible controls of any models tested, porcelain top and lid, option for extra-rinse setting, and selectable automatic temperature control (can blend hot and cold water to obtain a preset temperature). But: Both have lids that open left, rather than back. Similar: to (5): 2684, $500. **Recommendations:** Both are very good machines. (5) is the better value, unless the quietness of (3) is worth an additional $100 to you.

4 GE WPSQ3120T6 $510
6 GE WWSR3090T6 $480

• 42x27x26 in. • Water used: 43 gal. (4), 41 gal. (6)
These models are similar. (4) is among the quietest machines tested; it's also among the most energy-efficient top-loaders and has some mechanical touchpad controls, an end-of-cycle signal, and continuously variable water levels. (6) has rotary controls and only 4 water levels. Both have 3 selectable wash/spin speed combinations, options for extra-rinse setting, and plastic inner tub. The best models for access to all major components for servicing. **Model availability:** Model designations have stayed the same but models have changed significantly. **Recommendations:** Very good machines; (4) is a slightly better choice.

7 Whirlpool LSL9345E $510

• 42x27x27 in. • Water used: 42 gal.
Has option for extra-rinse setting, end-of-cycle signal that can be turned off, 5 water levels, and some mechanical touchpad controls. But: Lacks lip on top to contain spills. **Recommendation:** A very good machine with some desirable features.

8 Maytag LAT9706AA $590
11 Maytag LAT9406AA $540

• 43x26x27 in. • Water used: 39 gal.
These are similar models, except (8) has selectable wash/spin speed combinations, option for extra-rinse setting, switch for extended spin setting, and "on" and cycle indicator lights. Both have porcelain top and lid, and a bleach dispenser that is easier to pour into than others. But: Both lack self-leveling rear legs. **Recommendation:** Very good machines.

9 Amana LW8203 $480

• 43x26x28 in. • Water used: 42 gal.
Has stainless-steel inner tub. 2-yr. parts-and-labor warranty. But: Compared to most, harder to ser-

vice and extracts less water from clothes. Lacks a warm rinse with the warm wash. **Model availability:** Discontinued. **Recommendation:** A very good machine.

10 KitchenAid KAWS677E $500

• 43x27x26 in. • Water used: 41 gal.
Has option for extra-rinse setting and some mechanical touchpad controls. 2-yr. parts-and-labor warranty. But: Lacks lip on top to contain spills. Has only 4 water levels. **Recommendation:** A very good machine.

12 Whirlpool LSR5233E $440

• 42x27x26 in. • Water used: 43 gal.
Has color-coded controls. But: Lacks lip on top to help contain spills, has only 3 water levels, and warm rinse not available with warm wash. **Recommendation:** A very good, if spartan, machine.

13 Admiral LATA300AA $440

16 Magic Chef W227L $460

• 44x27x27 in. • Water used: 41 gal. (13), 42 gal. (16)
These models are similar. (13) has 3 selectable wash/spin speed combinations, while (16) has 4 selectable wash/spin speed combinations and offers no warm rinse with a warm wash. Both have plastic inner tub. Both have a fabric-softener dispenser that can be used as a liquid-detergent dispenser during soak cycle. But: Bleach dispenser on both is more difficult to pour into than others and may allow bleach to spatter into inner tub. **Model availability:** Discontinued. **Recommendation:** Good machines, but be careful if you use bleach. Magic Chef has been among the less reliable brands of top-loading machines.

14 Hotpoint VWXR4100T5 $410

• 42x27x26 in. • Water used: 37 gal.
Has 4 selectable wash/spin speed combinations, option for extra-rinse setting. Inner tub is plastic. But: Has only 4 water levels, and bleach dispenser is more difficult to pour into than others. **Model availability:** Model designation has stayed the same but model has changed significantly. **Recommendation:** A good machine.

15 White-Westinghouse MWX645RE $430

• 43x27x27 in. • Water used: 39 gal.
Has 4 selectable wash/spin speed combinations. Door locks during and for a short time after spin. Inner tub is plastic. **Recommendation:** A good machine.

17 Speed Queen AWM472 $480

• 43x26x28 in. • Water used: 42 gal.
Fabric-softener dispenser is optional. But: Compared to most, harder to service and extracts less water from clothes. Warm rinse not available with warm wash. **Model availability:** Discontinued. **Recommendation:** A good machine.

18 Frigidaire FWS645RB $470

• 42x27x27 in. • Water used: 46 gal.
Has 4 selectable wash/spin speed combinations. Door locks during and for a short time after spin. Inner tub is plastic. But: The least water-efficient model tested. **Model availability:** Discontinued. **Recommendation:** A good, if spartan, machine from one of the less-reliable brands of top-loading washer.

Can't find a model? Call the manufacturer. See page 342.

Ratings *Full-sized clothes dryers*

& Recommendations

The tests behind the Ratings

Overall score is based mainly on performance, noise, and convenience. **Sensor type** is either a moisture sensor (M) or thermostat (T). **Drying** performance combines results from tests on four types of load. **Drum volume** ranges from about 5½ to 7 cubic feet. **Ease of use** includes how easy it is to use controls, load laundry, and maintain the lint filter. **Noise** was judged as a machine dried a 6-pound load. **Price** is approximate retail. Models similar to those we tested are noted in the Model details; features may vary.

Typical features for these models

• Rotary control with two or three automatic drying cycles. • Separate temperature control. • Timed-dry cycle and an air-fluff cycle of an hour or more. • Extended cool-down tumble on at least one cycle. • Venting from three or more places. • Door that can be adjusted to open left or right. • Optional end-of-cycle signal. • Drum light. • Raised edges on top to contain spills. • One-year warranty on parts and labor.

Recommendations

All full-sized dryers can dry clothes well, but models with moisture sensors—like the top eight electric and top five gas models—can gauge dryness a bit more accurately than models that use thermostats. If gas is an option, buy a gas model: The $40 to $50 extra you pay will quickly be offset by their cheaper operating costs.

See Buying Guide report, page 86. Last time rated in CONSUMER REPORTS: March 1997.

Overall Ratings

E VG G F P

Within types, listed in order of overall score

Key no.	Brand and model	Price	Sensor type	Overall score (0–100; P F G VG E)	Drying	Drum volume	Ease of use	Noise
	ELECTRIC DRYERS							
1	**Kenmore** (Sears) 6693	$500	M		VG	E	VG	E
2	**Kenmore** (Sears) 6681	420	M		VG	E	VG	VG
3	**General Electric** DDSR475ET	380	M		VG	E	VG	VG

Key no.	Brand and model	Price	Sensor type	Overall score (0–100: P F G VG E)	Drying	Drum volume	Ease of use	Noise
	ELECTRIC DRYERS *continued*							
4	**GE Profile** DPSQ495ET	$440	M		⊖	⊜	⊖	⊖
5	**Maytag** LDE9806	490	M		⊖	⊖	⊖	⊜
6	**Whirlpool** LEL8858E	460	M		⊖	⊜	⊖	●
7	**KitchenAid** KEYS677E	430	M		⊖	⊜	○	⊖
8	**Whirlpool** LER5848E	400	M		⊖	⊜	○	⊖
9	**Roper** RES7648E	330	T		○	⊜	○	⊖
10	**Hotpoint** NWXR473ET	320	T		○	⊖	⊖	⊖
11	**Admiral** LDEA200	300	T		○	⊜	○	⊖
12	**Magic Chef** YE225	330	T		○	⊜	○	⊖
13	**Maytag** LDE9306	400	T		○	⊖	○	⊜
14	**White-Westinghouse** MDE436RE	300	T		○	○	○	○
15	**Amana** LE8317	310	T		○	⊖	○	○
	GAS DRYERS							
16	**Kenmore** (Sears) 7681	470	M		⊖	⊜	⊖	⊖
17	**General Electric** DDSR475GT	420	M		⊖	⊜	⊖	⊖
18	**GE Profile** DPSQ495GT	470	M		⊖	⊜	⊖	⊖
19	**KitchenAid** KGYS677E	480	M		⊖	⊜	○	⊖
20	**Whirlpool** LGR5848E	450	M		⊖	⊜	○	⊖
21	**Hotpoint** NWXR473GT	360	T		○	⊖	⊖	⊖
22	**Maytag** LDG9306	440	T		○	⊖	○	⊖
23	**Amana** LG8319	360	T		○	⊖	○	⊖
24	**White-Westinghouse** MDG436RE	340	T		○	○	○	○

Model details

Notes on the details: The gas dryers are listed with their electric counterparts. Dimensions are to the nearest quarter-inch. Height includes the control panel; depth with door open includes the reach of the door open 90 degrees. More space may be needed for vent piping.

1 Kenmore (Sears) 6693 $500

• HxWxD: 43¼x27x28¼ in. (42¼ in. with door open)

Performed better—and more quietly—than most on our mixed loads, leaving them appropriately damp. It did a very good job with all-cotton shirts and an average job with delicates. It has a blocked-lint-filter signal and an adjustable end-of-cycle signal. It comes with a drying rack. The

Ratings continued ▸

Ratings, continued

optional extended cool-down tumble runs for up to four hours, nice if you won't be around when the load is done. The lint filter is in the drum. The door opens down. **Model availability:** Discontinued. **Recommendation:** A very good performer.

2 **Kenmore 6681** $420

16 **Kenmore 7681** $470

• HxWxD: 43x29x28 in. (41¾ in. with door open)

Performed as well as (1), though a little more noisily. They have an adjustable end-of-cycle signal. They come with a drying rack. The lint filter is on top. The door opens down. But: The air-fluff cycle runs for only 30 minutes, and the machine vents only from the rear. Similar: 6682, $420, and 7682, $470, both with a door that can be adjusted to open left or right. **Recommendation:** Very good performers.

3 **GE DDSR475ET** $380

17 **GE DDSR475GT** $420

• HxWxD: 42¼x27x28¼ in. (51½ in. with door open)

Performed very well with all loads, including delicates. They have an adjustable end-of-cycle signal and come with a drying rack. The lint filter in the drum can be cleaned without removal. Additional warranty: 5 years on the drum (parts only). **Recommendation:** Very good performers.

4 **GE Profile DPSQ495ET** $440

18 **GE Profile DPSQ495GT** $470

• HxWxD: 42¼x27x28¼ in. (51½ in. with door open)

Performed very well with all loads, including delicates. The end-of-cycle signal is a pleasant chime. They come with a drying rack. The lint filter in the drum can be cleaned without removal. Additional warranty: 5 years on the drum (parts only). But: The mechanical touchpad buttons are less convenient than rotary dials. **Recommendation:** Very good performers.

5 **Maytag LDE9806** $490

• HxWxD: 43¾x28½x27 in. (51 in. with door open)

Performed very well—and more quietly than most—with all loads, including delicates. Its end-of-cycle signal is a pleasant chime. The porcelain top is less prone to scratches, but it's not raised at the front. It comes with a drying rack. The lint filter is in the drum. Additional warranties: 2 years on parts, 5 years on the drum and solid-state controls and against cabinet rust. But: Clothes tend to catch on the lint filter as they're unloaded. **Model availability:** Discontinued. **Recommendation:** A very good performer.

6 **Whirlpool LEL8858E** $460

• HxWxD: 42½x29x28 in. (41¾ in. with door open)

Performed better than most dryers on our mixed loads, leaving them appropriately damp. It did a very good job with all-cotton shirts and an average job with delicates. The "Easy Clean 100" lint filter needn't be cleaned after every cycle and has a 5-year (parts only) warranty. The door opens down. But: It's very noisy. The mechanical touchpad buttons are less convenient than rotary dials. The air-fluff cycle runs for only 30 minutes and the machine vents only from the rear. There's no raised edge on top. **Recommendation:** A very good performer from one of the more reliable brands, but noisy.

7 **KitchenAid KEYS677E** $430

19 **KitchenAid KGYS677E** $480

• HxWxD: 42¾x29x28 in. (41¾ in. with door open)

Performance was very good with mixed and all-cotton loads and average with delicates. They have a blocked-lint-filter signal. The lint filter is on top. The warranty is 2 years for parts and labor; 5 years (limited) on the element/burner, motor, and controls; 10 years on the drum and against cabinet rust. The door opens down. But: The mechanical touchpad buttons are less convenient than rotary dials. The air-fluff cycle runs for only 20 minutes and the machine vents only from the rear. There's no raised edge on top. **Recommendation:** Very good performers and, for the electric, among the more reliable brands.

8 Whirlpool LER5848E $400

20 Whirlpool LGR5848E $450

• HxWxD: 42¼x29x28 in. (41¾ in. with door open)
Performance was very good with mixed loads and average with all-cotton shirts. With delicates, the electric did a very good job and the gas was average. The lint filter is on top. The door opens down. But: The color-coded rotary dial is somewhat difficult to set. The air-fluff cycle runs for only 30 minutes and the machine vents only from the rear. There's no raised edge on top. **Recommendation:** Very good performers from one of the more reliable brands.

9 Roper RES7648E $330

• HxWxD: 42½x29x28 in. (41¾ in. with door open)
Performance was very good with our mixed loads and average with all-cotton shirts and delicates. The lint filter is on top. The door opens down. But: The air-fluff cycle runs for only 30 minutes and the machine vents only from the rear. There's no raised edge on top. **Recommendation:** A good performer.

10 Hotpoint NWXR473ET $320

21 Hotpoint NWXR473GT $360

• HxWxD: 42½x27x25¼ in. (48¾ in. with door open)
Performance was very good with delicates and average with other loads. The lint filter in the drum can be cleaned without removal. Additional warranty: 5 years on the drum (parts only). **Recommendation:** Good performers.

11 Admiral LDEA200 $300

12 Magic Chef YE225 $330

• HxWxD: 43¾x27x27½ in. (49¾ in. with door open)
Having just one heat setting, these similar models did an average job with all types of loads. The lint filter is in the drum. But: There's no drum light, and you can't turn off the end-of-cycle signal. The door opens only to the right. Similar: Admiral LDEA400, $320, adds a low temperature setting and drying rack; Magic Chef YE226, $330, adds a low temperature setting and drum light. **Recommendation:** Good, but bare bones.

13 Maytag LDE9306 $400

22 Maytag LDG9306 $440

• HxWxD: 43¾x28½x27 in. (51 in. with door open)
Performance was average with all types of loads. The electric model was quieter than most. The porcelain top is less prone to scratches, but it's not raised at the front. Additional warranties: 2 years for parts, 5 years on the drum and against cabinet rust. But: Clothes tend to catch on the lint filter as they're unloaded. There's no drum light, and you can't turn off the end-of-cycle signal—which may be too short to hear, anyway. **Model availability:** Both are discontinued. **Recommendation:** Good, but other, less expensive models perform better.

14 White-Westinghouse MDE436RE $300

24 White-Westinghouse MDG436RE $340

• HxWxD: 43½x27x25½ in. (47½ in. with door open)
Performance was average with all types of loads. The lint filter is in the drum. But: There's no air fluff, no drum light, no extended cool-down tumble, and you can't turn off the end-of-cycle signal. Similar: Frigidaire FDE436RE, $310, Frigidaire FDG436RE, $350. **Recommendation:** Good, but bare bones and, for the electric, among the less reliable brands.

15 Amana LE8317 $310

23 Amana LG8319 $360

• HxWxD: 43¼x27x28¼ in. (51¾ in. with door open)
Performance was average with all types of loads. They have an adjustable end-of-cycle signal. The warranty is 2 years for parts and labor, 5 years against cabinet rust. But: There's no drum light. The lint filter in the drum can't be removed. The cycle-control dial turns only clockwise. **Model availability:** Both are discontinued. **Recommendation:** Good performers.

Can't find a model? Call the manufacturer. See page 342.

Ratings *Compact electric dryers*

& Recommendations

The tests behind the Ratings

Compacts are rated on the same scale as full-sized dryers. **Overall score** is based mainly on drying performance, noise, and ease of use. **Price** is approximate retail. **Sensor** is a moisture sensor (M) or thermostat (T). Compacts operate on 120 or 240 volts as noted.

Typical features for these models

• One auto-dry cycle and no temperature control. • Timed-dry cycle that runs up to 105 minutes; air fluff, up to 10 minutes. • Lint filter at the rear of the drum (which has no light), so you have to reach inside the small opening to get at it. • Controls on the front. • Door that opens only to the right. • One-year parts-and-labor warranty. **Additional features:** • 120-volt models have wheels (optional on the GE). • The Kenmore (Sears) 8518 has three heat settings, an extended cool-down, and a 30-minute air fluff, but timed dry goes up to only 70 minutes. • The Whirlpool LER3622D has a 30-minute air fluff, but timed dry goes up to only 80 minutes.

Recommendations

All the compacts dried clothes well and were very quiet. All were very inconvenient. The GE DSKP233ET ($390) edged out the other models by a slight margin because it handled men's cotton shirts fairly well.

See Buying Guide report, page 86. Last time rated in CONSUMER REPORTS: March 1997.

Overall Ratings

Listed in order of overall score

Brand and model	Price	Overall score (0–100; P F G VG E)	HxWxD	Depth, door open	Sensor/ voltage
General Electric DSKP233ET	$390		31½x24x22 in.	38 in.	M/120
Whirlpool LDR3822D	350		32¾x24x22	38	M/120
Kenmore (Sears) 8518 (now 8818)	380		31½x24x21	36½	T/240
Kenmore (Sears) 8572 (now 8872)	380		32¾x24x22	38	M/120
Whirlpool LER3622D	370		31½x24x21	36½	T/240

Can't find a model? Call the manufacturer. See page 342.

Ratings *Gas ranges*

& Recommendations

The tests behind the Ratings

Overall score is based primarily on ease of cleaning, convenience, oven size, and cooking performance. **Cooktop speed** is based on how quickly the largest burner brought six liters of water from room temperature to a near-boil. **Cooktop controls** assesses the burner knobs—how smoothly and evenly they adjusted the flame, and the clarity of their markings. **Oven controls** considers ease of use and whether they're electronic or dial. **Price** is approximate retail. Bracketed numbers or letters in the model designation change according to the range's color. Models similar to those we tested are noted in the Model details; features may vary.

Typical features for these models

• Push-to-turn burner dials. • Spark igniters to light the cooktop burners and glow-type igniters to light the oven/broiler. • Can be converted to liquified-petroleum (LP) gas. • Porcelain cooktop, more durable than a painted surface. • Oven window and interior light. • Two adjustable oven shelves. • One-year parts-and-labor warranty. **Self-cleaning models:** • Broiler within the oven. • Four sealed cooktop burners. • A storage or warming drawer. **Manual-clean models:** • A separate, shallow broiling compartment below the oven. • Dial oven controls.

Recommendations

Most of these models would make fine choices. The top three models offer excellent countertop controls and very good cooktop design for $650 to $750, substantially less then many other models. Among the manual-clean models, the Kenmore 7518[1] ($400) is a good value, particularly if you prepare most of your food on the cooktop.

See Buying Guide report, page 90. Last time rated in CONSUMER REPORTS: May 1997.

Ratings continued ▸

Ratings, continued

Overall Ratings

E = Excellent symbol, VG = Very good symbol, G = Good symbol, F = Fair symbol, P = Poor symbol (legend: E VG G F P)

Within types, listed in order of overall score

Key no.	Brand and model	Price	Overall score (0–100: P F G VG E)	Cooktop: Speed	Cooktop: Controls	Cooktop: Cleaning	Oven: Size	Oven: Controls	Oven: Self-clean
	SELF-CLEANING MODELS								
1	**Kenmore** (Sears) 7557[1]	$650		VG	E	VG	E	E	F
2	**General Electric** JGBP30WEW[WW]	670		VG	E	VG	E	VG	F
3	**Amana** ARG7600[WW]	750		G	E	VG	VG	G	VG
4	**General Electric Profile** JGBP80MEV[BC]	1030		VG	E	F	E	VG	F
5	**Kenmore** (Sears) 7597[0]	930		VG	E	G	E	G	F
6	**Frigidaire Gallery Professional** FGF379WE[S]	1450		G	G	G	VG	G	E
7	**Tappan** TGF357CC[S]	760		G	G	G	VG	G	E
8	**Whirlpool** SF395LEE[Q]	710		G	G	G	E	VG	G
9	**Whirlpool** SF375PEE[N]	650		G	F	G	E	G	VG
10	**Tappan** TGF365BE[W]	700		F	G	G	VG	G	VG
11	**Maytag** CRG9700CA[E]	675		G	G	G	VG	G	E
12	**Maytag** CRG9830CA[E]	950		G	G	G	VG	F	E
13	**Magic Chef** 3448XT[W]	610		F	F	G	E	F	E
	MANUAL-CLEAN MODELS								
14	**Kenmore** (Sears) 7518[1]	400		G	E	VG	E	G	—
15	**General Electric** JGBPS20WEW[WW]	420		G	VG	G	E	G	—
16	**Hotpoint** RGB528GEV[WH]	370		G	F	F	E	G	—
17	**Designer Series by Tappan** (Montgomery Ward) 28044[0]	300		G	F	F	E	G	—

Model details

Self-cleaning models

1 Kenmore (Sears) 7557[1] $650

• Cooktop burners, Btu/hr.: 5000, 2 @ 9500, 12,000.

Burner controls adjust flame smoothly. Faltered in tough self-cleaning test (but lengthening self-cleaning cycle should remove extra-tough soil). Removable burner heads for easy cleaning. Cooktop gets quite hot while cooking with all burners on high. Oven-temperature dial, digital clock and timer. Oven window gives very good view. Oven shuts off automatically after running 12 hours. Door latch gets hot during self-cleaning cycle. Porcelain cooktop control panel and storage door. **Model availability:** Discontinued. **Recommendation:** A very good range—our top choice in this group.

2 General Electric JGBP30WEW[WW] $670

• Cooktop burners, Btu/hr.: 5000, 2 @ 9500, 12,000.

Like top-rated (1), though oven dial is less convenient and window view isn't as good. Door latch gets hot during self-cleaning cycle. **Recommendation:** Very good. Scored just below the Kenmore (1).

3 Amana ARG7600[WW] $750

• Cooktop burners, Btu/hr.: 5000, 9100, 2 @ 12,500.

Burner controls adjust flame smoothly, but we had to lower the maximum setting of the small burner to prevent scorching in chocolate-melt test. Cooktop gets quite hot while cooking with all burners on high. Oven broiler seared steaks and burgers better than other tested models did. Electronic oven controls. Oven window gives very good view. Oven shuts off automatically after running 12 hours. During self-cleaning cycle, hot spots develop on cooktop and its controls, and oven window gets relatively hot; permanent stains formed on two white burner controls. Porcelain-coated cooktop control panel. Additional two-year parts warranty; five years on sealed burners. **Model availability:** Discontinued. **Recommendation:** Very good, overall, with some useful features.

4 General Electric Profile GBP80MEV[BC] $1030

• Cooktop burners, Btu/hr.: 5000, 2 @ 9500, 12,000.

Flashy "commercial" styling. Works like (1), but cooktop doesn't get as hot with all burners on high, has electronic oven controls, oven window doesn't give as good a view, and oven has three shelves instead of two. Door latch gets hot during self-cleaning cycle. Shiny panels show fingerprints vividly, and heavy burner grates are awkward to clean. **Recommendation:** Very good, overall, but a stiff price for glitzy styling.

5 Kenmore (Sears) 7597[0] $930

• Cooktop burners, Btu/hr.: 5000, 2 @ 9500, 12,000.

Another commercial-style model. Much like top-rated (1), except cooktop doesn't get as hot while cooking with all burners on high, has electronic oven controls, and oven has three shelves instead of two. Door latch gets hot during self-cleaning cycle. Shiny panels show fingerprints vividly. **Model availability:** Discontinued. **Recommendation:** Very good, overall, but a stiff price for glitzy styling.

6 Frigidaire Gallery Professional FGF379WE[S] $1450

• Cooktop burners, Btu/hr.: 2 @ 9000, 2 @ 11,000.

Yet another commercial-style model. Removable grate spans work space along middle of cooktop. Electronic oven controls. Compartment below oven is warming drawer rather than storage space. Oven window gives very good view. Oven control-panel area gets very hot during broiling and self-cleaning cycle. Stainless-steel panels show fingerprints vividly. Two-year warranty on parts and labor. Similar: Frigidaire Gallery Professional FGF378WC[-], $1350. **Recommendation:** A very good performer overall. But you pay an extravagant price for extravagant styling.

Ratings continued ▶

Ratings, continued

7 Tappan TGF357CC[S] $760

• Cooktop burners, Btu/hr.: 2 @ 9000, 2 @ 11,000.

Cooktop and its controls develop hot spots during self-cleaning cycle, and permanent stain formed on burner control panel. We couldn't remove a stain from another test on a burner cap. Electronic oven controls. **Recommendation:** A very good range, worth considering.

8 Whirlpool SF395LEE[Q] $710

• Cooktop burners, Btu/hr.: 6500, 7500, 2 @ 9500.

Porcelain-coated cooktop control panel and front of storage door. Electronic oven controls. You can't tell 7500-Btu/hr. and 9500-Btu/hr. burners apart visually. Cooktop gets quite hot while cooking with all burners on high. Burners set to low flame tended to blow out when we let oven door slam shut. Window gets relatively hot during self-cleaning cycle, and a permanent black stain appeared between control panel and backguard. **Similar:** Whirlpool SF385PEE[-], $660. **Recommendation:** A very good range; worth considering.

9 Whirlpool SF375PEE[N] $650

• Cooktop burners, Btu/hr.: 6500, 7500, 2 @ 9500.

Like (8), except cooktop dials turn only 90 degrees, flame adjusts only in steps, and oven window doesn't get as hot during self-cleaning cycle. **Recommendation:** Very good, if you can live with the hard-to-adjust burner controls.

10 Tappan TGF365BE[W] $700

• Cooktop burners, Btu/hr.: 4 @ 9000.

Oven window gives very good view. Dial controls, with analog clock and timer. Hot spots develop on cooktop and its controls during self-cleaning cycle. Compartment below oven is warming drawer. **Model availability:** Discontinued. **Recommendation:** A very good range, worth considering.

11 Maytag CRG9700CA[E] $675

• Cooktop burners, Btu/hr.: 2 @ 9200, 2 @ 12,000.

Cooktop space is tight; our 11-inch skillet could not be centered on either back burner, and our eight-quart covered pot on the right rear burner blocked the electronic oven controls. Cooktop gets quite hot while cooking with all burners on High. Oven window gives very good view. Oven shuts off automatically after running 12 hours. Door latch gets hot during self-cleaning cycle. Storage drawer has lift-out plastic liner, convenient for cleaning. Additional two-year warranty on parts; five years on electronic clock; 10 years on burners. **Model availability:** Discontinued. **Recommendation:** A very good range, worth considering.

12 Maytag CRG9830CA[E] $950

• Cooktop burners, Btu/hr.: 2 @ 9200, 2 @ 12,000.

Similar to (11), except that oven can cook by convection. Convection cooking was slightly faster; a fan circulates the hot air in the oven. Also, this model has four shelves instead of two. Door latch gets hot and oven window gets relatively hot during self-cleaning cycle. **Model availability:** Discontinued. **Recommendation:** A very good range, but the convection fan isn't worth the extra money.

13 Magic Chef 3448XT[W] $610

• Cooktop burners, Btu/hr.: 4 @ 9200.

Cooktop space is tight; our 11-inch skillet could not be centered on either back burner. Cooktop burner dials turn only 90 degrees, and flame adjusts only in steps. Cooktop gets quite hot while cooking with all burners on high. Hot spots develop on cooktop, control panel, oven window, and latch during self-cleaning. Additional five-year warranty on burners. **Model availability:** Discontinued. **Recommendation:** A good performer, but many drawbacks. One of the less reliable brands.

Manual-clean models

14 Kenmore (Sears) 7518[1] $400

• Cooktop burners, Btu/hr.: 4 @ 9500.

The only tested manual-clean model with sealed burners. Flame height can be adjusted smoothly. Removable burner heads for easy cleaning. Cooktop gets quite hot while cooking with all burners on high. Oven window gives very good view. Food didn't broil well near edges of large broiling pan. Porcelain-coated cooktop control panel and front of broiler compartment. **Recommendation:** A very good range, if you don't care about a self-cleaning oven.

15 General Electric JGBPS20WEW[WW] $420

• Cooktop burners, Btu/hr.: 4 @ 9000
Flame height can be adjusted smoothly, but all burners scorched chocolate in 10-minute melt test. Removable burner heads for easy cleaning; large, easy-to-clean wells under burners. Food didn't broil well near edges of large broiler pan. Porcelain-coated cooktop control panel and front of broiler compartment. Similar: General Electric JGBS20BEW[-], $390. **Recommendation:** A good overall performer, if you don't mind cleaning the old-fashioned way.

16 Hotpoint RGB528GEV[WH] $370

• Cooktop burners, Btu/hr.: 4 @ 9000.
Cooktop burner dials turn only 90 degrees, and flame adjusts only in steps. Three of the four burners scorched chocolate in 10-minute melt test. Removable burner heads for easy cleaning; large, easy-to-clean wells under burners. Food doesn't broil well near edges of large broiling pan. Porcelain-coated cooktop control panel and front of broiler compartment. **Recommendation:** A good range.

17 Designer Series By Tappan (Montgomery Ward) 28044[0] $300

• Cooktop burners, Btu/hr.: 4 @ 9000.
The most basic range we tested. Cooktop burner dials turn only 90 degrees, and flame adjusts only in steps. Front burners set to low flame tended to blow out when we let oven door slam shut. Removable burner heads for easy cleaning. No oven window or oven light. No clock. **Recommendation:** A good performer, but very basic, with no frills at all. By far the least expensive range in this group.

How to use the Ratings in the Buying Guide

- Read the Recommendations for information on specific models and general buying advice.
- Note how the rated products are listed—in order of performance and convenience, price, or alphabetically.
- The overall score graph gives the big picture in performance. Notes on features and performance for individual models are listed in the Comments column or "Model details."
- Use the handy key numbers to find out the details on each model.
- Before going to press, we verify model availability for most products with manufacturers. Some tested models listed in the Ratings may no longer be available. Discontinued models are noted in Model details or Comments. Such models may actually still be available in some stores for part of 1998. Models indicated as successors should perform similarly to the tested models, according to the manufacturer. Features may vary.
- Models similar to the tested models, when they exist, are indicated in Comments or Model details.
- To find our last full report on a subject, check the reference above the Ratings chart or the eight-year index, page 346.

Ratings *Freezers*

& Recommendations

The tests behind the Ratings

Cold-storage tests: For temperature uniformity, we filled the freezers with boxes of spinach and ran them in 70° and 90° F rooms; the best kept all parts within one degree of 0°. For temperature stability, we changed room temperatures to mimic the change of seasons, without changing freezer settings. For reserve capacity when pushed to limits, we turned controls to the coldest setting and put the room to 110°. Finally, we set them to manufacturers' recommendations and checked how close they stayed to 0°. **Energy efficiency:** We monitored the electricity consumed by each when full; our judgments take into account energy use and usable volume. For the **convenience** score, we checked storage arrangements, features, lighting, controls, and such. **Defrost convenience** takes into account the relative ease of defrosting each type.

Typical features for these models

Model details (page 118) list capacity as it is on the label. The usable capacity of the chests is the same as the labeled capacity; manual uprights are about 1¼ cubic feet smaller than labeled; self-defrost uprights are about 3 cubic feet smaller. Dimensions are HxWxD. Most models have a door lock. All have a one-year warranty for manufacturing defects. Frigidaire-made models have a five-year warranty and Woods models a ten-year warranty on the sealed refrigeration system. All have a warranty of at least $100 against food spoilage in the warranty period. Most prices are approximate retail; * indicates price paid.

Recommendations

Within a type, chest freezer or self-defrost upright, most models performed similarly, are similarly efficient, and offer similar conveniences—or inconveniences. Once you've chosen the type, it's safe to choose by capacity and price. Spending more usually buys extra features, which may add to convenience.

See Buying Guide report, page 98. Last time rated in CONSUMER REPORTS: October 1997.

Overall Ratings by type

E = Excellent, VG = Very good, G = Good, F = Fair, P = Poor

Typical performance is listed by freezer type

	Cold storage	Energy efficiency	Convenience	Defrost convenience
Manual-defrost chest	E	E	F	G
Manual-defrost upright	G	VG	G	F
Self-defrost upright	VG	F	VG	E

Model details

Notes on the details: Models are listed by type and in order of increasing capacity.

Manual-defrost chests

Whirlpool EH070FXEN $320
- 7.0 cu. ft. • $25 annual energy cost
- 35x32x24 in.

Pricey for such a small model. Less energy-efficient than larger chests. 1 hanging basket. Company says don't run in ambient temperature of less than 55°.

Kenmore (Sears) 15711 $280
- 7.2 cu. ft. • $24 annual energy cost
- 35x36x24 in.

Good price, but lack of drain makes defrosting even more of a chore. Less energy-efficient than larger chests. 1 hanging basket.

Gibson GFC09M3EW $280
- 8.8 cu. ft. • $27 annual energy cost
- 34x42x24 in.

Holds a bit more than the most compact chests. Less energy-efficient than larger chests. Temperature stability was only very good; all other chests were excellent. 1 hanging basket.

General Electric FH10DX $320
- 10 cu. ft. • $29 annual energy cost
- 35x43x24 in.

Less energy-efficient than larger chests. Temperature alarm, interior light, 1 hanging basket.

Amana C150FW $400
- 14.8 cu. ft. • $35 annual energy cost
- 35x47x29 in.

No hanging basket. Company says don't run in ambient temperature above 90° or below 65°.

Kenmore (Sears) 16551 $450
- 14.8 cu. ft. • $38 annual energy cost
- 35x48x30 in.

Full-featured model. "Quick freeze" runs compressor continuously. "Flash defrost" slightly quickens defrosting. Exterior power-on light, temperature alarm, interior light, 3 hanging baskets.

Whirlpool EH220FXEN $590*
- 21.7 cu. ft. • $38 annual energy cost
- 35x65x29 in.

Enormous home freezer, more than 5 feet wide. Exterior power-on light, interior light, 2 hanging baskets. Company says don't run in ambient temperature of less than 55°.

Manual-defrost uprights

General Electric FP9SX $350
- 8.7 cu. ft. • $34 annual energy cost
- 54x22x26 in.

Very quiet but otherwise undistinguished. Less energy-efficient than larger upright manual models, but better than a typical self-defrost upright. Bottom door shelf retainer can let things drop out when door opens. Condenser coil on rear of unit, harder to clean. No drain; drip-pan bottom shelf. No interior light. No door lock.

Can't find a model? Call the manufacturer. See page 342.

Ratings continued

Ratings, continued

White-Westinghouse MFU09M2BW $420*
- 8.7 cu. ft. • $33 annual energy cost
- 52x24x27 in.

A small, plain model. Less energy-efficient than larger upright manuals, but better than self-defrost uprights. Less convenient than others in day-to-day use. No interior light. No door lock.

Tappan TFU12M4EW $340*
- 11.7 cu. ft. • $38 annual energy cost
- 56x28x27 in.

Mid-sized model performed well enough. But temperatures were far too warm when set according to manufacturer's recommendations. 1 bottom shelf has gate. No interior light.

Whirlpool EV120FXEN $430
- 11.8 cu. ft. • $40 annual energy cost
- 61x24x28 in.

Good performer: Kept temperatures more uniform and had better reserve capacity than other upright manuals. Less energy-efficient than other upright manuals. 1 bottom shelf has gate. No interior light. Company says don't run in ambient temperature of less than 55°.

Kenmore (Sears) 26411 $350
- 14 cu. ft. • $44 annual energy cost
- 60x28x29 in.

Good and inexpensive. 1 bottom shelf has gate.

Frigidaire FFU17D9CW $480
- 17 cu. ft. • $50 annual energy cost
- 66x32x27 in.

Fairly full featured. "Quick freeze" runs compressor continuously. "Flash defrost" slightly quickens defrosting. 2 bottom shelves have gate. Exterior power-on light, temperature alarm.

General Electric FP17DX $450
- 17 cu. ft. • $43 annual energy cost
- 66x32x27 in.

Unlike other manual uprights, has 1 adjustable shelf. Bottom shelf is slide-out basket. Temperature alarm. More convenient in day-to-day use than other manual-defrost uprights.

Frigidaire FFU21D9CW $500
- 20.7 cu. ft. • $48 annual energy cost
- 71x32x29 in.

A very large unit that should satisfy big storage needs. Most energy-efficient of tested upright manual models. "Quick freeze" runs compressor continuously. "Flash defrost" slightly quickens defrosting. 2 bottom shelves have gate. Exterior power-on light, temperature alarm.

Self-defrost uprights

Whirlpool EV150NXEN $500
- 15 cu. ft. • $61 annual energy cost
- 61x30x29 in.

Unusually quiet for a self-defrosting freezer. Temperature stability only good. Temperatures were too warm when set according to manufacturer's recommendations. Condenser coil on bottom may need occasional cleaning. Shelves not adjustable; 1 shelf has gate. Company says don't run in ambient temperature of less than 55°.

Kenmore (Sears) 26641 $560
- 15.7 cu. ft. • $70 annual energy cost
- 63x32x27 in.

A medium-sized model with an impressively flexible interior. As good as a chest model at keeping temperatures uniform. Reserve capacity only fair. Some shelves are adjustable as well as removable. "Quick freeze" runs compressor continuously. Exterior power-on light. Temperature alarm. Controls are on rear wall.

Amana ESUF20JW $660
- 19.6 cu. ft. • $75 annual energy cost
- 67x33x29 in.

More energy-efficient than other self-defrost models. Temperature uniformity only good. Shelves not adjustable; 1 bottom shelf has gate. Condenser coil on bottom, may need occasional cleaning. Company says don't run in ambient temperature above 90° or below 65°.

Kenmore (Sears) 26041 $650
- 20.3 cu. ft. • $75 annual energy cost
- 71x32x29 in.

More energy-efficient than other self-defrost models. Impressively flexible storage arrangements. "Quick freeze" runs compressor continuously. Exterior power-on light. Temperature alarm. Controls are on rear wall.

SMALL APPLIANCES

Vacuum cleaners

You don't have to pay a lot to get a vacuum that cleans well. Uprights are generally cheaper and more convenient, but a canister is more nimble for above-the-floor jobs.

Last CR reports: Uprights and canisters, January 1997; wet/dry vacs, July 1996; deep-cleaners, July 1997
Ratings: pages 132 (vacuums), 137 (wet/dry vacs), 141 (deep-cleaning vacs)
Brand repair histories: page 14
Expect to pay: $20 to more than $1000

What's available

Uprights. Uprights outsell canisters by more than seven to one. They usually cost less, weigh less, and require less storage space. One basic design uses a soft, outer bag, the other a stiff housing to hold the disposable dust bag.

Uprights have a rotating brush, which beats the dust and dirt out of pile carpet. On hard surfaces, however, they're generally less effective than canisters—their brushes may disperse debris rather than vacuum it up. Most uprights come with a long hose and an assortment of attachments for vacuuming stairs, upholstery, under furniture, and such. Uprights weigh only 13 to 18 pounds. Price range: $70 to more than $1000.

Canisters. Superior suction makes a full-sized canister the choice for vacuuming bare floors. Most come with a power-nozzle attachment with a rotating brush to clean carpets. (Usually, the rotating brush can be switched off when vacuuming floors.) Even with this bulky attachment, a canister can still maneuver around furniture more easily than an upright.

Full-sized canisters weigh more than uprights—most are more than 20 pounds. And the hose and numerous detachable wands can be cumbersome to store. A canister's bag is often smaller than an upright's, but it's usually easier to change. Compact canister vacuums are easier to carry than full-sized canisters, but their cleaning performance in our tests hasn't been as good. Price range for canisters of all sizes: $75 to $1100; most sell for $300 or less.

Carpet deep-cleaners. This type of vacuum (also known as extractors or steam cleaners) typically sprays on a detergent, sometimes working it in with moving brushes, and then vacuums up the dirty solution. Extractors come as canisters or uprights. Canisters are much easier to maneuver and easier to set up and store. Small, portable canister extractors in general don't perform well. Another variation scrubs but doesn't vacuum, much like old-style rug shampooers that work with a moist powder, but no water. These "scrubbing machines" must be used with a conventional vacuum.

To remove stains, you'll get better results using sponges, towels, and elbow grease. Price range: $90 to $390.

Wet/dry vacuums. Also known as "shop vacs," these specialty machines are for the garage, workshop, or basement. They tackle chores that are beyond the typical household vacuum, such as gobbling up nails or bailing out a wet basement. But they're noisy, and they exhaust much of the dust back into the room.

Basically, these cleaners are little more than a hose and nozzle attached to a plastic tank with a motor on top. Tank size varies from 6 to 20 gallons. Small models store easily and hold enough for most chores, but larger models are generally quieter and less likely to tip over. Price range: $40 to $150.

Handheld and stick vacuums. For quick pickups of the occasional spill or floating dust bunny, handheld and stick vacs are convenient. They're lightweight and require minimal storage space. Both types come in plug-in and battery-powered models. The plug-in variety tends to be more powerful. Some rechargeables can pick up wet as well as dry spills. Price range: $10 to $75.

What's new

Cleaning appliances have become specialized products: You'll find wet/dry vacs, handheld vacs, car vacs, stick vacs, battery-powered stick vacs, deep-cleaning vacs, and rug shampooers. At the same time, traditional canister vacuum cleaners are becoming harder to find. One reason: wall-to-wall carpeting, a surface on which upright models excel. Another reason: Uprights have appropriated the functions of canisters, often with more success than canisters have mimicked uprights. Many upright vacuums now include an onboard extension hose, which makes tools easy to connect. A power-nozzle attachment can give a canister the carpet-cleaning power of an upright, but canisters so equipped are still heavy and hard to handle.

Reliability

For the first time since we've been testing vacuums, we have reliability information on brands of full-sized upright and canister vacuum cleaners bought new by our readers between 1991 and 1996. Overall, vacuum cleaners are troublesome machines, with one of four in our survey needing repair, usually a belt replacement. Eureka and Panasonic had the worst repair records for canisters; Regina (now owned by Oreck), the worst for uprights. Electrolux and Hoover were among the better brands of uprights. Electrolux also did well among canisters, as did Rainbow. For more information, see the brand repair histories on page 14.

Shopping strategy

The layout of your house and what you vacuum will affect your choice of vacuum cleaner. If you have carpets of medium or deeper pile, an upright with tools at the ready is the best choice. If you have a lot of bare floor or if you have low-pile carpets or flat-weave rugs, choose a model that excels at surface cleaning. A canister might be a better choice than an upright that doesn't allow you to shut off the rotating carpet brush.

Stairs present a problem for any type, but canisters are sized and shaped to sit on a stair while you work. On an upright, look for a long hose or a "stair handle" on the body.

Rather than relying on one vacuum, you might decide to have two: one for upstairs and one for downstairs, or one for carpets and one for bare floors.

Handheld vacuums are versatile picker-uppers when they're stored accessibly. Plug-in models are less mobile but more powerful than rechargeables.

Choose a wet/dry vacuum mainly by size, noise level, stability, and features. The small models we tested were all very noisy, very unstable, or both, but they're suitable for occasional use.

Decide what to spend. There's no clear correlation between price and performance. Spending more typically gets you more power and more features (many of them not worthwhile), sturdier attachments, and occasionally, heftier construction. Brands sold through at-home demonstrations, like Kirby and Rainbow, carry high price tags mainly because of large sales commissions.

Manufacturers often make several lines of canisters and uprights, each with as many as six models priced in $10 to $30 steps, according to features. You'll pay $100 or so extra for self-propulsion in an upright or for a power nozzle in a canister. A high-efficiency filter is another premium feature.

What's in the stores. Eureka, Hoover, Kenmore (Sears), and Royal Dirt Devil account for 70 percent of all upright vacuums sold. Kenmore dominates the canister market. Black & Decker and Royal Dirt Devil sell three-fourths of all handheld vacuums. Two brands, Sears Craftsman and Shop Vac, account for most wet/dry vacuums sold.

Using the Ratings. The Ratings of uprights and canisters are based mainly on overall cleaning performance on carpets and hard surfaces. Wet/dry models were judged on different criteria. All picked up debris well enough, but two-thirds of those tested were judged poor for noise, stability, or both. If you can't find a model, call the manufacturer; see page 342.

Key features

Amps and horsepower. Regardless of type, all vacuums are labeled with claimed amperage, peak horsepower, or cleaning effectiveness per amp. We've found no correlation between those factors and performance in our tests.

Controls. An on/off switch that's high on an upright's handle is easy to use. On/off switches on most canisters are positioned low for foot operation. Most canisters have a separate foot switch to turn off the power nozzle.

Cord. Usually, the longer the power cord, the better. Standard lengths are 15 to 30 feet for a regular vacuum, 6 to 15 for a wet/dry vacuum. Canisters sometimes have a convenient built-in device that rewinds the cord. Uprights generally have two hooks for winding the cord. If one or both hooks swivel, you can release the cord quickly.

Dirt bags. Most full-sized vacuums collect dirt in a disposable paper bag. Some models signal when the bag is full or airflow is blocked. Soft-body uprights have the largest bags, but clogged pores in the bags decrease suction, so bags often have to be changed before they're full.

Installing a bag is easiest if its cardboard collar drops into a slot. Sliding the bag's sleeve over a tube and securing it with a spring band isn't as easy. And removing the bag from a soft-body upright without dumping the contents is a challenge. The plastic dust-collectors on most electric brooms and handheld vacuums are easy enough to remove and empty.

Dirt sensor. Some models offer a "dirt sensor" that indicates when a surface has been deep-cleaned. But this device merely tells you when the machine has stopped picking up dirt, not if all the dirt has been picked up.

Dust control. Despite what ads may say, even the best vacuum won't capture all dust and debris. Uprights with the fan in front of the dust bag tend to capture more. Canisters generally emit more dust in their exhaust. Wet/dry vacuums emit the most, by far.

As a rule, machines that use paper dust bags are cleaner than models with a bagless dust-collector or a water collection system. Microfiltration dust bags that supposedly minimize exhaust dirt are an option on some vacuums. Our tests have shown that most are no more effective than standard, cheaper bags.

On wet/dry vacuums, a cartridge filter is easier to install and remove than paper-over-foam or cloth-over-foam bag

Vacuum cleaners as air cleaners

For decades, vacuum-cleaner vendors have sold very expensive machines by playing on the fear of dirt. The modern version of this sales pitch draws on a real problem for some people: Most vacuum cleaners emit some dust and, with it, allergens such as dust-mite particles. To solve this problem, many manufacturers offer special filtration, sometimes involving $100 filters or other complex dirt-collection methods.

Our tests show that some vacuums release more dirt into the air than others, but some fairly ordinary models, not just the ones with the special HEPA (high-efficiency particulate-arresting) filters, were among the cleanest. In particular, the Hoover Dimension Supreme U5227-930 (similar to the U5221-930) scored highest among a recent test of allergen-trapping vacuums. And at a reasonable $195, this Hoover was also judged a CR Best Buy. Other allergen-trapping models to consider are the Nilfisk GS90 ($800), Miele White Pearl 5434i ($700), and the Fantom Fury F1005Z01 ($300). For details, see the Ratings on page 132.

filters. Unlike bags, cartridge filters don't have to come off when you switch from dry to wet pickup.

Hoses. The most convenient ones swivel. Nonswiveling ones can kink annoyingly as you vacuum. On a wet/dry vacuum, a 2½-inch hose can pick up more and bigger debris than the standard 1¼-inch hose.

Noise. No vacuum cleaner can be called quiet, but the canister models we tested were slightly less noisy than the uprights. Electric brooms and handheld vacuums tend to whine at a higher pitch than their full-sized cousins. Wet/dry vacuums are the noisiest.

Carpet-height adjustment. Look for a vacuum cleaner that raises or lowers the motorized beater brush with a dial, sliding lever, or pedal. Some models claim to adjust height automatically, but they usually aren't as effective as those that adjust manually. On a few uprights, the beater brush can be turned off, so you can avoid scattering dirt on uncarpeted portions of your floor. That improves carpet cleaning, but it might fling coarse soil about instead of sucking it in.

Pushing and carrying features. Big wheels or rollers make uprights easier to push, especially when the beater brush is set to the proper height. Self-propelled vacuums require very little effort.

Stair-climbing features. The longer the hose, the better the reach. Uprights usually have too large a "footprint" to fit securely on a stair; canisters tend to be more cooperative. Some vacuum cleaners come with a small power nozzle for vacuuming carpet on stairs.

Suction adjustment. When you vacuum loose or billowy objects, excessive suction can cause the vacuum to inhale the fabric. Most canisters and some uprights let you reduce suction by uncovering a hole or valve near the handle. Some models have more than one speed to let you vary suction.

• ***Features specific to wet/dry vacuums:***

Drain spout. This eliminates the need to lift the unit to dump out wet waste. You can roll the vacuum to a suitable spot and open the spout.

Easy-on, easy-off tank lid. A lid that sits atop the tank is easier to install and remove than one that requires you to line up locking points in specific notches, which may not be clearly marked.

Automatic coffeemakers

All automatic-drip machines make very good coffee. Some models are much easier to use than others.

Last CR report: November 1996
Expect to pay: $20 to $100

What's available

Automatic-drip machines are the predominant way Americans make coffee, beating out manual-drip systems, coffee presses, espresso machines, and the like. Automatic-drip machines range from single-cup models to full-sized units that brew up to 12 cups at a time. The biggest sellers are 10-cup and 12-cup machines.

Programmable or basic. It's nice to wake up to the smell of coffee, but a programmable coffeemaker's built-in timer adds to its price. You can brew your coffee in 15 minutes or less even with a basic coffeemaker. Price range: $20 and up for a basic model; $30 and up for a programmable model.

What's new

The continued popularity of specialty coffee and coffee bars has translated into sales of more coffeemakers. Manufacturers have responded to the demand with models that have more features and style. Built-in grinders, water filters, auto shutoff, and 24-hour programmable functions are not uncommon.

There's also a selection of color and shape. Color choices for coffeemakers have expanded from the standard black or white to green or blue. Carafes now come as sleek globes or angular hour-glasses, as well as the basic cylinder.

Shopping strategy

Our tests over the years show that all automatic-drip coffeemakers are capable of making very good coffee. Choose a machine by price, convenience, and styling.

Decide what to spend. A programmable coffeemaker can cost $20 to $40 more than a basic model. You can pay even more for additional features or styling. The Krups Crystal Arome Time, with its globelike carafe, costs $90—about $70 more than a good, basic model. Stylish carafes also cost more to replace. That Krups carafe costs about $20, compared with $10 for a plain one.

What's in the stores. Black & Decker, Mr. Coffee, and Proctor-Silex are the biggest-selling brands. Mass merchandisers, including Target and Wal-Mart, sell low-priced brands such as Mr. Coffee. Department stores sell prestige brands like Krups and Braun. Coffeemaker sales are highest—and prices often lowest—in November and December.

Key features

• *Recommended:*

Auto shutoff. Turns off the carafe's hot plate, usually after two hours. On some models, the shut-off time is adjustable up to four or five hours. But coffee is all but ruined after about an hour.

Home espresso machines: *Steam or pump?*

Espresso machines that rely on steam pressure make very good cappuccino and latté and good espresso, according to our tests. Machines that use an electric pump deliver much better espresso, but they're also much more expensive. Steam machines cost $50 to $100; pump machines, $140 to $250. If you drink straight espresso, buy a pump machine. Only a pump will deliver coffee that's smooth, full-bodied, and crowned by rich crèma. If the machine will be used mostly to make milk-based drinks, a steam espresso-maker will make cappuccinos and lattes that are almost as pleasing as those from a pump machine.

Three top-rated pump models from our November 1996 report are still available: the DeLonghi Bar 19 FU, $170, Saeco Super Idea, $190, available only at Starbucks coffee bars; and the Gaggia Espresso, $150.

Clear markings. Marks on the carafe and inside the reservoir make it easier to add the amount of water you need. Instead of reservoir markings, some models have a narrow window or tube that shows the water level, sometimes with a floating ball to mark the cups as you load the water.

Drip-stop. This prevents drips after the pot is removed at the end of the brew cycle. It also allows you to sneak a cup before the whole pot is brewed.

Easy-loading lid. A big flip-top lid makes it easiest to pour in water.

Hot plate with nonstick coating. Helps with cleanup after a spill. Most models have it.

• *Not recommended:*

Brew-strength control. In past tests, we've found this has little effect.

Built-in water filter. If excess chlorine is a problem, a filter at the tap may prove more useful than a filter inside your coffeemaker. Braun claims its filters also remove the minerals that cause calcification.

Descaling rod. Those with hard tap water must occasionally descale the machine, but that's easily done by running white vinegar or a special solution through the coffeemaker.

Small-batch setting. Some machines have a setting that adjusts the hot-plate temperature for smaller quantities, to avoid overheating the coffee. Others have a setting that changes water flow, supposedly to saturate the smaller quantity of coffee grounds for a longer time. Neither feature is really necessary.

Food processors

Mid-priced processors can do basic tasks; expensive models have more power and more functions.

Last CR Report: August 1997
Ratings: page 144
Expect to pay: $35 to $300

What's available

Processors vary by capacity of the bowl, which can range from less than a cup to nine cups or so. Large processors are useful for ambitious menus or the large quantities required for feeding many. Mid-sized models handle four to seven cups, good for most uses. And mini processors are essentially choppers with accessories, suitable for chopping an onion, a half-cup of nuts, or cheese.

Price range: large-sized, $50 to $300; mid-sized, $35 to $100; mini, $15 to $40.

What's new

The product hasn't changed much over the past five years. What has changed are the players. The Moulinex and Panasonic brands are no longer around, and West Bend has limited its distribution to Wal-Mart stores. Betty Crocker, KitchenAid, and Krups have added food processors to their kitchenware lineups.

Shopping strategy

Cooking enthusiasts who want to knead bread dough and make food in quantity may want to consider a pricey large model. A mid-sized model may suit you if you simply want the basics—pureeing, chopping, shredding. Mid-sized models require only slightly less counter space. The real space-savers are mini processors, but their skills are rudimentary.

Keep in mind that a food processor can't handle all tasks. An electric mixer is a better appliance for making mashed potatoes or whipped cream; a standard blender is more suited to liquefying vegetables, pureeing baby food, or concocting drinks.

Decide what to spend. You needn't pay top dollar to get a good, basic performer. Spending more than $70 for a mid-priced model or more than $100 for a large model buys features such as an extra, small bowl, a wide feed tube, or special attachments for whipping cream or mixing dough. In our tests, the more expensive models were typically better slicers and quieter in use.

What's in the stores. Mass merchandisers like Kmart and kitchen stores like Lechter's usually carry brands like Betty Crocker, Black & Decker, and Hamilton Beach. Look for top-of-the-line brands in department stores, gourmet shops, and mail-order catalogs.

Using the Ratings. The Ratings from our most recent tests include large and mid-sized models; there are only a few mini processors.

Many models remain on the market for a number of years—several of the models we rated in 1992 are still around. If you can't find a model, call the manufacturer; see page 342.

Key features

• ***Standard features on most models:***

Blades and disks. An S-shaped metal chopping blade and a slicing/shredding disk are standard for large and mid-sized models. Some models come with separate slicing and shredding disks.

Bowl. All standard food processors have a clear plastic bowl and lid and a plastic food-pusher. A bowl can hold more dry food than liquid.

Continuous feed. A chute that expels shredded or sliced food into a separate bowl or container.

Dishwasher-safe components. Even so, it's best to place them on the top rack, away from the heating element.

Feed tube. Some are wide enough to fit a medium-sized tomato. Some incorporate a slender inner tube for holding narrow foods like carrots upright.

Pulse. This control keeps the machine running as long as you hold it down.

Smooth, clean design. A simple housing is easier to wipe clean. Touchpad controls also expedite cleanup.

Speed controls. One speed is all you really need.

Blenders

Look for a model whose container and controls will be easy to use. More speed settings won't necessarily improve performance.

Last CR report: February 1997
Ratings: page 129
Expect to pay: $15 to $125

What's available

Handheld models. A handheld blender is used for making drinks or milk shakes and pureeing soups. It works like a simplified portable mixer: You simply plunge the blade into a container of ingredients. Handheld models can be can be corded or rechargable. The latter are convenient for whipping items on the range top. The typical handheld model has variable speeds that you control with a switch or dial and weighs only a couple of pounds, so it's easy to maneuver and store. Price range: $20 to $45.

Countertop models. A countertop blender, which consists of a base with a motor, a rotating blade, and a container, is larger and much more powerful than the handheld variety. Some blenders excel at crushing ice, even without added liquid. A countertop model also boasts more speed settings than you'll ever need. Containers range in size from 32 ounces to 48 ounces. Price range: $15 to $125.

What's new

Touchpad controls, found on high-end models, simplify cleanup considerably. A new KitchenAid model features an electronic sensor that's supposed to adjust power automatically to the workload. But even with this feature, the KitchenAid couldn't make a decent milk shake, chop ice evenly, or successfully puree carrots and potatoes in broth in our tests. One Waring model has a special disk attachment to make whipped cream. It helped somewhat, but don't expect it to transform a blender into a mixer. The basic design of a blender just doesn't allow enough air into the container to produce fluffy, aerated whipped cream.

Shopping strategy

Handheld models are limited to making shakes and drinks. Our most recent tests showed only slight differences between models. If your blending needs go beyond mixing liquids, consider a countertop blender.

For best value, look for a mid-priced model with the features you need.

Decide what to spend. High-end blenders aren't necessarily better performers than midpriced models. Overall, countertop blenders priced at $30 to $55 performed best.

What's in the stores. Hamilton Beach/Proctor Silex and Sunbeam/Oster are the leading brands. Braun offers only handheld models.

Using the Ratings. In our last test, we rated countertop blenders. Blender models typically remain available for a year or longer. New models are introduced gradually. If you can't find a model, call the manufacturer; see page 342.

Key features

Cleanup. Well-spaced buttons or touchpad controls make a blender easy to clean. Containers are almost always dishwasher-safe, but plastic may not hold up as well as glass. Blades shouldn't be hard to clean, but they may rust if not dried right away.

Containers. Containers may be plastic, glass, or stainless steel. Plastic is lighter and durable, but glass is more stable and stays cleaner-looking. Some manufacturers claim their containers have unique designs that increase blending effectiveness. We found no particular benefit in our tests. Markings that aid measuring, an opening in the lid for adding ingredients, a pouring spout, a handle, and a wide mouth are common conveniences. A blend-and-store container makes leftovers easy to tuck away and minimizes cleanup.

Controls. Most blenders have push buttons. Touchpad controls make cleaning easier. A few models have a sliding-speed control with a lighted display.

Speeds. Handheld models typically have one or two speeds—enough for mixing liquids. Some have a continuously variable speed. On countertop models, a wide range of speed is more important than the number of speeds. A few speeds are enough for most chores. A pulse control, which keeps the blades spinning only as long as you depress the control, is especially useful when it works with more than one speed.

Breadmakers

They all bake great-tasting bread, but some do it with less fuss.

Last CR report: November 1997
Ratings: page 130
Expect to pay: $90 to $250

A breadmaker is a mixer and an oven all in one. At the bottom of a nonstick pan inside the breadmaker is a kneading paddle. To make bread, you pour in carefully measured fresh ingredients or a packaged bread mix, select a program, press "start," and walk away. The machine's paddle mixes and kneads the dough. After the dough rises, it bakes in the same pan. From start to finish, it takes about 2½ to 4 hours to make the bread, depending on the machine.

What's available

Breadmakers come in sizes that refer to the approximate weight of the largest loaf the machine makes: 1, 1½, 2, or 2½ pounds. The smallest loaves yield 8 to 10 slices of bread; the largest, about twice that many.

Price range: 1-pound models, $90 to $120; 1½- to 2½-pound models, $100 to $250.

What's new

Most models make a tall, square loaf of bread, but more and more models are designed to turn out a loaf that somewhat resembles store-bought bread. The average retail price has fallen from $150 or so five years ago to $120 in 1996. Sale prices can be as little as $60 for a basic model.

Shopping strategy

All breadmakers make good or very good bread as long as the ingredients are correctly measured and fresh. A model with well-designed controls and simple loading and cleanup makes the task easier. Comparison-shop if you can, and don't settle for manufacturer's list price.

Decide what to spend. Basic machines of all sizes sell for less than $150 and are likely to have all the features most people need. Spending more buys extra features and special cycles.

What's in the stores. Most breadmakers are sold in discount stores like Wal-Mart and Kmart and in department stores like Sears and Macy's. There are more than two dozen brands of breadmaker, but the major players in the marketplace are Oster, Regal, Welbilt, and West Bend. Several brands have dropped out: Mr. Coffee, Hitachi, and Hamilton Beach/Proctor Silex.

Using the Ratings. We tested large-sized models. If you can't find a model, call the manufacturer; see page 342.

Key features

• *Standard features on most models:*

Digital controls. A digital display indicates the stage of preparation and time left. Setting the controls is usually easy; you push a few touchpad buttons and a start button.

Delay-start timer. Most breadmakers let you add the ingredients and select a time, up to 13 hours ahead, for the bread to be ready. A timer is useful if you like to wake up to fresh bread in the morning or come home to it in the evening.

Mix-in signal. A buzzer lets you know when to add raisins for raisin bread, caraway seeds for rye, and so forth. (If you add them at the start, some machines pulverize them by the end of the mixing.)

Nonstick bread pan. This makes the loaf easier to get out and the cleanup less of a chore.

Special cycles. Most breadmakers have a rapid cycle that cuts an hour or so off the kneading and rising time. However, bread made that way is generally not as high or fluffy as the standard-cycle bread. A dough cycle mixes and kneads, but does not bake, so you can remove the dough to shape it and bake it in a conventional oven. Programmed cycles adjust the time, temperature, or handling for special breads, such as fruit and nut or batter breads.

Viewing window. This small window lets you watch the action.

Ratings *Vacuum cleaners*

& Recommendations

The tests behind the Ratings

Cleaning is given the greatest weight. **Deep** cleaning reflects how much embedded sand and talcum powder the cleaner could extract from a medium-pile carpet. The best removed around four times as much as the worst. **Surface** cleaning measures how much air flows through the hose. Machines that produced fewer breathable dust particles were rated better in **emissions. Price** is approximate retail.

Typical features for these models

• 4- to 10-foot hose and a 15- to 30-foot power cord. • Onboard tool storage.

Recommendations

Many models would make a good choice. Among uprights, the top-rated Sharp Twin Energy is noteworthy for its superior performance. At $160, we judged it a CR Best Buy. Slightly less expensive and almost as good is the Eureka Powerline Plus ($140), but that brand has proved troublesome . Among canisters, the Nilfisk and Miele models sell in the $700-to-$800 range. The best performer at the most reasonable price is Eureka World Vac 6865B ($210).

See Buying Guide, page 121. Last time rated in CONSUMER REPORTS: August 1997, January 1997, and March 1996.

Overall Ratings

E VG G F P

Within types, listed in order of overall score

Key no.	Brand and model	Price	Overall score (0–100; P F G VG E)	Cleaning: Deep	Cleaning: Surface	Emissions	Noise
	UPRIGHTS						
1	**Sharp** Twin Energy EC-12TWT4 **A CR Best Buy**	$160		E	VG	VG	VG
2	**Hoover** Power Drive Supreme U6323-930	320		E	G	VG	F
3	**Kirby** G4	1350		VG	E	E	F
4	**Eureka** Powerline Plus 7680AT	140		E	VG	VG	F
5	**Hoover** Power Drive U6311-930	270		E	G	F	F
6	**Eureka** Bravo! II The Boss 7625AT	90		VG	G	VG	F
7	**Hoover** Turbo Power 4000-U5101-930	195		E	F	VG	G
8	**Hoover** Dimension Supreme U5227-930	195		VG	F	E	F

Key no.	Brand and model	Price	Overall score (0–100: P F G VG E)	Cleaning DEEP	Cleaning SURFACE	Emissions	Noise
	UPRIGHTS						
9	**Hoover** Dimension U5209-930	$180		⊖	○	⊜	◒
10	**Fantom** F11051	300		○	○	⊜	○
11	**Bissell** Plus 3550A	230		◒	⊖	⊖	◒
12	**Electrolux** Epic Series 3500 SR	650		⊖	◒	◒	◒
13	**Hoover** Preferred U4655-930	150		⊖	◒	○	●
14	**Hoover** Encore Supreme Soft & Light U4293-930	100		○	○	○	◒
15	**Miele** Powerhouse Plus S174i	320		◒	○	⊖	○
16	**Eureka** Powerline Plus Victory 4441AT	150		◒	○	◒	◒
17	**Royal** Dirt Devil Impulse 085400	90		○	◒	⊖	●
18	**Eureka** The Boss Victory 4335BT	100		◒	⊖	●	○
19	**Singer** SB12720	90		◒	●	⊖	●
20	**White-Westinghouse** Millenium WWU2020	100		◒	◒	⊖	●
	Singer Poweramp HB1412	180		○	●	●	●
21	**CANISTERS**						
22	**Nilfisk** GS90	800		⊖	⊜	⊜	⊖
23	**Miele** White Pearl S434i	700		○	⊜	⊜	⊖
24	**Eureka** Excalibur 6975A	300		⊖	⊖	⊖	⊖
25	**Eureka** World Vac 6865B	210		⊜	⊖	●	○
26	**Hoover** PowerMax Supreme S3611	300		⊖	○	●	○
27	**Panasonic** Eagle Eye Dirt Sensor MC-V9635	320		◒	⊜	◒	○
28	**Hoover** Futura S3567	200		⊖	○	●	○
29	**Electrolux** Epic Series 6500 SR	700		⊖	◒	⊖	○
30	**Rainbow** Performance Edition SE	1400		⊖	⊖	●	○
31	**White-Westinghouse** V.I.P. WWP9500	200		⊖	○	◒	○
32	**Electrolux** Renaissance C104A	900		○	○	◒	○
	Hoover Encore Supreme S3395-040	150		○	◒	●	◒
33	**COMPACT CANISTERS**						
34	**Sharp** EC-7311	100		◒	○	◒	⊖
35	**Sanyo** SC-585	80		◒	◒	⊖	⊖
36	**Hoover** Portapower II Supreme S1353	150		◒	●	◒	◒
37	**Eureka** Worldvac Mighty Mite II 3651A	120		●	◒	●	○
38	**Eureka** The Boss Mighty Mite II 3621A	75		●	●	●	○
39	**Hoover** Portapower II S1337	80		●	●	◒	○

Can't find a model? Call the manufacturer. See page 342.

Ratings continued ▶

Ratings, continued

Model details

Uprights

1 Sharp Twin Energy EC-12TWT4 $160
Hard-body upright with stair handle; fan pulls dirt into bag. Hose ready for use with onboard tools. **Recommendation:** Convenient and relatively quiet, this is a superior performer at a moderate price, though the sturdiness of the power-head housing is a worry.

2 Hoover Power Drive Supreme U6323-930 $320
Self-propelled hard-body upright with stair handle; fan pushes dirt into bag. Good side edge cleaner. Onboard tools are covered. Easy-to-maneuver hose. Manual carpet-height adjustment. **Recommendation:** Superior cleaner, but heavy and bulky.

3 Kirby G4 $1350
Self-propelled, soft-body upright with stair handle; fan pushes dirt into bag. Good side edge cleaner. No tools or hose on board; hard to convert for use with tools. Easy-to-maneuver hose. Suction control. Manual carpet-height adjustment. Low emissions. **Model availability:** Discontinued. **Recommendation:** Inconvenience, heft, and price more than counter this model's fine performance.

4 Eureka Powerline Plus 7680AT $140
Hard-body upright with stair handle; fan pushes dirt into bag. Good side edge cleaner. Onboard tools. Easy-to-maneuver but flimsy hose. Manual carpet-height adjustment. **Model availability:** Discontinued; successor: Bravo II 7677BT, $100. **Recommendation:** Low price and fine performance, but durability is a worry.

5 Hoover Power Drive U6311-930 $270
Very similar to (2), except for minor features. **Recommendation:** Good value for a self-propelled model.

6 Eureka Bravo! II The Boss 7625AT $90
• Soft-body upright with stair handle
Good side-edge cleaner. Onboard tools. Manual carpet-height adjustment. Doesn't exhaust much dust; very good choice for those with allergies. But: Flimsy hose. Noisy. Dirt disposal difficult and messy. **Recommendation:** Very good performance, but not among the most reliable brands.

7 Hoover Turbo Power 4000 U5101-930 $195
Hard-body upright with stair handle. Good side-edge cleaner. Doesn't exhaust much dust; very good choice for those with allergies. Onboard tools are covered. Easy-to-maneuver hose. Manual carpet-height adjustment. Among the most reliable brands. But: Mediocre suction. Noisy. **Recommendation:** Good overall.

8 Hoover Dimension Supreme U5227-930 $195
Hard-body upright with stair handle; fan pushes dirt into bag. Good side edge cleaner. Onboard tools are covered. Easy-to-manuever hose ready for use with tools. Manual carpet-height adjustment. Low emissions. **Recommendation:** Good performance and convenient design at a moderate price.

9 Hoover Dimension U5209-930 $180
Very similar to (8), except for minor features. **Recommendation:** Good performance and convenient design at a moderate price. Models in this line offer good value.

10 Fantom F11051 $300
Hard-body upright; fan pulls dirt into plastic dirt container. Good side edge cleaner. Suction control. Easy-to-maneuver hose ready for use with onboard tools. Manual carpet-height adjustment. Low emissions. **Model availability:** Discontinued. **Recommendation:** A good choice.

11 Bissell Plus 3550A $230
Hard-body upright with detachable handheld canister unit and stair handle; fan pulls dirt into bag. Hose ready for use with onboard tools. On/off switch for beater brush. **Recommendation:** A good choice if you have stairs, low-pile, or flat-weave rugs.

12 Electrolux Epic Series 3500 SR $650
Hard-body upright with stair handle; fan pulls dirt into bag. Easy-to-maneuver hose, but hose and tools are not onboard; hard to convert for use with tools. Suction control. Special power nozzle for stairs. On/off switch for beater brush. **Recommendation:** Expensive for what you get.

13 Hoover Preferred U4655-930 $150
Soft-body upright with stair handle; fan pushes dirt into bag. Good side edge cleaner. Onboard tools. Manual carpet-height adjustment. **Recommendation:** Good performer but noisy.

14 Hoover Encore Supreme Soft & Light U4293-930 $100
Soft-body upright with stair handle; fan pushes dirt into bag. Good side edge cleaner. Manual carpet-height adjustment. **Recommendation:** Good performer but not very convenient.

15 Miele Powerhouse Plus S174i $320
Hard-body upright with stair handle; fan pulls dirt into bag. Onboard tools are covered; hose ready for use with tools. Suction control. On/off switch for beater brush. Retractable cord. **Recommendation:** A good, if expensive, choice if you don't have deep carpets.

16 Eureka Powerline Plus Victory 4441AT $150
Hard-body upright with comfortable, contoured handle and stair handle; fan pulls dirt into bag. Hose ready for use with tools. Manual carpet-height adjustment. Easy to service. **Model availability:** Discontinued. **Recommendation:** A good choice if you don't have deep carpets.

17 Royal Dirt Devil Impulse 085400 $90
Hard-body upright; fan pushes dirt into bag. **Model availability:** Discontinued. **Recommendation:** Good, inexpensive performer, but noisy and not very convenient.

18 Eureka The Boss Victory 4335BT $100
Hard-body upright; fan pulls dirt into bag. Good side edge cleaner. Hose ready for tools. Awkward cord handling. Manual carpet-height adjustment. Easy to service. But: high emissions. **Model availability:** Discontinued; successor: The Boss Victory 4335DT, $90. **Recommendation:** Good, inexpensive performer, but not very convenient.

19 Singer SB12720 $90
Soft-body upright with stair handle; fan pushes dirt into bag. Good side edge cleaner. Hose ready for use with tools. Awkward cord handling. Manual carpet-height adjustment. **Model availability:** Discontinued. **Recommendation:** There are better choices.

20 White-Westinghouse Millenium WWU2020 $100
Soft-body upright with stair handle; fan pushes dirt into bag. Hose ready for use with tools. Awkward cord handling. Manual carpet-height adjustment. **Model availability:** Discontinued. **Recommendation:** There are better choices.

21 Singer Poweramp HB1412 $180
Hard-body upright with stair handle; fan pushes dirt into bag. Good side edge cleaner. Hose ready for use with onboard tools. Manual carpet-height adjustment. But: bulky, heavy, and high emissions. **Model availability:** Discontinued. **Recommendation:** There are better choices.

Canisters

22 Nilfisk GS90 $800
Good side edge cleaner. No tools on board or provision for cord storage. Suction control. On/off switch for beater brush. High-efficiency filter. Price includes optional power nozzle and special filter. **Model availability:** Discontinued. **Recommendation:** Superior cleaner with low emissions but inconvenient and extremely expensive.

23 Miele White Pearl S434i $700
Good side edge cleaner. Tools on board are covered. Easy-to-maneuver hose and retractable cord. Suction control. On/off switch for beater brush. Manual carpet-height adjustment. High-efficiency filter. Price includes optional power nozzle and special filter. **Recommendation:** Superior cleaner with low emissions but pricey..

24 Eureka Excalibur 6975A $300
Good side edge cleaner. Onboard tools are covered. Retractable cord. Suction control. On/off switch for brush. **Model availability:** Discontinued. **Recommen-dation:** More features than (24), but motor and wiring may not be as sturdy.

Ratings continued ▶

Ratings, continued

25 Eureka World Vac 6865B $210

Good side edge cleaner. Onboard tools. Easy-to-maneuver hose and retractable cord. Suction control. But: high emissions. **Recommendation:** Low price and very good performance make this a good value if emissions are not a problem.

26 Hoover PowerMax Supreme S3611 $300

Onboard tools are covered. Easy-to-maneuver hose and retractable cord. Suction control. On/off switch for beater brush. But: high emissions. **Recommendation:** Good performer if emissions are not a problem.

27 Panasonic Eagle Eye Dirt Sensor MC-V9635 $320

Dirt sensor. Onboard tools are covered. Easy-to-maneuver hose and retractable cord. Suction control. On/off switch for beater brush. Manual carpet-height adjustment. **Recommendation:** A good choice if you don't have deep carpets.

28 Hoover Futura S3567 $200

Onboard tools. Easy-to-maneuver hose and retractable cord. Suction control. But: high emissions. **Recommendation:** Good value if emissions are not a problem.

29 Electrolux Epic Series 6500 SR $700

Onboard tools. Retractable cord. Suction control. On/off switch for brush. Special power nozzle for stairs. **Recommendation:** Expensive for what you get.

30 Rainbow Performance Edition SE $1400

Dirt collected in water instead of disposable bag. Suction control. On/off switch for beater brush. Manual carpet-height adjustment. Easy to service. But: high emissions and water-filled tank is heavy. **Recommendation:** Emissions, inconvenience, and price outweigh its cleaning ability.

31 White-Westinghouse V.I.P. WWP9500 $200

Onboard tools. Awkward cord handling. Suction control. **Model availability:** Discontinued. **Recommendation:** Good, inexpensive performer but not very convenient.

32 Electrolux Renaissance C104A $900

Good side edge cleaner. Onboard tools are covered. Retractable cord. Suction control. On/off switch for beater brush. Special power nozzle for stairs. **Model availability:** Discontinued. **Recommendation:** Very expensive for what you get.

33 Hoover Encore Supreme S3395-040 $150

Onboard tools. No cord-storage provision. Suction control. But: High emissions. **Recommendation:** A good, inexpensive choice if you don't have deep carpets and emissions are not a problem.

Compact canisters

34 Sharp EC-7311 $100

Onboard tools. No power nozzle. Retractable cord. **Recommendation:** Quietness and good surface cleaning make this compact model top-rated.

35 Sanyo SC-585 $80

Onboard tools fall off easily. No power nozzle. Dirt collected in plastic compartment, very messy to dump out. Retractable cord. **Model availability:** Discontinued; successor: SC-535, $70. **Recommendation:** Inconvenient and messy.

36 Hoover Portapower II Supreme S1353 $150

Awkward cord handling. Power nozzle. Suction control. **Recommendation:** Fair performer.

37 Eureka Worldvac Mighty Mite II 3651A $120

Good side edge cleaner. No power nozzle. Awkward cord handling. Suction control. But: high emissions. **Model availability:** Discontinued; successor: 3679A, $100. **Recommendation:** There are better choices.

38 Eureka The Boss Mighty Mite II 3621A $75

Very similar to (36), but with less powerful motor. **Model availability:** Discontinued; successor: 3670A, $70. **Recommendation:** Keep looking.

39 Hoover Portapower II S1337 $80

Similar to (35), but with less powerful motor, no power nozzle, and no suction control. **Recommendation:** Keep looking.

Ratings *Wet/dry vacuums*

& Recommendations

The tests behind the Ratings

Overall score is based mostly on performance, stability, and convenience. **Dry performance** was tested using dense items—nails, bolts, and the like. **Wet performance** measured how quickly and thoroughly each model could pick up specific amounts of water. **Stability** is based mainly on results from tests in which the vacs were pulled across an uneven floor and placed on a board that was progressively inclined until the machine tipped over. **Ease of use** is based mostly on maintenance (including cleaning the filter and emptying the tank), maneuverability, and ease of storage. **Price** is approximate retail. Models similar to those we tested are noted in the Model details; features may vary.

Typical features for these models

• Onboard tools. • Cartridge or bag filter.

Recommendations

The highest-rated vacs in both size groups are very good machines, but they're pricey. A step down, models perform nearly as well: the small Craftsman (Sears) 17744 ($40), and the large Shop Vac QSP QM30A/925-59 ($80) and Hoover S6631 ($90). The Shop Vac is a CR Best Buy.

See Buying Guide report, page 121. Last time rated in CONSUMER REPORTS: July 1996.

Overall Ratings

E VG G F P

Within size groups, listed in order of overall score

Key no.	Brand and model	Price	Overall score (0–100; P F G VG E)	Performance: DRY	Performance: WET	Noise	Stability	Ease of use
	LARGE MODELS							
1	**Craftsman** (Sears) 17706	$140		E	E	F	VG	VG
2	**Royal** Dirt Devil 081600	150		E	G	P	E	VG
3	**Shop Vac** QSP QM30A/ 925-59 **A CR Best Buy**	80		VG	VG	G	G	G
4	**Hoover** S6631	90		G	VG	G	G	G
5	**Hoover** S6755	130		VG	VG	F	F	G
6	**Genie** PRO20-4031	90		E	VG	P	F	G

Can't find a model? Call the manufacturer. See page 342.

Ratings continued

Ratings, continued

Key no.	Brand and model	Price	Overall score (0–100: P F G VG E)	Performance DRY	Performance WET	Noise	Stability	Ease of use
	LARGE MODELS *continued*							
7	**Shop Vac** 8040/870-64-2	$130		⊖	○	◒	◒	○
8	**Eureka** Shop Boss Quiet Kleen 2832A	100		◒	⊖	○	◒	○
9	**Genie** SV12-200-20	60		○	⊖	●	●	◒
10	**Shop Vac** 800M/808-32-9	100		⊖	○	●	●	◒
	SMALL MODELS							
11	**Craftsman** (Sears) 17701	70		⊜	⊜	◒	◒	○
12	**Royal** Dirt Devil 08900	85		⊜	○	●	⊜	○
13	**Craftsman** (Sears) 17744	40		⊖	◒	◒	●	○
14	**Eureka** Shop Boss 2812A	60		◒	⊖	●	⊖	○
15	**Shop Vac** 3332.0E/333-32-8	65		○	○	○	●	◒
16	**Genie** BV6-150-22	50		○	⊖	◒	●	◒
17	**Shop Vac** 700M/707-02-6	40		○	○	○	●	◒
18	**Shop Vac** 700E/707-21-6	50		○	○	◒	●	◒
19	**Hoover** S6529	50		◒	⊖	○	●	◒

Model details

Large models

1 Craftsman (Sears) 17706 $140

• 16 gal. • Detachable blower. • Cartridge filter. • Wide hose. • Onboard tools. • 20-ft. cord. • 26 lb. • 6 hp.

This vac can pick up just about anything; the best model for fine dust and among the best for water. Very stable. Tank drain. Easy-on, easy-off lid. Utility and squeegee nozzles. But: Fairly noisy. High in dust emissions. **Recommendation**: An excellent performer.

2 Royal Dirt Devil 081600 $150

• 16 gal. • Detachable blower. • Cartridge filter. • Wide hose. • Onboard tools. • 20-ft. cord • 23 lb. • 5 hp.

Picks up just about anything well—except fine debris. Among the most stable machines. Tank drain. Floor, utility, and squeegee nozzles. But: Very noisy. **Model availability:** Discontinued; successor: 081600B, $90. **Recommendation**: An excellent performer.

3 Shop Vac QSP QM30A/925-59 $80

• 12 gal. • Bag filter. • Wide hose. • Onboard tools. • 18-ft. cord. • 18 lb. • 3 hp.

No other model better combines solid performance with respectable scores for noise, stability, and convenience. Tank drain. Floor, utility, and squeegee nozzles. Crevice tool. But: Only fair for fine dust. Can't be used as a blower. Similar: 925-60, $90, 16 gal.; 925-58, $70, 10 gal., no tank drain; 925-57, $60, 8 gal., no tank drain. **Recommendation**: A very good performer; excellent value. **A CR BEST BUY.**

4 Hoover S6631 $90

• 12.5 gal. • Cartridge filter. • Onboard tools • 6-ft. cord. • 20 lb. • 27,500 rpm.

Though a little less adept at dry debris than (3), this Hoover similarly combines solid performance with respectable scores for noise, stability, and convenience. Tank drain. Unique dual-tank system. Floor, utility, and squeegee nozzles. Crevice tool. But: Only fair for fine dust. **Recommendation**: A good performer; very good value.

5 Hoover S6755 $130

• 16 gal. • Detachable blower. • Cartridge filter. • Wide and narrow hoses. • 12-ft. cord. • Onboard tools. • 26 lb. • 28,000 rpm.
Larger in capacity than (4), a little better for dry pickup, and (as you'd expect at this price) with additional accessories. Floor, utility, and squeegee nozzles. Crevice tool. But: Also a bit noisier and a bit less stable than its brandmate. **Recommendation**: A good performer.

6 Genie PRO20-4031 $90

• 20 gal. • Wide and narrow hoses. • Cartridge filter. • 10-ft. cord. • 21 lb. • 4 hp.
An outstanding performer, especially on dry debris. Easy-on, easy-off lid. Floor, utility, and squeegee nozzles. Crevice tool. But: Emits a noisy screech. Quite unstable. High in dust emissions. **Model availability:** Discontinued. **Recommendation**: A good performer.

7 Shop Vac 8040/870-64-2 $130

• 20 gal. • Wide hose. • Bag filter. • 12-ft. cord. • 19 lb. • 4 hp.
A solid performer. Utility nozzle. But: Fairly noisy. Quite unstable. **Recommendation**: There are better choices.

8 Eureka Shop Boss Quiet Kleen 2832A $100

• 13 gal. • Wide and narrow hoses. • Bag filter. • Onboard tools. • 6-ft. cord. • 17 lb. • 5 hp.
True to its name, one of the quietest machines. Easy-on, easy-off lid. Floor, utility, and squeegee nozzles. But: Otherwise undistinguished, at best. **Recommendation**: There are better choices.

9 Genie SV12-200-20 $60

• 12 gal. • Bag filter. • 6-ft. cord. • 15 lb. • 2 hp.
Picked up debris competently. Easy-on, easy-off lid. Floor and squeegee nozzles. But: Among the noisiest and most unstable models. **Model availability:** Discontinued. **Recommendation**: There are better choices.

10 Shop Vac 800M/808-32-9 $100

• 12 gal. • Bag filter. • 6-ft. cord. • 13 lb. • 3 hp.
Picked up competently. Floor and squeegee nozzles. But: Among the noisiest and most unstable models. High in dust emissions. **Recommendation**: There are better choices.

Small models

11 Craftsman (Sears) 17701 $70

• 8 gal. • Wide hose. • Cartridge filter. • Onboard tools. • 6-ft. cord. • 13 lb. • 3 hp.
This vac can pick up just about anything—among the best models for water, and better than most at fine-dust pickup. Utility and squeegee nozzles. Crevice tool. But: Fairly noisy and fairly unstable. Can't be used as a blower. **Model availability:** Discontinued. **Recommendation**: Very good in performance and value.

12 Royal Dirt Devil 08900 $85

• 8 gal. • Detachable blower. • Wide hose. • Cartridge filter. • 14-ft. cord. • Onboard tools. • 22 lb. • 3.5 hp.
Among the best for dry, large debris, and among the most stable. Floor, utility, and squeegee nozzles. But: Very noisy. Heavy for its size. **Model availability:** Discontinued; successor: 08900B, $70. **Recommendation**: A very good performer.

13 Craftsman (Sears) 17744 $40

• 6 gal. • Wide hose. • Cartridge filter. • Onboard tools. • 6-ft. cord. • 12 lb. • 2 hp.
Though competent and inexpensive, this Sears can't match the overall performance of its larger brandmates. Better than most for fine dust. Utility nozzle. But: Very unstable. Fairly noisy. Among the worst for water. Can't be used as a blower. **Model availability:** Discontinued. **Recommendation**: A good—if limited—performer.

14 Eureka Shop Boss 2812A $60

• 9 gal. • Bag filter. • Onboard tools. • 6-in. cord. • 14 lb. • 1.5 hp.
A solid performer on water, and among the most

Can't find a model? Call the manufacturer. See page 342.

Ratings continued

Ratings, continued

stable. Easy-on, easy-off lid. Floor and squeegee nozzles. But: Among the worst for dry debris. Very noisy. **Recommendation**: A good—if limited—performer.

15 Shop Vac 3332.0E/333-32-8 $65

• 6 gal. • Detachable blower. • Bag filter. • 6-ft. cord. • 10 lb. • 2 hp.
Among the quietest machines. Floor and squeegee nozzles. But: Very unstable and quite inconvenient. Similar: 333-33-6, $75, 10 gal.; 333-34-4, $85, 12 gal. **Recommendation**: There are better choices.

16 Genie BV6-150-22 $50

• 6 gal. • Detachable blower. • Bag filter. • 6-ft. cord. • 13 lb. • 1.5 hp.
A solid performer. Easy-on, easy-off lid. Floor and squeegee nozzles. But: Very unstable, fairly noisy, and inconvenient. Similar: BV8-150-22, $65, 8 gal. **Recommendation**: There are better choices.

17 Shop Vac 700M/707-02-6 $40

• 6 gal. • Bag filter. • 6-ft. cord. • 9 lb. • 1.5 hp.
Much like (15), but with a smaller motor, no blower, fewer tools—and a much lower price. Similar: 707-03-4, $45, 8 gal.; 707-01-8, $35, 5 gal. **Recommendation**: There are better choices.

18 Shop Vac 700E/707-21-6 $50

• 8 gal. • Bag filter. • 6-ft. cord. • 10 lb. • 2 hp.
Much like (18), but with a larger capacity, no blower, and fewer tools. Similar: 707-22-4, $60,10 gal. **Recommendation**: There are better choices.

19 Hoover S6529 $50

• 6 gal. • Bag filter. • Onboard tools. • 6-ft. cord. • 10 lb. • 23,500 rpm.
The quietest vac tested, and very good for water. Floor nozzle. But: The worst for picking up dry debris and for dust emissions. **Recommendation**: There are better choices.

For the most recent product Ratings

See the monthly issues of CONSUMER REPORTS magazine. Or check out Consumer Reports Online. Our Web site *(www.ConsumerReports.org)* covers autos, appliances, electronics gear, more. Free areas provide useful listings, recalls, shopping guidance. Members pay $2.95 per month for unlimited use, including searchable access to test reports and product Ratings.

Ratings *Carpet deep-cleaners*

& Recommendations

The tests behind the Ratings

Overall score gives greatest weight to results of our **soil** test—how well a machine cleaned ground-in potting soil from carpeting. **Stains** shows how well the machine cleaned coffee, red wine, tomato sauce, and mud. **Ease of use** is a judgment of 14 factors, including setup and storage. **Dryness** indicates how damp the carpet was after cleaning; it was measured by weighing the carpet before and after each test. **Price** is the national average based on a survey or, where marked with an *, the price we paid. Models similar to those we tested are noted in the Model details; features may vary.

Typical features for these models

• 17-foot or longer power cord. • Hose that isn't long enough to clean a whole flight of stairs. • Shut off automatically when the dirty-water tank is full. • One-year warranty. **Most canisters:** • Capacity of two gallons of cleaning solution. • Weigh 33 to 43 pounds (with solution). • Shut off automatically when the dirty-water tank is full. **Most uprights:** Capacity of one gallon of cleaning solution. • Weigh 25 to 31 pounds (with solution).

Recommendations

Before you buy a machine, consider renting one. The canister-style Rinse 'N Vac/Carpet Magic or the upright-style Rug Doctor Mighty Pack will give you a feel for what the machines can do, for $20 a day. If you do decide to buy one, the Bissell Big Green Powerbrush canister ($210) and the Kenmore Cleaning Machine scrubber ($170) did the best job.

See Buying Guide Report, page 121. Last time rated in CONSUMER REPORTS: July 1997.

Overall Ratings

E VG G F P

Within types, listed in order of overall score

Key no.	Brand and model	Price	Overall score (0–100; P F G VG E)	Cleaning: Soil	Cleaning: Stains	Ease of use	Dryness
	LARGE CANISTER EXTRACTORS						
1	**Bissell** Big Green Powerbrush 1680-3	$210		VG	G	VG	G
2	**Rinse 'N Vac/Carpet Magic** CM-3H (rental)	$20/day		G	G	F	F
3	**Kenmore** (Sears) 86909	300		P	G	VG	G
4	**Bissell** Powerlifter 16603	165		P	F	VG	VG

Ratings continued

Ratings, continued

Key no.	Brand and model	Price	Overall score (0–100; P F G VG E)	Cleaning: Soil	Cleaning: Stains	Ease of use	Dryness
	LARGE CANISTER EXTRACTORS *continued*						
5	**Bissell** Big Green 1671	$170		●	◒	⊖	⊖
	UPRIGHT EXTRACTORS						
6	**Hoover** Steam Vac Deluxe F5857	230		○	○	○	⊖
7	**Rug Doctor** Mighty Pack EZ MP-R (rental)	$20/day		○	◒	◒	●
8	**Eureka** Dream Machine 2450B	190		◒	●	○	⊖
9	**Hoover** Steam Vac Supreme F5833	200		●	◒	◒	⊖
10	**Hoover** Steam Vac F5805	130		●	◒	◒	⊖
11	**Eureka** Dream Machine 2430A	140		●	●	●	⊖
	SMALL CANISTER EXTRACTORS						
12	**Bissell** Little Green Plus 1653-5	90		●	●	⊖	○
13	**Kenmore** (Sears) 3-in-1 86603	100		●	●	⊖	○
14	**Hoover** Steam Vac Jr. F5411	90		●	◒	○	⊖
	SCRUBBING MACHINES						
15	**Kenmore** (Sears) Cleaning Machine 88973	170		⊖	◒	●	●
16	**Windsor** Dri-Matic	*390		◒	●	○	⊖

Model details

Large canister extractors

1 Bissell 1680-3 $210

The machine works effectively, using moving brushes to scrub. The brushes can jam on shag carpeting. Two-year warranty. **Recommendation:** Good; the best of an unimpressive group of cleaners.

2 Rinse 'N Vac CM-3H $20/day

This rental worked just well enough to rank good. It holds more solution than other machines, and its vacuum hose should reach up a flight of stairs. That's fortunate; at 69 pounds when filled, it's not easy to tug along. **Model availability:** Discontinued. **Recommendation:** Good; a useful way to see if you want to buy a deep-cleaner.

3 Kenmore (Sears) 86909 $300

The machine uses either moving brushes or a clear nozzle, and has an attachment for bare floors. It can be used as a wet/dry (shop) vac. **Model availability:** Discontinued. **Recommendation:** Fair; look for one of the few choices rated good.

4 Bissell 16603 $165

The machine lacks the moving brush found on (1). It has a clear nozzle. Two-year warranty. **Recommendation:** Fair; there are better choices.

5 Bissell 1671 $170

Similar in performance to (4). It can also be used as a wet/dry (shop) vac and has an attachment for bare floors. Two-year warranty. Similar: Bissell Big Green 1672, $170. **Recommendation:** Fair; there are better choices.

Upright extractors

6 Hoover F5857 $230

The machine's moving brushes give a good scrub. Its long power cord is convenient. It has an attachment for bare floors. **Model availability:** Discontinued. **Recommendation:** Good overall performance; (1) rated better.

7 Rug Doctor EZ MP-R $20/day

This rental's brushes give a good scrub, but the machine is hard to use. It has twice the capacity of other uprights; it's also twice as heavy as some. The spray won't turn off while the brushes are on. The upholstery attachment should reach up a flight of stairs. **Recommendation:** A good way to see if you want to buy a deep-cleaner.

8 Eureka 2450B $190

The machine's moving brushes are soft and barely touch the carpeting. In our soil test, it left streaks. It converts easily to clean upholstery. It has an attachment for bare floors. The Eureka Dream Machine 2450A, an earlier model, performed similarly. **Recommendation:** Fair; choose one of the few better choices.

9 Hoover F5833 $200

It has no moving brushes, and can't handle heavy dirt. It has an attachment for bare floors. **Model availability:** Discontinued. **Recommendation:** Fair; there are better choices.

10 Hoover F5805 $130

A bare-bones version of (9). **Recommendation:** Fair; there are better choices.

11 Eureka 2430A $140

A bare-bones version of (8). **Model availability:** Discontinued. **Recommendation:** Fair; there are better choices.

Small canister extractors

12 Bissell 1653-5 $90

The machine is easy to use, but it's not effective. The dirty-solution tank doesn't shut off when full and can overflow. **Model availability:** Discontinued. **Recommendation:** Fair; no machine in this category did well.

13 Kenmore (Sears) 86603 $100

Like (12), it's convenient but not effective, and the dirty-solution tank can overflow. **Recommendation:** Fair; there are better choices.

14 Hoover F5411 $90

It does a little better with stains than other portables, but its power cord is shorter than most, making it inconvenient. **Recommendation:** Fair; there are better choices.

Scrubbing machines

15 Kenmore (Sears) 88973 $170

This old-style shampooer is one of the best soil-removers tested. But it doesn't vacuum, and takes two hands to control. It has attachments for bare floors but no tools for cleaning in tight spots. The solution tank can fall off during use. **Recommendation:** Very good for heavy soil, but inconvenient. Barely ranked good overall.

16 Windsor $390

The machine's moist powder doesn't wet carpeting. But it doesn't clean carpeting either, unless you use a lot more powder than recommended. You sprinkle the powder, use the machine to scrub it in, then pick up the dirt with a regular vacuum. The brushes can jam on shag carpeting. **Recommendation:** There are better, less expensive choices.

Can't find a model? Call the manufacturer. See page 342.

Ratings *Food processors*

& Recommendations

The tests behind the Ratings

Overall score is based mainly on our judgment of how the machines performed key processor chores—chopping, slicing, shredding, and pureeing. We also considered **noise, features,** and convenience (ease of setup, use, and cleaning). **Price** is the national average. Models similar to those we tested are noted in the Model details; features may vary.

Typical features for these models

• Excellent or very good at routine chopping. • Clear plastic bowl and lid and plastic food pusher. • S-shaped chopping blade and at least one slicing disk. • One motor speed that's adequate for most tasks (the motor is powerful enough for heavy chores like brioche dough only in some large models). • Come with a one-year warranty.

Recommendations

For basic tasks we recommend two mid-sized food processors: the Cuisinart Little Pro Plus and the Betty Crocker BC-2427. Each is priced at $90. For heavy-duty tasks like kneading dough, the clear choice is the top-rated KitchenAid Professional KFP650WH ($230). It's well equipped, capable, convenient to use, and quiet. The less expensive Braun UK280 ($130) is nearly as good but has been discontinued. For chopping or shredding small amounts, the Sunbeam 4817-8 mini processor ($40) was capable and efficient.

See Buying Guide report, page 127. Last time rated in CONSUMER REPORTS: August 1997.

Overall Ratings

E VG G F P

Within types, listed in order of overall score

Key no.	Brand and model	Price	Overall score (0–100; P F G VG E)	Performance: SLICING	Performance: SHREDDING	Performance: PUREEING	Noise	Features
	LARGE MODELS							
1	**KitchenAid** Professional KFP650WH	$230		E	VG	E	E	E
2	**Cuisinart** Pro Custom 11 DLC-8S	190		E	VG	E	E	VG
3	**Braun** UK280	130		E	VG	VG	VG	E
4	**Braun** UK11	85		G	E	VG	G	G

Key no.	Brand and model	Price	Overall score (0–100: P F G VG E)	Performance: SLICING	Performance: SHREDDING	Performance: PUREEING	Noise	Features
	LARGE MODELS *continued*							
5	**Black & Decker** FP1000	$55		○	⊖	⊖	◒	○
6	**Krups** 706	100		○	⊖	○	○	○
	MID-SIZED MODELS							
7	**Cuisinart** Little Pro Plus	90		○	⊖	⊜	⊜	⊖
8	**Betty Crocker** BC-2427	90		⊖	⊖	⊖	⊜	○
9	**Krups** 704	70		⊖	⊖	○	⊖	○
10	**Hamilton Beach** 70700	55		○	⊖	○	◒	○
11	**Hamilton Beach** 70100	35		○	⊖	◒	◒	○
12	**Regal** K813	40		◒	⊖	⊖	◒	○
	MINI PROCESSORS							
13	**Sunbeam** 4817-8	40	[1]	◒	⊖	⊖	●	–
14	**Betty Crocker** Micro Food Processor BC-1424	25	[1]	◒	○	○	◒	–
15	**West Bend** High Performance 41022	30	[1]	◒	⊖	◒	●	–

[1] *The mini processors are not comparable to the full-sized models and couldn't be rated on the same scale.*

Model details

Notes on the details: Dimensions (height, width, depth) are to the nearest inch. Bowl capacity is based on the amount of dry ingredients it holds when not in use and may not agree with manufacturer's rated capacity; actual capacity is lower when machine is running. Weight is to the nearest pound.

Large models

1 KitchenAid Professional KFP650WH $230

• 15x9x11 in. • 9½-cup capacity • 17 lb.
Easy to use, very powerful, quiet. Has very useful mini bowl, effective dough blade, so-so whipping paddle, extra slicing/shredding disks, storage box for disks and blades. Similar: KFP600WH, has plastic housing instead of metal and lacks whipping paddle. **Recommendation:** Excellent—does it all very well.

2 Cuisinart Pro Custom 11 DLC-8S $190

• 15x8x11 in. • 9¼-cup capacity • 13 lb.
Very powerful and quiet. Easy-to-use controls. Assembling the large feed tube, shredding blade, and slicing disk can be tricky. Dough blade works well. Has extra thin-slicing disk. 3-yr. overall warranty; 5-yr. motor warranty. **Recommendation:** Excellent—does everything very well. But it could be a bit more convenient to use.

3 Braun UK280 $130

• 14x14x7 in. • 10¾-cup capacity • 6 lb.
Feature-laden, powerful, variable speed, fairly quiet. Superb slicing disk and french-fry disk are adjustable for thickness. Has very useful mini bowl, cheese-grating disk, and effective whipping attachment. Wide feed tube is tricky to use. **Model availability:** Discontinued. **Recommendation:** Excellent. A talented performer, fine features.

4 Braun UK11 $85

• 14x14x7 in. • 10¾-cup capacity • 7 lb.
Very powerful two-speed machine. Whipping attachment is effective. Has extra thin-slicing/shredding disk, but its slicing didn't work well. Manu-

Ratings continued ▶

Ratings, continued

facturer recommends hand-washing components. **Model availability:** Discontinued. **Recommendation:** Very good. And a good value, if you don't mind convenience compromises.

5 Black & Decker FP1000 $55

• 13x11x8 in. • 9-cup capacity • 5 lb.
Powerful, user friendly, and lightweight—but noisy. Not great at chopping beef cubes or almonds. But very good at pureeing and shredding. 2-yr. warranty. **Recommendation:** Good. Lots of machine for the money.

6 Krups 706 $100

• 13x15x8 in. • 9¼-cup capacity • 9 lb.
Powerful two-speed motor. But didn't turn out tidy thin slices, very smooth purees, or voluminous whipped cream. **Recommendation:** Good—but too little for too much.

Mid-sized models

7 Cuisinart Little Pro Plus $90

• 13x6x9 in. • 4-cup capacity • 7 lb.
Very good, very quiet performer. Continuous-feed chute. Easy-to-use controls. Has juicer attachment that spins disconcertingly fast and sprays droplets on you and the countertop. 3-yr. overall warranty; 5-yr. motor warranty. **Recommendation:** Very good. Best and smallest of the mid-sized batch.

8 Betty Crocker BC-2427 $90

• 15x8x10 in. • 6¾-cup capacity • 10 lb.
A good performer overall, but purees weren't as smooth or almonds chopped as consistently as they could be. Very quiet. Manufacturer says bowl can go in microwave oven. 2-yr. warranty. **Model availability:** Discontinued. **Recommendation:** Good. A decent choice.

9 Krups 704 $70

• 11x12x7 in. • 6-cup capacity • 5 lb.
Variable-speed motor is noisy. Performance is good, although purees weren't as smooth as they could be. Plastic parts have to be hand-washed. **Recommendation:** Good. Worth considering.

10 Hamilton Beach 70700 $55

• 13x16x9 in. • 7½-cup capacity • 7 lb.
Continuous-feed chute. Two-speed motor is noisy. **Recommendation:** Good. A decent, no-frills machine.

11 Hamilton Beach 70100 $35

• 13x7x13 in. • 7¼-cup capacity • 5 lb.
Came up short in a couple of basic skills. Tricky to assemble. Noisy. Blades must be hand-washed. **Recommendation:** Good. There are better—though not cheaper—choices.

12 Regal K813 $40

• 15x7x11 in. • 6-cup capacity • 6 lb.
Noisy. Not a good slicer. Lid shifts easily in the middle of a chore, shutting off motor. **Recommendation:** Good, but there are better choices.

Mini processors

13 Sunbeam 4817-8 $40

• 15x8x8 in. • 2½-cup capacity • 4 lb.
Bowl mounted on tall, narrow base. Good for shredding and thick purees (hummus, for example) but not liquids, which leaked with less than ¼ cup of water. You must twist the lid to operate. Very noisy. Inconvenient to operate slicer/shredder chute. 2-yr. warranty. **Recommendation:** Best of the minis tested.

14 Betty Crocker Micro Food Processor BC-1424 $25

• 11x9x8 in. • 3-cup capacity • 3 lb.
Looks like a miniversion of a standard food processor. Not quite as noisy as others. 2-yr. warranty.

15 West Bend High Performance 41022 $30

• 14x10x6 in. • 3-cup capacity • 3 lb.
Bowl mounted on tall, narrow base. To operate, you must hold the "on" switch. Very noisy. Chopped herbs unevenly. Poor pureeing. 1-yr. warranty. **Model availability:** Discontinued.

Can't find a model? Call the manufacturer. See page 342.

Ratings *Blenders*
& Recommendations

The tests behind the Ratings

We challenge blenders with a range of tasks—from making soups and shakes to grating Parmesan cheese and cloves. The **overall score** includes our assessment of how convenient each blender is to use, as well as how well each handles tasks. Those with plastic containers became etched and cloudy after grating cloves, a hard test. The number of **speeds** is listed to help identify a model; more speeds aren't necessarily better. **Price** is approximate retail.

Typical features for these models

All the blenders have an opening in the lid to add ingredients in mid-operation.

Recommendations

Most of these models would make good choices. The three top-rated blenders performed particularly well and are convenient to use and moderately priced. The Waring TB701 ($45) offers easy-to-clean touchpad controls and an automatic pulse. The Cuisinart CB-4 ($60) has a glass container—the type we prefer—with an extra-wide opening for easy loading of food. The Osterizer 4100 ($40) performed as well as or better than any other blender tested at all speeds, but its chrome base and push buttons make cleaning less convenient. Note, however, that all three have been discontinued, and availability is uncertain.

See Buying Guide report, page 129. Last time rated in CONSUMER REPORTS: February 1997.

Overall Ratings

Listed in order of overall score

Key no.	Brand and model	Price	Overall score (0–100; P F G VG E)	Container	Speeds
1	**Waring** Touchblend TB701	$45		Plastic	4
2	**Cuisinart** Vari-Speed CB-4	60		Glass	Variable
3	**Osterizer** 4100	40		Glass	14
4	**Hamilton Beach** BlendMaster 54200	35		Glass	14
5	**Hamilton Beach** BlendMaster 50200	30		Glass	10
6	**Krups** Power X Plus 239	50		Glass	Variable

Ratings continued ▶

Ratings, continued

Key no.	Brand and model	Price	Overall score (0–100; P F G VG E)	Container	Speeds
7	**Osterizer** Professional Bartender 4135	$125		Stainless	2
8	**Osterizer** 4108	35		Plastic	10
9	**Hamilton Beach** BlendMaster 50100	25		Plastic	10
10	**Sunbeam** 4142	30		Plastic	6
11	**Hamilton Beach** BlendMaster 600WP	20		Plastic	7
12	**KitchenAid** Ultra Power KSB5	100		Glass	5

Model details

1 Waring Touchblend TB701 $45

Excels at many tasks, including crushing ice without liquid. It has an auto-pulse feature. Grating takes fancy pulse-work, but the results are very good. Touchpad controls are easy to clean. But: A hinged cover in the lid for adding ingredients is hard to open. The optional disk for whipping cream isn't worth the extra $8. Warranty: 5 yr. on the motor, 1 yr. on the rest. **Model availability:** Discontinued. **Recommendation:** A very good blender.

2 Cuisinart Vari-Speed CB-4 $60

Though it blends drinks a little less smoothly than (1), this blender performs most tasks, including crushing ice without liquid, very well. The lever control is easy to clean around, and the container has a wide mouth. But: Four samples developed black residue on top of the motor housing. The container lid doesn't fit very well. Warranty: 18 mo. **Model availability:** Discontinued. **Recommendation:** A very good blender, with a convenient glass container.

3 Osterizer 4100 $40

It doesn't make smooth milk shakes, but otherwise this blender performs as well as or better than any other we tested. It pulses on all speeds, a nice plus. But: The base may be hard to keep clean; its chrome finish shows fingerprints, and its push buttons are hard to clean around. And by the end of our tests, there was a tiny spot of rust on the blades. Warranty: 1 yr.; doesn't cover normal wear of parts. **Model availability:** Discontinued. **Recommendation:** A very good blender, but you have to be extra careful to dry the blades to avoid tiny rust spots.

4 Hamilton Beach Blendmaster 54200 $35

It grates and purees with the best, and does an OK job of crushing ice. The wide-mouthed container has easy-to-read measurements. But: The push-button controls may be hard to clean around. Warranty: 2 yr.; doesn't cover glass container. **Model availability:** Discontinued; successor: 54200R. **Recommendation:** A very good blender.

5 Hamilton Beach Blendmaster 50200 $30

Looks and performs like (4), but does a better job of crushing ice without liquid; (4) grates better. But: By the end of our tests, the blades were rusty. The push-button controls may be hard to clean around. Warranty: 2 yr.; doesn't cover glass container. **Recommendation:** A very good blender, but you have to be extra careful to dry the blades to avoid rust spots.

6 Krups Power X Plus 239 $50

Quietest blender we tested. It has power boost, and it pulses on all speeds; that's fortunate, because grating takes fancy pulse-work. It does an OK job of crushing ice without liquid. But: It leaks a lot when operated full. And by the end of our tests, the blades were a little rusty. Warranty: 1 yr.;

doesn't cover glass container. **Recommendation:** A very good performer when the container isn't full; you have to be extra careful to dry the blades to avoid rust spots.

7 Osterizer Professional Bartender 4135 $125

Overall performance is very good, though grating lemon zest takes fancy pulse-work. (You can pulse on both speeds, however.) Has a three-prong grounded plug, an extra safety feature. But: You can't see into the opaque, handle-less container, and the chrome-finished base shows fingerprints. Container and top can't go in dishwasher. Warranty: 5 yr.; doesn't cover normal wear of parts. **Model availability:** Discontinued. **Recommendation:** A very good performer, but the container is not very convenient.

8 Osterizer 4108 $35

Doesn't puree quite as well as most higher-rated blenders, but makes slightly smoother milk shakes than most. An optional ice blade, $13 extra, works well. But: The push-button controls may be hard to clean around. Warranty: 1 yr.; doesn't cover normal wear of parts. **Model availability:** Discontinued; successor: 6631. **Recommendation:** A very good blender.

9 Hamilton Beach Blendmaster 50100 $25

Does most things well, including crushing ice without liquid. Container has easy-to-read measurements. But: Container leaks a lot when operated full. One sample couldn't puree soup. Warranty: 2 yr. **Recommendation:** Good—but only if you get a good sample, and only if you use it with the container less than full.

10 Sunbeam 4142 $30

The power-boost feature and the wide-mouthed container with easy-to-read measurements are nice. But: Grating is a chore, and pureeing soup takes a long time. To use the highest speed, you must turn the dial control through the lower speeds. By the end of our tests, the blades were a little rusty. Warranty: 2 yr.; doesn't cover normal wear of parts. **Recommendation:** Good on most tasks—but you have to be extra careful to dry the blades to avoid rust spots.

11 Hamilton Beach Blendmaster 600WP $20

On the whole, it grates, purees, and makes drinks well. Container has easy-to-read measurements. But: It leaks a lot when operated full, and one sample broke pureeing soup. By the end of our tests, the blades were a little rusty. The push-button controls may be hard to clean around. Warranty: 2 yr. **Recommendation:** Good overall, but there are inconveniences—and you have to be careful to dry the blades to avoid rust spots.

12 KitchenAid Ultra Power KSB5 $100

Modern design. Has a three-prong grounded plug, an extra safety feature. But: This posh model spatters and leaves food unchopped. It's inconvenient to use: The container has no spout and is heavier than other glass containers. Warranty: 1 yr. **Recommendation:** There are better choices.

Can't find a model? Call the manufacturer. See page 342.

Ratings Breadmakers
& Recommendations

The tests behind the Ratings

The **overall score** is based on bread quality, convenience (including quiet operation during kneading cycle), and versatility, which we judged based on the number of useful features. Number of cycles gives an idea of versatility. Cycle times are for a basic white load on the regular cycle and on the rapid cycle. The dough cycles are usually shorter; the whole-wheat, longer. **Price** is the national average.

Typical features for these models

• Measures 14 inches high, 14 wide, and 11 deep. • Cycles for basic, basic rapid, and whole-wheat bread, and for basic bread dough. • Bakes a loaf that is shaped like a square column. • Lid that's removable, for easier cleaning. • Bakes a 2-lb. loaf. • Has a delay-start timer. • Has an "add ingredients" signal for fruit. • A bread pan and paddle that will cost from $40 to $60 to replace. • One-year warranty for parts and labor.

Recommendations

Any breadmaker should bake good bread, but some make it easier or are quieter than others. The two top-rated models—the Panasonic SD-YD205 ($190) and the Breadman TR800 ($150)—made the best bread and boast lots of special cycles that make them versatile. More basic machines that are easier to use and very quiet are the Goldstar HB202CE and the Toastmaster 1188 (each $100).

See Buying Guide report, page 130. Last time rated in CONSUMER REPORTS: November 1997.

Overall Ratings

Listed in order of overall score

Key no.	Brand and model	Price	Overall score (0–100; P F G VG E)	No. of cycles	Cycle times (hrs:mins) BASIC	RAPID
1	**Panasonic** Bread Baker SD-YD205	$190	▬▬▬▬▬▬▬	12	4:00	3:00
2	**Breadman** TR 800	150	▬▬▬▬▬▬▬	14	3:00	2:30
3	**Zojirushi** Home Baker Super BBCC-Q20	150	▬▬▬▬▬▬▬	5	3:50	2:00
4	**Goldstar** HB202CE	100	▬▬▬▬▬▬▬	7	3:40	2:00
5	**Toastmaster** Breadbox 1188	100	▬▬▬▬▬▬	7	3:40	2:00
6	**Regal** Kitchen Pro K6743	100	▬▬▬▬▬▬	6	2:40	—
7	**Breadman** Ultra TR700	100	▬▬▬▬▬	7	2:40	—

Key no.	Brand and model	Price	Overall score (0–100; P F G VG E)	No. of cycles	Cycle times (hrs:mins) BASIC	RAPID
8	**Pillsbury** Automatic Bread/ Dough Maker 1021	$120		6	3:40	—
9	**West Bend** Baker's Choice Plus 41090	200		8	3:40	3:20
10	**Black & Decker** All in One Deluxe B1630	110		6	3:50	2:00
11	**West Bend** Automatic Bread/ Dough Maker 41044	100		7	3:40	3:00
12	**Welbuilt** The Bread Machine ABM4100T	95		6	3:00	2:30

Model details

1 Panasonic Bread Baker SD-YD205 $190

Extra cycles: Basic and whole-wheat (each with regular, rapid, "sandwich," and rasin bread and dough settings); multigrain bread and dough.
Better bread, even on rapid cycle. Rectangular loaf. Lots of useful features: "on" light, 10-min. power-outage protection, measuring cup and spoon, yeast dispenser. But: Less convenient than others—no window, timer sets in only 1 direction, "ready" signal too quiet, lid not removable. **Recommendation:** A very good, versatile bread-lover's machine—but pricey.

2 Breadman TR800 $150

Extra cycles: French, sweet, whole-wheat regular and rapid breads; "quick" breads; pizza and bagel dough; jam; "Bake-only."
Better bread. Rectangular loaf. Lots of cycles. Useful features: independent crust setting, cycle-progress timer light, 1-hr. power-outage protection, warning when ambient temperature is too low to bake bread, instructional video. But: Raucous motor, "ready" signal too quiet, only 90-day warranty on bread pan, paddle. Complaints about customer service. **Recommendation:** A very good but noisy machine.

3 Zojirushi Home Baker Super BBCC-Q20 $150

Extra cycles: Mixed and whole-grain breads.
Very fast rapid cycle. Useful features: independent crust settings, "on" light, 20-sec. power-outage protection, instructional video, measuring cup and spoon. Clear display. Loud "ready" signal. But: New pan is $67. **Recommendation:** A very good machine with no big drawbacks.

4 Goldstar HB202CE $100

Extra cycles: French and specialty bread, cake.
Programs easily. Very convenient to use. Very quiet. Fast rapid cycle. Independent crust settings, measuring cup. But: LED display is barely visible in bright light. **Recommendation:** A very good machine at a very nice price.

5 Toastmaster Breadbox 1188 $100

Extra cycles: French and sweet breads; jam.
Similar to (4) in looks, programming layout, accessories, and results. Has a 3-year warranty. But: Keypad, in French and English, is cluttered. **Recommendation:** A very good machine at a very nice price.

6 Regal Kitchen Pro K6743 $100

Extra cycles: French, sweet, and "quick" breads.
Basic cycle is fast; no rapid cycle. Programs easily. Slightly smaller "footprint" than other machines. Useful features: cycle-progress display, 10-min. power-outage protection, warning when ambient temperature is too low to bake bread, instructional video. But: Lid not removable, "ready" signal too quiet. Similar model: K6747 Pro, $120. **Recommendation:** A very good machine, and very fast.

7 Breadman Ultra TR700 $100

Extra cycles: French bread; fruit and nut bread; cake; jam.
Basic cycle is fast; no rapid cycle. Programs easily and has a clearer, more intuitive keyboard lay-

Ratings continued ▸

Ratings, continued

out than others. Useful features: warning when ambient temperature is too low to bake bread, instructional video. But: Very noisy. Similar model: TR700DL, $140. **Recommendation:** A very good, fast machine—but noisy.

8 Pillsbury Automatic Bread/Dough Maker 1021 $120

Extra cycles: French, sweet, and "quick" breads. Useful features: independent crust settings, cycle-progress display, warns when ambient temperature is too low to bake bread, 10-min. power-outage protecton. But: Controls not clearly coded, "ready" signal too quiet, lacks keep-warm feature and "add ingredients" signal. **Recommendation:** Good.

9 West Bend Baker's Choice Plus 41090 $200

Extra cycles: Whole-wheat rapid bread; French, sweet, and quick breads.
Opens from front; shorter but much wider than others. Clear LED display. Useful features: independent crust settings, cycle-progress display, "on" light, 10-min. power-outage protection, warning when ambient temperature is too low to bake bread, interior light, loud "ready" signal, extended rise settings. But: Bread tended to be pale, and sometimes lopsided. Harder to clean. Controls not clearly color coded. **Recommendation:** Only good—at a hefty price tag.

10 Black & Decker All in One Deluxe B1630 $110

Extra cycles: Sweet and whole-grain breads; pasta. Generic recipe made bread of lower quality. Timer hard to set. Has independent crust settings on most cycles, "on" light, timer light, 20-sec. power-outage protection, instructional video, loud "ready" signal, fast rapid cycle. Slightly smaller footprint than others. Has 2-yr. warranty. **Similar model:** B1620, $100. **Recommendation:** Good, but finicky with recipes other than its own.

11 West Bend Automatic Bread/Dough Maker 41044 $100

Extra cycles: French and sweet breads; whole-wheat rapid bread.
Claims to make a 2-lb. loaf, but makes a 1½-lb. loaf. Noisy. Keypad layout not clear. Pan hard to insert, remove. Harder to clean. Has independent crust settings, cycle-progress display, warning when ambient temperature is too low to bake bread, "on" light. New pan only $25. **Recommendation:** Only good. There are better choices.

12 Welbilt The Bread Machine ABM4100T $95

Extra cycles: Sweet regular and sweet rapid breads; sweet dough. (No whole-wheat.)
Keyboard layout is less intuitive than others. Harder to clean than other machines. Lid not removable. No warranty. Has independent crust settings, cycle-progress displays, loud "ready" signal, quiet motor. Similar model: ABM4400, $95. **Recommendation:** Only good. There are better choices.

Can't find a model? Call the manufacturer. See page 342.

AROUND THE HOME

Bicycles

Expensive bikes are generally lighter, better made, and more enjoyable to ride, but kids and casual riders may be happy with cheaper models.

Last CR reports:
Kids' bikes, November 1996;
Mountain bikes, June 1997
Expect to pay: $50 to $3000

What's available

Mountain bikes. The most widely sold type, mountain bikes have fat, knobby tires; 26-inch wheels; flat handlebars; a sturdy frame; and 18 gears or more. The ride is comfortable but somewhat sluggish on pavement.

Prices range from less than $100 to thousands of dollars. In our tests, we've found that design and performance relate to price to some extent.

Low-priced models—those priced around $100 to $200—have a thick steel-tube frame and fork. At 35 pounds or more, they are hard to pedal.

Mid-priced models weigh about 30 pounds and typically have a host of features that make riding easier—longer pedal cranks, a wider selection of low gears, and brakes and shifters that operate much more smoothly than those on lower-priced models. Price range: $200 to $340.

Higher-priced models are best suited for rugged use. Their frames are typically made of steel alloys or aluminum, which are lightweight, strong, and durable. Tires have aggressive treads that get good grip on rough terrain. The front and, possibly, the rear suspension provide sure handling and comfort on bumps and lumps. Price: $350 and up.

Cruiser bikes. These are a throwback to the thick-tired, thick-framed models of yesteryear, but sometimes with more gears. They're heavy, low-maintenance bikes that are best suited for occasional use, a cruise around the neighborhood, or a shopping trip. They aren't for fast rides or steep hills. Price range: $100 to $500.

Road bikes. These lightweight bikes, designed for recreation or touring, come with narrow tires and drop handlebars. The design is fast and efficient, but casual riders may find the riding position uncomfortable and the ride jarring on rough surfaces. Although road bikes are the best choice for riding fast or far, they've declined in popularity. Price range: $450 to $3000 or more.

Hybrid bikes. Introduced in the late 1980s, these bikes attempt to marry a mountain bike's strength and comfort with a road bike's efficiency. Hybrids typically combine aspects of both: a medium-weight frame, "antler" handlebars for an upright riding position, and tires that are somewhat knobby and narrow. A hybrid should suit riders who commute or enjoy moderate fitness rides, even on hilly roads. Price range: $180 to $700.

Kids' bikes. This category includes models with training wheels and downsized mountain bikes. If your child is younger than 7 or so, you'll most likely be choosing from various sizes of single-speed, coaster-brake BMX-style bikes, suited to short hops around the neighborhood. For older children, a kids' mountain bike, with multiple speeds and hand brakes, would be more suitable. Price range: $50 to more than $250.

Other types. There are also special bikes for special needs: recumbents for people with back problems; folding bikes for travelers; electric-powered bikes; child trailers and tandems for adults with children.

What's new

Bicycle models and components change every year, like car models. Usually, changes are slight. The previous year's model may prove a good buy, with no compromise in performance or features.

Full-suspension frames, with shock absorbers front and back, are a major step-up feature on mountain bikes. Wheels with three or four fat spokes provide better aerodynamics. Gear shifts are now integrated with brake levers for easier use.

Shopping strategy

We recommend buying from a specialty bike store that's close to home, since a bike (like a car) needs regular tune-ups and occasional repairs. Better bike shops will fit the bike correctly to your size or will change a shifter or seat and make other initial adjustments to the bike. Try before you buy. (If the store doesn't permit test rides, shop elsewhere.) Ride over varying terrain, check the handling, and make sure that your posture and the seat feel comfortable. Test brakes to see that they respond evenly, without grabbing, as you increase pressure.

To find the right size, straddle the bike with both feet flat on the floor. Allow three inches of clearance between the top tube and crotch for mountain bikes, two inches for hybrids, and one inch for road bikes. (For women who ride more than just casually, we recommend a "men's" frame, which is sturdier than a step-through "women's" frame.)

Decide what to spend. Adult bicycles that are safe and satisfying cost at least $200 to $400, according to our tests. Spending more buys a lighter frame and higher-quality components, which make it easier to ride off-road, climb hills, and ride long distances. Adult bikes costing less than $200 typically are clunky and hard to ride.

What's in the stores. Huffy, Murray, Pacific, and Roadmaster are low-priced brands available at toy stores, discounters, warehouse clubs, and mass merchandisers like Wal-Mart, Kmart, and Toys 'R' Us. Moderate-to-high-priced brands like Schwinn, Trek, Diamondback, and Specialized are typically sold at specialty bike stores or chains.

Key features

Brakes. Hand brakes are typically either side-pull brakes, mounted on either side of the wheel, or cantilever brakes, mounted above the wheel. According to our tests, both types can stop a bike quickly and controllably.

If you ride in wet weather, avoid bikes with shiny steel wheel rims and side-pull brakes. In our wet-braking tests, such bikes have taken much farther to stop than have bikes equipped with aluminum alloy rims.

Frame. The frame material is a key factor in a bike's weight and quality of ride. The cheapest bikes have a thick steel frame that makes them heavy and provides a harsh ride. More expensive bikes have a frame made of high-strength steels, aluminum, carbon fiber, or exotic metals like titanium. These frames are lighter and can be better at soaking up shock.

Gears. These let you pedal comfortably despite changes in road slope. Using three sprocket wheels in front and six to eight in the rear, most mountain bikes and hybrids offer 18 to 24 speeds. Road bikes usually have 14 to 18 speeds (two sprocket wheels in front, seven to nine in the rear).

On mountain bikes, the number of gears matters less than their range, from low (for hills) to high (for fast riding).

Handlebars. Their size and shape influence riding efficiency and comfort. The bent-over posture required the drop handlebars on road bikes and the low, flat bars of some performance-oriented mountain bikes lessens wind resistance, reduces shocks from bumps, and improves handling. That posture also lets muscles work efficiently. For off-road riding, where you use your arms to navigate bumps and lumps, a flat handlebar is best. For casual rides on pavement and dirt roads, antler-style bars allow for an upright position.

Saddle. Seats are easy to change—don't let an uncomfortable one stop you from buying an otherwise good bike. Men's saddles tend to be long and narrow; women's, short and wide. Some manufacturers claim that seats filled with gel reduce shock and vibration. But in our tests with seats of all kinds, riders of both sexes found that the shape of the seat was the most important factor in determining whether a ride would be comfortable.

Shifters. Old-fashioned friction shifters were difficult to master until you developed a feel for them. Today's bikes use indexed shifters that make changing gears far easier. The three main types used on hybid and mountain bikes are: a *twist shift* (usually the Grip Shift brand), which is a collar encircling each end of the handlebar; a set of *levers underneath* each end of the handlebar (Shimano EZ-Fire Plus or Rapid Fire Plus); or, least desirable, a *thumb shifter*, a lever above each end of the handlebar. Shifters for road bikes include frame-mounted levers and, for more expensive bikes, handlebar-mounted brake/shift levers.

Tires. How a bike handles depends greatly on the tires. For rough trails, a mountain bike's tires should have big, widely spaced knobs for traction. Such tires produce a sluggish, "buzzy" ride on pavement. Hybrid-bike tires have smaller and closer-spaced knobs and sometimes a ridge down the middle. That reduces off-road traction but improves rolling resistance on pavement. Road-bike tires, smooth or with a fine tread, are designed for low rolling resistance. Note that wheels and tires are easily changed if they are not what you want.

Bicycle helmets

Most helmets provide more impact protection than required by the most stringent safety standards.

Last CR report: June 1997
Ratings: page 216
Expect to pay: $10 to $135

Safety

Laws and regulations. Although helmet use is still not mandated by the federal government, at least 15 states now have some type of helmet law. Helmets made after March 16, 1995, are required to meet at least one of the voluntary safety standards issued by groups like the Snell Memorial Foundation, the American National Standards Institute (ANSI), and the American Society for Testing and Materials (ASTM). These standards cover everything from impact protection to buckle and strap strength to how much of the head the helmet covers. Federal safety standards are expected to take effect over the next few years.

The importance of fit. A helmet can offer maximum protection only if it's the right size and correctly fitted. Helmets come in adult, youth, and toddler sizes, which vary from brand to brand and, sometimes, model to model.

Once you've narrowed the selection to a couple of models, fine-tune the fit using the foam pads that are usually supplied. A helmet should be level, covering your forehead, and all straps should be tight when the chin strap is buckled. If the helmet can move enough to expose your forehead when you push up firmly on the helmet's front edge, shorten the front straps. If the helmet can move enough to cover your eyes when you pull it toward the front, shorten the back straps. Chin straps should be tight enough so you can feel the helmet's top when you open your mouth. If you can't achieve a satisfactory fit, choose another helmet.

The buckle problem. When we most recently tested helmets, we found two types of buckle that broke apart in a significant number of samples. We recommend you avoid helmets from the 1997 model year that have "ITW Nexus TSK63" marked on the end of the buckle housing in small script under the strap or "Pinchguard" on the face of the buckle housing. Instead, look for a helmet with a raised dot on the face of the buckle housing or a buckle housing marked with either "ITW Nexus Shockloc" (on the end of housing) or "National Molding Co. HDSS-3/4" (on the face of the housing). Those models with buckles that broke apart have been called out in the Ratings (page 216).

If you already own a helmet with either of the problem buckles, contact the helmet manufacturer. In the meantime, it's better to continue using the helmet than wearing no helmet at all.

Our tests also uncovered some strap guides that didn't hold straps in place. To keep those helmets properly fitted, you'll have to adjust their straps frequently. When soaked by rain or sweat, some helmet straps elongated farther in our tests than is allowed under helmet safety standards. Whenever your straps get wet, it's a good idea to periodically check the tension of the chin strap.

When to replace. In general, you should discard a helmet after any accident—whether it looks damaged or not—because it may no longer protect adequately. Many manufacturers (noted in the Ratings) will replace a helmet after a crash, usually for a fee that's one-third or less of the cost of a new helmet. Manufacturers also suggest that helmets be replaced every three to five years, because weathering and air pollution can cause deterioration.

What's new

Over the years, we've seen dramatic improvements in helmet ventilation. The Giro Helios RL in our most recent test was so well ventilated that panelists actually felt cooler when wearing it than when they were bare headed. Unfortunately, the best-ventilated new helmets don't come cheap. The Helios costs $135.

More and more helmets claim to be specially made for multiple sports: bicycling, in-line skating, and skateboarding. Our tests show that most "multisport" helmets are no different from the typical bike helmet, which works just fine for in-line skating and skateboarding. Some multisport helmets do provide more protection at the back of the head in case of a backward fall.

Shopping strategy

Any helmet that meets Snell, ANSI, or ASTM safety standards should offer adequate protection, provided it's fitted correctly. We think you'll gain an additional measure of protection if you limit your selection to helmets with buckles that consistently passed our tests.

Decide what to spend. A good, basic helmet costs $10 to $30. To get good ventilation and easier adjustments, you may have to pay more. Helmets for youths and toddlers are less expensive than adult helmets—$10 to $40—but range more widely in quality, especially ventilation and strap adjustability.

What's in the stores. Toy stores and mass merchandisers like Kmart and Price Costco tend to sell helmets that cost less than $30. Some brands are carried exclusively by such retailers. Specialty bicycle shops, on the other hand, tend to carry only helmets that cost $30 or more. You're more likely to find help in fitting a helmet at such a store.

Using the Ratings. Wearing any of the helmets in the Ratings is better than wearing no helmet, but we think those buckles that consistently passed our tests warrant first consideration. If you can't find a model, call the manufacturer; see page 342.

Key features

Pads. Removable hook-and-loop (Velcro) pads in several thicknesses make it easiest to get a good fit. Pads in a single thickness or with adhesive backing make it harder to get the best fit.

Rear stabilizer. This encourages correct positioning of the helmet and helps prevent it from bouncing and shifting on your head. Some stabilizers are held by the straps; the strap-independent design is a bit more secure. Retrofit stabilizers are available at bike stores for $20 or so. A rear stabilizer won't keep a helmet in place during an accident. Properly adjusted straps do that.

Straps. Look for straps that can be easily pulled from side to side across the helmet and for guides that lock the straps in place.

Vents. The coolest helmets to wear tend to have many large air vents and a contoured interior that actually channels air over and around the head.

Mattress sets

Durability is pretty much a given in all but low-end mattresses and box springs.

Last CR report: March 1997
Expect to pay: $200 to $1350 for a full-sized set

What's available

Innerspring mattresses, the most widely purchased type of bedding, have coiled steel springs sandwiched between layers of padding. The padding, identical on top and bottom so you can flip the mattress, is usually made of several materials, including polyurethane foam, puffed-up polyester or cotton batting.

What's new

Sales of larger mattresses, especially queen-size, have increased in recent years. Mattresses are also thicker. They used to be about 7 inches thick; now, they're 9 to 15 inches. Such mattresses require sheets dubbed "deep pocketed," "high profile," or "high contour." Thicker mattresses pose another problem that our tests revealed: The thicker the mattress, the greater the sagging will become.

Telephone-based businesses like Dial-A-Mattress and Sleepy's are going head-to-head with chain stores and independent bedding stores. That means there are more places to shop.

Because most manufacturers make nearly identical mattresses to be sold under different names, comparison-shopping isn't easy. For example, a mattress called the Simmons Beautyrest Jewel of the Universe at Montgomery Ward was claimed to be the World Class Coventry Wool at Sleepy's and the Milan at Dial-A-Mattress. This name game allows each retailer to vary the price of similar mattresses by hundreds of dollars. To comparison-shop, you may have to learn various construction details to be sure you're comparing the same mattress.

Most major manufacturers will have nationally available models, sold through independent stores, and store-specific models, those available only in a particular chain like Sears, Montgomery Ward, or Bloomingdale's.

Shopping strategy

You likely need a new mattress if your current mattress is more than 10 years old, if it has formed annoying peaks, valleys, or lumps, or if you wake up stiff or sore. When you buy a mattress, buy a box spring, too—they perform as a unit.

Putting a new mattress on an old box spring could void your warranty.

Take time to comparison-shop—it can save you hundreds of dollars. Choose retailers that have served you well in the past or have been recommended by friends.

Use prices from competitors to bargain for a good price. Make sure there's a free-trial period and a generous warranty. Insist that no substitutions be made without your consent, and read the terms of your contract carefully.

Ask about disposal of your old mattress. Some companies will bring it to the curb for municipal pickup; others will cart it away for a nominal fee upon delivery of your new mattress.

Once it's delivered, carefully inspect your mattress. Refuse delivery if there's damage or if the store has substituted another mattress. Be sure to keep your receipt, and leave that "do not remove" tag attached to the mattress; you'll need both to make a warranty claim.

Decide what to spend. Durable and well-made mattresses are available in all but low-end sets. You can spend as little as $450 for a fine twin-size set, $600 for a full-size, $800 for a queen-size, and $1000 for a king-size. Sales are common, so there's no reason to pay list price. And deeper savings are often possible if you bargain. Mattress-by-phone businesses claim to offer rock-bottom prices, but you have to bargain hard to get them. If you buy the bed unseen and untried, be sure you can exchange it.

Spending more for a mattress gets you thicker padding, damask ticking, and perhaps a pillowtop—a cushion on both sleep surfaces that's filled with foam, wool, silk, or a down blend.

What's available. Sealy, Serta, and Simmons account for nearly three of every four mattresses sold, but there are more than 35 other brands. Although the big makers offer no-frills models, most people are more familiar with their flagship lines: the Sealy Posturepedic, Simmons Beautyrest, and Serta Perfect Sleeper.

Key features

Box spring or foundation. A box spring may be a wood frame containing heavy-gauge springs or a metal frame with springs. The plain wood frame, called a foundation, is usually used only in cheaper mattress sets. Placing a mattress atop a plain wooden frame can make the mattress seem harder than it actually is. Split box springs on foundations are available for second-floor bedrooms reached by narrow stairs.

Coils. In our tests, a higher coil count didn't necessarily mean less sagging, what we define as any permanent depression that becomes apparent as the mattress ages. Nor did a firmer mattress resist sagging better than a softer one. Any sagging that occurred in our tests was primarily in the padding, not in the springs. Coil design doesn't affect a mattress's ability to withstand use and abuse, but it can shape the bed's overall "feel." The minimum number of coils recommend for a full bed is 360.

Corner guards. They help keep the box spring's fabric from chafing against the metal corners of the bed frame.

Extra edge support. Added rigidity is useful to have at the head, foot, or sides.

Firmness. Terms defining firmness, such as "pillow soft," "plush," "cushion firm," and "superfirm," are of little value. Trying the mattresses out in the store is the best way to shop for a desired feel. If you select a model that carries no firmness label (few do), be aware that the firmness selected in the store may not be what is delivered to your home.

Handles. These let you reposition the

mattress on the box spring. Best are handles that go through the sides of the mattress and are anchored to the springs. Next best are fabric handles sewn vertically to the tape edging of the mattress. The weakest handles are inserted through the fabric and clipped to a plastic or metal strip on the mattress.

Padding. The innermost layers of padding prevent you from feeling the springs. Plastic webbing, nonwoven fabric, or a metal grid directly atop the springs can help keep them from chewing the pad above. The next layers of padding often start with egg-carton foam or soft, resilient foam. Other padding material includes foam of varied thicknesses and densities combined with garnetted cotton, thick wads of rough batting that provide loft but compress quickly. In some mattresses, one side may be firmer than the other, or a middle section may be firmer than the head or foot. The only way to know if it's right for you is to try it.

Quilting and top padding. In most cases, stitches attach the top layers of padding to the ticking. Stitch design varies and is largely an aesthetic consideration. Make sure stitches are uniform and unbroken; broken threads can allow the fabric to loosen and pucker. Top padding is generally polyurethane foam, with or without polyester batting. Batting provides a uniform, soft feel but tends to lose its loft faster than does a soft foam.

Ticking. On most models, the fabric covering is made of polyester or a cotton-polyester blend. Low-end mattresses may have vinyl ticking, which can eventually stretch and sag, but most materials should last the life of the mattress. More expensive mattresses have damask ticking, which has its design woven into the fabric, not just printed on. Some also contain a bit of silk, but that's more a marketing gimmick than a useful addition.

Latex wall paint

Our tests show that pricey paints don't always do the best job.

Last CR report: September 1997
Ratings: page 198
Expect to pay: $10 to $30 a gallon

What's available

Wall paints are all-purpose paints that can be used in just about any room. They typically come in a variety of sheens—flat, satin, and semigloss. Names and the degree of glossiness aren't uniform from one manufacturer to another.

Flat paint keeps reflections to a minimum and hides surface imperfections. As a rule, flat paint is harder to clean and picks up more dirt than does glossier paint.

A semigloss paint is easier to clean than a flat paint, but it may be too shiny for an entire room. In addition, some semigloss paints can remain sticky long after the paint feels dry to the touch, making them poor choices for painting trim and shelving.

A low-luster finish—often called eggshell or satin—is the middle ground between semigloss and flat. It's easy to clean and reflects less light than semigloss.

Glossy trim enamels are meant for windowsills, woodwork, and the like. "Kitchen and bath" paints are wall paints supposedly formulated to perform well in humid areas and to withstand mildew.

Colors are usually custom-mixed by

adding colorant to one of several tint bases—pastel for lighter colors; medium for deeper colors; and so on. The tint base, not the specific hue, largely determines a paint's performance: its toughness, its resistance to dirt and stains, and its ability to withstand scrubbing. Most brands of paint come in several tint bases to create a full range of colors.

What's new

In response to government anti-smog regulations limiting the amount of volatile organic compounds (VOCs) in paints—VOCs from applied paint contribute to ground-level ozone—paint manufacturers are producing more low- or zero-VOC paints. These new paints also claim to produce little or no odor.

Manufacturers are producing new paints that don't "block," or stick. If you've ever pried a glass off a painted bookshelf or tried to open a painted door in humid weather, you know what blocking is.

Getting rid of unused paint can be a problem. Some communities and paint providers have teamed up to create unused-paint distribution programs. Kelly-Moore has three recycling facilities in Texas, Green Paint Co. one in New England, and Major Paint Co. (Cycle II paint) one in California. In Seattle, latex paint is collected by the city, mixed, and sold as "Seattle Beige" to local schools and hospitals.

For consumers looking for a bargain, returned paint or mismatched colors can often be purchased inexpensively at Home Depot stores.

Shopping strategy

First, choose the type of paint and the color. Then, calculate how much paint you'll need. Paint manufacturers estimate that a gallon of paint should cover 400 to 450 square feet of wall space. If you're covering a very dark or contrasting color, or a very old or glossy surface, you'll probably need to buy primer to reduce the contrast between the old color and the new or to provide a sound surface for the new paint to adhere to.

Some manufacturers claim that their products are one-coat paints, but our tests over the years have shown that few paints, especially whites, do a very good job of one-coat hiding.

Colorfastness is important in sunny rooms, where sunlight can quickly blanch the wall's original color. The colorants added to tint the paint determine how much fading you'll see. Whites and browns don't fade, so they're a safe choice for a sunny room. Red and blue colorants don't fade very much, but bright green and yellow pigments do. In a mixture of pigments, the other colors will begin to stand out as the greens and yellows fade.

Decide what to spend. Premium latex wall paints all performed very well overall, as you'd expect. But in our tests, the costliest paints weren't always the best performers. You should be able to find a good paint for less than $15 a gallon.

Whether you buy paint from an independent paint retailer that stocks several brands, a company store like Sherwin-Williams, a home center, or a mass merchandiser like Wal-Mart, be sure to ask about discounts or deals on high-quantity purchases. In our experience, retailers often give a 10 to 15 percent discount. All else being equal, you can expect better service from a local paint store, but better prices from a home center.

What's in the stores. The two top-selling brands of interior latex paint, Sears and Sherwin-Williams, are sold exclusively in their stores. Other companies have tied their fortunes to specific retailers. For example, Behr is sold mostly through Home Depot, United Coatings through Wal-Mart. True Value and Ace, national hardware chain stores, manufacture their own paint.

Using the Ratings. For each brand of paint, we tested white, as well as a pastel and medium tint base in flat, low-luster, and semigloss. If you can't find a paint, call the manufacturer; see page 342.

Ceiling fans

Bigger isn't necessarily better. Shop according to the size of your room.

Last CR report: July 1997
Ratings: page 179
Expect to pay: $30 to $400 or more

A ceiling fan cools by forcing air down to the floor, where it spreads sideways to the walls before moving upward. It can make a room feel six or seven degrees cooler—enough to provide comfort on a moderately hot day. On a very hot or humid day, it can be used in conjunction with an air-conditioner, letting you lower the temperature setting on the air-conditioner.

The energy saved can be substantial. Based on a national average electricity rate of 8.31 cents per kilowatt-hour, it would cost about $1.50 to operate an energy-efficient ceiling fan at its highest speed for 12 hours a day for a month, versus about $20 to run a 6000-Btu/hr. air-conditioner.

What's available

Ceiling fans range 32 to 60 inches in diameter, measured from blade tip to blade tip. The two most widely sold sizes are 42-inch and 52-inch models. Manufacturers generally recommend 42-inch fans for rooms up to 225 square feet; 52-inch fans for rooms up to 400 square feet. For larger spaces, you might consider installing multiple fans. A 52-inch fan can weigh 15 to 40 pounds; a 42-inch fan, 10 to 15 pounds.

What's new

Manufacturers' emphasis in recent years on the decorative aspects of fans and lights has helped renew sales and made for a wider choice of colors, styles, and finishes. Some blades are reversible, with a different finish on each side. Styles include "themed" and novelty designs, such as baseball and basketball fans.

Safety

Although most ceiling fans can be turned on and off with a pull-chain switch or a handheld remote, installing a properly grounded wall switch is a good safety precaution. A fan is often easiest to install in place of an existing overhead light. Make sure the existing ceiling outlet box is replaced with one that's UL-approved and labeled "acceptable for fan support." Consider having a licensed electrician install the fan.

A ceiling fan shouldn't hang lower than seven feet above the floor, especially in areas where people may raise their arms, as when dressing. The tips of the blades should be no closer than 24 inches from any wall, away from curtains and draperies that could get tangled. Never install a fan in an area where it's likely to become wet, unless the fan is labeled "suitable for use in damp locations."

Shopping strategy

Measure the area of your room to determine the size you need. Decide whether you want to hang the fan from a swiveling downrod or flush against the ceiling. A downrod provides better air circulation, but the fan may wobble.

Decide what to spend. Spending more doesn't necessarily get you a better fan. You can buy a very good large fan for about $100 or a very good small one for as little as $30. Spending more buys "designer" styles and options such as a wall-mounted control or a remote.

What's in the stores. Ceiling fans are available at home centers, mass-market outlets, lighting and hardware stores, and electrical distributors.

Using the Ratings. We tested 42-inch and 52-inch ceiling fans to see how much air they moved, how fast, and how easy they were to install. Similar models should perform much the same as the tested models; features may vary. If you can't find a model, call the manufacturer; see page 342.

Key features

• *Standard on most models:*

Blades. Most fans come with four or five; a few have six. The number of blades produced no significant effect on airflow, although the extra blade made the fan run a bit slower in our tests.

Controls. Typically, three speeds controlled by a pull chain.

Reverse. Besides blowing air down, fans reverse direction to blow air up to the ceiling. Supposedly, reversing direction is useful in winter, to better circulate the warmer air near the ceiling. In our past tests, however, the wind-chill effect from the upward draft more than offset any heat saving.

• *Recommended if available:*

Hanger bracket. Most fans use a J-hook mount that requires lifting the fan twice. A hanger bracket lets you secure the downrod immediately.

• *Useful for some installations:*

Balance kit. Some fans come with small weights fastened with adhesive tabs to balance blades that wobble. The procedure isn't difficult, but some models may require more adjusting than others.

Wall-mounted control. A necessity for a fan on a cathedral ceiling.

Remote control. This comes with some top-of-the-line fans. Remotes that operate most fans are also available as aftermarket products.

Light kit. Some ceiling fans come with attached light fixtures. Others can be fitted with lights sold separately for $15 to $150.

Variable-speed control. Nice to have, but not very common.

Air-conditioners

Most air-conditioners do a good job of cooling and dehumidifying. Be sure to match a model's cooling capacity to your needs.

Last CR reports:
Small and medium-sized models, June 1997; Large models, June 1996
Ratings: page 189 (all sizes)
Expect to pay: $200 to $850

What's available

All window air-conditioners contain pretty much the same components. The part facing outdoors contains a compressor, fan, and condenser; the part facing indoors, a fan and an evaporator.

Models differ in cooling capacity, measured in British thermal units (Btu) per hour. How much cooling you need depends on the size of the room, its exposure, the number of windows, and the local climate. Use the chart opposite to determine what you need. An air-conditioner with too little capacity won't cool adequately. One that's too big can make you feel clammy, since the air-conditioner will tend to cycle off before it can adequately dehumidify the room. Ideally, an air-conditioner should allow temperature swings of no more than one-and-a-half degrees above or below the set point and should keep relative humidity fairly constant.

The smallest models are suitable for a small bedroom and have a cooling capacity of about 5000 Btu/hr. Price range: $200 to $500.

Models for medium-sized rooms have a cooling capacity of about 6000 to 10,000 Btu/hr. and can cool a living room or master suite. Price range: $400 to $700.

Large models, those rated at 11,000 to 12,000 Btu/hr., can cool about 500 square feet—a large room, or areas that run together, such as a living room and dining room. Price range: $500 to $850. Models rated larger than 12,000 Btu/hr. usually require a 240-volt line instead of the normal 120-volt line.

Models also differ in how efficiently they run. All else being equal, the higher the energy-efficiency rating (EER), the lower the energy consumption and the lower your electricity bill. For instance, a unit with an EER of 11 will cost 18 percent less to operate than a similar sized one with an EER of 9.

What's new

Over the years, our tests have shown that air-conditioners are getting quieter, based on measurements indoors with the units set on low.

"Low profile" models are designed to maximize window views by hanging much of the machinery below the sill. Such designs do not compromise performance or energy efficiency, as tests of mid-sized units from Gibson and Carrier recently demonstrated.

Shopping strategy

Shop early in the season for the best selection and sales. Before you set out, consider whether you need an air-conditioner, or if a ceiling fan (see page 162) will do the job.

If your mind is made up to buy an air-conditioner, your first step is to figure out the cooling capacity you need. Use the chart on page 165.

Once you've narrowed the selection to a couple of models with the cooling capacity needed, choose the one with the higher EER on the bright yellow tag required by federal law. We recommend an EER of at least 10.

Installing or removing an air-conditioner remains a two-person job. The small and medium-sized models in our tests weighed from 46 to 101 pounds.

Decide what to spend. The greater the capacity, the more an air-conditioner is apt to cost. At a given size, there's no correlation between price and performance.

What's in the stores. There are more than two dozen brands of air-conditioner.

How much cooling do you need?

Use the chart below to determine how much cooling you'll need for a space with an eight-foot ceiling.

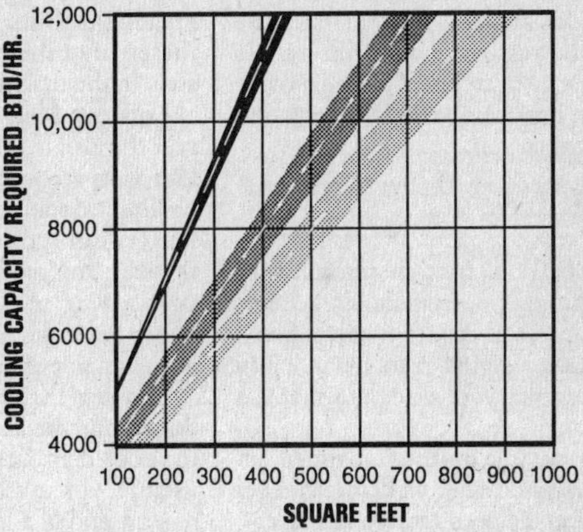

1. At the bottom of the chart, find the square footage you need to cool.

2. From there, move up the chart until you reach the correct band for what's above your room: the thickest band for an occupied area above; medium-width for an insulated attic; the thinnest for a noninsulated attic.

3. Within the band, move down for rooms facing mostly north or east, up for mostly south or west.

4. Read across to the appropriate Btu/hr.

5. From that Btu/hr., subtract up to 15 percent if you live in a cool Northern climate; add up to 10 percent for a hot Southern climate. Subtract 30 percent if the unit will be used only at night. If more than two people regularly occupy the area, add 600 Btu/hr. for every additional person. Add 4000 Btu/hr. if the area includes the kitchen.

Many come from the same manufacturers. Fedders, for instance, makes Emerson Quiet Kool. Frigidaire makes Gibson and White-Westinghouse. Matsushita Electric makes Panasonic and Quasar. Fedders, Kenmore (Sears), General Electric, and Whirlpool account for almost half of all sales in the U.S.

Using the Ratings. All the air-conditioners in the Ratings were good to excellent performers overall. They differed most in their ability to direct cool air to the left or the right. Some cope better with low voltage than others. And some are more energy efficient than others. Similar models should perform much the same as the tested models; differences exist primarily in styling. Choose a room model that performs well in the ways that matter most to you.

Key features

Controls. Look for a thermostat with clear markings. Controls should be logically arranged and easy to operate. Some models have a digital readout; it shows the temperature you've set and that the power is on.

Energy-saving options. A timer can turn an air-conditioner on before you get home, saving the need for it to run all day. An energy-saver setting, included on many models, is less useful. It cycles the fan and compressor on and off together, instead of letting the fan run continuously. It doesn't save much energy, and the change in noise levels can be jarring.

Installation features. Most room air-conditioners are designed to fit in a double-hung window. A limited selection of models fit in casement windows. Some models are made for through-the-wall installation.

Some models come fully assembled; others require you to add their side panels, usually an easy job. A slide-out chassis greatly simplifies installation: You secure the empty cabinet in the window, then slide in the machine's innards.

Louvers. Many room models can't direct the air effectively—important if the unit is in a corner or if you want spot-cooling. Models that let you close some louvers can redirect air more forcefully through the ones that remain open. A vent setting blows some room air outdoors. Some models also draw in fresh air, although not effectively.

"Power thrust." Also called "super thrust" and the like, this fan control sends the cooled air farther into the room. It's useful if you must mount the unit at the narrow end of a long room.

CO detectors

A plug-in model with digital display is best.

Last CR report: October 1997
Expect to pay: $30 to $95

Every year carbon monoxide (CO) causes deaths that could have been prevented by a detector. CO detectors should be in any home with a fuel-fired furnace, appliance or space heater, a wood-burning stove or fireplace, or an attached garage—all common sources of carbon monoxide. At relatively low levels CO can cause headache, dizziness, nausea, blurred vision, chest pain, and fainting—symptoms often mistaken for ailments like the flu. Continued exposure to high levels can bring on unconsciousness, brain damage, and even death.

What's available

A home CO detector is about the size of a smoke detector. Some models have a digital display of the level of carbon monoxide. All have horns that sound an 85-decibel alarm in response to an unsafe level of CO. If the alarm sounds, the detector should reset itself once the area is ventilated and the danger is past.

Plug-in. Most models are the AC-powered plug-in type; a few can be hard-wired into household circuitry. Plug-in models work by heating a metal-oxide sensor that reacts with CO. The major benefit of plug-in technology is that the detector is able to cleanse and reset itself in a relatively short time. Some plug directly into a wall socket; others have a six-foot power cord. Only a few offer battery backup. Price range: $30 to $95.

Battery-powered. This type usually uses a chemically treated disk that darkens upon prolonged exposure to CO. That method is slower than the sensor of the plug-in type. In addition, false alarms have been a problem. Price range: $40 to $80.

What's new

AIM recently introduced a battery-powered detector that employs a fuel-cell sensor instead of a chemically treated disk. It sounded an audible warning within a minute or so of exposure to CO.

Shopping strategy

To reduce the chance of CO poisoning, make sure that all combustion appliances are properly installed, well maintained, and checked yearly; have chimneys checked for blockage and cleaned once a year. And buy a plug-in CO detector with a digital display. Install a dectector in or near bedrooms—preferably at eye level, where it's easy to read a digital display.

Decide what to spend. A good plug-in model costs about $50. Make sure it can detect and display low levels of CO—less than 100 parts per million.

What's in the stores. The First Alert brand dominates the market. Most hardware stores and home centers carry them. Other brands, like Nighthawk, AIM, and S-Tech, are readily available and worked better in our most recent tests.

Recommendations. In our most recent tests, AC-powered plug-in detectors with digital displays from Nighthawk (model numbers 900-0046, 900-0014, 900-0056, 900-0057) were very impressive. Their digital displays were accurate, and they sounded full alarms well within the time limits. The S-Tech STCO-500LC, $45, also deserves serious consideration.

If you heat with wood, it's a good idea to have a detector with a battery backup or a battery-powered detector with digital display, such as the AIM Safety SAS6-96, $70, that will keep going in a blackout.

Key features

• *Standard on typical models:*

Hush/reset button. The "hush" button can temporarily silence the horn yet leave the CO sensor active.

LED light. Indicates the power is on.

Test button. Lets you verify that the detector's electronics are working.

• *Recommended:*

Digital display. This lets you monitor the CO level. It can tip you off to a potential carbon monoxide problem before it becomes severe.

Recall or memory. Models with this feature can provide the highest CO level sensed since the last resetting of the unit.

Child gates

Child gates are an essential tool in childproofing a home. All but one of the tested gates provided adequate safety.

Last CR report: January 1997
Ratings: page 214
Expect to pay: $15 to $70

Child gates block off staircases or potentially dangerous rooms, such as kitchens or workshops.

What's available

Mounted gates. To install these, you drill holes in the door frame or wall and mount the gate with screws. Once installed, a hardware gate is hard to dislodge. This type is the best choice where safety is paramount, such as at the top of a stairway. But many such gates aren't suitable for stairs, because they can swing outward over the stairs.

Pressure gates. Setting up these portable child barriers is usually as simple as sliding two panels past each other to fill up the opening. A pressure bar or other locking mechanism then wedges the gate in place. Pressure gates may mar the door frame or walls, but will leave no permanent holes.

Unfortunately, a child may be able to dislodge a pressure gate. That confines its use to less hazardous locations, such as an opening between two rooms, or the bottom of a stairway.

What's new

The childproofing industry is a relatively new and fast-growing segment of the product market, pioneered in 1981 by Safety 1st, the company that introduced "Baby on Board" signs for automobiles. Now, you can buy devices to aid in childproofing, where once there were only home remedies.

Shopping strategy

Decide what to spend. Gates cost anywhere from about $20 to $70. Our tests of gates showed no correlation between price and safety or quality. A child gate can run you as much as $70; the two top-rated models were priced at $50 and $35.

What's in the stores. Major brands of child gates are Fisher-Price, Gerry Baby, Kidco, Seymour, and North States. Safety 1st has an extensive line of other childproofing products. Other brands include First Years, Gerber, KinderGard, and Mericon.

Using the Ratings. We tested a dozen or so gates, primarily for how easily the gates were to install, open, and close. All the gates provided adequate safety, with the exception of the Seymour Keepsafe Expansion Gate 13-036-60. That model (and three larger variations) was downrated for having a jagged protrusion on top that might snag a child's clothing or a string or necklace around a child's neck.

If you can't find a model, call the manufacturer; see page 342.

Other childproofing products

Toilet lid locks. These are intended to keep children out of the toilet bowl.

Bathtub products. Cushioned covers for bathtub spouts and knobs are designed to reduce the risk of head injury.

Cabinet and drawer latches. These

are intended to keep children out of cabinets or drawers or from pulling drawers free.

Corner and edge bumpers. Cushions for the edges of furniture.

Door guards. Prevents a child from opening or closing a door.

Electrical-cord products. These secure excess cord to reduce the risk of injury to children who may trip, tug, or chew on it. An inexpensive alternative is to bind up excess cord with a twist tie—but not too tight, or you may damage the cord insulation.

Electrical-outlet covers. These block unused sockets so a child can't poke objects into them.

Electrical-switch locks. These products are designed to prevent a child's use of a wall switch that controls a hazarous appliance such as a garbage disposal.

Medicine-cabinet latches. These are designed to secure the doors of a medicine cabinet.

Stove guards. These block accress to the stove top or oven interior and keep stove knobs from being turned on.

Window-blind products. These keep window-blind cords out of the way to reduce the risk of strangulation.

Window locks. These prevent windows from being opened high enough for a child to get out, or from being closed on a child's head, hands, or neck. Most of the tested models were hard to use or install.

Not Acceptable childproofing products

The following products, listed alphabetically within types, were judged Not Acceptable in recent tests of childproofing products. For details, see CONSUMER REPORTS, January 1997.

Electrical-outlet covers small enough to pose a choking hazard:

- **AmerTac Style Safety Outlet Caps**
- **Brainerd 565XC Electrical Outlet Plugs**
- **Eagle Academy BP292CL Safety Caps**
- **GE 2501 Saf-T-Gard Safety Caps**
- **Gem 6025BL Safety Caps**
- **KinderGard 412 Outlet Plugs**
- **Leviton's 837-12777 Kiddy Cop Outlet Caps**
- **Safety 1st 117N Outlet Cap (translucent only)**
- **True Value 474239 Master Electrician Outlet Caps**

Stove guard can be defeated by a child older than about 2:

- **Safety 1st 242R Stove Knob Cover**

Lawn mowers

Buying the right type can save you hundreds of dollars.

Last CR reports:
Manual and electric, June 1995;
Gasoline push-type, June 1995;
Self-propelled, June 1996;
Tractors & riding mowers, June 1997
Ratings: page 203 (tractors & riding mowers)
Brand repair histories: pages 18 and 19
Expect to pay: $65 to $5000

What's available

Manual reel mowers. The reel mower has been brought up-to-date with lightweight alloys and plastic parts, but the way it works hasn't changed. A series of blades linked to wheels slice the grass.

Manual reel mowers are quiet, inexpensive, and relatively safe to operate. They require no maintenance aside from occasional sharpening or blade adjustment. Most can't cut grass higher than 1½ inches—those we've tested had a hard time plowing through thick, high grass—nor cut closer than three inches around obstacles. The cutting swath ranges from 14 to 18 inches. Reel mowers are practical for small, flat lawns. Price range: $70 to $100.

Electric mowers. These use an electric motor to drive a rotary blade, and you usually do the pushing. The motors are less powerful than the engines on gasoline-powered mowers, but in our tests, a few still performed better than some gas models at cutting tall grass.

Electric mowers run on standard house current. They're quiet and require little maintenance. They tackle tall and thick grass or weeds as well as most gasoline-powered mowers do. Many electrics mulch—chop up grass extra fine so clippings can decompose naturally in the lawn. They run on standard house current. Such models are practical for lawns of about a quarter-acre—typically, what can be reached by the 100-foot cord. Price range: $125 to $250.

Gasoline-powered mowers. Push-type gasoline-powered mowers are free to roam as long as there's fuel in the tank. Many can gobble up tall and thick grass or weeds; most can mulch. Generally, handling ranges from easy to very easy.

On the down side: Gasoline-powered mowers are noisy, and they require regular maintenance. The push type is practical for lawns of up to a half-acre and for trimming larger lawns. Their engines are typically a one-cylinder, four-stroke design that spins a 20-inch to 22-inch blade; power ranges from 3.5 to 5.5 hp. (A few models use a two-stroke engine, which uses a gasoline/oil fuel mixture and emits more pollutants.) Price range: $100 to $650.

Self-propelled models cost anywhere from $150 to $225 extra. The premium is worthwhile if your lawn is a half-acre or larger or if it's hilly. The engine, typically the same size as those in push-type models, powers either the front or rear wheels. Front-wheel-drive models are sometimes easier to maneuver, but rear-wheel drive provides better traction for climbing hills and better steering control. Price range: $300 to $850.

Riding mowers and lawn tractors. Riding mowers and small tractors are suitable for lawns about a half-acre and larger. If you're going to ride, a lawn tractor is the better buy, unless your lawn has lots of obstacles such as trees and rocks. There, a riding mower's small size would be an advantage.

Tractors have a front-mounted engine, while riding mowers typically have a rear-mounted engine. Both usually have five to seven forward speeds and one reverse speed. The more expensive tractors tend to have a convenient hydrostatic transmission with continuously variable speed adjustment. That design frees you from having to use a clutch. The deck of most riding mowers ranges from 28 to 33 inches, although a pair of unusual "zero turn radius" riding mowers we tested measure 40 and 42 inches. Many tractors cost no more than riding mowers, and their deck tends to be larger—anywhere from 36 to 48 inches.

Tractors are also more versatile. Add-on attachments enable them to plow, throw snow, or tow a cart. Riding mowers can't accept the same variety of add-ons.

With either type of machine, you need a measure of mechanical ability and strength to cope with the controls and upkeep. Figure on a space at least four feet wide and seven feet deep for storage.

Price range: $900 to $4000 for a riding mower or a lawn tractor.

What's new

Zero-turn-radius mowers promise better maneuverability, which helps reduce mowing and trimming time. You steer by pushing or pulling two control levers, rather than by turning a steering wheel. Each lever controls a rear drive wheel; you can make one wheel turn forward and the other wheel backward, for example. At the end of each run, you can turn 180 degrees for the next row without swinging wide or making several partial turns. You can also mow close to and around obstacles like trees and rock gardens. This comes at a steep price: about $3500.

We've noted one problem with zero-turn-radius mowers in our most recent tests: Because they have most of their weight in back, they tend to rear up when their optional rear-mounted grass-catcher bags are full. We strongly advise against using a zero-turn-radius mower with its optional grass-catcher.

Reducing air pollution. Gasoline-powered outdoor equipment, including mowers of all types, contributes to air pollution. California has led the way in reducing such emissions by requiring manufacturers to make engines that pollute less. Since the fall of 1995, new engines powering such equipment sold in that state have had to be certified that they meet a standard that should reduce hydrocarbon emissions by 30 percent. The Environmental Protection Agency began enforcing a similar standard nationwide in August 1997. Expect even tougher standards in years to come.

To meet the new standards, manufacturers often use engines with overhead valves instead of side valves. Although side-valve engines can be made to run cleanly, overhead-valve engines are considered better able to maintain a low pollution level over their lifetime. Battery-powered mowers may ultimately be the most environmentally friendly choice. So far, such models are expensive and limited in power.

Safety

Power mowers can cause serious injury. All walk-behind power mowers have what's called a "deadman" control, a safety control that stops the blade when you let go of the handle. That and other safety features have made mowing less hazardous. Injuries due to walk-behind mowers have dropped to about half of what they were 10 years ago. Still, thousands of people head to hospital emergency rooms every year from injuries caused by a power mower.

When you mow, keep the following safety tips in mind:

- Mow only when and where it's safe. Don't mow when the grass is wet; your foot could slip under the mower. Push a mower across a slope, not up and down it. (But *ride* a mower up and down, not across.) If the slope is more than about 15 degrees, don't mow at all; on slopes that steep, a push mower can get away from you, and a riding mower can tip over.
- Wear sturdy shoes and close-fitting clothes. Consider wearing ear protection.
- Before mowing, pick up toys, hoses, rocks, and twigs. Make sure no people or pets are nearby; a mower can hurl objects.
- Keep hands and feet away from moving parts.
- Don't defeat safety devices.
- Don't let children use or ride a mower.

Reliability

The more complex the mower, the more likely it will be to need repair, according to our surveys of readers. In our 1996 survey, readers reported on their experience with lawn mowers bought new between 1991 and 1996. Honda and Sears were among the more reliable brands of push-type mowers. Lawn-Boy and Snapper were among the least reliable. Snapper was among the least reliable brands of self-propelled mower.

Lawn tractors and riding mowers needed repairs more often than other types of mower. John Deere and Sears were among the most reliable brands of tractors; Cub Cadet, among the least reliable. Among riding mowers, Snapper, again, was among the least reliable brands. For more information, see the brand repair histories on pages 18 and 19.

Shopping strategy

Let the size and the terrain of your lawn determine the type of mower you buy. If you mow a quarter-acre or less of flat lawn, consider a manual reel mower; for a half-acre or less, a gasoline or electric mower that you push; for a half-acre to an acre, especially if the land is hilly, a self-propelled model; and for a half-acre or more, a lawn tractor.

How to handle clippings is another important choice. One option is to collect them, something walk-behind mowers do with a bag at the back or side. Rear bags are generally bigger than side bags and make a mower more maneuverable. A side-bagging model is apt to be less expensive, however. You can discharge the clippings, then rake them up. But the most convenient and environmentally friendly method is to mulch the clippings as you mow. Many models are sold as mulchers, and mulching kits are available to retrofit older mowers.

Don't try to predict performance by claims for motor or engine size. Our tests show no correlation between power and mowing ability.

Decide what to spend. Expect to pay top dollar for a reel mower that's easy to use, like the Agri-Fab 45-0193, $185. Our most recent tests of reel mowers found a couple of models nearly as good and half the price—the Great States Deluxe Light 815-18, $90, and Craftsman 3764, $90.

For an electric mower, expect to spend $200 or more, depending on battery capacity and features.

You can buy a gasoline-powered mower for as little as $100, but you'll probably have to spend $140 to $190 to get a decent model, according to our most recent tests. First choice among rear-baggers was the Murray Mark IV 2nOne, $175. Self-propelled models cost anywhere from $150 to $225 extra. Conveniences like an electric starter and a blade-brake/clutch safety system add about $100 each.

You can spend $4000 for a lawn tractor, but there's no need—competent machines cost less than $2000. Look for a hydrostatic transmission—it frees you from the need to use a clutch and provides continuous speed adjustment, for $200 to $400 extra. See the Ratings on page 203.

What's in the stores. Models are usually available for a couple of years; new models are introduced from winter into spring. You'll find low-priced mowers from brands like MTD, Murray, Rally, and private labels at discount stores like Kmart, Wal-Mart, and Target. Medium-priced models from Craftsman, Lawn-Boy, Lawn Chief, MTD, Yard-Man, and White are sold at home centers, hardware chains, and Sears. Independent dealers often sell the more expensive brands: Ariens, Cub Cadet, Honda, John Deere, Snapper, and Troy-Bilt.

Using the Ratings. Our most recent tests were of riding tractors. Similar models should perform much the same as the tested models, but features may vary. Models are usually available for a couple of years; new models are introduced from winter into spring. If you can't find a model, call the manufacturer; see page 342.

Key features

• *Recommended for electric mowers:*

Cord handling. The inconvenience of the power cord can be minimized with a sliding clip that lets the cord flip from side to side. The clip design is better than one that uses a handle you flip every time you reverse direction.

• *Recommended for gasoline-powered mowers:*

Blade-brake/clutch safety system. This system provides the safety of a "deadman" handle, which ensures that the blade stops turning as soon as you release it, without making you restart the engine every time. When you release the safety handle, the clutch releases the blade and a brake halts it, but the engine keeps running. More common—and less expensive—is a simple engine-kill system.

Choke at the throttle. The most convenient design is set simply by adjusting the throttle control. Most mowers use a simpler device to help start the engine—a primer, a little rubber bulb located on the engine. You press the bulb several times before you pull the cord.

Clutch that's easy to reach. The control should be within easy reach of your fingers as you mow.

Cutting-height adjustment that does all four wheels at once. Most mowers have spring-loaded adjusters on each wheel. They're easy enough to use, but easier yet is a single lever or crank handle that adjusts all four wheels at once. Such a feature adds $50 to $75 to the price.

Electric start. This is much easier than tugging on a rope. It adds $50 to $100 to the mower price.

Mowing modes that are easy to change. The most convenient design lets you change from bagging to mulching mode by removing the bag and inserting a plate or plug, and change from bagging to discharging by letting a chute fall into place. Watch out for models that make you use a wrench to change the blade.

Overhead-valve engine. This type of engine tends to be the least polluting. The two-stroke engine tends to be the dirtiest, partly because it burns a mixture of oil and gasoline.

Rear grass bag. The rear-bag design

makes it easier for a mower to maneuver and to do close trimming than a side-bag design. Make sure the bag is easy to install, remove, and empty.

Speeds. Some mowers have one speed, usually about 2½ mph; others have several; still others have a continuous range, typically from 1 to 3 mph. One speed is fine, but two speeds let you adjust to the terrain and the grass. Extra speeds are nice, but note that some six-speed mowers aren't as versatile as they seem—some of their low speeds are virtually the same.

• ***Recommended for tractors:***

Hydrostatic transmission. This $200-to-$400 feature frees you from the need to use a clutch, and it lets you continuously adjust the speed.

Snow throwers

If snowfall is typically light in your area, a smaller, less expensive single-stage model should be good enough.

Last CR report: October 1997
Ratings: page 208
Expect to pay: $300 to $1000 or more

Snow throwers use a gasoline-powered engine to propel a metal or rubber-tipped auger. That auger paddles snow through a discharge chute and helps move the machine forward. The chute can be rotated, so you can cast snow left, right, or straight ahead, and adjusted, to determine the height of the snow discharge.

What's available

Single-stage throwers. These generally come with a 3-hp to 5-hp two-stroke engine that requires an oil-and-gasoline mixture. The rubber-tipped auger touches the ground, leaving a surface cleaner than a two-stage model. It also has a deadman control similar to that on many lawn mowers, one that disengages the auger once you release the handle. This type of thrower is relatively easy to handle and compact to store. Price range: $300 to $750.

Two-stage throwers. Bigger and more powerful than single-stage models, this type typically comes with a 5-hp to 9-hp four-stroke engine that runs on gasoline alone. The metal auger picks up snow and moves it to a fast-spinning impeller that sends the snow out the chute—the two "stages" that give this type its name. Most two-stage machines are self-propelled, with at least four forward and two reverse speeds. (The range of speeds matters more than the number of speed settings.)

Two-stage machines have independent "deadman" controls: one lever governs power to the auger, another power to the wheels. Initially you must squeeze both, but then you can operate the machine one-handed, which lets you adjust the discharge chute, and in some cases, the snow deflector as you go. Adjustable skid shoes let you determine how close to the ground the machine cleans. Plan on plenty of space to store one of these bulky units. Price range: $600 to $1000 or more.

Shopping strategy

Horsepower typically translates into performance, we found, regardless of type. The models in our test with higher horsepower had a more powerful engine, and they tended to clear a wider swath. In addition, a larger engine provides the power needed to handle deep or wet snow.

For serious snow-clearing, consider a two-stage snow thrower. Typically, they're hard to handle and manuever. They're also heavy, weighing anywhere from 100 to more than 250 pounds.

For light snowfall—six to eight inches—one of the smaller, less expensive single-stage machines should do fine. These machines shouldn't be used to clean gravel walkways or driveways.

Decide what to spend. Single-stage models range from about $300 to $750; two-stage models, from around $600 to more than $2000. Spending more usually gets you a more powerful engine and the ability to clear a wider swath. The only notable feature that costs extra is an electric starter, which adds about $100 to the price.

What's in the stores. MTD, Sears Craftsman, and Toro are the most commonly purchased brands, accounting for about two-thirds of all snow throwers purchased.

Dealers that sell mowers and snow throwers also assemble the equipment and usually offer service. Mass merchandisers and home centers may charge for assembly, if they even offer that service, and usually leave it to you to find a service shop.

Using the Ratings. For our most recent test, we used single-stage machines in four to five inches of dry, powdery snow. Some did a good job of clearing it, but only two could throw it very far. Two-stage machines were used in 9 to 11 inches of dry, powdery snow, and again in a wetter accumulation. The best were quick and thorough; the worst were still better than the best single-stage machines. If you can't find a model, call the manufacturer; see page 342.

Water filters

Identifying the impurities in your water with a water test is the first step to getting the right filter.

Last CR report:
Filters, July 1997; Carafes, March 1996
Ratings: page 185 (filters)
Expect to pay: $10 to $900 or more

If you believe there's something wrong with your water—if it tastes bad or looks dirty, or it has a strong chlorine odor—ask your water system for a copy of its official water-quality report. You can also have your water tested to determine the problem. For about $20 to $150, you can obtain a water-testing kit from a mail-order laboratory (see "Testing the water" on page 177).

Water from private wells or small systems should be tested for bacteria, for nitrate and pesticides if you live in an intensive agricultural area, or for volatile organic compounds if you live near a landfill or factory. If you live in an older house in an older neighborhood, it's a good idea to test your kitchen tap for lead.

Should testing reveal contamination of your tap water, you have several options that include using bottled water; boiling the water to kill bacteria and parasites; using a distiller—a device that boils and condenses water to remove microbes, most minerals and metals, and some organic chemicals; using a carbon filter to remove contaminants, including lead;

or using special filters to eliminate iron and manganese.

What's available

Carafe filters. This type consists of a filter and a half-gallon pitcher. You pour the water through the top of the pitcher, wait 5 to 10 minutes for the water to be processed, then pour out the filtered water through the pitcher spout. Carafes do a reasonably good job at filtering out lead and chloroform. They also are the type to try first if your water passes tests but doesn't taste good. But carafes won't eliminate biological hazards, like *giardia* cysts, or fine sediment particles.

This type is costly if you use a lot of water. Filters must be changed after less than 100 gallons, so gallon for gallon, you pay more for filters than for other water-filter systems. Price range: $10 to $30. Annual cost of carafes: $20 to $200 (for one gallon of water daily).

Faucet-mounted models. These fist-sized devices screw onto the faucet spigot. A push-in or twist valve diverts water through the unit and out its own spigot, for filtered water on demand. In our tests, all faucet-mounted models improved the taste of water. The best excelled at removing organic chemicals, but did not do as well filtering lead. Installation is easy, but filters must be changed after less than 100 gallons. Price range of hardware: $20 to $50. Annual cost of filters: $20 to $75.

Countertop models. These often rely on a single cartridge that sits on your kitchen counter (and can take up as much space as a coffeemaker). Typically, you engage a diverter valve, and flexible tubes carry water from faucet to filter and back again, albeit at reduced flow. Do-it-yourselfers can easily install and maintain these filters. The best models removed more than 95 percent of the chloroform and lead in our tests; even runners-up cut more than 85 percent of the lead. Most countertop models can process hundreds of gallons of water before the filter needs to be changed. Price range: $40 to $300. Annual cost: $10 to $125.

Under-sink models. These solid performers are bigger than most other types and often use two or three cartridges in a series. Under-sink models must be connected to the cold-water line and usually come with a separate spigot, which is mounted on the sink.

These filters are slightly harder to maintain, since there are multiple cartridges to change. In our tests, they did a good job screening pollutants, but not necessarily better than countertop units. You may need a plumber for installation. Under-sink models can process hundreds of gallons of water before the filters need to be changed. Price range: $40 to $500. Annual cost: $10 to $200.

Reverse-osmosis models. These cumbersome units can take up most of the space under the sink; a separate spigot is mounted on the sink. This type combines a conventional filter with a reverse-osmosis unit so that water is forced through a special cellophanelike membrane. This removes many organic and inorganic substances, including industrial chemicals that regular filters cannot purge—lead, nitrate, and such heavy metals as arsenic, barium, and chromium—along with fluoride. An under-sink tank holds the output, which typically is about two gallons.

The initial cost is steep, and you'll have to pay a plumber or a dealer for installation. These systems also work slowly and waste several gallons of water for every gallon they purify. Reverse-osmosis models can process hundreds of gallons of water before the filters need to be changed.

Testing the water

The only certain way to find out if you need a water filter for health reasons is to have your water tested by a reliable laboratory. We evaluated four mail-order labs to see how quickly and how well they sized up lead and chloroform problems we deliberately concocted. All did a good job of analysis; the primary variations were in how the services operated.

Here's what we found.

- Services vary. Some labs test for only a few pollutants, others for many. Some offer tests piecemeal, while others offer packages tailored to a specific environment (rural, city) or specific concerns.
- Some lead-test kits include two, not one, sample vials. We suggest you use those kits, since it's best to measure lead twice, first when the tap is turned on in the morning and then after water has flowed for a few minutes. (If a kit provides only one vial for lead testing, buy two kits.)
- Some labs want their money up front, when you order the kit; some want to be paid when you send your water in for analysis.

There are hundreds of labs. To find one certified by your state, call your state health department or environmental protection agency. The U.S. EPA Safe Drinking Water Hotline, 800 426-4791, offers information on testing.

Here are details on the four services we evaluated. The labs are listed alphabetically.

- Clean Water Lead Testing, Asheville, N.C. (704 251-6800). $17 for two-sample lead test; does not offer chloroform test. Payment (check only) must accompany order for kit. Least expensive and quickest lab for lead testing. Affiliated with University of North Carolina.
- Daily Analytical Laboratories, Peoria, Ill. (800 752-6651). $20 for single lead test; $100 for chloroform-only kit. Payment (check or money order only) must accompany samples.
- Spectrum Laboratories, St. Paul, Minn. (800 447-5221). $18 for single lead test; $75 for chloroform-only kit. Payment (check or credit card) must accompany samples.
- Suburban Water Testing Laboratories, Temple, Pa. (800 433-6595). $35 for two-sample lead test; $145 for "The Basics" kit, the lab's cheapest package that tests for both chloroform and lead (it also tests pH, and for coliform bacteria, fluoride, nitrate, and other substances). Payment (check, money order, or credit card) must accompany order for kit. Filling lead-sample vials was a little harder than for other labs. Lab sent an "early warning" before final results, to tell us our lead levels were high.

Price range: $450 to $900. Annual cost: $100 to $175.

Shopping strategy

Official reports and lab tests can tell you if you need a water filter for health reasons. If your water passes tests but doesn't taste, smell, or look right, choose a filter meeting NSF International's Standard 42 for "aesthetic" problems. If testing has detected organic compounds or lead in the water, choose a filter meeting Standard 53 for that *specific* contaminant. If you need a filter capable of blocking parasites, look for one with a certification label that reads "absolute one micron".

Estimate your water needs by using gallon jugs for a few days. Then consider each type of filter's capacity and processing time.

Decide what to spend. What you spend depends primarily on the type of filter you choose. Carafes are the cheapest, reverse-osmosis filters the most expensive. Don't overlook annual operating costs, which vary by type and model.

What's in the stores. Filter systems are sold in water-treatment stores, hardware stores and home centers, department stores, and mass merchandisers.

Using the Ratings. We tested filters equipped with basic cartridges that remove off-tastes, lead, and organic chemicals. We spiked filtered water with roughly 80 parts per billion (ppb) of lead and 150 ppb of chloroform, demanding but not unrealistic levels. We sent about a gallon through each filter once every 90 minutes and determined its lifetime. The best models cut lead and organic contaminants by more than 95 percent, the worst by only 40 percent. All reduced chlorine and improved taste somewhat. If you can't find a model, call the manufacturer; see page 342.

How to use the Ratings in the Buying Guide

- **Read the Recommendations for information on specific models and general buying advice.**
- **Note how the rated products are listed—in order of performance and convenience, price, or alphabetically.**
- **The overall score graph gives the big picture in performance. Notes on features and performance for individual models are listed in the Comments column or "Model details."**
- **Use the handy key numbers to find out details on the models.**
- **Before going to press, we verify model availability for most products with manufacturers. Some tested models listed in the Ratings may no longer be available. Discontinued models are noted in Model details or Comments. Such models may actually still be available in some stores for part of 1998. Models indicated as successors should perform similarly to the tested models, according to the manufacturer. Features may vary.**
- **Models similar to the tested models, when they exist, are indicated in Comments or Model details.**
- **To find our last full report on a subject, check the reference above the Ratings chart or the eight-year index, page 346.**

Ratings *Ceiling fans*

& Recommendations

The tests behind the Ratings

Overall score is based mainly on air-moving ability and freedom from wobble. **Range** is the difference in airflow between fastest and slowest fan speeds. **Maximum** flow is at the highest speed. **Efficiency** is a measure of airflow versus power consumed at the highest speed. Freedom from **wobble** indicates steadiness at highest speed. Scores aren't comparable between size groups. **Price** is the estimated average, based on a national survey. Models similar to those we tested are noted in the Model details; features may vary. An * indicates that light kit is included.

Typical features for these models

• Three speeds. • Pull-chain speed control. • Four or five blades. • Switch to reverse direction of rotation. • Downrod or flush mount.

Recommendations

Among the large fans, the Hunter Sojourn 25874 ($190) and Casablance Panama 12222T ($370) top the Ratings. The Hampton Bay St. Claire 413-769 ($100) performed nearly as well in our tests. We judged it a CR Best Buy. Among the smaller fans, the Harbor Breeze Vandelle EF5171PB and the Hunter Coastal Breeze 23506 (each $60) led the Ratings by slight margins. The Hampton Bay Bridgeton 357-633, which scored nearly as high, sells for about $45. And its Home Depot brandmate, the Hampton Bay The Littleton 270-614, a flush-mounted model, sells for just $30. We judged each of those Hampton Bay models a CR Best Buy.

See Buying Guide report, page 162. Last time rated in CONSUMER REPORTS: July 1997.

Overall Ratings

E VG G F P

Within size groups, listed in order of overall score

Key no.	Brand and model	Price	Overall score (0–100; P F G VG E)	Air-moving ability: RANGE	Air-moving ability: MAXIMUM	Air-moving ability: EFFICIENCY	Wobble
	LARGE FANS *Recommended for rooms between 225 and 400 square feet*						
1	**Hunter** Sojourn 25874	$190		VG	E	VG	E
2	**Casablanca** Panama 12222T	370		E	E	F	VG
3	**Hampton Bay** St. Claire 413-769 **A CR Best Buy**	100*		G	E	E	E
4	**J.C. Penney** 832-1218	119*		G	E	VG	E

Ratings continued

Ratings, continued

Key no.	Brand and model	Price	Overall score (0–100: P F G VG E)	Air-moving ability: RANGE	Air-moving ability: MAXIMUM	Air-moving ability: EFFICIENCY	Wobble
	LARGE FANS *Recommended for rooms between 225 and 400 square feet (continued)*						
5	**Patton** 978A-WBR [1]	$140		G	VG	VG	E
6	**Hampton Bay** The Redington II Pinnacle 175-718	125*		G	E	VG	VG
7	**Hunter** Infiniti 25286	125		G	VG	VG	E
8	**Harbor Breeze** Colonial EF5006PB Item 37774	100*		G	VG	E	E
9	**Kenmore** (Sears) 99024	100*		G	VG	VG	E
10	**Patton** 994BR [2]	200		VG	E	F	VG
11	**Kenmore** (Sears) 99013	50		G	VG	VG	VG
12	**Hunter** The Original 23856	200		VG	E	F	G
13	**Casablanca** Clairemont 5192D	220		G	E	E	G
14	**Kenmore** (Sears) 99022	80*		F	VG	VG	E
15	**Hunter** Studio Series Remote 25736	200		F	VG	VG	E
16	**Encon** Empress 5EM-52PBE	90*		F	G	VG	E
17	**Windmere** UL52W	60*		G	VG	G	G
18	**Lasko** Preferred Design & Light 6505L	90*		G	VG	VG	F
19	**Emerson** Northwind Designer CF755AB	140		F	F	P	E
	SMALL FANS *Recommended for rooms up to 225 square feet*						
20	**Harbor Breeze** Vandelle EF5171PB Item 37813	60*		G	E	E	E
21	**Hunter** Coastal Breeze 23506	60		G	E	E	E
22	**Hampton Bay** Bridgeton 357-633 **A CR Best Buy**	45*		G	E	E	E
23	**Hunter** Low Profile II 23800	85		G	VG	VG	E
24	**Hampton Bay** The Littleton 270-614 **A CR Best Buy**	30*		G	E	VG	E
25	**Lasko** Decor 4205L America with Light	75*		G	E	G	E
26	**Casablanca** Four Seasons 75U11D	95		G	E	E	VG
27	**Encon** Traditional 5TD-42WHC	60*		G	E	VG	E
28	**Hunter** Summer Breeze 23684	100		G	VG	VG	E
29	**Hampton Bay** The Landmark 460-249	35		F	E	E	E
30	**Emerson** Northwind Snugger CF704SPB	110		G	VG	G	E
31	**J.C. Penney** 852-1841	100*		G	E	E	G
32	**Patton** 979A-42BR [3]	95		P	VG	G	E
33	**Windmere** MD42AW5C3TL	50*		F	G	P	P

[1] *Previously named Fasco Gulf Stream 978A-WBR.* [2] *Previously named Fasco Gilespie 994BR.*
[3] *Previously named Fasco The Snugger 979A-42BR.*

Model details

Large fans (about 52 inches)

1 Hunter Sojourn 25874 $190

• Weight: 20 lb. • 40 to 160 rpm • 5 reversible blades

A very efficient fan with excellent air-moving ability and a wide range in airflow. Comes with a blade-balance kit. But: Judged harder to assemble and install than most. Options: light kit, handheld remote, wall-mount control, different-length downrod, slanted-ceiling adapter. Warranty: 1-yr. full on fan, 25-yr. limited on motor. Similar: 25870; 25875; 25876; 25879. Kenmore (Sears) 99412. Lowe's Item 84996. **Recommendation:** A very good overall performer—our top choice among the large fans.

2 Casablanca Panama 12222T $370

• 50-inch diameter • Weight: 21 lb. • 25 to 180 rpm • Choice of 4 or 5 blades • Downrod-mount only

Excellent air-moving ability and a wide range of airflow, with 6 fan speeds. Wall-mounted control can be programmed to turn lights on and off and change fan speeds at preset times. Attaches with a convenient hanger bracket. Blades are packaged and sold separately. Options: light kit, flush-mount kit, different-length downrod, slanted-ceiling adapter. Warranty: 90-day in-home service, 1-yr. on fan, lifetime on motor. **Model availability:** Discontinued. **Recommendation:** Very good overall, but expensive and not as energy-efficient as most others.

3 Hampton Bay St. Claire 413-769 $100

• Weight: 22 lb. • 55 to 170 rpm • 5 reversible blades • 4-globe light assembly • Available only at Home Depot stores

A highly efficient fan with excellent air-moving ability. Attaches with a convenient hanger bracket. Comes with a blade-balance kit and different-length downrods. But: Fan and light-switch pull chains are hard to tell apart. Option: wall-mount control. Warranty: 1-yr. limited on fan, 30-yr. limited on motor. Similar: 270-449; 390-114. **Recommendation:** A very good choice. **A CR Best Buy.**

4 J.C. Penney 832-1218 $119

• Weight: 24 lb. • 90 to 205 rpm • Choice of 4 or 5 reversible blades • Swiveling 4-globe light assembly • Available only through store catalog

A very efficient fan with excellent air-moving ability. Attaches with a convenient hanger bracket. Comes with a blade-balance kit and different-length downrods. Options: handheld remote, slanted-ceiling adapter. Warranty: 1-yr. full on fan, lifetime replacement on motor. **Model availability:** Discontinued. **Recommendation:** A very good choice, although faster and a little noisier than most at high speed.

5 Patton 978A-WBR $140

• Weight: 14 lb. • 55 to 160 rpm • 5 reversible blades • Downrod-mount only • Previously named Fasco Gulf Stream 978A-WBR

A very efficient fan. Attaches with a convenient hanger bracket. Options: light kit, flush-mount kit, different-length downrod, slanted-ceiling adapter. Warranty: 1-yr. full on fan, 10-yr. limited on motor. **Model availability:** Discontinued. **Recommendation:** Very good overall.

6 Hampton Bay The Redington II Pinnacle 175-718 $125

• Weight: 23 lb. • 50 to 140 rpm • 5 reversible blades • 4-globe light assembly • Available only at Home Depot stores

A very efficient fan with excellent air-moving ability. Attaches with a convenient hanger bracket. Comes with a blade-balance kit, different-length downrods, and handheld remote speed and light control. But: Blades harder to balance than most. Warranty: 1-yr. limited on fan, lifetime limited on motor. Similar: 175-620; 175-652; 175-702. **Recommendation:** A very good choice.

7 Hunter Infiniti 25286 $125

• Weight: 16 lb. • 55 to 155 rpm • 5 blades

A very efficient fan. Comes with a blade-balance kit. Options: light kit, handheld remote, wall-mount control, different-length downrod, slanted-ceiling adapter. Warranty: 1-yr. full on fan, 20-yr. parts on motor. Similar: 25280; 25284; 25285; 25289. Kenmore (Sears) models 99406; 99407.

Can't find a model? Call the manufacturer. See page 342.

Ratings continued

Ratings, continued

Lowe's Items 31768; 31769. **Recommendation:** A very good choice.

8 Harbor Breeze Colonial EF5006PB Item 37774 $100

• Weight: 20 lb. • 65 to 155 rpm • 5 reversible blades • 4-globe light assembly • Available only at Lowe's stores

A highly efficient fan. Attaches with a convenient hanger bracket. Options: wall-mount control, handheld remote, different-length downrod, slanted-ceiling adapter. Warranty: 15-yr. limited on fan and motor. **Recommendation:** A very good choice.

9 Kenmore (Sears) 99024 $100

• Weight: 24 lb. • 55 to 150 rpm • 6 reversible blades • 5-globe light assembly

A very efficient fan. Comes with a blade-balance kit. But: Blades were harder to balance than most. Options: different-length downrod, slanted-ceiling adapter. Warranty: 20-yr. replacement on fan and motor. **Recommendation:** A very good performer overall.

10 Patton 994BR $200

• Weight: 18 lb. • 40 to 185 rpm • Choice of 4 or 5 reversible blades • Downrod-mount only • Previously named Fasco Gilespie 994BR

Excellent air-moving ability and a wide range in airflow. Attaches with a convenient hanger bracket. Options: light kit, flush-mount kit, different-length downrod, slanted-ceiling adapter. Warranty: 1-yr. full on fan, plus limited lifetime on fan and motor. **Model availability:** Discontinued. **Recommendation:** A very good performer, though less efficient and a little noisier than most at high speed.

11 Kenmore (Sears) 99013 $50

• Weight: 16 lb. • 70 to 210 rpm • Choice of 4 or 5 reversible blades

A very efficient fan with very good air-moving ability. Comes with a blade-balance kit. Options: light kit, different-length downrod, slanted-ceiling adapter. Warranty: 20-yr. replacement on fan and motor. Similar: 99014; 99015. **Recommendation:** A very good and relatively inexpensive choice, though faster and a little noisier than most at high speed.

12 Hunter The Original 23856 $200

• Weight: 39 lb. • 45 to 200 rpm • Choice of 4 or 5 blades • Downrod-mount only

Excellent air-moving ability and a wide range in airflow. Attaches with a convenient hanger bracket. Comes with a blade-balance kit. But: Its weight makes it harder than most to assemble and install. Blades were harder to balance than most. The motor requires lubrication. Options: light kit, handheld remote, wall-mount control, different-length downrod, slanted-ceiling adapter. Warranty: 1-year full on fan, lifetime parts on motor. Similar: 23850; 23852; 23854; 23855; 23859. **Recommendation:** A very good performer, but less efficient and noisier than most at high speed, and less convenient.

13 Casablanca Clairemont 5192D $220

• Weight: 24 lb. • 85 to 180 rpm • 5 blades • Downrod-mount only

A highly efficient fan with excellent air-moving ability. Attaches with a convenient hanger bracket. Blades are packaged and sold separately. Comes with a blade-balance kit. But: Blades were harder to balance than most. Options: light kit, wall-mount control, different-length downrod, slanted-ceiling adapter. Warranty: 1-yr. on fan, lifetime on motor. **Model availability:** Discontinued. **Recommendation:** A very good performer, although a little noisier than most at high speed.

14 Kenmore (Sears) 99022 $80

• Weight: 19 lb. • 80 to 175 rpm • 5 reversible blades • 4-globe light assembly

A very efficient fan. Warranty: 20-yr. replacement on fan and motor. **Recommendation:** Very good overall, but with a limited range in airflow.

15 Hunter Studio Series Remote 25736 $200

• Weight: 17 lb. • 75 to 170 rpm • 5 reversible blades

A very efficient fan. Comes with a blade-balance kit and handheld remote speed (and light) control. Options: light kit, wall-mount control, different-length downrod, slanted-ceiling adapter. Warranty: 1-yr. full on fan, 20-yr. parts on motor. Similar: 25730; 25734; 25739. Kenmore (Sears) 99416. Lowe's Items 37157; 37158, 37159. **Recommendation:** Very good, but with a limited range in airflow.

16 Encon Empress 5EM-52PBE $90

• Weight: 19 lb. • 70 to 150 rpm • Choice of 4 or 5 reversible blades • 5-globe light assembly
A very efficient fan. But: Judged harder to assemble and install than most. Options: different-length downrod, slanted-ceiling adapter. Warranty: 1-yr. full on fan, 10-yr. on motor. **Recommendation:** Good overall, but with a limited range in airflow.

17 Windmere UL52W $60

• Weight: 17 lb. • 55 to 160 rpm • Choice of 4 or 5 blades • Swiveling 4-globe light assembly
Comes with a blade-balance kit. Warranty: 1-yr. full on fan, 5-yr. on motor. **Recommendation:** A good performer.

18 Lasko Preferred Design & Light 6505L $90

• Weight: 20 lb. • 60 to 165 rpm • 5 reversible blades • 3-globe light assembly.
A very efficient fan. But: Blades were harder to balance than most, and the reverse switch, above the housing, is inconvenient. Warranty: 1-yr. limited on fan, 25-yr. limited on motor. Similar: 6502L; 6507L. **Recommendation:** A good performer, but wobbled more than most.

19 Emerson Northwind Designer CF755AB $140

• Weight: 18 lb. • 55 to 180 rpm • 5 reversible blades • Downrod-mount only
Mediocre air-moving ability for a large fan. Attaches with a convenient hanger bracket. Comes with a blade-balance kit. Warranty: 1-yr. full on fan, 20-yr. limited on motor. Similar: CF755BK; CF755DB; CF755G; CF755GS; CF755H; CF755NW; CF755OB; CF755PB; CF755PT; CF755TG; CF755TWW; CF755V; CF755W; CF755WPB; CF755WW. **Recommendation:** A good performer, but there are better choices.

Small fans (about 42 inches)

20 Harbor Breeze Vandelle EF5171PB Item 37813 $60

• Weight: 14 lb. • 65 to 200 rpm • 6 reversible blades • 3-globe light assembly • Available only at Lowe's stores
A highly efficient fan with excellent air-moving ability. Attaches with a convenient hanger bracket. Comes with a blade-balance kit. Options: handheld remote, wall-mount control, different-length downrod, slanted-ceiling adapter. Warranty: 10-yr. limited on fan and motor. **Recommendation:** A very good performer, and our top-rated small fan.

21 Hunter Coastal Breeze 23506 $60

• 44-inch diameter • Weight: 11 lb. • 75 to 230 rpm • 4 blades
A highly efficient fan with excellent air-moving ability. Comes with a blade-balance kit. Options: light kit, handheld remote, wall-mount control, different-length downrod, slanted-ceiling adapter. Warranty: 1-yr. full on fan, 20-yr. parts on motor. Similar: 23500, 23504, 23509, 23677. **Recommendation:** A very good performer.

22 Hampton Bay Bridgeton 357-633 $45

• Weight: 14 lb. • 110 to 210 rpm • Choice of 4 or 5 reversible blades • 3-globe light assembly • Available only at Home Depot stores
A highly efficient fan with excellent air-moving ability. Comes with a blade-balance kit and an extra downrod. Option: wall-mount control. Warranty: 1-yr. limited on fan, 30-yr. limited on motor. **Recommendation:** A very good performer at an exceptional price. **A CR Best Buy.**

23 Hunter Low Profile II 23800 $85

• Weight: 10 lb. • 85 to 225 rpm • 4 reversible blades • Flush-mount only
A very efficient fan. Attaches with a convenient hanger bracket. Comes with a blade-balance kit. Option: light kit. Warranty: 1-yr. full on fan, 20-yr. limited on motor. Similar: 23804; 23806. **Recommendation:** A very good choice for low ceilings.

24 Hampton Bay The Littleton 270-614 $30

• Weight: 11 lb. • 100 to 230 rpm • 4 reversible blades • 1-globe light assembly • Flush-mount only • Available only at Home Depot stores
A very efficient fan with excellent air-moving ability. Comes with a blade-balance kit. Option: wall-mount control. Warranty: 1-yr. limited on fan, 15-yr. limited on motor. **Recommendation:** A very good, very inexpensive choice for low ceilings. **A CR Best Buy.**

Ratings continued ▶

Ratings, continued

25 Lasko Decor 4205L America with Light $75

• Weight: 15 lb. • 85 to 230 rpm • 4 reversible blades • 3-globe light assembly

An excellent air-mover. Attaches with a convenient hanger bracket. But: Reverse switch, above the housing, is inconvenient. Warranty: 1-yr. limited on fan, 10-yr. limited on motor. Similar: 4202L; 4207L. **Recommendation:** A very good performer overall.

26 Casablanca Four Seasons 75U11D $95

• Weight: 11 lb. • 105 to 220 rpm • 5 reversible blades • Downrod-mount only

A highly efficient fan with excellent air-moving ability. Attaches with a convenient hanger bracket. Comes with extra downrod and a blade-balance kit. Options: light kit, handheld remote, wall-mount control, flush-mount kit, different-length downrod, slanted-ceiling adapter. Warranty: 1-yr. parts on fan, 25-yr. parts on motor. **Model availability:** Discontinued. **Recommendation:** A very good performer.

27 Encon Traditional 5TD-42WHC $60

• Weight: 15 lb. • 80 to 195 rpm • Choice of 4 or 5 reversible blades • 3-globe light assembly.

A very efficient fan with excellent air-moving ability. Options: handheld remote, wall-mount control, extra downrod, slanted-ceiling adapter. Warranty: 1-yr. full on fan, 10-yr. full on motor. **Recommendation:** A very good performer.

28 Hunter Summer Breeze 23684 $100

• Weight: 12 lb. • 75 to 225 rpm • 5 reversible blades

A very efficient fan. Comes with a blade-balance kit. Options: light kit, handheld remote, wall-mount control, different-length downrod, slanted-ceiling adapter. Warranty: 1-yr. full on fan, 20-yr. limited on motor. Similar: 23680; 23686. **Recommendation:** Very good overall.

29 Hampton Bay The Landmark 460-249 $35

• Weight: 10 lb. • 120 to 180 rpm • 4 reversible blades • Available only at Home Depot stores

A highly efficient fan with excellent air-moving ability. Comes with a blade-balance kit and extra downrod. Options: light kit, wall-mount control. Warranty: 1-yr. limited on fan, 15-yr. limited on motor. Similar: 460-281; 460-303. **Recommendation:** Very good, but limited airflow range, and faster than most at low speed.

30 Emerson Northwind Snugger CF704SPB $110

• Weight: 11 lb. • 80 to 205 rpm • 5 reversible blades • Flush-mount only

Comes with a blade-balance kit. Options: light kit, wall-mount control. Warranty: 1-yr. full on fan, 15-yr. limited on motor. Similar: CF704SAB, CF704SW, CF704SWW. **Recommendation:** Very good, suitable for low ceilings.

31 J.C. Penney 852-1841 $100

• Weight: 14 lb. • 115 to 260 rpm • 5 reversible blades • 3-globe light assembly • Available only through store catalog

A highly efficient fan with excellent air-moving ability. But: Blades were harder to balance than most. Option: slanted-ceiling adapter. Warranty: 1-yr. replacement on fan and motor. **Model availability:** Discontinued. **Recommendation:** A good performer, but faster than most at low speed.

32 Patton 979A-42BR $95

• Weight: 11 lb. • 130 to 205 rpm • Choice of 4 or 5 reversible blades • Flush-mount only • Previously named Fasco The Snugger 979A-42BR

A very good air-mover. Attaches with a convenient hanger bracket. Option: light kit. Warranty: 1-yr. full on fan, 10-yr. limited on motor. **Model availability:** Discontinued. **Recommendation:** A good fan for low ceilings, but limited range in airflow, and faster than most at low speed.

33 Windmere MD42AW5C3TL $50

• Weight: 12 lb. • 110 to 210 rpm • 5 reversible blades • 3-globe light assembly

Warranty: 1-yr. on fan, 5-yr. on motor. **Recommendation:** A generally poor performer that wobbled more than most.

Ratings *Water filters*

& Recommendations

The tests behind the Ratings

Overall score is based mainly on ability to remove the two contaminants and improve taste; filters lost points for clogging before they were spent and for difficult installation. **Annual cost** is our estimate to run a filter for a year, based on using one gallon of water daily. We recommend changing cartridges at least once a year, even if they are not exhausted. **Organics** summarizes results from chloroform tests. For **lead,** the best filters when relatively new removed more than 95 percent; the worst, less than 65 percent. **Taste** shows reduction of sulfur taste in dilute cabbage water. **Parasites** identifies filters certified as "absolute one micron." **Flow rate** is based on processing of a half-gallon. High: less than 30 seconds. Average: 30-60 seconds. Low: more than 60 seconds. **Price** is approximate retail and includes initial set of cartridges.

Recommendations

If your water passes tests but it doesn't taste good, first try using a carafe filter: The Ecowater 25001 ($22) did a very good job improving taste and was very convenient. If testing detects specific pollutants in your water, get a water-filter system that's effective at removing those pollutants. The top faucet model—the Culligan WaterWare FM-2 ($55)—was easy to install and better than average at removing lead. The best countertop model—the Amway E-84 ($310)—has a useful cartridge-replacement indicator. The number-two countertop model—the Shaklee BestWater MTS2000 ($230)—performed nearly as well and costs less. Under-sink filters worth considering: the Rainsoft Hydrefiner 9878 P-12 ($500) and, at less than one-third the price, the Ametek Kleen-Plus SY5197 ($155), a CR Best Buy. If you need the heavy-duty filtering ability of a reverse-osmosis unit, consider the Kinetico 518 ($900).

See Buying Guide report, page 175. Last time rated in CONSUMER REPORTS: July 1997.

Overall Ratings

E VG G F P

Within types, listed in order of overall score

Key no.	Brand and model	Price	Overall score (0–100; P F G VG E)	Annual cost	Organics	Lead	Taste	Parasites	Flow rate
	CARAFE MODELS								
1	**Ecowater** 25001	$22		$44	VG	G	VG	—	low
2	**Glacier Pure** GPB1	10		18	E	VG	E	—	low
3	**Brita** Standard 35507	20		64	G	F	G	—	low

Ratings continued ▶

Ratings, continued

Key no.	Brand and model	Price	Overall score (0–100: P F G VG E)	Annual cost	Organics	Lead	Taste	Parasites	Flow rate
	CARAFE MODELS *continued*								
4	**Shaklee** BestWater 51100	$26		$146	○	◒	○	—	low
5	**Teledyne** Water Pik WF-1	6		183	◒	⊖	⊜	—	low
	FAUCET-MOUNTED MODELS								
6	**Culligan** WaterWare FM-2	55		55	⊜	⊖	⊖	✔	low
7	**PUR** FM-1000C	40		61	⊜	○	⊖	✔	low
8	**NordicWare** 78100	30		78	○	◒	⊜	✔	low
9	**Ametek** FF-100	16		20	○	◒	◒	—	high
10	**Sears** WaterWorks Deluxe 625.345300	45		66	●	○	⊖	—	low
11	**Teledyne** Instapure F-2C	20		37	○	●	○	—	avg.
12	**Pollenex** WP300	20		63	●	●	○	—	low
	COUNTERTOP MODELS								
13	**Amway** E-84	310		85	⊜	⊜	⊖	✔	avg.
14	**Shaklee** BestWater MTS2000	230		95	⊜	⊖	⊜	✔	avg.
15	**PUR** CT-6000	70		22	⊜	⊖	○	✔	avg.
16	**Kinetico** 6500	250		87	⊜	⊖	⊜	—	avg.
17	**Home Water** CB50C	66		27	⊜	⊖	○	✔	avg.
18	**Ametek** Kleen-Plus CTR-210	42		10	⊜	○	○	—	avg.
19	**Omni** Total OT1	64		61	○	○	○	—	low
20	**Singer** WF-26	74		122	◒	○	⊜	—	avg.
	UNDER-SINK MODELS								
21	**Rainsoft** Hydrefiner 9878 P-12	500		55	⊜	⊜	⊜	✔	high
22	**Ametek** Kleen-Plus SY5197, **A CR Best Buy**	155		45	⊜	⊖	⊜	✔	low
23	**Omni** Total Plus OT-5	145		99	⊜	⊜	⊜	✔	low
24	**Everpure** H-200	285		95	⊖	⊖	⊖	✔	high
25	**Culligan** System 201	210		32	⊖	⊖	⊖	—	avg.
26	**Teledyne** Instapure IF-10A	45		11	⊜	◒	⊖	—	high
27	**Omni** Total II OT-2	105		62	○	○	⊖	—	avg.
28	**Teledyne** Instapure IF-100A	130		186	●	⊖	⊜	—	avg.

Key no.	Brand and model	Price	Overall score (0–100; P F G VG E)	Annual cost	Organics	Lead	Taste	Parasites	Flow rate
	REVERSE-OSMOSIS MODELS								
29	**Kinetico** 518	$900		$82	⊜	⊜	⊜	✔	high
30	**Sears** 625.347050	450		135	⊜	⊖	⊜	—	avg.
31	**Rainsoft** 9591	900		108	⊜	⊖	⊜	—	high
32	**Ecowater** ERO292E	700		118	⊖	⊜	⊖	—	high

Model details

Notes on the details: Total price, number, model number of replacement cartridge(s) used. Capacity is the volume processed before chloroform removal dipped below 60 percent or before the flow slowed to a trickle.

Carafe models

1 Ecowater 25001 $22

• Cartridge price: $12. • No. needed: 1. • Replacement cartridge: 50006. • Capacity: 100 gal. **Comment:** Very convenient.

2 Glacier Pure GPB1 $10

• Cartridge price: $5. • No. needed: 1. • Replacement cartridge: 62247. • Capacity: 100 gal. **Comments:** Least convenient carafe. Very slow.

3 Brita Standard 35507 $20

• Cartridge price: $7. • No. needed: 1. • Replacement cartridge: OB03. • Capacity: 40 gal. **Comment:** Very convenient.

4 Shaklee BestWater 51100 $26

• Cartridge price: $12. • No. needed: 1. • Replacement cartridge: 51101. Capacity: 30 gal. **Comment:** Very convenient.

5 Teledyne Water Pik WF-1 $6

• Cartridge price: $.50. • No. needed: 2. • Replacement cartridge: WR-1. • Capacity: 1 gal. **Comment:** Less convenient carafe; funnel with replacable filter discs; revamped model now more convenient.

Faucet-mounted models

6 Culligan WaterWare FM-2 $55

• Cartridge price: $12. • No. needed: 1. • Replacement cartridge: FM2RR. • Capacity: 80 gal.

7 PUR FM-1000C $40

• Cartridge price: $15. • No. needed: 1. • Replacement cartridge: RF2050. • Capacity: 90 gal. **Model availability:** Discontinued. **Comment:** Hard to change filtér.

8 NordicWare 78100 $30

• Cartridge price: $15. • No. needed: 1. • Replacement cartridge: 78110. • Capacity: 70 gal.

9 Ametek FF-100 $16

• Cartridge price: $5. • No. needed: 1. • Replacement cartridge: FC1. • Capacity: 90 gal. **Comment:** Does not claim to remove lead.

10 Sears Waterworks Deluxe 625.345300 $45

• Cartridge price: $9. • No. needed: 1. • Replacement cartridge: 4234532. • Capacity: 50 gal.

11 Teledyne Instapure F-2C $20

• Cartridge price: $6. • No. needed: 1. • Replacement cartridge: R2C. • Capacity: 60 gal. **Comment:** Does not claim to remove lead.

12 Pollenex WP300 $20

• Cartridge price: $12. • No. needed: 1. • Replacement cartridge: FWP300. • Capacity: 70 gal.

Countertop models

13 Amway E-84 $310

• Cartridge price: $85. • No. needed: 1. • Replacement cartridge: E85. • Capacity: 800 gal. **Comment:** Useful filter-change indicator.

Ratings continued ▶

Ratings, continued

14 Shaklee BestWater MTS2000 $230
• Cartridge price: $95. • No. needed: 1. • Replacement cartridge: 52301. • Capacity: 800 gal.

15 PUR CT-6000 $70
• Cartridge price: $15. • No. needed: 1. • Replacement cartridge: CTR5050. • Capacity: 250 gal.

16 Kinetico 6500 $250
• Cartridge price: $50. • No. needed: 1. • Replacement cartridge: 7268. • Capacity: 210 gal.

17 Home Water CB50C $66
• Cartridge price: $27. • No. needed: 1. • Replacement cartridge: CB50HMR. • Capacity: 500 gal. **Comment:** Hard to change filter.

18 Ametek Kleen-Plus CTR-210 $42
• Cartridge price: $10. • No. needed: 1. • Replacement cartridge: CC-10. • Capacity: 450 gal.

19 Omni Total OT1 $64
• Cartridge price: $37. • No. needed: 2.• Replacement cartridge: TC1, TC2. • Capacity: 220 gal. Discontinued. **Comment:** Hard to change filers.

20 Singer WF-26 $74
• Cartridge price: $30. • No. needed: 1. • Replacement cartridge: RWF6. • Capacity: 90 gal. **Comment:** Clogged very prematurely. Hard to change filter.

Under-sink models

21 Rainsoft Hydrefiner 9878 P-12 $500
• Cartridge price: $55. • No. needed: 1. • Replacement cartridge: 9875. • Capacity: 500 gal.

22 Ametek Kleen-Plus SY5197 $155
• Cartridge price: $45. • No. needed: 2. • Replacement cartridge: CC-10, CMR10R. • Capacity: 800 gal. **Comment:** Useful filter-change indicator. **A CR Best Buy.**

23 Omni Total Plus OT-5 $145
• Cartridge price: $54. • No. needed: 3. • Replacement cartridge: GAC1, TC3, BC1. • Capacity: 200 gal. Discontinued. **Comment:** Hard to change filters.

24 Everpure H-200 $285
Cartridge price: $95. • No. needed: 1. • Replacement cartridge: H-200. • Capacity: 500 gal. **Comment:** Hard to change filter.

25 Culligan System 201 $210
• Cartridge price: $32. • No. needed: 1. • Replacement cartridge: 01005582. • Capacity: 440 gal.

26 Teledyne Instapure IF-10A $45
• Cartridge price: $11. • No. needed: 1. • Replacement cartridge: IR10A. • Capacity: 500 gal. **Comment:** Does not claim to remove lead. Hard to change filter.

27 Omni Total II OT-2 $105
• Cartridge price: $34. • No. needed: 2. • Replacement cartridge: GAC1, TC3. • Capacity: 200 gal. Discontinued. **Comment:** Hard to change filters.

28 Teledyne Instapure IF-100A $130
• Cartridge price: $51. • No. needed: 2. • Replacement cartridge: IR10A, R70. • Capacity: 100 gal. **Comment:** Clogged very prematurely. Hard to change filters.

Reverse-osmosis models

29 Kinetico 518 $900
• Cartridge price: $165. • No. needed: 3. • Replacement cartridge: 7273, 7034, 5305. • Capacity: 400 gal. **Comment:** Hard to change filters.

30 Sears 625.347050 $450
• Cartridge price: $135. • No. needed: 2. • Replacement cartridge: 42-34709, 42-34706. • Capacity: 400 gal. **Comment:** Useful filter-change indicator. Hard to change filters.

31 Rainsoft 9591 $900
• Cartridge price: $145. • No. needed: 4. • Replacement cartridge: 9565, 9547, 9757, 9798. • Capacity: 400 gal. **Comment:** Hard to change filters.

32 Ecowater ERO292E $700
• Cartridge price: $118. • No. needed: 4. • Replacement cartridge: CF1512TBD, 7111381, 7150809, 7111399. • Capacity: 400 gal. **Comment:** Useful filter-change indicator. Hard to change filters.

Ratings *Room air-conditioners*

& Recommendations

The tests behind the Ratings

Overall score is based mostly on comfort, performance, and noise. **Comfort** scores reflect both cooling and dehumidification in our environmental chambers, with the units running on low speed in the regular and the "energy saver" mode, when available. **Flow control** shows how well each unit directs cool air to the left and to the right (as you face the unit). **Brownout** shows how well the unit performs on a sweltering day with reduced voltage. **Noise** is measured indoors on low speed. **Price** is the estimated average, based on a national survey. Models similar to those we tested are noted in the Model details; features may vary.

Typical features for these models

• Rating for 115-volt operation, on a three-wire, 15-amp circuit protected by a time-delay fuse or circuit breaker. • Power cord at least 60 inches long. • Design for installation in a double-hung window. • Removable air filter. • R-22 HCFC refrigerant, which has relatively low ozone-depleting potential. • Three cooling speeds. • Sash lock to keep window from being opened when air-conditioner is in place. • Adjustable horizontal and vertical louvers. • Vent for exhausting some room air. • Plastic expandable side panels. • One-year parts-and-labor warranty on entire unit, five-year parts-and-labor warranty on sealed refrigeration system.

Recommendations

All the tested models were good to excellent performers overall. Match cooling capacity (measured in Btu's per hour) to your space using the sizing graph on page 165. Then consider performance, price, convenience, and features. In the 5000-to-5800-Btu/hr. size, the Amana 5QZ21RC ($385), Gibson GAC056Y7A ($360), and Panasonic CW-606TU ($360) stood out as the top performers. The Kenmore (Sears) 75055 ($290) offers good value. In the 6000-to-6600-Btu/hr. group, the Amana 7QZ21RC ($425) clearly outperformed all others. The Whirlpool ACQ062XF ($310) lost points for noise and poor airflow to the right. Among the 7800-to-8600-Btu/hr. models, the top-rated Panasonic CW-806TU ($420) offers the best performance at an attractive price. In the larger sizes, the Friedrichs make good choices if price is not an issue. The less expensive GEs have been discontinued, but other moderately priced models such as the Sharp AF-T1106X ($500) and the Carrier XCB121E ($520) are still available.

See Buying Guide report, page 164. Last time rated in CONSUMER REPORTS: June 1997 and June 1996.

Ratings continued ▶

Ratings, continued

Overall Ratings

E = Excellent, VG = Very good, G = Good, F = Fair, P = Poor

Within types, listed in order of overall score

Key no.	Brand and model	Price	Overall score (0–100: P F G VG E)	Comfort	Flow control LEFT	Flow control RIGHT	Brownout	Noise
	5000 TO 5800 BTU/HR. MODELS							
1	**Amana** 5QZ21RC	$385		E/E	G	E	E	E
2	**Gibson** GAC056Y7A	360		E/E	VG	P	E	E
3	**Panasonic** CW-606TU	360		E/E	G	F	E	E
4	**Sharp** AF-505M6B	285		E	—	—	E	E
5	**Kenmore** (Sears) 75055	290		E/E	VG	P	F	E
6	**Carrier** UCA051B	320		VG	E	G	G	E
7	**Fedders** A3Q05F2AG	240		VG	VG	F	E	E
8	**Emerson** 5GC53	260		VG	G	G	E	E
9	**Whirlpool** ACQ052XF	300		E/E	E	P	F	G
10	**Friedrich** SQ05J10	380		G/VG	F	G	G	E
	6000 TO 6600 BTU/HR. MODELS							
11	**Amana** 7QZ21RC	425		E/E	G	E	E	E
12	**Whirlpool** ACQ062XF	310		E/E	E	P	E	G
13	**Gibson** GAB067F7B	395		E	VG	VG	E	VG
14	**Fedders** A3Q06F2BG	300		VG	E	P	E	VG
15	**Carrier** LCA061P	370		G	VG	P	E	VG
16	**Friedrich** SQ06J10	400		G/G	F	G	G	VG
17	**General Electric** AQV06LA	300		E	—	—	G	VG
	7800 TO 8600 BTU/HR. MODELS							
18	**Panasonic** CW-806TU	420		E/VG	G	F	E	E
19	**Friedrich** SS08J10A	670		E/VG	VG	F	E	VG
20	**Kenmore** (Sears) 75089	440		E/G	P	F	E	VG
21	**Whirlpool** ACQ082XD	410		E/E	VG	P	G	VG
22	**Carrier** TCA081P	400		VG/E	G	E	E	G
23	**General Electric** AQV08AA	400		E	F	VG	E	VG
24	**Sharp** AF-M807X	390		E	F	VG	E	VG
25	**Carrier** TCA081D	380		VG	G	E	E	G
26	**Fedders** A3Q08F2BG	340		VG	E	P	E	VG
27	**Gibson** GAC086Y7A	415		VG/E	VG	P	G	VG

Key no.	Brand and model	Price	Overall score 0–100 (P F G VG E)	Comfort	Flow control LEFT	Flow control RIGHT	Brownout	Noise
	7800 TO 8600 BTU/HR. MODELS *continued*							
28	**Frigidaire** FAC083W7A	$375		⊖	○	◒	○	⊖
29	**Amana** 9P2MY	440		⊖	⊖	⊜	○	○
	8900 TO 9200 BTU/HR. MODELS							
30	**Amana** 9QZ22RC	480		⊜/⊜	⊜	⊜	◒	○
31	**Friedrich** SS09J10A	700		⊜/⊜	⊖	○	●	⊖
32	**Gibson** GAX098Y1A	460		⊖/⊜	◒	○	●	⊜
	10,000 TO 10,500 BTU/HR. MODELS							
33	**General Electric** AMD10AB	500		⊜/⊜	⊜	○	⊜	⊖
34	**Friedrich** SS10J10A	770		⊜/⊜	○	◒	⊜	⊖
35	**Sharp** AF-T1106X	500		⊜/⊜	●	⊖	⊜	⊖
36	**Amana** 10QZ22RC	520		⊜/⊜	⊖	⊜	○	⊖
37	**Quasar** HQ2101KH	470		⊜/⊜	○	◒	○	⊖
38	**Whirlpool** ACQ102XD	480		⊜/⊜	⊖	○	○	○
39	**Kenmore** (Sears) 76109	450		⊖/⊖	○	◒	◒	⊖
40	**White-Westinghouse** WAL103Y1A	440		⊖	⊜	○	◒	⊖
41	**Fedders** A2Q10F2BG	380		○	⊜	●	⊜	⊖
42	**Carrier** TCA101D	480		⊜	○	⊖	●	○
	11,500 TO 12,000 BTU/HR. MODELS							
43	**Friedrich** SS12J10A	770		⊜/⊜	○	◒	⊜	⊖
44	**General Electric** AMH12AB	550		⊜/⊜	⊖	◒	⊜	⊜
45	**Carrier** XCB121E	520		⊖/⊜	⊜	◒	○	⊜
46	**Sharp** AF-T1206X	520		⊜/⊜	●	⊖	⊜	○
47	**Gibson** GAX128Y1A	500		⊖/⊖	◒	○	○	⊖
48	**White-Westinghouse** WAL126Y1A	480		⊖	⊜	◒	⊜	⊖
49	**Quasar** HQ2121KH	520		⊖/⊜	⊖	◒	○	⊖
50	**Amana** 12QZ22RC	580		⊖/⊜	○	⊜	●	⊖
51	**Fedders** A3J12E2AG	450		⊖	⊜	●	⊜	⊖
52	**Emerson** 12HT13	440		⊖	⊜	●	⊜	○
53	**Whirlpool** ACQ122XD	530		⊖/⊖	⊜	⊜	○	○
54	**Kenmore** (Sears) 72129	530		○/◒	◒	●	◒	○
55	**Goldstar** LW-L1210CL	500		◒	○	●	◒	⊖

Ratings continued ▶

Ratings, continued

Model details

5000 to 5800 Btu/hr. models

1 Amana 5QZ21RC $385
• 5400 Btu/hr. • 9.7 EER • 1.1 pt./hr. moisture removal • 61 lb. • Fits 23-to-40-in. windows
Longer warranty than others: 2 yr. on entire unit, 3rd through 5th yr. parts-and-labor warranty on refrigeration system. Exterior support bracket. But: No slide-out filter or up/down louver control. **Model availability:** Discontinued. **Recommendation:** Excellent performance overall.

2 Gibson GAC056Y7A $360
• 5450 Btu/hr. • 10 EER • 1.1 pt./hr. moisture removal • 54 lb. • Fits 22-to 36-in. windows
Extra 6th through 10th yr. parts-only warranty on compressor. But: Fan-only setting doesn't disable compressor. Only parts warranty on sealed system, 2nd through 5th yr. **Recommendation:** Excellent performance overall.

3 Panasonic CW-606TU $360
• 5800 Btu/hr. •10 EER • 0.9 pt./hr. moisture removal • 67 lb. • Fits 22-to-37-in. windows
Slide-out chassis. No upper sash lock. Only 2 fan speeds on "cool." **Model availability:** Discontinued. **Recommendation:** Very good overall.

4 Sharp AF-505M6B $285
• 5100 Btu/hr. • 9.7 EER • 1.2 pt./hr. moisture removal • 46 lb. • Fits 23-to-36-in. windows
No left-right louver control, vent, or upper sash lock. Only 1 fan-only setting. Only parts warranty on sealed system, 2nd through 5th yr. **Recommendation:** Very good performance overall, but no airflow directional control.

5 Kenmore (Sears) 75055 $290
• 5450 Btu/hr. • 10 EER • 1.1 pt./hr. moisture removal • 55 lb. • Fits 24-to-37-in. windows
No fan-only setting. Thermostat not marked with numbers. **Model availability:** Discontinued. **Recommendation:** Very good performance overall.

6 Carrier UCA051B $320
• 5200 Btu/hr. • 10 EER • 2.1 pt./hr. moisture removal • 73 lb. • Fits 25-to-38-in. windows
Slide-out chassis. Comes with through-wall instructions. But: Filter pulls out from bottom and may hit windowsill. Only 2 fan speeds on "cool." No upper sash lock or vent. Only parts warranty on sealed system, 2nd through 5th yr. **Recommendation:** Very good performance overall and good moisture removal for this size class, but some drawbacks.

7 Fedders A3Q05F2AG $240

8 Emerson 5GC53 $260
• 5100 Btu/hr. • 9.5 EER • 1.0 pt./hr. moisture removal • 60 lb. • Fits 23-to-39-in. windows
2-yr. warranty on fan motor. Exterior support bracket. But: Only parts warranty on sealed system, 2nd through 5th yr. No slide-out filter. No up/down louver control on (7). **Model availability:** Both are discontinued. **Recommendation:** Very good performance overall.

9 Whirlpool ACQ052XF $300
• 5000 Btu/hr. • 9.5 EER • 1.4 pt./hr. moisture removal • 54 lb. • Fits 25-to-43-in. windows
Only 1 fan-only setting. No up/down louver control. Thermostat not marked with numbers. **Recommendation:** Very good performance overall.

10 Friedrich SQ05J10 $380
• 5600 Btu/hr. • 10 EER • 1.5 pt./hr. moisture removal • 71 lb. • Fits 26-to-42-in. windows
Slide-out chassis. Comes with through-wall instructions. But: Thermostat not marked with numbers. **Recommendation:** Very good performance overall, but comfort score only middling.

6000 to 6600 Btu/hr. models

11 Amana 7QZ21RC $425
• 6600 Btu/hr. • 10 EER • 2.0 pt./hr. moisture removal • 65 lb. • Fits 23-to-40-in. windows
Longer warranty than others: 2 yr. on entire unit,

3rd through 5th yr. parts-and-labor on refrigeration system. Exterior support bracket. But: No slide-out filter or up/down louver control. **Model availability:** Discontinued. **Recommendation:** Excellent performance overall.

12 Whirlpool ACQ062XF $310
• 6000 Btu/hr. • 9.5 EER • 1.9 pt./hr. moisture removal • 57 lb. • Fits 25-to-41-in. windows
Only 1 fan-only setting. No up/down louver control. Thermostat not marked with numbers. **Recommendation:** Very good performance overall.

13 Gibson GAB067F7B $395
• 6100 Btu/hr. • 10 EER • 1.4 pt./hr. moisture removal • 53 lb. • Fits 26-to-38-in. windows
Longer warranty than others: 6th through 10th year parts-only on compressor. Low-profile design blocks little of window. Has handles for easier carrying. But: Thermostat not marked with numbers. Sharp corners on grille. **Similar:** Frigidaire FAB067W7B, $400. **Recommendation:** Very good performance overall.

14 Fedders A3Q06F2BG $300
• 6000 Btu/hr. • 10 EER • 1.6 pt./hr. moisture removal • 60 lb. • Fits 24-to-41-in. windows
2-yr. warranty on fan motor. Exterior support bracket. But: No slide-out filter, up/down louver control, or upper sash lock. Only parts warranty on sealed system, 2nd through 5th yr. **Model availability:** Discontinued. **Recommendation:** Very good performance overall.

15 Carrier LCA061P $370
• 6050 Btu/hr. • 9.1 EER • 2.0 pt./hr. moisture removal • 55 lb. • Fits 26-to-41-in. windows
Has handles for easier carrying, exterior support bracket. Low-profile design blocks little of window. But: No vent. Only 1 fan-only setting. Only parts warranty on sealed system, 2nd through 5th yr. **Recommendation:** Very good performance overall, but comfort score only middling.

16 Friedrich SQ06J10 $400
• 6600 Btu/hr. • 10 EER • 2.0 pt./hr. moisture removal • 74 lb. • Fits 26-to-42-in. windows
Slide-out chassis. Comes with through-wall instructions. But: Thermostat not marked with numbers. **Recommendation:** Very good performance overall and high moisture removal for this size class, but comfort score only middling.

17 General Electric AQV06LA $300
• 6000 Btu/hr. • 9 EER • 1.5 pt./hr. moisture removal • 46 lb. • Fits 24-to-35-in. windows
Lightest unit in this size class. But: No left/right louver control or vent. Only 1 fan-only setting. 2nd through 5th yr. warranty on compressor only. **Recommendation:** Very good performance overall, but no airflow directional control.

7800 to 8600 Btu/hr. models

18 Panasonic CW-806TU $420
• 7800 Btu/hr. • 10 EER • 2.3 pt./hr. moisture removal • 69 lb. • Fits 22-to-37-in. windows
Slide-out chassis. Only 2 fan speeds on "cool." No upper sash lock. **Model availability:** Discontinued. **Recommendation:** Very good performance overall.

19 Friedrich SS08J10A $670
• 8200 Btu/hr. • 10.8 EER • 1.5 pt./hr. moisture removal • 101 lb. • Fits 28-to-42-in. windows
Has 4 fan speeds, auto fan-speed control, timer, electronic controls. 5-yr. warranty on electronics. Comes with through-wall instructions. But: Hard to install despite slide-out chassis and exterior support bracket. Doesn't use expandable side panels—you must cut panels to fit. **Recommendation:** Very good performance overall, but heavy and requires more work to install.

20 Kenmore (Sears) 75089 $440
• 8000 Btu/hr. • 9.7 EER • 2.4 pt./hr. moisture removal • 80 lb. • Fits 25-to-45-in. windows
Louvers can be partially closed to increase air velocity. But: No fan-only setting. Thermostat not marked with numbers. **Model availability:** Discontinued. **Recommendation:** Very good performance overall.

21 Whirlpool ACQ082XD $410
• 8250 Btu/hr. • 9.6 EER • 1.7 pt./hr. moisture removal • 88 lb. • Fits 28-to-48-in. windows
Slide-out chassis. Comes with through-wall instructions. But: Only 1 fan-only setting. Thermostat not marked with numbers. **Recommendation:** Very good performance overall.

Ratings continued ▶

Ratings, continued

22 Carrier TCA081P $400

• 8600 Btu/hr. • 10 EER • 2.1 pt./hr. moisture removal • 66 lb. • Fits 26-to-38-in. windows
Has handles for easier carrying, exterior support bracket. But: Only 1 fan-only setting. Only parts warranty on sealed system, 2nd through 5th yr. **Recommendation:** Very good performance overall.

23 General Electric AQV08AA $400

• 8000 Btu/hr. • 9 EER • 1.9 pt./hr. moisture removal • 66 lb. • Fits 26-to-37-in. windows
Slide-out chassis. But: Only 1 fan-only setting. Shorter power cord than most. **Model availability:** Discontinued. **Recommendation:** Very good performance overall.

24 Sharp AF-M807X $390

• 8000 Btu/hr. • 9 EER • 1.8 pt./hr. moisture removal • 66 lb. • Fits 26-to-37-in. windows
Slide-out chassis. But: Only 1 fan-only setting. Shorter power cord than most. Only parts warranty on sealed system, 2nd through 5th yr. **Recommendation:** Very good performance overall.

25 Carrier TCA081D $380

• 8000 Btu/hr. • 9.2 EER • 2.0 pt./hr. moisture removal • 63 lb. • Fits 26-to-38-in. windows
Has handles for easier carrying, exterior support bracket. But: Only 2 fan speeds on "cool." No vent. Only parts warranty on sealed system, 2nd through 5th yr. **Recommendation:** Very good performance overall.

26 Fedders A3Q08F2BG $340

• 8000 Btu/hr. • 9.5 EER • 2.5 pt./hr. moisture removal • 69 lb. • Fits 24-to-40-in. windows
2-yr. warranty on fan motor. Exterior support bracket. But: No slide-out filter, up/down louver control, or upper sash lock. Only parts warranty on sealed system, 2nd through 5th yr. **Model availability:** Discontinued. **Recommendation:** Good performance overall.

27 Gibson GAC086Y7A $415

• 8000 Btu/hr. • 9.5 EER • 1.9 pt./hr. moisture removal • 61 lb. • Fits 23-to-37-in. windows
Only parts warranty on compressor, 6th through 10th yr. **Recommendation:** Good performance overall.

28 Frigidaire FAC083W7A $375

• 8000 Btu/hr. • 9.5 EER • 2.0 pt./hr. moisture removal • 61 lb. • Fits 22-to-36-in. windows
Only parts warranty on sealed system, 2nd through 5th yr. **Model availability:** Discontinued. **Recommendation:** Good performance overall.

29 Amana 9P2MY $440

• 8600 Btu/hr. • 9 EER • 3.0 pt./hr. moisture removal • 76 lb. • Fits 23-to-39-in. windows
Has exterior support bracket. But: No slide-out filter or up/down louver control. **Model availability:** Discontinued. **Recommendation:** Good performance overall. Highest dehumidification tested.

8900 to 9200 Btu/hr. models

30 Amana Quiet Zone 9QZ22RC $480

• 9100 Btu/hr. • 10.8 EER. • 2.5 pt./hr. moisture-removal. • 94 lb. • Fits 30-to-45-in. window
A very good, efficient performer. Slide-out chassis; exterior support bracket with leveling provision; outside drain hole. But: No slide-out filter. **Model availability:** Discontinued **Recommendation:** A very good choice.

31 Friedrich Quietmaster Electronic SS09J10A $700

• 9,200 Btu/hr. • 11.5 EER. • 1.7 pt./hr. moisture-removal. • 108 lb. • Fits 28-to-42-in. window.
Very efficient—but bulky and expensive. Has a slide-out chassis, exterior support bracket with leveling provision, 4 fan speeds on "cool," 24-hr. timer, digital readout. But: Hard to install; no upper-sash lock; no expandable side panels, no slide-out filter. **Recommendation:** Very good unless your area often has brownouts, but expensive.

32 Gibson Air Sweep GAX098Y1A $460

• 8900 Btu/hr. • 9.5 EER. • 2.3 pt./hr. moisture-removal. • 88 lb. • Fits 29-to-45-in. window.
A good, quiet unit—but mediocre directional control. Fairly quiet outdoors and at "high" indoors. Slide-out chassis, exterior support bracket with leveling provision, power louvers, outside drain hole. But: Short cord; filter pulls out from bottom and may hit sill. **Model availability:** Discontinued. **Recommendation:** A good choice unless your area often has brownouts.

10,000 to 10,500 Btu/hr. models

33 GE Premium AMD10AB $500

• 10,000 Btu/hr. • 10.0 EER. • 3.2 pt./hr. moisture removal. • 96 lb. • Fits 27-to-43-in. window. A very good, efficient performer—quiet indoors on High and quieter outdoors than most. Slide-out chassis, power louvers, 12-hr. timer, outside drain hole. But: No upper sash lock. **Model availability:** Discontinued. **Recommendation:** A very good choice, especially if you have nearby neighbors.

34 Friedrich Quietmaster Electronic SS10J10A $770

• 10,200 Btu/hr. • 11.7 EER. • 2.6 pt./hr. moisture removal. • 112 lb. • Fits 28-to-42-in. window. Very efficient—but bulky and expensive. Has a slide-out chassis, exterior support bracket with leveling provision, 4 fan speeds on "cool," 24-hr. timer, digital readout. But: Hard to install; no upper-sash lock; no expandable side panels, no slide-out filter. **Recommendation:** Very good, but expensive.

35 Sharp Comfort Touch AF-T1106X $500

• 10,500 Btu/hr. • 9.5 EER. • 3.2 pt./hr. moisture removal. • 78 lb. • Fits 26-to-37-in. window. A very good, efficient unit that's easy to install in a small window. Slide-out chassis, 12-hr. timer, digital readout. But: Short cord; no upper-sash lock. **Recommendation:** A very good choice unless you need to direct airflow to the left.

36 Amana Quiet Zone 10QZ22RC $520

• 10,200 Btu/hr. • 10.1 EER. • 3.0 pt./hr. moisture removal. • 102 lb. • Fits 30-to-45-in. window. A very good, highly efficient performer. Slide-out chassis; exterior support bracket with leveling provision, outside drain hole. But: No slide-out filter. **Recommendation:** A very good choice.

37 Quasar HQ2101KH $470

• 10,000 Btu/hr. • 9.1 EER. • 3.2 pt./hr. moisture removal. • 94 lb. • Fits 27-to-44-in. window. A very good performer, but not very efficient. Slide-out chassis, outside drain hole. But: No upper-sash lock. Similar: Panasonic Standard CW-1005FU, $530. **Recommendation:** A good performer, though not as efficient as others.

38 Whirlpool DesignerStyle ACQ102XD $480

• 10,000 Btu/hr. • 9.0 EER. • 2.6 pt./hr. moisture removal. • 96 lb. • Fits 28-to-46 in. window. A good performer, but not very efficient. Slide-out chassis and an outside drain hole. But: Thermostat settings have no numbers; short power cord. **Recommendation:** An OK—and low-priced—choice, but may cost more to operate than others.

39 Kenmore (Sears) 76109 $450

• 10,000 Btu/hr. • 9.0 EER. • 2.9 pt./hr. moisture removal. • 88 lb. • Fits 26-to-44-in. window. A good performer, but not very efficient. Hard to install; thermostat settings have no numbers. **Model availability:** Discontinued. **Recommendation:** An OK choice, but less efficient—may cost more to operate than others.

40 White-Westinghouse Continental WAL103Y1A $440

• 10,000 Btu/hr. • 9.5 EER. • 2.5 pt./hr. moisture removal. • 84 lb. • Fits 29-to-40-in. window. A good, efficient unit—but it doesn't dehumidify as well as others. Slide-out chassis, exterior support bracket with leveling provision. But: Lacks energy-saver mode; very noisy outdoors; short cord. **Similar:** Frigidaire Custom FAL103Y1A, $480. **Recommendation:** An OK choice in an area that doesn't get too humid.

41 Fedders Portable A2Q10F2BG $380

• 10,000 Btu/hr. • 9.2 EER. • 3.3 pt./hr. moisture removal. • 74 lb. • Fits 25-to-39-in. window. Low-priced, relatively lightweight, suited for small windows. Exterior support bracket with leveling provision. But: Hard to install; lacks energy-saver mode; very noisy outdoors; no upper-sash lock; no slide-out filter. Similar: Emerson Quiet Kool Compact Q 10GC13. **Recommendation:** OK unless you need to direct airflow to the right.

42 Carrier Siesta TCA101D $480

• 10,000 Btu/hr. • 9.0 EER. • 3.2 pt./hr. moisture removal. • 67 lb. • Fits 27-to-36-in. window. Lightweight, ideal for small windows—but less efficient than others. Outside drain hole. But: Lacks energy-saver mode; very noisy outdoors. **Recommendation:** An OK choice unless your area often has brownouts.

Ratings continued ▶

Ratings, continued

11,500 to 12,000 Btu/hr. models

43 Friedrich Quietmaster Electronic SS12J10A $770

• 12,000 Btu/hr. • 10.5 EER. • 3.5 pt./hr. moisture removal. • 111 lb. • Fits 28-to-42-in. window. Very efficient—but bulky and expensive. Has a slide-out chassis, exterior support bracket with leveling provision, 4 fan speeds on "cool," 24-hr. timer, digital readout. But: Hard to install; no upper-sash lock; no expandable side panels, no slide-out filter. **Recommendation:** Very good, but expensive.

44 GE Premium AMH12AB $550

• 11,500 Btu/hr. • 10.0 EER. • 3.6 pt./hr. moisture removal. • 96 lb. • Fits 27-to-43-in. window. A very good, efficient air-conditioner—and quieter than others. Features a slide-out chassis and such niceties as power louvers, a 12-hour timer, and an outside drain hole for condensation. But: No upper-sash lock. **Model availability:** Discontinued. **Recommendation:** A very good unit—quiet, too.

45 Carrier Electronic XCB121E $520

• 12,000 Btu/hr. • 10.0 EER. • 4.4 pt./hr. moisture removal. • 115 lb. • Fits 31-to-47-in. window. A very good, efficient unit—tops at removing moisture. Among its niceties: a slide-out chassis, power louvers, 24-hr. timer, digital readout, outside drain hole. But: Heavier than most; no upper-sash lock; filter pulls out from bottom and may hit sill. **Recommendation:** A very good choice, especially for a large window.

46 Sharp Comfort Touch AF-T1206X $520

• 12,000 Btu/hr. • 9.2 EER. • 3.6 pt./hr. moisture removal. • 80 lb. • Fits 26-to-37-in. window. Relatively lightweight to handle and install—but smaller and less efficient than others in this group. Niceties: slide-out chassis, 12-hr. timer, digital readout. But: No upper-sash lock; has short power cord. **Recommendation:** Very good for a small window—unless you want airflow to the left.

47 Gibson Air Sweep GAX128Y1A $500

• 12,000 Btu/hr. • 9.5 EER. • 3.5 pt./hr. moisture removal. • 93 lb. • Fits 29-to-45-in. window A good, efficient performer, despite mediocre directional control. Quiet indoors on "high." Slide-out chassis, exterior support bracket with leveling provision, power louvers, outside drain hole. But: Expensive; short cord; filter pulls out from bottom and may hit sill. **Recommendation:** A good choice, unless you will mount the unit in a corner.

48 White-Westinghouse Custom WAL126Y1A $480

• 12,000 Btu/hr. • 9.5 EER. • 3.4 pt./hr. moisture removal. • 89 lb. • Fits 29-to-40-in. window A good, efficient performer overall—and fairly low in price. Slide-out chassis, exterior support bracket with leveling provision, outside drain hole. But: Lacks energy-saver mode; has short cord. **Model availability:** Discontinued. **Recommendation:** A good value.

49 Quasar HQ2121KH $520

• 12,000 Btu/hr. • 9.1 EER. • 3.6 pt./hr. moisture removal. • 96 lb. • Fits 27-to-44-in. window. Good overall performance—but less efficient than others in this group. Slide-out chassis, power louvers, outside drain hole. But: No upper sash lock. **Recommendation:** A good choice.

50 Amana Quiet Zone 12QZ22RC $580

• 11,800 Btu/hr. • 10.0 EER. • 3.3 pt./hr. moisture removal. • 104 lb. • Fits 30-to-45-in. window. A very efficient model, good for large windows. Slide-out chassis, exterior support bracket with leveling provision, outside drain hole. But: Very noisy outdoors; no slide-out filter. **Recommendation:** A good choice unless your area often has brownouts.

51 Fedders Regency A3J12E2AG $450

• 12,000 Btu/hr. • 9.5 EER. • 3.9 pt./hr. moisture removal. • 102 lb. • Fits 26-to-39-in. window. Good, efficient performance; inexpensive. Slide-out chassis, exterior support bracket with leveling provision. But: Hard to install; lacks energy-saver mode; very noisy outdoors; no upper-sash lock; no expandable side panels. **Similar:** Emerson Quiet Kool Modulaire 12GJ14, $470. **Recom-**

mendation: A good choice unless you need to direct airflow to the right.

52 Emerson Quiet Kool Modulaire 12HT13 $440

• 12,000 Btu/hr. • 9.5 EER. • 3.9 pt./hr. moisture removal. • 95 lb. • Fits 29-to-45-in. window. Good, efficient performance; inexpensive. Slide-out chassis; exterior support bracket with leveling provision. But: Hard to install; lacks energy-saver mode; very noisy outdoors; no upper-sash lock; no expandable side panels. **Similar:** Fedders Whisperer A3T12F2AG, $400. **Recommendation:** A good choice unless you need to direct airflow to the right.

53 Whirlpool DesignerStyle ACQ122XD $530

• 12,000 Btu/hr. • 9.0 EER. • 4.0 pt./hr. moisture removal. • 99 lb. • Fits 28- to-46 in. window. Very good at dehumidifying, though less efficient than others. Slide-out chassis; outside drain hole. But: Very noisy outdoors; short cord; thermostat settings have no numbers. **Recommendation:** A good choice, but less efficient than others—and may cost more to operate.

54 Kenmore (Sears) 72129 $530

• 12,000 Btu/hr. • 9.0 EER. • 3.9 pt./hr. moisture removal. • 90 lb. • Fits 26-to-44-in. window. A mediocre performer and less efficient than others. Didn't keep room comfortable in energy-saver mode. Hard to install; very noisy outdoors. **Model availability:** Discontinued. **Recommendation:** There are better choices.

55 Goldstar LW-L1210CL $500

• 12,000 Btu/hr. • 9.0 EER. • 3.2 pt./hr. moisture removal. • 92 lb. • Fits 26-to-40-in. window. Mediocre at dehumidifying, and less efficient than others. Slide-out chassis, exterior support bracket with leveling provision, outside drain hole. But: Lacks energy-saver mode; no upper sash lock. **Model availability:** Discontinued. **Recommendation:** There are better choices.

How to use the Ratings in the Buying Guide

- **Read the Recommendations for information on specific models and general buying advice.**
- **Note how the rated products are listed—in order of performance and convenience, price, or alphabetically.**
- **The overall score graph gives the big picture in performance. Notes on features and performance for individual models are listed in the Comments column or "Model details."**
- **Use the handy key numbers to find out more about a product.**
- **Before going to press, we verify model availability for most products with manufacturers. Some tested models listed in the Ratings may no longer be available. Discontinued models are noted in Model details or Comments. Such models may actually still be available in some stores for part of 1998. Models indicated as successors should perform similarly to the tested models, according to the manufacturer. Features may vary.**
- **Models similar to the tested models, when they exist, are indicated in Comments or Model details.**
- **To find our last full report on a subject, check the reference above the Ratings chart or the eight-year index, page 346.**

Ratings *Latex wall paint*

& Recommendations

The tests behind the Ratings

Overall score summarizes our tests. Scores for **stain removal, two-coat hiding, toughness,** and **leveling** are averages of the performance of the white, pastel, and medium tint bases. See Model details for differences by color. Leveling describes the ability to dry to a smooth, texture-free coating. **Price** is the average per gallon, based on a survey. (Sico paint, a Canadian brand, is priced in U.S. dollars.)

Typical performance for these paints

• Good to excellent toughness (ability to withstand scrubbing and marring). • Ability to cover paint in two coats. • Almost no sticking for flat paints. • Excellent stain-resistance for semigloss paints. • Little change in glossiness or color after touch-up and rubbing, with semigloss paints generally standing up better than flats and low-luster paints.

Recommendations

Pratt & Lambert Accolade flat paint ($32), Behr Premium Plus Satin Enamel low-luster paint ($19), and Behr Premium Plus Enamel semigloss paint ($20) earned top scores for their type. Three Wal-Mart brands were each judged a CR Best Buy: Wal-Mart ColorPlace flat ($8); House Beautiful satin low-luster ($13); and House Beautiful Kitchen & Bath semigloss ($14).

See Buying Guide report, page 160. Last time rated in CONSUMER REPORTS: September 1997.

Overall Ratings

E VG G F P

Within types, listed in order of overall score

Key no.	Brand and model	Price	Overall score 0–100 (P F G VG E)	Stain removal	2-coat hiding	Toughness	Leveling
	FLAT PAINTS						
1	**Pratt & Lambert** Accolade	$32		E	VG	VG	G
2	**Pittsburgh** Manor Hall	22		E	VG	VG	F
3	**Glidden** Dulux Soft Matte	19		VG	E	VG	F
4	**Ace** Royal Touch	15		G	E	E	F
5	**Behr** Premium Plus Eggshell	18		VG	VG	E	F
6	**Wal-Mart** ColorPlace **A CR Best Buy**	8		VG	VG	VG	F

Key no.	Brand and model	Price	Overall score (0–100; P F G VG E)	Stain removal	2-coat hiding	Toughness	Leveling
	FLAT PAINTS *continued*						
7	**Sherwin-Williams** Super Paint	$23		○	◓	⊜	◓
8	**Dutch Boy** Renaissance	19		◒	⊜	◓	◓
9	**Behr** Premium Plus	17		◒	◓	⊜	◒
10	**Tru-Test** E-Z Kare	13		○	⊜	○	◓
11	**Benjamin Moore** Regal Wall Satin	22		◓	◒	○	◓
12	**Sears Best** Easy Living	18		●	⊜	⊜	◓
	LOW-LUSTER PAINTS						
13	**Behr** Premium Plus Satin Enamel	19		⊜	◓	⊜	○
14	**Pratt & Lambert** Accolade Velvet	33		⊜	○	◓	○
15	**House Beautiful** Satin (Wal-Mart), **A CR Best Buy**	13		⊜	◓	⊜	◒
16	**Pratt & Lambert** Accolade Satin	33		⊜	◓	◓	○
17	**Tru-Test** E-Z Kare Satin	18		⊜	◓	⊜	◓
18	**Sears Best** Easy Living Satin	20		⊜	○	⊜	◓
19	**Tru-Test** E-Z Kare Flat Enamel Eggshell	18		⊜	◓	⊜	○
20	**Benjamin Moore** Regal Aquapearl	26		⊜	◓	◓	◒
21	**Ace** Royal Touch Satin	18		⊜	◓	⊜	○
22	**Glidden** Dulux Satin Glow	21		⊜	◓	◓	◒
23	**Pittsburgh** Manor Hall Eggshell	23		⊜	○	◓	◒
24	**Benjamin Moore** Regal Aquavelvet Eggshell	26		⊜	○	◓	◒
25	**Sico** Supreme Velvet	25		⊜	○	○	◒
26	**Dutch Boy** Renaissance Satin	20		◓	⊜	⊜	◓
27	**Sherwin-Williams** Super Paint Satin	25		⊜	◓	◓	◓
	SEMIGLOSS PAINTS						
28	**Behr** Premium Plus Enamel	20		⊜	◓	⊜	○
29	**House Beautiful Kitchen & Bath** (Wal-Mart), **A CR Best Buy**	14		⊜	◓	⊜	○
30	**Tru-Test** E-Z Kare	19		⊜	◓	◓	◓
31	**Pittsburgh** Manor Hall	23		⊜	◓	⊜	○
32	**Sears Best** Easy Living	22		⊜	◓	◓	○
33	**Glidden** Dulux Silk Enamel	22		⊜	○	◓	◒

Ratings continued ▶

Ratings, continued

Key no.	Brand and model	Price	Overall score (0–100; P F G VG E)	Stain removal	2-coat hiding	Toughness	Leveling
	SEMIGLOSS PAINTS *continued*						
34	**Benjamin Moore** Regal Aquaglo Enamel	$26		⊜	○	⊖	○
35	**Sherwin-Williams** Super Paint	26		⊜	⊖	⊖	○
36	**Dutch Boy** Renaissance	22		⊜	○	⊖	⊖
37	**Ace** Royal Touch	19		⊜	○	⊖	○
38	**Pratt & Lambert** Accolade	36		⊜	○	○	⊖

Model details

Notes on the details: Here are instances in which a particular color of paint was markedly different from the average noted in the Overall Ratings.

Flat paints

1 Pratt & Lambert Accolade $32
White: Gloss change from touch-up ◒. **Pastel:** Color change from rubbing ●. **Medium:** Color changes from touch-up and rubbing ●; marring ⊖.

2 Pittsburgh Manor Hall $22
Generally not a good bet for sunny rooms. **White:** Hiding ◒. A good bet for bathrooms and other wet areas. **Pastel:** A good bet for bathrooms and other wet areas. **Medium:** Marring ⊖; color change from rubbing ●.

3 Glidden Dulux Soft Matte $19
White: High-sheen flat. Hiding ○. **Pastel:** Color and gloss changes from rubbing ◒; color change from touch-up ●. **Medium:** Color change from rubbing ◒. Not a good bet for windows and doors.

4 Ace Royal Touch $15
Generally not a good bet for sunny rooms. A good bet for bathrooms and other wet areas. **White:** Hiding ○. **Pastel:** Gloss change from rubbing ○; color change from rubbing ●; marring ◒. **Medium:** Stain removal ⊜.

5 Behr Premium Plus Eggshell $18
White: Hiding ◒; gloss change from rubbing ●. **Pastel:** Stain removal, gloss and color changes from rubbing ◒. **Medium:** Color change from rubbing ●; leveling ⊖.

6 Wal-Mart ColorPlace $8 **A CR Best Buy**
White: Hiding ◒. **Pastel:** Gloss change from rubbing ◒; color change from rubbing ●. **Medium:** Marring ○; color change from rubbing ●.

7 Sherwin-Williams Super Paint $23
Medium: Color changes from touch-up and rubbing ●.

8 Dutch Boy Renaissance $19
Generally not a good bet for sunny rooms. **White:** Marring, gloss change from rubbing ◒. **Pastel:** Color changes from touch-up and rubbing ●. **Medium:** Color changes from touch-up and rubbing ●.

9 Behr Premium Plus $17
White: Hiding ◒; leveling ●. **Pastel:** Gloss and color changes from rubbing ◒. **Medium:** Color change from rubbing ◒. A good bet for bathrooms and other wet areas.

10 Tru-Test E-Z Kare $13
White: Hiding ○. **Pastel:** Color change from touch-up ●; toughness ◒; scrubbability ◒. **Medium:** Color change from touch-up ●; color change from rubbing ◒; marring ○.

11 Benjamin Moore Regal Wall Satin $22
Pastel: Color change from touch-up ●; color change from rubbing ◒. **Medium:** Color change from touch-up ●.

12 Sears Best Easy Living $18
Generally not a good bet for sunny rooms. **Pastel:** Color changes from touch-up and rubbing ●. **Medium:** Color change from touch-up ●; color change from rubbing ◒.

Low-luster paints

13 Behr Premium Plus Satin Enamel $19
Product is a low semigloss. A good bet for bathrooms and other wet areas. **White:** Hiding and gloss change from rubbing ◒. **Pastel:** Gloss change from rubbing ◒. **Medium:** Gloss change from rubbing ○; leveling ⊜. Not a good bet for windows and doors.

14 Pratt & Lambert Accolade Velvet $33
Generally not a good bet for windows and doors. A good bet for bathrooms and other wet areas. **Pastel:** Hiding ⊜; gloss change from rubbing ◒. A good bet for windows and doors. **Medium:** Gloss change from rubbing ◒.

15 House Beautiful Satin (Wal-Mart) $13 **A CR Best Buy**
White: Not a good bet for windows and doors. A good bet for bathrooms and other wet areas. Gloss change from rubbing ●. **Pastel:** Marring ◒; color change from rubbing ●. **Medium:** Gloss and color changes from rubbing ◒.

16 Pratt & Lambert Accolade Satin $33
Generally not a good bet for windows and doors. Product is a low semigloss. **White, pastel:** Gloss change from rubbing ◒. **Medium:** Color change from rubbing ◒.

17 Tru-Test E-Z Kare Satin $18
Generally not a good bet for windows and doors. **White:** Marring ◒.

18 Sears Best Easy Living Satin $20
Generally not a good bet for windows, doors, or sunny rooms. **Pastel:** A good bet for windows and doors. **Medium:** Hiding ⊜; marring ◒.

19 Tru-Test E-Z Kare Flat Enamel Eggshell $18
Generally not a good bet for windows and doors. Gloss change from rubbing ●. **White:** Dead flat, not low-luster. Hiding ◒. A good bet for bathrooms and other wet areas. **Pastel, medium:** Not a good bet for bathrooms and other wet areas.

20 Benjamin Moore Regal Aquapearl $26
White: Gloss change from rubbing ●. **Pastel:** Not a good bet for windows and doors. Gloss change from rubbing ◒. Marring ●. **Medium:** Gloss change from rubbing ●.

21 Ace Royal Touch Satin $18
Generally not a good bet for windows, doors, or sunny rooms. Gloss change from rubbing ●.

22 Glidden Dulux Satin Glow $21
Generally not a good bet for windows and doors. Gloss change from rubbing ◒. **White:** Hiding ◒. A good bet for windows and doors. **Medium:** Color change from touch-up ●.

23 Pittsburgh Manor Hall Eggshell $23
Generally not a good bet for sunny rooms. **White:** Gloss change from rubbing ●. A good bet for bathrooms and other wet areas. **Pastel:** Hiding ⊜. Gloss change from rubbing ●. **Medium:** Dead flat, not low-luster. Toughness ◒.

24 Benjamin Moore Regal Aquavelvet Eggshell $26
Generally not a good bet for windows and doors. **White:** Marring ●. A good bet for windows and doors. **Pastel:** Flat, not low-luster. Marring ○; gloss change from rubbing ◒. **Medium:** Flat, not low-luster. Hiding ⊜. Gloss change from rubbing ●.

25 Sico Supreme Velvet $25
Sold in Canada. **White:** Gloss change from rubbing ●. **Pastel:** Hiding ⊜; gloss change from rubbing ●. **Medium:** Toughness, scrubbability ●; gloss change from rubbing ◒.

26 Dutch Boy Renaissance Satin $20
Generally not a good bet for windows, doors, or sunny rooms. **White:** A good bet for windows and doors. Gloss change from rubbing ●. **Pastel:** Gloss change from rubbing ●. **Medium:** Toughness ○; gloss and color changes from rubbing ◒.

Ratings continued ▶

Ratings, continued

27 Sherwin-Williams Super Paint Satin $25
Generally not a good bet for windows and doors. **White:** Hiding ◒. A good bet for windows and doors. **Pastel:** Color change from touch-up ●; gloss change from rubbing ◒. **Medium:** Color change from touch-up ●.

Semigloss paints

28 Behr Premium Plus Enamel $20
A good bet for bathrooms and other wet areas. **White:** Hiding, marring ◒. Not a good bet for windows and doors.

29 House Beautiful Kitchen & Bath (Wal-Mart) $14 **A CR Best Buy**
Generally not a good bet for windows and doors. Product is a low semigloss. **White:** A good bet for bathrooms and other wet areas. **Medium:** Color change from touch-up ●.

30 Tru-Test E-Z Kare $19
Generally not a good bet for windows and doors. **White:** Product is low luster. Hiding, marring ◒. **Medium:** A good bet for windows and doors.

31 Pittsburgh Manor Hall $23
Generally not a good bet for sunny rooms. **White:** Not a good bet for windows and doors. A good bet for bathrooms and other wet areas. **Pastel:** Marring ○. **Medium:** Color change from touch-up ●; color change from rubbing ◒; marring ⊖.

32 Sears Best Easy Living $22
Not a good bet for sunny rooms.

33 Glidden Dulux Silk Enamel $22
Medium: Hiding ⊖.

34 Benjamin Moore Regal Aquaglo Enamel $26
Generally not a good bet for windows and doors. **White, pastel:** A good bet for bathrooms and other wet areas. **Medium:** Hiding ⊖.

35 Sherwin-Williams Super Paint $26
Generally not a good bet for windows and doors. Pastel and medium bases are low semigloss. **White:** Hiding ◒. **Pastel:** Marring ○. **Medium:** Toughness ◒; leveling ●.

36 Dutch Boy Renaissance $22
Generally not a good bet for windows, doors, or sunny rooms. Product is a low semigloss. **Pastel:** Marring ○. **Medium:** Hiding ⊖; toughness ◒.

37 Ace Royal Touch $19
Generally not a good bet for windows, doors, or sunny rooms. **White:** Marring ◒. **Medium:** Hiding ⊖.

38 Pratt & Lambert Accolade $36
Generally not a good bet for windows and doors. Scrubbability ◒. **Pastel:** Marring ⊖. **Medium:** Hiding ⊖; toughness ◒; gloss change from rubbing ◒. A good bet for bathrooms and other wet areas.

Can't find a model? Call the manufacturer. See page 342.

For the most recent product Ratings

Ratings *Tractors & riding mowers*

& Recommendations

The tests behind the Ratings

Overall score is based on stability, mowing performance, handling, and convenience. **Stability** measures how likely each model was to rear up. Mowing modes are: **side discharge** (clippings sprayed to the side); **mulching** (clippings chopped fine and blown into the grass); and **bagging. Cutting** scores evenness of cut. **Dispersal** is how evenly clippings were spread. **Vacuuming** shows how free of clippings the lawn was after clippings were bagged. **Price** is a national average, based on a survey. Grass-catcher price is manufacturers' list. A mulching kit is included with some models, $19 to $160 with others.

Typical features for these models

• Electric starter. • Safety interlocks that prevent starting when drive or blades are engaged and that stop blades and forward motion when operator dismounts. • Adjustable seat. • Easy switch from bagging to side discharge. • Difficult switch to mulching. • Bags that hold 70 to 105 pounds. • Overhead-valve engine. • Single pedal for brake and clutch. • Headlights. • 2-year parts/labor warranty.

Recommendations

The Honda Harmony ($2350) scored highest of the models with a hydrostatic transmission. It isn't the best cutter in any mode, but it's at least competent in all three. The Sabre by John Deere 1538HS ($1800) is quite a bit cheaper. It scored quite close to the Honda, and according to our readers' experiences, John Deere has been among the more reliable brands. Among the models with a gear drive, the Murray 40530X92A scored highest in our tests—and its price, $935, makes it especially attractive. It's available mainly in Wal-Mart stores in Southern states. If a riding mower is the size you want, the John Deere GX85 ($1800) is a fine choice. The zero-turn-radius riding mowers—Ariens EZ Rider EZR 1440 ($3300) and Dixon ZTR 4423 ($3700)—offer undeniably superior maneuverability. But they're expensive. And because of their tendency to rear up when their bagging system is attached, we recommend against that option.

See Buying Guide report, page 170. Last time rated in CONSUMER REPORTS: June 1997.

Ratings continued

Overall Ratings

E = ⊜, VG = ⊖, G = ○, F = ◒, P = ●

Within types, listed in order of overall score

Key no.	Brand and model	Price, mower/ catcher	Overall score (0–100; P F G VG E)	Stability	Side discharge: CUTTING / DISPERSAL	Mulching: CUTTING/ DISPERSAL	Bagging: CUTTING / VACUUMING
	TRACTORS WITH HYDROSTATIC DRIVE						
1	**Honda** Harmony H2013HDA	$2350/371		VG	VG/G	G/G	G/VG
2	**Cub Cadet** by MTD HDS2135 136-214-100	2800/269		E	G/G	VG/G	G/VG
3	**John Deere** STX38 Hydro	2200/320		G	G/G	VG/VG	VG/VG
4	**Sabre** by John Deere 1538HS	1800/300		G	G/G	VG/VG	VG/G
5	**Toro** Wheel Horse 14-38HXL	2100/309		VG	G/G	G/VG	G/VG
6	**Husqvarna** YTH150	2100/240		VG	VG/G	VG/F	G/G
7	**Ariens** Sierra 1440H	2700/479		G	VG/VG	G/F	G/G
8	**Simplicity** Regent 14H	2700/395		VG	VG/G	G/G	G/P
9	**Kubota** T1560-40	3500/441		G	G/VG	G/G	G/G
10	**Yard-Man** by MTD X694G	1700/239		F	G/G	G/G	G/VG
11	**Sears** 917.258530 Hydro	1450/200		F	VG/G	G/F	G/G
12	**Murray** 42560X92A	1055/219		VG	G/G	G/G	G/G
	TRACTORS WITH GEAR DRIVE						
13	**Murray** 40530X92A	935/219		E	G/G	G/G	G/G
14	**Sabre** by John Deere 1338GS	1500/300		G	G/G	VG/G	VG/G
15	**Yard-Man** by MTD 1674G	1300/239		VG	G/G	G/G	G/VG
16	**Murray** 38500X92A	795/219		VG	G/G	G/G	G/VG
17	**Sears** 917.258520 Gear	1300/200		F	VG/G	G/F	G/VG
18	**Yard Machines** by MTD H450F 13AH450F302	820/239		VG	G/G	G/G	G/G
19	**Sears** 25851	1000/199		F	G/G	VG/F	VG/G
20	**Toro** Wheel Horse 13-38XL	1850/309		F	F/G	G/VG	F/G
	RIDING MOWERS						
21	**John Deere** GX85	1800/330		E	VG/E	G/F	E/VG
22	**Snapper** 331416BVE	2200/350		F	VG/G	F/VG	VG/E
	ZERO-TURN-RADIUS RIDING MOWERS *Not suitable for use with grass-catcher.*						
23	**Ariens** EZ Rider EZR 1440	3300/479		P	G/G	VG/VG	VG/G
24	**Dixon** ZTR 4423	3700/670		P	VG/VG	G/G	VG/G

Model details

Hydrostatic-drive tractors

1 Honda Harmony H2013HDA $2350
• 13-hp Honda engine • 38-in. swath • Top speed, 4.1 mph
Less noisy than most. Drive engages smoothly. Relatively tight turns. Ample leg room. Comfortable seat. California emissions sticker. But: Getting on and off can be awkward. No headlights. **Recommendation:** A very good machine, easy to operate. But pricey.

2 Cub Cadet by MTD HDS2135 136-214-100 $2800
• 13-hp Kohler engine • 38-in. swath • Top speed, 3.8 mph
Stops smoothly. Has both a pedal and a lever for speed control; lever serves as automotive-like cruise control during mowing. Comfortable seat. Large fuel tank. Easy to change oil. California emissions sticker. But: Drive pedal hard to operate in reverse. Brake pedal too close for tall users; reach is too far for short users. Doesn't cut in reverse. Catcher bags are hard to empty. Fuel level is hard to check. **Recommendation:** Very good but pricey—and there are tractor brands with a better repair record.

3 John Deere STX38 Hydro $2200
• 13-hp Kohler engine • 38-in. swath • Top speed, 5.7 mph
Drive engages smoothly. Relatively tight turns. Ample leg room. Easy to change oil. California emissions sticker. But: No headlights. **Recommendation:** Very good, especially at mulching and at cutting with a catcher. Among the more reliable tractor brands.

4 Sabre by John Deere 1538HS $1800
• 15-hp Briggs & Stratton engine • 38-in. swath• Top speed, 5.6 mph
Drive engages smoothly. Relatively tight turns. Ample leg room. Easy to change oil. California emissions sticker. **Recommendation:** A very good entry from John Deere's "affordable" line. Very good at mulching and at cutting with a catcher.

5 Toro Wheel Horse 14-38HXL $2100
• 14.5-hp Briggs & Stratton engine • 38-in. swath • Top speed, 4.6 mph
Less noisy than most. Precise steering. Relatively tight turns. Easy to convert to mulching. But: Stops abruptly. Brake pedal too close for tall users; reach is too far for short users. Drive pedal hard to use in reverse. Catcher bags hard to attach, and hold less than most. **Recommendation:** A very good machine, but with shortcomings.

6 Husqvarna YTH150 $2100
• 15-hp Kohler engine • 42-in. swath • Top speed, 4.6 mph
Ample leg room. Comfortable seat. Easy to convert to mulching. Large fuel tank. Easy to change oil. California emissions sticker. But: Stops abruptly. Brake-pedal reach is too far for short users. Cover makes catcher buckets hard to remove. Fuel level is hard to check. **Recommendation:** Very good if you don't mulch.

7 Ariens Sierra 1440H $2700
• 14-hp Briggs & Stratton engine • 40-in. swath• Top speed, 4.1 mph
Stops smoothly. Steers precisely. Ample leg room. Has automotive-like cruise control. Large fuel tank. Easy to change oil. California emissions sticker. 5-yr. warranty on ignition system; additional 3-yr. warranty on parts for mower. But: Tended to clog in tall-grass cutting test. Getting on and off can be awkward. Drive pedal hard to operate in reverse. Difficult to fuel. **Recommendation:** Very good, and one of the best in side-discharge mode. But at this price, you have better choices.

8 Simplicity Regent 14H $2700
• 14-hp Briggs & Stratton engine • 38-in. swath• Top speed, 5.1 mph
Drive engages smoothly. Relatively tight turns. Easy to change oil. California emissions sticker. 5-yr. warranty on ignition system. But: Stops abruptly. Brake pedal too close for tall users; reach is too far for short users. Seat must be tipped to remove catcher bags. Complex conversion between modes. **Recommendation:** Very good if you don't bag clippings. Expensive.

Can't find a model? Call the manufacturer. See page 342.

Ratings continued

Ratings, continued

9 **Kubota T1560-40** $3500

• 14-hp Kawasaki engine • 40-in. swath • Top speed, 5.2 mph

Less noisy than most. Drive engages smoothly. Ample leg room. Comfortable seat. Easy to fuel. Large fuel tank. California emissions sticker. But: Stops abruptly. Drive pedal too far for short users. Complex conversion to mulching. Fuel level is hard to check. Oil changing is messy. **Recommendation:** A good, convenient model, but there are better ones for much less money.

10 **Yard-Man by MTD X694G** $1700

• 15-hp Kohler engine • 42-in. swath • Top speed, 5.0 mph

Relatively tight turns. Ample leg room. Easy to convert to mulching. California emissions sticker. But: Front can rear up with full catcher. Brake pedal too close for tall users; reach is too far for short users. Awkward to get on and off. Catcher bags are hard to empty. Oil changing is messy. Doesn't cut in reverse. **Model availability:** Discontinued. **Recommendation:** A good tractor, overall, except for the worrisome rearing-up potential.

11 **Sears 917.258530 Hydro** $1450

• 15.5-hp Briggs & Stratton engine • 42-in. swath• Top speed, 4.6 mph

Ample leg room. Comfortable seat. Easy to convert to mulching. Easy to change oil. But: Front can rear up with full catcher. Stops abruptly. Brake-pedal reach is too far for short users. Cover makes catcher buckets hard to remove. **Model availability:** Discontinued. **Recommendation:** A good machine, but there are better choices.

12 **Murray 42560X92A** $1055

• 14.5-hp Briggs & Stratton engine • 42-in. swath • Top speed, 5.6 mph

Deck easy to level. But: Starts abruptly. Difficult to steer. Drive pedal too close for tall users. Getting on and off can be awkward. Drive pedal hard to operate in reverse. Seat must be tipped to remove catcher buckets. **Recommendation:** Good, and inexpensive, but has shortcomings.

Gear-drive tractors

13 **Murray 40530X92A** $935

• 14.5-hp Briggs & Stratton engine • 40-in. swath • 6 speeds from 1.0 to 4.5 mph

Stops smoothly. Precise shifting. Deck easy to level. But: Brake pedal too close for tall users. Getting on and off can be awkward. Seat must be tipped to remove catcher buckets. Buckets are hard to empty. **Recommendation:** A very good performer at a great price. But it's sold mostly in the South, in Wal-Mart stores.

14 **Sabre by John Deere 1338GS** $1500

• 13-hp Briggs & Stratton engine • 38-in. swath • 5 speeds from 1.5 to 4.8 mph

Relatively tight turns. Ample leg room. Easy to change oil. California emissions sticker. But: Starts and stops abruptly. Side-valve engine. **Recommendation:** A good choice. Among the more reliable tractor brands.

15 **Yard-Man by MTD 1674G** $1300

• 15.5-hp Briggs & Stratton engine • 42-in. swath • 7 speeds from 1.4 to 6.6 mph

Relatively tight turns. Ample leg room. Precise shifting. Easy to convert to mulching. California emissions sticker. But: Starts abruptly. Twin shift levers can suddenly send you speeding backward. Direction-control lever hard to move out of Neutral. Brake pedal too close for tall users; reach is too far for short users. Awkward to get on and off. Catcher bags hard to empty. Oil changing is messy. Doesn't cut in reverse. Very noisy. **Model availability:** Discontinued. **Recommendtion:** A good machine, if you can live with the shortcomings.

16 **Murray 38500X92A** $795

• 12.5-hp Briggs & Stratton engine • 38-in. swath • 5 speeds from 1.0 to 4.3 mph

Deck easy to level. But: Starts and stops abruptly. Brake pedal too close for tall users. Getting on and off can be awkward. Vague shifting. Seat must be tipped to remove catcher buckets. Buckets hard to empty. Side-valve engine. **Recommendation:** Inexpensive and good, if you can live with the shortcomings.

17 **Sears 917.258520 Gear** $1300

• 15.5-hp Briggs & Stratton engine • 42-in. swath • 6 speeds from 1.1 to 5.5 mph

Ample leg room. Comfortable seat. Easy to convert to mulching. Easy to change oil. But: Front rears up with full catcher. Starts abruptly. Brake-pedal reach is too far for short users. Cover makes catcher buckets hard to remove. **Model availability:** Discontinued. **Recommendation:** A good machine, except for the worrisome rearing-up tendency.

18 Yard Machines by MTD H450F 13AH450F302 $820

• 12.5-hp Briggs & Stratton engine • 38-in. swath • 5 speeds from 1.3 to 6.8 mph

Ample leg room. Easy to convert to mulching. But: Starts abruptly. Twin shift levers can suddenly send you speeding backward. Direction-control lever hard to move in and out of Neutral. Difficult to steer. Uncomfortable steering wheel. Relatively wide turns. Brake pedal too close for tall users; reach is too far for short users. Catcher bags hard to empty. Oil changing is messy. Doesn't cut in reverse. Very noisy. Side-valve engine. **Model availability:** Discontinued. **Recommendation:** A good machine at a good price, if you can live with the shortcomings.

19 Sears 25851 $1000

• 14.5 hp Briggs & Stratton engine • 42-in. swath • 6 speeds from 1.0 to 5.0 mph

Stops smoothly. Ample leg room. Easy to convert to mulching. Easy to change oil. But: Front rears up with full catcher. Starts abruptly. Shifting is imprecise. Brake-pedal reach is too far for short users. Awkward to get on and off. Cover makes catcher buckets hard to remove. **Model availability:** Discontinued. **Recommendation:** Good except for the worrisome rearing-up tendency.

20 Toro Wheel Horse 13-38XL $1850

• 13-hp Briggs & Stratton engine • 38-in. swath • 5 speeds from 1.3 to 5.5 mph

Less noisy than most. Ample leg room. Precise steering. Relatively tight turns. Precise shifting. Easy to convert to mulching. But: Front rears up with full catcher. Starts and stops abruptly. Brake pedal too close for tall users; reach is too far for short users. Catcher bags hard to attach, and they hold less than most. Side-valve engine. **Recommendation:** A good but pricey machine. Has worrisome rearing-up tendency.

Riding mowers

21 John Deere GX85 $1800

• 13-hp Briggs & Stratton engine • 30-in. swath • 5 speeds from 1.0 to 4.8 mph

Starts smoothly. Precise steering. Relatively tight turning circle. Easy to convert to mulching. Easy to fuel. Easy to change oil. California emissions sticker. But: Limited leg room. Confusing clutch and brake pedals. Clutch pedal too close. No headlights. Side-valve engine. **Recommendation:** A very good rider, worth considering.

22 Snapper 331416BVE $2200

•14-hp Briggs & Stratton engine • 33-in. swath • 5 speeds from 1.9 to 4.3 mph

Blade stops very quickly. Stops smoothly. Relatively tight turns. Easy to fuel. 5-yr. warranty. But: Front rears up when catcher is full. Starts abruptly. Imprecise steering. Limited leg room. Clutch pedal too close. Awkward to get on and off. No headlights. Similar: 331416KVE, $2200. **Recommendation:** A good machine, but way too expensive, and one of the less reliable brands of riding mowers.

Zero-turn-radius mowers

23 Ariens EZ Rider EZR 1440 $3300

• 14-hp Briggs & Stratton engine • 40-in. swath • Top speed, 5.4 mph

Zero turn radius makes back-and-forth mowing very easy. Hydrostatic drive. Ample leg room. Comfortable seat. Large fuel tank. Easy to change oil. California emissions sticker. 5-yr. warranty on ignition system; additional 3-yr. warranty on mower parts. But: Front rears up when catcher is full, and deck won't stay down on hills. A bit unstable when turning on a hill. Hard to maintain straight course. No headlights. Fuel level is hard to check. **Recommendation:** A good performer at a high price. Don't use with a catcher—too unstable.

24 Dixon ZTR 4423 $3700

• 14-hp Briggs & Stratton engine • 42-in. swath • Top speed, 4.5 mph

Zero turn radius makes back-and-forth mowing very easy. Mechanical drive. Ample leg room. Comfortable seat. Large fuel tank. Easy to change oil. California emissions sticker. 5-yr. warranty on ignition system. But: Front rears way up when catcher is full. Cover makes catcher bags hard to remove. Bags are hard to empty. Switching modes is very complex. Fuel level is hard to check. **Recommendation:** A good performer at a steep price. Don't use with a catcher—too unstable.

Ratings *Snow throwers*

& Recommendations

The tests behind the Ratings

The **overall score** covers both snow removal and convenience. In scoring single-stage models, we considered the fact that they aren't self-propelled and can't clear deep snow. **Clearing** reflects how quickly each machine could move snow. The two-stage machines were tested in 9 to 11 inches of dry snow and again in deeper snow; single-stage machines, in 4 to 5 inches of snow. **Throwing** reflects how high and how far each machine threw dry snow. **Surface cleaning** indicates how thoroughly each machine could remove snow in its path. We judged the **handling** of each machine as it was throwing snow. **Ease of use** covers starting, handle height, discharge-chute adjustment, and the like. **Price** is the national average, based on a survey.

Typical features for these models

• Electric start, powered by plugging into a wall outlet. • Handle that's 36 to 40 inches high. • Crank on the side to turn the discharge chute. • Chute deflector that must be adjusted by first loosening a knob or wing nut. Good to Fair performance in wet snow. **Most two-stage models:** • 4-stroke engine. • 1-gal. fuel tank. • Interlock between the drive and auger deadman controls for one-hand operation. • A release to depower one wheel, to make turning easier in light snow. • Adjustable, replaceable skid shoes and steel scrapers. • Fuel shutoff valve. **Most single-stage models:** • 2-stroke engine. • 1.2- to 1.5-qt. fuel tank. • Handle that can be folded without tools. • Replaceable plastic scraper.

Recommendations

The two-stage machines outperformed the single-stage models in snow-clearing and throwing. Any of the two-stage models would make a fine choice. Among them, the Toro 824 Power Shift ($1350) was the best all-around snow thrower. The powerful Honda HS828K1TAS ($2050) scored next highest, but it's very expensive and hard to handle. The MTD E640F ($770) offers the best combination of performance and value; we've judged it a **CR Best Buy.** The John Deere TRS21 ($640) and the Honda HS621A ($740) were our top-scoring single-stage models. The John Deere is the better value, and **a CR Best Buy.**

See Buying Guide report, page 174. Last time rated in CONSUMER REPORTS: October 1997.

Overall Ratings

E = Excellent, VG = Very good, G = Good, F = Fair, P = Poor (E VG G F P)

Key no.	Brand and model	Price	Overall score (0–100: P F G VG E)	Clearing	Throwing	Surface cleaning	Handling	Ease of use
	TWO-STAGE MODELS							
1	**Toro** 824 Power Shift	$1350		E	E	G	F	E
2	**Honda** HS828K1TAS	2050		VG	E	VG	P	E
3	**MTD** E640F **A CR Best Buy**	770		E	VG	VG	G	VG
4	**Noma** Performance G2794010	920		VG	E	G	F	VG
5	**Yard-Man** E623D	750		G	VG	G	G	E
6	**Ariens** ST824DL	1500		VG	VG	F	F	E
7	**Sears** Craftsman 247.88569	1200		VG	VG	G	F	E
8	**Troy-Bilt** 42010	1200		G	VG	G	G	VG
9	**Toro** 622 Power Throw	850		G	VG	P	G	G
10	**Simplicity** 860E	1420		G	VG	VG	F	VG
11	**John Deere** 826D	1240		G	VG	P	G	E
12	**Sears** Craftsman 536.88665	1150		VG	VG	G	F	VG
13	**Snapper** I5223	900		G	VG	G	G	G
14	**Sears** Craftsman 536.88612	750		G	VG	F	G	G
15	**Simplicity** 555M	960		G	VG	G	G	G
16	**MTD** 611D	600		G	VG	VG	G	G
17	**Troy-Bilt** 42000	800		G	VG	G	G	F
	SINGLE-STAGE MODELS							
18	**John Deere** TRS21 **A CR Best Buy**	640		G	VG	E	E	G
19	**Honda** HS621A	740		G	VG	E	VG	F
20	**Toro** CCR3000GTS	750		G	G	E	VG	G
21	**Murray** Ultra G2145060	410		G	F	E	VG	VG
22	**MTD** 140	310		F	F	E	E	G
23	**Sears** Craftsman 536.88468	550		F	G	VG	VG	VG
24	**White** Snow Boss 50	500		F	F	VG	VG	VG
25	**Snapper** LE317R	420		F	F	G	E	VG
26	**Sears** Craftsman 536.88458	450		F	F	G	VG	VG
27	**Ariens** SS522	550		P	P	VG	VG	E
	NOT ACCEPTABLE *This model lacks a deadman safety control for its auger (see the Model details).*							
28	**Toro** CCR Powerlite	430	Not scored	—	—	—	—	—

Ratings continued ▶

Model details

Notes on the details: Performance in wet snow was judged on 6 to 7 inches of loose granular snow and on the same depth of freshly fallen wet and heavy packed snow.

Two-stage models

1 Toro 824 Power Shift $1350

• 8 hp • 235 lb. • 24-in. swath • 4 forward speeds, 0.5 to 2.7 mph • 2 reverse speeds, 1.1 and 1.8 mph • 2-yr. warranty • 40x26x55 in.
Better than most in deep snow and clearing wet snow. Has a weight-forward setting to handle dense, compact snow. Chute deflector can be adjusted without loosening hardware. Partial guard helps keep hands out of the discharge chute. Electric start optional. But: Slightly noisier than most. **Recommendation:** Excellent overall. A good first choice if you need a big snow thrower.

2 Honda HS828K1TAS $2050

• 8 hp • 211 lb. • 28-in. swath • Continuously adjustable speeds, from 0.3 to 2.1 mph forward and from 0.4 to 1.3 mph in reverse • 1.6-gal. gas tank with gauge • 2-yr. warranty • 41x28x59 in.
No other model could throw snow as far or match the smoothness of the hydrostatic transmission. Better than most in deep snow and clearing wet snow. Has weight-forward settings for dense, compact snow. Quiet. Moves on tracks instead of tires. Convenient lever controls chute deflector. But: Very hard to handle; nearly impossible to move when engine is off. The 35-inch-high handle is a bit low for tall users. Similar: HS828K1TA, $1900. **Recommendation:** Excellent performance, but unwieldy and expensive.

3 MTD E640F $770

• 8 hp • 194 lb. • 26-in. swath • 6 forward speeds, 0.7 to 3.2 mph • 2 reverse speeds, 1.1 and 1.4 mph • 2-yr. warranty, plus 90-day no-fault coverage • 43x27x53 in.
We found little to fault in this fine machine. But: Scraper isn't adjustable. Similar: MTD Gold 31A-E640F-382, $800. **Recommendation:** Excellent performance, low price. **A CR Best Buy.**

4 Noma Performance G2794010 $920

• 9 hp • 217 lb. • 27-in. swath • 6 forward speeds, 0.9 to 2.7 mph • 2 reverse speeds, 0.9 and 1.1 mph • 2-yr. warranty • 48x29x58 in.
Cleared wet snow very well. Convenient lever controls chute deflector. But: Had trouble with deep snow. Slightly noisier than most. Deadman controls are stiff and relatively hard to hold down. Handle may be too high even for tall users. **Model availability:** Discontinued. **Recommendation:** Very good overall.

5 Yard-Man E623D $750

• 5.5 hp • 166 lb. • 22-in. swath • 6 forward speeds, 0.8 to 2.3 mph • 2 reverse speeds, 0.7 and 1.1 mph • 2-qt. gas tank • 2-yr. warranty; 90-day no-fault coverage • 43x23x53 in.
A small, moderately powered machine that gives away little in performance. Better than most in deep snow and clearing wet snow. Slightly quieter than most. Convenient lever controls chute deflector. But: Scraper isn't adjustable. **Recommendation:** Very good overall, and a very good value.

6 Ariens ST824DL $1500

• 8 hp • 246 lb. • 24-in. swath • 6 forward speeds, 1 to 2.9 mph • 2 reverse speeds, 1.2 and 1.3 mph • 5-yr. warranty on parts, 2-yr. on labor • 41x26x60 in.
This very heavy machine cleared and threw snow well. Better than most in deep snow and clearing wet snow. Handling left something to be desired. Chute-turning crank conveniently mounted atop the console. Chute deflector can be adjusted without loosening hardware. Comes with wheel chains. Electric start optional. **Recommendation:** Very good, but expensive.

7 Sears Craftsman 247.88569 $1200

• 9 hp • 210 lb. • 26-in. swath • 6 forward speeds, 0.4 to 1.8 mph • 2 reverse speeds, 0.7 and 1 mph • 2-yr. warranty • 44x27x53 in.
Performed better than most in deep snow. Has weight-forward settings for dense, compact snow. Moves on tracks instead of tires. Convenient lever controls the chute deflector. But: Hard to handle. Control-cable adjustment mechanism is

hard to get at. No fuel-shutoff valve. Scraper isn't adjustable. **Model availability:** Discontinued; successor: 247.88850, $1100. **Recommendation:** Very good, but it takes muscle to manage.

8 Troy-Bilt 42010 $1200

• 8 hp • 270 lb. • 24-in. swath • 5 forward speeds, 0.8 to 2 mph • 2 reverse speeds, 0.1 and 0.7 mph • 7-yr. warranty • 41x25x61 in.

Better than most at clearing wet snow. Unusual features include a heated handle, an easily adjusted chute deflector, and an automatic differential to make turning easier, although it tended to lose traction in deep or icy snow. Included wheel chains may help improve traction in those conditions. Electric start optional. But: Auger often stayed engaged even though we released the handlebar controls, which poses a safety hazard; mechanical adjustment can remedy the problem. Console-mounted chute-turning crank didn't move very smoothly. Handle is a bit low for tall users. **Recommendation:** Very good performance, but some annoying and dangerous quirks.

9 Toro 622 Power Throw $850

• 6 hp • 158 lb. • 22-in. swath • 3 forward speeds, 0.8 to 1.9 mph • 1.2-mph reverse speed • 2-yr. warranty • 44x24x55 in.

Chute deflector can be adjusted without loosening hardware. Partial guard helps keep hands out of the discharge chute. Slightly quieter than others. Electric start optional. But: Deadman controls aren't interlocked for one-hand operation, and they're rather stiff and hard to hold down. Scraper isn't adjustable. **Recommendation:** Very good overall.

10 Simplicity 860E $1420

• 8 hp • 253 lb. • 24-in. swath • 5 forward speeds, 0.3 to 2.3 mph • 2 reverse speeds, 1 and 1.5 mph • 2-yr. warranty • 42x26x56 in.

Cleared wet snow very well. Chute-turning crank conveniently mounted atop the console. Partial guard helps keep hands out of the discharge chute. Comes with wheel chains. But: Deadman controls are rather stiff and hard to hold down. Slightly noisier than most. **Recommendation:** Very good overall.

11 John Deere 826D $1240

• 8 hp • 192 lb. • 26-in. swath • 6 forward speeds, 0.6 to 2 mph • 2 reverse speeds, 0.5 and 0.8 mph • 2-yr. warranty • 42x28x51 in.

Performed better than most in deep snow. Convenient console-mounted lever controls chute deflector. But: Deadman controls aren't interlocked for one-hand operation. No provision to free a drive wheel for easier turning. Chute-turning crank sticks out from the back and can get in your way. Scraper isn't adjustable. **Recommendation:** Very good overall.

12 Sears Craftsman 536.88665 $1150

• 8.5 hp • 227 lb. • 28-in. swath • 6 forward speeds, 0.7 to 2.5 mph • 2 reverse speeds, 1 and 1.7 mph • 2-yr. warranty • 49x31x62 in.

Better than most at clearing wet snow. Only machine tested with both chute-turning crank and chute-deflector lever conveniently mounted on the console. But: Deadman controls are rather stiff and hard to hold down. Handle may be too high even for tall users. Lacks fuel-shutoff valve. **Model availability:** Discontinued. **Recommendation:** Very good overall.

13 Snapper I5223 $900

• 5 hp • 139 lb. • 22-in. swath • 4 forward speeds, 0.8 to 2.1 mph • 0.7-mph reverse speed • 2-qt. gas tank • 2-yr. warranty • 44x24x52 in.

Handle height can be adjusted somewhat. Engine is slightly quieter than most. Comes with wheel chains. But: Deadman controls aren't interlocked for one-hand operation. No provision to free a drive wheel for easier turning. Speed-control lever is low and hard to reach. Scraper isn't adjustable. **Recommendation:** Very good overall.

14 Sears Craftsman 536.88612 $750

• 5 hp • 142 lb. • 22-in. swath • 6 forward speeds, 0.7 to 2.7 mph • 2 reverse speeds, 1.1 and 1.9 mph • 2-qt. gas tank • 2-yr. warranty • 45x23x47 in.

Slightly quieter than most. But: Performance in deep snow was worse than most. Deadman controls aren't interlocked, but inconvenient one-hand operation is still possible. Speed-control lever is low and hard to reach. No fuel-shutoff valve. **Model availability:** Discontinued, but may still be available. **Recommendation:** Very good overall, but there are better choices.

15 Simplicity 555M $960

• 5 hp • 173 lb. • 22-in. swath • 5 forward speeds, 0.6 to 2.5 mph • 2 reverse speeds, 1.1 and 1.6

Can't find a model? Call the manufacturer. See page 342.

Ratings continued ▶

Ratings, continued

mph • 2-qt. gas tank • 2-yr. warranty • 42x25x49 in.
Chute-turning crank conveniently mounted atop the console. Partial guard helps keep hands out of the discharge chute. Slightly quieter than others. Comes with wheel chains. Electric start optional. But: Performance in deep snow was worse than most. Deadman controls aren't interlocked for one-hand operation, and they're rather stiff and hard to hold down. Scraper isn't adjustable. **Recommendation:** Good, but there are better choices.

16 **MTD 611D** $600

• 5 hp • 147 lb. • 22-in. swath • 5 forward speeds, 0.7 to 2.4 mph • 2 reverse speeds, 0.7 and 1.1 mph • 2-qt. gas tank • 2-yr. warranty, plus 90-day no-fault coverage • 43x24x52 in.
Slightly quieter than most. But: Performance in deep snow was worse than most. Deadman controls aren't interlocked for one-hand operation. Speed-control lever is low and hard to reach. Scraper isn't adjustable. **Recommendation:** Good, but there are better choices.

17 **Troy-Bilt 42000** $800

• 5 hp • 158 lb. • 21-in. swath • 3 forward speeds, 0.6 to 2.2 mph • 1.1-mph reverse speed • 2-qt. gas tank • 7-yr. warranty • 43x22x58 in.
Easily adjusted chute deflector. Quiet. Comes with wheel chains. Electric start optional. But: Deadman controls aren't interlocked for one-hand operation, require large hands to hold, and are rather hard to hold down. No provision to free a drive wheel for easier turning. Speed-control lever doesn't have positive engagement. Chute-turning crank didn't turn very smoothly. **Model availability:** Discontinued. **Recommendation:** Good, but there are better choices.

Single-stage models

18 **John Deere TRS21** $640

• 5 hp • 83 lb. • 21-in. swath • 2-yr. warranty • 37x22x46 in.
Auger propels this model briskly. Very easy to handle, threw snow quite far. But: Slightly noisier than most. Chute-turning crank didn't turn smoothly. Lacks fuel-shutoff valve. Similar: TRS21 without electric start, $540. **Recommendation:** Good overall. **A CR Best Buy.**

19 **Honda HS621A** $740

• 5.5 hp • 91 lb. • 20-in. swath • 2-yr. warranty • 38x23x47 in.
Threw snow farthest of all single-stage units. Has four-stroke engine. Auger propels the machine briskly. Slightly quieter than most. Adjustable scraper. Chute deflector can be adjusted without loosening hardware. Has fuel-shutoff valve. Electric start optional. But: Chute-turning crank became stiff during use. Folding the handle requires tools. Similar: HS621AS, $830. **Recommendation:** Good overall, but expensive.

20 **Toro CCR3000GTS** $750

• 5 hp • 75 lb. • 20-in. swath • 2-yr. warranty • 41x21x42 in.
Auger propels this machine briskly. Chute deflector can be adjusted without loosening hardware. But: Extremely stiff chute-turning crank (even when we installed a new gear). Folding the handle requires tools. **Recommendation:** Good, but expensive.

21 **Murray Ultra G2145060** $410

• 4.5 hp • 65 lb. • 21-in. swath • 2-yr. warranty • 37x22x39 in.
A notch below the top single-stage machines. Auger propels machine weakly. Slightly noisier than others. Hard to access spark plug. **Model availability:** Discontinued, but may still be available. Succeeded by 621450x4, $400. **Recommendation:** Fair.

22 **MTD 140** $310

• 3 hp • 54 lb. • 21-in. swath • 1-qt. gas tank • 2-yr. warranty plus 90-day no-fault coverage • 35x21x41 in.
Adjustable and reversible scraper. Electric start optional. But: Engine is slightly noisier than most. Handle a bit low for tall users. Auger control-cable adjuster is hard to get at. Similar: MTD Gold 31A-142-382, $320. **Recommendation:** Fair overall.

23 **Sears Craftsman 536.88468** $550

• 5 hp • 65 lb. • 21-in. swath • 1.6-qt. gas tank • 2-yr. warranty • 39x22x42 in.
Hard to access spark plug. **Model availability:** Discontinued. **Recommendation:** Fair overall.

24 White Snow Boss 50 $500

• 5 hp • 73 lb. • 20-in. swath • 2-yr. warranty • 40x22x42 in.

Chute deflector can be adjusted without loosening hardware. Handle can be adjusted to three positions. Engine slightly quieter than most. Electric start optional. But: Auger provides weak propulsion. Chute-turning crank didn't turn very smoothly. Cover must be unscrewed to adjust control cables. **Recommendation:** Fair overall.

25 Snapper LE317R $420

• 3 hp • 49 lb. • 17-in. swath • 2-yr. warranty • 35x19x44 in.

Cleared wet snow poorly. Auger provides weak propulsion. Chute-turning crank inconveniently mounted on the chute itself. Handle is a bit low for tall users. Slightly noisier than others. Electric start optional. **Recommendation:** Fair overall.

26 Sears Craftsman 536.88458 $450

• 3 hp • 52 lb. • 21-in. swath • 1-qt. gas tank • 1-yr. warranty • 35x22x39 in.

Cleared wet snow poorly; nearly stalled. Handle is a bit low for tall users. Hard to access spark plug. **Recommendation:** Fair overall. There are better choices.

27 Ariens SS522 $550

• 5 hp • 73 lb. • 22-in. swath • 5-yr. warranty • 40x22x42 in.

Convenient lever turns the discharge chute. Chute deflector can be adjusted without loosening hardware. Engine is slightly quieter than most. Handle can be adjusted to three positions. Electric start optional. But: Auger provided very weak propulsion. Hard to access spark plug. Similar: SS522E, $660. **Recommendation:** Fair overall. There are better choices.

Not Acceptable

28 Toro CCR Powerlite $430

• 3 hp • 37 lb. • 16-in. swath • 1-qt. gas tank • 2-yr. warranty • 36x16x41 in.

The Toro has no deadman control—as all other tested snow throwers do—to disengage the rapidly spinning auger while the engine is running. Someone reaching in to clear the discharge chute could seriously injure his or her hand.

How to use the Ratings in the Buying Guide

- Read the Recommendations for information on specific models and general buying advice.
- Note how the rated products are listed—in order of performance and convenience, price, or alphabetically.
- The overall score graph gives the big picture in performance. Notes on features and performance for individual models are listed in the Comments column or "Model details."
- Use the handy key numbers to find out more about a product.
- Before going to press, we verify model availability for most products with manufacturers. Some tested models listed in the Ratings may no longer be available. Discontinued models are noted in Model details or Comments. Such models may actually still be available in some stores for part of 1998. Models indicated as successors should perform similarly to the tested models, according to the manufacturer. Features may vary.
- Models similar to the tested models, when they exist, are indicated in Comments or Model details.
- To find our last full report on a subject, check the reference above the Ratings chart or the eight-year index, page 346.

Ratings *Child gates*

& Recommendations

The tests behind the Ratings

Overall score is based primarily on how easy the gate is to install, open, and close. **Ease of use** reflects tests by panelists whose hand strength varied. **Security** reflects how well the gate resisted being dislodged when we tried to knock or push it out of place. **Safety** reflects both the gate's adherence to the published standards and other safety considerations—including how easily the gate can be climbed. **Price** is approximate retail.

Recommendations

A mounted gate is the best choice for any location where safety is paramount. The safest choice we found for stairs is the Kidco Safeway Gate G20 ($60), followed by the North States Supergate III ($20). Of the pressure gates we tested, the Kidco Gateway G10 ($70) would best resist a child's buffeting and has a convenient door that you can open with one hand.

See Buying Guide Report, page 168. Last time rated in CONSUMER REPORTS: January 1997.

Overall Ratings

E ⊜ VG ⊖ G ○ F ◒ P ●

Within types, listed in order of overall score

Key no.	Brand and model (similar models)	Price	Overall score (0–100; P F G VG E)	Max. width measured	Ease of use	Security	Safety
	MOUNTED GATES						
1	**Kidco** Safeway Gate G20	$60		43½ in.	⊜	⊜	⊜
2	**Fisher-Price** AutoLock Gate 9263	35		42	⊜	⊜	⊖
3	**Gerry** Extra Wide Expansion Gate 160	30		60	⊖	⊜	○
4	**Gerry** Wood Slat Security Gate 1048 (1096)	18		48	⊖	⊜	⊖
5	**North States** Supergate III 8615	20		42	○/⊖[1]	⊜/●[1]	⊖/⊖[1]
6	**North States** Supergate V 8645 (8648)	45		62	○	⊜	○
	DOWNRATED						
7	**Seymour** Keepsafe Expansion Gate 13-036-60	20	Not scored	37	⊖	⊜	●
	PRESSURE-MOUNTED GATES						
8	**Kidco** Gateway G10	70		34	⊜	○	⊜
9	**Gerry** Soft Gate 524 (526)	22		42	⊖	◒	⊜

[1] *Judgment when used as a pressure-mounted gate.*

Key no.	Brand and model (similar models)	Price	Overall score (0–100; P F G VG E)	Max. width measured	Ease of use	Security	Safety
	PRESSURE-MOUNTED GATES *continued*						
10	**Gerry** Quick-Release Gate 222	$18		42 in.	⊖	◒	⊖
11	**Gerry** 4 Sure Gate 525	18		42	⊖	●	⊖
12	**Gerry** Plastic Mesh Security Gate 202 (662)	12		42	⊖	●	○
13	**Seymour** Guardmaster Security Gate 13-276-55 (13-378-11)	15		41	⊖	●	○
14	**Fisher-Price** QuickLock Gate 9262	30		42	○	●	⊖

Model details

Mounted gates

1 Kidco Safeway Gate G20 $60

Best gate for use at top of stairs. Poor instructions.

2 Fisher-Price AutoLock Gate 9263 $35

Convenient; good value. **Model availability:** Discontinued.

3 Gerry Extra Wide Expansion Gate 160 $30

Good choice for wide openings, but lock hard to use.

4 Gerry Wood Slat Security Gate 1048 (1096) $18

Excellent value, but lock hard to use.

5 North States Supergate III 8615 $20

Can be safely used at top of stairs. Hard to install. Lock hard to open. Can also be pressure-mounted.

6 North States Supergate V 8645 (8648) $45

Better in wide openings than narrow ones. **Model availability:** Discontinued; successor: V8648, $40.

Downrated

7 Seymour Keepsafe Expansion Gate 13-036-60 $20

This gate may snag a child's clothing. Comes in three larger widths. All are downrated.

Pressure gates

8 Kidco Gateway G10 $70

Expensive, but the most secure pressure-mounted gate (and only swing-design one). 6-inch extensions available ($20). Poor instructions.

9 Gerry Soft Gate 524 (526) $22

Especially good for uneven openings, traveling.

10 Gerry Quick-Release Gate 222 $18

Has quick release. Hard to set proper width.

11 Gerry 4 Sure Gate 525 $18

Good choice for uneven openings.

12 Gerry Plastic Mesh Security Gate 202 (662) $12

Using lock requires strong hands.

13 Seymour Guardmaster Security Gate 13-276-55 (13-378-11) $15

Using lock requires strong hands.

14 Fisher-Price QuickLock Gate 9262 $30

Easiest gate to dislodge. **Model availability:** Discontinued.

Ratings *Bicycle helmets*

& Recommendations

The tests behind the Ratings

Overall score is primarily based on impact absorption, with roll-off resistance, ventilation, strap adjustment, and weight also considered. **Impact protection** reflects how well the helmet fared when dropped from a succession of heights onto metal blocks of various shapes. **Roll-off** reflects how well the helmet stayed in place after it was fitted correctly on the head. **Venting** reflects judgments from three expert riders. Toddler models were judged by assessing design. **Straps** reflects both ease of adjustment and how well the strap guides stayed in place. **Price** is based on a national survey. Models similar to those we tested are noted in the Model details; features may vary.

Typical features for these models

• Removable sizing pads in several thicknesses, held in place by hook-and-loop (Velcro) fasteners. • Side straps that adequately maintain their adjustments. • One-year warranty.

Recommendations

For now, you should limit your choices to models with a buckle type that passed our tests—models without a footnote. Some good choices: The two Bell models, the EVO2 Pro ($100) and the Psycho Pro ($85); and the Pro-Action Illusion ($25), **a CR Best Buy.** The Illusion is sized "for women only," but it would fit males with small heads. Another fine choice is the Specialized Air Wave Mega ($35), a youth helmet that also comes in an adult version, the Specialized Air Wave.

See Buying Guide report, page 156. Last time rated in CONSUMER REPORTS: June 1997.

Overall Ratings

E VG G F P

Within types, listed in order of overall score

Key no.	Brand and model	Price	Overall score (0–100; P F G VG E)	Impact protection	Roll-off	Venting	Straps
	ADULT MODELS						
1	**Giro** Helios RL [1]	$135		VG	E	E	E
2	**Bell** EVO2 Pro	100		VG	E	VG	E
3	**Bell** Psycho Pro	85		VG	E	VG	E

Key no.	Brand and model	Price	Overall score (0–100; P F G VG E)	Impact protection	Roll-off	Venting	Straps
	ADULT MODELS *continued*						
4	**Pro-Action** Illusion **A CR Best Buy**	$ 25		VG	E	G	G
5	**Bell** Tsunami Pro [2]	50		VG	VG	G	E
6	**Bell** Image Pro	60		G	E	VG	E
7	**Rollerblade** City Gear [1]	35		G	E	G	G
8	**Specialized** Air Cut	45		VG	G	F	G
	YOUTH MODELS						
9	**Specialized** Air Wave Mega	35		VG	E	G	G
10	**Bell** Maniac Pro [2]	40		VG	E	F	VG
11	**Bell** Warped [2]	25		VG	E	F	E
12	**Pro-Action** Radio Active [1]	10		G	E	F	G
13	**PTI** Hydrogen	20		VG	P	F	P
14	**PTI** Cool Cats Deluxe	13		VG	F	P	P
	TODDLER MODELS						
15	**Bell** Li'l Bell Shell Pro [2]	30		VG	E	P	E
16	**Pro-Action** Ocean Friends	20		G	E	P	G
17	**PTI** Kid Cats	15		G	E	P	P

[1] Buckle didn't fail in our tests of this helmet, but is a buckle type that failed on some other 1997 helmets (see report, page 156). [2] Buckle failed on some 1997 samples of this helmet (see report).

Model details

Adult models

1 Giro Helios RL $135 [1]
Strap-independent rear stabilizer (used to adjust fit). Locking strap guides. $40 crash-replacement charge; 3-yr. limit. 10-oz. weight. 1996 models have buckle that passed tests. **Model availability:** Discontinued.

2 Bell EVO2 Pro $100
Strap-independent rear stabilizer. Brow pad. Locking strap guides. Detachable visor. $30 crash-replacement charge. 11-oz. weight. Similar: EVO Pro, $90.

3 Bell Psycho Pro $85
Strap-independent rear stabilizer. Locking strap guides. Detachable visor. $30 crash-replacement charge. 11-oz. weight.

4 Pro-Action Illusion $25
Claimed "for women only"; smaller sizes than most, liner accommodates ponytails. 2-yr. warranty. Free crash replacement. 10-oz. weight. **A CR Best Buy.**

5 Bell Tsunami Pro $50 [2]
Strap-independent rear stabilizer. Locking strap guides, detachable visor. $30 crash-replacement charge. 12-oz. weight. 1996 models have buckle that passed tests.

6 Bell Image Pro $60
Strap-independent rear stabilizer. Locking strap

Ratings continued

Ratings, continued

guides. Detachable visor. $30 crash-replacement charge. 11-oz. weight.

7 Rollerblade City Gear $35 [1]

Has extended rear coverage for multisport use. Strap-dependent rear stabilizer. 2-yr. warranty; free crash replacement. 10-oz. weight. Similar: City Gear Jr., $30 (youth model). 1996 models have buckle that passed tests.

8 Specialized Air Cut $45

Strap-dependent rear stabilizer. $20 crash-replacement charge. 9-oz. weight. But: When wet, straps stretched slightly more in tests than standards allow.

Youth models

9 Specialized Air Wave Mega $35

Strap-independent rear stabilizer. Detachable visor. $10 crash-replacement charge. 10-oz. weight. But: When wet, straps streched slightly more in tests than standards allow. Similar: Air Wave, $35 (adult model).

10 Bell Maniac Pro $40 [2]

Strap-dependent rear stabilizer. Locking strap guides. Detachable visor. 11-oz. weight. Similar: Jumpstart Pro, $35. Adult models: Vertigo Pro, $40; Oasis Pro, $30. 1996 models have buckle that passed tests.

11 Bell Warped $25 [2]

Available only at Price Costco stores. Locking strap guides. Detachable visor. 10-oz. weight. Similar: Copper Canyon Sedona, $25 (available only at Target stores); Havoc, $30; Comet, $15. Adult model: Laguna, $25.

12 Pro-Action Radio Active $10 [1]

Claimed suitable for multisport use, but design similar to typical bike helmet. 2-yr. warranty. $4.50 crash-replacement charge. 9-oz. weight. Comes in adult sizes.

13 PTI Hydrogen $20

Straps must be adjusted very tight to prevent roll-off. Claimed suitable for multisport use, but design similar to typical bike helmet. No warranty, but free crash replacement. 9-oz. weight.

14 PTI Cool Cats Deluxe $13

Straps must be kept very tight to prevent roll-off. Strap guides tend to slip. No warranty, but free crash replacement. 9-oz. weight.

Toddler models

15 Bell Li'l Bell Shell Pro $30 [2]

Locking strap guides. 9-oz. weight. 1996 models have buckle that passed tests.

16 Pro-Action Ocean Friends $20

No warranty, but free crash replacement. 9-oz. weight.

17 PTI Kid Cats $15

No warranty, but free crash replacement. 10-oz. weight. Similar: Kid Cats Fun Prints, $17.

For the most recent product Ratings

See the monthly issues of CONSUMER REPORTS magazine. Or check out Consumer Reports Online. Our Web site *(www.ConsumerReports.org)* covers autos, appliances, electronics gear, more. Free areas provide useful listings, recalls, shopping guidance. Members pay $2.95 per month for unlimited use, including searchable access to test reports and product Ratings.

Home Office

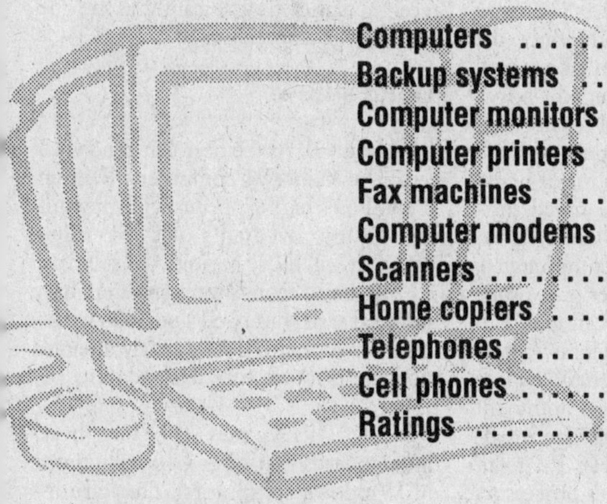

Computers

Most computers perform at a commendably high level. Base your choice on features, speed, reliability, and service.

Last CR report: September 1997
Price range: $1000 to $3000

What's available

Family PC or office PC? Family computers come with educational, financial, and entertainment software, a sound system, and a modem. Many manufacturers also offer computers for the home office that are virtually identical to family machines, but with more business software and less of a sound system. If you intend to use the computer primarily for work, a package like this is the better choice.

Macintosh or Windows? A PC running Windows and a Mac OS machine are comparable, though Macs still have the edge in ease of setting up and converting peripherals. You need not worry if you use Windows at the office and a Mac at home; most files and documents can be translated from one system to the other. (It's easier to translate PC to Mac than vice versa.)

Desktop or notebook? A desktop computer gives you the most capability for the money. But it takes up precious room and is hard to move from place to place. If space or portability is important to you, a notebook computer may be a better choice, though you'll have to spend several hundred dollars extra to get the speed and memory that a desktop model offers.

Big name or custom clone? A number of lesser-known manufacturers sell computers through mail-order ads in computer magazines. But unless you know that the company offers good service, the few dollars you'll save won't be worth the trouble if repairs are needed.

Some computer stores and repair shops assemble customized computers. Such clones may cost more than a major brand and probably won't include much software besides Windows 95, but they can give you a broad choice of components.

How powerful? Computer processors, chips whose speeds are designated in megahertz (MHz), are twice as fast as they were a year ago—an incredible blaze of computer power. Intel, the dominant processor-maker, began 1997 by introducing 166- and 200-MHz Pentium MMX chips (MMX identifies processors designed to speed up certain new multimedia software). Just a few month later, Intel added 233-MHz MMX processors, plus a new generation the company dubbed Pentium II, with speeds of 233 MHz and up. Meanwhile, the Mac OS market kept pace, featuring new PowerPC processors that run at 250 MHz and higher. But computers powered by the newest chips won't offer value until computer and software allow Pentium II processors to achieve their full potential.

Reliability

Last year's Annual Questionnaire asked readers to tell us about their computers. Among desktop computers purchased new between 1993 and 1996, 5 percent became completely inoperable within their first month; another 18 percent had problems but still worked in that first month. Among seven brands of computers, Apple's repair history was among the best; Gateway 2000's among the worst. For more information, see brand repair histories and overall Ratings on page 10. But reader's satisfaction with the service they received mattered significantly, as the sidebar on page 221 shows.

What's new

Pentium II. As the next-generation processor for Windows computers, Pentium II combines higher speeds with the multimedia improvements of the Pentium MMX. It will likely become the standard.

USB port. Windows computers have universal serial bus (USB) ports, new outlets for easy connection of newly designed modems, printers, scanners and other peripherals.

PC98. This is a new set of long-overdue standards that Microsoft will impose on Windows computers. They are intended to standardize and improve the compatibility and convenience of Windows-based computers and peripherals.

Troubleshooting software. The AST and Packard Bell computers in our most recent test featured "system wizard" troubleshooting software. If the software can't solve a problem, it accesses a database on the Internet. In our tests, it did that even for what we thought were fairly simple problems.

Shopping strategy

For those who are in the market for a computer, first decide on the type: desktop or notebook, "family" or "office," Mac OS or Windows PC.

Another important decision is where to buy the computer. In a recent survey, only 60 percent of readers said they were completely or very satisfied with a retailer.

(Office Depot and Staples were among the retailers besting that overall average—see CONSUMER REPORTS, September 1997, for details.) By contrast, 77 percent of readers who ordered direct from a company like Dell or Gateway were satisfied.

Whenever you buy, be sure to check the store or mail-order company's return policy. Our survey showed that 23 percent of computers develop a problem within the first 30 days after purchase.

Since most computers perform at a commendably high level, you should consider reliability and servicing as much as—if not more than—raw processing speed.

Decide what to spend. If you're replacing an older computer, these features give the best performance and value: 200-MHz Pentium MMX processor (Windows) or 180-MHz PowerPC processor (Mac OS); 32 megabytes (MB) of RAM, 3.2-gigabyte (GB) hard drive, 256-kilobyte (K) cache memory; 8X CD-ROM drive, 28.8- or 33.6-kbps modem; 15-inch monitor; 100-megabyte removable storage disk. Such a computer starts at around $2000.

Those people can easily get along on something as "slow" as a 166-MHz Windows computer or a 132-MHz PowerPC Mac OS machine. You can probably still find such a machine at a

Satisfaction with service

In a recent survey of readers, satisfaction with the manufacturer's servicing was closely tied to overall rating. The findings for how easily reached by phone presented here closely parallel our own experience when we've phoned the companies for technical support. Overall, 28 percent said the problem was never fixed; 19 percent said it took over a week to fix the problem; and over 40 percent said the manufacturer was hard to reach.

Brand	Satisfaction with service (0–100)	Specifics: Able to fix problem	Fixed problem promptly	Easily reached by phone
Apple	75	⊖	⊖	⊜
Dell	71	○	○	○
Gateway 2000	69	⊖	○	○
IBM	68	○	○	⊖
Compaq	62	○	○	○
AST	61	○	○	●
Packard Bell	57	◒	◒	●

Based on more than 9000 reader responses to the 1996 Annual Questionnaire, describing the most recent problem with a desktop computer that led them to call the manufacturer for help. Data refer only to problems in 1995 and the first third of 1996. A score of 100 would mean all consumers were completely satisfied. Differences of less than 4 points in satisfaction with service aren't meaningful.

significant discount.

What's in the stores. Many brands are sold through mail-order catalogs. Brands like Dell and Gateway 2000 are sold primarily by mail or at their own Web sites. The rest are sold at various retail outlets. New models are introduced in the spring and may still be available—at more attractive prices—when the new lines appear in the fall.

Key features

• ***Standard on typical models:***

Processor. The standard processor for Windows machines is the Pentium; for Mac OS, it's the PowerPC. Last year, the typical computer's processor ran at a speed of 133 to 200 MHz. This year, the typical processor runs at 166 to 300 MHz.

Memory. These days, memory is fairly cheap. Buy at least 32 MB of RAM and 256 K of cache memory.

Hard drive. The typical storage capacity now exceeds 2 GB, or about 2000 MB. Many models offer a 4-GB or even a 6-GB hard drive.

Fax/modem. More and more, computers can be used like a telephone for voice messages and conversation, as well as for transfer of data. A 33.6-kbps modem with voice and fax capability is pretty much standard. Newer 56-kbps modems work with a growing number of Internet providers.

Software. Many computers come with full-fledged business applications, including a word processor, spreadsheet program, and graphics package. Others skimp with a useful but less versatile "works" package. Unfortunately, some computers we tested wasted huge amounts of hard-drive and menu space on promotional software of questionable value. A few Windows computers come with instructional software called a shell.

A computer needs no more than 300 megabytes of preinstalled software—100 MB for the operating system, 100 MB for core applications, and 100 MB for everything else. Most manufacturers provide a way to uninstall software. Some advise deleting the promotional software manually. But that's not a good idea, since manual deletion leaves residual pieces of the software on the hard drive.

Technical support. Most companies provide free support during the one-year warranty period; some offer three years.

Internet access. Computers typically include sign-up kits for online services and Internet providers.

• ***For special needs:***

Monitors, 17 inches and up. A 15-inch monitor is large enough for most needs. A 17-inch screen offers 28 percent more viewing area in theory but often not in reality. See page 225.

Multimedia. Some models include speakers intended for the manufacturer's multimedia monitors. In our tests, most Windows computers were able to properly recognize and set up a monitor when it was designed for "plug and play," the new standard to simplify installing peripherals. The Apple Macintosh has long been known for easy-to-install peripherals and its unfailing ability to recognize them.

Features for upgrading

Expansion bays. For Windows computers, the PC case should have at least two empty spaces for hard drives and the like, so you can add more or newer drives. At least one empty bay should have front-panel access for removable disks. External hard drives can easily be added to a Mac with an SCSI connector on the back panel.

Expansion slots. These are spaces for plug-in cards and most other add-ons. On PCs, look for a combination of PCI and ISA slots, so you can use current and future plug-in cards. Many Macs have spare PCI slots.

Graphics adapter. This determines the resolution, color range, and speed with which images display on the monitor. It typically includes at least 2 MB of its own memory (DRAM or the faster and costlier VRAM), which will display millions of colors at a resolution of 800x600 pixels. To allow for higher resolution in the future, look for a board that accepts at least 4 MB of video memory. A plug-in graphics card is better than one built into the motherboard, because it's easier to replace later on with a better one.

I/O ports. These are sockets for connecting an external device such as a printer or modem. An enhanced parallel port will communicate with external devices at higher speeds than a conventional parallel port on a Windows machine The new USB port will allow future devices to be connected.

Memory sockets. Part of the motherboard, these determine how much memory (RAM) you can add to speed up your computer and enhance its performance. Machines have memory chips mounted on small plug-in boards called SIMMS or DIMMS, usually in denominations of 8, 16, or 32 MB. The motherboard should have enough empty memory sockets to let you double memory without removing existing plug-in boards.

Motherboard. The design of this main circuit board largely determines how fast your computer can run and what types of components you can plug in. Most computers from major manufacturers are designed around each manufacturer's own motherboard, limiting how much they can be upgraded. Clone machines often use a universal motherboard known as ATX.

The motherboard should also have a "flash BIOS" that supports such industry standards as "plug and play" and power management. A typical motherboard has two integrated drive electronics (IDE) sockets to plug in an additional hard drive, CD-ROM drive, or the like.

Processor. As a rule, a 200-MHz processor is sufficient for most needs. If it exceeds your budget, drop down a notch or two in speed. But if you run the newest games or do a lot of graphics, you'll be happier with a faster processor.

Backup systems

A backup system lets you protect important files or store gigantic ones. There are many useful types.

Last CR report: March 1997
Expect to pay: $200 to $500

It's risky to keep critical records on the hard drive of your computer without backing them up. If you haven't made an independent copy and your computer crashes, you could lose important files.

Floppy disks can be used to back up a couple of files, but for copying the entire hard drive, backup systems are a better safety net. They have the capacity to store large amounts of data, and in the event of a crash, it's easier to restore several programs from a single backup than to reinstall each one from the original disks.

What's available

Tape. This is the oldest type of backup system. It consists of a drive, installed inside or connected by cable to the computer, that reads and writes data on a tape cassette. (The cassettes are incompatible with audiocassette players.)

A popular format, known as Travan, can store and retrieve large amounts of information—as much as an entire hard drive—at relatively low cost. But Travan drives are pretty slow, according to our tests. The slowest ones took at least two minutes to restore an individual file from tape and two hours to back up everything on a 1-GB (gigabyte) hard drive (the drive can do that while you sleep). A tape drive usually comes with its own backup software to copy and restore files.

Removable disk. This choice has gained in popularity and dropped in price during the past year. The drive, located inside or next to your computer, performs much like a hard drive. It reads and writes magnetic-disk cartridges and can back up a hard drive or restore a file more quickly than tape can. While a floppy disk holds a mere 2 megabytes (MB), a Zip disk holds 100MB; a Jaz disk holds 1 GB, equal to about 1000 MB.

Our tests showed a direct correlation between price and backup speed: Slower, less costly drives may back up data no faster than a typical tape drive.

Macintosh computers have long treated "external" hard drives as just another drive. Copying files to a PC peripheral has been trickier. But if your computer uses a new version of Windows, you don't need special software. You can copy files to a removable drive just as if it were a hard drive.

Adding a backup software program will make backups easier, however. Windows 95 includes such software, but it can't use more than one disk in a backup. Several stand-alone backup programs do. Seagate Backup, Cheyenne Backup, and Hewlett-Packard Colorado Backup programs all can handle Windows 95's longer file names, an essential requirement.

Hard drive. This is similar to your computer's hard drive. Adding a second 2-GB hard drive can cost as little as $200 for Windows computers, a bit more for Mac OS machines. You can choose an internal hardd drive (if there's a place for it inside the computer) or an external drive.

Some drawbacks to keep in mind: Because it's inside your computer, an internal hard drive won't protect against fire or theft. An external hard drive, which has a protective shell, may be awkward or too bulky to take along when you travel.

Internal or external. An internal drive is less expensive than an external drive and saves space, but it isn't always easy to install—you may need to have the dealer do the work.

An external drive can be easy to install; it's the only choice if the computer has no spare drive bay. Some external drives connect to a computer's printer port; the printer then connects to the backup drive, not directly to the computer.

Although easy to install, drives that use the printer port can take two hours to back up 1-GB of data—too slow for full backup purposes.

A backup drive is about the size of a large paperback book. It can be internal or external for Windows computers; Mac OS computer nearly always use external disk cartridges for backup. External backup drives get their power from an AC adapter and attach to the computer by cable.

Internal ones fit into an empty drive bay in the computer case.

Shopping strategy

People using a Windows machine have many options available. If you just need an inexpensive way to back up an entire hard drive now and then and you don't mind having slow hardware, look for a tape drive that backs up 1 GB or more on a single $20 tape.

If you intend to back up data on a weekly or monthly basis, consider a system with 1 to 2 GB of capacity. A smaller-capacity system will work if it uses removable tape cassettes or disk cartridges. If you think you can forgo full backups, you'll need less than 1 GB of capacity—just enough to store your important files. For daily backups, a low-capacity removable disk system should suffice.

Mac OS users usually are limited to removable disks. For backing up an entire drive quickly, consider a removable disk like the SyQuest SyJet ($500). It can also substitute for a hard drive with essentially unlimited capacity.

Decide what to spend. The greater the storage capacity and the faster the backup speed, the more you can expect to pay. If you need a backup drive mostly to save new work or important files, consider a removable-disk drive priced between $150 and $300.

What's in the stores. Iomega and SyQuest are the most widely sold brands of backup system.

Key features

Backup software. Lets you manage the process by which files are stored to and retrieved from the backup media. Tape backup drives come with software, while disk backup drives often rely on existing or user-provided software.

Capacity. Some manufacturers claim their backup systems have capacities twice as large as the numbers we found. Those claims are based on the assumption that backup software will be able to compress many files to less than half their original size, but not all files are so pliant.

Computer monitors

A 15-inch screen is a good choice for most uses—and a far better value than a 17-inch monitor.

Last CR report: September 1997
Expect to pay: $300 to $1000

What's available

Desktop monitors, like TV sets, come in sizes based on the diagonal measurement of the tube; 14, 15, 17, and 21 inches are available, but 15-inch models are the biggest sellers. The advertised size may be substantially larger—often, about an inch—than the actual size of the image. It depends on how much tube the housing reveals and how the electronics "size" the image. Some manufacturers have begun to comply with voluntary standards by stating the visual image size (VIS). But the only sure way you'll know the actual screen size is to measure it in the store.

The 15-inch size is a good choice for most home offices. A 17-inch monitor is useful if you need to view as much of a full page of text as possible or if you need to view several items simultaneously. But a 17-inch model can be considerably more expensive than a 15-inch monitor, and it's heavier and bulkier, limiting where you can place it.

What's new

Thin, lightweight monitors are the latest design, based on the technology used in notebook-computer displays. They're expensive—$1000 to $3000—but prices are expected to drop within a year.

Shopping strategy

If your 14-inch monitor is on the blink or seems too small to display the software you use when doing routine work, it's worth upgrading to a 15-inch monitor. First-time buyers should also consider that size first. Bigger monitors—17 inches or larger—don't give as much bang for the buck, but they do present larger images and show more of the image you're working with. When shopping, measure the dimensions yourself.

Good bets for monitors include the 15-inch NEC MultiSync XV15+ ($400) and the 17-inch XV17+ ($700), both rated excellent in our most recent tests and still available. In the store, look at a page of fine text on the screen, making sure the center and edges are uniformly clear and bright. Check for contrast by looking at a graphic or picture. If a screen has high contrast, images and text will be bright and crisp, and the difference between black and white will be dramatic.

Decide what to spend. A 15-inch monitor costs between $300 and $500; a 17-inch monitor, between $600 and $1000. Within a size category, spending more gets you features useful to professional and sophisticated users: high-resolution modes, advanced-display controls. Don't pay extra for high-resolution modes that aren't supported by the video card or monitor driver in your computer. Check with the monitor manufacturer to be sure you have the latest version of its software specific to your monitor.

You need at least one megabyte of video memory to show 65,536 colors at 800x600 resolution for a good display on a 15-inch monitor. More memory is needed when you use a higher resolution or more colors. If you want your monitor to produce more colors (useful if you work with photos), you might need more video memory or, for $100 to $250, a new video card.

Some discounters and mail-order dealers may keep prices down by bundling computers with inferior monitors. Don't buy if the dealer won't let you compare monitors in the store, won't allow a reasonable time to try the monitor at home, or won't provide the size and features you want.

What's in the stores. Major computer makers—Apple, Compaq, IBM, Packard Bell—all market their own brand of monitors. Other leading brands include NEC, Samsung, Sony, and View-Sonic. Superstores like CompUSA offer a wide selection and return privileges.

Key features

Standard features include adjustments for screen height and width, picture centering and picture geometry, and controls for brightness and contrast.

• ***Also standard on most models:***

Power management. This allows the computer to regulate the electricity use by, for example, turning the screen off when you're not using it. Virtually all new monitors have this feature, but it may not be supported by older video cards.

• *Recommended if available:*

Dot pitch. This refers to the spacing between phosphor dots on the picture tube that produce an image. Look for a model with a dot pitch of 0.28 mm or less. The smaller, the better, but also the more expensive.

Plug and play. This feature allows you to quickly install the monitor for best performance.

Refresh rate. This tells you how many times per second the full image is redrawn on the picture tube. A monitor used at a refresh rate of 70 hertz (Hz) or more will produce images without any noticeable flicker.

Resolution. This measures the number of picture elements, or pixels, on the screen. All else being equal, the higher the resolution, the sharper the image, and often the higher the price. If you choose a 15-inch monitor, look for one with a resolution of 800x600 or higher.

Viewable image size. Look for a model where the VIS is closest to the nominal size.

• *For special uses:*

Color control. If you use the computer for projects like drawing, look for controls such as color temperature or color balance, which fine-tune colors.

Computer printers

If speed is most important, consider a laser printer. Ink-jet printers print black-and-white text that's comparable—and they print in color.

Last CR report: October 1996
Expect to pay: $200 to $1000

What's available

Ink-jet printers. Ink-jet machines use a print head that moves across the page, spraying liquid ink through ultrafine jets as rollers scroll the page up. To produce an array of colors and tones, most ink-jet printers mix four colors—cyan (blue-green), magenta, yellow, and black. The quality of black-and-white text is almost as good as that of a laser printer. Graphics are better from a laser (or the laser's close relative, the LED printer). Ink-jets also print in color, something only very expensive lasers can do.

You can expect two to three pages of text per minute from the typical ink-jet model, more at the low-resolution setting. Printing graphics usually takes much longer, up to several minutes per page. Color photos are typically the slowest to print.

Paper and ink costs, while low for printing plain text, can be quite high if you print a lot of densely colored pages. Price range for ink-jets: $100 to $500.

Laser and LED printers. These printers produce images with a scanning laser or an array of LEDs (light-emitting diodes). Like photocopiers, they create images using toner, quickly reproducing an almost limitless variety of type forms and sizes. They don't do as good a job as ink-jets in reproducing gray areas, so graphics and photos are rendered less clear. Home laser models print only in black and white; color capability is still limited to high-priced business machines. Laser printers are fast. Pages typically print at a rate of four to eight pages per minute.

Laser and LED models typically take

up less space than ink-jet models or older laser printers. Price range: $200 to $500 for a black-and-white model; color lasers start at $3000.

What's new

Text pages printed on plain copier paper by the best new ink-jet printers are as crisp as those from laser printers. You'll find some good quality ink-jets priced as low as $230, at least $100 less than low-end ink-jets from a few years ago. Prices for laser printerss haven't fallen quite so dramatically.

Shopping strategy

If print speed is not a priority, we recommend an ink-jet model.

If work space is at a premium and you also need a fax machine, consider a multifunction machine—a fax machine that also serves as a printer (see "Fax machines," page 229). Make sure the printer you choose is compatible with your computer.

Most printers work exclusively with either the Windows or Macintosh operating system. A few will work with both. Many PC-compatible printers work in both Windows and DOS, though you lose some features in DOS. DOS users should pay attention to the number of fonts that reside in the printer, since you may be limited to using only those. Windows and Macintosh models let you use any fonts stored on the hard drive.

Decide what to spend. A good color ink-jet printer can cost as little as $200. Entry-level laser machines cost less than $400. High-end laser or LED printers usually provide a bit more speed, more resident memory, network connectivity, and improved graphics performance, while higher-priced ink-jets usually offer better color quality. You'll also pay extra to get a printer that uses PostScript, a printer language used for desktop publishing.

Cost per page. Ink-jets typically use 3 or 4 cents' worth of ink to print a page of text, compared to 1 or 2 cents' worth of toner for laser printers. With color printing, ink-jet costs can increase to several dollars per page, especially when printing photographs.

That's partly because most ink-jet printers use a color cartridge that must be replaced entirely, at $20 to $30, when any one color runs out. There are kits that let you refill the cartridges yourself to cut costs, but they may affect print quality. And if you break something in the process, your warranty probably won't cover those repairs.

Using specialty papers to print photos and graphics may enhance quality, but will add more to the cost per page. Glossy paper that gives crisp color and resolution can cost up to $2 per sheet; less expensive coated papers can run 5 to 15 cents per page.

What's in the stores. Hewlett-Packard leads the market; other brands include Apple, Canon, Epson, and Lexmark. Color ink-jet printers are the most widely sold type; black-and-white-only ink-jets have all but disappeared. Most printers are purchased from electronics and computer stores, office and supply chains like Staples, or discount outlets like Wal-Mart.

Key considerations

Dots per inch (dpi). This reflects the fineness of detail the printer can reproduce. Most new printers deliver 600 dpi, some as many as 1440 dpi. However, more is not necessarily better. Print quality also depends on the type of paper you use, the speed of printing, the quality of inks in the printer, and the type of file you're printing. Six hundred dpi is enough for most users.

Label printing. All lasers can do this. Some ink-jet printers cannot.

Memory. It's no longer so important that a printer have the memory to download an entire print order. That's because many PCs run in Windows, which allows users to regain control of their computer soon after sending a document to print. The Macintosh operating system has long had such a "background" arrangement. Computers with a large memory can speed up the printing of large files, such as graphics, by letting the printer handle the file piecemeal.

Printer languages. Most consumer-level printers use the Hewlett-Packard Printer Control Language. Like PostScript, a cheaper printer language used for desktop publishing, PCL helps ensure that documents will look the same when printed on any PCL-compatible machine.

Speed of printing. Most ink-jet units print between one and three pages per minute (ppm) of black text in "letter quality" mode, although some manufacturers say that their machines can attain six to eight ppm in draft mode. Ink-jets can't outpace laser printers—although the speediest ink-jets are nearly as fast (three ppm) as the slowest lasers.

Two-sided printing. Some computer software allows two-sided printing: You print the odd-numbered pages of a document, flip the paper, and then print the even-numbered pages.

Fax machines

Fax performance is fairly uniform. Multifunction machines can copy, print, and scan, but you sacrifice quality for the compact "footprint."

Last CR report: September 1997
Ratings: page 244
Expect to pay: $200 to $800

What's available

Fax-only or multifunction? A fax-only machine is an inexpensive and space-efficient choice for sending or receiving faxes and even making photocopies. Multifunction machines also serve as a printer for IBM-compatible computers (multifunction models aren't available for Macintosh computers), a scanner for importing text or images into your computer, and a telephone answering machine. Price range of fax-only models: $200 to $400. Price range of multifunction models: $300 to $800.

Thermal or plain paper? Both fax-only and multifunction models print on either thermal or plain paper. The type of paper a machine uses doesn't affect the quality of the faxes it produces, but it does affect how long the faxes last and what they cost to print.

Thermal paper yellows and fades over time, making it unsuitable for archiving. For faxes that don't fade, you need a plain-paper machine. These print in one of three ways. The best models (all multifunction machines) use either ink-jet or laser printing like a computer printer.

Plain-paper fax-only models use a technology known as thermal transfer, in which a heated printhead sears images onto a continuous heat-sensitive film, which then transfers them onto the paper. Machines that use thermal technology—either thermal paper or thermal-transfer printing—are relatively expensive to use. Expect per-and-printing costs of about 6 to 8 cents per page, compared with 3 to 5 cents for many fax machines that use ink-jet or laser printing.

What's new

More and more multifunction fax models are available. Features continue to proliferate, particularly on the combo machines.

Shopping strategy

If you only send and receive faxes informally, a fax-only thermal-paper machine generally makes the best choice. For business use, a fax-only machine that uses plain paper may be a better, if slightly bulkier, alternative. Consider a multifunction machine if you're short on space and can live with a slightly lower-quality printing than most dedicated computer printers provide.

Decide what to spend. Fax-only machines range in price from about $200 to $400, with plain-paper models usually more expensive. Multifunction machines range in price from $300 to about $800. Fax performance is fairly uniform, but higher-end machines were markedly better at printing than low-priced ones in our tests.

What's in the stores. Office discount outlets often have broad selections at low prices. Retail office-supply dealers may provide better service. Prices at mail-order outlets can be low, but you can't look goods over before you buy. For mail-order sources, consult a computer magazine such as Computer Shopper.

Using the Ratings. We tested multifunction and fax-only machines, rating factors such as the appearance of received faxes and how well faxes resisted fading and curling. Similar models should perform much the same as the tested models; features may vary. If you can't find a model, call the manufacturer; see page 342.

Key features

• *Standard on most models:*

Copier capability. All models can be used to make photocopies, at about 30 seconds per page. None copy as well as any home copier we've tested.

Fax/tel switch enables operation on a phone line used for voice calls.

Remote start to initate reception from extension phones.

Transmission-resolution switch, with fine, photo, and standard settings.

• *Standard on most multifunction machines:*

Digital clock to schedule delayed-send feature.

Scanning. Most multifunction models let you import text or images scanned by the machine into your computer. Photos—albeit only in black and white—can be used immediately by a graphics program. Text requires a two-stage process. After scanning, it has to be "read" by an optical-character-recognition (OCR) program before it can be edited on the computer. In our tests, multifunction machines with scanning were accurate enough. But as with copying, none was as good as a dedicated device.

Speaker to hear transmissions.

Telephone handset.

• *Useful for some:*

Ability to "poll," or call another machine in order to receive a document from it, and to be polled.

Broadcast capability. The ability to send the same fax (as long as memory permits) to many destinations without having to scan it over and over.

Built-in telephone answering machine. Typical features include automatic message count, personal mailboxes, time-and-date stamp, and remote retrieval of messages.

Caller ID. Fax number of the sender (or, for voice calls, phone number of the caller) is displayed, providing you subscribe to your phone company's caller-ID service.

Delayed sending. Delays transmitting a document until a programmed time, say, when phone rates are lower.

Distinctive-ring detection. Allows the machine to take advantage of a phone-company service that gives you distinctive rings for multiple phone numbers on an existing single phone line.

Document feeder. Holds pages for copying or feeding. Large capacity is useful for long documents.

Dual access. Allows you to set a fax to transmit while the machine is receiving a fax or (with multifunction models) printing a document.

Error-correction mode (ECM). Helps the machine maintain high accuracy on a noisy line.

Memory. Lets you store a number of fax pages—typically 20 to 30—that are received after the machine jams or its paper runs out. Memory also lets you create broadcast lists or lets you use another fax machine to retrieve faxes sent to your machine. Memory usually must be shared with the fax machine's built-in answering machine, if it has one, but you often can elect to store only faxes or only voice calls.

OCR programs. Provided with some multifunction machines that have a scanner, this software allows you to edit scanned text. (You can also buy OCR software for $200 or more.)

Output tray. Holds faxed or printed pages; eliminates a paper heap on the floor or your desk.

Pager notification. This feature allows the machine to page you when a fax arrives.

PC fax. Allows many functions of the fax machine to be controlled from a personal computer. Also lets the PC itself send faxes.

Shortcut calling aids. One-touch keys and speed-dial numbers allow connection to frequently called numbers with the press of a button or two.

Computer modems

The fastest ones cost more, but it can be money well spent.

Last CR report: May 1996
Expect to pay: $100 to $250

What's available

Transmission speeds. To enter cyberspace, you need a modem to translate digital data from the computer into an analog signal for the phone line, and vice versa. Modems can generally do that at speeds from 14.4 to 33.6 kilobits per second (kbps). The fastest modems on the market now claim to operate at speeds up to 56 kbps (see "What's new," next page). More common modems (known as V.34bis) operate at speeds up to 33.6 kbps. Modems any slower than that may be unsatisfactory for surfing the net.

Under ideal conditions, a 28.8 modem communicates twice as fast as a 14.4 one.

But ideal conditions rarely happen over real telephone lines. On the best-performing modems tested, we had to lower their receiving speed a little to overcome interference on the line.

Internal/external. Modems can be bought as a separate box or can be added to the inside of the computer. An internal modem usually costs less than a comparable external one, but internal modems can be difficult to install. Instructions are often poor.

"Plug and play" is supposed to make it easier to install an internal modem in an IBM-compatible computer. But the system doesn't always work well, particularly in computers not running Windows 95.

What's new

56-kbps modem. Available now, this is supposedly twice as fast as a 28.8-kbps modem. (It's fast, but it can't really deliver 56 kbps on existing phone lines.) It has several hitches, though: It works only with an Internet provider that supports it (many don't yet), and it requires high-quality phone connections between you, the phone company, and the Internet provider to support its needs. There are currently two competing protocols that are incompatible with each other. If you buy one of these modems, make sure it can be upgraded to whatever 56-kbps standard the industry chooses.

Shopping strategy

On the basis of our experience, we recommend considering an external modem. Consider an internal modem only if your computer has no spare high-speed serial port or you're willing to pay extra for installation.

Decide what to spend. Speed and price are linked. It's worthwhile to buy the fastest modem you can afford. Modems that operate at 33.6 kbps cost $50 to $200. Many claim to be upgradeable to one of the 56-kbps protocols.

What's in the stores. U. S. Robotics is the biggest-selling brand. Motorola and Zoom Telephonics are also major manufacturers. Modems are sold mostly by computer stores, but mail-order sources and electronics stores are also places to look.

Key features

Card length. Internal modems come in the form of "cards." Half-length cards take up less space in your PC than full-length ones.

Display. On external modems, look for LEDs that are clear and easy to read.

Power switch. Without this, you have to plug and unplug an external modem to turn it on and off.

Serial-port cable. Most external modems don't come with this cable. For an IBM-compatible computer, make sure you buy a cable that fits your machine's particular serial port. For a Macintosh, be sure to use a high-speed cable.

Software support. Terminal and fax support is basic. Some models also support voice mail, file sharing, a speakerphone, and caller ID.

Voice/data communication. Modems with this feature allow voice/data exchange in addition to sending data and faxes. Such models usually include a speakerphone, voice mail, and features associated with telephone-answering machines.

Scanners

A color flatbed scanner is more versatile than the sheet-fed type.

Last CR report: July 1997
Expect to pay: $150 to $400

A scanner can capture the image of nearly anything you can put on a flat surface. You can use it to add photos or drawings to your computer files, or to scan in documents for archive purposes or to avoid retyping them. Many scanners come with "OCR software," which can interpret a page of scanned words as text.

All scanners work essentially the same way: A light-sensitive charged-coupled device (CCD) converts light reflected from a scanned image into an electronic signal. The signal is then digitized and stored on the computer's hard drive.

Scanners typically come with three basic types of software: one to control the scanning, one to adjust an image's appearance after it has been scanned, and one to recognize text.

What's available

Flatbed scanner. This type, which resembles a photocopier, is the most versatile. You can use it with documents that are bound or unbound, smooth or textured, or items that vary in size or thickness. It scans by moving its CCD past whatever is placed on a fixed, transparent scanning surface. Most flatbeds connect to a small computer system interface (SCSI) port, which requires adding a plug-in card (usually supplied) to most Windows computers. Mac scanners connect to the printer output port on the back of the computer. Price range: $200 to $400.

Sheet-fed scanner. This type uses a fixed CCD to scan single sheets fed through a friction-roller system. As a result, most sheet-fed scanners can't scan bound documents, and their rollers may scratch items like glossy photographs. Sheet-fed scanners are generally smaller and less expensive than flatbeds. Most sheet-fed scanners we've tested connect to a computer's parallel port, often shared by a printer. Price range: $200 to $300.

Photo scanner. This is a small sheet-fed machine that scans things that are only four to five inches wide. Price range: $150 to $200.

Handheld scanner. Once the most popular type in the consumer market, it has given way to more automated types that don't require a steady hand. Price range: $100 to $150

What's new

Not long ago, scanners were "professional" desktop publishing equipment. Now, lower prices are attracting home-computer users. In late 1996, the average price for flatbed scanners dropped to about $550; for sheet-fed units, to about $250.

Shopping strategy

Scanners are typically available in both PC and Mac versions. Although all of the scanners we tested produced acceptable pictures, a color flatbed model deserves first consideration because of its versatility, if you have room for it.

Look for these minimum specifications: a parallel or SCSI interface; a TWAIN driver and TWAIN-compliant software;

at least 24-bit color depth; and 300x300 dots-per-inch (dpi) optical resolution. Make sure your computer has the right type of empty slot for a scanner that includes a plug-in card. If the included card is the older, ISA type, you may need to buy a new card if you buy a new computer in a year or two.

Decide what to spend. A flatbed scanner priced at $200 to $300 offers the best value. For some flatbeds, you can get a multisheet feeder, but it costs $350 to $500 extra and adds to the amount of space a scanner takes up. We found that many of the software packages that came with the scanners we tested were not state-of-the-art—they were scaled-down or older versions. Software upgrades for scanners or OCR software can cost $100 or more.

What's in the stores. Sheet-fed scanners are more prevalent than flatbed models. Hewlett-Packard, Logitech, Storm, and Visioneer are the most widely available brands. Computer stores and mail-order catalogs will have the biggest selection, but office-supply stores, TV/ appliance stores, and warehouse clubs also carry scanners.

Key features

Brightness control. This adjusts the black level in a scanned picture. Increasing brightness lightens blacks; decreasing it richens and deepens them.

Contrast control. This adjusts the maximum difference between the lightest and darkest areas in a scanned picture.

Driver software. This software essentially determines the quality of the images, because it controls the quality and the amount of information captured by a scanner.

Gamma control. This lets you emphasize an image's highlights or darker areas.

Image-editing software. This lets you manipulate an image to change its brightness or contrast, say, or to create a soft border rather than a hard edge. You can use the manufacturer's software or a third-party product like Adobe PhotoDeluxe. (Some scanners come with both.)

Optical-character-recognition (OCR) software. This comes with both flatbed and sheet-fed models. It reads images of typewritten pages and converts text to a word-processing file with a certain level of errors. In our tests, the best OCR software produced text that could easily be edited to match the scanned document. The worst models' output required too much work to re-create the original. If you need to scan a lot of highly formatted pages, plan to upgrade to the full version of the software.

Power switch. Look for one mounted where it can be reached easily, not on the back panel.

Preview controls. This lets you see the image while you scan it.

Home copiers

Even the most basic models produce crisp, clear copies. Choose according to features and cost of copies.

Last CR report: September 1997
Ratings: page 248
Expect to pay: $300 to $1000

What's available

Moving or fixed platen? The platen is the glass plate on which you put the material to be copied. In less expensive copiers, the platen moves, shuttling the page to be copied over a lighted slot. A moving-platen copier can be much cheaper and smaller than a machine with a fixed platen. Some have a carrying handle and fold to the size of an attaché case. But a copier with a moving-platen has a few distinct disadvantages:

• Moving-platen machines don't reduce or enlarge, something many fixed-platen machines can do.

• Machines with a moving platen take longer to make copies: 19 to 30 seconds for the first and 12 to 20 seconds per copy thereafter, according to our most recent tests. Those with a fixed platen took 9 to 22 seconds for the first copy, then just 6 to 8 seconds per copy.

• A moving platen makes it awkward to copy from bulky materials like books. On a copier with a fixed platen, the machine's optics move, not your original (or you).

• Although cheaper to buy, moving-platen copiers can be more expensive to run. The operating cost of the moving-platen machines we tested was at least 9 cents per copy; a few of the fixed-platen machines cost only 3 cents per copy.

Price range for moving-platen models: $300 to $500. For fixed-platen models: $600 to $1000.

Drum and toner cartridge, separate or combined? A copier's optics project an image onto an electrically charged revolving drum. The drum remains charged where the image is dark and attracts toner in those areas. As paper presses against the drum, the toner is transferred from drum to paper. Finally, a fuser softens the toner and bonds it to the paper.

In some copiers, drum and toner reside inside a single cartridge, so you change both at the same time. In Sharp and Xerox models, drum and toner cartridges are separate, and you can change them as needed. Generally, replacing the cartridge is easy and neat, but if you pick up a Sharp or Xerox cartridge the wrong way, you'll get messy black toner on your hands.

Whether combined or separate, drums and toner cartridges are expensive. In the copiers we tested, drums cost $120 to $140; toner cartridges, $90 to $125; combination units, $90 to $125. Because a drum can last thousands of copies longer than the toner, using a combination cartridge means that you may have to throw out a drum before it's worn out.

What's new

A few home copiers now come equipped with a document feeder, previously available only on office copiers. Fixed-platen models with a document feeder cost about $1000. Similar models without a feeder are $600 to $700.

Shopping strategy

Small home-office copiers are more about convenience than saving money.

Owning a copier isn't necessarily cheaper than using a copy shop.

Fixed-platen copiers are the better choice if you make, say, 10 or more copies a day. They're big, boxy, and heavy—40 to 50 pounds. Moving-platen copiers, smaller and more limited, make sense for fairly light use.

Decide what to spend. Even a basic model makes excellent copies. Let features and cost per copy determine your choice. Cost per copy ranged from 3 cents to 14 cents in our most recent tests.

Beyond that is the expense of replacing drum and toner cartridges, which cost about $100 to $150.

In our tests, fixed-platen models using a combined drum-and-toner cartridge needed a new one after as few as 1000 copies. Models with separate drum and toner catridges produced 11,500 copies before needing replacement. Moving-platen units with separate drum and toner cartridges delivered from 750 to 1350 copies before requiring a new toner cartridge and 10,000 to 12,000 copies before needing a new drum. Combination cartridges lasted about 750 copies.

What's in the stores. In the past five years, some companies—Mita, Sanyo, and Tandy—have stopped selling small copiers. Virtually the only surviving brands are Canon, Sharp, and Xerox (and some Sharp and Xerox copiers are essentially twins under their nameplates).

Using the Ratings. We tested both fixed-platen and moving-platen copiers using the optimal exposure settings. Trained panelists judged the copy quality. All of the models did an excellent job reproducing text. Our figures for cost per copy are based on the use of a densely printed original—a severe test. If text on your originals is often sparse, your costs will be substantially lower.

Similar models should perform much the same as the tested models; features may vary. If you can't find a model, call the manufacturer; see page 342.

Key features

• ***Standard on most models:***

Copy-darkness control. You generally set darkness by moving a wheel or a sliding control to compensate for especially light or dark originals.

Multiple copies. Moving-platen copiers typically can be set to make up to nine copies from one original. Some have a continuous mode, which lets you make up to 20 copies at a time or until the paper runs out. Fixed-platen copiers can be set to run up to 99 copies.

Paper tray. Copiers typically hold 50, 100, or 250 sheets. More expensive copiers hold blank paper in an internal drawer; less expensive ones store it in an open tray hanging to one side.

Warranty. Xerox copiers come with a longer warranty than Canon or Sharp machines—three years versus one.

• ***Recommended:***

Autoexposure setting. This sets darkness automatically—important for originals that aren't simply black text on white paper. In our tests, it worked well with most copiers and can keep you from wasting paper as you tweak the controls to get things right.

Toner-saver. On some Sharp and Xerox models, this feature reduces the amount of toner that sticks to the drum, substantially stretching the life of the toner cartridge.

In our tests, text looked slightly less crisp when we used the toner-saver, but the difference was barely perceptible. And toner-saver actually made photos look better.

• ***Useful for particular needs***

Book mode. This feature, also called

"two-page separation," automatically copies adjacent bound pages onto separate sheets in one pass.

Copy size. Not all machines accept paper in both letter size (8½x11 inches) and legal size (8½x14 inches). Some moving-platen models make only letter-size.

Document feeder. Some copiers come equipped with a document feeder that lets you feed up to 20 original pages at a time without lifting the lid. This feature, while convenient, adds substantially to a copier's cost.

Enlarge/reduce settings. Almost all the copiers with this feature let you make adjustments in 1 percent increments and have other helpful settings—for fitting a legal-size original onto letter-size paper, for example.

Second paper tray. It's useful for colored paper, label sheets, and letterhead. But even copiers without a second tray will accept such special papers, and some have a manual-feed slot for inserting them.

Telephones

Cordless phones are convenient, but corded models still sound better.

Last CR reports: Corded phones, November 1995; Cordless phones, November 1996
Expect to pay: $10 to $250

No matter how many telephones a household has, it should have at least one corded phone in case of a power outage. Cordless phones require household current, and so will not work when the power goes out.

Both cordless and corded phones are bedecked with functions that can often can add substantially to the price.

Corded phones

The typical corded phone has two components: a base that plugs into a telephone jack, and a handset.

In our most recent tests, most performed quite capably, conveying voices intelligibly under normal conditions. The variations in sound quality that we found are likely to matter only in very noisy environments.

What's available

Console models. These are updated versions of the traditional Bell desk phone. Price range: $50 to more than $200.

Trim-style models. These are space-savers; the push buttons are on the handset itself, and the base is about half as wide as a console's. Price range: $20 to $75.

What's new

As cordless and cellular models soar in popularity, prices for some corded models have taken a nosedive. Bargains abound.

Shopping strategy

Since good sound quality is pretty much a given, your main considerations should be features and price. Before you buy, make sure the handset is comfortable to hold in your hand and to your ear.

Decide what to spend. For as little as $25 or so, you can buy a corded phone with speed-dialing and other features. For $50 or more, you get a speakerphone and two-line capability.

What's in the stores. AT&T is still the dominant brand of conventional telephones. Lucent Technologies is an AT&T spin-off company that markets phones. Major chains, such as Best Buy and Circuit City, generally offer the lowest prices. Phones usually go on sale during November and December.

Cordless phones

Sound-quality problems with cordless phones have steadily decreased. Our most recent tests indicated much improvement and far less static and interference.

Besides standard phone features, cordless phones have several features unique to cordless transmission. For instance, you'll find them in varying configurations: with dual keypads and a speakerphone to let you make calls from the base; dual handsets (both a corded and a cordless handset are integrated into the base); extra charging base (for charging the handset in a second room); and multihandset base (which supports more than one cordless handset).

The types

Cordless phones vary in how they transmit their signals:

10- and 25-channel models. Also known as 43/49-megahertz (MHz) models. Ten channels are sufficient for a neighborhood that's not densely populated. Models with 25 channels have a better chance of finding a clear channel in areas where neighbors' phones, garage-door openers, and the like can interfere. Price range: $50 to $100.

900-MHz models. These have anywhere from 25 to 100 channels and a greater range than 43/49-MHz models. They are also less vulnerable to interference and static. Price range: $150 to $250. Digital versions cost an extra $50 or so; they're static-free and virtually impossible to eavesdrop on without special equipment.

What's new

Recently 900-MHz cordless phones commanded a substantial premium. Now, prices have fallen to as low as $150 for some models, not much more than full-featured 43/49-MHz models.

Manufacturers have responded to consumers' peeves with cordless phones with user-friendly designs: easy-to-pocket handsets akin to cellular phones; chargers for an extra battery, so there's always a fresh spare; antenna-less handsets; and headphones that plug into the handset for hands-free use.

Shopping strategy

The sound quality of cordless phones has varied more than that of corded models in our tests. Even so, you aren't likely to go far wrong—the worst cordless models in our most recent tests were still good. Most people would be satisfied with a 43/49-MHz model, with or without an answering machine. Consider a 900-MHz model if you need more range or more security.

Decide what to spend. Basic 900-MHz cordless models cost $150 to $250; 43/49-MHz models, $50 to $100.

Expect to pay an additional $50 for a digital 900-MHz model. Features that cost extra include an answering machine ($100 or so), an extra line, a speakerphone, a pager/intercom, a keypad on the base, and an LCD display on the base or the handset.

What's in the stores. Besides AT&T, the major brands of cordless models include GE, Panasonic, and Sony. You'll find them in the same stores that carry corded phones.

Phone features

Corded and cordless phones share many features.

• *Recommended:*

Batteries. All cordless handsets use replaceable batteries. A typical 43/49-MHz phone's fully charged battery will last about eight hours in continuous use, according to our tests; a 900-MHz phone's battery may not last as long.

Easy-to-see keys. Keys that are lighted let you dial in the dark. Big keys make dialing easy for kids and for people with poor eyesight or limited finger dexterity.

Low-battery indicator. Lets you know when to recharge the battery.

Out-of-range warning. Gives an audible alert when the handset is too far from the base.

One-touch speed-dialing. Stores a number so you can dial by touching a single key.

Power-off switch. Located on the handset, it can lengthen battery time.

Redial. Repeats the dialing of the last number. Some models can redial a busy number several times automatically or continuously.

Ringer in base. When you're near the base, alerts you to an incoming call, no matter where the handset may be.

Save. For storing a number just dialed.

Storing numbers. Most phones can store from 3 to 15 numbers of 16 digits or longer—generally sufficient even for international dialing.

Volume controls. Typically, one control raises or lowers the volume at the handset; another, at the phone's ringer. Speakerphones also have a volume control for the speaker in the base. "Mute" disconnects the microphone so a caller can't hear sounds from your end. "Hold" disconnects both microphone and earpiece.

• *Optional:*

Answerer. Built-in answering machines are increasingly common, especially on cordless phones.

Autoscan. Automatically finds the clearest channel on a cordless phone.

Caller ID compatibility. Can be built into a phone or bought as a stand-alone device. With it, subscribers to the phone company's service can see the phone number and, in some locations, the name of the person calling.

Flash. It briefly disconnects a call so you can take another call on the same line.

Keypad on base. Allows you to dial a cordless phone or to receive calls when the handset is in another room.

LCD display. May include the number dialed, time of day, time spent talking, channel being used, and low-battery signal.

Paging/intercom. One-way paging lets you send a signal from the base to a misplaced handset, so you can find it. Two-way lets you send the signal in both directions; on models with an intercom, you can talk as well.

Signal scrambling. The digital technology found on 900-MHz cordless phones offers the greatest security against eavesdropping. Some 43/49-MHz models have a signal-scrambling feature that should also thwart casual snoops.

Two-line capability. Allows you to handle a second phone line and to "conference" two callers in a three-way conversation. It's especially useful in homes that frequently use online services.

Cellular phones

The service plan matters most. Select the plan that fits your needs and budget, then compare handsets.

Last CR report: November 1997
Ratings: page 245
Expect to pay: Nothing to $200 or more

Nearly 50 million Americans now use a cell phone, and another 7 million or so are expected to take to the airwaves over the coming year. Cell-phone boutiques and kiosks have popped up on nearly every Main Street and mall in the U.S. Newspapers are full of ads. The product has taken off faster than fax machines, faster than cable TV, and just as fast as the now ubiquitous VCR.

The marketplace is as chaotic as any bazaar. Labyrinthine pricing schemes disguise rates that are sometimes 10 times higher than that of conventional phone service. In addition, the technology is changing and consumers will have to choose between phones that operate on an analog system or a digital one.

What's available

Analog phones. These now range in size from small fold-up models to larger units that resemble a walkie-talkie and in weight from 5 to 9 ounces or more—a significant difference for something that's carried on your person. Basic models are available—some designed for use only in emergencies don't even have a normal keypad—but most models are loaded with features. Price: Depends on the service contract.

Digital phones. New digital cellular and PCS (Personal Communications Service) models produce less static than analog models. Their batteries allow more talk time and standby time, because a digital transmitter turns off and on as needed during a conversation. (Analog transmitters must stay on throughout the call.) And digital models offer features not found on analog models, such as e-mail and paging capabilities.

However, a digital phone may not deliver the service you bargained for, however, because the network of antennas and base stations that connects digital handsets to the landline telephone system covers most big metro areas but little of the space in between. When you roam outside your digital service area, your phone might revert to analog service, or it might not work at all unless you have a dual-mode phone, one with both a digital and analog transmitter/receiver. But having to pack two phones into one makes for a larger handset. Digital phones can also be expensive. They wholesale for between $400 and $600—about twice what analog units cost.

Choosing a service plan

Service providers like AT&T Wireless, AirTouch, and Bell Atlantic have turned the process of buying a cell phone into something akin to a shell game. Typically, they and retailers like Circuit City, Radio Shack, and Staples, who act as their commissioned agents, will give you the handset—which wholesales for between $150 and $300—for little or no charge when you sign up for their service.

"Special" deals offer low initial monthly costs that lock subscribers into contracts that are hard to escape. You may be lured by "free" minutes of airtime that can turn out to be pretty expensive, or by promotions of cut-rate cellular-phone handsets. What the brochures may not mention, or may bury in the fine print, is that you pay for the low-cost hardware through the monthly access charge or a stiff early-termination fee. Advertised per-minute rates as low as 2 cents can end up costing 60 times more when all fees and real usage patterns are taken into account.

Even a straightforward list of a plan's fees won't reveal much about the ultimate cost until those fees are applied to an actual usage pattern. For a realistic idea of cost, you'll need to estimate:

• When you'll be placing calls—during peak or off-peak hours.

• Where you'll be when you call—in your home area, in extended home areas, in a variety of "roaming" areas away from your home base.

• Where you'll be calling to—across town, outside your home zone, in-state, across the country.

The worksheet on page 243 can help.

Plans also share certain features and fees, which can help you compare them:

Monthly access charge. The basic monthly fee you will be expected to pay your carrier to maintain your wireless account. Access charges typically range from around $15 to as much as several hundred dollars a month, depending mainly on how much airtime is included.

Airtime charges. The cost for that portion of the time you spend on the phone when your transmission signal travels between your wireless phone and the cellular station that sends and receives it. These charges typically run from around 20 cents to $1 per minute, and you incur them whether you initiate or receive the call.

Landline charges. The charge you incur when a call you've made is passed from a cellular station to a regular phone line. You pay these charges, which usually range from 5 cents to 12 cents per minute, even when you are making cellular calls that are part of the basic monthly service or when making "free" weekend cell-phone calls.

Included minutes. Airtime allotted to you each month under your rate plan for which you pay no additional per-minute charges. Generally, the higher your monthly access charge, the more included minutes you get. But these minutes are usually limited to calls made from or received in your home area.

Peak time. The higher-priced calling periods encompassing weekday business hours, when most people want to use the phone. Peak time generally lasts from 7 A.M. to 9 P.M., but may begin as early as 6 A.M. and end as late as 10 P.M.

Off-peak time. Periods of slack demand for phone use, when per-minute airtime costs are lower, including weekdays from 9 or 10 P.M. to 6 or 7 A.M. and weekends.

Home area. The territory where you travel and use your phone most—usually where you live—and where your calls will cost the least. You may want to choose a "home area away from home," if you tend to spend a lot of time traveling and calling an out-of-town location.

Extended home area. Usually, but not always, the territory surrounding or adjacent to your home area, where your carrier charges airtime at your home rate.

Roaming area. Generally, everywhere outside your home or extended home areas, where rates are higher. The display on the cellular phone will indicate when you are roaming.

Key features

Alphanumeric directory. This feature allows you to store the names and numbers of people you most frequently call. It's easiest to use with scroll- and alphabetic-search features.

Any-key answer. This lets you answer an incoming call by hitting any key, rather than only the "send" key, something older phones used to send and receive calls.

Authentication. This system of secret codes is designed to foil thieves who would steal your phone's electronic identification number, "clone" it, and fraudulently bill calls to you. Many models have this feature, but not all cellular service providers support it yet. Check to see if yours does.

Call timer. This feature keeps track of the time spent talking on the current call, as well as cumulatively. Some timers will beep at preset intervals to remind you how long you've been talking. They're useful if you're trying to stick to a monthly included-minutes budget.

Dot-matrix display. Either light-emitting diode (LED) or liquid-crystal display (LCD) produces detailed, easy-to-read numbers and letters. "Union Jack" displays, so called because their lights are laid out in a pattern similar to that of a British flag, are less legible.

Nickel-metal-hydride or lithium-ion batteries. Unlike older nickel-cadmium batteries, these power units do a better job of holding a charge, and when partially drained will recharge fully.

"Smart" backup power options. Some models come with a spare battery, to double your talk time. Others allow you to swap batteries while you talk, or they come with an alkaline battery adapter—useful for when an emergency doesn't allow time to recharge. Models that have a rapid charger can replenish the battery in 1 or 2 hours instead of the 7 to 12 hours required by an ordinary "trickle" charger. An automobile adapter allows you to power the phone by plugging it into your car's cigarette lighter.

Vibrating alert. Instead of ringing, the handset vibrates to let you know discretely that you have an incoming call.

Shopping strategy

Look for a service plan suited to the way you intend to use the phone. Then select a handset that will perform reliably when and where you expect to make your calls.

Choose the service plan first. Your yearly service bills will probably dwarf what you pay for the handset. Average users can face as much as a threefold difference in rates charged by competing carriers.

Expect to be offered a wide selection of cell-phone models with any plan you choose. But the prices charged by each carrier—or electronics retailer—for the same handsets will vary, too. Don't conclude that the merchant charging the least for the handset will offer the lowest total cost for the handset and service. Use the worksheet on page 243 to compare plan costs.

Make performance a priority. Each cell-service provider will be able to provide clear signals in most parts of the territory its transmission antennas cover, but there will be pockets where cell signals will be spotty. You'll want to choose a phone that can ably compensate for a degraded transmission. Our tests have shown that not all phones perform equally well.

A good cell phone must have a receiver with sufficient RF (radio frequency) sensitivity to "hear" signals sent out by the phone company's base-station transmitters, then pluck those radio waves out of the air. Most handsets don't have to work very hard to do this in the urban heart of a cellular service area because

Which combination of cell phone and service costs less?

Use this worksheet to estimate the cost of the service, your biggest expense. From the service providers' rate sheets, fill in the basic monthly service charge; the per-minute charge for calls made during peak hours, off-peak hours, and while "roaming" outside your home area; and the number of minutes included at no charge each month in each category. If you aren't sure how you'll use your cell phone, assume you'll behave like an average user and make 42 minutes of calls per month—17 peak and 23 off-peak in your home area and 2 minutes "roaming." Use those figures to compute your total annual cost of service. Then add the price of the cell phone.

What you pay for service	Estimated number of minutes used (National average)		Number of "free" minutes included in plan		Per-minute charge *		Cost
During PEAK periods	17 min.	–		X		=	Add
During OFF-PEAK periods	23 min.	–		X		=	Add
While ROAMING	2 min.	–		X		=	Add

* If number of free minutes equals or exceeds your estimated use, enter zero; otherwise multiply the difference by the per-minute charge.

Basic monthly service charge

Total MONTHLY cost of service

Multiply by 12

Total ANNUAL cost of service

Add

Price of cell phone

First-year cost of cellular

signal transmissions are strong, thanks to lots of closely spaced base stations located to handle the high volume of calls. But a good receiver is of paramount importance on the remote and rural fringes of a service area where transmitters are spaced farther apart.

A good handset should also compensate for "multipath" signals. When reflections of the signal arrive at your phone nanoseconds late, after bouncing off buildings, mountains, even passing trucks, you hear a rapid "pft-pft-pft" sound while moving or a static noise as you shift from spot to spot.

Focus on features. While some features add to the usefulness of the phone you buy, don't compromise quality reception and call handling to get a phone packed with extras you may not need. Some salespeople may try to persuade you to spend as much as $250 to $400 more for a fancier model, but if you're a first-time cell-phone user, opt for a simpler model that performs reliably. You can always switch to a model equipped with features you decide you need when you renew your service contract. You'll probably discover that you can upgrade your handset for free with a new contract.

However, you won't know how well a phone works until you start using it in a variety of settings. If you choose a model that doesn't work well, you're stuck with it—unless you're willing to pay a steep fee to prematurely terminate your service plan or to buy a new phone if the old one was purchased independent of a service contract.

Decide what to spend. The same cellular handset can cost you $29 or $229—or nothing at all. That's because cellular providers and electronics retailers commonly "bundle" the handsets with a service plan that lets you send and receive calls with the phone. What you ultimately pay—and whether you get a sleek, feature-laden model or a bulkier basic handset—will depend on the monthly service plan you select.

Most cellular plans offer a choice of one or more cheap or "free" models—each a basic cell phone. Of course, you don't really get something for nothing. What you pay for the handset is buried inside your monthly service charges. We calculate that for the one-time $150-to-$300 cost of each "giveaway" phone, a service provider can expect to earn revenues of more than $500 a year from the subscriber.

What's in the stores. You don't have to buy a cell phone from a cellular service provider. Electronics stores, wholesale price clubs, office supply stores, and other retailers sell handsets, and any of them can hook you up with service from one of the carriers in your area. About half of all cell phones sold are Motorola products. Nokia, which also manufacturers Radio Shack phones, is the next most widely sold brand.

Using the Ratings. We tested only handsets that use analog radio technology. Beyond sizing up how well each handset performed, we looked at the usefulness of features that purportedly make cell phones more convenient. Our tests of cellular phones found a dozen that rated very good overall. However, each had performance strengths and weaknesses. We found no relationship between price and performance.

Some cell phones excel at establishing and holding on to calls, an especially critical factor in remote areas where you'd most need reliable performance in an emergency. Another factor, talk time between battery charges, also varies widely. If you can't find a model, call the manufacturer; see page 342.

Ratings *Cell phones*
& Recommendations

The tests behind the Ratings

Overall score is based on the quality of reception, battery life, and ease of use. **Call setup** measures the signal level needed to establish a call connection. **Call maintenance** indicates the phone's ability to maintain an established call, generally requiring a lower signal level than a call setup. **Multipath** indicates a phone's immunity to interference caused by reflections of a received signal off nearby objects under varying conditions. We developed a computer-controlled simulation of this interference under five scenarios: highway travel at 60 mph, on roads at 45 mph, over hills at 30 mph, and through city streets at 15 mph and at a walking pace. **Battery life** indicates how long the battery allows you to talk and how long the phone can be left on to receive incoming calls. **Ease of use** reflects our evaluation of various features and their utility. These included display legibility, keyboard layout and feel, ease of entering and recalling stored numbers, and portability. **Price range** reflects prices gathered from cellular service providers and retailers from May through July 1997.

Typical features

• Numeric memory. • Received-signal-strength indicator. • Own-phone-number display. • Last-number redial. • Authentication. • Battery-strength indicator. • Roaming indicator. • Name storage. • Any-key answer. • Call timer. • One-touch dialing. • One-year warranty.

Recommendations

When shopping for a cellular phone, find a service plan suited for the way you intend to use the phone, and select a handset that will perform reliably when and where you expect to make calls. Don't conclude that the merchant charging the least for the handset will offer the lowest total cost for the handset and service—crunch the numbers yourself. If you need to stay in touch but spend most of your time in meetings where a ringing phone would be disruptive, consider the Radio Shack CT-500 or the Motorola Micro TAC Elite, which have a silent, vibrating alert. If you want to store many numbers in the cell phone's memory, don't buy the Motorola Populous, which can hold only nine numbers and whose memory banks can be erased accidentally.

See Buying Guide report, page 240. Last time rated in CONSUMER REPORTS: November 1997.

Ratings continued ▶

Overall Ratings

E · VG · G · F · P

Listed in order of overall score

Key no.	Brand and model	Price range	Overall score (0–100; P F G VG E)	Call setup	Call maintenance	Multipath	Battery life	Ease of use
1	**AudioVox** MVX-855	$150-380		VG	VG	E	F	VG
2	**Nokia** 638	0-60		VG	E	VG	G	VG
3	**NEC** TalkTime 820	0-29		G	E	VG	E	G
4	**Oki** 1430	19-89		VG	E	VG	F	VG
5	**Radio Shack** CT-500	0.01		VG	VG	VG	F	VG
6	**Nokia** 232	0-249		E	P	VG	F	VG
7	**Ericsson** AH618	1-199		G	G	VG	G	G
8	**Motorola** Micro TAC Elite	30-619		G	G	G	F	VG
9	**Philips** Fizz	0-20		VG	F	VG	F	VG
10	**Sony** CM-RX100	0-370		E	P	F	G	VG
11	**Mitsubishi** AH-350	30-60		G	G	VG	F	VG
12	**Motorola** Populous	0-149		VG	G	E	G	F
13	**AudioVox** MVX-401	0-29		F	F	P	F	G
14	**Ericsson** AF738	35-330		G	P	P	G	G
15	**Panasonic** EB-H65S	25-300		G	P	P	F	VG

Model details

1 AudioVox MVX-855 $150-$380

• 5¾x1¾x⅞ in. • 6 oz. • Nickel-metal-hydride battery • 74-min. talk time • 13-hr. standby.
Excellent overall immunity to signal reflections, and among the best in hilly terrain. Very good call setup. Among the most portable. But: Battery life was among the shortest. Additional useful features: Advanced battery technology, spare battery, beeps to indicate elapsed talk time, 3-yr. warranty. **Recommendation:** An excellent phone with many features, but pricey.

2 Nokia 638 $0-$60

• 7½x2⅛x1¼ in. • 9 oz. • Nickel-cadmium battery • 117-min. talk time • 26-hr. standby.
Very good call setup and overall immunity to signal reflections. One of the best at holding on to a call. But: One of the heaviest. Additional useful feature: Large display. **Recommendation:** An excellent phone.

3 NEC TalkTime 820 $0-$29

• 7¾x2x1⅜ in. • 9 oz. • Nickel-cadmium battery • 218-min. talk time • 47-hr. standby.
Very good overall immunity to signal reflections, though only fair in hilly terrain; longest battery life by far of models tested. Among the best at holding on to a call. But: A less readable display, one of the heaviest, and can't store names. Similar models: TalkTime 810 and 840. **Recommendation:** An excellent performer with few features.

4 Oki 1430 $19-$89

• 7½x2⅛x1¼ in. • 8 oz. • Nickel-metal-hydride battery • 62-min. talk time • 10-hr. standby.
Very good call setup and immunity to signal re-

flection. One of the best at holding a call and in immunity to signal reflections. Additional useful features: Beeps to indicate elapsed talk time. Similar model: Oki 1435. **Recommendation:** Very good.

5 **Radio Shack CT-500** $0.01

• 5⅝x2⅜x1⅛ in. • 8 oz. • Nickel-cadmium battery • 55-min. talk time • 10-hr. standby.
Very good call setup and immunity to signal reflection. But: Battery life among the shortest. LED display disappears after several seconds. Additional useful features: Vibrating call alert, beeps to indicate elapsed talk time. **Recommendation:** A very good phone.

6 **Nokia 232** $0-$249

• 6⅜x2⅛x⅞ in. • 7 oz. • Nickel-metal-hydride battery • 50-min. talk time • 17-hr. standby.
Among the best call setup; very good immunity to signal reflection. But: Poor at holding a call, battery life among the shortest. Additional useful features: Rapid charger included. **Recommendation:** Very good, but can be expensive.

7 **Ericsson AH618** $1-$199

• 6⅝x1⅞x1⅜ in. • 7 oz. • Nickel-cadmium battery • 124-min. talk time • 27-hr. standby.
Very good immunity to signal reflection and good call setup. But: Less readable display. **Recommendation:** A very good phone.

8 **Motorola Micro TAC Elite** $30-$619

• 6x2¼x⅞ in. • 5 oz. • Lithium-ion battery • 94-min. talk time • 18-hr. standby.
Good call setup and good overall immunity to signal reflection. One of the lightest models tested. But: LED display disappears after several seconds. Additional useful features: Vibrating call alert, beeps to indicate elapsed talk time, rapid charger included, battery can be swapped while phone is on, 3-yr. warranty. **Recommendation:** Very good performer, but can be very expensive.

9 **Philips Fizz** $0-$20

• 7⅝x2½x⅞ in. • 8 oz. • Nickel-cadmium battery • 71-min. talk time • 14-hr. standby.
Very good immunity to signal reflections and very good call setup. But: Only fair handling of multipath in hilly terrain, and battery life among the shortest. **Recommendation:** Very good.

10 **Sony CM-RX100** $0-$370

• 2½x3⅝x1⅛ in.• 7 oz. • Lithium-ion battery • 99-min. talk time • 27-hr. standby.
Among the best call setup. But: Among the worst at holding a call, immunity to signal reflection only fair, and among the worst in hilly terrain. Additional useful features: Beeps to indicate elapsed talk time. **Recommendation:** Very good, but can be expensive.

11 **Mitsubishi AH-350** $30-$60

• 7⅛x2⅛x1⅜ in. • 8 oz. • Nickel-metal-hydride battery • 104-min. talk time • 13-hr. standby.
Very good overall immunity to signal reflection, and good at setting up calls. Additional useful features: Rapid charger included. **Recommendation:** Very good.

12 **Motorola Populous** $0-$149

• 7¼x2¼x1⅛ in. • 8 oz. • Nickel-cadmium battery • 123-min. talk time • 19-hr. standby.
Excellent overall immunity to signal reflection, and among the best in hilly terrain; very good call setup. But: Less legible display that disappears after several seconds. Additional useful feature: Can use alkaline batteries. **Recommendation:** Very good, but basic.

13 **AudioVox MVX-401** $0-$29

• 6⅞x2⅜x1⅛ in. • 8 oz. • Nickel-cadmium battery • 97-min. talk time • 15-hr. standby.
Rated good overall. But: One of the worst for immunity to signal reflection. Ability to establish a call judged only fair, less legible display, and can't store names. Additional useful feature: Beeps to indicate elapsed talk time. Similar model: MVX-401A. **Recommendation:** An older design; there are better alternatives.

14 **Ericsson AF738** $35-$330

• 5⅛x2x1 in. • 5 oz. • Nickel-metal-hydride battery • 124-min. talk time • 26-hr. standby.
Good call setup. One of the lightest models tested. But: Among the worst for immunity to signal reflection and at holding calls. Less legible display. Additional useful features: Beeps to indicate elapsed talk time, rapid charger included. **Recommendation:** A good phone, but can be expensive.

15 **Panasonic EB-H65S** $25-$300

• 5½x1¾x1¼ in. • 5 oz. • Nickel-metal-hydride battery • 77-min. talk time • 10-hr. standby.
Good call setup. One of the lightest models tested. But: One of the worst for immunity to signal reflection and at holding on to calls; battery life among the shortest. **Recommendation:** Fair.

Ratings *Home copiers*
& Recommendations

The tests behind the Ratings

Overall score is based mainly on performance with printed text and, to a smaller degree, on supply costs, speed, and performance with photos. We used the optimal exposure setting and based scores on trained panelists' judgments of copy quality. **Text** shows how well text was reproduced. All models did an excellent job. **Photo** shows how well the copiers reproduced a photograph, thin lines, and shades of gray. **Speed** combines the time required to make the first copy and the time per copy after that. **Cost per copy** uses the cost of supplies (paper, drum, and toner) and the life of the drum and toner cartridge to calculate per-copy expenses. Your costs will probably be less than ours: Our densely printed test documents used more toner than sparsely printed documents would have. **Price** is the estimated average, based on a national survey.

Typical features for these models

• Standby mode to power up instantly when the start button is pressed. • Automatic shut-off if idle for a few minutes. • Can create labels and transparencies. • Hinged cover.

Recommendations

If your needs are modest—maybe five copies a day, with no enlarging or reducing—you can get by with a moving-platen copier. Good choices include the Canon PC320 and the Xerox 5305—each $350—but neither handles legal-size paper. If you need to make legal-size copies, consider the Xerox XC580 ($470). If you're outfitting a more elaborate home office and plan to make many copies, invest in a fixed-platen machine. The fixed-platen Xerox XC830 ($650), which has a toner-saver mode, makes copies at a comparatively lower cost.

See Buying Guide Report, page 235. Last time rated in CONSUMER REPORTS: September 1997.

Overall Ratings

E VG G F P

Within types, listed in order of overall score

Key no.	Brand and model	Price	Cost per copy	Text	Photo	Speed
	FIXED-PLATEN COPIERS					
1	**Xerox** XC830 [1]	$650	3¢	E	VG	G
2	**Sharp** Z-835 [1]	1000 [2]	3	E	VG	G
3	**Canon** PC770	900	14	E	G	VG
4	**Canon** PC720	650	14	E	G	VG
	MOVING-PLATEN COPIERS					
5	**Xerox** XC580	470	9	E	G	F
6	**Canon** PC320	350	13	E	G	G
7	**Canon** PC300	300	13	E	G	G
8	**Xerox** 5305	350	13	E	G	F

[1] *We scored these models based on a best-case scenario: cost per copy and photo quality in toner-saver mode; text quality in regular mode. Text remained nearly as crisp in toner-saver mode.*
[2] *Comes with a document feeder, which adds substantially to a copier's price.*

Model details

Notes on the details: If you often copy double-spaced pages of text, you may get two or three times as many copies per toner cartridge as we did in our fairly demanding tests.

Fixed-platen copiers

1 Xerox XC830 $650

• First copy: 19 seconds • 9 copies per minute • 100-sheet paper drawer

Letter- or legal-size copies; reduces 30 percent and enlarges 40 percent. Book mode copies adjacent bound pages onto separate sheets. Manual feed for cards, labels, and letterhead. Autoexposure to set copy darkness. Toner-saver stretches cartridge life and improves copies of photos. Three-year warranty. **Supplies:** Toner cartridge, about $125, good for 11,500 copies in tests, with toner-saver on; drum, about $140, rated by manufacturer for 12,000 copies. Similar: Xerox XC820, $640, has no book mode; Sharp Z-820, $700. **Recommendation:** Excellent overall. Especially consistent copy quality, and low per-copy cost.

2 Sharp Z-835 $1000

• First copy: 22 seconds • 10 copies per minute • 250-sheet paper drawer

Has 20-sheet document feeder. Letter- or legal-size copies; reduces 30 percent and enlarges 40 percent. 50-sheet alternate paper tray for letterhead or legal-size paper. Autoexposure to set copy darkness. Toner-saver stretches cartridge life and improves copies of photos. However, toner-saver control is hard to set. One-year warranty. **Supplies:** Toner cartridge, about $120, good for 11,500 copies in tests, with toner-saver on; drum, about $140, rated by manufacturer for 12,000 copies. Similar: Xerox XC1045, $1000. **Recommendation:** Excellent overall. Features you'll appreciate if you make a lot of copies, and low per-copy cost.

Ratings continued

Ratings, continued

3 Canon PC770 $900

• First copy: 10 seconds • 11 copies per minute • 250-sheet paper drawer

Letter- or legal-size copies; reduces 30 percent and enlarges 40 percent. 50-sheet alternate paper tray for letterhead or legal-size paper. Autoexposure to set copy darkness. One-year warranty with on-site repairs. Supplies: Single cartridge, including toner and drum, about $125; good for 1000 copies in tests; very easy to change. Similar: Canon PC790, $1100, has 30-sheet document feeder. **Recommendation:** Excellent overall, but high per-copy cost.

4 Canon PC720 $650

• First copy: 9 seconds • 8 copies per minute • 250-sheet paper drawer

Letter- or legal-size copies; reduces 30 percent and enlarges 40 percent. Manual feed for cards, labels, transparencies, and letterhead. Autoexposure to set copy darkness. One-year warranty with on-site repairs. **Supplies:** Single cartridge, including toner and drum, about $125; good for 1000 copies in tests; very easy to change. Similar: Canon PC710, $600; enlarge/reduce limited to 70, 78, 86, or 141 percent. **Recommendation:** Excellent overall, but high per-copy cost and a bit slower than competitors.

Moving-platen copiers

5 Xerox XC580 $470

• First copy: 30 seconds • 5 copies per minute • 100-sheet paper tray

Letter- or legal-size copies. Continuous copy mode. Autoexposure to set copy darkness. Three-year warranty. **Supplies:** Toner cartridge, about $90, good for 1350 copies in tests; drum, about $120, rated by manufacturer for 12,000 copies. Similar: Xerox XC540, $430; paper tray holds only 40 sheets. **Recommendation:** Excellent overall, and most economical to operate among its class.

6 Canon PC320 $350

• First copy: 20 seconds • 4 copies per minute • 50-sheet paper tray

Letter-size copies only. Carrying handle. Continuous copy mode. Autoexposure to set copy darkness. One-year warranty, and Canon will ship a replacement overnight, free. **Supplies:** Single cartridge, including toner and drum, about $90, good for 750 copies in tests; easy to change. Similar: Canon PC325, $400, takes legal-size as well as letter-size paper. **Recommendation:** Excellent overall, but high per-copy cost.

7 Canon PC300 $300

• First copy: 19 seconds • 4 copies per minute • Manual paper feed—no paper tray

Letter-size copies only. Carrying handle. One-year warranty, and Canon will ship a replacement overnight, free. **Supplies:** Single cartridge, including toner and drum, about $90; good for 750 copies in tests; easy to change. **Recommendation:** Excellent overall, but high per-copy cost, and copy paper must be fed by hand, sheet by sheet—an inconvenience.

8 Xerox 5305 $350

• First copy: 24 seconds • 3 copies per minute • 50-sheet paper tray

Letter-size copies only. Carrying handle. Continuous copy mode. Autoexposure to set copy darkness. Three-year warranty. **Supplies:** Toner cartridge, about $90, good for 950 copies in tests; drum, about $120, rated by manufacturer for 10,000 copies. **Model availability:** Discontinued. **Recommendation:** Excellent overall, but high per-copy cost, and the slowest copier tested.

Can't find a model? Call the manufacturer. See page 342.

Ratings *Fax machines*
& Recommendations

The tests behind the Ratings

Overall score is based primarily on appearance of received faxes and how well they resist fading and curling. **Appearance of pages** scores reflect their crispness and clearness. **Fax** pages were compared to a high-quality reference fax; **copier** and **scanner** pages to the original images; **printer** pages to pages of text from a good stand-alone laser printer. Incoming **fax speed** is based on time required to print a double-spaced page; outgoing, on time to transmit a double-spaced fax from the machine to our test computer. All tests were at a data-transfer rate of 9.6 kilobits per second (kbps). **Ease of use** reflects particular advantages and disadvantages. **Price** is a national average.

Typical features for these models

• Copier capability. • Automatic redial. • Data-transfer rate of at least 9.6 kbps. • Fax/tel switch, enabling operation on a phone line used for voice calls. • Transmission-resolution switch, with fine, photo, and standard settings. • Remote start to initiate reception from extension phones. • On thermal machines, a paper cutter. • Telephone handset. • Ability to poll—to call another machine in order to receive a document from it—and to be polled. • Broadcast capability. • Ability to enlarge and reduce copies, and to allow up to 99 copies to be ordered. • Delayed sending. • Ability to detect "distinctive ringing." • Technical support via a toll-free telephone number. **Multifunction machines:** • Operate only with IBM-compatible computers. • Speaker to hear transmissions. • Digital clock to schedule delayed sendings. • Ability to accept telephone-answering device. **All scanners:** Compatible with "TWAIN"—a software standard that enables scanned images to be imported directly into text and graphics programs on your computer.

Recommendations

The top-rated multifunction machine, the Brother MFC-4550 ($790), performs all its functions well and has a very low per-page cost. But better buys for most people include the Hewlett-Packard OfficeJet 300 ($460) and the Samsung Multijet FX-4100 ($450). A fax-only machine is an inexpensive and space-efficient choice. For faxes that don't fade, buy a machine that prints on plain paper. The two such models we tested—the Sharp UX-1100 ($340) and Brother Intellifax-1270 ($360)—vary mostly in a few features. The best value in a fax-only machine that uses thermal paper is the Brother FAX-290MC ($250).

See Buying Guide Report, page 229. Last time rated in CONSUMER REPORTS: September 1997.

Ratings continued ▶

Ratings, continued

Overall Ratings

E VG G F P

Listed within types in order of overall score

Key no.	Brand and model	Price	Overall score (0–100; P F G VG E)	Appearance of pages: FAX	COPIER	PRINTER	SCANNER	Fax speed IN/OUT	Ease of use
	MULTIFUNCTION MACHINES								
	PLAIN-PAPER MODELS								
1	**Brother** MFC-4550	$790		VG	VG	E	VG	E/E	VG
2	**Hewlett-Packard** OfficeJet 300	460		VG	G	VG	—	VG/E	G
3	**Samsung** Multijet FX-4100	450		G	F	VG	—	F/E	VG
4	**Sharp** UX-1400	450		G	F	G	G	E/E	VG
5	**Panasonic** KX-F1050	390		G	F	G	G	F/VG	G
	THERMAL-PAPER MODEL								
6	**Brother** MFC-390MC	300		G	G	F	G	VG/VG	VG
	FAX-ONLY MACHINES								
	PLAIN-PAPER MODELS								
7	**Sharp** UX-1100	340		G	G	—	—	VG/E	VG
8	**Brother** Intellifax-1270	360		G	G	—	—	G/VG	VG
	THERMAL-PAPER MODELS								
9	**Brother** FAX-290MC	250		G	G	—	—	VG/VG	VG
10	**Brother** FAX-190	200		VG	G	—	—	VG/VG	F
11	**Panasonic** KX-F780	290		G	G	—	—	VG/VG	F
12	**Radio Shack** TFX-1032	380		VG	G	—	—	VG/G	F
13	**Sharp** UX-177	200		VG	G	—	—	G/G	G

Model details

Notes on the details: Cost per page includes ink, toner, and plain paper, at 1 cent per sheet. **Memory** is in double-spaced typed pages. **Small-sized** machines take up a space of about 1 foot wide by 1 to 1½ feet deep; **medium,** about 15 inches wide by about 2 feet deep; and **large,** about 1½ feet by 2 feet deep. **Printer speed** is given in pages per minute (ppm). **Fast-dial number** is the total number of one-touch keys and speed-dial numbers; both allow you to program buttons to call frequently used numbers.

Multifunction machines

1 Brother MFC-4550 $790

• Laser printing • 3¢/page • Printer (5.7 ppm), PC fax, scanner • 44-pg. memory • Large-sized • 1-yr. warranty

The sole laser-printing multifunction machine tested. The best scanner of all, though less convenient than others to set up. Can activate pager upon receipt of fax. Has fax forwarding, 14.4-kbps speed, dual access, ECM, 60 fast-dial numbers, 30-page feeder, and 200-page paper tray. But: Deeper than others (32 in.). **Recommendation:** An excellent machine, but a good value only if you must have the superb appearance of laser-printed pages.

2 Hewlett-Packard OfficeJet 300 $460
• Ink-jet printing • 5¢/page • Printer (3 ppm) • 22-pg. memory • Large-sized • 1-yr. warranty
The faster at printing of the two ink-jet models tested—though (3), the other ink-jet, was quicker with faxes. Has ECM, 65 fast-dial numbers, 20-page feeder, and 100-page paper tray. But: Lacks toll-free telephone support and telephone handset. Transmitted faxes, especially photos, not as well as most. Exorbitant post-warranty repair cost ($263 flat charge). **Recommendation:** A very good machine, though with fewer capabilities than most multifunctions.

3 Samsung Multijet FX-4100 $450
• Color ink-jet printing • 4¢/page • Printer (1.3 ppm) • 26-pg. memory • Large-sized • 1-yr. warranty
Among the few color-capable machines sold. Has ECM, dual access, 70 fast-dial numbers, 30-page feeder, and 100-page paper tray. Will operate in DOS. But: Transmitted faxes, especially photos, not as well as most. Slower than most at copying. The black print it uses when printing color pages is mixed from three colors, and so is a bit muddy. **Model availability:** Discontinued. **Recommendation:** A very good machine, and the only one tested that prints in color. But has fewer capabilities than most multifunctions, and performs slowly.

4 Sharp UX-1400 $450
• Thermal-transfer printing • 7¢/page • Printer (2.1 ppm), PC fax, scanner, OCR, telephone answering machine • 30-page memory • Medium-sized • 90-day warranty
Has 14.4-kbps speed, ECM, caller ID, 99 fast-dial numbers, 20-page document feeder, and 300-page paper tray. But: Did not fax photos as well as others. Slower than most at copying. Cannot connect an answering machine. **Recommendation:** A very good machine, especially if you don't anticipate sending many photographs or fine-resolution graphics. But pricey for a thermal-transfer model.

5 Panasonic KX-F1050 $390
• Thermal-transfer printing • 7¢/page • Printer (2.4 ppm), PC fax, scanner • 26-page memory • Large-sized • 1-yr. warranty
This model received faxes at one of the slowest rates in our tests. Can activate pager upon receipt of fax. Has dual access, 126 fast-dial numbers, 15-page feeder, and 250-page paper tray. Will operate in DOS. But: Can make only one copy at a time, and lacks broadcast capability. **Model availability:** Discontinued, though may still be available in stores. **Recommendation:** A good machine, as long as neither fast fax reception nor multiple copies are priorities.

6 Brother MFC-390MC $300
• Thermal printing • 8¢/page • Printer (1.3 ppm), PC fax, scanner, telephone answering machine, OCR • 22-page memory • Small-sized • 1-yr. warranty
Rich in features at a modest price. Can activate pager upon receipt of fax. Has fax forwarding, dual access, ECM, 14.4-kbps speed, caller ID, 10-page feeder, and 55 fast-dial numbers. But: Lacks copy enlargement/reduction, output tray for originals and for incoming faxes. Not as good as others on extremely noisy lines. **Recommendation:** A good machine, but only a fair printer.

Fax-only machines

7 Sharp UX-1100 $340
• Thermal-transfer printing • 7¢/page • 26-page memory • Medium-sized • 90-day warranty
The fastest fax-only machine at transmitting faxes. Has ECM, caller ID, 99 fast-dial numbers, 20-page feeder, and 300-page paper tray. But: Not as good as most at faxing photos. **Model availability:** Discontinued. **Recommendation:** A very good machine.

8 Brother Intellifax-1270 $360
• Thermal-transfer printing • 8¢/page • 23-page memory • Medium-sized • 90-day warranty
This machine transmits faxes at a very good speed. Can activate pager upon receipt of fax. Can add printing, PC fax, and scanner functions with Missing Link, $80. Has fax forwarding, dual access, ECM, caller ID, 200-page paper tray, 20-page document feeder, and 60 fast-dial num-

Ratings continued

Ratings, continued

bers. Less deep than other medium-sized models. But: Not as good as others on extremely noisy lines. Similar: Intellifax-1170, lacks fax forwarding and pager activation. **Recommendation:** A very good machine.

9 **Brother FAX-290MC** $250

• Thermal printing • 8¢/page • Telephone answering machine • 22-pg. memory • Small-sized • 1-yr. warranty

This model, which sends and receives at very good speeds, is essentially identical to (6), except it lacks the Missing Link hardware that allows it to be used as a printer and scanner. **Recommendation:** A very good machine—and a good value.

10 **Brother FAX-190** $200

• Thermal printing • 8¢/page • Small-sized • 90-day warranty

A very basic machine that has dual access, caller ID, 10-page document feeder, and 25 fast-dial numbers. But: Can make only one copy at a time and, lacking memory, cannot receive faxes when out of paper. Also lacks copy enlargement/reduction, and an output tray for originals and for incoming faxes. Not as good as others on extremely noisy lines. Similar: FAX-170, has five fewer fast-dial numbers. **Recommendation:** A very good machine, and a good value if your needs are very basic.

11 **Panasonic KX-F780** $290

• Thermal printing • 8¢/page • Telephone answering machine • Small-sized • 1-yr. warranty

The fastest fax-only machine for making copies. Has pager activation upon receipt of fax, ECM, 60 fast-dial numbers, and a 15-page document feeder. Can accept a 164-ft. paper roll, rather than usual 98 ft. But: Cannot be connected to an answering machine. Can make only one copy at a time and, lacking memory, cannot receive faxes when out of paper. Also lacks copy enlargement/reduction, and output tray for originals and for incoming faxes. Faxes more prone to curl than with others. **Model availability:** Discontinued, though may still be available in stores. **Recommendation:** A good machine but a poor value.

12 **Radio Shack TFX-1032** $380

• Thermal printing • 6¢/page • Small-sized • 90-day warranty

This is the most expensive fax-only model—and the slowest at both faxing and copying. Has 10-page document feeder and 28 fast-dial numbers. But: Can make only one copy at a time and, lacking memory, cannot receive faxes when out of paper. Also lacks broadcast capability, toll-free support, delayed sending, distinctive-ring detection, output tray for originals and for incoming faxes. Not as good as others on extremely noisy lines. Cannot be polled. **Model availability:** Discontinued. **Recommendation:** A good machine but a poor value.

13 **Sharp UX-177** $200

• Thermal printing • 7¢/page • Small-sized • 90-day warranty

Can accept 164-ft. paper roll, rather than the usual 98 ft. Has caller ID, 20-page document feeder, and 50 fast-dial numbers. But: Lacks copy enlargement/reduction; output tray for original. Can make only one copy at a time and, lacking memory, cannot receive faxes when out of paper. Faxes more prone to curl than with others. **Model availability:** Discontinued. **Recommendation:** A good machine, and a reasonable value if your needs are very basic.

Can't find a model? Call the manufacturer. See page 342.

AUTOS

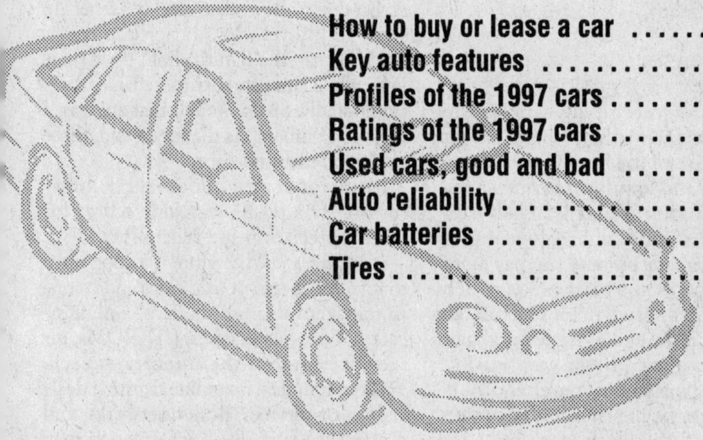

How to buy or lease a car

Shopping for a car can be a rational process or an emotional odyssey. There are practical considerations like overall performance, safety, and reliability. And there are personal considerations like aesthetics and image. Whether you buy or lease, new or used, the more your practical side prevails, the better your chances of getting the best transportation at the lowest price.

New or used?

Nearly three out of every four cars sold last year were used cars. It's easy to see why. Compared with a good-quality used car, a new car is a poor investment.

New cars cost a lot and lose much of that value in their first three years. With a used car, the previous owner has taken the biggest hit in depreciation. In the years that follow, cars depreciate much more slowly. Since a used car costs less, you may also save money by paying cash and avoiding finance costs. And insurance coverage on a used car is cheaper.

But the choice of new versus used goes beyond dollars and cents. Important benefits of buying new include the reliability that the car's newness conveys and the warranty the car comes with. A used car may have been driven abusively by its previous owner, or vital maintenance may have been neglected. A used car will have used up at least part of the factory warranty. (Dealers may provide their own warranty on a used car, but it's often not as comprehensive.) And if you buy from a private owner, you buy as is. Another pitfall in buying used is that important safety features like dual air bags and antilock brakes were less common a few years ago. That puts an added burden on you to search out a used car that has all the latest safety equipment.

Buy or lease?

One out of three new cars will be leased rather than bought this year—no doubt because of the lure of low monthly payments and low down payments featured so prominently in lease advertising. Lease payments are lower than car-loan payments because you pay mostly for the amount the car depreciates during the time you have it, plus an interest charge. But at the end of the lease, you no longer have a car. If you keep leasing, your monthly payments never end.

A lease may be the cheapest way to get behind the wheel, but it may not be the cheapest way to stay there. Leasing may hold a clear advantage if you lease an expensive car for business use. You may then be able to deduct more of the cost than if you buy the car. Leasing may also make sense if you need transportation immediately but lack a down payment to buy a car. And it may make sense if you want to drive a car you can't afford to buy—or if you don't want to go through the hassle of selling the car eventually.

Narrowing your choices

To be successful in any purchase or lease transaction, new or used, you need good information. Begin by choosing several models to focus on. Check the profiles of the 1997 cars, beginning on page 266. For used models, see our list of good bets, as well as used cars to avoid, on pages 284 to 286. See also our Frequency-of-Repair charts, starting on page 289.

Talk to your insurance agent. Insuring some kinds of cars—sports cars, for instance—can be very expensive.

If you're buying a new car and expect to get rid of it in a few years, look for a model that doesn't depreciate quickly. Generally, sport-utility vehicles and pickup trucks (and one car, the Saturn) hold their value best, while large and luxury sedans depreciate rapidly. So do models that are leased in large numbers. As the leases end, those cars flood the used-car market.

Also, look at a model's reliability record. The profiles include scores for both depreciation and reliability.

Manufacturers' literature is a good place to find out about specifications and colors. Automakers also use modern communication tools—videotapes, CD-ROMs, interactive sites on the Internet—to sell. You can find dealers online through dealer-locator services, dealer networks, and dealer Web sites. Such information may be helpful—but it's still an advertisement, and it's probably missing key facts such as the dealer costs of the car and options.

CONSUMER REPORTS offers detailed price information through our New Car Price Service (see page 257). A printout lists sticker and invoice prices for a specific model and all its factory options. It also tells of factory "incentives"—rebates or low interest rates. That service can also give you the trade-in value of your current car, or you can call our Used Car Price Service direct (see page 257).

You can also get such information, in different levels of detail, from other sources. Printed price guides are available at bookstores, newsstands, and libraries, but frequent price changes can quickly make such guides obsolete. Information is also available from auto clubs and on the Internet.

Be wary of promises of "wholesale" or "preferred" prices offered by online ser-

MORE AUTO INFORMATION

Consumer Reports Online
Our Web site *(www.ConsumerReports.org)* covers autos, appliances, electronics gear, and more. Free areas provide useful listings, recalls, and shopping guidance. Members pay $2.95 per month for unlimited use, including searchable access to road test reports and auto Ratings, with an interactive car selector, profiles, and our unique reliability information for nearly 200 1998 models and hundreds of used 1989 to 1997 models.

Cars: The Essential Guide on CD-ROM
This interactive CD-ROM covers new and used cars, minivans, pickups, and sport-utility vehicles from 1989 through 1998 in an easy-to-use database. It includes an interactive video for practicing negotiating with dealers. You'll also find Ratings and buying advice on auto products and accessories. For more information, see page 358.

New Car Price Service
This service provides the latest consumer advice and price information for cars, minivans, sport-utility vehicles, and light trucks. Sticker prices and dealer-invoice costs for the vehicle, factory options and packages show you how much room you have to negotiate. You also receive the latest information on customer and dealer incentives along with advice on getting the best price. To order, see back cover.

Used Car Price Service
With a touch-tone phone, you can get purchase and trade-in prices for cars, minivans, sport-utility vehicles, and light trucks, 1988 to 1997 models. Prices for used 1997 models are available as of January 1998. Prices take into account the vehicle's age, mileage, major options, condition, and the region you live in. A Trouble Summary, based on Consumer Reports Frequency-of-Repair data, is available for many models. To order, see page 357.

Auto Insurance Price Service
You receive a personalized report this lists up to 25 of the lowest-priced policies for the drivers in your household. This service helps you compare policies, and also includes our how-to-buy insurance guide and money saving tips. To order, see page 359.

vices such as Auto-By-Tel and AutoVantage. Our car-buying experience tells us you can often beat their prices by bargaining with dealers face-to-face. Note, too, that dealers pay substantial fees to services to get the referrals in their region. Those dealers may not be the ones who'll give you the best deal.

New-car buying strategy

For most people, car-shopping is an unfamiliar and daunting experience, made worse because bargaining about price is expected. If you want to avoid the negotiating process, you can buy a Saturn. That make has a one-price, take-it-or-leave-it policy. But if you don't happen to want a Saturn, the haggle-free choices are limited. Some other automakers have established a one-price policy for a few specific models, but those models are usually the less popular ones.

Truth is, you needn't be a skilled haggler to negotiate a good deal. You do, however, have to do a little homework. And you have to be willing to shop around—that's the most basic tenet for getting the best price.

It goes without saying that falling in love with one specific car is a sure way to overpay. Have two or three models in mind. That way, if one dealer won't give you a good deal, you can price a competing make. Note that some models have "twins"—similar models with different nameplates—that increase your shopping opportunities. If you're considering, say, a Dodge Caravan, you can check out the similar Plymouth Voyager as well.

Visit dealers' showrooms to get a close look at the models you're considering. Sit inside and check the fit. Ask for a test drive, and pick up any available brochures. But don't let the salesperson talk price just yet. First, determine how much room you have for negotiating.

Learn the dealer's cost. If you have the invoice price in hand when you walk into the showroom, the salespeople may not be pleased, but they'll treat you with more respect. Bargain up from the invoice price, not down from the sticker price.

Make a worksheet. Whichever price source you use, write down the make, model, and trim line of each car you want to price. List each option or options package by name and manufacturer's code number (price guides give that information). Write down the prices of the basic car and each extra-cost item—the wholesale prices in one column, retail prices in another. Add the destination charge to both columns, since there's no markup on it. Then total the columns, and subtract any factory rebate from the wholesale column. The difference between the two totals—wholesale and retail—is your bargaining room.

The art of the deal. The simplest and most effective approach is to present your figures to the salesperson and say you want the lowest markup over invoice the dealership will accept. If your figures are challenged, ask to see the dealer's figures; that's only fair.

Keep the transaction simple. Don't discuss a trade-in or financing until you have arrived at a firm price for the new car.

Explain immediately that you'll be pricing that model—or other, similar models—at several more dealerships, so you won't be buying right away. But make it clear that when you do buy—sometime in the next few days—the lowest bid will win the sale.

The dealer won't want to let you leave the showroom, but never mind. Resist any efforts to pressure you to buy the car immediately. Ask the dealer for the best price, and leave.

What constitutes a good deal depends on supply and demand. Generally, about 2 to 5 percent over invoice is reasonable. If the dealer is overstocked with a particular model, you may be able to do even better. But for new and popular models in short supply, you may have to pay more. Ultimately, the only way to find out the going purchase price is to shop around.

Don't feel too guilty about squeezing the dealer's profit. The domestic automakers and some foreign ones give their dealers an additional "holdback" of 2 or 3 percent of the sticker price for each vehicle sold.

One tricky item is advertising charges, imposed on some dealers by manufacturers' zone offices. Those charges—typically, from $200 to $400—vary from region to region and model to model, and they don't show up in price guides. Advertising charges should be added to the dealer's cost, as long as they're legitimate. Before you pay, ask to see documentation.

Late in the model year, a dealer may offer a tempting deal on a "leftover" model. But realize that as soon as you drive such a car out of the showroom, it will instantly undergo a year's worth of depreciation. Two years from now, it will be a three-year-old car, and its resale value will reflect that fact. If the car is stolen or wrecked soon after you've bought it, your insurance will pay you much less than if you'd bought the latest model. If you keep the car a long time—say, six or eight years—depreciation is not a significant factor.

After you think you've agreed on a purchase price, the salesperson or the business manager may try to sell you dealer-installed "packs" such as rustproofing, paint sealant, or fabric protection, or an extended-service contract. Refuse them. They're generally overpriced or worthless. Some, like dealer rustproofing, may actually do more harm than good.

Trading in your old car. Once you've agreed on the price of the new car, you can discuss the trade-in separately with the dealer. You can usually get a better price by selling your old car privately. But that's a hassle that may mean staying home to wait for calls and allowing strangers to drive your car and enter your home.

To get an idea of what you should get for your old car, whether from a dealer or in a private sale, use the Consumer Reports Used Car Price Service (see page 257 for details) or other guides available at libraries, newsstands, and bookstores, and on the Internet.

Leasing strategy

A lease deal could be as good as a purchase deal—but it often isn't. Besides using confusing language, some salespeople use unethical sales tactics—like convincing people to pay what amounts to more than the full sticker price for their leased car. Some of the tricks reported to consumer-protection agencies are downright illegal—like cheating people out of the credit for the car they trade in, or even leading them to believe they're negotiating a loan when they're actually signing a lease deal.

New disclosure language mandated by the government took effect in late 1997. It's a step in the right direction, but it still won't force leasing companies to disclose all the information you need to comparison-shop.

How leasing works. When you sign a lease, you make the deal with a car dealer, who acts as a representative of a leasing company. That company may be the finance arm of an automaker (Chrysler Credit, Ford Credit, GMAC), or it may be a bank or other financial institution.

After you sign the lease, the dealer sells the car to the leasing company for the price you negotiated. Your monthly payments—which cover depreciation, interest charges, and any state taxes—go to the leasing company, not to the dealer.

The lease spells out a term, typically two or three years, and the amount of each monthly payment. Usually, it also quotes a "residual value"—nominally, an estimate of what the car will be worth at the end of the lease term. Your monthly payments are calculated roughly on the basis of the difference between the car's initial price and its residual value.

With a standard "closed end" lease, you can walk away from the car at the end of the lease or, if the lease includes a buying option, you can buy the car. Don't sign an "open end" lease, which requires you to make up any shortfall between the residual value of the car, as projected in the lease, and the actual value at the end of the lease.

Automakers that want to boost sales can subsidize leases ("subvent," in leasing parlance) by having their captive finance companies offer a high residual value. That means lower monthly payments, which can be a good deal for you if you walk away from the car at the end of the lease.

Be prepared to live with the terms of the contract. For example, if you exceed the mileage limit, you may have to pay as much as 25 cents per mile for the excess. So estimate your mileage needs carefully. A 12,000-mile limit is typical, but you can negotiate a higher limit if necessary. Resolve to take good care of your car to avoid steep "excess wear and tear" charges. And be prepared to stick it out for the full term of the lease, since terminating prematurely can set you back thousands of dollars.

Shopping for a lease. It's best to keep an open mind, approaching a leasing deal as if you're buying the car. Follow the buying advice we give on page 258. Ask several dealers for their best purchase price, and bring up leasing only after you have the lowest price. Then you can compare and decide which is best for you.

Also, check the newspapers for ads offering factory-subsidized leases. Even if the car models offered aren't ones you want, the ads will give you an idea of the deals that are available.

Throughout the negotiations, make sure the capitalized cost—the price of the car—is no higher than the purchase price you negotiated. Ask what "money factor" is used to work out the monthly payments. Multiplying the money factor by 2400 gives the approximate interest rate. Make sure GAP (guaranteed auto protection) insurance is included at no extra cost. If the car is stolen or destroyed, GAP insurance will cover the difference between the book value of the car and what you owe on the lease.

Before you sign the contract, ask to take it home for careful study or expert advice. Be sure you understand everything. The vehicle identification number in the contract should match that of the car you want. And see that the automaker's warranty covers the full term of the lease. If important information is missing, have it added. Terms like "excess wear and tear" should be defined clearly.

Used-car leasing. Although it's growing even faster than new-car leasing, used-car leasing still accounts for a very small proportion of used-car transactions.

A used-car lease offers the major attraction of a new-car lease: low monthly payments. But it also combines the disadvantages of leasing with the disadvantages of buying a used car. You may have scanty information about what you're really paying and how it's derived. And you're taking a chance on the car's reliability. You also give up the thrill of driving a new car, one of leasing's major selling points. Before you consider leasing a used car, calculate how much it would cost you to buy the car instead.

Used-car buying strategy

New-car leasing has been a boon to used-car buyers. As those leases expire, more and more two- and three-year-old cars are flooding the market, increasing your choices. Check used-car prices before you shop. Such information is available from our Used Car Price Service (see page 257); from printed guides at bookstores, newsstands, libraries, and banks; and on the Internet.

The reliability record of a car model is important—and that's where CONSUMER REPORTS readers can help. Their experience with the half-million or more cars they tell us about each year in our Annual Questionnaire serves as a unique guide to how well those cars have held up over the years, and how well they're likely to hold up in the years to come. Refer to the tables starting on page 289 for specifics on more than 200 cars and light trucks, going back as many as eight years.

The National Highway Traffic Safety Administration (800 424-9393) can tell you whether a model has been recalled. Also, the Buying Guide lists all auto recalls published in CONSUMER REPORTS during the last year. See page 329.

Where to buy

Superstores and new-car dealers. Used-car superstores have huge lots. Typically, you sit in the office and choose from hundreds of vehicles on a computer monitor. Also typically, superstores feature no-haggle pricing and on-site financing. Chains such as CarMax, Auto-Nation USA, Car America, SmartCars, and Driver's Mart Worldwide are regional, but they may be national soon. Others are independent.

Superstores and new-car dealers often feature the cream of the crop in used cars. But prices may be high.

A relatively new development is the "certified" used car, sold with a special warranty from the automaker rather than the dealer. These are supposed to be the very best used vehicles, reconditioned to the automaker's specifications.

Independent used-car dealers. Prices are apt to be lower here, but quality may be lower, too.

Service stations. If they've serviced the car, they can recount its history—a plus. If you're a regular customer, that may be an added incentive to give you a fair deal. Selection will be limited, however.

Private owners. Expect the lowest prices and the biggest risks.

Checking it out

A car sold by a dealer must have a "buyer's guide" sticker with warranty information. Read it carefully. If you're buying from a private party, ask to see service records and the warranty booklet. Such records are an indication that the car has been serviced and maintained properly.

No matter how clean the car looks, have a mechanic inspect it thoroughly (cost: about $60 to $100). If the mechanic finds flaws, ask for a written repair estimate. In your negotiations, you can ask that the cost of repairs be deducted from the car's price.

Before you take a car to your mechanic,

you can perform a few simple tests to eliminate an obvious clunker:

• See that body panels line up properly. Misalignment indicates accident damage.

• Check for rust, especially under the doors, in the trunk, and in the wheel wells.

• Watch out for odometer readings that don't jibe with the car's condition. The odometer may have been rolled back illegally. Loose door hinges, sagging springs in the driver's seat, severe pedal wear—all may indicate high mileage.

• Try all the controls, check the displays, and make sure all the accessories do what they're supposed to do.

• Check under the car for leaks.

• With the engine idling, jiggle the steering wheel back and forth. There should be no more than a couple of inches of play in the steering wheel before the front wheels turn.

• On a level road, the car should track straight without constant steering corrections or adjustments.

• The engine should accelerate smoothly. Coast from about 15 mph to 5 mph in low gear, then floor the accelerator. A cloud of blue exhaust smoke indicates an oil-burner.

• Signs of transmission wear: in an automatic, a lag between the engine's acceleration and the car's; in a manual, a clutch that slips or doesn't engage smoothly.

• On a straight, level road, try a series of gentle stops from 30 mph. Watch for pulling to one side.

Key auto features

Options are sold two ways: individually and in packages, with names like Preferred Equipment Group. The price per item in a package is usually lower than the individual price, so a package can be a good deal, if you want most of the equipment. But packages can sometimes force you to buy equipment you don't want or need.

Here's a guide to key options. A check (✔) indicates an option we recommend because it adds to safety, convenience, or comfort.

✔ **Adjustable steering column.** $58 to $235. Lets you position the steering wheel comfortably for driving and helps you slip in and out of the driver's seat easily. Some have power tilt and telescoping features; some, a programmable memory. Recommendation: Especially useful for cars with more than one driver.

✔ **Air bags.** Driver and passenger air bags are standard in all cars and most other passenger vehicles. (The conventional design protects in a head-on crash, but not in a side-impact accident. More and more automakers, however, are offering side air bags.) A driver's air bag is standard or optional (about $400) in some trucks. Recommendation: A must for both front seats.

✔ **Air-conditioning.** Standard on many vehicles; $460 to $1980 option on some. Add $100 to $200 for automatic temperature control. Improves comfort, reduces outside noise, and prevents window fogging year-round. Reduces fuel economy, particularly in stop-and-go traffic. Costly to repair. Recommendation: A must in the South and Southwest. It's difficult to sell a used car, anywhere, without it.

✔ **All-wheel drive.** Standard in some vehicles; $1000 to $3800 option in others. Greatly improves traction and directional stability in rain, snow, and mud. Full-time all-wheel drive, which is always in use, also improves handling on dry roads.

Selectable four-wheel drive works almost as easily and as well. Part-time four-wheel drive can't be used on dry roads. Recommendation: Makes a vehicle more surefooted but reduces fuel economy. Costly to repair.

✔ **Antilock brakes (ABS).** Standard in many vehicles; $500 to $950 option in some. Maintains control during hard stops and provides shorter stops on slippery roads. The brakes do the pumping; the driver just stomps and steers. Recommendation: An important safety item, but must be used properly.

✔ **Automatic transmission.** Standard or optional in virtually all vehicles; costs up to $1450 as an option. Today's automatics are practical even with a small engine. Some models now have a five-speed automatic or continuously variable transmission (CVT). Overdrive gear and lock-up torque converter improve fuel economy. Recommendation: Manual transmissions usually deliver better fuel economy, but automatics are much easier to drive, especially in heavy traffic.

Cellular phone. $650 to $790. Lets you call police, ambulance, or tow truck—or just to tell someone you'll be late. Monthly and per-call charges are dropping. Recommendation: Expensive, but useful in an emergency. Get a "hands-free" system so you can drive safely. Voice-activated dialing is another good feature.

✔ **Central locking system.** $25 to $225 (keyless entry costs $135 to $250). Lets you lock and unlock all doors at once, inside or out, with a remote control. Variations abound. The best design depends on how comfortable you are about where you travel. Possible nuisances: automatic systems that don't let you open your door from inside; systems that automatically unlock all the doors when the car is put in park (as in many GM cars). Recommendation: Soon becomes an indispensable convenience.

Cruise control. $175 to $475. Helps maintain the speed limit and may reduce driver fatigue. But it can also lull you into inattention. Impractical in heavy traffic. Recommendation: Best for long distances on open roads.

Dealer "packs," or add-ons. Cost varies. Packs include dealer-installed rustproofing, pinstripes, paint and upholstery preservatives, and the like. At best, they're unnecessary or no better than aftermarket products that you apply yourself. Improperly applied rustproofing can hasten corrosion. Recommendation: A waste of money.

Extended-service contract. Cost varies. Extends manufacturer's warranty, which typically runs for three years. Recommendation: May be worthwhile for an unreliable model—but you wouldn't want to buy one of those cars anyway.

Full-sized spare. Not widely available, but about $80 to $260 when it is. Adds a fifth, full-sized tire to the rotation and has none of the speed or distance limitations of a small, limited-service spare. Heavy and awkward to handle. Recommendation: Worthwhile if available.

✔ **Integrated child seat.** $100 to $250. More expensive than separately sold seats, but there are no installation problems. When not open for a child, the safety-seat hardware may reduce passenger-seat comfort. Recommendation: Worthwhile for families with small children.

Leather upholstery. $475 to $1525. Looks and feels luxurious, but is often slippery and clammy. Feels hot in the summer and cold in winter, unless you spend another $225 to $580 for a seat heater. Recommendation: Durable and easy to clean, but an indulgence.

Limited-slip differential. $95 to $1900. On slippery roads, improves traction but can cause difficulty turning. Recommendation: Traction control or all-wheel drive does the job better.

Optional engine. Additional horsepower for can add hundreds or even thousands of dollars. A larger engine is usually less noisy at highway speeds, but it's typically less fuel efficient. May be available only with other equipment upgrades. Recommendation: Most base engines are adequate in passenger cars. Light trucks, minivans, and SUVs may benefit, especially for trailer-towing.

✔ **Power mirrors.** $70 to $140. Easy-to-adjust mirrors contribute to safety. Recommendation: Especially useful for cars with more than one driver.

✔ **Power seat.** $203 to $955. A variety of adjustments enhance driver comfort and view. A "memory" allows programming different settings for different drivers. Some cars also offer power adjustments for the front passenger seat. Recommendation: Especially useful in cars with otherwise low front seats.

Power windows. $265 to $340. Some give you one-touch lowering of the driver's window and driver's control of all windows. Lock-out feature reduces hazard to children. Switches can be confusing and hard to find at night. Recommendation: An indulgence, perhaps, but after you've lived with power, turning a window crank seems a burden.

✔ **Rear-window defroster.** Standard in most cars; $70 to $330 option in some. Keeps the rear window clear of fog, frost, and snow. Recommendation: Practical.

✔ **Rear-window wiper/washer.** Standard in many vehicles; $125 to $280 option in some. Clears dew, rain, snow, and grime. Recommendation: Important for station wagons, hatchbacks, and SUVs.

Sound system. $25 to $2075, depending on components, from simple ra-

Air-bag safety

Air bags markedly reduce the chances of serious injury or death in a head-on crash. With children and short adults (under 5 feet 2 inches), the explosive force of an inflating air bag has caused numerous injuries and a small number of deaths in low-speed crashes. In most documented instances, the occupants were not buckled up, or improperly belted, which is an important factor in the effectiveness of an air bag.

The government is considering various modifications to air bags that would make them safer for vehicle occupants of all ages and sizes. But with or without an air bag, it's always preferable to place children in a car's rear seat (the center rear seat is safest of all). That's especially important when using a child safety seat, vital when using a rear-facing infant seat.

Adults can best protect themselves from air-bag injury by properly fastening the safety belt, so the shoulder portion crosses the chest, and by moving the front seat as far back as comfortable. The driver's chest should be as far from the steering wheel as possible while still allowing the driver to control the car comfortably.

dios to CD players. The best systems approach room acoustics. Recommendation: A personal preference.

Sunroof/moonroof. $595 to $1550. Generally, a sunroof lets in light only when open; a moonroof is like a tinted window in the roof. Improves ventilation, brightens the interior. Can help resale value. Recommendation: Check head room before you buy.

Theft-deterrent system. $60 to $695 gets you some combination of loud noise and flashing lights. May deter theft and reduce your insurance rates, but alarms disturb the neighbors and are often ignored. Recommendation: Buy the car from the dealer and the device from an auto-supply or car-alarm store, where it's likely to cost less.

✔ **Traction control.** Standard on some cars; $175 to $202 option on others. Improves traction and directional stability on slippery roads, though not as effectively as all-wheel drive. Sophisticated systems work at all speeds; others, typically, below 25 mph. Recommendation: Worthwhile, especially in rear-wheel-drive cars.

Motor oil and oil additives

Buy the grade of oil recommended in your owner's manual, and shop for price, not brand.

Motor oil. **Motor oil should be thin enough to flow easily when the engine is cold and remain thick enough to protect the engine when it's hot. Its ability to flow—or viscosity—is translated into grades. The two most commonly recommended are 10W-30 and 5W-30. Automakers specify grades according to the temperature range expected in the climate where the car is used. The lower the number, the thinner the oil and the more easily it flows.**

In our tests, we found no difference between 5W-30 and 10W-30 brandmates under high-temperature, high-stress conditions. At low temperatures, the 5W-30 oil flowed more easily.

Oil additives. **Slick 50 and STP Oil Treatment boast that they reduce engine friction and wear. In our tests, we found no discernible benefits from either product. In fact, the STP Oil Treatment increased the oil viscosity, so 10W-30 oil acted more like 15W-40, a grade not often recommended. In very cold weather, that might pose a risk of engine damage.**

Shopping strategy. **Buy the viscosity grade recommended in your owner's manual. Look for the American Petroleum Institute "starburst" emblem on the container. The starburst indicates that the oil meets the latest industry requirements for protection against deposits, wear, oxidation, and corrosion. Expensive synthetic oil is worth considering only for extreme driving conditions, such as very hot or very cold weather. Skip the additives.**

Profiles of the 1997 cars

Here, listed alphabetically by make and model, you'll find descriptions of nearly all the 1997 models of cars, minivans, sport-utility vehicles, and pickups. For most of these models, our comments are based on a recent test, if not of the '97 model itself, then of its very similar recent predecessor (most models don't change significantly from year to year).

At the end of each entry, you'll find the date of the last full road test published in CONSUMER REPORTS. These detailed reports are available at libraries or by fax or mail from our Consumer Reports by Request 24-hour service. To use the service, note the four-digit fax number at the end of the model's entry and call 800 896-7788 from a touch-tone phone. The cost is $7.75 per report.

Predicted reliability is a judgment based on our Frequency-of-Repair data for past models (see page 287). If a vehicle has been recently redesigned, only data for models relevant to the 1997 models are considered. **Depreciation** predicts how well a new model will keep its value, based on the difference between a model's original sticker price and its resale value after three years. The average depreciation for all cars was 28 percent. As a group, sport-utility vehicles had the lowest rate (21 percent). Pickup trucks also tend to hold their value. Large cars have a relatively high depreciation (36 percent, on average).

Throughout, ✔ indicates a model recommended by CONSUMER REPORTS; **NA** means data not available; ⬆ means a model is promising; **New** means there's no data because the car is new or has been redesigned.

⊜	⊖	○	◒	●
Much better than average				Much worse than average

Model	Predicted reliability	Depreciation	Comments
Acura CL	○	NA	This fairly upscale model is based on the Honda Accord Coupe and comes with either a powerful 2.2-liter "VTEC" Four or a 3.0-liter V6. Either engine is a good choice. Expect good handling and a refined, quiet ride, but rather cramped quarters. **Last report/fax: ——**
✔ Acura Integra	⊜	⊖	A refined and good-handling small car with a proven record of reliability. The cabin feels a bit cramped and is somewhat noisy. **Last report/fax: August 95/9597**
✔ Acura RL	⊜	NA	The RL is Acura's flagship sedan. It handles well and delivers a smooth, quiet ride, but is not as capable, overall, as outstanding competitors like the BMW 5-Series or Mercedes E-class. **Last report/fax: November 96/9513**
Acura SLX	NA	NA	A rebadged Isuzu Trooper that we rate Not Acceptable because of its tendency to roll over. It's big and boxy, and a handful to maneuver. **Last report/fax: October 96/9507**
✔ Acura TL	⊖	NA	Handles competently, with a firm yet supple ride. Good ergonomics and room for four, but not five. Nice but not outstanding all around. **Last report/fax: February 96/9456**
✔ Audi A4	⊖	NA	A European sports sedan with quick, precise handling and a firm but comforatble ride. The interior is well laid out but a bit cramped, especially in the rear. All-wheel drive is available. **Last report/fax: February 96/9456**

Model	Predicted reliability	Depreciation	Comments
Audi A6	⊖	◒	The A6 is a German sports sedan with a roomy interior and comfortable seats. All-wheel drive is available. A redesign is due for 1998. **Last report/fax: ——**
Audi A8	New	NA	The A8 is a full-sized V8-powered German luxury sedan with an all-aluminum body. It competes with the best cars from BMW, Jaguar, Mercedes-Benz, and Lexus. **Last report/fax: ——**
✔ BMW 3-Series	⊖	○	Delivers sports-car handling and tenacious tire grip. A firm but comfortable ride and good noise insulation give a sense of quality. A good alternative to similar Japanese sports sedans. **Last report/fax: March 97/9558**
BMW 318ti	NA	NA	The 318ti is a small hatchback, similar to the regular 318 but shorter. Expect excellent sports-carlike handling and tenacious tire grip, plus a firm but comfortable ride. **Last report/fax: ——**
✔ BMW 5-Series	⊖	○	The new 5-Series offers pure, functional precision. It handles particularly well and gives you a good feel of the road. The ride is firm but quiet and comfortable. Excellent seats. **Last report/fax: November 96/9513**
BMW 740i	NA	◒	BMW's luxury V8 sedan competes with the world's finest and costliest cars. It delivers exceptional power, smoothness, quietness, and comfort, and comes loaded with accessory gadgets. **Last report/fax: ——**
BMW Z3	○	NA	This sleek roadster is built in South Carolina. It's based on components from the 3-Series sedans. It's big enough for tall people. The Six is the engine of choice but it's costly. **Last report/fax: ——**
Buick Century	New	NA	The Century was redesigned for 1997 but still feels dated and outclassed. Lots of standard equipment but not a well-integrated package. The brakes are unimpressive, and it handles rather clumsily. **Last report/fax: October 97/9618**
Buick LeSabre	○	◒	A quiet, softly sprung freeway cruiser. Expect the Le Sabre to handle sloppily and its body to lean sharply in turns. An optional firmer suspension helps a lot. **Last report/fax: January 96/9447**
Buick Park Avenue	New	NA	This quiet, roomy sedan was redesigned for 1997. The transmission is as smooth as any you'll find and acceleration is effortless, particularly in the supercharged version. **Last report/fax: ——**
Buick Regal	New	NA	The redesigned Regal delivers sprightly acceleration and acceptable handling, along with a soft, fairly well-controlled ride. Similar: Oldsmobile Intrigue and Pontiac Grand Prix. **Last report/fax: ——**
Buick Riviera	○	NA	This large, heavy coupe accelerates well and is very quiet. Tall drivers need more head room, and short drivers must sit too close to the wheel. Some controls and displays are awkward. **Last report/fax: July 95/9423**
Buick Skylark	⊖	◒	This basically unimpressive car responds slowly to its steering, and the body leans sharply in turns. The V6 is a better choice than the Four. **Last report/fax: ——**
Cadillac Catera	◒	NA	Small for a Cadillac but big for some European cars, the roomy, German-made Catera handles with agility and grace. The ride is firm but well controlled and supple. **Last report/fax: March 97/9558**
Cadillac DeVille	○	◒	The DeVille is big, plush, and roomy, with side air bags and electronic stability control. The upscale Concours version comes with GM's sophisticated aluminum Northstar V8. **Last report/fax: ——**
Cadillac Eldorado	○	◒	A plush coupe with a powerful aluminum engine and good automatic transmission, this car is cumbersome to maneuver in sharp turns. The ride isn't luxury-car smooth. **Last report/fax: ——**
Cadillac Seville	○	◒	A powerful aluminum V8 helps this luxury sedan accelerate very quickly. The ride is smooth except on poor roads. The rear seat is not very comfortable. Will be redesigned for 1998. **Last report/fax: ——**

Model	Predicted reliability	Depreciation	Comments
Chevrolet Astro	◒	○	The Astro has an enormous cargo area, but the design is dated. Drawbacks also include ponderous handling and an uncomfortable ride. All-wheel drive is available. Similar: GMC Safari. **Last report/fax: July 96/9489**
Chevrolet Blazer	●	⊖	The Blazer (and similar GMC Jimmy) are roomy and quiet. Still, they have mediocre brakes, a so-so ride, and a cramped rear seat. Full-time all-wheel-drive (without low range) is available on high-trim versions. **Last report/fax: August 95/9421**
Chevrolet C/K 1500	○	⊖	The Chevy (and similar GMC Sierra) offers a smooth powertrain and a quiet cabin, but a stiff ride. The third (rear) door on extended-cab versions is a worthwhile option. **Last report/fax: September 96/9499**
Chevrolet Camaro	●	○	One of the last rear-wheel-drive muscle cars. Seating is decent for two, but the driver can't see out well. The optional V8 is the engine of choice. Convertible versions are also available. **Last report/fax: October 93/7341**
✔ Chevrolet Cavalier	○	NA	The Cavalier is a competitive, if not outstanding, small car. But engine whine, imprecise steering, and a cramped rear seat limit one's enjoyment. Ergonomics are good, and seating is fairly comfortable. Similar: Pontiac Sunfire. **Last report/fax: January 97/9539**
Chevrolet Corvette	New	◒	The legendary two-seat sports car was redesigned for 1997, and added more power, a roomier cockpit, improved controls, and a rear-mounted transmission. It's still muscular, but more refined than its predecessors. **Last report/fax: ——**
✔ Chevrolet Lumina	○	◒	The Lumina comes nicely equipped and performs competently but not outstandingly. The interior is well laid out and very quiet, but the seats are thinly padded and not very comfortable. **Last report/fax: February 97/9549**
✔ Chevrolet Malibu	○	NA	Replacing the Corsica, the Malibu is a cheaper alternative to Japanese nameplates like the Camry and Accord. While not as polished as those, it rides and handles soundly, and has a well-thought-out interior. **Last report/fax: May 97/9572**
Chevrolet Monte Carlo	○	NA	This coupe version of the Lumina sedan offers good ergonomics but an unimpressive combination of sloppy handling and bounding ride. The LS rides better than the sporty Z34 model. **Last report/fax: July 95/9423**
Chevrolet S-Series	●	⊖	This pickup is a fairly new design, with a quiet cabin and good powertrain. Ride and handling are unexceptional. Reliability has been poor, and this truck didn't do well in government crash tests. **Last report/fax: November 95/9434**
Chevrolet Suburban	○	⊜	This huge truck-based sport-utility vehicle especially emphasizes utility. It can carry nine people and tow a heavy trailer. Fuel economy is horrid. **Last report/fax: ——**
Chevrolet Tahoe	○	○	The spacious Tahoe is a shortened Suburban. The ride is not bad for a truck. It lends itself well to hauling and towing, but fuel economy is poor and the brakes mediocre. **Last report/fax: October 96/9508**
Chevrolet Venture	●	NA	Redesigned for 1997, the Venture minivan and its GM siblings ride comfortably and handle quite well. Rear seating is uncomfortable. The similar Trans Sport did poorly in an offset frontal crash test. **Last report/fax: July 97/9589**
Chrysler Cirrus	◒	NA	A roomy sedan with good acceleration, the Cirrus handles adequately and has a nicely designed interior, but the ride, noise, and reliablity could be better. **Last report/fax: October 97/9618**

Model	Predicted reliability	Depreciation	Comments
✔ Chrysler Concorde	○	○	This large sedan handles as nimbly as a much smaller car, yet it seats five adults comfortably. Reliability has improved of late. A redesign is due for 1998. **Last report/fax: March 93/7948**
✔ Chrysler LHS	○	●	A stretched version of the Chrysler Concorde, the LHS handles well and boasts a limousine-like rear seat. **Last report/fax: March 94/9714**
Chrysler Sebring	●	NA	This sporty coupe is based on the Mitsubishi Galant platform. The Sebring is similar to its Dodge Avenger cousin. Both are stylish but a little humdrum. **Last report/fax: July 95/9423**
Chrysler Sebring Convertible	NA	NA	As a convertible, stylish and fun; but acceleration and braking are just adequate. The ride is jittery. The front seats are ample and supportive.The soft top's glass rear window is a plus. **Last report/fax: August 97/5598**
Chrysler Town & Country	◒	◒	This is a loaded version of the Dodge Grand Caravan and Plymouth Grand Voyager minivans. A well-designed package with good ride and handling and many useful details. **Last report/fax: July 97/9589**
Dodge Avenger	●	NA	This sporty coupe performs adequately in most ways. It's fairly nimble and quick. We'd choose the 2.5-liter Mitsubishi V6 over the noisy Chrysler 2.0-liter Four. **Last report/fax: July 95/9423**
✔ Dodge Caravan	○	◒	The Dodge Caravan/Plymouth Voyager minivan twins, redesigned for 1996, perform exceptionally well, overall. The second, left-side, sliding door is very handy. Reliability is average so far. **Last report/fax: July 96/9489**
✔ Dodge Dakota	○	○	Redesigned for 1997, the Dakota is greatly improved. It handles well for a pickup, but as with other trucks, ride comfort is only so-so. The cab is roomy, and the cargo bed is large. **Last report/fax: July 97/5591**
Dodge Grand Caravan	◒	◒	The Grand Caravan is a longer-bodied version of the Caravan minivan. Overall, it's well-designed—comfortable, quiet, roomy, and nice to drive. The long-wheelbase versions have not been as reliable as the short versions. **Last report/fax: July 97/9589**
Dodge Intrepid	◒	○	This large sedan handles as nimbly as a much smaller car, yet it seats five adults comfortably. Reliability problems cloud the fine overall performance. A redesign is due for 1998. **Last report/fax: January 95/9981**
Dodge Neon	◒	NA	This small car has a roomy interior and choice of two 2.0-liter engines. We prefer the double-overhead-cam version and manual transmission. The ride is choppy. Handling is predictable, but not exactly sporty. **Last report/fax: March 96/9457**
Dodge Ram 1500	○	⊜	The big Ram still won't ever let you forget it's a truck. Handling is ponderous but steady. Presently, extended-cab versions lack a third (rear) door. (The Ford F-150 is far more up-to-date.) **Last report/fax: September 96/9499**
Dodge Stratus	◒	NA	The Stratus is a roomy sedan that handles fairly well; the ride is so-so. The V6 accelerates better than the Four. The seats are a little lumpy but not uncomfortable. **Last report/fax: December: 95/9433**
Eagle Talon	●	⊖	The Talon comes from a joint venture of Chrysler and Mitsubishi. Turbocharging and all-wheel drive are available for extra performance and traction. **Last report/fax: ——**
Eagle Vision	◒	◒	This large sedan handles as nimbly as a much smaller car, yet it seats five adults comfortably. There will be no 1998 model. **Last report/fax: March 93/7948**
Ford Aerostar	○	◒	This aged rear-drive minivan is a sound choice for heavy-duty work such as pulling a trailer. All-wheel-drive is available and preferred. It will disappear after 1997. **Last report/fax: September ——**

Model	Predicted reliability	Depreciation	Comments
Ford Aspire	NA	◒	This little commuter car is a chore to drive. Good fuel economy, head room, and luggage space don't make up for poor acceleration, handling, and ride. Discontinued after 1997. **Last report/fax: October 94/9921**
✔ Ford Contour	○	NA	A good, solid family sedan. It handles nimbly and has comfortable front seats, but the rear is cramped. The four-cylinder engine is noisy; choose the V6 if you can. Similar: Mercury Mystique. **Last report/fax: August 96/9493**
✔ Ford Crown Victoria	○	◒	An old-fashioned V8-powered freeway cruiser. It handles decently, especially with the upgraded handling package. Expect a serene ride and a huge trunk. Will receive a facelift for 1998. Similar: Mercury Grand Marquis. **Last report/fax: March 94/9714**
✔ Ford Escort	○	◒	Much improved since its 1997 redesign. The engine is lively. It corners fairly nimbly. The ride is still a little choppy but handles bumps quite well. Cramped cabin for tall people. Similar: Mercury Tracer. **Last report/fax: January 97/9539**
✔ Ford Expedition	○	NA	This large SUV, based on the F-150 pickup, handles surprisingly well for its bulk and can carry nine people or lots of cargo. The high step-up gets old fast. Fuel economy is abysmal. **Last report/fax: June 97/9575**
✔ Ford Explorer	○	⊖	Lots of cargo space for a mid-sized SUV. The ride could be better, but handling, acceleration, and braking are all good. Full-time all-wheel drive, a major plus, is optional. **Last report/fax: June 97/9575**
✔ Ford F-150	○	⊖	This new-for-1997 model has set moden standards for ride, handling, and comfort among big pickup trucks. The F-150 has good ergonomics, a third (rear) door on extended-cab models, and dual airbags. **Last report/fax: September 96/9499**
Ford Mustang	◒	⊖	This old-fashioned muscle car has a rigid body and a fairly usable interior. But even with the optional V8, the Mustang doesn't feel sporty to drive. The V6 version falls particularly short. **Last report/fax: ——**
✔ Ford Probe	○	○	A nicely balanced sporty hatchback. In GT trim, it accelerates powerfully and handles well, though its ride is stiff and jittery. The Mazda MX-6 is a similar coupe version. Discontinued after 1997. **Last report/fax: ——**
✔ Ford Ranger	○	○	Rides and handles quite well, particularly for a pickup truck. The interior is quiet, comfortable, and well-laid-out. Redesigned for 1998. Similar: Mazda B-Series. **Last report/fax: November 95/9434**
Ford Taurus	◒	NA	This is a good, well-rounded family sedan. It corners responsively and offers a firm ride. The front is roomy and comfortable; head room is scarce in the rear. Similar: Mercury Sable. **Last report/fax: January 96/9447**
Ford Thunderbird	◒	◒	Expect a decent ride, but handling is not nimble. Standard equipment includes a wealth of power accessories. The 4.6-liter V8 is the better engine choice. Discontinued after 1997. Similar: Mercury Cougar. **Last report/fax: July 95/9423**
Ford Windstar	◒	NA	This minivan is a commendable performer, but reliability has been troublesome. Expect a comfortable ride and roomy interior, but ponderous handling. A large driver's door is available instead of a left-side sliding door. **Last report/fax: July 97/9589**
GMC Jimmy	●	⊖	The Jimmy (and similar Chevy Blazer) are roomy and quiet SUVs. But expect mediocre brakes, a so-so ride, and a cramped rear seat. Full-time all-wheel-drive (without low range) is available on high-trim versions. **Last report/fax: August 95/9421**
GMC Safari	◒	○	Though the Safari minivan has an enormous cargo area, the design is dated. Drawbacks also include cramped foot room, ponderous handling, and an uncomfortable ride. All-wheel drive is available. Similar: Chevy Astro. **Last report/fax: July 96/9489**

Model	Predicted reliability	Depreciation	Comments
GMC Sierra C/K 1500	○	⊖	The Sierra (and similar Chevy C/K pickup) offers a smooth powertrain. But the handling is trucklike, and the ride is stiff. The third (rear) door on extended-cab versions is a worthwhile option. **Last report/fax: September 96/9499**
GMC Sonoma	●	○	The Sonoma and similar Chevy "S" pickup is fairly new but not especially carlike. The ride is quiet but stiff, and handling is unexceptional. Reliability and crash-worthiness remain concerns. **Last report/fax: November 95/9434**
GMC Suburban	○	⊜	This huge truck-based sport-utility vehicle especially emphasizes utility. It can carry nine people and tow a heavy trailer. Fuel economy is laughable. **Last report/fax: ——**
GMC Yukon	○	○	The Yukon is a shortened GMC Suburban. The ride is quiet, not bad for a truck. It lends itself well to hauling and towing, but fuel economy is poor and the brakes mediocre. **Last report/fax: October 96/9508**
Geo Metro	⊖	NA	A small economy car with a choppy ride and insufficient power. Fuel economy is only okay. The Geo name has died; all Geos will be rebadged as Chevrolets after 1997. Similar: Suzuki Swift. **Last report/fax: September 95/9429**
✔ Geo Prizm	⊜	○	A reliable small car. Expect decent ride and handling. Cramped rear seats. The Geo name has died; all Geos will be rebadged as Chevrolets after 1997. Similar: Toyota Corolla. Redesigned for 1998. **Last report/fax: ——**
Geo Tracker	○	○	This noisy and slow little SUV has a punishing ride. It's not suited for cruising long distances. Four-wheel drive is optional. All Geos will be rebadged as Chevrolets after 1997. Similar: Suzuki Sidekick. **Last report/fax: June 96/9478**
✔ Honda Accord	⊜	⊖	One of the best family sedans. Expect responsive acceleration, decent handling, a good ride, comfortable seats, and exceptional reliability. The EX version handles better than the DX or LX. Redesigned for 1998. **Last report/fax: January 96/9447**
✔ Honda CR-V	⊖	NA	A small but spacious SUV based on the Civic sedan. All-wheel drive is standard, as is an automatic transmission. Good ride, but handling is not nimble. The cabin layout is not well designed. **Last report/fax: November 97/9622**
✔ Honda Civic	⊖	○	A very good small car. The 1.6-liter Four is very well matched to the optional automatic transmission. The interior is thoughtfully designed, and the ride is exceptionally good for a small car. **Last report/fax: March 96/9457**
✔ Honda Odyssey	⊜	NA	This minivan has four doors, like a wagon. The only engine choice is a barely adequate Four. Ride and handling are carlike, and visibility and maneuverability are good. Similar: Isuzu Oasis. **Last report/fax: October 95/9431**
Honda Passport	○	⊖	This SUV is really an Isuzu Rodeo with a Honda badge. Four-wheel drive is available. The Passport leans sharply in turns, steers slowly, and delivers a mediocre ride. Redesigned for 1998. **Last report/fax: ——**
✔ Honda Prelude	⊜	○	This well-rounded sports coupe blends lively acceleration with nimble handling. It's easy and fun to drive. The cramped cabin grew a little roomier with its 1997 redesign. **Last report/fax: ——**
Honda del Sol	⊜	◒	It should drive like a sports car—but it doesn't. Instead, this pseudo-convertible feels more like a small sedan. The ride is busy, and the body flexes too much. Discontinued after 1997. **Last report/fax: ——**
Hyundai Accent	NA	NA	This entry-level Hyundai is a small, basic runabout with a well-equipped, modern interior and so-so ride. Reliability is unknown—but previous Hyundai models have been very troublesome. **Last report/fax: September 95/9429**

Model	Predicted reliability	Depreciation	Comments
Hyundai Elantra	NA	○	The Elantra fits between the small Accent and mid-sized Sonata. Nimble handling and a well-appointed cabin are long suits. The ride is jittery, and the transmission downshifts reluctantly. **Last report/fax: January 97/9539**
Hyundai Sonata	NA	○	The Sonata tries to imitate the better Japanese sedans, but with limited success. The ride is not well controlled. The body leans, and the tires squeal even during gentle cornering. **Last report/fax: February 95/9992**
Hyundai Tiburon	New	NA	An attractive sporty coupe based on the Elantra, the Tiburon is agile, quick, and fun to drive—if you're not too tall. The ride is sports-car stiff, the seats are low and very firm. **Last report/fax: August 97/9597**
✔ Infiniti I30	⊜	NA	This is an upscale version of the Nissan Maxima with more sound-deadening material and a plusher interior. The I30 is competent all around but the ride could be better. **Last report/fax: February 96/9456**
✔ Infiniti J30	⊜	◒	This rear-wheel drive, semi-luxurious sedan emphasizes near-absolute road isolation over sporty handling. The small back seat and trunk make it functionally a luxury coupe despite its four doors. Discontinued after 1997. **Last report/fax: ——**
✔ Infiniti Q45	⊜	●	A fine if costly luxury car, redesigned for 1997. The new V8 is strong and smooth. The interior is well laid out. Traction control is standard, useful in a rear-drive car. **Last report/fax: ——**
Infiniti QX4	New	NA	Basically, a fancy version of the Nissan Pathfinder with a sophisticated all-wheel-drive system. Expect a comfortable ride and responsive steering; the QX4 is more maneuverable than bulkier SUVs. Cargo space is slim. **Last report/fax: ——**
Isuzu Hombre	NA	NA	A basic Chevy compact pickup with slightly different sheet metal. Expect a stiff but quiet ride, unremarkable handling, and a weak and rough engine. **Last report/fax: ——**
✔ Isuzu Oasis	⊜	NA	A rebadged Honda Odyssey, it's a smallish minivan that rides and drives like a Honda Accord. Unlike most minivans, the Oasis has four doors, like a station wagon. The engine could be stronger. **Last report/fax: October 95/9431**
Isuzu Rodeo	○	⊖	A compact SUV that accelerates modestly and leans heavily during cornering. Four-wheel drive is available. It offers little more cargo space than does a standard station wagon. Similar: Honda Passport. Redesigned for 1998. **Last report/fax: ——**
Isuzu Trooper	⊜	NA	We have rated the Trooper Not Acceptable because of its rollover propensity in our tests. Even without that it is a tall, expensive box with ungainly handling and a so-so ride. **Last report/fax: October 96/9507**
Jaguar XJ6	NA	◒	A very refined sedan with a few quirks, it has powerful acceleration and a well-mannered ride. The control layout has been improved, though the cockpit remains a little cramped. Renamed XJ8 for 1998. **Last report/fax: ——**
Jeep Cherokee	○	○	Redesigned for 1997, the Cherokee kept its old looks, as well as many of the not-so-good aspects of earlier versions. The interior is cramped, the ride hard and noisy. Handling remains trucklike, too. **Last report/fax: November 97/9622**
✔ Jeep Grand Cherokee	○	○	A civilized sport-utility, with almost carlike handling and an okay ride. Acceleration and braking are sound. A sophisticated all-wheel drive system is available. Reliability has improved of late. **Last report/fax: June 97/9575**
Jeep Wrangler	○	⊜	The smallest, least expensive, and crudest Jeep. The ride is hard and noisy; the handling, primitive. Popular with off-roaders despite a poor reliability record. The new 1997 model is improved but still pretty rough. **Last report/fax: November 97/9622**

Model	Predicted reliability	Depreciation	Comments
Land Rover Discovery	●	⊜	Smaller and a lot cheaper than the Range Rover, but still roomy and well equipped. It feels slow and heavy. It gets miserable fuel economy and has had a poor reliability record. **Last report/fax: August 95/9421**
Land Rover Range Rover	NA	⊖	Power everything and leather galore festoon this luxurious large sport-utility. It rides comfortably for an SUV and handles adequately, but it doesn't accelerate briskly. Has all-wheel drive as standard equipment. **Last report/fax: ——**
✔ Lexus ES300	⊜	○	Redesigned for 1997, the ES300 is an upscale version of the Toyota Camry. It does everything well—but it's no bargain. Expect sound handling, strong and quiet performance, and lots of standard equipment. **Last report/fax: March 97/9558**
✔ Lexus GS300	⊜	○	Among luxury sports sedans, the rear-drive GS300 emphasizes the luxury end of the spectrum. Exceptionally quiet ride, but the steering feels too light. Displays and controls are first-rate. Will be redesigned for 1998. **Last report/fax: ——**
✔ Lexus LS400	⊜	◒	This is Toyota's flagship luxury car. Combines a sophisticated rear-drive powertrain with a lush, quiet, leather-wrapped interior. Side air bags are standard, traction control optional. Exceptional reliability record. **Last report/fax: ——**
Lexus LX450	New	NA	This is a big, imposing Toyota Land Cruiser with a slightly softer suspension and a Lexus badge. Leisurely acceleration and a busy ride detract a little from this luxury-truck's driving pleasure. **Last report/fax: ——**
✔ Lexus SC300/SC400	⊜	○	This two-door luxury coupe gets fine performance from its aluminum V8 in SC400 trim, but the much-cheaper SC300's Six accelerates well too. Handling is crisp. Quality and refinement are top-notch. **Last report/fax: July 93/9325**
Lincoln Continental	○	●	Redesigned for 1995, the well-equipped Continental picked up a fine-performing aluminum V8. As a luxury car it falls short. Ride, noise isolation, and general feel are rather ordinary. **Last report/fax: November 96/9513**
✔ Lincoln Mark VIII	○	●	A sophisticated, rear-drive luxury two-door with a spirited aluminum V8. Handling is agile for such a large car. The cockpit is modern, and the front seats are comfortable. **Last report/fax: ——**
Lincoln Town Car	⊖	●	A big, old-fashioned, rear-wheel-drive highway cruiser with a modern V8 and lots of luxury appointments. Expect a quiet, soft ride and seating for six. A redesign is due for 1998. **Last report/fax:**
✔ Mazda 626	○	○	A well-rounded and high-rated family sedan. The pricey V6 runs particularly smoothly and powerfully, but the Four is a better value. Will be redesigned for 1998. **Last report/fax: January 94/9392**
✔ Mazda B-Series	○	○	A Ford Ranger compact pickup under the Mazda nameplate. Quiet and comfortable, it's one of the best in the class, but still suffers from so-so ride and handling. Redsigned for 1998. **Last report/fax: November 95/9434**
Mazda MPV	NA	○	This minivan rides badly, handles awkwardly, and is a chore to convert from people-carrying to cargo hauling. The rear seat is cramped, and the engine can barely handle the vehicle's weight. **Last report/fax: July 96/9489**
✔ Mazda MX-5 Miata	⊜	○	A rear-wheel-drive convertible that's as fun to drive as any sports car on the road, despite a noisy, stiff ride and small trunk. Expect excellent handling and a smooth-running engine. **Last report/fax: ——**
✔ Mazda MX-6	○	◒	Similar to the Ford Probe, but with a coupe body instead of a hatchback. We prefer the V6 to the Four. Handling is smooth and predictable, the ride is decent. Discontinued after 1997. **Last report/fax: ——**

Model	Predicted reliability	Depreciation	Comments
✔ Mazda Millenia	⊖	NA	A refined and high-rated luxury sedan that's quiet and comfortable, pleasant to drive, and well put together. The high-line "S" model offers both high power and relatively good fuel economy. **Last report/fax: May 95/9401**
✔ Mazda Protegé	○	◒	The Protege´ is one of the best small sedans on the market, though it's a little pricey. A roomy car in a small package, it rides decently and handles well. **Last report/fax: June 95/9416**
✔ Mercedes-Benz C-Class	○	⊖	A strong engine, responsive handling, and a supple ride are strong points. The seats may be too firm for some, and it's pricey for its size. Expect good quality with a high resale value. **Last report/fax: March 97/9558**
✔ Mercedes-Benz E-Class	⊖	○	One of the world's finest cars, this model is a joy to drive. It's a fine balance of spirited acceleration, precise handling, and a luxurious ride. A wagon joins the E-Class in 1998. **Last report/fax: November 96/9513**
Mercedes-Benz SLK	New	NA	A roadster/coupe with a supercharged Four and many innovative technical and safety features. The hard-top electrically retracts into the trunk. Sadly for sports car fans, the only available gearbox is a five-speed automatic. **Last report/fax: ——**
Mercury Cougar	◒	○	A slightly up-market version of the Ford Thunderbird. Expect a decent ride, but so-so handling. Many power accessories are standard. The 4.6-liter V8 is the better engine choice. Discontinued after 1997. **Last report/fax: July 95/9423**
✔ Mercury Grand Marquis	○	◒	A big, old-fashioned V8 freeway cruiser. Expect a serene ride and a huge trunk. The Handling and Performance package is a worthwhile option. Receives a facelift for 1998. Similar: Ford Crown Victoria. **Last report/fax: March 94/9714**
Mercury Mountaineer	○	NA	A relabeled Ford Explorer. The single engine choice is the 5.0-liter V8. The optional all-wheel-drive system stays permanently engaged, but it has no low-range setting for serious off-roading. **Last report/fax: ——**
✔ Mercury Mystique	○	NA	This sedan has a well-controlled ride, handles exceptionally well, and is sensibly appointed, but the rear seat is cramped. The V6 is a much better choice than the noisy four-cylinder that comes standard. **Last report/fax: October 97/9618**
✔ Mercury Sable	○	NA	Redesigned for 1996, the Sable is improved in nearly every way from its predecessor. Expect good handling and decent comfort. Offers slightly more headroom in the rear than the similar Ford Taurus. **Last report/fax: February 97/9549**
✔ Mercury Tracer	○	◒	Much improved for 1997. The engine is lively, and handling is fairly nimble. The ride is still a little choppy. The cabin is cramped for tall people. Similar: Ford Escort. **Last report/fax: January 97/9539**
✔ Mercury Villager	○	○	The Villager and its twin the Nissan Quest are among the better minivans, carlike and pleasant to drive. Drawbacks include a relatively modest cargo area and the lack of a left-side sliding door. **Last report/fax: July 96/9489**
Mitsubishi 3000GT	○	◒	With all-wheel drive and twin turbochargers, this technological showpiece is fast and furious. But it's pricey—and not as much fun to drive as a Mazda Miata. The more basic versions are nothing special. **Last report/fax: ——**
Mitsubishi Diamante	New	●	Mitsubishi's flagship luxury car never stood out in the fast company with which it competed. It was redesigned, with a larger engine, for 1997. **Last report/fax: ——**
Mitsubishi Eclipse	●	○	This sporty coupe, a sibling of the Eagle Talon, was redesigned for 1995. The turbocharged versions are the ones to choose. All-wheel drive is also available. **Last report/fax: ——**

Model	Predicted reliability	Depreciation	Comments
✔ Mitsubishi Galant	○	○	A competent, good-performing family sedan. The Four delivers lively acceleration. Ride, handling, and braking are only okay, but the controls are easy to use. **Last report/fax: May 97/9572**
⬆ Mitsubishi Mirage	New	◒	One of the more capable small cars, with secure handling and a fairly comfortable, quiet ride. The inside feels airy and spacious. Sadly, antilock brakes are hard to find on this model. **Last report/fax: January 97/9539**
Mitsubishi Montero	NA	○	The best things about the high, boxy Montero are its sophisticated all-wheel-drive system and seven-passenger seating option. The worst is its cumbersome emergency handling. Receives a facelift for 1998. **Last report/fax: ——**
Mitsubishi Montero Sport	New	NA	A moderate-sized SUV that rides quietly but uncomfortably, and has only a part-time four-wheel-drive system. Sluggish even with the V6. Not a top choice. **Last report/fax: June 97/9575**
✔ Nissan 200SX	⊖	NA	This coupe version of the Nissan Sentra was new for 1995. Lower trimlines are inexpensive and a little dowdy. But look to the SE-R trimline for a nimble, good-performing sporty coupe. **Last report/fax: May 96/9471**
Nissan 240SX	NA	◒	A rear-wheel-drive sporty coupe. Expect sound handling and a fairly comfortable ride. As in other sporty coupes, the rear seat is best left uninhabited. **Last report/fax: ——**
✔ Nissan Altima	⊜	⊖	A mid-sized sedan that performs decently but unexceptionally overall. The sports-oriented SE version handles better than the top-line GLE, but the best value is the mid-level GXE. Redesigned for 1998. **Last report/fax: November 94/9923**
✔ Nissan Maxima	⊜	◒	Overall, we'd put the Maxima a notch below the Toyota Camry. The powertrain is first rate, but the ride, seat comfort, and handling are only good, not great. **Last report/fax: February 95/9992**
✔ Nissan Pathfinder	⊖	○	A 1996 redesign gave the Pathfinder carlike ride and handling. A top contender, but modest interior size compromises cargo space and rear-seat comfort. Its four-wheel-drive system is part-time only. **Last report/fax: October 96/9508**
✔ Nissan Quest	○	○	The Quest and its twin the Mercury Villager are among the better minivans, carlike and pleasant to drive. Drawbacks include a relatively modest cargo area and the lack of a left-side sliding door. **Last report/fax: July 96/9489**
✔ Nissan Sentra	⊖	○	The Sentra falls just a notch or two below the best competing small sedans, such as the Mazda Protegé and Honda Civic. The steering is a little sluggish, and the cockpit is cramped. **Last report/fax: June 95/9416**
Nissan Truck	⊖	○	A basic compact pickup made in Tennessee. The only engine is a four-cylinder, and four-wheel ABS is unavailable. A complete redesign is due for the 1998 model year. **Last report/fax: ——**
Oldsmobile 88	○	◒	A big, quiet, softly sprung freeway cruiser. Comes standard with a responsive V6—no need to opt for the supercharged V6 option.The optional touring suspension improves handling markedly. **Last report/fax: ——**
Oldsmobile Achieva	○	◒	Expect a quite interior and adequate power, but an unsettled ride. Handling and braking are merely mediocre. The interior looks bigger than it is. Discontinued after the1997 model year. **Last report/fax: August 96/9493**
Oldsmobile Aurora	○	NA	Overstyled and overweight. The V8 powertrain is top-notch, but its artificially weighted steering, poor visibility, lack of roominess, and middling ride quality put it behind the luxury competition. **Last report/fax: May 95/9401**
Oldsmobile Bravada	NA	NA	A loaded version of the Chevy Blazer. All-wheel drive is standard. The strong V6 delivers powerful acceleration, and the automatic transmission is smooth shifting. Handles with considerable body lean. Cargo space is generous. **Last report/fax: ——**

Model	Predicted reliability	Depreciation	Comments
✔ Oldsmobile Cutlass	○	NA	Similar to the good-performing Chevy Malibu. The only engine is a 3.1-liter V6. Ride, handling, and braking are sound, but still lacks the Mercury Mystique's sportiness and the Toyota Camry's polish. **Last report/fax: October 97/9618**
Oldsmobile Intrigue	New	NA	The 1998 Intrigue, introduced in 1997, competes with the Toyota Camry and Nissan Maxima. The Intrigue accelerates briskly and handles fairly well. Similar: Buick Regal and Pontiac Grand Prix. **Last report/fax: ——**
Oldsmobile Silhouette	●	NA	The GM minivan siblings are greatly improved for 1997. The ride is good. Handling is competent. The rear seats are uncomfortable. The similar Trans Sport did poorly in an offset frontal crash test. **Last report/fax: July 97/9589**
Plymouth Breeze	NA	NA	This cousin of the Dodge Stratus sedan has a roomy rear seat and well-designed controls and displays. Handling is sound; ride, braking, and acceleration about average. **Last report/fax: August 96/9493**
Plymouth Grand Voyager	◒	◒	The Grand Voyager is a longer-bodied Voyager minivan. It rides quietly, handles nimbly, and easily converts between people- and cargo-hauling duties. The long-wheelbase versions have not been as reliable as the short versions. **Last report/fax: July 97/9589**
Plymouth Neon	◒	NA	This small car has a roomy interior. Although both Neon engines are noisy, we prefer the double-overhead camshaft Four mated to a manual transmission. The ride is choppy. Handling is predictable, but not sporty. **Last report/fax: May 96/9471**
✔ Plymouth Voyager	○	◒	This minivan was redesigned for 1996. Expect nimble handling, a quiet ride, abundant cargo space and easy conversion between cargo-and people-moving. Best engine choice is the 3.3-liter V6. Reliability has been average. **Last report/fax: July 96/9489**
✔ Pontiac Bonneville	○	◒	Properly equipped, the Bonneville is one of GM's best large sedans. The optional firm suspension and touring tires markedly improve handling. Pass up the supercharged V6; the standard V6 does just fine. **Last report/fax: March 94/9714**
Pontiac Firebird	●	○	An old-fashioned rear-wheel-drive muscle car, like its cousin, the Chevrolet Camaro. The optional V8 provides effortless acceleration and makes the standard V6 seem sluggish by comparison. Convertible versions are also available. **Last report/fax: ——**
Pontiac Grand Am	○	○	The interior is quiet, the transmission shifts smoothly, and the control layout is improved. The ride remains mediocre, and handling is imprecise. A new model will be offered in 1998. **Last report/fax: August 96/9493**
✔ Pontiac Grand Prix	○	NA	One of GM's best sedans, the redesigned Grand Prix steers responsively and corners crsiply. It accelerates well and shifts smoothly. Front seating is fairly comfortable too. Similar: Buick Regal and Oldsmobile Intrigue. **Last report/fax: February 97/9549**
✔ Pontiac Sunfire	○	NA	The Sunfire aims to be a sporty and inexpensive small car, with some success. It's pleasant enough to drive, and comes with many useful amenities. Similar: Chevrolet Cavalier. **Last report/fax: May 96/9471**
Pontiac Trans Sport	●	NA	Redesigned and improved for 1997, the Trans Sport minivan has a comfortable ride. It handles competently. The rear seats are uncomfortable. The Trans Sport did poorly in an offset frontal crash test. **Last report/fax: July 97/9589**
Porsche Boxster	New	NA	The new-for-'97 Boxster is a rear-drive two-seater with a flat "boxer" engine mounted amidships. Precise, razor-sharp handling makes it a joy to drive. Considered "the affordable Porsche," at a mere $40,000. **Last report/fax: ——**

Model	Predicted reliability	Depre- ciation	Comments
Saab 900	●	○	This is an able if slightly quirky sports sedan. Handling, performance, and accommodations are all quite good. Offers abundant cargo space with rear seat folded down. Reliability has been a problem. **Last report/fax: August 94/9792**
Saab 9000	○	○	A well-designed and pleasant-to-drive European-style sports sedan. The control layout is a little inconvenient. The hatchback is roomy, and turbo versions are very quick. Will be replaced in mid-1998. **Last report/fax: ——**
Saturn	⊖	⊜	Not bad on balance, but its1996 freshening failed to hush the noisy engine or smooth out the transmission. The SL1 compromises handling for ride comfort; the SL2 does the opposite. **Last report/fax: March 96/9457**
✔ Subaru Impreza	⊜	◒	In uplevel trim, the Impreza handles well. Accommodations are slightly tight. It's one of the cheapest ways to get all-wheel-drive. The fun-to-drive Outback Sport is more of a hatchback than a small wagon. **Last report/fax: September 97/9603**
✔ Subaru Legacy	⊜	⊖	One of our top-rated cars, the Legacy is a competent, well-rounded sedan and one of the few that offer all-wheel drive. The regular wagon versions are better than the popular Outback. **Last report/fax: September 97/9603**
Suzuki Esteem	NA	NA	The Esteem offers good accommodations and reasonable performance and fuel economy. But it's slightly behind in interior noise and ride comfort. A wagon version will be offered for 1998. **Last report/fax: March 96/9457**
Suzuki Sidekick	○	○	This small SUV is noisy and uncomfortable. The four-door is a foot longer and commensurately roomier than the two-door. Four-wheel drive is available, but it's only a part-time system. Similar: Geo Tracker. **Last report/fax: June 96/9478**
Suzuki Swift	⊖	○	A very small economy car with a choppy, noisy ride and insufficient power. Not especially nimble nipping around town, and fatiguing on long trips. Fuel economy is only okay. Similar: Geo Metro. **Last report/fax: September 95/9429**
Suzuki X90	NA	NA	More of a conversation piece than a real car or serious SUV. To the basic impracticality of a two-seater add awkward handling and a harsh, noisy ride of an SUV. Not a good bet. **Last report/fax: June 96/9478**
✔ Toyota 4Runner	⊜	⊜	The 4Runner delivers good performance and fairly good fuel economy. The ride could be better, but it handles soundly, it's quiet inside, and it holds lots of cargo. Altogether, a good package. **Last report/fax: October 96/9508**
✔ Toyota Avalon	⊖	NA	Think of the Avalon as a V6-powered extended-length Camry. It's comfortáble, quiet, refined, and easy to drive. Though not sporty, the Avalon offers roomy seating for six and fine attention to interior details. **Last report/fax: May 95/9401**
✔ Toyota Camry	⊜	⊖	One of the best sedans on the market—quiet, refined, and easy to drive, with comfortable seating. It feels like a luxury car, and it has been exceptionally reliable. **Last report/fax: May 97/9572**
✔ Toyota Celica	⊜	○	A well-rounded sporty coupe, though not as fast as competitors like the Acura Integra. It handles well, gives good fuel economy, and has been very reliable. The rear seat is very cramped. **Last report/fax: June 94/9742**
✔ Toyota Corolla	⊜	○	An able overall performer with good reliability. The car handles predictably, though it's not nimble. Front seating is fine, but the rear is a little cramped. Redesigned for 1998. Similar: Geo Prizm. **Last report/fax: ——**
✔ Toyota Land Cruiser	⊖	⊖	The big, imposing Land Cruiser competes at the expensive end of the sport-utility-vehicle market. Expect leisurely acceleration and subpar fuel economy. You get a high, commanding view but a slightly busy, rubbery ride. **Last report/fax: ——**

Model	Predicted reliability	Depreciation	Comments
Toyota Paseo	NA	○	A sporty version of the Tercel. Acceleration is good, but the handling is not nimble. A soft suspension and numb steering rob it of true sportiness. The rear seat is very small. **Last report/fax: ——**
✔ Toyota Previa	⊜	○	A good though expensive minivan, with responsive steering and a good, quiet ride. The Previa has been the most reliable of any minivan. Will be replaced by the Camry-based Sienna for 1998. **Last report/fax: ——**
✔ Toyota RAV4	⊜	NA	A small SUV that rides well and handles nimbly. It offers full-time all-wheel-drive, but with no low range. The front seats are good. Cargo space is generous for such a small vehicle. **Last report/fax: November 97/9622**
✔ Toyota Supra	⊖	○	Lots of flash for lots of cash. The Supra is a muscular speedster with a bone-jarring ride. We think the Mazda Miata is more fun to drive—for half the price. **Last report/fax: June 94/9742**
Toyota T100	⊖	○	A full-sized pickup, designed for hauling and towing. If you plan to do much of either, opt for the V6 instead of the standard Four. A reliable truck, but pricey. **Last report/fax: ——**
Toyota Tacoma	⊖	NA	An unimpressive compact pickup. Has a responsive V6 and a quiet cabin. Expect slow steering and an awful ride. The non-antilock brakes perform poorly. The cargo box is rimmed with flimsy sheet metal. **Last report/fax: November 95/9434**
Toyota Tercel	⊖	○	First and foremost an economy car. Delivers a responsive powertrain and excellent fuel economy. Unfortunately, it also has a rough, noisy ride in a cramped cabin, and, without ABS, mediocre braking. **Last report/fax: September 95/9429**
✔ Volkswagen Golf	○	◒	A sporty, good-handling hatchback that's fun to drive. The ride is supple and reasonably quiet. The front seats are good, too. The V6-powered GTI version is especially quick. **Last report/fax: May 96/9471**
✔ Volkswagen Jetta	○	○	Think of the Jetta as a Golf with a very large trunk. Expect fine handling, a good ride, and comfortable seats. We prefer the manual transmission. **Last report/fax: November 94/9923**
✔ Volkswagen Passat	○	NA	VW's costliest car rides and handles very well. It has a roomy rear seat and big trunk. The automatic transmission blunts the engine's performance; we recommend the manual instead. Redesigned for 1998. **Last report/fax: February 95/9992**
Volvo C70	New	NA	A coupe based on the Volvo 850—now the S70. Combines sporty looks with a Volvo sedan's full functional and safety systems. Expect a stiff ride, and good acceleration in turbo versions. **Last report/fax: ——**
✔ Volvo S70/V70	⊖	⊖	Turbo versions are very quick. Large, comfortable front seats only partly make up for a stiff, jiggly ride. Renamed the S70 in 1997. **Last report/fax: September 97/9603**
✔ Volvo S90/V90	○	○	Formerly the 960 series. An expensive, rear-drive sedan and wagon. Traction-control is not available. Expect good seating and a huge trunk. The car rides and handles well, and the Six accelerates enthusiastically. **Last report/fax: ——**

Ratings of the 1997 cars

The Ratings include only cars for which we have recent test results. To earn our recommendation—marked by a ✔—a model has to perform well in our tests and must have been at least average in reliability. A promising label—marked by an ⬆—indicates a new model that performed well but whose reliability we can't yet predict. "Twins" and "triplets"—essentially similar models sold under different nameplates—are grouped in the charts below; each is marked with a ■. Typically, we've tested only one of those models. **Fuel usage** is overall mpg, based on our own tests on and off the track. **Tested model** notes the trim line, engine, and drivetrain of the model tested—items that can affect specific test results.

Model	Overall score	Fuel usage	Tested model
	P F G VG E		
SMALL CARS WITH MANUAL TRANSMISSION			
✔ Volkswagen Jetta		23 mpg	GLX 2.8 V6; man 5
✔ Acura Integra		30	LS 4-door 1.8 Four; man 5
✔ Volkswagen Golf		30	GL 2.0 Four; man 5
Dodge/Plymouth Neon		26	Sport 2.0 Four; man 5
Hyundai Accent		35	L 1.5 Four; man 5
Toyota Tercel		39	Base 1.5 Four; man 5
Ford Aspire		36	Base 1.3 Four; man 5
Geo Metro		35	LSi 2-door 1.0 Three; man 5
SMALL CARS WITH AUTOMATIC TRANSMISSION			
✔ Mazda Protegé		26	ES 1.8 Four; auto 4
✔ Honda Civic		31	LX 1.6 Four; auto 4
⬆ Mitsubishi Mirage		27	LS 1.8 Four; auto 4
✔ Nissan Sentra		28	GXE 1.6 Four; auto 4
✔ ■ Ford Escort		28	LX 2.0 Four; auto 4
✔ ■ Mercury Tracer		28	Ford Escort LX 2.0 Four; auto 4
Hyundai Elantra		25	GLS 1.8 Four; auto 4
✔ ■ Chevrolet Cavalier		26	LS 2.2 Four; auto 4
✔ ■ Pontiac Sunfire		26	Chevrolet Cavalier LS 2.2 Four; auto 4
Suzuki Esteem		29	GLX 1.6 Four; auto 4
Saturn		29	SL1 1.9 Four; auto 4
Toyota Tercel		32	DX 1.5 Four; auto 4

Model	Overall score (P F G VG E)	Fuel usage	Tested model
SMALL CARS WITH AUTOMATIC TRANSMISSION *continued*			
Dodge/Plymouth Neon		26 mpg	Highline 2.0 Four; auto 3
Hyundai Accent		28	Base 1.5 Four; auto 4
Geo Metro		29	LSi 4-door 1.3 Four; auto 3
SPORTY COUPES			
✔ Nissan 200SX		28	SE-R 2.0 Four; man 5
✔ Volkswagen Golf GTI		27	2.0 Four; man 5
✔ Acura Integra Coupe		31	LS 1.8 Four; man 5
✔ Honda Civic Coupe		34	EX 1.6 Four; man 5
Hyundai Tiburon		27	FX 2.0 Four; man 5
✔ Saturn SC		28	SC2 1.9 Four; man 5
✔ ▪ Chevrolet Cavalier		25	Pontiac Sunfire GT 2.4 Four; man 5
✔ ▪ Pontiac Sunfire		25	GT 2.4 Four; man 5
Dodge/Plymouth Neon		30	Sport 2.0 Four; man 5
SPORTS/SPORTY CARS			
✔ Toyota Supra		22	Turbo 3.0 Six; man 6
✔ Toyota Celica		28	GT 2.2 Four; man 5
COUPES			
▪ Chrysler Sebring		22	Dodge Avenger ES 2.5 V6; auto 4
▪ Dodge Avenger		22	ES 2.5 V6; auto 4
▪ Ford Thunderbird		20	LX 4.6 V8; auto 4
▪ Mercury Cougar		20	Ford Thunderbird LX 4.6 V8; auto 4
Chrysler Sebring Convertible		21	JXi 2.5 V6; auto 4
Chevrolet Monte Carlo		18	Z34 3.4 V6; auto 4
Buick Riviera		17	3.8 V6; auto 4
MEDIUM CARS UNDER $25,000			
✔ Toyota Camry		25/23	LE 2.2 Four/3.0 V6; auto 4
✔ Mercury Mystique (1998)		22	LS 2.5 V6; auto 4
✔ Nissan Maxima		24	GXE 3.0 V6; auto 4
✔ Subaru Legacy		24	L 2.2 Four; auto 4
✔ Volkswagen Passat		20	GLX 2.8 V6; auto 4
✔ Honda Accord		21	EX 2.7 V6; auto 4
✔ Oldsmobile Cutlass		24	GLS 3.1 V6; auto 4
✔ Chevrolet Malibu		24	Base 2.4 Four; auto 4
✔ Pontiac Grand Prix		21	SE 3.8 V6; auto 4

Model	Overall score P F G VG E	Fuel usage	Tested model
MEDIUM CARS UNDER $25,000 *continued*			
✔ Mitsubishi Galant		25 mpg	ES 2.4 Four; auto 4
✔ ■ Mercury Sable		22	GS 3.0 V6; auto 4
■ Ford Taurus		21	LX 3.0 V6; auto 4
✔ Ford Contour		24	GL 2.0 Four; auto 4
Chrysler Cirrus		22	LXi 2.5 V6; auto 4
✔ Nissan Altima		23	GLE 2.4 Four; auto 4
Plymouth Breeze		23	Base 2.0 Four; auto 4
Hyundai Sonata		21	GLS 3.0 V6; auto 4
✔ Chevrolet Lumina		22	LS 3.1 V6; auto 4
Dodge Stratus		20	Base 2.4 Four; auto 4
Pontiac Grand Am		24	SE 2.4 Four; auto 4
Oldsmobile Achieva		24	SL Series II 2.4 Four; auto 4
Buick Century		22	Limited 3.1 V6; auto 4
MEDIUM CARS OVER $25,000			
Cadillac Catera		20	3.0 V6; auto 4
✔ Lexus ES300		22	3.0 V6; auto 4
✔ Mercedes-Benz C280		24	2.8 Six; auto 5
✔ BMW 328i		24	2.8 Six; auto 4
✔ Mazda Millenia		22	S 2.3 V6; auto 4
✔ Infiniti I30		23	3.0 V6; auto 4
✔ Audi A4		22	2.8 V6; auto 5
✔ Acura 2.5TL		23	Premium 2.5 Five; auto 4
Saab 900		22	SE 2.5 V6; auto 4
Oldsmobile Aurora		17	4.0 V8; auto 4
LARGE CARS			
✔ Toyota Avalon		22	XLS 3.0 V6; auto 4
✔ Chrysler LHS		20	3.5 V6; auto 4
✔ ■ Chrysler Concorde		21	3.5 V6; auto 4
■ Dodge Intrepid		20	Base 3.3 V6; auto 4
■ Eagle Vision		21	TSi 3.5 V6; auto 4
✔ Pontiac Bonneville		18	SSEi 3.8 V6; auto 4
✔ ■ Ford Crown Victoria		19	LX 4.6 V8; auto 4
✔ ■ Mercury Grand Marquis		19	Ford Crown Victoria LX 4.6 V8; auto 4
Buick LeSabre		20	Custom 3.8 V6; auto 4

Model	Overall score (P F G VG E)	Fuel usage	Tested model
LUXURY CARS			
✔ Mercedes-Benz E320		22 mpg	3.2 Six; auto 5
✔ BMW 528i		20	2.8 Six; auto 4
✔ Acura 3.5RL		20	3.5 V6; auto 4
Lincoln Continental		18	4.6 V8; auto 4
STATION WAGONS			
✔ Volvo V70		21	GLT 2.4 Five Turbo; auto 4
✔ Subaru Legacy		21	GT 2.5 Four; auto 4
✔ Honda Accord		25	EX 2.2 Four; auto 4
■ Ford Taurus		20	LX 3.0 V6; auto 4
✔ ■ Mercury Sable		20	Ford Taurus LX 3.0 V6; auto 4
✔ Subaru Legacy		21	Outback 2.5 Four; auto 4
✔ Subaru Impreza		23	Outback Sport 2.2 Four; auto 4
✔ ■ Ford Escort		25	LX 2.0 Four; auto 4
✔ ■ Mercury Tracer		25	Ford Escort LX 2.0 Four; auto 4
SMALL SPORT-UTILITY VEHICLES			
✔ Toyota RAV4		22	2.0 Four; auto 4
✔ Honda CR-V		24	2.0 Four; auto 4
Jeep Cherokee		16	Sport 4.0 Six; auto 4
■ Suzuki Sidekick		23	JLX Sport 1.8 Four; man 5
■ Geo Tracker		24	LSi 1.6 Four; man 5
Jeep Wrangler		15	Sahara 4.0 Six; auto 3
SPORT-UTILITY VEHICLES			
✔ Ford Explorer		16	XLT 4.0 V6; auto 5
✔ Jeep Grand Cherokee		15	Laredo 4.0 Six; auto 4
✔ Toyota 4Runner		18	SR5 3.4 V6; auto 4
✔ Ford Expedition		13	XLT 4.6 V8; auto 4
✔ Nissan Pathfinder		15	LE 3.3 V6; auto 4
Mitsubishi Montero Sport		18	LS 3.0 V6; auto 4
■ Chevrolet Tahoe		13	LS 5.7 V8; auto 4
■ GMC Yukon		13	Chevrolet Tahoe LS 5.7 V8; auto 4
■ Chevrolet Blazer		17	LT 4.3 V6; auto 4
■ GMC Jimmy		17	Chevrolet Blazer LT 4.3 V6; auto 4
Land Rover Discovery		13	3.9 V8; auto 4

Model	Overall score	Fuel usage	Tested model
	P F G VG E		
MINIVANS			
■ Chrysler Town & Country		18 mpg	Plymouth Grand Voyager SE 3.3 V6; auto 4
■ Dodge Grand Caravan		18	Plymouth Grand Voyager SE 3.3 V6; auto 4
■ Plymouth Grand Voyager		18	SE 3.3 V6; auto 4
Ford Windstar (1998)		19	LX 3.8 V6; auto 4
✔ ■ Dodge Caravan		19	LE 3.3 V6; auto 4
✔ ■ Plymouth Voyager		19	Dodge Caravan LE 3.3 V6; auto 4
■ Chevrolet Venture		19	LS 3.4 V6; auto 4
■ Oldsmobile Silhouette		19	Chevrolet Venture LS 3.4 V6; auto 4
■ Pontiac Trans Sport		18	SE Montana 3.4 V6; auto 4
✔ ■ Honda Odyssey		21	EX 2.2 Four; auto 4
✔ ■ Isuzu Oasis		21	Honda Odyssey EX 2.2 Four; auto 4
✔ ■ Mercury Villager		19	GS 3.0 V6; auto 4
✔ ■ Nissan Quest		19	Mercury Villager GS 3.0 V6; auto 4
■ Chevrolet Astro		15	GMC Safari SLE 4.3 V6; auto 4
■ GMC Safari		15	SLE 4.3 V6; auto 4
Mazda MPV		16	LX AWD 3.0 V6; auto 4
COMPACT PICKUPS (EXTENDED CAB)			
✔ Dodge Dakota		16	SLT 3.9 V6; auto 4
✔ ■ Ford Ranger		18	XLT 4.0 V6; auto 4
✔ ■ Mazda B-Series		18	Ford Ranger XLT 4.0 V6; auto 4
■ Chevrolet S-10		17	GMC Sonoma SLE 4.3 V6; auto 4
■ GMC Sonoma		17	SLE 4.3 V6; auto 4
Toyota Tacoma		21	3.4 V6; auto 4
FULL-SIZED PICKUPS (EXTENDED CAB)			
✔ Ford F-150		16	XLT 4.6 V8; auto 4
■ Chevrolet C1500		15	Silverado 5.0 V8; auto 4
■ GMC Sierra C1500		15	Chevrolet C1500 Silverado 5.0 V8; auto 4
Dodge Ram 1500		13	Laramie SLT 5.2 V8; auto 4

Used cars, good & bad

Used cars are less of a gamble than they once were. Cars in general are growing more reliable. Better engineering and design have drastically reduced once-common problems like body rust and water leakage. Still, some cars are significantly more reliable than others. Once you've narrowed your search to a particular model, check the model's reliability history (Frequency-of-Repair charts begin on page 287).

About these lists. Derived from the trouble summaries, they cover 1989 through 1995 models with better- or worse-than-average reliability. Most 1996 cars were generally less than six months old when our readers reported on them for the 1996 survey and are considered too new to be included in the used-car lists. Problems with the engine, engine cooling, transmission, clutch, driveline, and body rust have been weighted more heavily than other problems.

Prices in the "reliable" list are average as of mid-1997 in the East for a car with average mileage, air-conditioning, and cassette stereo sound system. Luxury cars were priced with leather upholstery, sunroof, and CD player. We've assumed an automatic transmission for all but sporty cars.

Throughout, 2WD means two-wheel drive; 4WD is all- or four-wheel drive.

Reliable used cars

Listed alphabetically by price

Less than $6000

BUICK LeSabre, '89
DODGE Colt, Colt Wagon, '91
EAGLE Summit (except Wagon), '91
FORD Festiva, '89
HONDA Civic CRX, '89-90 • **Civic,** '89 • **Prelude,** '89
MAZDA Pickup 2WD, '89-90 • **626,** '89 [1] • **MX-6,** '89 [1]
MITSUBISHI Galant, '89-90 • **Mirage,** '91
NISSAN Sentra, '91 • **Stanza,** '89 • **240SX,** '89
OLDSMOBILE 98, '89
PLYMOUTH Colt, Colt Wagon, '91
TOYOTA Corolla, '89-90 • **Tercel,** '91 • **Pickup,** '89
VOLVO 240 Series, '89

$6000-$8000

ACURA Integra, '89-90 • **Legend,** '89 [2]
BMW 3-Series, '89
CADILLAC DeVille, '89 • **Eldorado,** '89
EAGLE Summit Wagon, '92
GEO Tracker, '91-92 • **Prizm,** '92
HONDA Accord, '89-90 • **CRX,** '91 • **Civic,** '91-92 • **Prelude,** '90
ISUZU Pickup, '92
MAZDA 323, '92-93 • **626,** '90-91 • **929,** '89 • **MX-6,** '91 • **Pickup 2WD,** '91-92 • **Protegé,** '92
MERCURY Tracer, '92
MITSUBISHI Galant, '91
NISSAN Pickup 2WD, '89 • **Maxima,** '89 [2] • **Sentra,** '92 • **Stanza,** '90-91 [2]
PLYMOUTH Colt Vista Wagon, '92
PONTIAC Bonneville, '89
SUZUKI Sidekick, '91
TOYOTA Camry, '89-91 • **Celica,** '89-90 • **Corolla,** '91-92 • **Paseo,** '92 • **Pickup,** '90-92 • **Tercel,** '92-93
VOLVO 240 Series, '90 • **740 Series,** '89

$8000-$10,000

ACURA Integra, '91-92
CADILLAC DeVille, '90
FORD Ranger Pickup 2WD, '93
GEO Prizm, '93-94
HONDA Accord, '91-92 • **Civic**, '93 • **Prelude**, '91
INFINITI G20, '91-92
LEXUS ES250, '90
MAZDA MX-5 Miata, '90-91 • **Protegé**, '94
MITSUBISHI Expo LRV, '92 • **Galant**, '92 • **Montero**, '90
NISSAN 240SX, '91-92 • **Altima**, '93 • **Maxima**, 90 [2], 91 • **Pickup 2WD**, '90-91 • **Sentra**, '93-94 • **Stanza**, '92 [2]
PLYMOUTH Colt Vista Wagon, '94
SATURN '94
SUBARU Impreza, '93
SUZUKI Sidekick, '92
TOYOTA Celica, '91 • **Corolla**, '93-94 • **Cressida**, '89-90 • **MR2**, '91 • **Tercel**, '94-95 • **Pickup**, '93-94
VOLVO 740 Series, '90

$10,000-$12,000

ACURA Integra, '93 • **Legend**, '90 [2]
BMW 3-Series, '90
EAGLE Summit Wagon, '94-'95
FORD Ranger Pickup 2WD, '94
GEO Prizm, '95
HONDA Accord, '93 • **Civic**, '94 • **Civic del Sol**, '93 • **Prelude**, '92
LEXUS ES250, '91
MAZDA MX-5 Miata, '92 • **Pickup 2WD**, '94
MERCURY Tracer, '95
MITSUBISHI Expo LRV, '94
NISSAN 200SX, '95 • **240SX**, '93 • **Altima**, '94-95 • **Maxima**, '92-93 • **Pathfinder**, '89 • **Pickup 2WD**, '92-93 • **Pickup 4WD**, '91 • **Sentra**, '95
OLDSMOBILE Cutlass Ciera, '95
SATURN '95
SUBARU Impreza, '95 • **Legacy**, '92-93
TOYOTA 4Runner,'89 • **Camry**, '92-93 • **Celica**, '92 • **Corolla**, '95 • **T100 Pickup**, '93
VOLVO 740 Series, '91

$12,000-$15,000

ACURA Integra, '94 • **Legend**, '91 • **Vigor**, '92-93
AUDI 100, '92
BUICK LeSabre, '94-95
HONDA Accord, '94-95 • **Civic**, '95 • **Civic del Sol**, '95 • **Prelude**, '93-94
INFINITI G20, '93-94
MAZDA MX-5 Miata, '93-94
MITSUBISHI Diamante, '92
NISSAN Maxima, '94 [2] • **Pathfinder**, '90-91 • **Pickup 2WD**, '94 • **Pickup 4WD**, '93
SUBARU Legacy, '94
TOYOTA Camry, '94-95 • **Celica**, '93-94 • **Previa Van**, '91-92 • **T100 Pickup**, '94
VOLVO 940 Series, '91

$15,000-$20,000

ACURA Integra, '95 • **Legend**, '92
HONDA Prelude, '95
INFINITI G20, '95 • **J30**, '93 • **Q45**, '91
LEXUS ES300, '92-93 • **LS400**, '90-91
MAZDA MX-5 Miata, '95
MERCEDES-BENZ S-Class, '89
MITSUBISHI Diamante, '94
NISSAN Maxima, '95 [2] • **Pathfinder**, '92-94
SUBARU Legacy, '95
TOYOTA 4Runner, '93 • **Celica**, '95 • **Previa Van**, '93-94
VOLVO 850, '93

$20,000-$25,000

ACURA Legend, '93-94
AUDI A6, '95
BMW 3-Series, '95
HONDA Odyssey, '95
INFINITI J30, '94-95
LEXUS ES300, '94-95 • **SC300/400**, '92 • **LS400**, '92
LINCOLN Town Car, '95
MAZDA Millenia, '95
MERCEDES-BENZ 300, '92
TOYOTA 4Runner, '94-95 • **Previa Van**, '95
VOLVO 850, '95

$25,000 and up

ACURA Legend, '95
BMW 5-Series 6, '95
INFINITI Q45, '94
LEXUS ES300, '95 • **GS300**, '93-94 • **LS400**, '93-95 • **SC300/400**, '93, '95
MERCEDES-BENZ E-Class, '94
TOYOTA Land Cruiser, '95

[1] Manual transmission only.
[2] Automatic transmission only.

Used cars to avoid

Listed alphabetically by make

BUICK Skylark, '90-91

CADILLAC Eldorado, '93-94 • **Fleetwood,** '94

CHEVROLET Astro Van, '93-95 • **Blazer,** '89-91 • **K-Blazer,** '92-94 • **Camaro** V6, '94 • **Camaro** V8, '93-95 • **Cavalier,** '89, '92 • **Corsica, Beretta,** '92-93, '95 • **Lumina APV Van,** '90, '92, '94 • **K1500-2500 Pickup,** '92, '95 • **S-10 Blazer,** '89-94 • **Blazer,** '95 • **S-10 Pickup** 4, '91, '94 • **S-10 Pickup V6 2WD,** '94 & **4WD,** '91-92, '94-95 • **Sportvan,** '89-91, '93-95 • **Suburban,** '89, '91-93

CHRYSLER Cirrus, '95 • **Concorde,** '93-94 • **LeBaron Coupe/ Convertible,** '90-95 • **New Yorker Fifth Ave.,** '92-93 • **New Yorker/LHS,** '94 • **Sebring,** '95 • **Town & Country Van 2WD,** '90-94 & **4WD,** '92-94

DODGE Avenger, '95 • **Caravan 4 Turbo,** '89 • **Caravan V6 2WD,** '89-93 • **Grand Caravan V6 2WD,** '89-94 & **4WD,** '91-94 • **Dakota Pickup 2WD,** '94 & **4WD,** '92-94 • **Daytona,** '89-90 • **Dynasty,** '92-93 • **Intrepid,** '93-94 • **Monaco,** '91 • **Neon,** '95 • **Omni,** '89 • **Ram Pickup 4WD,** '94-95 • **Ram Van/ Wagon,** '89-95 • **Shadow,** '89, '91, '93 • **Spirit,** '95 • **Stratus,** '95

EAGLE Premier, '89, '91 • **Talon,** '95 • **Vision,** '93-94

FORD Aerostar Van, '89-92 • **Bronco,** '89-95 • **Bronco** II, '89-90 • **Club Wagon,** Van, '89-94 • **Contour,** '95 • **Escort,** '89 • **Explorer,** '91-92 • **F150-250 Pickup 2WD,** '94 & **4WD,** '89-95 • **Mustang,** '93-94 • **Ranger Pickup 4WD,** '89, '91-92, '95 • **Taurus 4,** '89-90 • **Taurus V6,** '89-93 • **Taurus SHO,** '90-93, '95 • **Tempo,** '89-94 • **Thunderbird V6,** '95 • **Thunderbird** V8, '93-94 • **Windstar,** '95

GEO Storm, '90, '92

GMC Jimmy, '89-91 • **Yukon,** '92-94 • **S-15 Jimmy,** '89-91 • **Jimmy,** '92-95 • **S-15 Sonoma Pickup 4,** '91, '94 • **S-15 Sonoma Pickup V6 2WD,** '94 & **4WD,** '91-92, '94-95 • **Safari Van,** '93-95 • **Sierra K1500-2500 Pickup,** '92, '95 • **Suburban,** '89, '92-93

HYUNDAI Excel, '89, '91

ISUZU Rodeo V6, '92 • **Trooper,** '90-91

JAGUAR, '95

JEEP Cherokee 2WD, '93, '95 & **4WD,** '90 • **Grand Cherokee 2WD,** '93 • **Wrangler,** '89-95

LAND ROVER Discovery, '95

LINCOLN Continental, '89-91, '95

MAZDA 626, '94 • **Navajo 4WD,** '91 • **Pickup 4WD,** '95

MERCURY Capri 4, '91 • **Cougar V6,** '95 • **Cougar V8,** '93-94 • **Mystique,** '95 • **Sable,** '89-91 • **Topaz,** '89-94

MITSUBISHI Eclipse, '95

NISSAN Pickup 4WD, '95

OLDSMOBILE Achieva, '92-93 • **Cutlass Calais,** '89-91 • **Cutlass Supreme,** '94 • **98,** '93 • **Silhouette Van,** '90, '92, '94

PLYMOUTH Acclaim, '95 • **Voyager 4 Turbo,** '89 • **Voyager V6 2WD,** '89-93 • **Grand Voyager V6 2WD,** '89-94 & **4WD,** '91-94 • **Horizon,** '89 • **Neon,** '95 • **Sundance,** '89, '91, '93

PONTIAC Firebird V6, '94 • **Firebird V8,** '93-95 • **Grand Am,** '89-92 • **Grand Prix,** '90-91, '94 • **Sunbird,** '92-94 • **Trans Sport Van,** '90, '92, '94

SAAB 900, '94-95 • **9000,** '92

SUBARU Coupe, Sedan & Wagon, '89 • **Loyale,** '90

TOYOTA Tacoma Pickup 4WD, '95

VW Golf, '89 • **Golf GTI VR6,** '95 • **Jetta,** '92 • **Jetta GLX VR6,** '95

VOLVO 960 Series, '95

Auto reliability

Consumer Reports' unique Frequency-of-Repair records, 1989-1996

Cars are more reliable than they once were, American cars dramatically so. We know that because CONSUMER REPORTS has been collecting data and reporting on automobile reliability for more than 40 years. Each year, we ask readers to report on a year's worth of car troubles by answering our Annual Questionnaire. In the 1996 survey, they told us about significant troubles with 604,000 cars, minivans, sport-utility vehicles (SUVs), and pickup trucks. Problems that qualify as significant include those that are expensive to fix, that put the car out of commission for a time, or that cause a safety problem.

Each year, sorting the data by make, model, and year gives us a snapshot of each model's history. We know, for example, that in 1980, Chrysler, Ford, and General Motors cars showed, on average, about 100 problems per 100 cars. In 1995, that had dropped to about 35 problems per 100 cars. Japanese cars had a problem rate of 35 per 100 in 1980; 20 per 100 in 1995.

The cars most likely to be trouble-free are those from the three major Japanese manufacturers—Toyota/Lexus, Honda/Acura, and Nissan/Infiniti. The most reliable model of all in 1996 was the Lexus LS400; readers reported just 5 problems per 100 cars. The most reliable American make was the Saturn, with 19 problems per 100 cars.

Overall, SUVs and pickup trucks are more trouble-prone than sedans and minivans. The most reliable light truck had 1½ times as many problems as the best car.

From the reliability data, we also develop other information:

- The Frequency-of-Repair charts, which detail the reliability history of 216 models.
- The lists of reliable used cars and used cars to avoid on pages 284 to 286.
- The predicted reliability of new models in the auto profiles, starting on page 266.
- Trends and patterns.

How to read the charts

Behind all the symbols in these charts lie real problems experienced by real people. A black mark in a model's record doesn't mean all such cars will suffer a problem—it means that this model will probably suffer more than its share. Any car, as it ages, is likely to need some repair. But due to the quality of the parts, the nature of the design, or the craftsmanship in producing the car, some models suffer problems at a rate far lower or higher than what one might expect from sheer aging.

The Frequency-of-Repair charts detail the trouble spots. The symbols on these charts are on an absolute scale, from ⊖ (2 percent or fewer vehicles suffered a particular problem) to ● (nearly 16 percent or more—sometimes a lot more). The explanation at the head of the charts details what each trouble spot includes. Look at the column for the year you're interested in.

Since problems crop up as a car ages, before crossing a car off your list, check its trouble rate against the overall average. By comparing a model's score with what the average model showed for that year, you can tell exactly where it is much better than average.

The composite chart for "the average model" also shows which systems, overall, can be expected to deteriorate as the car ages. Not surprisingly, brakes wear out a lot.

Trouble spots

Use this chart to see how the overall averages for each model year compare with trouble spots on the model you're considering. You can get some idea of whether a model's problems are excessive for its age.

The Average Model

TROUBLE SPOTS	89	90	91	92	93	94	95	96
Engine	◒	○	○	⊖	⊖	⊖	⊜	⊜
Cooling	◒	○	○	○	⊖	⊜	⊜	⊜
Fuel	○	○	○	⊖	⊖	⊖	⊜	⊜
Ignition	○	○	⊖	⊖	⊖	⊜	⊜	⊜
Auto. trans.	○	○	○	⊖	⊖	⊖	⊖	⊜
Man. trans.	⊖	⊖	⊖	⊖	⊜	⊖	⊜	⊜
Clutch	◒	○	○	⊖	⊖	⊖	⊖	⊜
Electrical	●	●	●	◒	◒	◒	○	⊖
A/C	◒	◒	○	○	⊖	⊖	⊖	⊜
Suspension	○	○	○	○	⊖	⊖	⊖	⊜
Brakes	●	●	●	◒	◒	○	⊖	⊜
Exhaust	◒	◒	○	○	⊜	⊜	⊜	⊜
Body rust	○	○	⊖	⊜	⊜	⊜	⊜	⊜
Paint/trim	◒	◒	○	○	○	⊖	⊖	⊜
Integrity	◒	◒	○	○	○	○	○	○
Hardware	◒	◒	◒	◒	◒	◒	○	⊖

Key to problem rates

- ⊜ ....2.0% or less
- ⊖ 2.0%-5.0%
- ○ 5.0%-9.3%
- ◒ 9.3%-14.8%
- ● ....More than 14.8%
- * ....Insufficient data
- □ ....Not applicable

Overall average

What they include

Pistons, rings, valves, block, heads, bearings, camshafts, gaskets, turbocharger, cam belts and chains, oil pump.

Radiator, heater core, water pump, thermostat, hoses, intercooler and plumbing.

Choke, fuel injection, computer and sensors, fuel pump, tank, emissions controls, carburetion setting.

Spark plugs, coil, distributor, electronic ignition, sensors and modules, timing.

Transaxle, gear selector, linkage, coolers and lines.

Gearbox, transaxle, shifter, linkage.

Lining, pressure plate, release bearing, linkage and hydraulics.

Starter, alternator, battery, horn, switches, controls, instruments, lights, radio and sound system, accessory motors, electronics, wiring.

Compressor, condenser, evaporator, expansion valves, hoses, dryer, fans, electronics.

Linkage, power-steering gear, pump, coolers and lines, alignment and balance, springs and torsion bars, ball joints, bushings, shocks and struts, electronic or air suspension.

Hydraulic system, linings, discs and drums, power boost, antilock system; parking brake and linkage.

Manifold, muffler, catalytic converter, pipes.

Corrosion, pitting, perforation.

Fading, discoloring, chalking, peeling, cracking; loose trim, moldings, outside mirrors.

Seals, weather stripping, air and water leaks, wind noise, rattles and squeaks.

Window, door, seat mechanisms; locks, safety belts, sunroof, glass, wipers.

TROUBLE SPOTS	Acura Integra 89	90	91	92	93	94	95	96	Acura Legend 89	90	91	92	93	94	95	96
Engine	⊖	⊖	⊖	⊜	⊜	⊜	⊜	⊜	⊖	⊖	⊜	⊜	⊜	⊜	⊜	
Cooling	⊖	⊖	⊖	⊜	⊜	⊜	⊜	⊜	⊖	⊖	○	○	⊜	⊜	⊜	
Fuel	⊖	⊜	⊜	⊜	⊜	⊜	⊜	⊜	⊖	⊜	⊜	⊜	⊜	⊜	⊜	
Ignition	○	⊜	⊜	⊜	⊜	⊜	⊜	⊜	⊖	⊖	⊜	⊜	⊜	⊜	⊜	
Auto. trans.	⊖	⊖	⊜	⊜	⊜	○	⊜	*	⊖	⊖	⊖	⊖	⊜	⊜	⊜	
Man. trans.	⊜	⊜	⊜	⊜	⊜	⊜	⊜	⊜	⊜	⊜	*	*	*	*	*	
Clutch	◒	⊖	⊖	⊖	⊖	⊜	⊜	⊜	●	●	*	*	*	*	*	
Electrical	○	○	○	⊖	⊖	⊖	⊖	⊜	◒	◒	◒	◒	○	○	⊖	
A/C	◒	⊖	⊜	⊖	⊖	⊜	⊜	⊜	⊖	⊖	⊖	○	⊖	⊜	⊜	
Suspension	⊖	⊖	⊜	⊜	⊖	⊜	⊜	⊜	○	○	⊖	⊜	⊜	⊜	⊜	
Brakes	◒	◒	○	○	⊜	⊖	⊜	⊜	●	●	◒	○	⊖	⊜	⊜	
Exhaust	●	◒	○	◒	⊖	⊜	⊜	⊜	○	⊖	⊜	⊜	⊜	⊜	⊜	
Body rust	◒	⊖	⊜	⊜	⊜	⊜	⊜	⊜	○	⊜	⊜	⊜	⊜	⊜	⊜	
Paint/trim	◒	⊖	⊖	⊖	⊖	⊜	⊜	⊜	⊖	⊖	⊖	⊖	⊜	⊜	⊜	
Integrity	○	○	○	○	○	○	○	⊜	○	⊜	○	⊜	⊜	○	⊜	
Hardware	◒	○	○	⊖	⊖	○	⊖	⊜	○	○	◒	◒	⊖	○	⊖	

TROUBLE SPOTS	Acura TL 89	90	91	92	93	94	95	96	Acura Vigor 89	90	91	92	93	94	95	96
Engine								⊜				⊜	⊜	Insufficient data		
Cooling								⊜				⊜	⊜			
Fuel								⊜				⊜	⊜			
Ignition								⊜				⊜	⊜			
Auto. trans.								⊜				⊜	*			
Man. trans.												*	*			
Clutch												*	*			
Electrical								⊖				◒	⊜			
A/C								⊜				⊖	⊜			
Suspension								⊜				⊖	⊜			
Brakes								⊖				○	⊖			
Exhaust								⊜				⊖	⊜			
Body rust								⊜				⊜	⊜			
Paint/trim								⊜				⊖	⊜			
Integrity								⊖				○	⊖			
Hardware								⊖				⊖	⊖			

TROUBLE SPOTS	Audi 100, A6 89	90	91	92	93	94	95	96	Audi A4 89	90	91	92	93	94	95	96
Engine	Insufficient data	Insufficient data	Insufficient data	○	Insufficient data	Insufficient data	⊖	Insufficient data								⊜
Cooling				○			⊜									⊜
Fuel				○			⊜									⊜
Ignition				⊖			⊜									⊜
Auto. trans.				*			*									*
Man. trans.				*			*									*
Clutch				*			*									*
Electrical				◒			○									○
A/C				⊖			⊖									⊜
Suspension				⊜			⊜									⊜
Brakes				○			⊜									⊜
Exhaust				⊜			⊜									⊜
Body rust				⊜			⊜									⊜
Paint/trim				⊖			⊜									⊜
Integrity				⊖			⊖									⊜
Hardware				○			⊖									⊖

TROUBLE SPOTS	BMW 3-Series 89	90	91	92	93	94	95	96	BMW 5-Series 6 89	90	91	92	93	94	95	96
Engine	◒	○	●	○	⊜	⊜	⊜	Insufficient data	⊖	○	⊖	⊖	Insufficient data	Insufficient data	⊜	Insufficient data
Cooling	◒	◒	◒	○	⊖	⊜	⊜		●	●	◒	○			⊜	
Fuel	◒	⊖	○	○	⊖	⊖	⊜		⊖	⊖	⊖	○			⊜	
Ignition	⊖	⊜	⊜	⊖	⊜	⊖	⊜		⊖	⊜	⊜	⊜			⊜	
Auto. trans.	*	*	*	⊖	⊖	⊖	⊜		*	⊖	*	*			⊜	
Man. trans.	*	*	⊜	⊜	⊜	⊜	⊜		*	*	*	*			*	
Clutch	*	*	⊖	⊖	⊖	⊜	⊜		*	*	*	*			*	
Electrical	●	●	●	●	●	◒	○		●	●	◒	●			○	
A/C	○	○	○	◒	⊖	⊖	⊖		◒	⊖	○	◒			⊖	
Suspension	⊖	⊖	⊖	⊖	⊜	⊜	⊜		○	○	⊜	⊖			⊜	
Brakes	◒	◒	◒	○	○	○	⊜		○	○	○	⊖			⊜	
Exhaust	○	⊖	○	⊖	⊜	⊜	⊜		◒	○	⊖	○			⊜	
Body rust	⊜	⊜	⊖	⊜	⊜	⊜	⊜		⊜	⊜	⊖	⊜			⊜	
Paint/trim	⊖	⊖	○	⊖	⊜	⊖	⊖		⊖	⊜	⊜	⊖			⊜	
Integrity	○	⊖	○	◒	○	◒	⊖		⊖	⊖	⊜	○			⊖	
Hardware	○	○	◒	●	●	◒	○		◒	○	○	◒			⊖	

BMW 5-Series V8

Trouble spots	89	90	91	92	93	94	95	96 (Insufficient data)
Engine						⊖	◒	
Cooling						⊜	⊜	
Fuel						⊖	⊖	
Ignition						⊜	⊜	
Auto. trans.						○	*	
Man. trans.						*	*	
Clutch						*	*	
Electrical						◒	○	
A/C						⊖	⊖	
Suspension						⊖	⊖	
Brakes						⊖	⊜	
Exhaust						⊜	⊜	
Body rust						⊜	⊜	
Paint/trim						⊜	⊜	
Integrity						○	⊖	
Hardware						○	○	

Buick Century

Trouble spots	89	90	91	92	93	94	95	96 (Insufficient data)
Engine	○	⊖	⊜	⊜	⊜	⊖	⊖	
Cooling	◒	◒	◒	○	⊖	⊖	⊜	
Fuel	◒	○	○	⊖	⊖	⊖	⊖	
Ignition	○	⊖	⊖	⊜	⊜	⊜	⊜	
Auto. trans.	○	⊖	⊖	⊖	⊖	⊜	⊜	
Man. trans.								
Clutch								
Electrical	●	●	●	◒	○	◒	⊖	
A/C	◒	⊖	⊖	⊖	⊖	⊖	⊜	
Suspension	○	○	⊖	⊖	⊖	⊖	⊖	
Brakes	●	●	●	●	●	◒	⊖	
Exhaust	●	◒	◒	◒	○	⊜	⊜	
Body rust	○	○	○	⊖	⊜	⊜	⊜	
Paint/trim	●	◒	○	⊖	○	⊖	⊖	
Integrity	◒	○	○	○	○	◒	◒	
Hardware	●	◒	◒	○	◒	◒	◒	

Buick Electra, Park Avenue & Ultra

Trouble spots	89	90	91	92	93	94	95	96
Engine	⊖	⊖	⊖	⊖	⊜	⊖	⊖	⊜
Cooling	◒	○	○	○	⊖	⊖	⊜	⊜
Fuel	○	○	⊖	⊖	⊜	⊜	⊜	⊜
Ignition	○	○	○	○	⊜	⊜	⊜	⊜
Auto. trans.	○	⊖	⊖	⊖	⊖	⊖	⊜	⊜
Man. trans.								
Clutch								
Electrical	●	●	●	●	●	◒	◒	○
A/C	○	◒	●	◒	○	⊖	⊖	⊜
Suspension	○	⊖	○	○	⊖	⊖	⊖	⊜
Brakes	●	●	●	●	○	⊖	⊜	⊜
Exhaust	⊖	⊖	⊜	⊜	⊖	⊜	⊖	⊜
Body rust	○	⊖	⊖	⊜	⊜	⊜	⊜	⊜
Paint/trim	◒	○	○	○	⊖	⊜	⊖	⊜
Integrity	◒	○	◒	◒	◒	○	○	○
Hardware	◒	◒	●	◒	●	◒	○	⊖

Buick LeSabre

Trouble spots	89	90	91	92	93	94	95	96
Engine	⊖	⊖	⊖	⊖	⊖	⊖	⊜	⊜
Cooling	◒	◒	○	○	○	⊖	⊜	⊜
Fuel	○	○	⊖	⊖	⊖	⊜	⊜	⊜
Ignition	○	◒	◒	⊖	⊖	⊜	⊜	⊜
Auto. trans.	○	⊖	⊖	⊖	⊖	⊖	⊜	⊜
Man. trans.								
Clutch								
Electrical	●	●	●	●	◒	○	⊖	⊖
A/C	○	○	○	○	○	⊖	⊖	⊜
Suspension	○	○	⊖	○	⊖	⊖	⊖	⊖
Brakes	●	●	●	●	◒	⊖	⊖	⊜
Exhaust	⊖	⊜	⊜	⊖	○	⊜	⊜	⊜
Body rust	○	○	⊖	⊜	⊜	⊜	⊜	⊜
Paint/trim	◒	◒	○	○	⊖	⊖	⊖	⊜
Integrity	○	⊖	○	◒	◒	○	○	○
Hardware	◒	○	◒	◒	◒	○	○	⊖

Buick Regal

Trouble spots	89	90	91	92	93	94	95	96
Engine	◒	○	⊖	⊖	⊖	⊖	⊜	⊜
Cooling	◒	◒	○	○	⊖	⊖	⊜	⊜
Fuel	◒	○	⊖	⊜	⊖	⊜	⊜	⊜
Ignition	◒	○	⊖	⊜	⊜	⊜	⊜	⊜
Auto. trans.	◒	○	○	⊖	⊖	⊖	⊖	⊜
Man. trans.								
Clutch								
Electrical	●	●	●	●	◒	◒	○	⊖
A/C	◒	◒	○	○	⊖	⊖	⊜	⊜
Suspension	●	◒	○	⊖	⊖	⊖	⊜	⊖
Brakes	●	●	●	●	●	◒	○	⊖
Exhaust	○	⊖	⊜	⊜	⊖	⊜	⊜	⊖
Body rust	○	⊖	⊜	⊜	⊜	⊜	⊜	⊜
Paint/trim	◒	◒	⊖	⊖	⊖	⊖	⊖	⊖
Integrity	○	◒	○	○	○	◒	◒	○
Hardware	●	●	◒	◒	○	◒	◒	⊖

Buick Riviera

Trouble spots	89 (Insufficient data)	90	91 (Insufficient data)	92 (Insufficient data)	93 (Insufficient data)	94	95	96 (Insufficient data)
Engine		⊖					⊜	
Cooling		○					⊜	
Fuel		○					⊜	
Ignition		◒					⊜	
Auto. trans.		⊖					⊜	
Man. trans.								
Clutch								
Electrical		●					◒	
A/C		●					⊖	
Suspension		○					⊖	
Brakes		●					⊖	
Exhaust		⊜					⊜	
Body rust		⊜					⊜	
Paint/trim		○					⊖	
Integrity		○					◒	
Hardware		●					●	

Buick Roadmaster

Trouble spots	89	90	91 (Insufficient data)	92	93	94	95	96 (Insufficient data)
Engine				⊖	⊜	⊖	⊜	
Cooling				○	⊖	⊜	⊜	
Fuel				⊖	⊜	⊖	⊜	
Ignition				⊖	⊜	⊜	⊖	
Auto. trans.				⊖	⊖	⊖	⊖	
Man. trans.								
Clutch								
Electrical				●	◒	◒	◒	
A/C				◒	○	⊖	⊜	
Suspension				⊖	○	○	○	
Brakes				◒	○	○	○	
Exhaust				⊖	⊜	⊜	⊜	
Body rust				⊜	⊜	⊜	⊜	
Paint/trim				●	◒	○	○	
Integrity				◒	○	◒	◒	
Hardware				◒	◒	◒	◒	

Buick Skylark

Trouble spots	89	90	91	92	93	94	95	96 (Insufficient data)
Engine	●	◒	○	⊖	⊖	⊜	⊜	
Cooling	●	◒	○	◒	⊖	⊜	⊜	
Fuel	●	○	○	⊖	⊖	○	⊜	
Ignition	◒	⊖	○	⊖	⊜	⊖	⊜	
Auto. trans.	○	○	⊖	⊖	⊜	⊜	⊖	
Man. trans.								
Clutch								
Electrical	●	●	●	◒	○	◒	⊖	
A/C	◒	○	○	○	⊖	⊜	⊜	
Suspension	○	○	◒	○	○	⊖	⊜	
Brakes	◒	●	●	●	●	●	○	
Exhaust	●	●	●	⊖	⊖	⊜	⊜	
Body rust	●	●	○	⊜	⊜	⊜	⊜	
Paint/trim	●	●	●	○	○	⊖	⊖	
Integrity	◒	◒	◒	◒	◒	⊖	○	
Hardware	○	◒	◒	◒	◒	◒	○	

⊜ ⊖ ○ ◒ ●

Few ← **Problems** → Many

* Insufficient data

Cadillac Brougham, Fleetwood (RWD)

TROUBLE SPOTS	89	90	91	92	93	94	95	96
Engine	◒	⊖	⊜	Insufficient data	⊜	⊖	Insufficient data	Insufficient data
Cooling	●	○	○		○	⊜		
Fuel	○	⊖	○		⊜	⊖		
Ignition	⊖	⊖	⊜		⊖	⊖		
Auto. trans.	○	⊖	⊖		⊖	⊖		
Man. trans.								
Clutch								
Electrical	●	●	●		◒	◒		
A/C	●	●	◒		◒	⊜		
Suspension	○	◒	○		◒	○		
Brakes	◒	◒	◒		○	○		
Exhaust	◒	◒	○		⊜	⊜		
Body rust	○	⊖	⊜		⊖	⊜		
Paint/trim	◒	◒	⊖		●	●		
Integrity	○	◒	○		◒	●		
Hardware	○	●	●		◒	●		

Cadillac DeVille, Fleetwood (FWD)

TROUBLE SPOTS	89	90	91	92	93	94	95	96
Engine	○	○	◒	○	○	⊖	⊜	⊖
Cooling	○	○	○	○	⊖	⊜	⊜	⊜
Fuel	⊖	◒	◒	◒	⊖	⊖	⊖	⊜
Ignition	⊖	○	⊖	⊖	⊜	⊜	⊜	⊜
Auto. trans.	⊖	⊖	⊖	⊖	○	⊖	⊖	⊜
Man. trans.								
Clutch								
Electrical	●	●	●	◒	◒	◒	○	⊖
A/C	◒	◒	◒	◒	○	⊖	⊖	⊖
Suspension	○	⊖	○	○	◒	○	⊖	⊖
Brakes	●	●	●	●	◒	○	⊖	⊜
Exhaust	⊖	⊖	⊜	⊖	⊖	⊜	⊜	⊜
Body rust	⊜	⊜	⊜	⊜	⊜	⊜	⊜	⊜
Paint/trim	○	⊖	⊖	○	○	⊖	⊖	⊜
Integrity	○	○	○	○	○	○	○	⊖
Hardware	◒	◒	○	○	⊖	◒	◒	⊖

Cadillac Eldorado

TROUBLE SPOTS	89	90	91	92	93	94	95	96
Engine	○	◒	Insufficient data	◒	⊖	⊖	⊜	Insufficient data
Cooling	○	◒		○	○	⊜	⊜	
Fuel	⊖	●		⊖	⊖	⊖	⊜	
Ignition	⊖	○		⊜	⊖	⊜	⊜	
Auto. trans.	○	⊖		○	⊖	○	⊜	
Man. trans.								
Clutch								
Electrical	●	●		●	●	●	○	
A/C	●	◒		○	○	⊖	○	
Suspension	○	⊖		◒	○	○	⊖	
Brakes	●	●		○	◒	○	⊜	
Exhaust	⊜	○		⊖	⊜	⊜	⊖	
Body rust	⊜	⊜		⊜	⊜	⊜	⊜	
Paint/trim	◒	⊜		⊖	◒	○	◒	
Integrity	⊖	⊜		●	●	◒	◒	
Hardware	◒	◒		●	●	◒	●	

Cadillac Seville

TROUBLE SPOTS	89	90	91	92	93	94	95	96
Engine	◒	○	◒	◒	⊖	⊖	⊜	⊖
Cooling	●	⊖	○	○	⊖	⊖	⊜	⊜
Fuel	⊖	◒	⊖	⊖	○	⊜	⊖	⊖
Ignition	⊖	○	⊜	⊜	⊖	⊖	⊜	⊜
Auto. trans.	○	⊖	⊖	⊖	⊖	⊖	⊖	⊜
Man. trans.								
Clutch								
Electrical	●	●	●	◒	●	◒	◒	○
A/C	●	◒	●	◒	◒	○	⊖	⊖
Suspension	○	⊖	◒	○	○	⊖	⊖	⊖
Brakes	●	●	●	○	○	⊖	⊜	⊜
Exhaust	⊖	○	⊜	⊜	⊖	⊜	⊜	⊜
Body rust	⊖	⊜	⊜	⊜	⊜	⊜	⊜	⊜
Paint/trim	◒	⊖	⊖	⊖	⊖	⊖	○	⊖
Integrity	◒	○	○	◒	◒	◒	◒	⊖
Hardware	◒	◒	○	◒	◒	◒	●	⊖

Chevrolet Astro Van

TROUBLE SPOTS	89	90	91	92	93	94	95	96
Engine	◒	⊖	⊖	⊖	○	⊜	⊜	⊜
Cooling	◒	○	○	⊖	⊖	⊖	⊜	⊜
Fuel	○	○	⊖	○	○	⊖	⊖	⊖
Ignition	○	⊖	⊖	⊖	⊖	⊖	⊖	⊜
Auto. trans.	○	○	○	⊖	○	⊖	⊖	⊖
Man. trans.	*							
Clutch	*							
Electrical	●	●	●	◒	●	●	○	⊖
A/C	●	◒	○	○	○	◒	○	⊜
Suspension	◒	●	◒	○	○	⊖	⊖	⊖
Brakes	●	●	●	●	●	◒	○	○
Exhaust	●	◒	◒	⊖	⊖	⊖	⊜	⊜
Body rust	○	⊖	⊜	⊜	⊖	⊜	⊜	⊜
Paint/trim	●	●	◒	◒	○	○	⊖	○
Integrity	●	●	●	●	●	●	◒	○
Hardware	●	●	●	◒	●	●	◒	○

Chevrolet Blazer, K-Blazer, Tahoe

TROUBLE SPOTS	89	90	91	92	93	94	95	96
Engine	○	○	⊖	⊖	⊖	⊖	⊖	⊖
Cooling	◒	◒	○	●	○	⊜	⊜	⊜
Fuel	○	○	⊖	○	○	⊖	⊖	⊖
Ignition	⊖	○	⊖	○	⊖	⊖	⊜	⊜
Auto. trans.	○	○	⊖	○	○	⊖	⊜	⊜
Man. trans.	*	*	*	*	*	*	*	
Clutch	*	*	*	*	*	*	*	
Electrical	●	●	●	●	●	◒	○	⊖
A/C	◒	⊖	⊖	○	⊖	○	⊜	⊜
Suspension	○	◒	◒	○	⊖	⊖	⊜	⊜
Brakes	●	●	●	●	●	◒	○	⊜
Exhaust	◒	◒	◒	◒	○	⊜	⊜	⊜
Body rust	●	●	◒	⊜	⊖	⊖	⊜	⊜
Paint/trim	●	●	●	◒	◒	○	⊖	⊜
Integrity	●	●	●	◒	●	◒	○	○
Hardware	●	●	●	◒	●	●	○	○

Chevrolet C1500-2500 Pickup

TROUBLE SPOTS	89	90	91	92	93	94	95	96
Engine	○	○	⊖	⊖	○	⊖	⊖	⊜
Cooling	◒	○	○	⊖	⊖	⊜	⊜	⊜
Fuel	○	⊖	⊖	⊖	⊖	⊖	⊜	⊜
Ignition	○	○	○	⊖	⊖	⊖	⊜	⊜
Auto. trans.	○	○	○	○	⊖	⊖	⊜	⊜
Man. trans.	⊖	⊖	○	⊖	*	*	○	*
Clutch	●	●	◒	◒	*	*	◒	*
Electrical	●	●	●	●	◒	◒	○	⊖
A/C	◒	○	○	○	⊖	⊖	⊖	⊜
Suspension	◒	○	○	○	⊖	⊖	⊖	⊖
Brakes	●	◒	○	○	⊖	⊖	⊖	⊖
Exhaust	●	●	◒	◒	⊖	⊖	⊜	⊜
Body rust	⊖	⊖	⊜	⊜	⊜	⊜	⊜	⊜
Paint/trim	●	●	◒	○	○	⊖	⊖	⊜
Integrity	◒	○	○	○	○	○	○	⊖
Hardware	◒	○	○	○	◒	◒	◒	○

Chevrolet Camaro V8

TROUBLE SPOTS	89	90	91	92	93	94	95	96
Engine	◒	Insufficient data	⊜	Insufficient data	○	○	◒	Insufficient data
Cooling	●		○		○	⊖	⊖	
Fuel	◒		○		○	⊖	⊖	
Ignition	◒		○		○	⊖	⊖	
Auto. trans.	○		⊖		*	⊖	⊖	
Man. trans.	*		*		*	*	⊖	
Clutch	*		*		*	*	⊜	
Electrical	●		●		◒	●	●	
A/C	○		⊖		○	⊖	⊖	
Suspension	○		○		○	⊖	⊖	
Brakes	◒		○		◒	○	⊖	
Exhaust	◒		○		⊜	⊜	⊜	
Body rust	○		⊜		⊖	⊜	⊜	
Paint/trim	●		●		◒	○	○	
Integrity	●		●		●	●	●	
Hardware	●		◒		●	●	◒	

Chevrolet Caprice

Trouble spots	89	90	91	92	93	94	95	96
Engine	○	⊖	⊖	⊖	⊜	⊖	⊜	⊜
Cooling	◒	◒	○	⊖	⊖	⊜	⊜	⊜
Fuel	⊖	⊖	⊖	⊖	⊜	⊖	⊜	⊖
Ignition	⊖	⊖	○	○	⊜	⊖	⊖	⊜
Auto. trans.	○	○	⊖	⊖	⊜	⊖	⊖	⊜
Man. trans.								
Clutch								
Electrical	●	●	●	●	◒	◒	○	○
A/C	○	○	◒	◒	○	⊜	⊖	⊜
Suspension	○	○	○	○	○	○	○	⊖
Brakes	●	◒	●	●	○	○	○	⊖
Exhaust	●	●	●	⊜	⊜	⊜	⊜	⊜
Body rust	○	◒	⊖	⊜	⊜	⊜	⊜	⊜
Paint/trim	●	●	◒	○	○	⊖	○	○
Integrity	○	○	◒	○	○	○	◒	◒
Hardware	◒	◒	●	◒	◒	◒	○	○

Chevrolet Cavalier

Trouble spots	89	90	91	92	93	94	95	96
Engine	◒	○	○	○	⊖	⊜	⊖	⊜
Cooling	●	●	○	◒	⊖	⊖	⊜	⊖
Fuel	◒	○	⊖	⊖	⊖	⊖	⊜	⊜
Ignition	◒	⊖	○	⊖	⊜	⊖	⊜	⊜
Auto. trans.	○	⊖	⊖	⊖	⊖	⊜	⊜	⊜
Man. trans.	⊖	*	*	*	*	*	⊖	⊖
Clutch	○	*	*	*	*	*	⊖	⊜
Electrical	●	●	●	●	●	◒	○	○
A/C	◒	◒	○	○	○	⊖	⊜	⊜
Suspension	○	○	○	⊖	⊖	○	⊖	⊖
Brakes	●	●	●	●	●	●	⊖	⊜
Exhaust	●	○	○	⊖	⊜	⊜	⊜	⊜
Body rust	●	◒	○	⊖	⊖	⊖	⊜	⊜
Paint/trim	●	●	◒	○	○	○	⊖	⊖
Integrity	●	◒	◒	◒	◒	◒	◒	○
Hardware	◒	◒	◒	●	◒	◒	○	⊖

Chevrolet Corsica, Beretta

Trouble spots	89	90	91	92	93	94	95	96 (Insufficient data)
Engine	◒	◒	○	○	⊖	⊖	⊖	
Cooling	●	◒	◒	●	◒	⊖	⊖	
Fuel	●	○	○	⊖	⊖	⊖	⊜	
Ignition	◒	○	⊜	⊖	⊖	⊖	⊖	
Auto. trans.	○	⊖	⊖	⊖	⊖	⊖	⊖	
Man. trans.	⊜	*	*	*	*	*	*	
Clutch	◒	*	*	*	*	*	*	
Electrical	●	●	●	●	●	◒	◒	
A/C	◒	◒	○	○	○	⊜	⊖	
Suspension	○	○	○	⊖	○	○	⊖	
Brakes	●	●	●	●	●	◒	○	
Exhaust	●	●	⊖	⊖	⊖	⊜	⊖	
Body rust	○	○	⊖	⊜	⊜	⊜	⊖	
Paint/trim	●	●	●	◒	○	○	⊖	
Integrity	●	●	◒	◒	◒	◒	◒	
Hardware	●	●	◒	○	◒	◒	○	

Chevrolet K1500-2500 Pickup

Trouble spots	89	90	91	92	93	94	95	96
Engine	◒	⊖	○	⊖	⊖	⊖	⊖	⊜
Cooling	◒	○	○	○	⊖	⊜	⊜	⊖
Fuel	○	⊖	⊖	○	⊖	⊜	⊜	⊖
Ignition	○	○	○	○	⊖	⊖	⊜	⊜
Auto. trans.	○	○	◒	◒	○	⊖	⊖	⊖
Man. trans.	*	○	*	○	*	*	⊖	*
Clutch	*	●	*	◒	*	*	◒	*
Electrical	●	●	●	●	●	◒	○	⊖
A/C	○	○	○	⊖	⊖	⊖	⊖	⊜
Suspension	◒	○	○	○	⊖	⊖	⊖	⊜
Brakes	●	◒	◒	○	○	○	⊖	⊜
Exhaust	●	●	◒	◒	○	⊜	⊜	⊜
Body rust	○	⊖	⊖	⊜	⊜	⊜	⊜	⊜
Paint/trim	●	●	◒	○	○	⊖	⊖	⊜
Integrity	◒	○	○	○	○	○	○	○
Hardware	◒	○	○	○	◒	◒	◒	○

Chevrolet Lumina

Trouble spots	89	90	91	92	93	94	95	96
Engine		○	○	○	⊖	⊜	⊜	⊜
Cooling		◒	○	⊖	⊜	⊖	⊜	⊜
Fuel		○	○	⊖	⊖	⊜	⊜	⊜
Ignition		○	⊖	⊖	⊖	⊖	⊜	⊜
Auto. trans.		◒	⊖	⊖	⊖	⊖	⊖	⊜
Man. trans.			*	*	*			
Clutch			*	*	*			
Electrical		●	●	●	●	◒	○	⊖
A/C		○	○	⊖	⊖	⊖	⊜	⊜
Suspension		○	○	⊖	⊖	⊜	⊖	⊖
Brakes		●	●	●	●	●	⊖	⊜
Exhaust		⊖	⊖	⊜	⊜	⊜	⊜	⊜
Body rust		⊖	⊖	⊜	⊜	⊜	⊜	⊜
Paint/trim		●	○	○	⊖	⊜	⊖	⊜
Integrity		●	◒	○	◒	◒	○	⊖
Hardware		●	◒	◒	◒	○	○	⊖

Chevrolet Lumina APV Van

Trouble spots	89	90	91	92	93	94	95	96 (Insufficient data)
Engine		○	⊖	⊖	⊖	⊖	⊜	
Cooling		●	●	●	⊖	⊖	⊜	
Fuel		⊖	⊖	⊖	⊖	⊖	⊖	
Ignition		⊖	⊖	⊖	⊖	⊜	⊜	
Auto. trans.		○	⊖	⊖	○	⊖	⊜	
Man. trans.								
Clutch								
Electrical		●	●	●	●	◒	◒	
A/C		◒	○	○	⊖	⊖	⊜	
Suspension		◒	○	○	○	⊖	⊖	
Brakes		●	●	●	◒	○	⊜	
Exhaust		○	⊜	⊖	⊖	⊜	⊜	
Body rust		⊜	⊜	⊜	⊜	⊜	⊜	
Paint/trim		●	●	⊖	○	○	⊖	
Integrity		●	◒	○	○	◒	◒	
Hardware		●	●	●	●	●	●	

Chevrolet Monte Carlo

Trouble spots	89	90	91	92	93	94	95	96
Engine							⊖	⊜
Cooling							⊖	⊜
Fuel							⊜	⊖
Ignition							⊜	⊖
Auto. trans.							⊖	⊜
Man. trans.								
Clutch								
Electrical							⊖	○
A/C							⊖	⊜
Suspension							⊖	⊜
Brakes							○	⊖
Exhaust							⊜	⊜
Body rust							⊜	⊜
Paint/trim							○	⊖
Integrity							◒	○
Hardware							○	○

Chevrolet S-10 Blazer, Blazer

Trouble spots	89	90	91	92	93	94	95	96
Engine	○	○	○	○	○	⊖	⊖	●
Cooling	◒	◒	○	○	⊖	⊖	⊖	⊜
Fuel	○	○	⊖	○	●	○	○	⊜
Ignition	○	○	○	○	○	⊖	⊖	⊜
Auto. trans.	⊖	○	⊖	⊖	○	○	⊖	⊜
Man. trans.	*	*	*	*	*	*	*	*
Clutch	*	*	*	*	*	*	*	*
Electrical	●	●	●	●	●	●	◒	⊖
A/C	◒	⊖	○	⊖	○	⊖	⊖	⊜
Suspension	◒	◒	○	○	○	⊖	⊖	⊖
Brakes	●	●	●	●	●	●	◒	⊖
Exhaust	●	◒	◒	⊖	⊖	⊜	⊜	⊜
Body rust	●	●	●	○	⊖	⊖	⊜	⊜
Paint/trim	●	●	●	◒	◒	○	○	⊖
Integrity	●	●	●	●	●	●	●	○
Hardware	●	●	●	◒	●	◒	◒	○

⊜ ⊖ ○ ◒ ●
Few ◄— **Problems** —► Many

* Insufficient data

Chevrolet S-10 Pickup V6 (2WD)

TROUBLE SPOTS	89	90	91	92	93	94	95	96
Engine	○	○	○	⊖	⊖	⊖	⊖	◒
Cooling	◒	○	○	○	⊖	⊜	⊖	⊜
Fuel	○	○	⊖	⊖	○	⊖	⊖	⊖
Ignition	○	○	○	○	⊖	⊜	⊜	⊜
Auto. trans.	⊜	*	⊜	⊖	⊖	⊖	⊜	⊖
Man. trans.	*	*	⊖	⊖	⊖	*	⊜	*
Clutch	*	*	○	○	○	*	⊖	*
Electrical	●	●	◒	◒	◒	●	○	⊖
A/C	◒	*	⊖	⊖	⊖	⊖	⊖	⊜
Suspension	⊖	⊖	⊖	⊖	⊖	○	⊖	⊖
Brakes	◒	◒	○	◒	○	◒	○	⊖
Exhaust	◒	●	◒	○	⊜	⊜	⊜	⊜
Body rust	◒	●	◒	⊖	⊖	⊜	⊜	⊜
Paint/trim	●	●	●	●	◒	○	⊖	⊜
Integrity	●	◒	◒	○	○	○	◒	○
Hardware	●	◒	◒	○	○	◒	○	○

Chevrolet S-10 Pickup V6 (4WD)

TROUBLE SPOTS	89	90	91	92	93	94	95	96
Engine	○	Insufficient data	○	⊖	Insufficient data	○	⊖	Insufficient data
Cooling	◒		○	⊖		⊖	⊜	
Fuel	⊖		⊖	○		○	⊖	
Ignition	○		○	○		⊖	⊜	
Auto. trans.	⊖		○	*		○	⊖	
Man. trans.	*		*	*		*	*	
Clutch	*		*	*		*	*	
Electrical	●		●	◒		●	○	
A/C	⊖		○	*		⊖	⊖	
Suspension	●		○	○		○	⊖	
Brakes	◒		◒	●		●	◒	
Exhaust	◒		●	◒		⊜	⊜	
Body rust	●		●	○		⊜	⊜	
Paint/trim	●		●	●		○	○	
Integrity	◒		◒	○		●	◒	
Hardware	◒		●	○		◒	◒	

Chevrolet Sportvan

TROUBLE SPOTS	89	90	91	92	93	94	95	96
Engine	◒	○	○	⊖	⊖	⊖	⊜	Insufficient data
Cooling	◒	●	◒	⊖	⊖	⊖	⊜	
Fuel	○	○	⊜	○	⊖	○	⊜	
Ignition	○	⊖	⊜	⊜	⊜	⊖	⊜	
Auto. trans.	◒	○	○	◒	⊖	○	⊜	
Man. trans.	*							
Clutch	*							
Electrical	●	●	◒	◒	●	●	◒	
A/C	●	●	●	○	◒	◒	○	
Suspension	○	○	○	◒	◒	○	⊖	
Brakes	◒	●	●	●	●	●	○	
Exhaust	◒	●	◒	⊜	⊜	⊖	⊜	
Body rust	●	●	◒	⊖	⊖	⊖	⊜	
Paint/trim	●	●	●	◒	○	◒	○	
Integrity	●	●	●	◒	●	●	◒	
Hardware	●	●	●	◒	●	●	●	

Chevrolet Suburban

TROUBLE SPOTS	89	90	91	92	93	94	95	96
Engine	○	⊖	⊖	⊖	⊜	⊜	⊜	⊜
Cooling	●	◒	○	●	◒	⊜	⊜	⊜
Fuel	○	⊖	⊖	⊖	⊜	⊖	⊜	⊜
Ignition	⊖	⊖	○	⊖	⊜	⊜	⊜	⊜
Auto. trans.	◒	○	◒	◒	⊖	⊖	⊖	⊜
Man. trans.	*	*						
Clutch	*	*						
Electrical	●	●	●	●	●	◒	◒	⊖
A/C	◒	◒	○	○	⊖	○	⊖	⊖
Suspension	○	○	○	◒	⊖	⊖	⊖	⊖
Brakes	●	●	●	●	◒	◒	○	⊖
Exhaust	●	◒	○	◒	⊖	⊜	⊜	⊜
Body rust	●	○	⊖	⊜	⊖	⊜	⊜	⊜
Paint/trim	●	●	●	◒	○	⊜	⊖	⊖
Integrity	●	●	●	◒	◒	○	○	○
Hardware	●	●	●	●	●	◒	◒	○

Chrysler Cirrus

TROUBLE SPOTS	89	90	91	92	93	94	95	96
Engine							⊜	⊜
Cooling							⊜	⊜
Fuel							⊖	⊜
Ignition							⊖	⊜
Auto. trans.							⊖	⊜
Man. trans.								
Clutch								
Electrical							◒	⊖
A/C							◒	⊜
Suspension							○	⊜
Brakes							○	⊖
Exhaust							⊜	⊜
Body rust							⊜	⊜
Paint/trim							●	⊖
Integrity							●	○
Hardware							◒	⊖

Chrysler Concorde

TROUBLE SPOTS	89	90	91	92	93	94	95	96
Engine					⊖	⊖	⊜	⊜
Cooling					○	⊜	⊜	⊜
Fuel					○	⊖	⊜	⊜
Ignition					⊖	⊖	⊜	⊜
Auto. trans.					○	◒	⊖	⊜
Man. trans.								
Clutch								
Electrical					●	◒	○	⊖
A/C					●	◒	○	⊜
Suspension					○	⊖	⊖	⊜
Brakes					●	◒	○	⊜
Exhaust					⊜	⊜	⊜	⊜
Body rust					⊜	⊜	⊜	⊜
Paint/trim					⊖	⊖	⊖	⊜
Integrity					◒	○	○	⊖
Hardware					◒	○	○	⊖

Chrysler LeBaron Coupe & Conv.

TROUBLE SPOTS	89	90	91	92	93	94	95	96
Engine	●	◒	◒	○	⊖	○	⊜	
Cooling	●	●	○	○	⊖	⊜	⊜	
Fuel	◒	○	◒	⊖	⊖	⊖	⊖	
Ignition	○	⊖	⊜	⊖	⊜	⊜	⊜	
Auto. trans.	◒	●	●	●	◒	○	○	
Man. trans.	*	*	*	*	*			
Clutch	*	*	*	*	*			
Electrical	●	●	●	●	◒	○	○	
A/C	●	◒	⊖	○	○	⊖	⊖	
Suspension	●	○	○	⊖	⊖	⊖	⊖	
Brakes	●	●	○	◒	○	⊖	⊖	
Exhaust	○	⊖	◒	◒	⊜	⊜	⊜	
Body rust	○	⊖	⊜	⊖	⊜	⊜	⊜	
Paint/trim	◒	●	○	◒	◒	◒	○	
Integrity	●	●	●	●	●	●	●	
Hardware	●	●	●	●	●	◒	◒	

Chrysler LeBaron Sedan

TROUBLE SPOTS	89	90	91	92	93	94	95	96
Engine		◒	◒	○	○	⊖		
Cooling		◒	○	⊖	⊖	⊖		
Fuel		○	○	○	⊖	⊖		
Ignition		○	⊖	⊖	⊖	⊜		
Auto. trans.		◒	◒	○	○	○		
Man. trans.								
Clutch								
Electrical		●	◒	●	○	◒		
A/C		◒	○	○	◒	○		
Suspension		○	○	⊖	⊖	⊖		
Brakes		●	◒	○	○	⊜		
Exhaust		⊜	●	●	⊜	⊜		
Body rust		⊖	⊖	⊜	⊜	⊜		
Paint/trim		◒	◒	○	⊖	⊖		
Integrity		○	○	○	○	○		
Hardware		○	○	⊖	○	○		

Chrysler New Yorker Fifth Avenue

Insufficient data (89)

Trouble spots	89	90	91	92	93	94	95	96
Engine		○	⊖	○	○			
Cooling		◒	○	○	○			
Fuel		○	○	⊖	⊖			
Ignition		○	○	⊖	⊖			
Auto. trans.		●	●	●	◒			
Man. trans.								
Clutch								
Electrical		●	●	●	●			
A/C		◒	○	●	◒			
Suspension		◒	◒	◒	○			
Brakes		●	◒	◒	◒			
Exhaust		⊜	⊖	⊜	⊜			
Body rust		⊖	⊖	⊜	⊜			
Paint/trim		○	⊖	◒	⊖			
Integrity		○	○	○	◒			
Hardware		◒	○	◒	●			

Chrysler New Yorker, LHS

Trouble spots	89	90	91	92	93	94	95	96
Engine						⊖	⊜	⊜
Cooling						⊜	⊜	⊜
Fuel						⊖	⊜	⊜
Ignition						⊖	⊜	⊜
Auto. trans.						◒	⊖	⊖
Man. trans.								
Clutch								
Electrical						◒	○	⊖
A/C						●	○	⊜
Suspension						⊖	⊖	⊖
Brakes						●	○	⊜
Exhaust						⊜	⊜	⊜
Body rust						⊜	⊜	⊜
Paint/trim						⊖	⊖	⊜
Integrity						◒	○	⊜
Hardware						◒	○	⊖

Chrysler Sebring

Trouble spots	89	90	91	92	93	94	95	96
Engine							⊖	⊖
Cooling							⊖	⊜
Fuel							⊖	⊖
Ignition							⊖	⊜
Auto. trans.							⊖	⊖
Man. trans.							*	*
Clutch							*	*
Electrical							●	○
A/C							⊖	⊜
Suspension							○	○
Brakes							○	⊜
Exhaust							⊜	⊜
Body rust							⊜	⊜
Paint/trim							⊖	⊖
Integrity							●	○
Hardware							●	○

Chrysler Town & Country Van (2WD)

Trouble spots	89	90	91	92	93	94	95	96
Engine		○	○	○	○	⊖	⊜	⊜
Cooling		●	○	○	○	⊖	⊜	⊜
Fuel		○	○	⊖	⊖	⊖	⊜	○
Ignition		○	⊖	⊖	⊖	⊜	⊜	⊜
Auto. trans.		●	●	●	●	○	⊖	⊖
Man. trans.								
Clutch								
Electrical		●	●	●	◒	◒	○	○
A/C		◒	○	○	◒	⊖	⊖	⊜
Suspension		◒	○	○	○	⊖	⊖	⊖
Brakes		●	●	●	◒	○	⊖	⊖
Exhaust		⊖	●	⊖	⊜	⊜	⊜	⊖
Body rust		⊖	⊖	⊜	⊜	⊜	⊜	⊜
Paint/trim		◒	○	○	⊖	⊖	⊖	⊖
Integrity		◒	◒	◒	◒	●	◒	○
Hardware		●	◒	●	●	●	●	○

Chrysler Town & Country Van (4WD)

Insufficient data (95)

Trouble spots	89	90	91	92	93	94	95	96
Engine				○	○	⊖		
Cooling				○	⊖	⊖		
Fuel				◒	⊖	⊖		
Ignition				○	⊜	⊜		
Auto. trans.				●	●	◒		
Man. trans.								
Clutch								
Electrical				●	◒	◒		
A/C				○	○	⊖		
Suspension				○	◒	⊖		
Brakes				●	◒	○		
Exhaust				●	⊜	⊜		
Body rust				⊖	⊜	⊜		
Paint/trim				⊖	⊖	○		
Integrity				◒	○	◒		
Hardware				●	●	●		

Dodge Avenger

Trouble spots	89	90	91	92	93	94	95	96
Engine							⊖	⊖
Cooling							⊖	⊜
Fuel							⊖	⊖
Ignition							⊖	⊜
Auto. trans.							⊖	⊖
Man. trans.							*	*
Clutch							*	*
Electrical							●	○
A/C							⊖	⊜
Suspension							○	○
Brakes							○	⊜
Exhaust							⊜	⊜
Body rust							⊜	⊜
Paint/trim							⊖	⊖
Integrity							●	○
Hardware							●	○

Dodge Caravan 4

Insufficient data (96)

Trouble spots	89	90	91	92	93	94	95	96
Engine	◒	○	◒	○	○	⊖	⊖	
Cooling	●	◒	◒	○	⊖	⊜	⊜	
Fuel	○	○	○	○	⊖	○	⊜	
Ignition	⊖	○	⊖	⊖	⊜	⊖	⊜	
Auto. trans.	◒	○	○	○	○	⊖	⊖	
Man. trans.	*	*		*	*			
Clutch	*	*		*	*			
Electrical	◒	◒	●	◒	○	○	⊖	
A/C	●	●	⊖	⊖	◒	⊖	⊖	
Suspension	○	○	○	○	⊖	⊖	⊜	
Brakes	●	●	●	◒	○	⊖	⊜	
Exhaust	⊖	⊖	●	●	⊜	⊜	⊜	
Body rust	○	⊖	⊖	⊜	⊜	⊜	⊜	
Paint/trim	◒	◒	○	⊖	⊖	○	⊖	
Integrity	◒	◒	◒	◒	◒	◒	○	
Hardware	●	●	◒	◒	○	◒	◒	

Dodge Caravan V6 (2WD)

Trouble spots	89	90	91	92	93	94	95	96
Engine	●	●	◒	○	○	⊖	⊜	⊜
Cooling	●	◒	◒	○	⊖	⊖	⊜	⊜
Fuel	◒	◒	○	○	⊖	⊖	⊜	○
Ignition	⊖	⊖	⊖	⊖	⊜	⊜	⊜	⊜
Auto. trans.	●	●	●	◒	◒	○	⊖	⊖
Man. trans.								
Clutch								
Electrical	●	●	●	●	◒	○	○	⊖
A/C	●	○	⊖	○	◒	⊖	⊖	⊜
Suspension	○	○	○	○	⊖	⊖	⊖	○
Brakes	●	●	●	●	◒	⊖	⊖	⊖
Exhaust	⊖	⊖	●	○	⊜	⊜	⊜	⊜
Body rust	○	○	⊖	⊜	⊜	⊜	⊜	⊜
Paint/trim	●	◒	○	⊖	⊖	⊖	⊖	⊖
Integrity	◒	●	◒	◒	◒	◒	○	○
Hardware	●	●	◒	●	●	◒	◒	○

⊜ ⊖ ○ ◒ ●
Few ◄— **Problems** —► Many

*
Insufficient data

Dodge Colt, Colt Wagon

TROUBLE SPOTS	89	90	91	92	93	94	95	96
Engine	◒	●	○	○	⊜			
Cooling	○	⊖	⊜	⊖	⊖			
Fuel	⊖	○	⊖	⊜	⊜			
Ignition	⊖	⊖	⊖	⊜	⊖			
Auto. trans.	⊖	○	○	○	◒			
Man. trans.	⊖	⊖	⊖	⊖	*			
Clutch	⊖	⊖	○	○	*	Insufficient data		
Electrical	◒	○	○	⊜	○			
A/C	●	○	○	○	○			
Suspension	○	○	⊖	⊖	⊜			
Brakes	●	●	◒	◒	◒			
Exhaust	⊜	⊖	⊜	⊜	⊜			
Body rust	⊖	⊖	⊖	⊜	⊜			
Paint/trim	◒	○	○	○	○			
Integrity	◒	●	◒	◒	○			
Hardware	◒	◒	◒	◒	◒			

Dodge Dakota Pickup (2WD)

TROUBLE SPOTS	89	90	91	92	93	94	95	96
Engine	○	○	⊖	○	⊖	⊖	⊜	⊜
Cooling	◒	◒	◒	○	⊖	⊜	⊜	⊖
Fuel	○	○	○	◒	○	⊖	⊖	⊖
Ignition	◒	○	○	○	⊖	⊜	⊜	⊜
Auto. trans.	●	●	○	○	○	◒	○	○
Man. trans.	*	*	*	*	*	*	*	*
Clutch	*	*	*	*	*	*	*	*
Electrical	●	◒	◒	◒	○	○	⊖	○
A/C	◒	◒	◒	⊖	⊖	⊖	⊖	⊖
Suspension	○	⊖	◒	○	○	○	○	⊖
Brakes	●	●	●	●	○	○	⊖	⊖
Exhaust	○	⊖	◒	◒	⊜	⊜	⊜	⊜
Body rust	○	⊜	⊜	⊖	⊜	⊜	⊜	⊖
Paint/trim	◒	◒	○	●	○	⊖	⊖	○
Integrity	○	◒	○	○	○	◒	◒	○
Hardware	○	○	⊖	⊖	○	○	○	○

Dodge Dakota Pickup (4WD)

TROUBLE SPOTS	89	90	91	92	93	94	95	96
Engine				○	⊖	⊜	⊖	
Cooling				○	⊖	⊖	⊜	
Fuel				◒	○	⊖	○	
Ignition				○	⊜	⊜	⊜	
Auto. trans.				●	●	○	○	
Man. trans.				*	*	*	*	
Clutch	Insufficient data	Insufficient data	Insufficient data	*	*	*	*	Insufficient data
Electrical				◒	○	○	⊖	
A/C				⊖	⊖	⊖	⊜	
Suspension				○	○	⊖	⊖	
Brakes				●	◒	⊖	⊖	
Exhaust				●	⊖	⊜	⊜	
Body rust				⊖	⊖	⊜	⊖	
Paint/trim				◒	○	⊜	○	
Integrity				○	○	○	○	
Hardware				⊖	◒	○	⊖	

Dodge Dynasty

TROUBLE SPOTS	89	90	91	92	93	94	95	96
Engine	●	○	○	○	○			
Cooling	●	◒	○	⊖	○			
Fuel	◒	○	○	⊖	⊖			
Ignition	⊖	○	○	⊖	⊖			
Auto. trans.	●	●	●	●	●			
Man. trans.								
Clutch								
Electrical	●	●	●	◒	◒			
A/C	◒	◒	○	○	◒			
Suspension	◒	◒	○	○	○			
Brakes	●	●	◒	◒	◒			
Exhaust	⊜	⊖	●	●	⊜			
Body rust	⊖	⊖	⊜	⊖	⊜			
Paint/trim	○	○	○	○	⊖			
Integrity	◒	◒	◒	◒	◒			
Hardware	●	◒	⊖	○	○			

Dodge Grand Caravan V6 (2WD)

TROUBLE SPOTS	89	90	91	92	93	94	95	96
Engine	●	○	○	○	○	⊖	⊜	⊜
Cooling	●	●	○	○	○	⊖	⊜	⊜
Fuel	○	○	○	⊖	⊖	⊖	⊜	○
Ignition	⊖	○	⊖	⊖	⊖	⊜	⊜	⊜
Auto. trans.	●	●	●	●	●	○	⊖	⊖
Man. trans.								
Clutch								
Electrical	●	●	●	●	◒	◒	○	○
A/C	●	◒	○	○	◒	⊖	⊖	⊜
Suspension	◒	◒	○	○	○	⊖	⊖	⊖
Brakes	●	●	●	●	◒	○	⊖	⊖
Exhaust	⊜	⊖	●	⊖	⊜	⊜	⊜	⊜
Body rust	○	⊖	⊖	⊜	⊜	⊜	⊜	⊜
Paint/trim	●	◒	○	○	⊖	⊖	⊖	⊖
Integrity	●	◒	◒	◒	◒	●	◒	○
Hardware	●	●	◒	●	●	●	●	○

Dodge Grand Caravan V6 (4WD)

TROUBLE SPOTS	89	90	91	92	93	94	95	96
Engine			○	○	○	⊖		
Cooling			◒	○	⊖	⊖		
Fuel			○	◒	⊖	⊖		
Ignition			○	○	⊜	⊜		
Auto. trans.			●	●	●	◒		
Man. trans.								
Clutch							Insufficient data	
Electrical			●	●	◒	◒		
A/C			⊖	○	○	⊖		
Suspension			◒	○	◒	⊖		
Brakes			●	●	◒	○		
Exhaust			●	●	⊜	⊜		
Body rust			⊖	⊖	⊜	⊜		
Paint/trim			◒	⊖	⊖	○		
Integrity			●	◒	○	◒		
Hardware			●	●	●	●		

Dodge Intrepid

TROUBLE SPOTS	89	90	91	92	93	94	95	96
Engine					⊖	⊖	⊜	⊜
Cooling					⊖	⊜	⊜	⊜
Fuel					○	⊖	⊖	⊜
Ignition					⊖	⊖	⊜	⊜
Auto. trans.					◒	◒	⊖	⊖
Man. trans.								
Clutch								
Electrical					●	◒	○	⊖
A/C					●	◒	⊖	⊜
Suspension					○	⊖	⊖	⊜
Brakes					●	◒	○	⊜
Exhaust					⊜	⊜	⊜	⊜
Body rust					⊖	⊜	⊜	⊜
Paint/trim					●	○	○	⊜
Integrity					●	●	◒	○
Hardware					◒	◒	○	⊖

Dodge Neon

TROUBLE SPOTS	89	90	91	92	93	94	95	96
Engine							⊖	⊜
Cooling							⊜	⊜
Fuel							⊖	⊖
Ignition							⊖	⊜
Auto. trans.							⊖	⊖
Man. trans.							⊜	*
Clutch							⊜	*
Electrical							◒	○
A/C							⊖	⊖
Suspension							⊖	⊖
Brakes							○	⊖
Exhaust							⊜	⊜
Body rust							⊜	⊜
Paint/trim							⊖	⊖
Integrity							●	○
Hardware							◒	○

Dodge Ram Pickup (2WD)

Trouble spots	89	90	91	92	93	94	95	96
Engine						⊖	⊖	⊜
Cooling						⊜	⊜	⊜
Fuel						○	○	⊜
Ignition						⊜	⊜	⊜
Auto. trans.						○	⊖	⊖
Man. trans.						*	*	*
Clutch	Insufficient data	Insufficient data	Insufficient data	Insufficient data	Insufficient data	*	*	*
Electrical						○	⊜	⊖
A/C						⊜	⊜	⊜
Suspension						⊖	○	⊖
Brakes						○	○	○
Exhaust						⊜	⊜	⊜
Body rust						⊜	⊜	⊜
Paint/trim						○	⊜	⊖
Integrity						○	○	⊖
Hardware						○	⊜	⊖

Dodge Ram Pickup (4WD)

Trouble spots	89	90	91	92	93	94	95	96
Engine						○	⊖	⊜
Cooling						⊜	⊖	⊜
Fuel						○	○	⊖
Ignition						⊜	⊜	⊜
Auto. trans.						◒	○	○
Man. trans.						*	*	*
Clutch	Insufficient data	Insufficient data	Insufficient data	Insufficient data	Insufficient data	*	*	*
Electrical						○	○	⊖
A/C						⊖	⊜	⊜
Suspension						◒	○	⊖
Brakes						◒	◒	○
Exhaust						⊜	⊜	⊖
Body rust						⊖	⊜	⊜
Paint/trim						○	○	⊜
Integrity						◒	○	⊖
Hardware						◒	○	⊖

Dodge Ram Van B150-250

Trouble spots	89	90	91	92	93	94	95	96
Engine	◒	○	⊖	○		⊜	⊜	
Cooling	●	◒	○	○		⊜	⊜	
Fuel	○	○	○	○		⊖	⊖	
Ignition	○	⊖	○	⊖		⊖	⊜	
Auto. trans.	◒	◒	○	◒		○	⊖	
Man. trans.	*	*	*	*				
Clutch	*	*	*	*	Insufficient data			Insufficient data
Electrical	●	●	●	◒		◒	◒	
A/C	●	●	◒	◒		○	⊖	
Suspension	◒	◒	◒	⊖		⊖	⊖	
Brakes	●	●	●	◒		○	○	
Exhaust	◒	○	◒	○		⊜	⊜	
Body rust	●	◒	○	⊖		⊖	⊖	
Paint/trim	●	●	◒	◒		○	○	
Integrity	●	◒	◒	●		●	●	
Hardware	●	◒	◒	◒		◒	◒	

Dodge Shadow

Trouble spots	89	90	91	92	93	94	95	96
Engine	●	◒	◒	◒	⊖	⊖		
Cooling	●	●	◒	○	⊖	⊜		
Fuel	◒	◒	◒	○	⊖	⊖		
Ignition	○	○	○	⊖	⊖	⊖		
Auto. trans.	○	⊖	⊖	○	○	○		
Man. trans.	*	*	*	⊖	*	*		
Clutch	*	*	*	⊜	*	*		
Electrical	●	●	●	●	◒	◒		
A/C	●	●	●	○	◒	◒		
Suspension	●	○	○	⊖	⊖	⊜		
Brakes	●	●	◒	○	⊖	⊜		
Exhaust	○	⊖	●	●	⊜	⊜		
Body rust	○	○	○	⊖	○	⊜		
Paint/trim	●	◒	◒	◒	◒	⊖		
Integrity	●	◒	◒	◒	◒	◒		
Hardware	●	◒	◒	○	◒	◒		

Dodge Spirit

Trouble spots	89	90	91	92	93	94	95	96
Engine	●	◒	◒	○	○	⊖	⊖	
Cooling	●	◒	○	⊖	⊖	⊖	⊜	
Fuel	○	○	○	○	⊖	⊖	⊖	
Ignition	⊖	○	⊖	⊖	⊖	⊜	⊜	
Auto. trans.	○	◒	◒	○	○	○	⊖	
Man. trans.	*	*	*	*	*			
Clutch	*	*	*	*	*			
Electrical	●	●	◒	●	○	◒	○	
A/C	●	◒	○	○	◒	○	⊖	
Suspension	◒	○	○	⊖	⊖	⊖	⊖	
Brakes	●	●	◒	○	○	⊜	⊖	
Exhaust	⊖	⊜	●	●	⊜	⊜	⊜	
Body rust	○	⊖	⊖	⊜	⊜	⊜	⊜	
Paint/trim	●	◒	◒	○	⊖	⊖	⊖	
Integrity	○	○	○	○	○	○	○	
Hardware	○	○	○	⊖	○	○	◒	

Dodge Stealth

Trouble spots	89	90	91	92	93	94	95	96
Engine			○	○	⊜	⊜		
Cooling			⊜	⊖	⊖	⊜		
Fuel			⊖	⊖	⊖	⊖		
Ignition			⊖	⊜	⊜	⊜		
Auto. trans.			*	*	*	*		
Man. trans.			◒	○	⊖	*		
Clutch			○	◒	●	*	Insufficient data	Insufficient data
Electrical			●	●	●	●		
A/C			⊜	⊜	⊜	⊖		
Suspension			⊜	○	⊖	⊖		
Brakes			○	⊖	⊖	⊖		
Exhaust			⊜	⊜	⊜	⊜		
Body rust			⊖	⊜	⊜	⊜		
Paint/trim			○	○	◒	○		
Integrity			○	◒	●	○		
Hardware			○	●	◒	○		

Dodge Stratus

Trouble spots	89	90	91	92	93	94	95	96
Engine							⊜	⊜
Cooling							⊜	⊜
Fuel							⊖	⊜
Ignition							⊖	⊜
Auto. trans.							⊖	⊜
Man. trans.							*	*
Clutch							*	*
Electrical							◒	⊖
A/C							◒	⊜
Suspension							○	⊜
Brakes							○	⊖
Exhaust							⊜	⊜
Body rust							⊜	⊜
Paint/trim							●	⊖
Integrity							●	○
Hardware							◒	⊖

Eagle Summit (except Wagon)

Trouble spots	89	90	91	92	93	94	95	96
Engine	◒	●	○	○	⊖			
Cooling	○	⊖	⊜	⊖	⊖			
Fuel	⊖	○	⊖	⊜	⊜			
Ignition	⊖	⊖	⊖	⊜	⊖			
Auto. trans.	⊖	○	○	○	◒			
Man. trans.	⊖	⊖	⊖	⊖	*			
Clutch	⊖	⊖	○	○	*	Insufficient data	Insufficient data	Insufficient data
Electrical	◒	○	○	⊖	○			
A/C	●	○	○	○	○			
Suspension	○	○	⊖	⊖	⊜			
Brakes	●	●	◒	◒	◒			
Exhaust	⊜	⊖	⊜	⊜	⊜			
Body rust	⊖	⊖	⊜	⊜	⊜			
Paint/trim	◒	○	○	○	○			
Integrity	◒	●	◒	◒	○			
Hardware	◒	◒	◒	◒	◒			

⊜ ⊖ ○ ◒ ●

Few ◄— **Problems** —► Many

* Insufficient data

Eagle Summit Wagon

TROUBLE SPOTS	89	90	91	92	93	94	95	96
Engine				⊖	⊜	⊜	⊜	Insufficient data
Cooling				⊖	⊖	⊖	⊜	
Fuel				⊖	⊜	⊜	⊜	
Ignition				⊖	⊖	⊜	⊜	
Auto. trans.				⊖	○	⊖	*	
Man. trans.				*	*	*	*	
Clutch				*	*	*	*	
Electrical				○	◒	◒	○	
A/C				⊜	⊖	⊜	⊜	
Suspension				⊜	⊖	⊜	⊖	
Brakes				⊖	⊜	⊖	○	
Exhaust				⊖	⊜	⊜	⊜	
Body rust				⊖	⊜	⊜	⊜	
Paint/trim				⊖	○	⊖	⊜	
Integrity				○	◒	○	○	
Hardware				○	●	⊖	○	

Eagle Talon

TROUBLE SPOTS	89	90	91	92	93	94	95	96
Engine		●	◒	◒	○	○	○	Insufficient data
Cooling		○	⊖	⊖	⊖	⊖	⊜	
Fuel		⊖	○	⊖	⊖	⊖	⊖	
Ignition		⊖	○	⊖	⊖	⊜	○	
Auto. trans.		○	○	⊖	*	*	⊖	
Man. trans.		○	○	○	⊖	*	⊖	
Clutch		○	○	○	⊖	*	⊖	
Electrical		◒	●	◒	◒	◒	●	
A/C		⊖	⊖	⊖	⊜	⊖	⊜	
Suspension		⊖	⊖	⊖	⊖	⊖	⊖	
Brakes		●	◒	◒	○	⊖	⊖	
Exhaust		⊖	⊖	⊖	⊜	⊜	⊜	
Body rust		⊖	⊜	⊜	⊜	⊜	⊜	
Paint/trim		◒	○	◒	○	⊖	○	
Integrity		○	○	◒	◒	◒	●	
Hardware		●	●	●	◒	○	●	

Eagle Vision

TROUBLE SPOTS	89	90	91	92	93	94	95	96
Engine					⊖	⊖	⊜	Insufficient data
Cooling					⊖	⊖	⊜	
Fuel					○	⊜	⊜	
Ignition					⊖	⊜	⊜	
Auto. trans.					○	○	⊖	
Man. trans.								
Clutch								
Electrical					●	◒	○	
A/C					●	◒	⊖	
Suspension					⊖	⊖	⊖	
Brakes					●	◒	⊖	
Exhaust					⊜	⊜	⊜	
Body rust					⊜	⊜	⊜	
Paint/trim					⊖	⊖	⊖	
Integrity					◒	●	◒	
Hardware					◒	○	○	

Ford Aerostar Van

TROUBLE SPOTS	89	90	91	92	93	94	95	96
Engine	○	○	○	○	⊖	⊜	⊜	Insufficient data
Cooling	●	●	◒	○	⊖	⊖	⊖	
Fuel	○	○	⊖	⊖	⊖	⊜	⊜	
Ignition	○	○	⊖	⊖	⊜	⊜	⊜	
Auto. trans.	◒	◒	○	○	⊖	⊖	⊜	
Man. trans.	*	*	*	*	*	*		
Clutch	*	*	*	*	*	*		
Electrical	●	●	●	●	◒	◒	○	
A/C	●	●	●	●	○	⊖	⊖	
Suspension	●	●	◒	○	○	○	○	
Brakes	●	●	●	●	●	◒	○	
Exhaust	◒	●	●	●	○	⊜	⊜	
Body rust	●	◒	⊜	⊜	⊜	⊜	⊜	
Paint/trim	◒	○	⊖	⊖	⊖	⊖	⊖	
Integrity	●	◒	◒	◒	○	◒	◒	
Hardware	●	●	●	◒	◒	◒	◒	

Ford Bronco

TROUBLE SPOTS	89	90	91	92	93	94	95	96
Engine	●	○	○	⊖	⊜	⊖	⊖	Insufficient data
Cooling	◒	◒	○	⊖	⊖	⊖	⊜	
Fuel	●	◒	◒	○	○	⊜	⊜	
Ignition	○	⊖	⊖	⊖	⊜	⊜	⊜	
Auto. trans.	○	◒	*	⊖	⊖	○	⊖	
Man. trans.	*	*	*	*	*	*	*	
Clutch	*	*	*	*	*	*	*	
Electrical	●	●	◒	●	●	⊖	○	
A/C	●	◒	○	○	⊖	⊖	⊜	
Suspension	●	◒	○	○	⊖	○	○	
Brakes	●	●	●	●	●	●	●	
Exhaust	●	●	◒	○	⊖	⊜	⊜	
Body rust	●	●	○	⊖	⊜	⊖	⊜	
Paint/trim	●	●	◒	◒	◒	⊜	○	
Integrity	◒	◒	●	◒	◒	●	●	
Hardware	●	●	●	●	◒	◒	◒	

Ford Club Wagon, Van

TROUBLE SPOTS	89	90	91	92	93	94	95	96
Engine	◒	◒	○	○	⊖	⊖	⊜	Insufficient data
Cooling	●	◒	◒	○	○	⊖	⊜	
Fuel	◒	●	○	●	○	⊖	⊖	
Ignition	○	○	○	⊖	⊜	⊜	⊜	
Auto. trans.	○	◒	◒	○	⊖	⊖	⊜	
Man. trans.								
Clutch								
Electrical	●	●	◒	●	◒	◒	◒	
A/C	●	●	●	◒	◒	○	⊖	
Suspension	◒	◒	◒	●	●	◒	○	
Brakes	●	●	●	●	●	●	●	
Exhaust	●	◒	●	◒	⊖	⊜	⊜	
Body rust	◒	◒	○	⊖	⊖	⊜	⊜	
Paint/trim	◒	◒	○	○	○	○	⊖	
Integrity	●	●	◒	○	○	◒	⊖	
Hardware	●	◒	○	◒	◒	○	○	

Ford Contour

TROUBLE SPOTS	89	90	91	92	93	94	95	96
Engine							⊜	⊜
Cooling							⊜	⊜
Fuel							●	⊖
Ignition							⊜	⊜
Auto. trans.							⊖	⊜
Man. trans.							⊖	*
Clutch							⊜	*
Electrical							○	⊖
A/C							⊖	⊜
Suspension							⊖	⊜
Brakes							⊖	⊜
Exhaust							⊜	⊜
Body rust							⊜	⊖
Paint/trim							⊖	⊜
Integrity							◒	○
Hardware							●	○

Ford Crown Victoria, LTD Crown Victoria

TROUBLE SPOTS	89	90	91	92	93	94	95	96
Engine	○	○	⊖	⊖	⊜	⊜	⊜	⊜
Cooling	●	○	⊖	⊜	⊜	⊜	⊜	⊜
Fuel	○	○	○	⊖	⊖	⊖	⊖	⊜
Ignition	⊖	○	⊖	○	⊖	⊜	⊜	⊜
Auto. trans.	○	○	⊖	○	●	○	⊖	⊖
Man. trans.								
Clutch								
Electrical	●	●	●	●	◒	○	◒	⊖
A/C	●	◒	○	◒	⊖	⊖	⊖	⊜
Suspension	○	○	○	⊖	⊖	⊖	⊖	⊖
Brakes	●	●	●	●	●	○	○	⊖
Exhaust	●	◒	○	◒	⊜	⊜	⊜	⊜
Body rust	⊖	⊖	○	⊜	⊜	⊜	⊜	⊜
Paint/trim	○	○	○	○	⊜	⊖	⊖	⊜
Integrity	○	○	⊖	○	○	○	○	⊖
Hardware	◒	●	●	◒	○	○	○	⊖

Trouble spots	Ford Escort 89	90	91	92	93	94	95	96
Engine	◒	◒	○	⊖	⊖	⊖	⊜	⊜
Cooling	◒	◒	○	○	⊖	⊖	⊜	⊜
Fuel	●	●	○	○	⊖	⊜	⊜	⊜
Ignition	◒	◒	⊖	⊖	⊜	⊜	⊜	⊜
Auto. trans.	◒	⊖	○	⊖	⊖	⊖	⊖	⊜
Man. trans.	⊖	⊜	⊜	⊜	⊖	⊜	⊜	*
Clutch	◒	○	○	⊖	⊖	⊖	⊜	*
Electrical	●	●	●	◒	◒	○	○	⊜
A/C	●	●	●	○	⊖	⊜	⊜	⊖
Suspension	◒	◒	○	⊖	⊖	⊖	⊜	⊜
Brakes	●	●	●	◒	◒	○	⊖	⊜
Exhaust	○	○	⊖	⊜	⊜	⊜	⊜	⊜
Body rust	◒	○	⊖	⊖	⊜	⊜	⊜	⊜
Paint/trim	◒	○	○	⊖	⊖	⊖	⊖	⊜
Integrity	●	●	◒	○	○	○	○	○
Hardware	◒	◒	◒	◒	◒	○	○	⊖

Trouble spots	Ford Explorer 89	90	91	92	93	94	95	96
Engine			◒	◒	⊖	⊜	⊜	⊜
Cooling			◒	○	⊖	⊖	⊖	⊜
Fuel			⊖	⊖	⊜	⊖	⊜	⊜
Ignition			⊜	⊖	⊜	⊜	⊜	⊜
Auto. trans.			○	○	⊖	⊜	⊖	⊜
Man. trans.			○	◒	⊖	⊜	⊜	⊜
Clutch			○	○	○	⊖	⊜	⊜
Electrical			●	●	◒	○	○	⊖
A/C			●	●	⊖	⊖	⊖	⊜
Suspension			◒	◒	○	⊖	⊖	⊖
Brakes			●	●	●	◒	⊖	⊜
Exhaust			●	◒	○	⊜	⊜	⊜
Body rust			○	⊖	⊜	⊜	⊜	⊜
Paint/trim			○	○	⊖	⊖	⊖	⊜
Integrity			○	○	○	⊖	○	⊖
Hardware			◒	◒	◒	○	○	⊖

Trouble spots	Ford F150-250 Pickup (2WD) 89	90	91	92	93	94	95	96
Engine	◒	○	○	⊖	⊖	⊖	⊜	⊜
Cooling	◒	○	○	○	⊖	○	⊖	⊜
Fuel	◒	●	◒	◒	○	○	⊖	⊜
Ignition	○	○	○	⊖	⊖	⊜	⊜	⊜
Auto. trans.	◒	◒	◒	○	○	⊖	⊜	⊜
Man. trans.	○	⊖	⊖	⊖	⊖	⊖	⊖	*
Clutch	◒	○	○	◒	○	○	○	*
Electrical	●	●	◒	◒	◒	◒	○	⊜
A/C	●	◒	◒	○	⊖	⊖	⊜	⊜
Suspension	◒	◒	○	○	○	○	○	⊖
Brakes	●	●	●	●	●	●	○	⊖
Exhaust	●	●	◒	◒	⊖	⊜	⊜	⊜
Body rust	◒	○	○	⊖	⊖	⊜	⊜	⊜
Paint/trim	●	●	●	◒	○	⊖	⊖	⊖
Integrity	○	○	○	◒	○	◒	○	⊖
Hardware	◒	◒	◒	◒	◒	○	⊜	⊜

Trouble spots	Ford F150-250 Pickup (4WD) 89	90	91	92	93	94	95	96
Engine	◒	◒	◒	○	⊖	⊜	⊖	⊜
Cooling	●	◒	○	○	○	⊖	⊜	⊜
Fuel	●	●	◒	◒	◒	⊖	⊖	⊜
Ignition	◒	○	⊖	⊖	⊖	⊜	⊜	⊜
Auto. trans.	◒	●	◒	○	○	⊖	○	⊖
Man. trans.	○	⊖	⊖	⊖	⊖	○	⊜	*
Clutch	◒	○	⊖	○	○	◒	⊖	*
Electrical	●	●	◒	◒	◒	○	○	⊖
A/C	◒	○	○	○	⊖	○	⊜	⊜
Suspension	◒	◒	○	○	○	○	○	○
Brakes	●	●	●	●	●	●	◒	⊖
Exhaust	●	●	●	◒	○	⊜	⊜	⊜
Body rust	●	◒	○	⊖	⊖	⊜	⊜	⊜
Paint/trim	●	●	●	○	◒	⊖	⊖	⊜
Integrity	◒	◒	◒	○	◒	○	○	○
Hardware	◒	◒	◒	◒	◒	○	○	⊖

Trouble spots	Ford Festiva 89	90	91	92	93	94	95	96
Engine	○	○	⊖	Insufficient data	⊜			
Cooling	⊜	⊖	⊖		⊜			
Fuel	⊖	⊜	⊜		⊜			
Ignition	⊖	⊜	⊖		⊜			
Auto. trans.	*	*	*		*			
Man. trans.	⊖	⊜	⊜		⊖			
Clutch	⊖	⊖	⊜		⊜			
Electrical	◒	◒	○		○			
A/C	◒	*	*		*			
Suspension	○	⊖	⊖		⊖			
Brakes	●	●	●		◒			
Exhaust	●	●	●		◒			
Body rust	○	○	⊖		⊖			
Paint/trim	○	⊖	⊖		○			
Integrity	◒	◒	○		○			
Hardware	◒	◒	◒		◒			

Trouble spots	Ford Mustang 89	90	91	92	93	94	95	96
Engine	○	○	⊖	⊖	⊖	⊜	⊖	⊖
Cooling	◒	◒	○	⊜	○	⊜	⊜	⊜
Fuel	○	○	○	⊖	⊜	⊖	⊖	⊜
Ignition	⊖	○	⊜	⊖	⊖	⊖	⊜	⊜
Auto. trans.	◒	◒	◒	○	⊖	●	⊖	*
Man. trans.	○	○	*	*	*	⊖	⊜	*
Clutch	◒	○	*	*	*	○	⊜	*
Electrical	●	●	●	●	●	◒	○	○
A/C	●	●	●	○	○	⊖	⊖	⊖
Suspension	◒	○	◒	○	◒	○	⊖	⊜
Brakes	◒	◒	◒	◒	◒	○	⊖	⊖
Exhaust	◒	○	◒	○	⊜	⊜	⊜	⊜
Body rust	○	⊖	⊖	⊖	⊖	⊜	⊜	⊜
Paint/trim	●	●	●	◒	●	○	⊖	⊖
Integrity	●	●	●	◒	●	○	○	○
Hardware	●	●	●	●	●	◒	◒	⊖

Trouble spots	Ford Probe 89	90	91	92	93	94	95	96
Engine	○	○	⊖	⊖	⊖	⊖	⊜	Insufficient data
Cooling	◒	◒	◒	◒	⊖	⊜	⊜	
Fuel	⊖	⊖	○	⊖	○	⊖	⊜	
Ignition	⊖	⊖	⊖	⊜	○	⊖	⊜	
Auto. trans.	◒	○	⊖	⊖	⊖	⊖	⊜	
Man. trans.	⊖	⊖	⊜	*	⊖	⊜	⊜	
Clutch	○	⊖	⊜	*	⊖	⊜	⊜	
Electrical	●	●	●	●	●	●	○	
A/C	●	●	●	○	⊖	⊖	⊖	
Suspension	○	○	○	○	⊖	⊖	⊖	
Brakes	◒	●	●	◒	◒	○	⊖	
Exhaust	●	●	○	◒	○	⊜	⊜	
Body rust	⊖	⊖	⊜	⊜	⊜	⊜	⊜	
Paint/trim	◒	◒	◒	◒	○	○	⊖	
Integrity	◒	●	●	◒	●	●	●	
Hardware	●	●	●	○	●	◒	◒	

Trouble spots	Ford Ranger Pickup (2WD) 89	90	91	92	93	94	95	96
Engine	◒	◒	○	○	⊜	⊜	⊖	⊜
Cooling	◒	◒	○	○	⊖	⊜	⊜	⊜
Fuel	○	⊖	○	⊖	⊜	⊖	⊖	⊜
Ignition	⊖	⊖	⊖	⊖	⊖	⊜	⊜	⊜
Auto. trans.	○	○	○	⊖	⊖	⊖	⊖	⊖
Man. trans.	○	⊖	⊖	⊖	⊜	⊜	⊜	⊜
Clutch	○	○	⊖	⊖	⊖	⊖	⊖	⊜
Electrical	◒	◒	◒	○	○	○	◒	⊖
A/C	●	●	●	◒	⊖	⊖	⊜	⊜
Suspension	○	○	⊖	⊖	⊖	⊖	⊜	⊜
Brakes	◒	●	◒	○	◒	○	⊖	⊖
Exhaust	●	●	◒	○	⊖	⊜	⊜	⊜
Body rust	○	○	⊖	⊖	⊜	⊜	⊜	⊜
Paint/trim	●	●	○	○	⊖	⊖	⊖	⊖
Integrity	⊖	○	○	○	⊖	⊖	⊖	⊖
Hardware	○	○	○	○	⊖	⊖	○	⊖

⊜ ⊖ ○ ◒ ●

Few ← **Problems** → Many

* Insufficient data

Ford Ranger Pickup (4WD)

Trouble spots	89	90	91	92	93	94	95	96
Engine	●	◒	○	◒	⊖	⊜	⊖	⊖
Cooling	●	◒	◒	◒	⊖	⊜	⊖	⊖
Fuel	○	○	⊖	⊖	⊖	⊖	⊖	⊖
Ignition	○	⊖	○	⊖	⊖	⊜	⊜	⊜
Auto. trans.	*	○	*	*	⊖	⊖	○	*
Man. trans.	○	*	○	*	⊖	⊜	⊜	*
Clutch	○	*	◒	*	○	⊖	⊜	*
Electrical	◒	◒	◒	◒	○	○	○	⊖
A/C	●	●	●	◒	○	⊜	⊜	⊜
Suspension	○	○	○	○	⊖	⊖	○	⊜
Brakes	●	●	●	◒	●	○	○	⊜
Exhaust	●	●	●	◒	⊖	⊜	⊜	⊜
Body rust	◒	○	⊖	⊜	⊜	⊜	⊜	⊜
Paint/trim	●	●	○	○	⊖	⊖	⊖	⊜
Integrity	○	○	○	○	⊖	⊖	⊖	⊜
Hardware	○	⊖	○	◒	⊖	○	○	⊖

Ford Taurus SHO

Trouble spots	89	90	91	92	93	94	95	96
Engine	⊖	⊖	⊖	⊖	⊜	⊜	⊜	Insufficient data
Cooling	◒	●	◒	●	○	○	⊖	
Fuel	○	○	○	○	⊖	○	⊖	
Ignition	⊖	⊖	⊖	⊖	⊖	⊜	⊜	
Auto. trans.					○	⊖	○	
Man. trans.	○	*	⊜	⊜	*	*	*	
Clutch	●	*	●	●	*	*	*	
Electrical	●	●	●	●	●	○	○	
A/C	●	●	●	●	○	○	⊖	
Suspension	●	◒	●	◒	○	⊖	⊜	
Brakes	●	●	●	●	●	○	○	
Exhaust	⊜	⊖	⊖	⊖	⊜	⊜	⊜	
Body rust	○	⊖	○	⊜	⊜	⊜	⊜	
Paint/trim	◒	◒	◒	⊖	○	⊖	○	
Integrity	○	◒	●	◒	◒	◒	●	
Hardware	○	○	○	○	○	○	○	

Ford Taurus V6

Trouble spots	89	90	91	92	93	94	95	96
Engine	◒	○	⊖	⊖	⊖	⊜	⊜	⊜
Cooling	●	●	◒	●	◒	○	⊜	⊜
Fuel	◒	○	○	○	○	⊖	⊖	⊖
Ignition	○	⊖	⊖	⊖	⊖	⊜	⊜	⊜
Auto. trans.	◒	◒	●	⊖	⊖	⊖	⊜	⊖
Man. trans.								
Clutch								
Electrical	●	●	●	◒	◒	○	○	⊖
A/C	●	●	●	◒	○	⊖	⊖	⊜
Suspension	●	●	●	◒	○	⊖	⊖	⊖
Brakes	●	●	●	●	●	⊖	⊖	⊖
Exhaust	⊜	⊖	⊜	⊜	⊜	⊜	⊜	⊜
Body rust	◒	◒	○	⊜	⊜	⊜	⊜	⊜
Paint/trim	●	◒	○	⊖	⊖	⊖	⊖	⊖
Integrity	◒	◒	◒	◒	◒	◒	◒	◒
Hardware	◒	◒	◒	◒	◒	○	○	○

Ford Tempo

Trouble spots	89	90	91	92	93	94	95	96
Engine	●	●	◒	○	⊖	⊖		
Cooling	●	●	○	◒	○	○		
Fuel	●	◒	●	◒	◒	⊖		
Ignition	◒	○	○	⊖	⊖	⊜		
Auto. trans.	◒	○	○	○	⊖	⊖		
Man. trans.	⊜	*	*	*	*	*		
Clutch	◒	*	*	*	*	*		
Electrical	●	●	●	◒	◒	○		
A/C	●	●	●	○	⊖	⊖		
Suspension	●	●	◒	○	○	⊖		
Brakes	●	●	●	●	●	◒		
Exhaust	●	●	●	●	◒	⊖		
Body rust	◒	○	○	⊖	⊜	⊜		
Paint/trim	●	◒	●	◒	⊖	⊖		
Integrity	●	◒	◒	◒	◒	◒		
Hardware	●	●	●	●	●	○		

Ford Thunderbird V6

Trouble spots	89	90	91	92	93	94	95	96
Engine	○	○	⊜	⊖	⊖	⊜	⊖	Insufficient data
Cooling	◒	◒	○	○	⊖	⊜	○	
Fuel	◒	○	⊖	⊖	⊖	⊜	⊖	
Ignition	⊖	⊖	⊖	⊖	⊖	⊜	⊜	
Auto. trans.	○	○	⊖	⊖	⊖	○	⊖	
Man. trans.	*	*	*	*	*	*	*	
Clutch	*	*	*	*	*	*	*	
Electrical	●	●	●	◒	◒	○	○	
A/C	●	●	●	○	○	○	○	
Suspension	◒	◒	○	○	⊖	⊜	⊖	
Brakes	●	●	●	◒	●	●	●	
Exhaust	⊖	⊜	⊜	⊜	⊜	⊜	⊜	
Body rust	○	⊖	○	⊜	⊖	⊜	⊜	
Paint/trim	●	●	◒	◒	●	○	⊖	
Integrity	◒	◒	◒	○	◒	◒	○	
Hardware	●	●	◒	○	●	◒	◒	

Ford Thunderbird V8

Trouble spots	89	90	91	92	93	94	95	96
Engine			⊖	⊜	⊜	⊖	⊜	⊜
Cooling			○	○	○	⊜	⊜	⊜
Fuel			◒	⊖	⊜	⊖	⊜	○
Ignition			○	⊜	⊖	⊜	⊜	⊜
Auto. trans.			○	○	○	◒	⊖	○
Man. trans.								
Clutch								
Electrical			●	●	◒	◒	○	◒
A/C			●	○	○	⊖	⊖	◒
Suspension			○	⊖	○	○	⊖	○
Brakes			●	●	●	●	●	⊖
Exhaust			⊖	⊜	⊜	⊜	⊜	⊜
Body rust			⊖	⊜	⊖	⊜	⊜	⊜
Paint/trim			●	◒	●	○	⊖	⊖
Integrity			○	◒	◒	◒	○	○
Hardware			◒	○	●	○	⊖	⊖

Ford Windstar

Trouble spots	89	90	91	92	93	94	95	96
Engine							⊜	⊜
Cooling							⊜	⊜
Fuel							⊖	⊖
Ignition							⊜	⊜
Auto. trans.							⊖	⊖
Man. trans.								
Clutch								
Electrical							●	○
A/C							⊖	⊖
Suspension							⊖	⊖
Brakes							◒	⊖
Exhaust							⊜	⊜
Body rust							⊜	⊜
Paint/trim							⊖	⊖
Integrity							◒	○
Hardware							●	○

Geo Metro

Trouble spots	89	90	91	92	93	94	95	96
Engine	○	○	⊖	○	⊖	⊖	⊜	Insufficient data
Cooling	○	⊖	⊜	⊜	⊜	⊜	⊜	
Fuel	⊖	○	⊖	⊖	⊖	⊖	⊜	
Ignition	○	⊖	⊖	⊖	⊖	⊖	⊜	
Auto. trans.	*	*	*	⊖	*	*	*	
Man. trans.	*	⊖	⊜	⊜	⊜	⊜	⊜	
Clutch	*	○	⊖	⊖	⊖	⊖	⊖	
Electrical	◒	◒	◒	◒	◒	◒	⊖	
A/C	*	●	○	○	○	○	⊖	
Suspension	◒	⊖	⊖	⊖	⊖	⊖	⊜	
Brakes	●	◒	○	◒	⊖	○	⊖	
Exhaust	●	●	●	◒	⊖	⊖	⊜	
Body rust	⊖	○	⊖	⊖	⊜	⊜	⊜	
Paint/trim	○	○	○	○	⊖	⊖	○	
Integrity	●	●	●	◒	◒	◒	⊖	
Hardware	●	●	●	●	●	◒	◒	

Trouble spots	Geo Prizm 89	90	91	92	93	94	95	96
Engine		⊖	⊖	⊜	⊜	⊜	⊜	⊜
Cooling		◒	⊖	⊖	⊜	⊜	⊜	⊜
Fuel		⊖	⊜	⊜	⊜	⊜	⊜	⊜
Ignition		⊖	⊖	⊜	⊜	⊜	⊜	⊜
Auto. trans.		⊜	⊖	⊖	⊜	⊜	⊜	⊜
Man. trans.		⊜	⊖	*	⊜	⊜	⊜	*
Clutch		⊜	○	*	⊜	⊜	⊜	*
Electrical		◒	●	◒	◒	○	⊖	⊖
A/C		⊖	⊜	⊖	⊜	⊜	⊜	⊜
Suspension		⊖	⊖	⊖	⊖	⊜	⊜	⊜
Brakes		◒	○	◒	⊖	⊖	⊜	⊜
Exhaust		●	●	●	⊜	⊜	⊜	⊜
Body rust		○	⊖	⊜	⊜	⊜	⊜	⊜
Paint/trim		○	○	○	○	⊖	⊖	⊜
Integrity		●	○	⊖	○	⊖	⊖	⊖
Hardware		●	●	●	●	○	○	⊖

Trouble spots	Geo Storm 89	90	91	92	93	94	95	96
Engine		◒	○	○	Insufficient data			
Cooling		◒	◒	●				
Fuel		○	○	○				
Ignition		○	○	○				
Auto. trans.		*	*	*				
Man. trans.		*	⊖	*				
Clutch		*	⊖	*				
Electrical		●	○	○				
A/C		○	⊖	◒				
Suspension		◒	●	○				
Brakes		●	●	●				
Exhaust		●	●	●				
Body rust		●	⊖	⊖				
Paint/trim		●	○	◒				
Integrity		●	◒	◒				
Hardware		●	◒	○				

Trouble spots	Geo Tracker 89	90	91	92	93	94	95	96
Engine	Insufficient data	◒	⊖	○	⊖	⊜	⊜	Insufficient data
Cooling		⊖	⊖	⊜	⊜	⊖	⊜	
Fuel		⊖	⊖	⊖	⊜	⊖	⊜	
Ignition		⊖	⊖	○	⊜	○	⊜	
Auto. trans.		*	*	*	*	⊜	⊖	
Man. trans.		*	*	*	⊖	⊜	⊜	
Clutch		*	*	*	⊜	⊜	⊜	
Electrical		○	○	○	○	◒	○	
A/C		*	*	○	⊖	⊖	○	
Suspension		⊖	⊜	⊖	⊖	⊜	⊜	
Brakes		◒	●	○	○	○	⊖	
Exhaust		●	●	◒	⊖	⊜	⊜	
Body rust		○	○	⊜	⊜	⊜	⊜	
Paint/trim		○	○	⊖	⊖	⊖	⊖	
Integrity		○	○	○	○	◒	◒	
Hardware		●	○	○	◒	○	◒	

Trouble spots	GMC Jimmy, Yukon (4WD) 89	90	91	92	93	94	95	96
Engine	○	○	⊖	⊖	⊖	⊖	⊖	⊖
Cooling	◒	◒	○	●	○	⊜	⊜	⊜
Fuel	○	○	⊖	○	○	⊖	⊖	⊖
Ignition	⊖	○	⊖	○	⊖	⊖	⊜	⊜
Auto. trans.	○	○	⊖	○	○	⊖	⊜	⊜
Man. trans.	*	*	*	*	*	*	*	*
Clutch	*	*	*	*	*	*	*	*
Electrical	●	●	●	●	●	◒	○	⊖
A/C	◒	⊖	⊖	○	⊖	○	⊜	⊜
Suspension	○	◒	◒	○	⊖	⊖	⊜	⊜
Brakes	●	●	●	●	●	◒	○	⊜
Exhaust	◒	◒	◒	◒	○	⊜	⊜	⊜
Body rust	●	●	◒	⊜	⊖	⊖	⊜	⊜
Paint/trim	●	●	●	◒	◒	○	⊖	⊜
Integrity	●	●	●	◒	●	◒	○	○
Hardware	●	●	●	◒	●	●	○	○

Trouble spots	GMC S-15 Jimmy, Jimmy 89	90	91	92	93	94	95	96
Engine	○	○	○	○	○	⊖	⊖	●
Cooling	◒	◒	○	○	⊖	⊖	⊖	⊜
Fuel	○	○	⊖	○	●	○	○	⊜
Ignition	○	○	○	○	○	⊖	⊖	⊜
Auto. trans.	⊖	○	⊖	⊖	○	○	⊖	⊜
Man. trans.	*	*	*	*	*	*	*	*
Clutch	*	*	*	*	*	*	*	*
Electrical	●	●	●	●	●	●	◒	⊖
A/C	◒	⊖	○	⊖	○	⊖	⊖	⊜
Suspension	◒	◒	○	○	○	⊖	⊖	⊖
Brakes	●	●	●	●	●	●	◒	⊖
Exhaust	●	◒	◒	⊖	⊖	⊜	⊜	⊜
Body rust	●	●	●	○	⊖	⊖	⊜	⊜
Paint/trim	●	●	●	◒	◒	○	○	⊖
Integrity	●	●	●	●	●	●	●	○
Hardware	●	●	●	◒	●	◒	◒	○

Trouble spots	GMC S-15 Sonoma Pickup V6 (2WD) 89	90	91	92	93	94	95	96
Engine	○	○	○	⊖	⊖	⊖	⊖	◒
Cooling	◒	○	○	○	⊖	⊜	⊖	⊜
Fuel	○	○	⊖	⊖	○	⊖	⊖	⊖
Ignition	○	○	○	○	⊖	⊜	⊜	⊖
Auto. trans.	⊜	*	⊜	⊖	⊖	⊖	⊜	⊖
Man. trans.	*	*	⊖	⊖	⊖	*	⊜	*
Clutch	*	*	○	○	○	*	⊖	*
Electrical	●	●	◒	◒	◒	●	○	⊖
A/C	◒	*	⊖	⊖	⊖	⊖	⊖	⊜
Suspension	⊖	⊖	⊖	⊖	⊖	○	⊖	⊖
Brakes	◒	◒	○	◒	○	◒	○	⊖
Exhaust	◒	●	◒	○	⊜	⊜	⊜	⊜
Body rust	◒	●	◒	⊖	⊖	⊜	⊜	⊜
Paint/trim	●	●	●	●	◒	○	⊖	⊜
Integrity	●	◒	◒	○	○	○	◒	○
Hardware	●	◒	◒	○	○	◒	○	○

Trouble spots	GMC S-15 Sonoma Pickup V6 (4WD) 89	90	91	92	93	94	95	96
Engine	○	Insufficient data	○	⊖	Insufficient data	○	⊖	Insufficient data
Cooling	◒		○	⊖		⊖	⊜	
Fuel	⊖		⊖	○		○	⊖	
Ignition	○		○	○		⊜	⊜	
Auto. trans.	⊖		○	*		○	⊖	
Man. trans.	*		*	*		*	*	
Clutch	*		*	*		*	*	
Electrical	●		●	◒		●	○	
A/C	⊖		○	*		⊖	⊖	
Suspension	●		○	○		○	⊖	
Brakes	◒		◒	●		●	◒	
Exhaust	◒		●	◒		⊜	⊜	
Body rust	●		●	○		⊜	⊜	
Paint/trim	●		●	●		○	○	
Integrity	◒		◒	○		●	◒	
Hardware	◒		●	○		◒	◒	

Trouble spots	GMC Safari Van 89	90	91	92	93	94	95	96
Engine	◒	⊖	⊖	⊖	○	⊜	⊜	⊜
Cooling	◒	○	○	⊖	⊖	⊖	⊜	⊜
Fuel	○	○	⊖	○	○	⊖	⊖	⊖
Ignition	○	⊖	⊖	⊖	⊖	⊖	⊖	⊜
Auto. trans.	○	○	○	⊖	○	⊖	⊖	⊖
Man. trans.	*							
Clutch	*							
Electrical	●	●	●	◒	●	●	○	⊖
A/C	●	◒	○	○	○	◒	○	⊜
Suspension	◒	●	◒	○	○	⊖	⊖	⊖
Brakes	●	●	●	●	●	◒	○	○
Exhaust	●	◒	◒	⊖	⊖	⊖	⊜	⊜
Body rust	○	⊖	⊜	⊜	⊖	⊜	⊜	⊜
Paint/trim	●	●	◒	◒	○	○	⊖	○
Integrity	●	●	●	●	●	●	◒	○
Hardware	●	●	●	◒	●	●	◒	○

⊜ ⊖ ○ ◒ ●
Few ← Problems → Many

*
Insufficient data

Trouble spots	GMC Sierra C1500-2500 Pickup								GMC Sierra K1500-2500 Pickup							
	89	90	91	92	93	94	95	96	89	90	91	92	93	94	95	96
Engine	○	○	⊖	⊖	○	⊖	⊖	⊜	◒	⊖	○	⊖	⊖	⊖	⊖	⊜
Cooling	◒	○	○	⊖	⊖	⊜	⊜	⊜	◒	○	○	○	⊖	⊜	⊜	⊖
Fuel	○	⊖	⊖	⊖	⊖	⊖	⊜	⊜	○	⊖	⊖	○	⊖	⊜	⊜	⊖
Ignition	○	○	○	⊖	⊖	⊖	⊜	⊜	○	○	○	○	⊖	⊖	⊜	⊜
Auto. trans.	○	○	○	○	⊖	⊖	⊜	⊜	○	○	◒	◒	○	⊖	⊖	⊖
Man. trans.	⊖	⊖	○	⊖	*	*	○	*	*	○	*	○	*	*	⊖	*
Clutch	●	●	◒	◒	*	*	◒	*	*	●	*	◒	*	*	◒	*
Electrical	●	●	●	●	◒	◒	○	⊖	●	●	●	●	●	◒	○	⊖
A/C	◒	○	○	○	⊖	⊖	⊖	⊜	○	○	○	⊖	⊖	⊖	⊖	⊜
Suspension	◒	○	○	○	⊖	⊖	⊖	⊖	◒	○	○	○	⊖	⊖	⊖	⊜
Brakes	●	◒	○	○	⊖	⊖	⊖	⊖	●	◒	◒	○	○	○	⊖	⊜
Exhaust	●	●	◒	◒	⊖	⊖	⊜	⊜	●	●	◒	◒	○	⊜	⊜	⊜
Body rust	⊖	⊖	⊜	⊜	⊜	⊜	⊜	⊜	○	⊖	⊖	⊜	⊜	⊜	⊜	⊜
Paint/trim	●	●	◒	○	○	⊖	⊖	⊜	●	●	◒	○	○	⊖	⊖	⊜
Integrity	◒	○	○	○	○	○	○	⊖	◒	○	○	○	○	○	○	○
Hardware	◒	○	○	○	◒	◒	◒	○	◒	○	○	○	◒	◒	◒	○

Trouble spots	GMC Suburban								Honda Accord							
	89	90	91	92	93	94	95	96	89	90	91	92	93	94	95	96
Engine	○	⊖	⊖	⊖	⊜	⊜	⊜	⊜	⊖	⊖	⊖	⊜	⊜	⊜	⊜	⊜
Cooling	●	◒	○	●	◒	⊜	⊜	⊜	○	⊜	⊜	⊖	⊜	⊜	⊜	⊜
Fuel	○	⊖	⊖	⊖	⊜	⊖	⊜	⊜	⊖	⊜	⊜	⊜	⊜	⊜	⊜	⊜
Ignition	⊖	⊖	○	⊖	⊜	⊜	⊜	⊜	⊖	⊖	⊖	⊖	⊜	⊜	⊜	⊜
Auto. trans.	◒	○	◒	◒	⊜	⊖	⊖	⊜	⊖	⊖	⊜	⊜	⊜	⊜	⊜	⊜
Man. trans.	*	*							⊜	⊜	⊜	⊜	⊜	⊜	⊜	⊜
Clutch	*	*							⊖	○	⊖	⊜	⊜	⊜	⊜	⊜
Electrical	●	●	●	●	●	◒	◒	⊖	○	◒	○	○	○	⊖	⊖	⊜
A/C	◒	◒	○	○	⊜	○	⊖	⊖	◒	○	○	⊖	⊖	◒	⊖	⊜
Suspension	○	○	○	◒	⊜	⊜	⊖	⊖	○	○	⊖	⊜	⊜	⊜	⊜	⊜
Brakes	●	●	●	●	◒	◒	○	⊖	●	○	○	○	⊖	⊖	⊜	⊜
Exhaust	●	◒	○	◒	⊖	⊜	⊜	⊜	○	○	○	⊖	⊜	⊜	⊜	⊜
Body rust	●	○	⊖	⊜	⊖	⊜	⊜	⊜	○	⊖	⊜	⊜	⊜	⊜	⊜	⊜
Paint/trim	●	●	●	◒	○	⊜	⊖	⊖	⊖	⊖	⊖	⊖	⊜	⊖	⊜	⊜
Integrity	●	●	●	◒	◒	○	○	○	○	○	○	⊖	○	○	⊖	⊜
Hardware	●	●	●	●	●	◒	◒	○	◒	◒	◒	○	○	○	⊖	⊖

Trouble spots	Honda Civic								Honda Civic del Sol							
	89	90	91	92	93	94	95	96	89	90	91	92	93	94	95	96
Engine	○	○	⊖	⊜	⊜	⊜	⊜	⊜					⊜	⊜	⊜	
Cooling	⊖	⊖	⊜	⊜	⊜	⊜	⊜	⊜					⊜	⊖	⊜	
Fuel	⊖	⊖	⊜	⊜	⊜	⊜	⊜	⊜					⊜	⊜	⊜	
Ignition	○	○	⊖	⊜	⊜	⊜	⊜	⊜					⊜	⊜	⊜	
Auto. trans.	⊖	⊖	⊖	⊜	⊜	⊜	⊜	⊜					⊜	*	*	
Man. trans.	⊜	⊜	⊜	⊜	⊜	⊜	⊜	⊜					⊜	*	*	
Clutch	○	⊖	⊖	⊜	⊜	⊜	⊜	⊜					⊜	*	*	
Electrical	◒	◒	○	⊖	⊖	⊖	⊖	⊖					⊖	⊖	⊖	Insufficient data
A/C	◒	◒	○	⊖	⊖	○	⊖	⊜					⊜	⊖	*	
Suspension	⊖	⊖	⊖	⊖	⊖	⊜	⊜	⊜					⊜	⊜	⊜	
Brakes	●	●	●	⊖	⊖	⊖	⊜	⊜					⊖	⊖	⊜	
Exhaust	●	●	●	⊖	⊜	⊜	⊜	⊜					⊜	⊜	⊜	
Body rust	○	○	⊜	⊜	⊜	⊜	⊜	⊜					⊜	⊜	⊖	
Paint/trim	⊖	⊖	⊖	○	⊖	⊖	⊜	⊖					⊖	⊖	⊖	
Integrity	○	◒	○	○	⊖	⊖	⊖	○					●	●	○	
Hardware	◒	◒	○	○	⊖	⊖	⊖	⊖					●	●	○	

Trouble spots	Honda CRX								Honda Odyssey							
	89	90	91	92	93	94	95	96	89	90	91	92	93	94	95	96
Engine	○	○	⊖												⊜	
Cooling	⊖	⊖	⊖												⊜	
Fuel	⊖	⊖	⊜												⊜	
Ignition	⊖	⊖	⊖												⊜	
Auto. trans.	*	*	*												⊜	
Man. trans.	⊜	⊜	⊜													
Clutch	○	⊖	⊜													
Electrical	◒	◒	○												⊖	Insufficient data
A/C	◒	○	○												⊜	
Suspension	⊖	⊖	⊜												⊖	
Brakes	◒	◒	○												⊜	
Exhaust	●	●	●												⊜	
Body rust	◒	⊖	⊖												⊜	
Paint/trim	○	⊖	⊖												⊜	
Integrity	⊖	○	⊖												⊖	
Hardware	◒	◒	◒												⊖	

Honda Passport V6

TROUBLE SPOTS	89	90	91	92	93	94	95	96 (Insufficient data)
Engine						○	⊜	
Cooling						⊜	⊜	
Fuel						⊜	⊜	
Ignition						⊜	⊜	
Auto. trans.						⊖	⊖	
Man. trans.						*	*	
Clutch						*	*	
Electrical						○	○	
A/C						⊖	⊖	
Suspension						⊖	⊖	
Brakes						⊖	⊜	
Exhaust						⊜	⊜	
Body rust						⊖	⊜	
Paint/trim						⊖	○	
Integrity						○	◒	
Hardware						◒	◒	

Honda Prelude

TROUBLE SPOTS	89	90	91	92	93	94	95	96 (Insufficient data)
Engine	○	⊖	⊖	⊜	⊖	⊜	⊜	
Cooling	⊖	⊖	○	⊜	⊜	⊜	⊜	
Fuel	⊖	⊜	⊜	⊜	⊜	⊜	⊜	
Ignition	⊜	⊜	⊜	⊜	⊖	⊜	⊜	
Auto. trans.	○	*	*	⊜	*	*	*	
Man. trans.	⊜	⊜	⊜	⊜	*	*	*	
Clutch	◒	◒	○	⊖	*	*	*	
Electrical	◒	○	○	⊖	○	⊖	⊜	
A/C	●	○	⊖	⊖	○	⊖	⊖	
Suspension	○	⊖	⊜	⊜	⊜	⊜	⊜	
Brakes	●	◒	○	⊖	⊜	⊜	⊜	
Exhaust	◒	○	○	⊜	⊜	⊜	⊜	
Body rust	⊖	⊜	⊜	⊖	⊜	⊜	⊜	
Paint/trim	○	⊖	⊜	○	○	⊖	⊜	
Integrity	○	⊖	⊖	◒	○	○	○	
Hardware	◒	○	⊖	⊖	○	⊜	◒	

Hyundai Excel

TROUBLE SPOTS	89	90	91	92 (Insufficient data)	93 (Insufficient data)	94 (Insufficient data)	95	96
Engine	●	◒	◒					
Cooling	●	○	○					
Fuel	○	◒	○					
Ignition	◒	○	◒					
Auto. trans.	⊖	*	*					
Man. trans.	●	*	*					
Clutch	●	*	*					
Electrical	●	●	◒					
A/C	●	*	*					
Suspension	○	○	◒					
Brakes	●	●	●					
Exhaust	●	●	●					
Body rust	●	○	○					
Paint/trim	●	○	●					
Integrity	●	◒	◒					
Hardware	●	●	●					

Infiniti G20

TROUBLE SPOTS	89	90	91	92	93	94	95	96
Engine			⊜	⊜	⊜	⊜	⊜	⊜
Cooling			⊜	⊜	⊜	⊜	⊜	⊜
Fuel			⊖	⊜	⊜	⊜	⊜	⊜
Ignition			⊜	⊜	⊜	⊜	⊜	⊜
Auto. trans.			⊜	⊜	⊜	⊜	⊜	*
Man. trans.			*	*	⊜	*	⊖	*
Clutch			*	*	⊖	*	⊜	*
Electrical			◒	○	⊖	⊖	⊖	○
A/C			⊖	⊖	⊖	⊜	⊜	⊜
Suspension			⊜	⊖	⊜	⊖	⊖	⊜
Brakes			⊖	○	⊖	⊜	⊜	⊜
Exhaust			⊖	⊜	⊜	⊜	⊜	⊜
Body rust			⊜	⊜	⊜	⊜	⊜	⊜
Paint/trim			⊖	⊖	⊖	⊜	⊜	⊜
Integrity			⊜	⊜	⊖	⊖	⊖	⊖
Hardware			◒	◒	○	⊜	⊖	⊜

Infiniti I30

TROUBLE SPOTS	89	90	91	92	93	94	95	96
Engine								⊜
Cooling								⊜
Fuel								⊜
Ignition								⊜
Auto. trans.								⊜
Man. trans.								*
Clutch								*
Electrical								⊜
A/C								⊜
Suspension								⊜
Brakes								⊜
Exhaust								⊜
Body rust								⊜
Paint/trim								⊜
Integrity								⊜
Hardware								⊜

Infiniti J30

TROUBLE SPOTS	89	90	91	92	93	94	95	96 (Insufficient data)
Engine					⊜	⊜	⊜	
Cooling					⊜	⊜	⊜	
Fuel					⊖	⊖	⊜	
Ignition					⊖	⊜	⊜	
Auto. trans.					⊜	⊜	⊜	
Man. trans.								
Clutch								
Electrical					○	○	⊜	
A/C					⊖	⊜	⊜	
Suspension					⊖	⊜	⊜	
Brakes					○	⊖	⊜	
Exhaust					⊜	⊜	⊜	
Body rust					⊜	⊜	⊜	
Paint/trim					⊖	○	⊖	
Integrity					⊖	○	⊜	
Hardware					◒	○	⊖	

Infiniti Q45

TROUBLE SPOTS	89	90	91	92 (Insufficient data)	93 (Insufficient data)	94	95 (Insufficient data)	96 (Insufficient data)
Engine		○	⊖			⊜		
Cooling		○	⊖			⊜		
Fuel		◒	⊖			⊖		
Ignition		⊖	⊜			⊜		
Auto. trans.		◒	○			⊜		
Man. trans.								
Clutch								
Electrical		◒	◒			◒		
A/C		●	○			⊜		
Suspension		◒	○			○		
Brakes		●	●			○		
Exhaust		⊜	⊜			⊜		
Body rust		⊖	⊜			⊜		
Paint/trim		⊜	⊜			⊖		
Integrity		⊖	⊖			⊖		
Hardware		●	●			⊖		

Isuzu Pickup

TROUBLE SPOTS	89	90	91 (Insufficient data)	92	93 (Insufficient data)	94 (Insufficient data)	95 (Insufficient data)	96
Engine	◒	◒		○				
Cooling	◒	⊖		⊖				
Fuel	⊖	○		⊖				
Ignition	⊖	○		⊜				
Auto. trans.	*	*		*				
Man. trans.	⊜	⊖		*				
Clutch	○	⊜		*				
Electrical	◒	○		○				
A/C	*	*		*				
Suspension	⊖	⊖		⊜				
Brakes	○	●		○				
Exhaust	●	◒		⊖				
Body rust	●	○		⊖				
Paint/trim	○	⊖		○				
Integrity	⊖	⊖		○				
Hardware	◒	○		○				

⊜ ⊖ ○ ◒ ●
Few ← **Problems** → Many

*
Insufficient data

Trouble spots	Isuzu Rodeo V6 89	90	91	92	93	94	95	96
Engine			Insufficient data	⊖	○	○	⊜	Insufficient data
Cooling				◒	⊖	⊜	⊜	
Fuel				⊖	⊖	⊜	⊜	
Ignition				⊖	⊖	⊜	⊜	
Auto. trans.				*	*	⊜	⊖	
Man. trans.				*	*	*	*	
Clutch				*	*	*	*	
Electrical				●	○	○	○	
A/C				◒	⊖	⊖	⊜	
Suspension				⊖	⊜	⊖	⊖	
Brakes				◒	○	⊖	⊜	
Exhaust				○	⊜	⊜	⊜	
Body rust				⊖	⊖	⊜	⊜	
Paint/trim				○	●	⊖	○	
Integrity				◒	●	○	◒	
Hardware				●	●	◒	◒	

Trouble spots	Isuzu Trooper II, Trooper 89	90	91	92	93	94	95	96
Engine	●	◒	◒	○	⊖	⊖	⊜	Insufficient data
Cooling	◒	◒	○	⊜	⊖	⊜	⊜	
Fuel	○	○	○	⊜	○	⊖	⊜	
Ignition	⊖	⊖	⊖	⊜	⊜	⊜	⊜	
Auto. trans.	*	*	*	*	*	⊜	⊜	
Man. trans.	⊖	⊖	○	*	*	*	*	
Clutch	●	●	◒	*	*	*	*	
Electrical	◒	○	◒	●	◒	⊖	⊖	
A/C	○	○	○	⊖	⊖	⊖	⊜	
Suspension	⊖	○	○	○	⊖	⊜	⊜	
Brakes	●	●	●	⊖	⊖	⊖	⊜	
Exhaust	●	●	●	○	⊖	⊖	⊜	
Body rust	●	◒	◒	⊖	⊖	⊜	⊜	
Paint/trim	○	○	○	⊖	⊖	⊖	○	
Integrity	◒	◒	◒	○	○	○	○	
Hardware	○	◒	○	○	◒	○	○	

Trouble spots	Jeep Cherokee, Wagoneer (4WD) 89	90	91	92	93	94	95	96
Engine	○	○	○	○	⊖	⊖	⊜	⊜
Cooling	●	●	⊖	⊖	○	⊖	⊜	⊜
Fuel	○	◒	⊖	⊖	⊜	⊜	⊜	⊜
Ignition	○	○	⊖	⊜	⊜	⊖	⊜	⊜
Auto. trans.	○	○	○	⊖	⊜	⊖	⊖	⊜
Man. trans.	⊖	*	*	*	*	*	*	*
Clutch	●	*	*	*	*	*	*	*
Electrical	●	●	●	◒	◒	◒	○	○
A/C	◒	○	○	⊖	⊖	⊖	⊖	⊜
Suspension	◒	○	○	○	⊜	⊖	⊜	⊖
Brakes	●	●	●	◒	○	⊖	○	⊜
Exhaust	●	●	●	◒	⊖	⊜	⊜	⊜
Body rust	○	○	⊖	⊜	⊜	⊜	⊜	⊜
Paint/trim	●	◒	○	○	⊖	⊖	⊖	⊜
Integrity	●	◒	●	◒	◒	◒	◒	◒
Hardware	●	●	◒	○	◒	◒	○	○

Trouble spots	Jeep Grand Cherokee (4WD) 89	90	91	92	93	94	95	96
Engine					⊖	⊖	⊜	⊜
Cooling					⊖	⊜	⊜	⊜
Fuel					⊖	⊖	⊜	⊜
Ignition					⊖	⊖	⊜	⊜
Auto. trans.					○	○	⊖	⊜
Man. trans.					*	*	*	
Clutch					*	*	*	
Electrical					◒	◒	○	○
A/C					○	⊖	⊖	⊜
Suspension					○	⊜	⊜	⊖
Brakes					◒	○	○	⊜
Exhaust					⊜	⊜	⊜	⊜
Body rust					⊜	⊜	⊜	⊜
Paint/trim					⊖	⊖	⊖	⊜
Integrity					◒	○	○	⊖
Hardware					◒	○	○	⊖

Trouble spots	Jeep Wrangler 89	90	91	92	93	94	95	96
Engine	○	Insufficient data	○	◒	⊖	⊖	⊖	Insufficient data
Cooling	◒		○	⊖	○	⊜	⊜	
Fuel	●		◒	○	⊖	○	⊖	
Ignition	◒		⊖	⊖	⊖	⊖	⊜	
Auto. trans.	*		*	*	*	*	*	
Man. trans.	*		*	*	⊖	⊜	⊖	
Clutch	*		*	*	○	⊖	⊖	
Electrical	●		●	◒	○	○	○	
A/C	*		*	*	*	*	*	
Suspension	◒		⊖	⊖	○	⊖	⊖	
Brakes	●		○	○	○	⊖	⊖	
Exhaust	●		◒	○	○	○	⊜	
Body rust	◒		○	◒	⊖	⊖	⊖	
Paint/trim	◒		◒	◒	○	○	⊜	
Integrity	●		●	●	●	●	◒	
Hardware	●		●	●	●	●	◒	

Trouble spots	Land Rover Discovery 89	90	91	92	93	94	95	96
Engine						Insufficient data	○	Insufficient data
Cooling							⊖	
Fuel							○	
Ignition							⊖	
Auto. trans.							*	
Man. trans.							*	
Clutch							*	
Electrical							●	
A/C							⊖	
Suspension							⊖	
Brakes							○	
Exhaust							⊜	
Body rust							⊜	
Paint/trim							⊖	
Integrity							◒	
Hardware							●	

Trouble spots	Lexus ES250 89	90	91	92	93	94	95	96
Engine		⊖	⊖					
Cooling		○	⊖					
Fuel		⊜	⊜					
Ignition		⊖	⊜					
Auto. trans.		⊖	⊖					
Man. trans.		*	*					
Clutch		*	*					
Electrical		◒	○					
A/C		⊖	⊖					
Suspension		◒	⊖					
Brakes		○	⊖					
Exhaust		⊜	⊜					
Body rust		⊖	⊜					
Paint/trim		⊖	⊜					
Integrity		○	⊖					
Hardware		◒	◒					

Trouble spots	Lexus ES300 89	90	91	92	93	94	95	96
Engine				⊜	⊜	⊜	⊜	⊜
Cooling				⊖	⊖	⊜	⊜	⊜
Fuel				⊜	⊜	⊜	⊜	⊜
Ignition				⊜	⊜	⊜	⊜	⊜
Auto. trans.				⊖	⊜	⊜	⊜	⊜
Man. trans.				*	*			
Clutch				*	*			
Electrical				◒	○	⊖	⊖	⊜
A/C				⊖	⊜	⊜	⊜	⊜
Suspension				⊖	⊖	⊜	⊖	⊜
Brakes				○	⊜	⊖	⊖	⊜
Exhaust				⊜	⊜	⊜	⊜	⊜
Body rust				⊜	⊜	⊜	⊜	⊜
Paint/trim				⊜	⊜	⊜	⊜	⊜
Integrity				⊖	⊖	○	○	⊖
Hardware				○	⊖	⊖	⊜	⊜

Lexus GS300

Trouble spots	89	90	91	92	93	94	95 (Insufficient data)	96 (Insufficient data)
Engine					⊜	⊜		
Cooling					⊜	⊜		
Fuel					⊜	⊜		
Ignition					⊜	⊜		
Auto. trans.					⊜	⊜		
Man. trans.								
Clutch								
Electrical					⊖	⊖		
A/C					⊜	⊜		
Suspension					⊖	⊜		
Brakes					⊖	○		
Exhaust					⊜	⊜		
Body rust					⊜	⊜		
Paint/trim					⊖	⊜		
Integrity					⊖	○		
Hardware					○	⊜		

Lexus LS400

Trouble spots	89	90	91	92	93	94	95	96
Engine		⊖	⊜	⊜	⊜	⊜	⊜	⊜
Cooling		⊖	⊜	⊜	⊜	⊜	⊜	⊜
Fuel		⊜	⊜	⊜	⊜	⊜	⊖	⊜
Ignition		⊜	⊜	⊜	⊜	⊜	⊜	⊜
Auto. trans.		⊜	⊜	⊜	⊜	⊜	⊖	⊜
Man. trans.								
Clutch								
Electrical		○	○	○	○	⊖	○	⊜
A/C		○	○	○	⊜	⊜	⊖	⊜
Suspension		◒	○	⊖	⊖	⊖	⊖	⊜
Brakes		○	⊖	⊖	⊖	○	⊖	⊜
Exhaust		⊜	⊜	⊜	⊜	⊜	⊜	⊜
Body rust		⊜	⊜	⊜	⊜	⊜	⊜	⊜
Paint/trim		⊜	⊜	⊜	⊖	⊜	⊜	⊜
Integrity		⊖	⊖	⊜	⊖	⊖	⊖	⊜
Hardware		⊖	⊖	⊖	⊖	⊖	○	⊜

Lexus SC300/400

Trouble spots	89	90	91	92	93	94 (Insufficient data)	95	96 (Insufficient data)
Engine				⊜	⊜		⊜	
Cooling				⊜	⊜		⊜	
Fuel				⊜	⊜		⊜	
Ignition				⊜	⊜		⊜	
Auto. trans.				⊜	⊜		⊜	
Man. trans.				*	*		*	
Clutch				*	*		*	
Electrical				◒	○		⊖	
A/C				⊖	⊖		⊜	
Suspension				⊜	⊜		⊖	
Brakes				⊜	⊜		⊜	
Exhaust				⊜	⊜		⊜	
Body rust				⊜	⊜		⊜	
Paint/trim				⊜	○		⊖	
Integrity				⊖	○		○	
Hardware				○	○		⊖	

Lincoln Continental

Trouble spots	89	90	91	92	93	94	95	96
Engine	●	●	◒	○	⊖	⊜	⊜	⊜
Cooling	◒	◒	○	○	⊜	⊜	⊜	⊜
Fuel	○	◒	⊖	⊖	○	⊖	◒	⊜
Ignition	○	○	⊖	⊜	⊜	⊜	⊖	⊜
Auto. trans.	●	◒	●	⊖	⊖	⊜	⊜	⊜
Man. trans.								
Clutch								
Electrical	●	●	●	●	◒	◒	●	◒
A/C	●	●	●	◒	◒	○	⊖	⊖
Suspension	●	●	●	●	◒	⊖	○	⊜
Brakes	●	●	●	●	◒	○	⊖	⊜
Exhaust	⊖	⊖	⊖	⊜	⊜	⊜	⊜	⊜
Body rust	○	⊖	⊜	⊜	⊜	⊜	⊜	⊜
Paint/trim	◒	◒	○	⊜	⊜	⊖	⊖	⊜
Integrity	◒	◒	○	○	○	○	◒	⊖
Hardware	●	●	●	◒	◒	◒	◒	⊖

Lincoln Mark VII, Mark VIII

Trouble spots	89	90	91 (Insufficient data)	92 (Insufficient data)	93	94	95	96 (Insufficient data)
Engine	○	⊜			⊖	⊜	⊜	
Cooling	○	○			⊖	⊜	⊜	
Fuel	○	◒			⊖	⊜	⊜	
Ignition	⊖	⊖			⊖	⊜	⊜	
Auto. trans.	○	⊜			●	○	⊖	
Man. trans.								
Clutch								
Electrical	●	●			●	●	◒	
A/C	●	◒			⊖	⊜	⊖	
Suspension	●	◒			○	○	⊖	
Brakes	●	●			○	○	○	
Exhaust	●	◒			⊜	⊜	⊜	
Body rust	○	⊖			⊜	⊜	⊜	
Paint/trim	◒	●			⊜	⊜	⊜	
Integrity	○	○			○	○	○	
Hardware	●	●			◒	○	○	

Lincoln Town Car

Trouble spots	89	90	91	92	93	94	95	96
Engine	○	⊖	⊖	⊖	⊜	⊜	⊜	⊜
Cooling	●	○	⊖	⊜	⊜	⊜	⊜	⊜
Fuel	○	⊖	○	⊖	⊖	⊖	⊖	⊜
Ignition	⊖	○	◒	○	⊖	⊜	⊜	⊜
Auto. trans.	◒	⊖	⊖	◒	●	○	⊜	⊖
Man. trans.								
Clutch								
Electrical	●	●	●	●	◒	○	◒	○
A/C	●	◒	◒	○	⊖	⊖	⊜	⊜
Suspension	◒	◒	○	⊖	⊖	⊖	⊜	⊖
Brakes	◒	●	●	●	◒	○	⊖	⊜
Exhaust	◒	◒	○	⊜	⊜	⊜	⊜	⊜
Body rust	○	⊜	⊜	⊜	⊜	⊜	⊜	⊜
Paint/trim	◒	○	○	○	⊖	⊖	⊜	⊜
Integrity	○	○	○	⊖	○	○	○	○
Hardware	●	●	●	◒	◒	○	○	⊖

Mazda 323

Trouble spots	89	90	91	92	93	94 (Insufficient data)	95	96
Engine	○	○	⊖	⊜	⊖			
Cooling	○	⊖	○	⊜	⊜			
Fuel	⊜	⊜	⊖	⊜	⊜			
Ignition	⊖	⊜	⊜	⊜	⊜			
Auto. trans.	●	⊖	○	*	*			
Man. trans.	⊜	⊜	⊜	*	*			
Clutch	⊖	⊖	⊖	*	*			
Electrical	◒	◒	○	○	○			
A/C	◒	○	○	*	*			
Suspension	○	○	○	○	⊖			
Brakes	●	●	◒	◒	○			
Exhaust	●	●	◒	○	⊖			
Body rust	⊖	⊖	⊜	⊖	⊜			
Paint/trim	○	◒	○	○	⊖			
Integrity	○	◒	◒	◒	○			
Hardware	◒	●	◒	○	○			

Mazda 626

Trouble spots	89	90	91	92	93	94	95	96
Engine	○	⊖	⊖	⊜	⊖	⊖	⊜	⊜
Cooling	⊖	⊖	⊖	⊖	⊜	⊜	⊜	⊜
Fuel	⊜	⊖	⊖	⊜	⊖	⊖	⊜	⊜
Ignition	⊜	⊜	⊖	⊜	⊖	⊖	⊜	⊜
Auto. trans.	●	○	⊖	○	⊖	○	⊖	⊖
Man. trans.	⊜	⊜	⊜	⊜	⊖	⊜	⊖	*
Clutch	⊜	⊖	⊖	⊖	⊖	⊖	⊜	*
Electrical	◒	◒	◒	⊖	◒	●	⊖	⊜
A/C	○	◒	⊖	⊖	⊖	⊖	⊜	⊜
Suspension	⊖	○	○	◒	○	⊖	⊖	⊜
Brakes	◒	●	●	◒	◒	○	⊜	⊜
Exhaust	●	●	○	○	⊖	⊜	⊜	⊜
Body rust	⊖	⊜	⊜	⊜	⊜	⊜	⊜	⊜
Paint/trim	○	○	○	○	○	○	⊖	⊜
Integrity	◒	◒	◒	◒	●	●	◒	⊜
Hardware	●	◒	◒	◒	●	●	○	⊜

⊜ ⊖ ○ ◒ ●
Few ← **Problems** → Many

* Insufficient data

Mazda 929

TROUBLE SPOTS	89	90	91	92	93	94	95	96
Engine	◒	○	◒	◒	⊖			
Cooling	○	⊖	○	○	⊜			
Fuel	○	⊖	⊖	⊖	⊖			
Ignition	⊖	○	⊖	⊖	⊜			
Auto. trans.	◒	○	◒	⊖	○			
Man. trans.						Insufficient data	Insufficient data	
Clutch								
Electrical	◒	◒	○	●	●			
A/C	○	⊖	○	⊖	⊖			
Suspension	○	○	⊖	○	⊜			
Brakes	●	●	●	●	●			
Exhaust	◒	●	●	⊖	⊜			
Body rust	⊜	⊜	⊜	⊜	⊜			
Paint/trim	⊖	○	○	◒	○			
Integrity	○	○	○	◒	○			
Hardware	●	●	◒	●	●			

Mazda Millenia

TROUBLE SPOTS	89	90	91	92	93	94	95	96
Engine							⊖	
Cooling							⊜	
Fuel							⊜	
Ignition							⊜	
Auto. trans.							⊜	
Man. trans.								Insufficient data
Clutch								
Electrical							○	
A/C							⊖	
Suspension							⊜	
Brakes							⊜	
Exhaust							⊜	
Body rust							⊜	
Paint/trim							⊖	
Integrity							⊖	
Hardware							⊖	

Mazda MPV Van V6 (2WD)

TROUBLE SPOTS	89	90	91	92	93	94	95	96
Engine	●	●	◒	◒	●			
Cooling	○	◒	○	○	⊜			
Fuel	⊖	⊖	⊖	⊜	⊜			
Ignition	○	⊖	⊖	⊖	⊜			
Auto. trans.	◒	○	○	○	○			
Man. trans.	*	*				Insufficient data	Insufficient data	Insufficient data
Clutch	*	*						
Electrical	◒	○	◒	◒	○			
A/C	◒	◒	○	⊖	⊜			
Suspension	○	○	○	○	○			
Brakes	●	●	●	◒	○			
Exhaust	●	◒	○	⊖	⊜			
Body rust	⊜	⊖	⊖	⊜	⊜			
Paint/trim	⊖	○	◒	○	⊖			
Integrity	⊖	○	⊖	⊖	⊖			
Hardware	●	●	◒	○	○			

Mazda MX-5 Miata

TROUBLE SPOTS	89	90	91	92	93	94	95	96
Engine		⊖	⊜	⊖	⊜	⊜	⊜	
Cooling		⊜	⊜	⊜	⊖	⊜	⊜	
Fuel		⊜	⊜	⊜	⊖	⊜	⊜	
Ignition		⊖	⊖	○	○	⊜	⊜	
Auto. trans.			*	*	*	*	*	
Man. trans.		⊖	⊜	⊖	⊖	⊜	⊜	Insufficient data
Clutch		○	⊖	⊜	⊜	⊜	⊜	
Electrical		◒	◒	○	◒	○	○	
A/C		⊖	⊜	⊜	⊜	⊜	⊖	
Suspension		⊜	⊜	⊜	⊜	⊜	⊜	
Brakes		⊖	○	⊖	⊜	⊜	⊜	
Exhaust		⊖	⊜	⊜	⊜	⊜	⊜	
Body rust		⊜	⊜	⊜	⊜	⊜	⊜	
Paint/trim		◒	○	○	⊜	⊖	⊖	
Integrity		○	○	○	◒	⊖	⊜	
Hardware		○	○	◒	○	⊖	⊖	

Mazda MX-6

TROUBLE SPOTS	89	90	91	92	93	94	95	96
Engine	○	○	⊖		⊖	⊜	⊜	
Cooling	○	⊖	○		⊜	⊜	⊜	
Fuel	⊖	⊖	⊖		⊖	⊜	⊖	
Ignition	⊜	⊖	⊜		⊖	⊜	⊜	
Auto. trans.	●	◒	*		⊖	*	*	
Man. trans.	⊜	⊜	⊜	Insufficient data	⊜	⊖	*	Insufficient data
Clutch	⊖	⊖	⊜		⊜	⊜	*	
Electrical	●	◒	○		●	◒	○	
A/C	◒	◒	○		○	⊜	⊜	
Suspension	○	○	⊖		⊖	⊖	⊜	
Brakes	◒	●	◒		○	⊖	⊜	
Exhaust	●	●	◒		○	⊜	⊜	
Body rust	⊖	⊖	⊜		⊜	⊜	⊜	
Paint/trim	◒	◒	◒		◒	○	○	
Integrity	○	●	◒		●	●	●	
Hardware	●	●	●		●	●	◒	

Mazda Pickup (2WD)

TROUBLE SPOTS	89	90	91	92	93	94	95	96
Engine	◒	⊖	○	⊖	○	⊜	⊖	⊜
Cooling	○	⊖	⊖	⊖	○	⊜	⊜	⊜
Fuel	○	⊖	⊜	⊖	⊜	⊖	⊖	⊜
Ignition	⊖	⊜	⊖	⊖	⊜	⊜	⊖	⊜
Auto. trans.	*	⊜	⊜	*	*	⊖	⊖	⊖
Man. trans.	⊜	⊜	⊜	⊜	⊜	⊜	⊜	⊜
Clutch	⊖	⊖	⊜	⊜	⊜	⊖	⊖	⊜
Electrical	○	○	⊖	⊖	⊖	○	◒	⊖
A/C	○	⊖	⊖	⊖	○	⊖	⊜	⊜
Suspension	⊖	⊜	⊜	⊜	⊜	⊖	⊜	⊜
Brakes	●	◒	◒	◒	○	○	⊖	⊖
Exhaust	●	●	●	◒	○	⊜	⊜	⊜
Body rust	○	⊖	⊖	⊜	⊖	⊜	⊜	⊜
Paint/trim	○	○	○	⊖	⊖	⊜	⊖	⊖
Integrity	⊖	⊖	⊖	○	⊖	⊖	⊖	⊖
Hardware	⊖	⊖	○	⊖	⊖	⊖	○	⊖

Mazda Pickup (4WD)

TROUBLE SPOTS	89	90	91	92	93	94	95	96
Engine						⊜	⊖	⊖
Cooling						⊜	⊖	⊖
Fuel						⊖	⊜	⊖
Ignition						⊜	⊜	⊜
Auto. trans.						⊖	○	*
Man. trans.	Insufficient data	Insufficient data	Insufficient data	Insufficient data	Insufficient data	⊜	⊜	*
Clutch						⊖	⊜	*
Electrical						○	○	⊖
A/C						⊜	⊜	⊜
Suspension						⊖	○	⊜
Brakes						○	○	⊜
Exhaust						⊜	⊜	⊜
Body rust						⊜	⊜	⊜
Paint/trim						⊜	⊖	⊜
Integrity						⊖	⊜	⊜
Hardware						○	○	⊖

Mazda Protege

TROUBLE SPOTS	89	90	91	92	93	94	95	96
Engine		○	○	⊜	⊖	⊜	⊜	⊜
Cooling		○	⊖	⊖	⊖	⊜	⊜	⊜
Fuel		⊖	⊖	⊖	⊜	⊜	⊜	⊜
Ignition		⊖	⊖	⊜	⊖	⊜	⊜	⊜
Auto. trans.		⊖	⊖	⊖	⊖	⊖	⊜	*
Man. trans.		⊜	⊜	⊜	⊜	⊖	⊜	*
Clutch		⊜	⊖	⊖	⊖	⊜	⊜	*
Electrical		◒	◒	◒	○	⊖	◒	⊖
A/C		○	⊖	○	⊖	⊖	⊖	⊖
Suspension		○	⊖	⊖	⊜	⊖	⊜	⊜
Brakes		◒	◒	◒	○	⊖	⊖	⊜
Exhaust		●	●	○	⊜	⊜	⊜	⊜
Body rust		⊖	⊜	⊖	⊜	⊜	⊜	⊜
Paint/trim		◒	○	○	⊖	⊖	⊜	⊖
Integrity		○	○	○	○	○	○	⊖
Hardware		◒	◒	◒	◒	○	◒	⊖

TROUBLE SPOTS	Mercedes-Benz C-Class 89	90	91	92	93	94	95	96
Engine						⊖	⊖	
Cooling						⊜	⊜	
Fuel						⊖	⊖	
Ignition						⊖	⊜	
Auto. trans.						⊖	⊖	
Man. trans.								
Clutch								
Electrical						◒	●	Insufficient data
A/C						○	○	
Suspension						⊜	⊖	
Brakes						⊖	⊖	
Exhaust						⊖	⊜	
Body rust						⊜	⊜	
Paint/trim						⊖	⊜	
Integrity						○	⊖	
Hardware						●	◒	

TROUBLE SPOTS	Mercedes-Benz E-Class 89	90	91	92	93	94	95	96
Engine	○	○	◒	⊖	○	⊖	⊜	
Cooling	●	●	◒	○	⊖	⊜	⊜	
Fuel	○	○	⊖	⊖	○	⊜	⊜	
Ignition	⊖	⊜	⊖	⊜	○	⊜	⊜	
Auto. trans.	⊖	○	⊖	⊖	⊜	⊜	⊖	
Man. trans.								
Clutch								
Electrical	◒	○	◒	●	●	◒	◒	Insufficient data
A/C	◒	◒	⊖	○	⊜	⊜	⊖	
Suspension	⊖	⊖	⊜	⊖	○	⊖	⊖	
Brakes	◒	◒	⊜	○	◒	○	○	
Exhaust	○	○	⊜	⊜	⊖	⊜	⊜	
Body rust	⊜	⊜	⊜	⊜	⊜	⊜	⊜	
Paint/trim	⊜	⊖	⊜	⊜	⊖	⊜	⊖	
Integrity	⊖	⊜	⊜	⊜	◒	⊖	⊖	
Hardware	◒	○	○	⊖	◒	○	○	

TROUBLE SPOTS	Mercury Cougar V6 89	90	91	92	93	94	95	96
Engine	○	○	⊜	⊖	⊖	⊜	⊖	
Cooling	◒	◒	○	○	⊖	⊜	○	
Fuel	◒	○	⊖	⊖	⊖	⊜	⊖	
Ignition	⊖	⊖	⊖	⊖	⊖	⊜	⊜	
Auto. trans.	○	○	⊖	⊖	⊖	○	⊖	
Man. trans.	*	*						
Clutch	*	*						
Electrical	●	●	●	◒	◒	○	○	Insufficient data
A/C	●	●	●	○	○	○	○	
Suspension	◒	◒	○	○	⊖	⊜	⊖	
Brakes	●	●	●	◒	●	●	●	
Exhaust	⊖	⊜	⊜	⊜	⊜	⊜	⊜	
Body rust	○	⊖	○	⊜	⊖	⊜	⊜	
Paint/trim	●	●	◒	◒	●	○	⊖	
Integrity	◒	◒	◒	○	◒	◒	○	
Hardware	●	●	◒	○	●	◒	◒	

TROUBLE SPOTS	Mercury Cougar V8 89	90	91	92	93	94	95	96
Engine			⊖	⊜	⊜	⊖	⊜	⊜
Cooling			○	○	○	⊜	⊜	⊜
Fuel			◒	⊖	⊜	⊖	⊜	○
Ignition			○	⊜	⊖	⊜	⊜	⊜
Auto. trans.			○	○	○	◒	⊖	○
Man. trans.								
Clutch								
Electrical			●	●	◒	◒	○	◒
A/C			●	○	○	⊖	⊖	◒
Suspension			○	⊖	○	○	⊖	○
Brakes			●	●	●	●	●	⊖
Exhaust			⊖	⊜	⊜	⊜	⊜	⊜
Body rust			⊖	⊜	⊖	⊜	⊜	⊜
Paint/trim			●	◒	●	○	⊖	⊖
Integrity			○	◒	◒	◒	○	○
Hardware			◒	○	●	○	⊖	⊖

TROUBLE SPOTS	Mercury Grand Marquis 89	90	91	92	93	94	95	96
Engine	○	○	⊖	⊖	⊜	⊜	⊜	⊜
Cooling	●	○	⊖	⊜	⊜	⊜	⊜	⊜
Fuel	○	○	○	⊖	⊖	⊖	⊖	⊜
Ignition	⊖	○	⊖	○	⊖	⊜	⊜	⊜
Auto. trans.	○	○	⊖	○	●	○	⊖	⊖
Man. trans.								
Clutch								
Electrical	●	●	●	●	◒	○	◒	⊖
A/C	●	◒	○	◒	⊖	⊖	⊖	⊜
Suspension	○	○	○	⊖	⊖	⊖	⊖	⊖
Brakes	●	●	●	●	●	○	○	⊖
Exhaust	●	◒	○	◒	⊜	⊜	⊜	⊜
Body rust	⊖	⊖	○	⊜	⊜	⊜	⊜	⊜
Paint/trim	○	○	○	○	⊜	⊖	⊖	⊜
Integrity	○	○	⊖	○	○	○	○	⊖
Hardware	◒	●	●	◒	○	○	○	⊖

TROUBLE SPOTS	Mercury Mystique 89	90	91	92	93	94	95	96
Engine							⊜	⊜
Cooling							⊜	⊜
Fuel							●	⊖
Ignition							⊜	⊜
Auto. trans.							⊖	⊜
Man. trans.							⊖	*
Clutch							⊜	*
Electrical							○	⊖
A/C							⊖	⊜
Suspension							⊖	⊜
Brakes							⊖	⊜
Exhaust							⊜	⊜
Body rust							⊜	⊜
Paint/trim							⊖	⊜
Integrity							◒	○
Hardware							●	○

TROUBLE SPOTS	Mercury Sable 89	90	91	92	93	94	95	96
Engine	◒	○	○	○	⊖	⊜	⊜	⊜
Cooling	●	◒	○	◒	○	○	⊜	⊜
Fuel	◒	○	○	○	○	⊖	⊖	⊜
Ignition	○	⊖	⊖	⊖	⊖	⊜	⊜	⊜
Auto. trans.	◒	◒	●	⊖	⊖	⊖	⊖	⊖
Man. trans.								
Clutch								
Electrical	●	●	●	●	●	○	○	⊖
A/C	●	●	●	◒	○	○	⊖	⊜
Suspension	●	●	●	◒	○	⊖	⊖	⊖
Brakes	●	●	●	●	●	○	⊖	⊖
Exhaust	⊖	⊖	⊜	⊜	⊜	⊜	⊜	⊜
Body rust	◒	○	⊖	⊜	⊜	⊜	⊜	⊜
Paint/trim	●	◒	○	⊖	⊖	⊖	⊖	⊜
Integrity	◒	○	○	◒	◒	◒	◒	○
Hardware	◒	◒	◒	◒	◒	○	○	⊖

TROUBLE SPOTS	Mercury Topaz 89	90	91	92	93	94	95	96
Engine	●	●	◒	○	⊖	⊖		
Cooling	●	●	○	◒	○	○		
Fuel	●	◒	●	◒	◒	⊖		
Ignition	◒	○	○	⊖	⊖	⊜		
Auto. trans.	◒	○	○	○	⊖	⊖		
Man. trans.	⊜	*	*	*	*	*		
Clutch	◒	*	*	*	*	*		
Electrical	●	●	●	◒	◒	○		
A/C	●	●	●	○	⊖	⊖		
Suspension	●	●	◒	○	○	⊖		
Brakes	●	●	●	●	●	◒		
Exhaust	●	●	●	●	◒	⊖		
Body rust	◒	○	○	⊖	⊜	⊜		
Paint/trim	●	◒	●	◒	⊖	⊖		
Integrity	●	◒	◒	◒	◒	◒		
Hardware	●	●	●	●	●	○		

⊜ ⊖ ○ ◒ ●
Few ← **Problems** → Many

*
Insufficient data

Mercury Tracer

Trouble spots	89	90	91	92	93	94	95	96
Engine	◒		○	⊜	⊖	⊖	⊜	Insufficient data
Cooling	●		○	⊖	⊖	⊖	⊜	
Fuel	⊖		⊖	○	⊖	⊖	⊜	
Ignition	⊖		⊖	⊜	⊜	⊖	⊜	
Auto. trans.	⊖		⊖	⊜	⊖	⊖	⊜	
Man. trans.	⊜		⊜	*	*	*	*	
Clutch	⊖		○	*	*	*	*	
Electrical	◒		●	◒	●	●	○	
A/C	●		●	⊖	⊖	⊜	⊖	
Suspension	○		○	⊖	⊖	⊖	⊖	
Brakes	●		◒	◒	○	○	⊜	
Exhaust	●		⊖	⊜	⊜	⊜	⊜	
Body rust	○		⊖	⊜	⊜	⊜	⊜	
Paint/trim	○		○	○	⊖	⊖	⊜	
Integrity	○		◒	○	○	⊖	⊖	
Hardware	◒		◒	○	◒	●	○	

Mercury Villager Van

Trouble spots	89	90	91	92	93	94	95	96
Engine					⊖	⊖	⊖	⊖
Cooling					⊖	⊖	⊜	⊜
Fuel					⊖	⊖	⊜	⊜
Ignition					⊜	⊜	⊜	⊜
Auto. trans.					⊖	⊜	⊜	⊜
Man. trans.								
Clutch								
Electrical					●	◒	○	○
A/C					○	○	⊖	⊖
Suspension					○	⊖	⊖	⊖
Brakes					◒	○	○	⊖
Exhaust					○	⊜	⊜	⊜
Body rust					⊜	⊜	⊜	⊜
Paint/trim					⊖	⊖	⊜	⊜
Integrity					◒	◒	○	○
Hardware					●	◒	◒	○

Mitsubishi 3000GT

Trouble spots	89	90	91	92	93	94	95	96
Engine			○	○	⊜	⊜	Insufficient data	Insufficient data
Cooling			⊜	⊖	⊖	⊜		
Fuel			⊖	⊖	⊖	⊖		
Ignition			⊖	⊜	⊜	⊜		
Auto. trans.			*	*	*	*		
Man. trans.			◒	○	⊖	*		
Clutch			○	◒	●	*		
Electrical			●	●	●	●		
A/C			⊜	⊜	⊜	⊖		
Suspension			⊜	○	⊖	⊖		
Brakes			○	⊜	⊜	⊜		
Exhaust			⊜	⊜	⊜	⊜		
Body rust			⊖	⊜	⊜	⊜		
Paint/trim			○	○	◒	○		
Integrity			○	◒	●	○		
Hardware			○	●	◒	○		

Mitsubishi Diamante

Trouble spots	89	90	91	92	93	94	95	96
Engine				⊖	⊖	⊜	Insufficient data	Insufficient data
Cooling				⊜	⊖	⊜		
Fuel				⊖	⊖	⊖		
Ignition				⊖	⊖	⊜		
Auto. trans.				⊖	○	⊖		
Man. trans.								
Clutch								
Electrical				◒	◒	◒		
A/C				⊖	⊜	⊜		
Suspension				⊖	⊖	⊖		
Brakes				◒	○	○		
Exhaust				⊜	⊜	⊜		
Body rust				⊜	⊜	⊜		
Paint/trim				⊖	⊖	⊜		
Integrity				⊖	○	○		
Hardware				○	○	◒		

Mitsubishi Eclipse

Trouble spots	89	90	91	92	93	94	95	96
Engine		●	◒	◒	○	○	○	Insufficient data
Cooling		○	⊖	⊖	⊖	⊖	⊜	
Fuel		⊖	○	⊖	⊖	⊖	⊖	
Ignition		⊖	○	⊖	⊖	⊜	○	
Auto. trans.		○	○	⊖	*	*	⊖	
Man. trans.		○	○	○	⊖	*	⊖	
Clutch		○	○	○	⊖	*	⊖	
Electrical		◒	●	◒	◒	◒	●	
A/C		⊖	⊖	⊖	⊜	⊖	⊜	
Suspension		⊖	⊖	⊖	⊖	⊖	⊖	
Brakes		●	◒	◒	○	⊖	⊖	
Exhaust		⊖	⊖	⊖	⊜	⊜	⊜	
Body rust		⊖	⊜	⊜	⊜	⊜	⊖	
Paint/trim		◒	○	◒	○	⊖	○	
Integrity		○	○	◒	◒	◒	●	
Hardware		●	●	●	◒	○	●	

Mitsubishi Expo LRV

Trouble spots	89	90	91	92	93	94	95	96
Engine				⊖	⊜	⊜		
Cooling				⊖	⊖	⊖		
Fuel				⊖	⊖	⊜		
Ignition				⊖	⊖	⊜		
Auto. trans.				⊖	○	⊖		
Man. trans.				*	*	*		
Clutch				*	*	*		
Electrical				○	◒	◒		
A/C				⊜	⊖	⊜		
Suspension				⊜	⊖	⊜		
Brakes				⊖	⊖	⊖		
Exhaust				⊖	⊜	⊜		
Body rust				⊖	⊜	⊜		
Paint/trim				⊖	○	⊖		
Integrity				○	◒	○		
Hardware				○	●	⊖		

Mitsubishi Galant

Trouble spots	89	90	91	92	93	94	95	96
Engine	◒	◒	⊖	○	Insufficient data	⊜	⊜	Insufficient data
Cooling	○	⊖	⊖	⊖		⊜	⊜	
Fuel	⊖	⊖	⊜	⊖		⊜	⊜	
Ignition	⊖	⊖	⊜	⊜		⊜	⊜	
Auto. trans.	○	⊖	⊖	⊖		⊖	⊜	
Man. trans.	*	*	*	*		*	*	
Clutch	*	*	*	*		*	*	
Electrical	◒	◒	○	○		◒	⊖	
A/C	●	⊖	⊖	⊖		⊖	⊖	
Suspension	○	○	⊖	⊖		⊖	○	
Brakes	◒	◒	◒	○		◒	○	
Exhaust	⊖	⊖	⊜	⊜		⊜	⊜	
Body rust	⊜	⊜	⊜	⊜		⊜	⊜	
Paint/trim	○	○	○	⊖		⊖	⊖	
Integrity	○	○	⊖	○		◒	○	
Hardware	◒	○	⊖	○		●	◒	

Mitsubishi Mirage

Trouble spots	89	90	91	92	93	94	95	96
Engine	◒	●	○	○	⊖	Insufficient data	Insufficient data	Insufficient data
Cooling	○	⊖	⊜	⊖	⊖			
Fuel	⊖	○	⊖	⊜	⊜			
Ignition	⊖	⊖	⊖	⊜	⊖			
Auto. trans.	⊖	○	○	○	◒			
Man. trans.	⊖	⊖	⊖	⊖	*			
Clutch	⊖	⊖	○	○	*			
Electrical	◒	○	○	⊖	○			
A/C	●	○	○	○	○			
Suspension	○	○	⊖	⊖	⊜			
Brakes	●	●	◒	◒	◒			
Exhaust	⊜	⊖	⊜	⊜	⊜			
Body rust	⊖	⊖	⊖	⊜	⊜			
Paint/trim	◒	○	○	○	○			
Integrity	◒	●	◒	◒	○			
Hardware	◒	◒	◒	◒	◒			

Key: ⊜ = Few problems, ⊖, ○, ◒, ● = Many problems (Few ← Problems → Many); * = Insufficient data

Nissan 200SX

Trouble spots	89	90	91	92	93	94	95	96
Engine							⊜	
Cooling							⊖	
Fuel							⊖	
Ignition							⊜	
Auto. trans.							*	
Man. trans.							*	
Clutch							*	Insufficient data
Electrical							○	
A/C							⊜	
Suspension							⊖	
Brakes							⊜	
Exhaust							⊜	
Body rust							⊜	
Paint/trim							○	
Integrity							○	
Hardware							○	

Nissan 240SX

Trouble spots	89	90	91	92	93	94	95	96
Engine	○	⊖	⊖	⊜	⊜			
Cooling	⊖	⊖	⊜	⊜	⊜			
Fuel	⊖	⊖	⊜	⊖	⊖			
Ignition	⊜	⊖	⊜	⊜	⊜			
Auto. trans.	◒	*	*	*	*			
Man. trans.	○	⊖	⊖	*	*			
Clutch	●	◒	○	*	*	Insufficient data	Insufficient data	Insufficient data
Electrical	●	●	○	◒	○			
A/C	○	◒	⊖	⊜	⊜			
Suspension	⊖	⊖	○	⊜	⊖			
Brakes	●	●	◒	○	⊜			
Exhaust	●	●	○	⊜	⊜			
Body rust	⊖	○	⊖	⊜	⊜			
Paint/trim	○	⊖	⊖	○	⊖			
Integrity	◒	○	⊖	○	◒			
Hardware	●	◒	○	○	○			

Nissan Altima

Trouble spots	89	90	91	92	93	94	95	96
Engine					⊜	⊜	⊜	⊜
Cooling					⊜	⊜	⊜	⊜
Fuel					⊖	⊜	⊜	⊜
Ignition					⊜	⊜	⊜	⊜
Auto. trans.					⊜	⊜	⊜	⊜
Man. trans.					⊜	⊜	⊜	*
Clutch					⊖	⊜	⊜	*
Electrical					○	○	○	⊖
A/C					○	⊖	⊖	⊜
Suspension					⊜	⊖	⊜	⊜
Brakes					○	⊖	⊜	⊜
Exhaust					⊜	⊜	⊜	⊜
Body rust					⊜	⊜	⊜	⊜
Paint/trim					⊖	⊖	⊖	⊜
Integrity					○	⊖	⊖	⊖
Hardware					○	○	○	⊜

Nissan Maxima

Trouble spots	89	90	91	92	93	94	95	96
Engine	⊖	⊖	⊖	⊖	⊜	⊜	⊜	⊜
Cooling	⊖	⊖	⊜	⊜	⊜	⊜	⊜	⊜
Fuel	⊖	○	⊜	⊖	⊖	⊜	⊜	⊜
Ignition	⊜	⊜	⊜	⊜	⊜	⊜	⊜	⊜
Auto. trans.	○	⊖	⊖	⊖	⊜	⊖	⊜	⊜
Man. trans.	⊖	○	⊖	⊜	⊜	*	⊜	⊜
Clutch	●	●	○	⊖	⊖	*	○	⊜
Electrical	●	●	◒	○	○	⊖	⊖	⊖
A/C	○	⊖	⊜	⊜	⊖	⊖	⊜	⊜
Suspension	⊖	⊖	⊖	⊖	⊜	⊜	⊜	⊜
Brakes	●	●	●	●	◒	○	⊜	⊜
Exhaust	◒	○	⊖	⊜	⊜	⊜	⊜	⊜
Body rust	⊖	⊖	⊖	⊜	⊜	⊜	⊜	⊜
Paint/trim	○	⊖	○	⊖	⊖	⊖	⊜	⊜
Integrity	⊖	⊖	⊖	⊖	⊖	⊖	⊖	⊖
Hardware	●	◒	◒	○	○	○	⊖	⊜

Nissan Pathfinder

Trouble spots	89	90	91	92	93	94	95	96
Engine	⊖	⊖	⊜	⊖	⊜	⊜	⊖	
Cooling	⊖	⊖	⊖	⊜	⊜	⊜	⊜	
Fuel	○	⊖	⊜	⊖	⊖	⊜	⊜	
Ignition	⊖	⊜	⊜	⊜	⊜	⊜	⊜	
Auto. trans.	*	◒	○	○	⊖	⊜	⊖	
Man. trans.	*	⊜	⊖	⊜	⊜	⊜	⊖	
Clutch	*	○	○	⊜	⊜	⊜	○	Insufficient data
Electrical	◒	◒	◒	◒	◒	○	○	
A/C	○	○	⊜	⊖	⊖	⊖	⊖	
Suspension	⊖	⊖	○	⊖	○	○	⊖	
Brakes	○	○	◒	○	○	⊖	⊜	
Exhaust	●	●	●	○	⊜	⊜	⊜	
Body rust	○	○	○	⊖	⊜	⊜	⊜	
Paint/trim	⊖	⊖	⊖	⊖	⊖	⊖	⊖	
Integrity	○	○	○	○	○	○	⊖	
Hardware	●	◒	○	○	○	○	○	

Nissan Pickup (2WD)

Trouble spots	89	90	91	92	93	94	95	96
Engine	⊖	⊖	⊜	⊜	⊖	⊜	⊖	
Cooling	⊖	⊖	⊜	⊜	⊜	⊜	⊜	
Fuel	○	⊖	⊜	⊖	⊖	⊖	⊜	
Ignition	⊖	⊜	⊜	⊖	⊜	⊖	⊜	
Auto. trans.	○	◒	○	⊖	⊖	⊜	⊜	
Man. trans.	⊜	⊖	⊖	⊜	⊜	⊖	⊖	
Clutch	○	◒	○	⊖	○	○	○	Insufficient data
Electrical	◒	○	○	◒	○	⊖	⊖	
A/C	○	○	○	⊖	⊖	⊜	⊜	
Suspension	⊖	⊖	⊖	⊖	○	⊖	⊖	
Brakes	◒	⊖	○	○	⊖	⊜	⊜	
Exhaust	◒	●	◒	○	⊜	⊜	⊜	
Body rust	●	◒	⊖	⊖	⊜	⊖	⊜	
Paint/trim	●	◒	◒	○	⊖	⊜	⊖	
Integrity	○	○	○	○	⊖	○	○	
Hardware	◒	●	○	⊖	○	⊖	⊖	

Nissan Pickup (4WD)

Trouble spots	89	90	91	92	93	94	95	96
Engine	⊖	⊖	⊜		⊜	⊖	⊖	
Cooling	⊖	⊜	⊜		⊜	⊜	⊜	
Fuel	○	⊖	⊜		⊜	⊖	⊖	
Ignition	○	⊖	⊖		⊜	⊜	⊜	
Auto. trans.	*	*	*		*	*	*	
Man. trans.	⊖	⊖	○		⊜	⊖	⊖	
Clutch	○	○	○	Insufficient data	⊖	⊖	◒	Insufficient data
Electrical	○	◒	○		⊖	⊖	○	
A/C	*	*	*		*	⊖	⊜	
Suspension	○	◒	○		◒	○	○	
Brakes	◒	⊖	○		⊖	⊖	⊜	
Exhaust	●	●	◒		⊜	⊜	⊜	
Body rust	●	●	○		⊜	⊜	⊖	
Paint/trim	●	●	○		⊖	⊖	⊜	
Integrity	◒	○	⊖		○	○	○	
Hardware	●	●	○		○	⊖	⊖	

Nissan Quest Van

Trouble spots	89	90	91	92	93	94	95	96
Engine					⊖	⊖	⊖	⊖
Cooling					⊖	⊖	⊜	⊜
Fuel					⊖	⊖	⊜	⊜
Ignition					⊜	⊜	⊜	⊜
Auto. trans.					⊖	⊜	⊜	⊜
Man. trans.								
Clutch								
Electrical					●	◒	○	○
A/C					○	○	⊖	⊖
Suspension					○	⊖	⊖	⊖
Brakes					◒	○	○	⊖
Exhaust					○	⊜	⊜	⊜
Body rust					⊜	⊜	⊜	⊜
Paint/trim					⊖	⊖	⊜	⊜
Integrity					◒	◒	○	○
Hardware					●	◒	◒	○

⊜ ⊖ ○ ◒ ●
Few ← **Problems** → Many

*
Insufficient data

Nissan Sentra 89	90	91	92	93	94	95	96	Nissan Stanza 89	90	91	92	93	94	95	96	TROUBLE SPOTS
◒	○	⊜	⊜	⊜	⊜	⊜	⊜	○	○	⊖	⊖					Engine
○	⊖	⊜	⊜	⊜	⊜	⊜	⊜	⊖	⊜	⊜	⊜					Cooling
⊖	⊖	○	○	⊖	⊜	⊖	⊜	⊖	⊖	○	⊖					Fuel
⊖	⊖	⊜	⊜	⊜	⊜	⊜	⊜	⊖	⊖	⊖	⊖					Ignition
◒	○	○	⊖	⊖	⊜	⊜	⊖	⊖	○	⊖	⊜					Auto. trans.
⊖	⊜	⊖	⊜	⊜	⊜	⊜	*	*	⊖	⊖	⊜					Man. trans.
◒	○	○	⊖	⊖	⊜	⊜	*	*	●	●	◒					Clutch
◒	◒	◒	○	○	⊖	○	⊖	◒	◒	◒	◒					Electrical
◒	○	○	⊖	⊖	⊜	⊜	⊜	○	○	○	⊖					A/C
◒	○	⊖	⊖	⊜	⊜	⊜	⊜	○	⊖	⊖	⊜					Suspension
●	●	●	◒	◒	○	⊖	⊜	●	●	●	◒					Brakes
●	●	◒	⊖	⊜	⊜	⊜	⊜	●	○	⊖	⊜					Exhaust
●	◒	⊖	⊜	⊜	⊜	⊜	⊜	○	⊖	⊜	⊜					Body rust
●	◒	◒	○	○	⊖	⊖	⊜	◒	○	○	○					Paint/trim
◒	◒	○	○	○	⊜	○	⊜	◒	○	○	⊜					Integrity
●	◒	○	○	○	○	○	⊜	●	○	○	○					Hardware

TROUBLE SPOTS	Oldsmobile 88 89	90	91	92	93	94	95	96	Oldsmobile 98 89	90	91	92	93	94	95	96
Engine	⊖	⊖	⊖	⊖	⊖	⊜	⊜	⊜	⊖	⊖	⊖	⊖	○	⊖	⊜	Insufficient data
Cooling	◒	◒	○	◒	○	⊖	⊜	⊜	◒	◒	○	◒	○	⊜	⊜	
Fuel	◒	○	○	⊖	⊖	⊜	⊜	⊜	○	○	⊖	⊜	⊖	⊜	⊖	
Ignition	◒	◒	◒	○	⊖	⊜	⊜	⊜	○	◒	○	⊖	⊖	⊜	⊖	
Auto. trans.	○	○	○	⊖	⊜	⊖	⊜	⊜	○	○	○	⊖	○	⊜	⊜	
Man. trans.																
Clutch																
Electrical	●	●	●	●	●	◒	○	○	●	●	●	●	●	●	◒	
A/C	◒	◒	◒	○	○	⊖	⊖	⊜	●	◒	●	◒	○	⊖	⊖	
Suspension	○	⊖	⊖	○	⊖	⊖	⊖	⊜	○	○	⊖	⊖	⊖	⊜	⊖	
Brakes	●	●	●	●	◒	⊖	⊜	⊖	●	●	●	●	●	⊖	⊜	
Exhaust	⊖	⊖	⊜	⊖	○	⊜	⊖	⊖	⊖	⊖	⊜	⊜	○	⊜	⊖	
Body rust	○	⊖	⊖	⊜	⊜	⊜	⊜	⊜	⊖	⊖	⊜	⊜	⊖	⊜	⊜	
Paint/trim	◒	◒	○	○	⊖	⊖	⊖	⊜	◒	○	○	⊖	⊖	⊖	⊖	
Integrity	○	○	○	◒	○	○	◒	○	○	○	○	○	◒	○	○	
Hardware	◒	◒	○	◒	◒	◒	○	⊖	◒	◒	◒	◒	◒	●	◒	

Oldsmobile Achieva 89	90	91	92	93	94	95	96	Oldsmobile Aurora 89	90	91	92	93	94	95	96	TROUBLE SPOTS
			○	⊖	⊖	Insufficient data	Insufficient data							⊜	⊜	Engine
			●	○	⊜									⊜	⊖	Cooling
			⊖	⊖	⊖									⊖	⊜	Fuel
			⊖	⊖	⊜									⊜	⊜	Ignition
			⊜	⊖	⊜									⊜	⊖	Auto. trans.
			*	*	*											Man. trans.
			*	*	*											Clutch
			●	●	○									◒	○	Electrical
			○	⊖	⊖									⊖	⊖	A/C
			○	◒	⊖									⊜	⊜	Suspension
			●	●	●									⊜	⊜	Brakes
			⊜	⊜	⊜									⊜	⊜	Exhaust
			⊖	⊜	⊜									⊜	⊜	Body rust
			◒	○	⊖									⊖	⊖	Paint/trim
			●	●	◒									◒	○	Integrity
			●	●	●									◒	⊖	Hardware

TROUBLE SPOTS	Oldsmobile Cutlass Calais 89	90	91	92	93	94	95	96	Oldsmobile Cutlass Ciera 89	90	91	92	93	94	95	96
Engine	●	●	◒						○	○	⊖	⊖	⊜	○	⊜	Insufficient data
Cooling	●	◒	○						◒	◒	●	○	⊖	⊜	⊜	
Fuel	●	○	○						○	○	⊖	⊖	⊖	⊖	⊜	
Ignition	●	◒	○						○	⊖	⊖	⊖	⊜	⊜	⊜	
Auto. trans.	◒	○	○						○	⊖	⊖	⊖	⊖	⊖	⊜	
Man. trans.	*	*	*													
Clutch	*	*	*													
Electrical	●	●	●						●	●	●	◒	○	◒	○	
A/C	○	◒	○						○	○	○	⊖	⊖	⊖	⊜	
Suspension	◒	○	◒						○	○	○	○	⊖	⊖	⊖	
Brakes	●	●	●						●	●	●	●	●	◒	⊖	
Exhaust	●	●	●						◒	◒	●	◒	○	⊜	⊜	
Body rust	●	●	◒						●	○	⊖	⊖	⊜	⊜	⊜	
Paint/trim	●	●	●						●	◒	○	○	⊖	⊖	⊖	
Integrity	◒	○	◒						○	○	○	○	○	◒	◒	
Hardware	◒	◒	◒						●	◒	◒	○	○	◒	○	

Oldsmobile Cutlass Supreme

Trouble spots	89	90	91	92	93	94	95	96
Engine	○	◒	○	⊖	⊜	○	⊜	⊜
Cooling	◒	◒	○	○	⊖	⊖	⊜	⊜
Fuel	◒	◒	○	⊜	⊖	⊖	⊖	⊜
Ignition	◒	○	⊖	⊖	⊖	⊜	⊜	⊜
Auto. trans.	○	○	⊖	⊖	⊖	⊖	⊜	⊜
Man. trans.	*	*	*	*				
Clutch	*	*	*	*				
Electrical	●	●	●	●	●	●	◒	○
A/C	●	◒	○	○	⊖	⊖	⊖	⊜
Suspension	●	◒	○	⊖	⊜	⊖	⊖	⊜
Brakes	●	●	●	●	●	●	⊖	⊜
Exhaust	⊖	⊖	⊖	⊖	⊜	⊜	⊜	⊜
Body rust	⊖	⊖	⊖	⊜	⊜	⊜	⊜	⊜
Paint/trim	●	●	◒	○	◒	○	○	⊜
Integrity	◒	◒	◒	◒	◒	◒	◒	○
Hardware	●	●	●	●	◒	●	◒	⊖

Oldsmobile Silhouette Van

Trouble spots	89	90	91	92	93	94	95	96
Engine		○	⊖	⊖	⊖	⊖	⊜	Insufficient data
Cooling		●	●	●	⊖	⊖	⊜	
Fuel		⊖	⊖	⊖	⊖	⊖	⊖	
Ignition		⊖	⊖	⊖	⊖	⊜	⊜	
Auto. trans.		○	⊖	⊖	○	⊖	⊜	
Man. trans.								
Clutch								
Electrical		●	●	●	●	◒	◒	
A/C		◒	○	○	⊖	⊖	⊜	
Suspension		◒	○	○	○	⊖	⊖	
Brakes		●	●	●	◒	○	⊜	
Exhaust		○	⊜	⊖	⊖	⊜	⊜	
Body rust		⊜	⊜	⊜	⊜	⊜	⊜	
Paint/trim		●	●	⊖	○	○	⊖	
Integrity		●	◒	○	○	◒	◒	
Hardware		●	●	●	●	●	●	

Plymouth Acclaim

Trouble spots	89	90	91	92	93	94	95	96
Engine	●	◒	◒	○	○	⊜	⊖	
Cooling	●	◒	○	⊖	⊖	⊖	⊜	
Fuel	○	○	○	○	⊜	⊖	⊖	
Ignition	⊖	○	⊖	⊖	⊖	⊜	⊜	
Auto. trans.	○	◒	◒	○	○	○	⊖	
Man. trans.	*	*	*	*	*			
Clutch	*	*	*	*	*			
Electrical	●	●	◒	●	○	◒	○	
A/C	●	◒	○	○	◒	○	⊖	
Suspension	◒	○	○	⊖	⊖	⊖	⊖	
Brakes	●	●	◒	○	○	⊜	⊖	
Exhaust	⊖	⊜	●	●	⊜	⊜	⊜	
Body rust	○	⊖	⊖	⊜	⊜	⊜	⊜	
Paint/trim	●	◒	◒	○	⊜	⊖	⊖	
Integrity	○	○	○	○	○	○	○	
Hardware	○	○	○	⊖	○	○	◒	

Plymouth Colt Vista Wagon

Trouble spots	89	90	91	92	93	94	95	96
Engine	◒	Insufficient data	Insufficient data	⊖	⊜	⊜		
Cooling	◒			⊖	⊖	⊖		
Fuel	○			⊖	⊖	⊜		
Ignition	⊖			⊖	⊖	⊜		
Auto. trans.	*			⊖	○	⊖		
Man. trans.	*			*	*	*		
Clutch	*			*	*	*		
Electrical	●			○	◒	◒		
A/C	*			⊜	⊖	⊜		
Suspension	◒			⊜	⊖	⊜		
Brakes	◒			⊖	⊖	⊖		
Exhaust	⊖			⊖	⊜	⊜		
Body rust	⊖			⊖	⊜	⊜		
Paint/trim	⊖			⊖	○	⊖		
Integrity	○			○	◒	○		
Hardware	○			○	●	⊖		

Plymouth Colt, Colt Wagon

Trouble spots	89	90	91	92	93	94	95	96
Engine	◒	●	○	○	⊖	Insufficient data		
Cooling	○	⊖	⊜	⊖	⊖			
Fuel	⊖	○	⊖	⊜	⊜			
Ignition	⊖	⊖	⊖	⊜	⊖			
Auto. trans.	⊖	○	○	○	◒			
Man. trans.	⊖	⊖	⊖	⊖	*			
Clutch	⊖	⊖	○	○	*			
Electrical	◒	○	○	⊖	○			
A/C	●	○	○	○	○			
Suspension	○	○	⊖	⊖	⊜			
Brakes	●	●	◒	◒	◒			
Exhaust	⊜	⊖	⊜	⊜	⊜			
Body rust	⊖	⊖	⊖	⊜	⊜			
Paint/trim	◒	○	○	○	○			
Integrity	◒	●	◒	◒	○			
Hardware	◒	◒	◒	◒	◒			

Plymouth Grand Voyager V6 (2WD)

Trouble spots	89	90	91	92	93	94	95	96
Engine	●	○	○	○	○	⊖	⊜	⊜
Cooling	●	●	○	○	○	⊖	⊜	⊜
Fuel	○	○	○	⊖	⊖	⊖	⊜	○
Ignition	⊖	○	⊖	⊖	⊖	⊜	⊜	⊜
Auto. trans.	●	●	●	●	●	○	⊖	⊖
Man. trans.								
Clutch								
Electrical	●	●	●	●	◒	◒	○	○
A/C	●	◒	○	○	◒	⊖	⊖	⊜
Suspension	◒	◒	○	○	○	⊖	⊖	⊖
Brakes	●	●	●	●	◒	○	⊖	⊖
Exhaust	⊜	⊖	●	⊖	⊜	⊜	⊜	⊜
Body rust	○	⊖	⊖	⊜	⊜	⊜	⊜	⊜
Paint/trim	●	◒	○	○	⊖	⊖	⊖	⊖
Integrity	●	◒	◒	◒	◒	●	◒	○
Hardware	●	●	◒	●	●	●	●	○

Plymouth Grand Voyager V6 (4WD)

Trouble spots	89	90	91	92	93	94	95	96
Engine			○	○	○	⊖	Insufficient data	
Cooling			◒	○	⊜	⊖		
Fuel			○	◒	⊖	⊖		
Ignition			○	○	⊜	⊜		
Auto. trans.			●	●	●	◒		
Man. trans.								
Clutch								
Electrical			●	●	◒	◒		
A/C			⊖	○	○	⊖		
Suspension			◒	○	◒	⊜		
Brakes			●	●	◒	○		
Exhaust			●	●	⊜	⊜		
Body rust			⊖	⊖	⊜	⊜		
Paint/trim			◒	⊖	⊜	○		
Integrity			●	◒	○	◒		
Hardware			●	●	●	●		

Plymouth Laser

Trouble spots	89	90	91	92	93	94	95	96
Engine		●	◒	◒	○	○		
Cooling		○	⊖	⊖	⊖	⊖		
Fuel		⊖	○	⊖	⊖	⊖		
Ignition		⊖	○	⊖	⊖	⊜		
Auto. trans.		○	○	⊖	*	*		
Man. trans.		○	○	○	⊖	*		
Clutch		○	○	○	⊖	*		
Electrical		◒	●	◒	◒	◒		
A/C		⊖	⊖	⊖	⊜	⊖		
Suspension		⊖	⊖	⊖	⊖	⊖		
Brakes		●	◒	◒	○	⊖		
Exhaust		⊖	⊖	⊖	⊜	⊜		
Body rust		⊖	⊜	⊜	⊜	⊜		
Paint/trim		◒	○	◒	○	⊖		
Integrity		○	○	◒	◒	◒		
Hardware		●	●	●	◒	○		

⊜ ⊖ ○ ◒ ●

Few ← **Problems** → Many

* Insufficient data

Plymouth Neon

TROUBLE SPOTS	89	90	91	92	93	94	95	96
Engine							⊖	⊜
Cooling							⊜	⊜
Fuel							⊖	⊖
Ignition							⊖	⊜
Auto. trans.							⊖	⊖
Man. trans.							⊜	*
Clutch							⊜	*
Electrical							◒	○
A/C							⊖	⊖
Suspension							⊖	⊖
Brakes							○	⊖
Exhaust							⊜	⊜
Body rust							⊜	⊜
Paint/trim							⊖	⊖
Integrity							●	○
Hardware							◒	○

Plymouth Sundance

TROUBLE SPOTS	89	90	91	92	93	94	95	96
Engine	●	◒	◒	◒	⊖	⊖		
Cooling	●	●	◒	○	⊖	⊜		
Fuel	◒	◒	◒	○	⊖	⊖		
Ignition	○	○	○	⊖	⊖	⊖		
Auto. trans.	○	⊖	⊖	○	○	○		
Man. trans.	*	*	*	⊖	*	*		
Clutch	*	*	*	⊜	*	*		
Electrical	●	●	●	●	◒	◒		
A/C	●	●	●	○	◒	◒		
Suspension	●	○	○	⊖	⊖	⊜		
Brakes	●	●	◒	○	⊖	⊜		
Exhaust	○	⊖	●	●	⊜	⊜		
Body rust	○	○	○	⊖	○	⊜		
Paint/trim	●	◒	◒	◒	◒	⊖		
Integrity	●	◒	◒	◒	◒	◒		
Hardware	●	◒	◒	○	◒	◒		

Plymouth Voyager 4

TROUBLE SPOTS	89	90	91	92	93	94	95	96
Engine	◒	○	◒	○	○	⊖	⊖	Insufficient data
Cooling	●	◒	◒	○	⊖	⊜	⊜	
Fuel	○	○	○	○	⊖	○	⊜	
Ignition	⊖	○	⊖	⊖	⊜	⊖	⊜	
Auto. trans.	◒	○	○	○	○	⊖	⊖	
Man. trans.	*	*		*	*			
Clutch	*	*		*	*			
Electrical	◒	◒	●	◒	○	○	⊖	
A/C	●	●	⊖	⊖	◒	⊖	⊖	
Suspension	○	○	○	○	⊖	⊖	⊜	
Brakes	●	●	●	◒	○	⊖	⊜	
Exhaust	⊖	⊖	●	●	⊜	⊜	⊜	
Body rust	○	⊖	⊖	⊜	⊜	⊜	⊜	
Paint/trim	◒	◒	○	⊖	⊖	○	⊖	
Integrity	◒	◒	◒	◒	◒	◒	○	
Hardware	●	●	◒	◒	○	◒	◒	

Plymouth Voyager V6 (2WD)

TROUBLE SPOTS	89	90	91	92	93	94	95	96
Engine	●	●	◒	○	○	⊖	⊜	⊜
Cooling	●	◒	◒	○	⊖	⊖	⊜	⊜
Fuel	◒	◒	○	○	⊖	⊖	⊜	○
Ignition	⊖	⊖	⊖	⊖	⊜	⊜	⊜	⊜
Auto. trans.	●	●	●	◒	◒	○	⊖	⊖
Man. trans.								
Clutch								
Electrical	●	●	●	●	◒	○	○	⊖
A/C	●	○	⊖	○	◒	⊖	⊖	⊜
Suspension	○	○	○	○	⊖	⊖	⊖	○
Brakes	●	●	●	●	◒	⊖	⊖	⊖
Exhaust	⊖	⊖	●	○	⊜	⊜	⊜	⊜
Body rust	○	○	⊖	⊜	⊜	⊜	⊜	⊜
Paint/trim	●	◒	○	⊖	⊖	⊖	⊖	⊖
Integrity	◒	●	◒	◒	◒	◒	○	○
Hardware	●	●	◒	●	●	◒	◒	○

Pontiac Bonneville

TROUBLE SPOTS	89	90	91	92	93	94	95	96
Engine	⊖	⊖	⊖	⊖	⊖	⊖	⊖	⊜
Cooling	◒	◒	○	○	○	⊖	⊜	⊜
Fuel	○	○	○	⊖	⊖	⊜	⊜	⊜
Ignition	○	◒	◒	○	⊜	⊜	⊜	⊜
Auto. trans.	⊖	○	○	⊖	⊖	⊜	⊜	⊜
Man. trans.								
Clutch								
Electrical	●	●	●	●	●	●	◒	◒
A/C	◒	◒	○	◒	⊖	⊖	⊜	⊜
Suspension	○	○	⊖	⊖	⊖	⊜	⊖	⊖
Brakes	●	●	●	●	◒	⊖	⊜	⊜
Exhaust	⊖	⊜	⊜	⊖	⊖	⊜	○	⊖
Body rust	○	⊖	⊖	⊜	⊜	⊖	⊜	⊜
Paint/trim	●	○	◒	○	⊖	⊖	⊖	⊖
Integrity	○	○	○	◒	○	◒	◒	○
Hardware	◒	○	◒	◒	◒	◒	○	○

Pontiac Firebird V8

TROUBLE SPOTS	89	90	91	92	93	94	95	96
Engine	◒	Insufficient data	⊜	Insufficient data	○	○	◒	Insufficient data
Cooling	●		○		○	⊖	⊖	
Fuel	◒		○		○	⊖	⊖	
Ignition	◒		○		○	⊖	⊖	
Auto. trans.	○		⊖		*	⊖	⊖	
Man. trans.	*		*		*	*	⊖	
Clutch	*		*		*	*	⊜	
Electrical	●		●		◒	●	●	
A/C	○		⊖		○	⊖	⊖	
Suspension	○		○		○	⊖	⊖	
Brakes	◒		○		◒	○	⊖	
Exhaust	◒		○		⊜	⊜	⊜	
Body rust	○		⊜		⊖	⊜	⊜	
Paint/trim	●		●		◒	○	○	
Integrity	●		●		●	●	●	
Hardware	●		◒		●	●	◒	

Pontiac Grand Am

TROUBLE SPOTS	89	90	91	92	93	94	95	96
Engine	●	●	◒	○	⊖	⊖	⊜	⊜
Cooling	●	◒	●	●	○	⊜	⊜	⊜
Fuel	◒	◒	○	⊖	⊖	⊖	⊜	⊜
Ignition	●	○	○	⊖	⊜	⊜	⊜	⊜
Auto. trans.	○	⊖	⊜	⊖	⊖	⊖	⊜	⊜
Man. trans.	*	*	*	*	*	*	*	*
Clutch	*	*	*	*	*	*	*	*
Electrical	●	●	●	●	◒	○	○	○
A/C	○	○	○	⊖	⊖	⊖	⊜	⊜
Suspension	◒	○	○	○	⊖	⊖	⊖	⊜
Brakes	●	●	●	●	●	●	○	⊜
Exhaust	●	●	●	⊜	⊜	⊜	⊜	⊜
Body rust	●	●	◒	⊖	⊜	⊜	⊜	⊜
Paint/trim	●	●	●	○	○	⊖	⊖	⊖
Integrity	●	◒	●	◒	◒	◒	○	○
Hardware	◒	◒	◒	◒	◒	◒	○	○

Pontiac Grand Prix

TROUBLE SPOTS	89	90	91	92	93	94	95	96
Engine	◒	◒	◒	⊖	⊖	○	⊜	⊜
Cooling	●	◒	◒	○	⊜	⊖	⊜	⊜
Fuel	●	◒	○	⊖	⊖	⊖	⊜	⊖
Ignition	◒	○	⊖	○	⊖	⊜	⊜	⊜
Auto. trans.	○	◒	⊖	⊖	⊖	○	⊖	⊜
Man. trans.	*	*	*	*	*			
Clutch	*	*	*	*	*			
Electrical	●	●	●	●	●	●	○	○
A/C	◒	◒	○	○	⊖	⊖	⊜	⊜
Suspension	●	◒	○	○	⊖	⊖	⊖	⊜
Brakes	●	●	●	●	●	◒	⊖	⊖
Exhaust	⊖	⊜	⊖	⊜	⊜	⊜	⊜	⊜
Body rust	⊖	⊖	⊜	⊜	⊜	⊜	⊜	⊜
Paint/trim	●	●	◒	○	○	○	○	⊖
Integrity	◒	◒	○	○	◒	◒	◒	◒
Hardware	◒	●	●	◒	●	●	◒	◒

Pontiac Sunbird

TROUBLE SPOTS	89	90	91	92	93	94	95	96
Engine	●	●	○	○	⊖	⊜		
Cooling	●	●	◒	◒	○	○		
Fuel	○	○	⊖	⊖	⊖	○		
Ignition	⊖	○	⊖	⊖	⊜	⊖		
Auto. trans.	⊜	⊜	⊖	⊖	⊖	*		
Man. trans.	*	*	*	*	*	*		
Clutch	*	*	*	*	*	*		
Electrical	●	●	●	●	●	○		
A/C	◒	◒	○	○	⊜	⊜		
Suspension	○	○	○	○	⊖	⊜		
Brakes	●	●	●	●	●	●		
Exhaust	●	●	○	○	⊜	⊖		
Body rust	●	◒	○	○	⊜	⊜		
Paint/trim	◒	◒	◒	○	◒	○		
Integrity	◒	◒	◒	●	●	●		
Hardware	◒	◒	○	●	●	◒		

Pontiac Sunfire

TROUBLE SPOTS	89	90	91	92	93	94	95	96
Engine							⊖	⊜
Cooling							⊜	⊖
Fuel							⊜	⊜
Ignition							⊜	⊜
Auto. trans.							⊜	⊜
Man. trans.							⊖	⊖
Clutch							⊖	⊜
Electrical							○	○
A/C							⊜	⊜
Suspension							⊖	⊖
Brakes							⊖	⊜
Exhaust							⊜	⊜
Body rust							⊜	⊜
Paint/trim							⊖	⊖
Integrity							◒	○
Hardware							○	⊖

Pontiac Trans Sport Van

TROUBLE SPOTS	89	90	91	92	93	94	95	96
Engine		○	⊖	⊖	⊖	⊖	⊜	Insufficient data
Cooling		●	●	●	⊖	⊖	⊜	
Fuel		⊖	⊖	⊖	⊖	⊖	⊖	
Ignition		⊖	⊖	⊖	⊖	⊜	⊜	
Auto. trans.		○	⊖	⊖	○	⊖	⊜	
Man. trans.								
Clutch								
Electrical		●	●	●	●	◒	◒	
A/C		◒	○	○	⊖	⊖	⊜	
Suspension		◒	○	○	○	⊖	⊖	
Brakes		●	●	●	◒	○	⊜	
Exhaust		○	⊜	⊖	⊖	⊜	⊜	
Body rust		⊜	⊜	⊜	⊜	⊜	⊜	
Paint/trim		●	●	⊖	○	○	⊖	
Integrity		●	◒	○	○	◒	◒	
Hardware		●	●	●	●	●	●	

Saab 900

TROUBLE SPOTS	89	90	91	92	93	94	95	96
Engine	◒	○	○	⊖	Insufficient data	○	⊜	Insufficient data
Cooling	●	◒	◒	◒		◒	⊖	
Fuel	◒	○	⊖	⊖		⊖	⊖	
Ignition	○	⊜	⊖	⊖		⊜	⊜	
Auto. trans.	*	*	*	*		⊖	⊜	
Man. trans.	⊖	*	*	*		◒	⊖	
Clutch	⊖	*	*	*		⊖	⊜	
Electrical	●	●	◒	◒		◒	●	
A/C	●	●	◒	⊖		⊖	⊖	
Suspension	◒	○	○	⊖		○	○	
Brakes	◒	◒	○	⊖		○	○	
Exhaust	●	●	○	⊖		⊖	⊜	
Body rust	⊖	○	⊖	⊜		⊜	⊜	
Paint/trim	○	○	⊖	⊖		○	⊜	
Integrity	◒	○	○	○		◒	○	
Hardware	◒	◒	◒	○		◒	●	

Saab 9000

TROUBLE SPOTS	89	90	91	92	93	94	95	96
Engine	◒	Insufficient data	○	○	○	Insufficient data	⊜	Insufficient data
Cooling	●		●	●	◒		○	
Fuel	○		⊖	⊖	○		⊖	
Ignition	⊖		⊖	⊖	○		⊖	
Auto. trans.	*		*	*	*		*	
Man. trans.	*		*	*	*		*	
Clutch	*		*	*	*		*	
Electrical	●		●	●	●		●	
A/C	●		○	⊖	⊖		⊖	
Suspension	⊖		○	⊜	⊜		⊜	
Brakes	●		○	◒	⊖		⊜	
Exhaust	○		◒	⊖	○		⊜	
Body rust	⊖		⊜	⊜	⊜		⊜	
Paint/trim	○		⊖	⊜	⊖		⊖	
Integrity	⊖		⊖	○	○		○	
Hardware	●		●	◒	○		○	

Saturn

TROUBLE SPOTS	89	90	91	92	93	94	95	96
Engine			○	◒	○	⊖	⊜	⊜
Cooling			⊖	⊖	⊖	⊜	⊜	⊜
Fuel			○	⊖	⊜	⊖	⊜	⊜
Ignition			⊜	⊜	⊜	⊜	⊜	⊜
Auto. trans.			○	○	⊖	⊖	⊖	⊜
Man. trans.			⊖	⊜	⊜	⊜	⊖	⊜
Clutch			⊖	⊖	○	⊖	⊜	⊜
Electrical			●	●	◒	○	○	⊖
A/C			⊖	⊖	⊖	⊜	⊜	⊜
Suspension			⊖	⊖	⊜	⊜	⊜	⊜
Brakes			◒	○	◒	○	○	⊜
Exhaust			⊖	⊖	⊜	⊜	⊜	⊜
Body rust			⊖	⊜	⊜	⊜	⊜	⊜
Paint/trim			○	⊖	⊜	⊜	⊜	⊜
Integrity			○	◒	◒	○	◒	⊖
Hardware			●	◒	◒	○	○	⊖

Subaru Impreza

TROUBLE SPOTS	89	90	91	92	93	94	95	96
Engine					⊜	Insufficient data	⊜	⊜
Cooling					⊜		⊜	⊜
Fuel					⊜		⊜	⊜
Ignition					⊜		⊜	⊜
Auto. trans.					⊜		⊜	*
Man. trans.					⊜		⊜	*
Clutch					⊜		⊜	*
Electrical					⊖		⊜	⊜
A/C					⊖		⊜	⊜
Suspension					⊖		⊜	⊜
Brakes					○		⊜	⊜
Exhaust					⊜		⊜	⊜
Body rust					⊜		⊜	⊜
Paint/trim					⊖		⊖	⊜
Integrity					⊖		○	⊖
Hardware					⊖		⊖	⊜

Subaru Legacy, Outback

TROUBLE SPOTS	89	90	91	92	93	94	95	96
Engine		⊖	⊖	⊜	⊜	⊜	⊜	⊜
Cooling		⊖	⊜	⊜	⊜	⊜	⊜	⊜
Fuel		⊖	⊜	⊜	⊜	⊜	⊜	⊜
Ignition		⊜	⊜	⊜	⊜	⊜	⊜	⊜
Auto. trans.		⊖	○	⊜	⊜	⊜	⊜	⊜
Man. trans.		⊜	⊖	⊜	⊜	⊜	⊜	⊜
Clutch		◒	◒	○	⊖	⊖	⊜	⊜
Electrical		○	○	⊖	⊖	⊖	○	⊖
A/C		◒	○	⊖	⊜	⊜	⊜	⊜
Suspension		○	○	⊖	⊖	⊜	⊜	⊜
Brakes		●	◒	◒	○	⊖	⊜	⊜
Exhaust		⊖	⊜	⊜	⊜	⊜	⊜	⊜
Body rust		○	⊖	⊖	⊜	⊜	⊜	⊜
Paint/trim		○	○	○	⊖	⊖	⊜	⊖
Integrity		○	⊖	○	○	⊖	⊖	⊜
Hardware		●	◒	○	○	○	○	⊖

⊜ ⊖ ○ ◒ ●
Few ◄— **Problems** —► Many

* Insufficient data

Key: ● much worse than average; ◒ worse than average; ⊖ average; ⊜ better than average; ○ much better than average; * not available (symbols as printed in the charts)

Subaru, Subaru Loyale

TROUBLE SPOTS	89	90	91	92	93	94	95	96
Engine	●	●	●	●	●			
Cooling	●	◒	○	⊖	⊖			
Fuel	○	⊖	⊖	⊖	○			
Ignition	⊖	○	⊖	⊖	⊖			
Auto. trans.	○	*	*	⊖	*			
Man. trans.	⊖	⊜	⊜	⊜	*			
Clutch	●	●	○	○	*			
Electrical	◒	◒	◒	○	○	Insufficient data		
A/C	◒	◒	⊖	⊜	⊖			
Suspension	○	○	⊖	⊖	⊖			
Brakes	●	◒	○	○	⊖			
Exhaust	●	●	◒	○	⊜			
Body rust	●	●	○	⊖	⊜			
Paint/trim	○	◒	⊜	⊖	○			
Integrity	●	◒	○	○	◒			
Hardware	◒	○	◒	○	○			

Suzuki Sidekick

TROUBLE SPOTS	89	90	91	92	93	94	95	96
Engine		◒	⊖	○	⊖	⊜	⊜	
Cooling		⊖	⊖	⊜	⊜	⊖	⊜	
Fuel		⊖	⊖	⊖	⊜	⊖	⊜	
Ignition		⊖	⊖	○	⊜	○	⊜	
Auto. trans.		*	*	*	*	⊜	⊖	
Man. trans.		*	*	*	⊖	⊜	⊜	
Clutch		*	*	*	⊜	⊜	⊜	
Electrical	Insufficient data	○	○	○	○	◒	○	Insufficient data
A/C		*	*	○	⊖	⊖	○	
Suspension		⊖	⊜	⊖	⊖	⊜	⊜	
Brakes		◒	●	○	○	○	⊖	
Exhaust		●	●	◒	⊖	⊜	⊜	
Body rust		○	○	⊜	⊜	⊜	⊜	
Paint/trim		○	○	⊖	⊖	⊖	⊖	
Integrity		○	○	○	○	◒	◒	
Hardware		●	○	○	◒	○	◒	

Suzuki Swift

TROUBLE SPOTS	89	90	91	92	93	94	95	96
Engine	○	○	⊖	○	⊖	⊖	⊜	
Cooling	○	⊖	⊜	⊜	⊜	⊜	⊜	
Fuel	⊖	○	⊖	⊖	⊖	⊖	⊜	
Ignition	○	⊖	⊖	⊖	⊖	⊖	⊜	
Auto. trans.	*	*	*	⊖	*	*	*	
Man. trans.	*	⊖	⊜	⊜	⊜	⊜	⊜	
Clutch	*	○	⊖	⊖	⊖	⊖	⊖	
Electrical	◒	◒	◒	◒	◒	◒	⊖	Insufficient data
A/C	*	●	○	○	○	○	⊖	
Suspension	◒	⊖	⊖	⊖	⊖	⊖	⊜	
Brakes	●	◒	○	◒	⊖	○	⊖	
Exhaust	●	●	●	◒	⊖	⊖	⊜	
Body rust	⊖	○	⊖	⊖	⊜	⊜	⊜	
Paint/trim	○	○	○	○	⊖	⊖	○	
Integrity	●	●	●	◒	◒	◒	⊖	
Hardware	●	●	●	●	●	◒	◒	

Toyota 4Runner

TROUBLE SPOTS	89	90	91	92	93	94	95	96
Engine	○	◒	◒	◒	⊖	⊜	⊜	⊜
Cooling	○	○	○	○	⊖	⊜	⊜	⊜
Fuel	⊖	⊖	⊜	⊖	⊜	⊜	⊜	⊜
Ignition	⊖	⊜	⊜	⊜	⊜	⊜	⊜	⊜
Auto. trans.	*	⊖	⊜	○	⊖	⊜	⊜	⊜
Man. trans.	⊜	⊖	⊜	⊜	⊖	⊜	⊜	*
Clutch	◒	◒	○	○	⊖	⊜	⊜	*
Electrical	○	◒	◒	○	○	⊖	⊖	○
A/C	⊖	●	◒	⊖	⊖	⊜	⊜	⊜
Suspension	⊖	⊖	⊖	○	⊖	⊖	⊖	⊖
Brakes	○	◒	◒	◒	○	⊖	⊜	⊜
Exhaust	●	○	⊖	⊜	⊜	⊜	⊜	⊜
Body rust	◒	○	⊖	⊜	⊜	⊖	⊜	⊜
Paint/trim	○	⊖	⊖	⊖	⊖	⊖	⊖	⊜
Integrity	⊖	⊖	⊖	⊖	⊖	⊖	⊖	⊜
Hardware	○	○	○	○	⊖	⊖	⊖	⊖

Toyota Avalon

TROUBLE SPOTS	89	90	91	92	93	94	95	96
Engine							⊜	⊜
Cooling							⊜	⊜
Fuel							⊜	⊜
Ignition							⊜	⊜
Auto. trans.							⊜	⊜
Man. trans.								
Clutch								
Electrical							⊖	⊖
A/C							⊜	⊜
Suspension							⊜	⊜
Brakes							⊖	⊜
Exhaust							⊜	⊜
Body rust							⊜	⊜
Paint/trim							⊜	⊜
Integrity							●	○
Hardware							○	⊖

Toyota Camry

TROUBLE SPOTS	89	90	91	92	93	94	95	96
Engine	○	⊖	⊖	⊜	⊜	⊜	⊜	⊜
Cooling	⊖	⊖	⊖	⊜	⊜	⊜	⊜	⊜
Fuel	⊖	⊖	⊜	⊜	⊜	⊜	⊜	⊜
Ignition	⊖	⊖	⊜	⊜	⊜	⊜	⊜	⊜
Auto. trans.	⊖	⊖	⊖	⊜	⊜	⊜	⊜	⊜
Man. trans.	⊖	⊖	⊜	⊜	⊜	⊜	⊜	*
Clutch	○	○	⊖	⊖	⊖	⊜	⊜	*
Electrical	◒	◒	◒	○	○	⊖	⊖	⊖
A/C	⊖	⊖	⊖	○	⊜	⊜	⊜	⊜
Suspension	○	○	⊖	⊖	⊖	⊖	⊖	⊜
Brakes	◒	◒	◒	○	○	⊖	⊖	⊜
Exhaust	●	◒	⊖	⊜	⊜	⊜	⊜	⊜
Body rust	◒	◒	⊖	⊜	⊜	⊜	⊜	⊜
Paint/trim	○	○	⊖	⊖	⊖	⊜	⊜	⊜
Integrity	○	○	⊖	⊖	⊖	⊖	⊖	⊖
Hardware	○	○	○	○	⊖	⊖	⊖	⊜

Toyota Celica

TROUBLE SPOTS	89	90	91	92	93	94	95	96
Engine	○	⊖	⊖	⊜	⊜	⊜	⊜	
Cooling	○	○	⊖	⊜	⊜	⊜	⊜	
Fuel	⊖	⊜	⊜	⊜	⊜	⊜	⊜	
Ignition	⊖	⊜	⊜	⊜	⊜	⊜	⊜	
Auto. trans.	⊖	⊜	⊜	⊜	⊜	⊜	⊜	
Man. trans.	⊖	⊜	⊜	⊜	*	⊜	*	
Clutch	○	○	⊖	⊖	*	⊜	*	
Electrical	◒	◒	◒	○	○	⊖	⊖	Insufficient data
A/C	⊖	●	◒	○	⊖	⊜	⊜	
Suspension	⊖	⊖	⊖	⊖	⊖	⊜	⊜	
Brakes	◒	○	○	⊖	⊖	⊜	⊜	
Exhaust	●	⊖	⊜	⊜	⊜	⊜	⊜	
Body rust	◒	⊜	⊜	⊜	⊜	⊜	⊜	
Paint/trim	◒	○	⊖	⊖	⊖	⊖	⊖	
Integrity	○	○	○	⊖	○	○	○	
Hardware	○	○	○	○	◒	⊜	⊖	

Toyota Corolla

TROUBLE SPOTS	89	90	91	92	93	94	95	96
Engine	○	⊖	⊖	⊖	⊜	⊜	⊜	⊜
Cooling	○	○	○	⊖	⊜	⊜	⊜	⊜
Fuel	⊖	⊜	⊜	⊜	⊜	⊜	⊜	⊜
Ignition	⊖	⊖	⊜	⊜	⊜	⊜	⊜	⊜
Auto. trans.	⊜	⊜	⊖	⊖	⊜	⊜	⊜	⊜
Man. trans.	⊜	⊜	⊜	⊜	⊜	⊜	⊜	*
Clutch	⊖	⊖	⊖	⊖	⊖	⊜	⊜	*
Electrical	◒	◒	●	◒	◒	○	⊖	⊖
A/C	⊖	⊖	⊖	⊖	⊖	⊜	⊜	⊜
Suspension	⊖	⊖	⊖	⊖	⊖	⊜	⊜	⊜
Brakes	●	◒	◒	○	⊖	⊜	⊜	⊜
Exhaust	●	●	●	◒	⊜	⊜	⊜	⊜
Body rust	○	⊖	⊖	⊜	⊜	⊜	⊜	⊜
Paint/trim	○	⊖	⊖	⊖	⊖	⊖	⊜	⊜
Integrity	○	○	○	⊖	○	⊜	⊖	⊜
Hardware	○	◒	◒	◒	◒	○	⊖	⊖

Toyota Cressida

Trouble spots	89	90	91	92	93	94	95	96
Engine	◒	○	○					
Cooling	○	○	◒					
Fuel	⊜	⊜	⊖					
Ignition	⊖	⊖	⊜					
Auto. trans.	⊖	⊜	⊜					
Man. trans.								
Clutch								
Electrical	◒	◒	◒					
A/C	●	●	●					
Suspension	⊖	⊜	⊖					
Brakes	●	◒	◒					
Exhaust	○	⊖	⊖					
Body rust	⊖	⊜	⊜					
Paint/trim	⊖	⊜	⊜					
Integrity	⊖	⊖	⊖					
Hardware	○	⊖	⊖					

92: Insufficient data

Toyota Land Cruiser

Trouble spots	89	90	91	92	93	94	95	96
Engine						⊜	⊜	
Cooling						⊜	⊜	
Fuel						⊜	⊜	
Ignition						⊜	⊜	
Auto. trans.						⊖	⊜	
Man. trans.								
Clutch								
Electrical						○	⊖	
A/C						⊜	⊖	
Suspension						⊜	⊖	
Brakes						●	⊖	
Exhaust						⊜	⊜	
Body rust						⊜	⊜	
Paint/trim						⊖	⊖	
Integrity						◒	○	
Hardware						⊖	⊖	

89, 90, 91, 92, 93, 96: Insufficient data

Toyota Pickup

Trouble spots	89	90	91	92	93	94	95	96
Engine	⊖	○	○	⊖	⊖	⊜		
Cooling	○	○	○	○	⊖	⊜		
Fuel	⊖	⊜	⊜	⊜	⊜	⊜		
Ignition	⊖	⊜	⊜	⊜	⊜	⊜		
Auto. trans.	⊖	⊖	⊖	⊜	⊖	⊖		
Man. trans.	⊖	⊖	⊜	⊜	⊜	⊜		
Clutch	○	⊖	⊖	○	⊖	⊜		
Electrical	○	○	⊖	⊖	⊖	⊖		
A/C	⊖	⊖	⊜	⊜	⊜	⊜		
Suspension	⊖	⊖	⊖	⊖	⊖	⊖		
Brakes	◒	◒	○	○	⊖	⊖		
Exhaust	◒	○	⊖	⊜	⊜	⊜		
Body rust	○	⊖	⊖	⊜	⊜	⊜		
Paint/trim	○	⊖	⊖	⊜	⊖	⊖		
Integrity	⊖	⊖	⊖	⊖	⊖	○		
Hardware	⊖	⊖	⊖	⊖	⊖	⊖		

Toyota Previa Van

Trouble spots	89	90	91	92	93	94	95	96
Engine			⊜	⊜	⊜	⊜	⊜	
Cooling			⊜	⊜	⊜	⊜	⊖	
Fuel			⊜	⊜	⊜	⊜	⊜	
Ignition			⊖	⊜	⊜	⊜	⊜	
Auto. trans.			⊜	⊜	⊜	⊖	⊜	
Man. trans.			*	*	*			
Clutch			*	*	*			
Electrical			●	◒	⊖	○	⊖	
A/C			●	◒	⊖	○	⊜	
Suspension			⊖	⊖	⊖	⊖	⊖	
Brakes			◒	◒	○	○	⊖	
Exhaust			⊜	⊜	⊜	⊜	⊜	
Body rust			⊜	⊜	⊜	⊜	⊜	
Paint/trim			⊖	⊜	⊜	⊖	⊜	
Integrity			○	⊖	⊖	⊖	⊖	
Hardware			◒	○	○	○	⊖	

96: Insufficient data

Toyota RAV4

Trouble spots	89	90	91	92	93	94	95	96
Engine								⊜
Cooling								⊜
Fuel								⊜
Ignition								⊜
Auto. trans.								*
Man. trans.								*
Clutch								*
Electrical								⊜
A/C								⊜
Suspension								⊜
Brakes								⊜
Exhaust								⊜
Body rust								⊜
Paint/trim								⊜
Integrity								⊜
Hardware								⊜

Toyota T100 Pickup

Trouble spots	89	90	91	92	93	94	95	96
Engine					⊖	⊜	⊜	⊜
Cooling					⊜	⊜	⊜	⊜
Fuel					⊜	⊜	⊜	⊜
Ignition					⊖	⊜	⊜	⊜
Auto. trans.					*	*	⊖	*
Man. trans.					⊜	*	⊜	*
Clutch					⊖	*	⊜	*
Electrical					⊖	○	⊖	⊜
A/C					⊜	*	⊜	⊜
Suspension					○	○	⊖	⊜
Brakes					⊖	⊜	⊖	⊜
Exhaust					⊜	⊜	⊜	⊜
Body rust					⊜	⊜	⊜	⊜
Paint/trim					⊖	○	⊜	⊜
Integrity					○	○	○	⊜
Hardware					○	○	○	⊖

Toyota Tacoma Pickup (2WD)

Trouble spots	89	90	91	92	93	94	95	96
Engine							⊜	⊜
Cooling							⊜	⊜
Fuel							⊜	⊜
Ignition							⊜	⊜
Auto. trans.							⊜	*
Man. trans.							⊜	*
Clutch							⊜	*
Electrical							⊖	⊖
A/C							⊜	*
Suspension							⊖	⊖
Brakes							⊖	⊖
Exhaust							⊜	⊜
Body rust							⊜	⊜
Paint/trim							⊜	⊜
Integrity							●	⊖
Hardware							◒	⊜

Toyota Tercel

Trouble spots	89	90	91	92	93	94	95	96
Engine	◒	◒	⊖	⊖	⊜	⊜	⊜	
Cooling	○	○	○	⊖	⊜	⊜	⊜	
Fuel	◒	●	⊜	⊜	⊜	⊜	⊜	
Ignition	○	○	⊜	⊜	⊜	⊜	⊜	
Auto. trans.	⊖	⊖	⊜	⊜	*	⊜	⊖	
Man. trans.	⊜	⊜	⊜	⊜	⊜	⊜	*	
Clutch	⊖	⊖	⊜	⊜	⊜	⊜	*	
Electrical	◒	◒	○	○	⊖	⊖	○	
A/C	○	⊖	○	○	⊖	⊜	⊜	
Suspension	⊖	⊖	⊜	⊜	⊜	⊜	⊖	
Brakes	●	●	○	○	⊖	⊖	⊜	
Exhaust	●	●	⊖	⊜	⊖	⊜	⊜	
Body rust	◒	○	⊜	⊖	⊜	⊜	⊜	
Paint/trim	○	○	⊖	○	⊜	⊖	⊜	
Integrity	◒	○	⊖	○	⊖	○	◒	
Hardware	○	○	⊜	○	⊖	○	○	

96: Insufficient data

⊜ ⊖ ○ ◒ ●
Few ← **Problems** → Many

*
Insufficient data

Volkswagen Golf, GTI, Golf III 4

TROUBLE SPOTS	89	90	91	92	93	94	95	96
Engine	◒					⊜	⊜	⊖
Cooling	●					⊖	⊜	⊜
Fuel	◒					⊖	⊖	⊜
Ignition	○					⊜	⊖	⊖
Auto. trans.	*					⊜	○	*
Man. trans.	⊜					⊜	⊜	*
Clutch	◒	Insufficient data	Insufficient data	Insufficient data	Insufficient data	⊜	⊜	*
Electrical	●					●	●	○
A/C	●					○	⊖	⊖
Suspension	○					⊖	⊖	⊜
Brakes	●					⊖	⊖	⊖
Exhaust	●					⊜	⊜	⊜
Body rust	◒					⊜	⊜	⊜
Paint/trim	◒					○	⊖	⊖
Integrity	●					◒	○	⊖
Hardware	●					●	●	◒

Volkswagen Jetta, Jetta III 4

TROUBLE SPOTS	89	90	91	92	93	94	95	96
Engine	○	○	○	○		⊜	⊜	⊖
Cooling	●	●	◒	○		⊖	⊜	⊜
Fuel	○	○	◒	◒		⊖	⊖	⊜
Ignition	○	○	○	○		⊜	⊖	⊖
Auto. trans.	*	*	*	*		⊜	○	*
Man. trans.	○	○	⊜	*		⊜	⊜	*
Clutch	◒	○	⊖	*	Insufficient data	⊜	⊜	*
Electrical	●	●	●	●		●	●	○
A/C	◒	◒	◒	○		○	⊖	⊖
Suspension	○	◒	◒	○		⊖	⊖	⊜
Brakes	◒	◒	○	○		⊖	⊖	⊖
Exhaust	●	●	○	○		⊜	⊜	⊜
Body rust	○	⊖	⊖	⊖		⊜	⊜	⊜
Paint/trim	◒	◒	○	◒		○	⊖	⊖
Integrity	◒	●	◒	●		◒	○	⊖
Hardware	●	●	●	●		●	●	◒

Volkswagen Passat

TROUBLE SPOTS	89	90	91	92	93	94	95	96
Engine		◒					⊜	
Cooling		○					⊜	
Fuel		○					⊖	
Ignition		○					⊖	
Auto. trans.		*					*	
Man. trans.		*					⊖	
Clutch		*	Insufficient data	Insufficient data	Insufficient data	Insufficient data	⊜	Insufficient data
Electrical		●					◒	
A/C		◒					⊖	
Suspension		◒					⊜	
Brakes		◒					⊖	
Exhaust		●					⊜	
Body rust		⊜					⊜	
Paint/trim		⊖					⊜	
Integrity		⊖					○	
Hardware		●					○	

Volvo 240 Series

TROUBLE SPOTS	89	90	91	92	93	94	95	96
Engine	⊖	⊖	⊖	⊜	⊜			
Cooling	◒	○	○	○	○			
Fuel	○	⊖	○	○	⊖			
Ignition	⊖	⊖	○	⊖	○			
Auto. trans.	○	⊖	⊖	⊖	⊖			
Man. trans.	*	*	*	*	*			
Clutch	*	*	*	*	*			
Electrical	●	●	●	◒	●			
A/C	●	◒	○	⊖	○			
Suspension	○	⊖	⊖	⊖	⊜			
Brakes	●	●	●	●	●			
Exhaust	●	◒	○	◒	⊖			
Body rust	⊜	⊜	⊜	⊜	⊜			
Paint/trim	⊖	○	⊖	⊖	⊖			
Integrity	○	○	○	○	○			
Hardware	○	◒	○	○	◒			

Volvo 740 Series

TROUBLE SPOTS	89	90	91	92	93	94	95	96
Engine	○	○	⊖	⊖				
Cooling	○	⊖	○	◒				
Fuel	◒	○	○	⊖				
Ignition	○	⊖	⊖	⊖				
Auto. trans.	⊖	⊜	⊖	⊖				
Man. trans.	*	*	*					
Clutch	*	*	*					
Electrical	●	◒	●	◒				
A/C	◒	○	○	⊖				
Suspension	⊖	○	○	⊖				
Brakes	●	●	◒	◒				
Exhaust	◒	◒	○	⊖				
Body rust	⊜	⊜	⊜	⊜				
Paint/trim	⊖	⊖	⊖	○				
Integrity	◒	○	⊖	⊖				
Hardware	◒	◒	◒	◒				

Volvo 850 Series

TROUBLE SPOTS	89	90	91	92	93	94	95	96
Engine					⊖	⊜	⊜	⊜
Cooling					⊜	⊜	⊜	⊜
Fuel					⊖	⊖	⊜	⊜
Ignition					⊜	⊜	⊜	⊖
Auto. trans.					⊖	⊜	○	⊜
Man. trans.					⊖	⊜	⊜	*
Clutch					○	⊖	⊜	*
Electrical					◒	◒	○	⊖
A/C					○	⊖	⊜	⊜
Suspension					⊖	⊜	⊜	⊜
Brakes					⊖	⊖	⊜	⊜
Exhaust					⊜	⊜	⊜	⊜
Body rust					⊜	⊜	⊜	⊜
Paint/trim					⊖	○	⊖	⊜
Integrity					○	○	⊖	⊖
Hardware					◒	◒	○	⊖

Volvo 940 Series

TROUBLE SPOTS	89	90	91	92	93	94	95	96
Engine			○	⊖	⊜	⊜	⊜	
Cooling			○	◒	○	⊖	⊜	
Fuel			⊖	⊖	⊖	⊜	⊜	
Ignition			⊜	⊜	⊖	⊜	⊜	
Auto. trans.			⊜	⊜	⊖	⊖	○	
Man. trans.								
Clutch								
Electrical			◒	◒	◒	○	○	
A/C			○	⊖	○	⊖	⊖	
Suspension			⊖	⊖	⊖	⊜	⊖	
Brakes			◒	○	○	○	⊖	
Exhaust			⊖	⊜	⊜	⊜	⊜	
Body rust			⊜	⊜	⊜	⊜	⊜	
Paint/trim			⊖	⊜	⊖	⊖	⊖	
Integrity			⊖	⊖	⊖	⊖	○	
Hardware			◒	○	○	○	⊖	

Volvo 960 Series

TROUBLE SPOTS	89	90	91	92	93	94	95	96
Engine						⊜	⊖	⊜
Cooling						⊖	⊜	⊜
Fuel						⊖	⊖	⊜
Ignition						⊖	⊜	⊜
Auto. trans.						⊖	○	⊜
Man. trans.								
Clutch								
Electrical				Insufficient data	Insufficient data	○	⊖	⊖
A/C						⊖	⊖	⊜
Suspension						⊖	◒	⊖
Brakes						○	⊖	⊖
Exhaust						⊜	⊜	⊜
Body rust						⊜	⊜	⊜
Paint/trim						○	○	⊜
Integrity						⊖	○	⊖
Hardware						○	◒	⊖

Car batteries

Buy the size and current rating specified for your car; some "one size fits all" types won't work as well.

Last CR report: October 1997
Ratings: page 317
Expect to pay: $35 to $75

What's available

The two main specifications are group size and cold-cranking amps. The specifications appropriate for your battery should be listed in the owner's manual for your vehicle or in a catalog at an auto-parts store.

Group size. Batteries within a given group have the same dimensions, and the terminals are in the same place (on the top or the side).

CCA (cold-cranking amps). Within each size, manufacturers typically offer batteries that vary in starting power. CCAs are basically a measure of how much current the battery can deliver to the starter motor for at least 30 seconds at 0°F. Car manufacturers typically specify CCA ranges from 500 to 600 amps.

Not every brand is made in every CCA level, so you may need to go a little above the recommended amperage in order to buy the brand you want. Resist any sales pitch to buy a battery with a CCA rating far above the recommended level. The higher rating generally isn't worth the extra money that's sometimes charged.

Maintenance. Batteries are described as maintenance-free or low-maintenance, which requires occasional refills through its plastic caps or covers; how often depends on the climate and the car. Maintenance-free models are sealed, so no refills are required.

Shopping strategy

When shopping for a new battery, get the right size group for your vehicle. The universal-fit batteries in our tests have not performed as well as some batteries with a specific group size.

Look for "fresh" models that are less than six months old. Deciphering the shipping/manufacturing code isn't easy and, sometimes, it isn't accurate. The shipping date may be printed on a sticker or other wrapping or stamped into the plastic case. One system uses a letter for the month ("A" for January) and a number for the year ("7" for 1997).

The longer a model's reserve, the better. Reserve capacity determines how long a battery can power the engine and electrical accessories should the car's charging system fail. In most batteries, it ranges from about one to two hours—the longer the better.

Consider replacing a battery that's more than about four years old if it's having trouble cranking the starter motor. A service center or auto center can recharge the battery, and perform a "load test" to determine if the battery is worth keeping.

Know where to shop. Large auto centers and parts stores, auto dealers, discount stores, and department stores are apt to stock a wider variety of sizes than a garage or service station. And merchandise is more likely to be fresh if business is brisk.

Using the Ratings. We rated the batteries according to cold-cranking performance and reserve capacity. If you can't find a model, call the manufacturer; see page 342.

Ratings *Car batteries*

& Recommendations

The tests behind the Ratings

Overall score is derived from our tests of cold-cranking performance and reserve capacity. **Cranking CCA** gives the manufacturer's specification for the cold-cranking amps a battery can put out; **cranking score** reflects results of our tests of cold-cranking power. **Reserve** tracks how long a car might continue running should its charging system suddenly fail. **Warranty** shows the period during which the manufacturer will replace the battery free of charge if it fails and the overall period during which any reimbursement applies. **Maintenance** categories are low, for models with removable caps (you add water occasionally), and none, for those that claim to be maintenance free. Those marked with an * say they're maintenance free yet have removable caps. **Price** is the estimated average, based on a national survey.

Recommendations

The best choice in group size 24 is the Motorcraft Silver Series BXT-24F ($70). Best in group size 75 are the Eveready 75-550 ($35) and the Delco 60 75-60 ($68), but the Eveready has a poor warranty. If you can't readily find the group size your car requires, look for the dual-terminal universal-fit Delco Freedom 70DT-60 ($62) or the DieHard Gold HeatHandler (Sears) 36180 ($80).

See Buying Guide report, page 317. Last time rated in CONSUMER REPORTS: October 1997.

Overall Ratings

E · VG · G · F · P

Key no.	Brand and model	Price	Overall score (0–100; P F G VG E)	Cranking CCA	Cranking SCORE	Reserve	Warranty REPLACE/OVERALL	Maintenance
	GROUP SIZE 24							
1	**Motorcraft** Silver Series BXT-24F	$70		600 amps	VG	E	24/84 mo.	Low
2	**Delco** 60 24-60	62		550	E	VG	12/60	None
3	**EverStart** (Wal-Mart) 24-5	38		525	E	G	12/60	Low
4	**Eveready** 24-525	35		525	E	G	3/72	None*
5	**Interstate** 24-50	53		460	E	G	18/50	Low
6	**Champion** 24-4	55		500	E	F	18/75	Low
7	**AutoZone** 24-5S	40		460	VG	F	3/60	Low
8	**NAPA** Power 60 6024	45		500	F	G	3/60	Low

Ratings continued

Ratings, continued

Key no.	Brand and model	Price	Overall score (0–100; P F G VG E)	Cranking CCA	Cranking SCORE	Reserve	Warranty REPLACE/OVERALL	Maintenance
	GROUP SIZE 24 *continued*							
9	**Exide** Mega Cell Classic 24-60	$56		525 amps	◒	○	3/60	None*
	GROUP SIZE 75							
10	**Eveready** 75-550	35		550	○	○	3/72	None*
11	**Delco** 60 75-60	68		550	⊖	○	12/60	None
12	**Interstate** Mega-Tron MT-75	74		650	○	○	18/60	Low
13	**EverStart** (Wal-Mart) 75-5	38		525	○	○	12/60	Low
14	**Interstate** 75-50	64		550	◒	○	18/50	Low
	DUAL-TERMINAL							
15	**Delco** Freedom 70DT-60 (26/70)	62		550	⊖	○	12/60	None
16	**DieHard** Gold HeatHandler (Sears) 36180 (26/70)	80		550	○	○	24/84	None
17	**Champion** UF-2 (35/75)	55		650	◒	○	12/72	Low
18	**Exide** Nascar Select 630 70DT-84N (26/70)	75		525	●	○	24/84	None*

Model details

Group size 24

1 Motorcraft Silver Series BXT-24F $70

Long free-replacement period.

2 Delco 60 24-60 $62

We had trouble finding fresh samples. Discontinued, but may still be available. Replacement: 24-6YR.

3 EverStart (Wal-Mart) 24-5 $38

Marked drop in reserve performance during tests. Rated models made by Johnson Controls (most Northern states). Four samples from Calif. made by GNB (also sold in most Southern states except Fla.) performed worse.

4 Eveready 24-525 $35

One of the poorest warranties.

5 Interstate 24-50 $53

6 Champion 24-4 $55

7 Autozone 24-5S $40

One of the poorest warranties. Sold in Southern U.S.

8 NAPA Power 60 6024 $45

Marked drop in reserve performance during tests. One of the poorest warranties.

9 Exide Mega Cell Classic 24-60 $56

Marked drop in reserve performance during tests. One of the poorest warranties. Manufacturer says improved design is being introduced at retail this fall.

Group size 75

10 Eveready 75-550 $35

One of the poorest warranties.

11 Delco 60 75-60 $68

We had trouble finding fresh samples. Discontinued, but may still be available. Replacement: 75-5YR.

12 Interstate Mega-Tron MT-75 $74

Similar dual-terminal model: MT-75DT (four samples tested), with slightly better reserve capacity, similar CCA.

13 EverStart (Wal-Mart) 75-5 $38

Rated models made by Johnson Controls (most Northern states). Four samples from Calif. made by GNB (also sold in most Southern states except Fla.) performed similarly.

14 Interstate 75-50 $64

Dual-terminal

15 Delco Freedom 70DT-60 (26/70) $62

We had trouble finding fresh samples. Discontinued, but may still be available. Replacement: 70DT-6YR, claims 555 CCA.

16 DieHard Gold HeatHandler (Sears) 36180 (26/70) $80

Long free-replacement period. Sold in Southern U.S. Discontinued, but may still be available. Replacement: 37180, made by a different manufacturer.

17 Champion UF-2 (35/75) $55

18 Exide Nascar Select 630 70DT-84N (26/70) $75

Long free-replacement period.

How to use the Ratings in the Buying Guide

- Read the Recommendations for information on specific models and general buying advice.
- Note how the rated products are listed—in order of performance and convenience, price, or alphabetically.
- The overall score graph gives the big picture in performance. Notes on features and performance for individual models are listed in the Comments column or "Model details."
- Use the handy key numbers to find more details about the models.
- Before going to press, we verify model availability for most products with manufacturers. Some tested models listed in the Ratings may no longer be available. Discontinued models are noted in Model details or Comments. Such models may actually still be available in some stores for part of 1998. Models indicated as successors should perform similarly to the tested models, according to the manufacturer. Features may vary.
- Models similar to the tested models, when they exist, are indicated in Comments or Model details.
- To find our last full report on a subject, check the reference above the Ratings chart or the eight-year index, page 346.

Tires

They help determine a car's handling and its safety. Our tests indicate that brands are not good guides to quality.

Last CR reports: All-season car tires, April 1997; Ratings: page 321
Expect to pay: $30 to $140

What's available

All-season tires. Standard equipment on most sedans, they're designed to perform reasonably well—but not to excel—in most conditions.

Performance tires. These are made to endure aggressive, high-speed driving. They tend to provide superior grip, although at the expense of tread life. This type also tends to ride harshly and noisily.

Light-truck tires. These have the letters LT, instead of P, preceding the size designation. They are biased toward general road use, off-road driving, or a combination of the two.

Snow tires. They're the best in heavy snow. But their sharp-edged, widely spaced tread blocks may make them noisy and skittish on dry pavement. Use them only during winter months.

Decoding a tire

The cryptic letters and numbers on a tire's sidewall conceal a wealth of information. A multipart designation like "P185/70R14" is typical. Here's what the codes mean.

Size. The P signifies a passenger-car tire. The next three digits are the tire's cross-section width in millimeters: 185 mm. Then comes the "aspect ratio"—the ratio of sidewall height to cross-section. The 70 means the sidewall height is 70 percent—about 130 mm in a tire 185 mm wide. The R means a radial tire (virtually the only design sold today). The next two digits represent the diameter of the wheel on which the tire fits, in inches.

Load index and speed rating. A three-figure code like "87S" is typical. The 87 is a numerical code associated with the maximum load a tire can carry. The speed rating, S, may follow the tire size, or may precede the R ("185/70SR14"). It specifies the top speed the tire can sustain.

Shopping strategy

Shop around. Sales are common in the competitive tire business. But a tire's list price is often inflated to begin with, so $25 off isn't necesarily a bargain.

Here are where tires are sold:

Tire dealers. Over half of all buyers shop at tire dealers, which offer a wide selection of brands and sizes.

Service stations. Your local garage will probably be very accommodating if you're a regular customer. But it may offer limited stock.

Department stores, warehouse clubs, and auto-parts stores. The quality and selection vary at chain stores such as Costco, Sam's Club, and Sears. If you find premium name-brand tires at such outlets, compare prices at other dealers.

Mail-order houses. These outlets generally offer the lowest prices and a very wide selection. Delivery generally takes only a few days, and you can have the tires shipped directly to your garage.

Using the Ratings. We test tires at our Auto Test Center in Connecticut, most recently all-season tires. If you can't find a model, call the manufacturer: see page 342.

Ratings *All-season tires*

& Recommendations

The tests behind the Ratings

We tested size P185/70R14, logical replacements for the standard tires on most new sedans, wagons, and minivans. The results should be broadly applicable to similar 15-inch, 70-series tires. The Pirelli P400 Touring has a T speed rating; the others, S. All have an A traction rating and a B temperature rating. We tested each tire in sets of four. **Prices** are approximate retail.

Recommendations

Where snow is infrequent, look for an all-season tire with at least a very good overall score in wet and dry conditions—the Pirelli P400 Touring, Dunlop SP40 A/S, Goodyear Regatta, or Cooper Lifeliner Classic II. For regions with occasional but serious snow, select an all-season tire with a very good score in snow—the Cooper Lifeliner Classic II, General Ameri G4S, Michelin XW4, or Goodyear WeatherHandler. In the Snow Belt, you generally need snow tires.

See Buying Guide report, page 320. Last time rated in CONSUMER REPORTS: February 1997.

Overall Ratings

E VG G F P

Listed by group; within groups, listed in order of overall score

Key no.	Brand and model	Price	Wet and dry overall score (0–100; P F G VG E)	Snow traction	Braking DRY/WET	Cornering DRY/WET	Emergency handling
1	**Pirelli** P400 Touring	$70		P	E/E	E/G	E
2	**Dunlop** SP40 A/S	66		F	VG/VG	VG/F	E
3	**Goodyear** Regatta	79		F	VG/VG	G/F	VG
4	**Cooper** Lifeliner Classic II	60		VG	VG/VG	G/P	G
5	**Kelly-Springfield** Navigator 800S	60		F	VG/VG	G/F	VG
6	**General** Ameri G4S	55		VG	G/G	G/F	VG
7	**Michelin** XW4	76		VG	G/G	VG/F	VG
8	**Goodyear** WeatherHandler	60		VG	VG/G	VG/P	VG
9	**BF Goodrich** The Advantage	60		G	VG/VG	G/F	VG

Ratings continued ▸

Ratings, continued

Model details

Notes on the details: Braking distance is the average for stopping on dry pavement from 60 mph (the average was 145 ft.), on wet pavement at 40 mph with anti-lock brakes (ABS) (average: 71 ft.) and without (average: 93 ft.).

1 Pirelli P400 Touring $70
Outperformed others in braking, cornering, resistance to hydroplaning. Taut handling. Noisy on coarse pavement. Relatively high rolling resistance. Poor grip in snow when starting off and maintaining speed. Braking: at 60 mph on dry pavement, 137 ft.; at 40 mph on wet pavement with ABS, 66 ft., and without ABS, 89 ft. Treadwear rating: 420.

2 Dunlop SP40 A/S $66
A nicely balanced performer. Brakes well on wet and dry pavement. Corners well on dry pavement. Taut handling. Low rolling resistance. Noisy on coarse pavement. Low grip in soft snow. Very gentle throttle required to move the vehicle in snow. Braking: at 60 mph on dry pavement, 142 ft.; at 40 mph on wet pavement with ABS, 69 ft., and without ABS, 92 feet. Treadwear rating: 420.

3 Goodyear Regatta $79
A tire that emphasizes comfort over handling. Soft ride, quiet on both smooth and coarse pavement. Overall, a good but not outstanding performer. Difficult to start off in snow, poor grip in soft snow. Braking: at 60 mph on dry pavement, 145 ft.; at 40 mph on wet pavement with ABS, 70 ft., and without ABS, 92 ft. Treadwear rating: 460.

4 Cooper Lifeliner Classic II $60
Relatively good braking. Soft and supple ride, quiet on rough roads. Good resistance to hydroplaning, but poor cornering grip on wet pavement, and handling is below par. Confident start-off on level snow. Good bite in soft snow. A good overall compromise. Braking: at 60 mph on dry pavement, 145 ft.; on wet pavement with ABS, 71 ft., and without ABS, 92 feet. Treadwear rating: 480.

5 Kelly-Springfield Navigator 800S $60
A competent tire, overall. Relatively good braking on wet pavement in cars without ABS. Noisy on coarse pavement. Relatively high rolling resistance. Difficult to start off in snow. Fair traction on either hard-packed or soft snow. Braking: at 60 mph on dry pavement, 145 ft.; on wet pavement with ABS, 72 ft., and without ABS, 91 ft. Treadwear rating: 480.

6 General Ameri G4S $55
Soft and supple ride, but longest braking distances. Generally crisp handling, but loses grip rather abruptly. Unusually noisy on coarse pavement. Low rolling resistance. Good on hard-packed snow, bogs down in soft snow. A good overall compromise. Braking: at 60 mph on dry pavement, 149 ft.; at 40 mph on wet pavement with ABS, 74 ft., and without ABS, 97 ft. Treadwear rating: 520.

7 Michelin XW4 $76
Good dry cornering. Long stopping distances on dry pavement and on wet without ABS. Very quiet on smooth pavement, noisy on coarse pavement. Low rolling resistance. Good grip in soft snow, less so in hard-packed snow. A good overall compromise. Braking: at 60 mph on dry pavement, 148 ft.; on wet pavement with ABS, 71 ft., and without ABS, 97 ft. Treadwear rating: 400.

8 Goodyear WeatherHandler $60
A quiet tire. Cornering grip is good on dry pavement, poor on wet pavement. With ABS, wet-pavement stops are a little long. This tire is sold only at Sears. Good grip on hard-packed and soft snow. A good overall compromise. Braking: at 60 mph on dry pavement, 146 ft.; on wet pavement with ABS, 74 ft., and without ABS, 95 ft. Treadwear rating: 460.

9 BF Goodrich The Advantage $60
Overall, an adequate tire, no more. The ride is the harshest in this group, and the cornering grip on both wet and dry pavement is unimpressive. Low rolling resistance. Good grip on packed snow, but bogs down in soft snow. Braking: at 60 mph on dry pavement, 146 ft.; on wet pavement with ABS, 70 ft., and without ABS, 94 ft. Treadwear rating: 440.

PRODUCT RECALLS

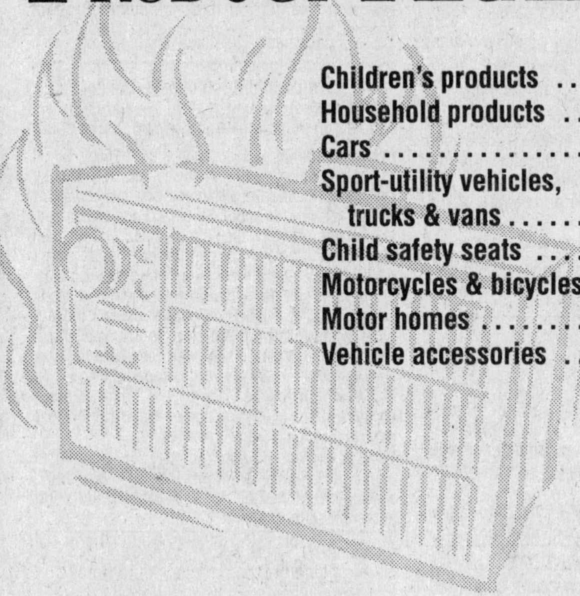

Products ranging from toy trains to snowmobiles are recalled when there are safety defects. Various Federal agencies—the Consumer Product Safety Commission (CPSC), the National Highway Traffic Safety Administration, the U.S. Coast Guard, and the Food and Drug Administration—monitor consumer complaints and, when there's a problem, issue a recall.

However, the odds of your hearing about an unsafe product are slim. Manufacturers are reluctant to issue a recall in the first place because they can be costly. And getting the word out to consumers can be haphazard.

A selection of the most far-reaching recalls appear monthly in CONSUMER REPORTS. The following pages gather together a year's worth of recalls from the November 1996 through October 1997 issues of CONSUMER REPORTS. For the latest information, see the current issue of the magazine or our Web site *(www.ConsumerReports.org)*.

If you wish to report an unsafe product or get recall information, call the CPSC's hotline, 800 638-2772.

Recall notices about your automobile can be obtained from a new-car dealer or by calling the NHTSA hotline at 800 424-9393. Questions about food and drugs are handled by the FDA's Office of Consumer Affairs, 301 443-3170.

You can better assure yourself of getting a recall notice by returning the warranty cards that come with many products.

Children's products

Gerry Deluxe Baby Monitor 602

Improperly wired monitor could cause a fire.

Products: 990,000 monitors sold between June 1988 and May 1990. The two-piece set resembles a pair of walkie-talkies. Embossed on the back of the affected transmitter are the words "GERRY DELUXE BABY MONITOR MODEL 602" and a date code that runs sequentially form 8806 to 9005. The date code may appear in the form of a clock with an arrow pointing to the month the monitor was made and the two digits of the year on either side of the arrow.

What to do: Call 800 672-6289 for how to return the monitor for a free replacement, or write to Gerry Baby Products Co., Attn: Building R-602 Recall, 1500 East 128th Ave., Thornton, Colo. 80241.

Evenflo play yards

Hinges could collapse, trapping a child in the play yard.

Products: 1.2 million Happy Camper, Happy Cabana, and Kiddie Camper play yards. Each play yard folds and comes with a carrying bag and mattress. Look for the word Evenflo and the model name on the top rail.

What to do: Call Evenflo at 800 447-9178 for a free hinge cover that prevents it from collapsing.

Go-karts (various brands)

Long hair or clothing could become entangled in exposed rear axle, causing injury or death.

Products: 127,000 gasoline-powered go-karts sold 8/76-3/97 for $500 to $2500, including: 75,000 go-karts made by Ken-Bar Mfg., Cornelia, Ga., and sold under Mud Hog, Salute to America, Sand Dog, Scorpion, and Streaker brands, models DD7, DD8, D680, D710, D720, D810,D840,S465, SC7,STA8, STA9, and SD11 (call 800 241-3557); 39,000 go-karts made by T&D Metal Prods., Watseka, Ill., and sold under Bird Mfg., Campout, Klipper Karts, Kool Kart, Pathwinder, and Pro-Kart brands, serial numbers EM001 through EM029 and 0030 through 39126 (call 888 465-2780); 7000 go-karts made by Bob's Kart Shop, Seridan, Ill., and sold under Grasshopper, Ground Hawg, and T.C. Go-fur brands, all models (call 815 496-2820 collect); 5000 go-karts made by Carter Brothers Mfg. and sold under Superwheels, Hotbodies, Kartwheels, Master Karts, and Desert Storm brands, model numbers beginning with 17 (call 800 523-5278); 750 go-karts made by Kartco Inc., Sebastopol, Miss., and sold under Kartco and Roadboss brands, model 445 (call 800 350-8739); and 83 go-karts made by Avenger Inc., Monroe, La., and sold under Yellow Jacket brand, model SST (call 318 322-2007 collect).

What to do: Call for free axle-guard kit. For safety, also check any go-kart model not listed above. With engine off, push go-kart from behind. If you see rear axle rotating, call U.S. Consumer Product Safety Commission at number listed below. (Also, see go-kart recall in Sept. 1996 issue, page 55.)

Binky Newborn Orthodontic pacifiers

Nipple can detach from shield and choke child.

Products: 13,000 pacifiers sold 8/94-8/95 by Target Stores and other stores nationwide and 5/95-8/95 by University Hospitals of Oklahoma City, individually or in sets of two, for about $1 each. Pacifier has red, mint-green, blue or white butterfly mouth shield, with star and crescent vent holes on each side. Some white shields have crescent vent holes on each side. Some white shields have crescents, stars, and hearts stenciled on front. Knob on pacifier doesn't move if twisted, and well around knob is 1/4 inch deep. Pacifier came in plastic shell with cardboard backing. label on back of package reads, in part, "Made***in Malaysia***Griptight Malaysia Ltd." English-made pacifiers whose knob moves when twisted and whose well is 3/8 inch deep aren't recalled.

What to do: Return pacifier to store for replacement or mail it to Binky-Griptight, Inc., P.O. Box 3307, Wallington, N.J. 07057 for replacement and reimbursement of postage.

Ohio Art Splash Off Water Rocket

During filling process, rocket could break into flying pieces that might injure bystanders.

Products: 67,800 toys sold 4/97-6/97 for $20. Rocket is made of red, yellow, and clear plastic. It measures 16 in. high and sits atop 18-in.-high launch pad. Words "Splash Off" appear on side of toy. To launch device, water from garden hose is fed through tube into launch pad. When filled, launch ring is depressed to execute liftoff.

What to do: Return to store for refund. For more information, call Ohio Art Co. at 800 641-6226.

Cosco metal cribs

Mattress platform may have been installed as side rail with wide-spaced slats that could trap a child's head.

Products: 390,000 full-size tubular metal cribs on wheels made since 1/95 and sold for $90 to $150, including the following models: 10T01 (red, white or blue); 10T04 (red or white); 10T05 (red or white); 10T06 (multiple colors); 10T08 (white and brass); 10T14 (white); 10T84 (multiple colors); 10T85 (white);10T94 (white); 10T95 (white and brass) 10M06 (multiple colors); 10M84 (multiple colors); 10M85 (white); and 10M94 (white). Affected models bear date code of 0195 (Jan. 1995) or newer, which appears on sticker on bottom of an end panel. Hazard exists because slats are spaced more than 2 3/8 in. apart, a violation of Federal Safety Standard. Such spacing could allow an infant's head, but not the body, to slip through leading to strangulation.

What to do: Inspect crib for misassembly by trying to pass a soda can through slats on side rail. If can passes through, stop using crib immediately and call Cosco at 800 221-6736 to arrange for free in-home repair. Alternatively, Cosco will provide instructions for proper do-it-yourself reassembly. Company is offering owners gift to encourage repair.

Klutz "Chinese Jump Rope" sold with activity book of same name

Metal fasteners that join elasticized ropes could come off, causing rope to snap back and, possibly, injure bystanders.

Products: 132,000 jump ropes, packaged with the 66,000 copies activity book by Anne Akers Johnson, sold since 3/97 through Klutz Catalog and by stores nationwide for $11. Each book comes with two elastic ropes, one short, one long. "Chinese Jump Rope" is colorful illustrated children's book that describes how to play variations of the popular jump rope game, including "Doubles," "American Ropes," Crazy Rope," and "Toothpicks."

What to do: Call Klutz collect at 415 857-0888 for free replacement ropes. Consumers can make the repair by cutting rope ends, removing metal crimps, and tying the ends together with square knot.

Century TraveLite Sport strollers

Restraint buckle could unlatch or stroller could fold suddenly and allow child to fall out.

Products: 166,000 strollers, models 11-171, 11-181, and 11-191, made 2/95-10/95 and sold for $60 to $80. Model number and date of manufacture are on stroller's side tubing.

What to do: Call 800 944-0039 for free repair kit and installation instructions.

Cosco Quiet Time wind-up infant swings

Seat could fall off and injure child.

Products: 355,500 swings, models 08-975 and 08-977, made 2/1/93 to 9/30/95 and sold for $45 to $49. Label under seat lists model number and date-of-manufacture code. Recalled swings have date codes 0593 (fifth week of '93) through 4095. Swing consists of four tubular white metal legs supporting plastic swing seat, which has vinyl or fabric cover. Seat can be set in two positions. Fully wound, swing operates for about 30 minutes. "Cosco Quiet Time" is printed on label on top of swing.

What to do: Call 800 221-6736 for free repair kit and installation.

ProCourt portable "basketball system" (backboard, rim, pole, and base)

Water, which adds weight to base, could leak out and allow set to fall.

Products: 29,800 portable basketball systems designed for residential use and sold 1/97-4/97 in department, discount, and sporting goods stores for $99. System consists of 3-inch-thick telescoping metal pole, 44-inch acrylic backboard, black metal rim with white net, and 26-gallon black polyethylene base on wheels. Numeral 4 is on bottom of base. Date code 970101 to 970873 is stamped on bottom of horizontal plate that attaches rim to pole.

What to do: Call 800 225-3865 for replacement base and installation instructions. Company will also provide free net. (Or, if you move system only occasionally, you can fill base with sand. When filled with sand, base does not leak.)

"Starfish" children's inflatable swimming vest

Buckles could unlatch and allow child to sink.

Products: 5000 vests sold 5/96-3/97 for about $14. Plastic vest has blue inner lining and collar, and yellow-and-pink body secured by two plastic buckles in front. "Starfish" logo and name appear on front of vest and on buckles. Vest came in sizes A to D, for children between one and eight years old.

What to do: Return vest to store for refund.

Carter's infant carrier

Adjustable shoulder strap could come loose and allow infant to fall out.

Products: 5400 infant carriers, style 89000, sold since 6/96 for about $30. Carrier is made of light blue quilted fabric with waist belt, padded shoulder strap, zippered leg openings with padding, and padded back and head supports. Padded fabric is light blue, white, green, and pink. Waist belt and shoulder strap are white nylon webbing with white stitching. "Carter's" brand label is sewn into seam. Carrier came in cardboard package labeled, in part, "Carter's Infant Carrier . . . 0-24 mos." Style number is on bottom of box. Infant carriers bearing style number 89200 (with black stitching at ends of shoulder strap, which are threaded through buckles) aren't being recalled.

What to do: Call 800 942-9442 for free replacement.

For the latest recalls See the monthly issues of CONSUMER REPORTS magazine or our Web site *(www.ConsumerReports.org)*.

Kid's Phone Beeper Combo toy

Antenna and pieces of plastic from around base could break off and choke child.

Products: 73,300 toys distributed 8/96-9/96 at Dollar General stores in Central U.S. for $5. Toy consists of plastic cellular phone and beeper. Telephone is yellow and white with red plastic flip-down bottom and blue trim. It measures 6 inches high and 2 1/2 inches wide. Beeper is white with yellow, red, and blue trim, and measures 2 1/2 inches high and 3 1/2 inches wide. Pushing buttons on either component causes flashing lights and telephone or beeper sounds. Cardboard box packaging says, in part: "KID'S PHONE BEEPER COMBO . . . ITEM NO. 63305/7-S."

What to do: Return toy to store for refund.

Toy water baton given as premium with kids' meals at Dairy Queen restaurants

If child chews on baton, cap could come off and release plastic balls. Cap and balls could choke child.

Products: 150,000 toys distributed 6/96-10/96. Baton is 9-inch water-filled clear plastic rod containing glitter and blue, purple, and green balls. Each end of toy has purple cap, and "Dairy Queen" is printed on rod.

What to do: Return toy to any Dairy Queen store for free kids' meal or ice cream sundae.

Children's novelty paperweights and pens

Contain kerosene or other petroleum products that are flammable and hazardous if swallowed or inhaled.

Products: 40,000 sets sold 10/96-12/96 through schools to children from kindergarten to sixth grade for $4 to $5. Plastic paperweights came in five styles: Ocean in the Box, Floating Eye, Antique Car, Magic Diamond, and Water Timer. Style name appears on cardboard box. Clear plastic pen, with eyeball in middle, came wrapped in cellophane without label.

What to do: Call 800 829-2647 for refund.

Felix the Cat "roller fun balls" distributed with kids' meals at Wendy's restaurants

Seams could open and release small toy fish, which could choke small child.

Products: 800,000 toys distributed 2/10/97-3/4/97. Clear plastic ball is 2 1/2 inches in diameter and contains four small plastic fish 5/8-inch long; fish are red, yellow, purple, and green. Toy came in plastic bag labeled, in part, "FELIX THE CAT. . . ROLLER FUN BALL. . . WENDY' S KIDS' MEAL."

What to do: Return to Wendy's for free replacement.

Playskool 1-2-3 high chair

Restraint bar could break off and allow unbelted child to fall out.

Products: 287,000 high chairs made 5/95-5/96 and bearing serial numbers TX 51321 through TX 61442. Number is on label on high-chair's seatback. Chair sold for about $65. Restraint bar, which holds tray in place, is at center front of seat.

What to do: Call 800 555-0428 for replacement restraint bar.

Tonka Soft Walkin' Wheels toy vehicles

Wheel hubs could come off axle and choke child.

Products: More than 1 million battery-powered toy vehicles, model 90165, sold since 1/94 for about $15. Toys are designed to move across floor in home. They are covered in brightly colored nylon fabric and come in five styles: dump truck, school bus, airplane, train, and fire truck. Affected toys have serial number 9527 or lower, or have no visible number at all; serial numbers are printed in blue ink on sewn-in label that lists cleaning instructions, brand name, and model number. Soft Walkin' Wheels dalmation, dinosaur, pig, "tugger," "Soft Squeeze 'n Shine," and "Soft Shakin' Wheels" are not recalled. Nor are toys with serial number higher than 9527.

What to do: Call 800 524-8107 for replacement toy, or return toy to store for refund or replacement.

Cabbage Patch Kids Snacktime Kids doll

When doll simulates chewing action, child's hair or finger could get caught in doll's mouth.

Products: 500,000 dolls sold since last fall. (Chewing action can be stopped by removing doll's battery pack.)

What to do: Return doll to Mattel Distribution Center, 14310 Ramona Ave., Chino, Calif., 91710, for $40 refund.

K-Line electric model trains

If train derails, coupler coil spring could overheat and create fire hazard.

Products: 20,000 "The Heavyweight" trains sold since late '91 at hobby and specialty stores for $75 to $125 per car. Trains include early-1900s coach, pullman, baggage, railway post office, diner, and observation cars in 1:48 scale, running on three-rail O-gauge track. All came individually boxed and include label listing the model name and number. Recalled models include: Baltimore and Ohio Railroad, car numbers K10-0004 and K10-0045;

Erie-Lackawanna Railroad six-car set (K-44251), car numbers K25-0001, K25-0002, K25-0098, K25-0316, K-25-0469, K-25-1813; Ringling Bros. and Barnum & Bailey, K83-0072, K83-0073, K83-0080, K83-0093, K83-0094, K83-0095, and K83-0096; Southern railroad, K86-0004 and K86-0042; Southern Pacific Railroad, K88-0112, K88-1918, and K88-5124; Union Pacific Railroad 6-car set (K-44911), K91-0100, K91-0101, K91-0102, K91-0103, K91-0104, and K91-0107. Additional trains were sold only at these outlets: Chesapeake & Ohio Railroad 6-car set (K-44151), car numbers K15-0110, K15-0385, K15-0727, K15-0827, K15-0972, and K15-2500 (sold by K-Line Collectors Club, Chapel Hill, N.C.); Lackawanna Railroad 6-car set (K-44381), K38-0001 through K38-0004, K38-0465, and K38-1812 (sold by The Train Station, Mountain Lakes, N.J.); Toy Train Museum cars, K85-1870, K85-1877, K85-1884, K85-1896, and K85-1899 (sold by Toy Train Museum, Strasburg, Pa.); Texas & Pacific Railroad 6-car set (K-44891), K89-0718, K89-1018, K89-1109, K89-1402, K89-1658, and K89-1818 (sold by Collectible Trains & Toys, Dallas); Pasadena Mutual Funds car, K99-1986 (sold by Pasadena Group of Mutual Funds, Greenwich, Conn.)

What to do: Call 800 866-9986 for repairs.

Evenflo Houdini portable play yard

Metal push caps (small metal washers) that connect components have small plastic covers that could break off and choke child. Also, exposed edges of push caps could cut child.

Products: 205,000 play yards sold '94-96 for $45. All Evenflo Houdini play yards whose model number begins with 332 are subject to recall; model number is on tag on bottom of play yard.

What to do: Inspect top rail. If plastic covers are loose, cracked, or missing, call 800 490-7549 and ask for free replacements and installation instructions. (Each play yard has 16 push caps and covers: three in each corner of top rails, and one in center of each top rail.) Even if plastic covers are intact, call for warning label to affix to play yard.

Speidel "My First ID" bracelet

Could choke small child.

Products: 211,000 gold- or silver-colored bracelets sold 6/95-12/96 at Cole Gift Centers, Hills, JC Penney, Meijer, Wal-Mart, and other department, discount, and jewelry stores for $11-$16. Cardboard gift box, shaped like wooden alphabet block, is labeled "MY FIRST ID by Speidel." Label on bracelet warns that product is not intended for children under age three—but label isn't visible at store. Some bracelets were also labeled ". . . Specially sized for little ones . . . Perfect for commemorative first occasions like . . . First Birthdays . . . First Words . . . First Steps . . . ." Bracelets, which are suitable for engraving, are 5 1/2 inches long and come in eight styles: model 2350—metal chain of small simulated pearls with heart-shaped charm; models 2351 through 2354—metal chain with thin curved plate (for engraving), with attached heart, cross, or bear charm; models 2355, 2589, and 2590— metal chain with thin curved plate. Model 2355 has heart-shaped cutout on plate. (Model number is on box.)

What to do: If child is less than three years old, return bracelet to store for refund.

All Our Kids portable playpens

Could collapse and strangle child in V formed by folding top rail.

Products: 13,000 playpens, models 741, 742, and 761, sold '92-95. Playpen comes in various colors, shapes (rectangular and square), and sizes. Some have detachable toy bag on one end. "All Our Kids" appears on two of four top rails.

What to do: Destroy playpen to prevent use. Since maker is out of business, refund is unavailable.

Baby Buzz stretchable crib mobile

If strung across crib or playpen, could strangle small child. Lacks required warning label.

Products: More than 26,000 mobiles sold 12/95-12/96 at Dollar Value and other discount stores for about $1. Toy consists of four 1 1/2-inch plastic balls and plastic animal figures strung on elastic, with white hook at either end for securing mobile to stroller, carriage, swing, or infant seat. Balls and figures come in various colors. Some plastic items are imprinted with word "China." Toy came in clear plastic bag with multicolored carboard top labeled, "Baby Buzz Baby Stretch Mobile." Picture of bee holding rattle appears on cardboard.

What to do: Return mobile to store for refund.

Century Fold-N-Go Travel Playard portable playpens.

Could collapse and strangle child in V formed by folded top rail.

Products: 212,000 portable playpens, models 10-710 and 10-810. Model number appears on label on floor or on one of support tubes under floor. Model 10-710, measuring 26 x 38 inches, was sold at Toys 'R' Us from 6/94 for $50. Model 10-810, measuring 28 x 41 inches, was sold at juvenile-product and discount stores from 2/93 for $80. Both models fold compactly and fit into nylon carrying case. Other Fold-N-Go models have different top rails and are not subject to recall.

What to do: Call 800 541-0264 for repair kit and installation instructions.

Various wooden bunk beds

Top bunk has openings that pose strangulation hazard. Spaces are large enough for child's body to pass through, but narrow enough to entrap head.

Products: 100,000 bunk beds made by following companies: Bedder Bunk Co. of Winlock, Wash. (both beds are twin sized), sold '84-92 in Northern Calif., Ore., and Wash.; Oakland Wood Shop Mfg. of Oakland, Calif. (phone: 510 536-4014), (both twin sized), sold 9/94-10/96 in Calif., Ore., and Wash.; P.J. Sleep Shop of Portland, Ore. (503 232-5222), (twin and double sized), sold '81-10/96 in Portland; Stoney Creek of Redmond, Wash. (both twin sized), sold '80-93 in Ore. and Wash.; and Wholesale Importers and Exporters of Los Angeles (213 563-3346), models 1040 Deluxe and 1051 Clover (both twin sized), sold '84-3/96 in Calif., Ore., and Wash. To be safe, all bunk beds should have guard rails on both sides of top bunk. in addition, all spaces between guard rail and bed frame and in headboard and footboard should be less than 3 1/2 inches.

What to do: Call manufacturer or retailer for free replacement guard rail, retrofit kit, or instructions to help eliminate hazard. (Bedder Bunk Co. and Stoney Creek are out of business; do not let small children use their bunk beds.) If you are unsure of manufacturer or have other questions, call Consumer Product Safety Commission, 800 638-2772. Additional safe-guard: Don't let children under age six sleep in top bunk.

Exploring Nature Funstation science-activity book kit

Compass could leak fluid containing kerosene, which is hazardous if swallowed or inhaled.

Products: 34,000 kits sold 3/96-8/96 for $13-$22. Kit, intended for ages 8 and older, contains book with science projects, magnifying glass, petri dish, crayons, tweezer, test tube, thermometer, and stickers.

What to do: Call 800 454-1625 to exchange kit.

Radio Flyer Little Wood Wagon

Red paint contains excessive lead, toxic if child swallows paint chips.

Products: 14,000 toy wagons sold 6/96-9/96 for $20-$25. Wagon has metal pull handle and body measures 12 1/2 x 7 1/2 x 4 inches. Black plastic wheels are 3 inches high and 1 inch thick.

What to do: If bottom of wagon has no decal (with date of manufacture), return wagon to store for refund or call 800 621-7613 for replacement.

Graco playpen

Mesh netting could unravel at seam and strangle child.

Products: 133,000 playpens sold in juvenile-products and discount stores for $35-$55. Drop-side playpen has vinyl-covered top rails and pad. Recalled units bear date-of-manufacture codes 111395 (Nov. 13, 1995) to 091296 (Sept. 12, 1996). Date-code is first six digits of serial number, listed on floor label under pad (see arrow).

What to do: Call 800 423-9078 for free repair kit and instructions. Discontinue use if netting has started to unravel.

Cooper catcher's helmet with faceguard

If wire faceguard is adjusted too low, ball could pass through and cause serious facial or head injuries.

Products: 8400 helmets sold 10/95-5/96 for $35. Helmets are red, navy, royal, or black, with "Cooper - Made in Canada - CL87" printed on both sides. Back of helmet has white warning label next to words, "Little League Approved - CL87."

What to do: Detach faceguard and return it to store for free replacement.

Gerber Flip Fingers rattle

Small parts could spill out and choke child.

Products: 60,000 rattles with red U-shaped handle marked "Gerber," sold 5/96-10/96 for about $1.40. Rattle is 5 1/4 inches long, 2 1/2 inches wide. Rattles with green handle are not being recalled.

What to do: Call 800 443-7237 for instructions on returning rattle to company for refund.

Household products

Halogen lamps

Heat from bulbs could cause nearby materials to burn.

Products: 40 million halogen floor lamps sold without a wire or glass guard over the bulb shield.

What to do: Free wire guard and instructions are available at Ames, B.J.'s Wholesale Club, Hechingers/Home Quarters, Home Base, Home Depot, Ikea, Kmart, Lowes, Montgomery Ward, Office Depot, Target, and Wal-Mart. Call 800 985-2220 if you can't get to a store.

Pfaltzgraff pizza stones

Oiling stone and later cleaning at high heat, per instructions, could cause fire.

Products: 123,500 unglazed clay pizza stones sold since '93 and deep-dish pizza stones sold since '95 for about $20. Regular pizza stone is flat disk about ½ in. thick and 13 in. wide. Floral design and "Pfaltzgraff USA" and "Baking Stone" are molded into bottom.

What to do: Call manufacturer at 800 999-2811 for refund or revised instruction booklet. Among other things, new instructions warn against cleaning stone in oven at temperatures higher than 425°F.

Series 400 Stargard AT dual-contact heat detector

May not reliably detect fire.

Products: 12,000 heat detectors sold nationwide 5/94-5/97 at stores that distribute fire-detection equipment. Heat detector, white plastic disk about 41/2 in. in diameter, is component in fire-detection alarm system. System is geared toward commerical, rather than residential use. At center of disk is smaller, three-tiered metal disk. Words "STARGARD AT" and "Chemetronics Caribe" (the manufacturer) appear beside it. Recalled detectors have one of following date codes stamped on side: 0594 (May '94) to 1294 (December '94); W1-Y95 (week one, year '95) to W52-Y95 (week 52, year '95); W1-Y96 to W52-Y96; and W1-Y97 to W22-Y97.

What to do: Call Chemetronics at 800 496-8383 for free replacement and to arrange for installation.

Homelite gasoline-powered back-pack blower

Fuel lines could leak, possibly causing fire and injuring user.

Products: 80,000 blowers, model BP-250, sold 10/94-12/96 for $200. Device is 2 1/2 ft. tall and 1 1/2 ft. wide, with 30 cc. engine. Blower is mostly red with black components and is mounted on black frame. Shoulder straps are attached to frame. Words "Homelite BP-250...Made in U.S.A." appear under blower's red support bar. Affected models bear "UT" nos. UT 08017F or UT 08017G, and serial nos. ranging from HP2000001 to HP3659999, HQ0010001 to HQ3659999, and HR0010001 to HR2109999. Nunbers appear on sticker on fuel tank.

What to do: Stop using blower immediately and take it to nearest Homelite servicing dealer for repair. For name of closest dealer, or more information, call 800 242-4672.

Pro Form R-930 Space Save Rider exercise machine

Could unexpectedly collapse during use, causing head, neck, and shoulder injuries.

Products: 78,000 black metal exercise machines, which resemble bicycle without wheels, sold 8/96-5/97 at retail stores nationwide for about $250. Affected units bear model number PFCR64060 and serial number beginning with GO4, G33, G43, G53, G63, G73, G83, or G93. Numbers appear on decal underneath seat frame near front of machine. Words "Pro Form R-930...Push Resistance...Pull Resistance" is written in yellow on each side of seat frame. "Space Saver" is written in gray on top of frame.

What to do: Stop using machine immediately and call distributor, Icon Health & Fitness Inc., at 800 999-3756 for free repair kit and installation instructions. Kit can also be obtained by writing to company's Customer Service Dept., 1500 South 1000 West, Logan, Utah 84321.

Coleman camp ax

Handle could break and allow steel head to fly off.

Products: 20,000 axes sold 1/96-6/97 at discount and sporting-goods stores for $20. Ax has black plastic handle about 13 1/2 inches long and steel ax head about 2 3/4 inches long. "Coleman" is imprinted on handle. Ax comes with black case for blade. Blister pack had green and red backing that reads, in part, "Coleman Deluxe Camp Axe . . . 836-430T."

What to do: Call 800 257-5299 for refund.

T-Fal Superclean deep fryers

Base could melt, posing burn hazard and damaging counter.

Products: 29,000 white plastic deep fryers with hinged lid, including Superclean Safety Fryer Midi 3350 and Superclean Safety Fryer Maxi 3358 and 3360, sold 5/96-12/96 for $50 to $70. Fryers were sold at stores such as Ames, Bradlees, and Hills, as well as on QVC TV shopping channel. Only models with nonremovable pot are subject to recall. Recalled Superclean Midi was made during 22nd through 30th week of '96; Maxi model 3358, during 45th week of '96; Maxi model 3360, during 26th and 46th weeks of '96. Date is indicated by three-digit number, with first two digits indicating week, third digit indicating year. Silver label under base includes date of manufacture, above words "MADE IN MEXICO," and code (model) number.

What to do: Call 888 397-6535 for inspection and, if necessary, replacement of fryer.

Handheld hair dryer

Poses electrocution hazard if dropped in water.

Products: 8000 hair dryers sold 12/94-2/97 at discount and variety stores for $11. White plastic dryer has "PROFESSIONAL STYLER . . . ASBESTOS FREE . . . HD-20 . . . MADE IN CHINA" printed on it. Instead of large rectangular ground-fault circuit-interrupter plug, which cuts off current if device is dropped in water, dryer has ordinary plug. Triangular cardboard box says, in part, "Professional HAIR DRYER HD-20." Picture of dryer is on box.

What to do: Return dryer to store for refund.

Carol and Ace outdoor extension cords

Exposed wire near receptacle end poses shock hazard.

Products: 2700 extension cords, 2 to 100 feet long and in various gauges. Cords were sold 4/97-5/97 for $6 to $90. Carol brand cords are orange, yellow, green, blue, or beige with matching or black plug and triple receptacle. Receptacle is labeled "CAROL" and "W-8." Cardboard wrapper said, in part, "CAROL . . . POWR-CENTER . . . Outdoor Cord . . . Made in USA." Ace brand cords are orange with black plug and triple receptacle imprinted with "W-8 " and on some samples "ACE". Cardboard wrapper said, in part, "ACE Outdoor 3 Outlet Power Center . . . Manufactured in USA for ACE." Both brands are UL listed.

What to do: Return extension cord to store or call 888 594-2600 for refund.

Gamo model AF-10 BB air pistol

Could discharge unexpectedly.

Products: 1335 compact air pistols sold 6/94-4/97 at gun shops and sporting-goods stores for about $80. Pistol, about 8 1/2 inches long and can discharge one BB or 10 in succession. It has adjustable rear sight, manual cross-bolt trigger safety, rifled steel barrel, and molded checkered grip.

What to do: Return air pistol to store or send COD via United Parcel Service to Gamo USA, 3911 S.W. 47th Ave., Suite 914, Fort Lauderdale, Fla. 33314. Company will modify pistol.

Eight-outlet power strip electrical surge protector

Poses fire and shock hazards.

Products: 30,000 surge protectors sold 1/95-10/96 at discount, variety, and hardware stores in Northeast for $6. Device is beige colored plastic with red power switch and black reset button. Switch and button are on raised end of surge protector, which is about 1/2 in. higher than outlets. Electrical cord is beige. Embossed on bottom is "8 Outlet Power Strip . . . MP8 . . . Made in China." Also on bottom is silver label that says: "UL Listed 50E8." Labeling on clear plastic bag says, in part, "Guard Security Hardware."

What to do: Return surge protector to store for refund.

Five-piece and six-piece wok sets sold at Pier 1 Import stores

Support stand poses severe laceration hazard.

Products: 7680 five-piece and six-piece wok sets sold 4/93-4/97. Five-piece set includes 9-inch aluminum lid, steel body, steel support stand with five circular cutouts, wire steamer rack, and frying rack. Box said, in part, "MINI WOK SET . . . The Market at Pier 1 . . . Contents made in Taiwan . . . SKU#119-5651." Set sold for $25 (later reduced to $9). Six-piece set sold for $35 (later reduced to $13). It includes 13-inch aluminum lid, steel body, steel support stand with nine circular cutouts, wire steamer rack, stainless-steel food turner with wooden handle, and pair of chopsticks. Set came in cardboard box labeled in part: "SIX PIECE WOK SET . . . The Market at Pier 1 . . . Contents made in Taiwan . . . SKU#119-5649."

What to do: Return set to store for refund.

Levi's and Dockers men's and women's fleece fabric garments

Dangerously flammable.

Products: 34,000 Levi's Jeans For Women junior-sized sweatshirts sold 10/96-2/97 at J.C. Penney, Levi's Only Store, Levi's Outlets by Designs, and other retailers for $30. Sweatshirts came in two styles: sleeveless pullover vest with drawstring hood (product code 55930) and a long-sleeve, crew-neck design, (code 55956). Code is on care label. Both styles have center embroidery. Label says "Levi's Jeans for Women . . . Made in Korea . . . 82% cotton/18% polyester . . . WPL 423." Also recalled are 23,000 sweatshirts sold 8/95-2/97 for $25 to $35 under "Dockers Khakis for Women" and "Dockers Authentics for Men" labels. Womens garments came as vests (product codes 53601 and 54601), cardigans (codes 53604 and 54604), and pullovers (codes 53605 and 54605). Garments came in small, medium, and large, and in various colors including ink, oatmeal heather, black, red, and natural. Men's garment is navy-colored shirt that laces up in front (product code 67191). It came in small, medium, large, and extra large. Label reads "Dockers Khakis for Women" or "Dockers Authentics for Men." and "Made in Korea . . . 80% cotton/20% polyester . . . WPL 423."

What to do: Return garment to store for refund.

"Lily" table lamps sold at Kmart stores

Could catch fire.

Products: 41,300 table lamps made of bronze-colored metal with two frosted white shades, sold 11/96-4/97. Lamp is 15 1/4 inches high. Base is shaped like lily pad; shades, like lily flowers. Gold sticker on bottom of lamp reads "Made in China." Clear sticker on bulb socket reads, in part, "Use 25 watt type B or smaller lamp . . . E123788."

What to do: Return lamp to Kmart for refund.

Stihl 029 and 039 gasoline-powered chain saws

Fuel cap could loosen and leak, posing fire hazard.

Products: 256,000 chain saws sold since 3/93 for $350 to $450. Only saws with a serial number of 235153631 or lower are subject to recall. Model number appears on top of engine; serial number is on housing, above bumper spikes, directly under front hand guard.

What to do: Have Stihl dealer replace fuel cap. Some Stihl saws were recalled in 1994 to repair ignition ground wire, so dealer will check for that problem as well. Call 800 467-8445 for location of nearest dealer.

Pomtrex electric iron

Could overheat and pose fire hazard.

Products: 40,000 irons sold 11/94-9/96 at discount, hardware, and variety stores for about $7. Irons are black, red, or beige with metal base and plastic handle. "Pomtrex" trademark appears above the settings markings. Packaging reads, in part, "POMTREX ELECTRIC AUTOMATIC IRON . . . MODEL NO. 600-00701."

What to do: Return iron to store for refund.

Peak 1 22-ounce fuel-storage canister for camping equipment

Defective threads in neck could allow fuel leak.

Products: 14,127 red aluminum canisters sold 5/96-9/96 at sporting-goods stores and through backpacking, mountain-climbing, and camping catalogs. Canisters were made during the first half of '96 and carry 1-96 date code stamped on bottom. They were included with purchase of Peak 1 Apex stoves or sold separately for $12.50.

What to do: Call 800 257-5299 for replacement and instructions for disposing of defective canister.

Six-outlet electrical surge protectors

Pose electrocution and fire hazards.

Products: 7500 surge protectors sold 8/95-10/96 by wholesalers and discount stores for $6 to $7. Two models are involved; neither is labeled, but both are made of beige metal with black cord and outlets. One model has single red power switch and came in blue cardboard box labeled, in part, " 6 Outlet AC Surge Protector. . . Clean Power Source With Spike Supressor. . . Built In Safety Circuit Breaker. . . Master Switch With Pilot Light. . . Durable Enamel Finished Housing. . . 15 AMPS Maximum Capacity." Picture of device appears on box. Other model has seven red power switches and came in red cardboard box labeled, in part, "6 Outlet Power Surge Protector Safety Circuit Breaker. . . Individual Switch. . . 15 AMPS. . . Built-In Brackets. . . Heavy-duty surge protection for computer systems and other sensitive electronic equipment." Device is visible through cutout in box.

What to do: Return surge supressor to store for refund. For information, call distributor, Supreme Premium Products, at 800 544-7710. In New York metropolitan area, phone 212 629-8527.

Mr. Coffee espresso/cappuccino maker

Filter holder is hard to secure. If not properly seated, holder could dislodge under pressure, break carafe, and cause cuts from glass and burns from hot coffee.

Products: 50,000 espresso/cappuccino makers sold 9/96-2/97 for $40. Only model ECM9 is being recalled; model number is imprinted on bottom of base. Device is black plastic and metal, 13 inches long, 7 1/2 inches wide, and 10 1/4 inches high, and comes with four-cup carafe. It came in carton labeled, in part, "Mr. Coffee Steam Espresso/ Cappuccino Maker ECM9."

What to do: Call 888 999-3934 toll-free for free replacement filter holder, filter basket, and coupons for disposable filters. Have espresso/cappuccino maker available at time of call to verify model number.

NNE electric steam iron

Could overheat and catch fire, even when in Off position!

Products: More than 5000 irons sold 12/95-2/96 at discount stores for about $10. Iron has white or red plastic housing and detachable water tank. Model number YPZ-100 is on sticker on back of iron. Light blue cardboard box says, "NNE Steam/Dry & Spray Electric Iron With Detachable Water Tank."

What to do: Return iron to store for refund.

Adapter plugs used to connect three-pronged plug into two-slot grounded outlet

Pose fire and shock hazards.

Products: 60,000 plugs sold 1/96-7/96 in blister packs of three for $1 at Dollar Tree and Only One Dollar stores in South, Midwest, and East. Plugs are orange with the following words imprinted in rubber housing: "CAUTION. . . CONNECT TAB TO GROUNDED SCREW. . . CHINA. . . 15A. . . 125V." Black cardboard backing on pack says, in part: "3 PK. . . GROUNDING ADAPTER PLUG. . . For connection of 3 pronged plug to a 2 slot grounded outlet. . . UL LISTED. . . MADE IN CHINA." (Adapters were incorrectly identified as being listed with Underwriters Laboratories.)

What to do: Return plugs to store for refund.

Sears water-filter cartridge

Could release nickel into water and cause stomach cramps, nausea, and diarrhea.

Products: 14,000 Sears water- filter cartridges, designed to fit most standard-sized under-sink and countertop water filter housings. Cartridges were sold since 3/96 at Sears stores as item number 42 34375 for $17. Cylindrical cartridge measures about

10x3 inches and has white plastic housing and 1½-inch-wide green end cap. Label on housing reads, in part, "WaterWorks Chemical Contaminant/Taste and Odor Filter Cartridge Premium Grade Granular Activated Carbon." When label is removed, no name or identifying number appears on cartridge; however, it's the only cartridge with green end cap sold at Sears. When first used, recalled cartridges give water metallic taste and make it turn green.

What to do: Call 800 945-0109 for instructions on returning cartridge for refund or replacement. If you experience symptons, seek medical attention for possible nickel ingestion. Pregnant women, small children, the elderly, and people with kidney problems may be most at risk.

Hydro-Air drain cover for spas, hot tubs, and swimming pools

Suction could draw hair into drain. Bather might not be able free hair and could drown.

Products: 206,000 drain covers installed '80-95. Cover is white plastic disk six inches in diameter, with 18 rectangular openings on top. Each opening is 3/4 inch long, 5/16 inch wide. "Hydro Air P/N 10-6200" is imprinted on top of cover.

What to do: Call 800 230-9560 for free replacement cover.

Various chenille sweaters

Could catch fire and burn more quickly than newspaper.

Products: 32,000 soft-textured sweaters sold '96 for $38 to $130 by boutiques and by major chains like BCBG, Bloomingdale's, Dillard's, Express, Foley's, Lerner of New York, Limited Too, Lord & Taylor, Macy's, Neiman Marcus, Nordstrom, Parisian, and Robinson-May. Most are 65 percent rayon and 35 percent nylon; a few are 90 percent rayon and 10 percent nylon, 67 percent rayon and 33 percent nylon, or all rayon. Most have long or short sleeves and crew neck or turtleneck; some are mock wrap-style sweaters or V-neck vests. Sweaters were made in China, Hong Kong, Taiwan, and U.S. and come in various colors. Labels carry following names and registration numbers: BCBG Maxazeria, RN 80734 (made or imported by BCBG Max Azria, Vernon, Calif., 213 589-2224); 525 Made in America, RN 61680 (525 Made in America, Inc., New York City, 212 921-5688); Maille ISHYU, RN78635 (Pretty Talk, Miami, 305 717-3180); Sisters, RN 84332 (Fredini, dba Miss LA, Los Angeles, 213 745-7921); Karen Kane, Karen Kane Lifestyle, and Karen Kane Lifestyle Petite, RN 59168 (Karen Kane, Los Angeles, 800 590-5263); The Limited, RN 54867 (Limited Inc. Limited Too, Columbus, Ohio, 800 723-8785); Express Tricot, RN 54867 (Limited Express [Limited Inc.], Columbus, Ohio, 614 479-4031); and N.Y. Jeans, RN 23243 (Lerner New York Inc. [Limited Inc.], New York, 800 723-5111).

What to do: Return sweater to store for refund or credit. Not all sweaters with brand names and RN numbers listed above are subject to recall; if retailer can't tell whether sweater is affected, phone appropriate manufacturer or importer. For more information and names of other retailers participating in recall, phone Consumer Product Safety Commission, 800 638-2772.

Electric hair dryers sold in New York Metropolitan area

Lack immersion-protection plug, to guard against electrocution if dryer is dropped in water while turned on. Also, inadequate wiring poses fire hazard.

Products: 5000 white plastic dryers, packaged in box labeled "International Hair Styling Set with 7 Attachments . . . HD-868" and sold 11/95-5/96 at discount stores for $10. "Professional Styler Asbestos Free" appears on device itself.

What to do: Return dryer to store for refund. On any dryer, look for large rectangular plug at end of cord. Certification mark of recognized testing organization (like UL) should also appear on dryer or package.

Admiral, Crosley, Magic Chef, Norge, and Signature gas clothes dryers

Dryer could overheat and catch fire.

Products: 73,000 dryers made by Maytag and sold '89-91. Recalled Admiral, Crosley, Magic Chef, and Norge dryers bear serial numbers beginning with letters AD, BD, CD, DC, DD, EC, ED, FC, GD, HD, JD, KD, LD, and MD. Recalled Signature models begin with code 09A, 09B, 09C, 09D, 09E, 09F, 09G, 09H, 09J, 09K, 09L 98K, 98L, and 98M. Number is inside dryer door. Dryers sold under Maytag name are not included in recall.

What to do: Call 800 955-6566 to arrange for inspection and, if necessary, repair.

AC adapter for Compaq Armada 4100 notebook computer

Poses shock hazard.

Products: 30,000 adapters sold 9/23/96-11/20/96. Adapters with three hollow pins in recessed male connector and part number 217984-001 printed on bar-code label are subject to recall. Adapters with the same part number but solid pins are not included. Adapters are black and measure about 2¾x 4 ½ inches. They were sold either separately or with Armada 4100 computers and associated convenience bases.

What to do: Call 800 322-9515 for replacement adapter.

SmartLite and RiteLite fluorescent work lights

Could cause shock.

Products: 11,400 work lights, model numbers. FL-600, FL-650, SL-600, SL-605, and SL-650, sold 6/95-7/96 at automotive, hardware, and home-improvement stores for $30 to $70. Lights measure 9 1/4 in. long and have twin-tube fluorescent bulb in clear plastic tubular case. Case has yellow plastic end caps and metal hook. Light comes with either 20- or 50-foot cord. Model number is on silver tag attached to retractable cord reel. Lights without retractable reel display model number on blue or black cardboard box labeled, in part: "Fluorescent Work Light with Retractable Reel. . . Stays Cool in Use. . . Tough Impact Resistant. . . On-Off Switch."

What to do: Call 800 655-8996 for plastic screw that you can substitute for metal one to eliminate shock hazard.

Cotton-polyester blend fleece men's and women's garments

Could catch fire and burn faster than newspaper.

Products: 138,100 garments made of fleece-type fabric (mostly 80 percent cotton, 20 percent polyester). Fabric, whose texture resembles inside-out sweatshirt material is sometimes called sherpa. Recall includes 116,700 womens garments, mostly tops in polo, crew, and tunic styles, sold 10/96-1/97 for $20 to $40 by J.C. Penney and other retailers such as Dayton's, Hudson's, Jean Nicole, Marshall Field, Petrie, and Stuarts. Some jackets and pants are also involved. Garments came in sage, peach, ivory, and gray, and have two sewn-in labels. One says "Jason Maxwell," other says , "Made in Turkey. . . RN 34570." Fiber content of gray garments is 55 percent cotton, 45 percent polyester. Regent International is distributor. Also recalled are 21,400 men's long-sleeved henley-style pullover fleece shirts with five-button closure at neck. Shirts came in navy, spruce green, olive green, natural, burgundy, and gray. They have two sewn-in labels. One says "Fast"; the other, "Made in Korea. . . RN 57336." Shirts were distributed by Tomen America and sold 7/96-1/97 by Ross Dress for Less for $10 to $20.

What to do: Return garment to store for refund. Recall does not involve other Jason Maxwell or Fast clothes. For more information, call Regent International at 800 536-1500 or Tomen America at 888 287-2207 toll-free.

American FarmWorks K-9 control box (controls electricity in electric fences)

Used outdoors in humid or wet environment, box could overheat and catch fire.

Products: 13,000 boxes that control electricity in electric fences. Controllers were sold at hardware and farm-supply stores since 4/96 for $28. Red, yellow, and black label on box lists model name. Affected units have serial number starting with MT08096 or MT09096. Device was sold individually or as part of pet and garden fence kit.

What to do: Call 800 962-2880 for replacement.

Garden Lavender Botanical Candle sold at Bath & Body Works stores

Dried flowers inside candle could catch fire as candle burns.

Products: 18,400 candles sold 5/96-8/96 for $15. Cylindrical white-wax candle measures 4 inches high and 4 inches in diameter and contains small purple lavender flowers. Label on bottom reads, "Garden Lavender Botanical Candle."

What to do: Return candle to store for refund plus $25 Bath & Body Works gift certificate.

Various electrical extension cords

Undersized wires pose electrocution and fire hazards.

Products: 31,000 extension cords, imported from China by Northeastern Plastics Inc., packaged in green and white sleeve labeled "JUMPOWER," and sold 4/96-7/96 in Mich., N.Y., N.J., and P.R. for $5. Recalled cords include models 441 (brown, 6 feet long); 442 (brown, 9 feet); 443 (brown, 12 feet); 445 (brown, 20 feet); 447 (white, 9 feet); and 448 (white, 12 feet). Markings "SPT-1 60C VW-1 18 awg X 2C YWC" appear in green ink on each cord. Also, 2000 extension cords, distributed by D-M Sales Corp. and sold 2/93-9/96 nationwide by wholesalers and discount stores for $1. Recalled cord is brown, 9 feet long, and carries imprinted code "SPT-2 VW-1 18 AWGX2C E135675 403801-001." Identification number E109853 is molded on plug. Cord came in green cardboard sleeve labeled, in part: "Supreme HOUSEHOLD EXTENSION CORD . . . 9 FT. . . UPC #0 18285 00422 4 . . . "

What to do: Return cord to store for refund. For information, call Northeastern Plastics at 800 989-2674, ext. 76., or D-M Sales Corp. (aka Supreme Import Export Inc.) at 800 551-1113 (or 718 499-5454 from New York metropolitan area).

Various hand-shaped Halloween candles

As candle burns, high flames pose fire hazard.

Products: About 228,000 hand-shaped novelty candles, with separate wick in each of five fingers. Recalled candles include: Decorative Novelty Candles sold 8/96-10/96 at Walgreens stores. Candle is pink-toned with red band around bottom of wrist. Purple, red, and yellow-shaded cardboard box has picture of candle; "Decorative Novelty

Candle" is printed on front of box, with $2.99 price in upper right corner. Also recalled: Glowing Gore and Dem Bones candles, sold 3/94-10/96 at gift, drug, and grocery stores for $6. Glowing Gore candle is pink-toned with red blotches; Dem Bones candle is pale green with dark green blotches. Each is 7 1/2 inches high. Label on plastic wrapping under hand says, "DEM BONES DRIPPING OOZE CANDLE," or "GLOWING GORE DRIPPING BLOOD CANDLE." Also recalled: Bleeding Hand candles sold during Halloween '95 and '96 at Caldor, gift, specialty, and drug stores for $4. Candle is pink-toned or dark green with red band around bottom of wrist and is 7 inches high. Plastic and purple-cardboard package says "Bleeding Hand Candle" and "C.R. Seasons LTD" on front and back.

What to do: Return candle to store for refund.

Velvety-textured chenille sweaters sold by J.C. Penney

Could catch fire and burn as quickly as newspaper.

Products: 26,240 sweaters, made of 67 percent rayon and 33 percent nylon, sold 9/96-10/96 at stores and through Penney's '96 Christmas Catalog for $29-$36 under name "M B MIXED BLUES CLOTHING CO." Short- and long-sleeved sweaters came in various colors: apple (kiwi or lime green); black; dark brown (chocolate); forest green; fuschia; ivory; plum; red; and royal blue. Sewn-in label has RN number 93677 on front and supplier number 701524 on back.

What to do: Return sweater to Penney's store for refund.

Ford, New Holland, and Toro yard and garden tractors

Brakes could fail.

Products: 6500 tractors made by Toro and sold 1/94-5/96 for about $2000, including: Toro Wheel Horse Yard and Garden Tractor, model 72040 (serial numbers 4900001 to 5999999); Ford or New Holland LS 25 Gear Yard Tractor (T4A0001 to T4A1201 and T5A0001 to T5A0617); and Ford or New Holland LS 45 Gear tractor (T4C0001 to T4C0581, and T5C0001 to T5C0168). Model and serial numbers are on fender under seat.

What to do: Toro owners can phone 800 348-2424 for name of nearest service center for free brake modification. Ford and New Holland owners should consult tractor owner's manual or Yellow Pages, under "tractors," for nearest service center.

Candle-lite Clearfire scented candles

Could flare up in use; glass holder could overheat, break, and burn or cut user.

Products: Three million candles, in textured, 3-inch vase-shaped clear glass jar, sold 10/95-4/96 for $4. Candles were made of clear, gel-like substance and came in five styles: red with apple cider scent; green with spruce scent; clear with floral vanilla scent; blue with mulberry scent; and yellow with sunflower scent. Label on bottom of jar has UPC number beginning with "076001" and ending with one of following numbers: 304737, 304744, 304959, 304966, 304997, 305000, 305192, 305208, 305222, 305239, 306878, 306885, 306892, 307356, 307363, 307554, 307561, 307745, 806712, 806729, 806750, 806767. Clearfire candles with plastic cover aren't being recalled.

What to do: Return candle wick and UPC label from bottom of jar to Candle-lite, P. O. Box 42486, Cincinnati, Ohio 45242 for $6 refund. For information, call 800 866-6654.

Lane cedar chests

Lock that latches automatically when lid is shut poses risk of suffocation to child playing inside.

Products: 12 million wooden chests in a variety of styles, sizes, and colors, made since 1912. Lane began using redesigned locks in 1987. To identify chest with old-style suspect lock, close lid and try to open it without depressing locking button. If lid opens, lock needn't be replaced. In addition, old-style lock clicks loudly when lid is shut.

What to do: Call 888 856-8758 for free replacement lock and installation instructions. Lane will make special arrangements for people who need help installing lock.

Hammocks (various models)

Lacking spreader bars to hold them open, hammocks hang like rope. They can twist around and strangle the occupant.

Products: 75,000 lightweight, portable hammocks measuring 5 to 7 feet wide, 7 to 20 feet long. Sporting-goods stores sold EZ Sales Hang Ten hammocks from '79-91 for $6 to $16. Outdoor-equipment stores and catalog houses sold Twin Oaks Backpack hammocks since early '80s for $8 to $14. Surplus and sporting-goods stores sold Safesport hammocks from '94-96 for about $8. (In August, we reported on 3 million other hammocks recalled for same problem.)

What to do: Return hammock to store or catalog house for refund. Dispose of any hammock that lacks a spreader bar if you can't identify its seller or manufacturer.

Global Industries Wood Tilter chair

Seat could break when occupant leans against seatback.

Products: 2500 chairs sold 7/15/96-10/5/96, primarily at Staples stores, for $80. Chair has gray or black upholstery, wooden arms with upholstered caps, and five-legged base with wooden caps.

Model number 8924 is on bottom of seat.

What to do: Call 888 242-4778 for replacement chair.

Sheer silk chiffon scarves

Extremely flammable—burn faster than newspaper.

Products: 40,000 long, flowing scarves sold 1/95-11/95 at Dress Barn, Caldor, Fashion Gal, Warehouse of Fashion, and other stores for $6-$10. Scarves, available in 11 styles, were made in China and are labeled, in part: "Pure Silk by 37 West, RN 62415."

What to do: Return scarf to store for refund or replacement. Retailer should help consumers identify scarves subject to recall. For more information, call distributor at 212 391-5252 or Government hotline, 800 638-2772.

'94-96 Polaris snowmobiles

Brakes could fail or handlebar could break.

Products: Brake problem: 19,320 snowmobiles sold 3/93-4/96 for $6000-$9000, including '94-96 Storm and Storm SKS (model numbers 0945582, E945582, 0945782, E945782, 0955582, E955582, 0955782, E955782, 0965582, E965582, 0965782, E965782); '96 Storm RMK (0965982); '96 Ultra, Ultra SKS, and Ultra RMK (0960578, E960578, 0960678, E960678, and 0960978); '96 600 XCR SP (0965677). Handlebar problem: 19,327 snowmobiles sold 3/95-4/96 for $5000-$7000, including following '96 models: XLT Touring (model numbers 0963357 and E963357); Classic (0963865); 500 SKS (0962564 and E962564); 500 EFI (0963774); 500 EFI RMK (0962974); Trail (0962761); Classic Touring (0963365 and E963365); 500 (Carb) (0962764); 500 RMK (0962964); 500 EFI SKS (0962574); Trail Touring (0962262 and E962262); and 440 (0962760). Serial number is on right side of tunnel where driver's right foot rests.

What to do: For brake problem, have Polaris dealer install support bracket to keep engine-coolant tank from expanding. For handlebar problem, have dealer check and, if necessary, replace handlebar. For nearest dealer, call 800 765-2747.

Wagner Power Steamer (model 700)

When filler cap is opened, steam and hot water could escape forcefully and burn user.

Products: 44,000 wallpaper-steamers sold 7/94-3/97 at hardware and home-supply stores for about $70. Plastic device is mostly gray and black with round one-gallon water tank that measures 6 1/2 inches high and 9 1/2 inches in diameter. Steamer has 11 1/2 - foot hose that connects steamplate to steamer. Yellow filler cap is attached to end of hose that connects to spout of water tank. Tank and steamplate have yellow labels displaying model number 700 and "Wagner Power Steamer" lettering. Model 700 steamers bear serial number beginning with K, L, or M and ending with N. Serial number is printed in blue ink on bottom of water container.

What to do: Phone 800 686-8525 for free replacement hose and filler cap.

Husqvarna gasoline-powered chain saws (various models)

If removable exhaust deflector isn't properly attached, heat from muffler could melt front hand guard, exposing user to risk of serious injury or death from contact with chain.

Products: 277,000 chain saws sold '90-95 for about $400 to $600. Recalled saws bear model number 42, 51, 55, 242, or 254, and have serial number beginning with 531 or lower. Recalled saws also include models 61 and 257, with serial number beginning with 324 or lower. Model number is on left side of engine and on serial-number plate on left front of engine. Saws are orange, with "Husqvarna" printed on both sides of engine. Hand guard is black, orange, or gray plastic.

What to do: Return chain saw to nearest Husqvarna dealer for free replacement muffler with deflector welded on. Company will also replace any hand guard with heat damage. For location of nearest dealer, call 800 438-7297.

K-Tel Deluxe food dehydrator with fan, model 80043

Could overheat and catch fire.

Products: 75,000 dehydrators sold 10/93-12/95 at stores and through telemarketers for $30 to $40. Round, white plastic device is 13 inches in diameter with 3-inch-thick base and gray plastic lid. Base is labeled, in part: "K-TEL . . . Style No. LD 1010 . . . ." Base is stacked with five trays (each with hole in center), on which food can be dried.

What to do: Phone 800 462-5292 for free replacement or comparable product.

Cars

'84-95 Jeep Cherokees and '93-95 Jeep Grand Cherokees

Unintended acceleration could occur..

Models: 2.2 million Jeep Cherokees and Jeep Grand Cherokees.

What to do: Have dealer install a free brake/transmission interlock.

'90-93 Chrysler, Dodge, and Plymouth minivans

Antilock brakes may fail to function properly.

Models: '90-93 Chrysler Fifth Avenue, Imperial, New Yorker, and Salon and Dodge Dynasty; '90-93

Dodge Monaco and Eagle Premier; '91-93 Dodge Caravan and Grand Caravan, Plymouth Voyager and Grand Voyager, and Chrysler Town & Country.

What to do: Have dealer check the braking system.

'96 Ford Taurus, Lincoln Continental, and Mercury Sable

Vehicle could roll away even though transmission shifter is in Park.

Models: 340,000 cars made 4/95-8/96.

What to do: Have dealer inspect and, if necessary, replace park-pawl shaft.

'89-91 Mazda RX7

Automatic shoulder belt could jam.

Models: 17,800 cars made 12/88-5/91.

What to do: Have dealer replace inoperative belt.

'91-92 Dodge Shadow and Plymouth Sundance

Driver's seat could come apart, causing possible loss of vehicle control and crash.

Models: 148,000 cars made 7/90-6/92.

What to do: Have dealer install redesigned lower seatback attaching bolt.

'93 Dodge Colt, Dodge Colt Vista minivan, Plymouth Colt, Eagle Summit and Eagle Summit wagon

Driver's safety belt may not provide adequate protection in crash.

Models: 24,000 cars and light trucks made 4/92-6/93.

What to do: Have dealer install new guide rail for shoulder belt.

'92-93 Dodge and Plymouth Colt, and Eagle Summit

Automatic shoulder belts may not slide back properly, increasing risk of injury in crash.

Models: 46,000 cars made 3/91-11/92.

What to do: Have dealer replace door-latch switches.

'91-96 Infiniti G20

Fuel-filler- tube assembly could rust and leak, posing fire hazard. Problem is most likely in areas where road salt is used.

Models: 85,000 cars made 7/90-5/96.

What to do: Have dealer replace filler tube and other assembly components as needed.

'91-92 Infiniti G20 and Nissan NX

Rear safety belts may not latch properly.

Models: 36,000 cars made 10/90-12/91.

What to do: Have dealer replace rear safety-belt buckles.

'92-93 Mitsubishi Expo and Expo LRV, and '93 Mirage

When doors close, automatic front shoulder belts may not slide back, leaving occupants unprotected.

Models: 38,948 cars, including Expos and Expo LRV s made 3/91-11/92 and Mirages made 4/92-11/92.

What to do: Have dealer replace shoulder-belt guide rail.

'95 Buick, Chevrolet, Oldsmobile, and Pontiac models

Center-rear safety belt could fail in crash.

Models: 50,709 cars made 2/95, including Buick Regal, Chevrolet Lumina and Monte Carlo, Oldsmobile Cutlass, and Pontiac Grand Prix.

What to do: Have dealer replace center-rear safety belt.

'97 Buick and Cadillac

Antilock-brake system could engage during routine braking and increase stopping distance.

Models: 77,449 cars made 4/96-12/96, including Buick Park Avenue and Cadillac Seville, Deville, and El Dorado.

What to do: Have dealer replace electronic brake-control module or electronic brake- and traction-control module.

'96-97 Hyundai models

Windshield wipers could fail.

Models: 74,965 cars made 4/95-10/96, including '96-97 Accent, Elantra, and Sonata and '97 Tiburon.

What to do: Have dealer clean contacts on wiper circuit breaker.

'91-95 Ford, Lincoln, and Mercury

Water could freeze in cruise-control cable and prevent driver from disengaging cruise control.

Models: 212,700 cars with 3.8-liter V6, including '91-94 Lincoln Continental and '91-95 Ford Taurus and Mercury Sable. Recall applies only to cars registered in Alaska, Colo., Idaho, Ill., Ind., Iowa, Kan., Maine, Mass., M ich., Minn., Mo., Mont., Neb., N.H., N.Y., N.D., Ohio., Pa., S.D., Vt., Wisc., and Wyo. Affected vehicles were made 7/90-11/94.

What to do: Have dealer install cable boot to keep out water.

'92-95 Ford, Lincoln, and Mercury

Snow could clog engine-cooling fan and make it overheat, posing fire hazard.

Models: 75,200 cars, with 2.3-liter Four, 3.0-liter

V6, or 3.8-liter V6, including '92-94 Ford Tempo, Mercury Topaz, and Lincoln Continental and '92-95 Ford Taurus and Mercury Sable. Recall applies only to cars registered in Alaska, Iowa, Minn., Neb., N.D., and S.D. are being recalled. Dates of manufacture are: Tempo, 8/5/91-5/20/94; Topaz, 8/5/91-5/16/94; Continental, 8/12/91-11/17/94; Taurus, 5/3/91-6/26/95; Sable, 6/19/91-6/16/95.

What to do: Have dealer install wiring with circuit breaker to prevent fan motor from overheating.

'96 Chrysler Sebring convertible

Water and road salt could short-circuit power mirror and pose fire hazard.

Models: 39,000 cars made 8/96.

What to do: Have dealer replace power-mirror switch.

'95-96 Buick Roadmaster, Cadillac Fleetwood, and Chevrolet Caprice

Wheels could come off.

Models: 21,582 cars made 8/95.

What to do: Have dealer tighten lug nuts to specifications.

'95-96 Chevrolet, Pontiac, and Oldsmobile (various models)

Four-way hazard-warning flashers may not work.

Models: 270,014 cars made 7/95-8/95 including '95-96 Chevrolet Cavalier and Pontiac Sunfire, and '96 Pontiac Gran Am and Oldsmobile Achieva.

What to do: Check whether flashers are working properly. If not, have dealer replace hazard switch.

'95 Honda Accord

Air bag could deploy unexpectedly and cause injury or loss of control.

Models: 164,139 cars made 4/94-2/95.

What to do: Have dealer replace air bag electronic control unit.

'91-94 Dodge Stealth

Front brake hose could leak and reduce stopping ability.

Models: 23,000 cars made 7/90-11/94.

What to do: Have dealer install redesigned front brake hoses.

'96-97 Ford, Lincoln, and Mercury (various models)

Vehicle could roll even though transmission shifter is in Park.

Models: 380,000 vehicles, including '96 Ford Windstar made 8/96; 96 Lincoln Continental made 4/95-8/96; and '96-97 Ford Taurus and Mercury Sable made 4/95-8/96.

What to do: Have dealer inspect and, if necessary, repair park pawl assembly.

'95-96 Ford Crown Victoria, Mercury Grand Marquis, and Lincoln Town Car

Front-suspension welds could break, causing creaking and clanking noises and pulling to one side during braking. Eventually, steering could deteriorate.

Models: 231,000 cars made 6/15/95-3/29/96.

What to do: Have dealer inspect and, if necessary, repair welds. (After 3/1/97, cars may not be eligible for recall program after basic warranty has expired.)

'95-96 Mitsubishi Eclipse

Fuel-tank gaskets could leak, posing fire hazard.

Models: 5731 cars made 3/94-7/96.

What to do: Have dealer inspect fuel tank and, if necessary, replace faulty parts.

'89-93 Porsche (various models)

Over time, steering could fail.

Models: 12,538 cars made 4/88-7/92, including '89-92 911 and Carrera 2/4 Turbo and '93 911 RS.

What to do: Have dealer inspect upper universal joint in steering column and replace it if it's cracked.

'93-95 Mazda RX-7

Oil mist could collect in brake vacuum check valve and reduce brakes' power assist, so that stopping would require more pedal effort.

Models: 13,900 cars made 12/91-12/95.

What to do: Have dealer replace two vacuum hoses and check valve.

'97 Saturn SC1 and SC2

Right front seat could slide forward in frontal crash, increasing risk of injury.

Models: 3472 cars made 5/96-7/96.

What to do: Have dealer replace seat's inboard fore-aft seat adjuster.

'96 Ford Taurus

Gasoline could be expelled from engine air cleaner or exhaust system, creating fire hazard.

Models: 4700 cars made 10/95-7/96.

What to do: Have dealer inspect and, if necessary, replace fuel-pressure regulator.

'95-96 Eagle Talon

Fuel-tank could leak, creating fire hazard.

Models: 9616 cars made 3/94-7/96.

What to do: Have dealer inspect and, if necessary, replace fuel tank, cap, and gaskets.

'96-97 Volvo 850 and 960 series cars

Engine may not slow to idle when accelerator is released.

Models: 13,221 late '96 and early '97 sedans and station wagons made 4/96-7/96. Affected cars can be identified by last six digits of vehicle identification number. 850 models bear numbers 256997 to 311340; 338213 to 380371; 332305 to 376485; and 339561 to 372831 (numbers run sequentially). 960 models bear numbers 036243 to 039442 and 098612 to 107701.

What to do: Have dealer replace throttle body in fuel system.

'93-96 Volvo 850 with engine-block heater

Heater could separate from engine and rub through fuel hose, creating fire hazard.

Models: 400 cars made through 8/96.

What to do: Have dealer inspect and secure or, if necessary, replace block heater.

'93-95 Geo Prizm and Toyota Corolla

If liquid should spill around center console box, air bag could deploy, creating accident hazard.

Models: 627,858 cars made 6/92-1/95.

What to do: Have dealer install protective cover over air-bag sensor and replace any sensor damaged by previous spill.

'96 Honda Civic

Brakes could lose power assist, making car harder to stop.

Models: 160,689 hatchbacks, sedans, and coupes made 8/95-5/96.

What to do: Have dealer clean soapy lubricant from inside of brake-booster vacuum hose with hot water.

'88-90 Volkswagen Passat and '89-90 Corrado

If engine overheats, hot coolant could leak into car and burn driver's feet or steam up interior.

Models: 8100 cars made 10/87-12/90.

What to do: Have dealer replace heat exchanger.

'91-95 Mitsubishis (various models)

Brake hose could crack, leak fluid, and reduce effectiveness of brakes.

Models: 93,000 coupes, sedans, and station wagons with antilock brakes, and sport-utility vehicles with or without ABS, made 7/90-5/95, including '91-94 3000GT; '92-95 Diamante; and '92-93 Montero.

What to do: Have dealer replace left and right front brake hoses.

'96-97 Buicks, Oldsmobiles, and Pontiacs

Engine backfire could break upper intake manifold and cause fire or prevent engine from running.

Models: 275,811 cars with 3.8-liter V6, including '96 Buick Park Avenue, Regal, and Riviera, Oldsmobile 88 and 98, and Pontiac Bonneville; also, '96-97 Buick LeSabre.

What to do: Have dealer reprogram engine control module. Until repair is made, don't start engine when hood is open.

'96 Chrysler Sebring JX convertible

Brakes could lose power assist, making car harder to stop.

Models: 22,500 cars with V6, made 8/95-5/96.

What to do: Have dealer make sure vacuum hose is firmly secured to engine manifold.

'90-95 BMWs (various models)

Brake lights may be lit continuously or not at all.

Models: 180,000 cars made 1/90-3/94, including '90-92 535i, 735i, 735iL, and 750i; '90-94 525i; '92-94 325i, 325iS, and 525iT; '93-94 740i and 740iL; '94 325iC, 530i, 530iT, and 540i; and '95 M3.

What to do: Have dealer replace brake-light switch.

'91-'92 BMWs (various models)

Air bag may not deploy in crash.

Models: 75,000 cars made 7/90-3/92, including '91-92 525i, 535i, 735i, 735iL, 750iL, 850i, and M5; and '92 318i, 318iS, 325i, 325iS, and 525iT.

What to do: Have dealer replace locking tab for air-bag contact ring in steering wheel.

'95 Ford Contour and Mercury Mystique

Fuel could leak from filler pipe and create fire hazard.

Models: 167,784 cars made 7/94-4/95.

What to do: Have dealer install redesigned fuel-tank assembly.

'96 Buick Skylark and Oldsmobile Achieva

During deployment, air bag could snag inside dash and provide inadequate protection in crash.

Models: 48,689 cars made 8/95-2/96.

What to do: Have dealer inspect dash and, if necessary, install plastic edge protector on dash reinforcement. On some models, dealer will replace entire dash-panel pad.

'97 Nissan Altima

Rear safety belts could fail in crash.

Models: 36,000 cars made 6/96-9/96.

What to do: Have dealer inspect buckle assemblies and replace buckles with lot no. 023 or 029.

Takata Corp. safety belts in '86-91 cars

The belt could fail to latch, stay latched, or unlatch.

Models: Acura: '86-91 Integra; '86-90 Legend; '91 NSX. Chrysler: Dodge—'86-91 Colt; '86-89 Conquest; '86-91 Ram/Ram D-50; '87-89 Raider; '91 Stealth. Eagle—'89-91 Summit; '90-91 Talon. Plymouth—'86-91 Colt; '90-91 Laser. Ford: '88-91 Festiva. General Motors (Geo): '89-91 Metro, Tracker; '90-91 Storm. Honda: '86-91 Accord, Civic, Prelude; '86-87, '89-91 Civic CRX. Infiniti: '90 to '91 M30, Q45. Isuzu: '90-91 Impulse, pickup; '91 Rodeo, Stylus. Mazda: '88-89 323 sedan and wagon; '88-89 MX-6, '88-91 929, MPV van. Mitsubishi: '86-88 Cordia; '90-91 Eclipse; '86-87, '89 Galant ; '86-91 Mirage, Montero, pickup; '88-90 Sigma; '86 Starion; '91 3000GT; '87-90 van/wagon. Nissan: '87-88 200SX; '89-91 240SX (manual lap belt); '88-91 Pathfinder; '87-91 Sentra; '88-91 D21 truck; '87-90 C22 van. Subaru: '87-91 Justy; '88-90 Loyale. Suzuki: '88-91 Samurai, Sidekick; '89-91 Swift.

What to do: Have the dealer check the affected belts, which carry a number beginning with TK52 or A7 on the lower part of the buckle or on the webbing. Automakers have agreed to replace broken belts and modify those that haven't broken.

Sport-utility vehicles, trucks & vans

'96-97 Isuzu Trooper

Brake fluid could leak from hose, lengthening stopping distances.

Models: 6667 sport-utility vehicles made 2/96-6/96.

What to do: Have dealer inspect clearance between brake hose and upper control arm and, if necessary, replace hose.

'92-94 Ford Explorer

Electrical short could occur in remote power-mirror circuit, resulting in fire or smoke.

Models: 61,000 sport-utility vehicles made 8/92-11/94.

What to do: Have dealer install in-line 10 amp fuse in positive battery feed to power mirror control-switch assembly.

'94-97 Dodge Ram

Under certain hard-driving conditions, overheated transmission fluid could melt hose connections and spray onto exhaust manifold, possibly causing a fire.

Models: 96,000 light-duty trucks made 1/94-2/97.

What to do: Have dealer replace high-temperature side of transmission-fluid cooler-hose connector fittings with connectors that incorporate stainless-steel retainer.

'92 Dodge and Plymouth minivans

Over time, bolts could weaken and break, allowing rear hatch to open suddenly.

Models: 436,000 minivans made 7/91-6/92, including Dodge Caravan and Grand Caravan, and Plymouth Voyager and Grand Voyager.

What to do: Have dealer inspect bolts used to attach gas strut to body and hatch. Dealer will replace strut and integral bolts or replace bolt and washer and tighten them properly.

'96-97 Chevrolet Astro and GMC Safari

Right-rear safety belt could fail in crash.

Models: 18,972 minivans made 7/95-6/96.

What to do: Have dealer install "protector" on frame of seat cushion to keep safety-belt webbing from coming apart.

'95-96 Land Rover Discovery

Right front door could open unexpectedly.

Models: 20,889 vehicles made 4/95-6/96.

What to do: Have dealer install hardware to make door latch properly. (Dealer will check other door latches as well.).

'96 Isuzu Trooper

Center rear safety belt may not latch properly.

Models: 2345 vehicles made 2/96.

What to do: Have dealer inspect center rear safety belt and, if necessary, replace buckle.

'97 Ford Expedition

Rear axle components could come loose from frame and cause accident.

Models: 25,000 sport-utility vehicles made 7/96-10/96.

What to do: Have dealer install track-bar bracket reinforcement kit. Dealer will also inspect axle tubes and replace those without stamped date code.

'95 Nissan Quest
Taillights and brake lights could fail.

Models: 25,000 minivans made 4/95-9/95. (Center high-mounted brake light is unaffected.)

What to do: Have dealer install redesigned sockets and wiring.

'97 Ford F-150
Safety belts could fail in a crash.

Models: 133,000 light-duty pickup trucks made 8/95-4/96.

What to do: Have dealer inspect and, if necessary, repair safety-belt anchorage attachments.

'95 Mercury Villager
Taillights and brake lights could fail. (High center-mounted brake light isn't affected.)

Models: 36,000 minivans made 4/95-9/96.

What to do: Have dealer install redesigned rear light sockets and wiring assemblies.

'89-91 Jeep Cherokee & Wagoneer
Antilock brake system (ABS) could fail. High brake-pedal effort might needed to stop vehicle. (If ABS fails, dashboard warning lights usually come on.)

Models: 52,000 SUVs made 7/88-6/91.

What to do: Have dealer test ABS and make necessary repairs. Manufacturer will extend warranty on all ABS components to 10 years or 100,000 miles—except for brake-actuator piston and pump-motor assemblies, which have lifetime coverage). Owners will also be reimbursed for previous ABS repairs.

'94 Honda Passport and Isuzu Amigo, Pickup, and Rodeo
Safety belts may not buckle securely.

Models: 13,004 Hondas made 1/94-7/94, and 49,079 Isuzus made 11/93-12/93.

What to do: Have dealer inspect and, if necessary, replace belt buckles.

'95-96 Dodge Ram diesel
Engine oil seeping into vacuum hose could make it collapse partially, making vehicle harder to stop.

Models: 58,000 light pickup trucks with diesel engines made 6/95-6/96.

What to do: Have dealer install check valve to keep oil out of hose. Also, have dealer replace vacuum hose with one that's oil-resistant.

'96-97 Ford trucks, minivans, and sport-utility vehicles
Rear tires could wear prematurely if inflated according to incorrect labeling.

Models: 134,770 vehicles made 12/95-3/96, including '96 Aerostar, F350, Explorer, and Ranger, and '96-97 F250.

What to do: Have dealer install correct label.

'91 Chevrolet Blazer, GMC Jimmy, and Oldsmobile Bravada
Rear safety belts may not latch properly.

Models: 97,351 sport-utility vehicles made 9/89-1/91.

What to do: Have dealer replace all three rear safety-belt buckles.

'96 Geo Tracker and Suzuki Sidekick
In rear-end crash, fuel tank could puncture, creating fire hazard.

Models: 18,121 Trackers and 4325 Sidekicks, four-door models only, made 8/95-6/96.

What to do: Have dealer install two shield gussets between fuel tank and attachment brackets.

'96 Ford Club Wagon and Econoline
Vehicle could roll when parked on incline, even with parking brake set.

Models: 53,400 light-duty vans made 2/96-5/96.

What to do: Have dealer adjust parking brake.

Child safety seats

Evenflo Travel Tandem child safety seats
When used with its base, the seat may not properly restrain a child in a crash.

Products: All Evenflo Travel Tandem infant seats made before April 1, 1996. (Seats made after that date have a modified design.)

What to do: Call 800 233-5921 or 937 773-3971 to receive a free reinforcement kit, which includes a reinforcement plate that easily attaches to the buckle-assembly area that connects the seat to the base.

Evenflo Champion, Trooper, and Scout child-safety seats
In front-facing position, child's head could swing too far in crash, increasing risk of injury.

Products: 150,000 safety seats, with model numbers beginning with digits 219, 224, 225, or 229, made 10/14/96-2/6/97. Model number and date of manufacture appear on label on seat's shell.

What to do: Call 800 233-5921 for replacement harness-adjuster assembly.

Evenflo Champion and Scout child safety seats
In most upright front -facing position, seat

may not provide adequate protection in crash.

Products: 1,122,000 Champion safety seats, whose model number begins with digits 224, made 6/1/93 to 11/22/96. Also 118,000 Scout seats, with model numbers begin ning with digits 229, made 6/1/93 to 12/16/96. Model number and date of manufacture are on label on seat shell.

What to do: Call 800 490-7497 for replacement recline arm that prevents seat from being used in most upright position.

Century child safety seats

Buckle could release on impact, resulting in increased risk of injury in crash.

Products: 376,000 infant seats (models 4525, 4535, 4560, 4565, 4575, and 4590) and 4-in-1 infant car-seat stroller systems (models 11-570, 11-597, 11-600, and 11-650) made 9/12/95-5/13/96. Date of manufacture and model no. appear on side of seat.

What to do: Call Century Products at 800 837-4044 for free replacement buckle and installation instructions. Seat owners can also obtain buckle by writing to company at 9600 Valley View Rd., Macedonia, Ohio 44056.

Motorcycles & bicycles

Various brands of bicycles with Shimano pedal cranks

Cranks could break, cutting rider and causing loss of control.

Models: More than one million cranks installed on at least 49 brands (including most major ones) and 200 bicycle models since 1994. Cranks may also have been installed as upgrade in Acera, Alivio and Altus group of components. Suspect cranks are numbered FC-CT90, FC-M290, or FC-MC12. Number is located on back or inner side of right crank arm.

What to do: Chech for number to see if crank is subject to recall. (Don't look for the Shimano name as it's unlikely to appear.) If it is, call Shimano at 800 353-4719 to arrange for free replacement at nearby authorized repair shop. Consumers can also arrange for free repair by contacting their bicycle dealer.

'96-97 Kawasaki motorcycles

Electrical system could fail, possibly resulting in accident.

Models: 5208 motorcycles, models VN1500 and Vulcan Classic, made 11/95-1/97.

What to do: Have dealer replace battery cable and inspect battery for damage.

1996 Raleigh M55 bicycle with Ballistic LE300A suspension fork

Fork could come apart and cause loss of control.

Models: 1400 bicycles sold 8/95-1/97. Bike frame is green; suspension fork is gray with black decals that read "BALLISTIC" and "L300A 6061 ALUMINUM" on sides. "BALLISTIC" decal also appears on brake yoke. Bicycles with SR DuoTrack 7006 suspension fork are not subject to recall.

What to do: Return bicycle to authorized Raleigh dealer for free replacement fork. For name of nearest dealer, call 800 222-5527.

'93 Giant mountain bicycles

Suspension fork could come apart and cause loss of control.

Models: 8500 bicycles, models ALM-1, ATX-780, and CFM-3, sold 9/92-6/94 for $650 to $1000. Dealers also sold forks as replacement parts and aftermarket equipment for up to $150. Legs of silver-colored steel fork have black "GIANT ZORBERS" decals.

What to do: Take bicycle to any authorized Giant dealer for inspection and, if necessary, fork replacement. For location of nearest dealer, call 800 874-4268.

Motor homes

'89-97 Intasca and Winnebago motor homes

Spare tire could fall off and cause accident.

Models: 10,590 motor homes made 7/88-9/96. Itasca models include '92-97 Adventurer, '91 Elandan, '93-95 and '97 Suncruiser, '93-94 Sundancer, '89-93 Sunflyer, and '95-96 Sunrise. Winnebago models include '92-97 Adventurer, '95-96 Brave, '94 Chieftain, '91 Elandan, '92-94 Elante, '93-94 Minnie-Winnie, '93 Shell, and '93-97 Vectra.

What to do: Have dealer install support bracket.

Vehicle accessories

Sears DieHard battery charger

Could overheat and cause fire.

Products: 100,000 battery chargers, model number 200.71310, sold for $65. Recalled chargers bear date codes H961 (1/96) through H972 (F2/97). Model number is on front of charger; date code is on plastic base on bottom of charger. Label on front of charger reads, in part: "Sears . . . Die Hard . . . Fully Automatic Battery Charger Engine Starter." Chargers with white sticker on back bearing number 1682 are not subject to recall.

What to do: Return to Sears for replacement.

For the latest recalls See the monthly issues of CONSUMER REPORTS magazine or our Web site *(www.ConsumerReports.org).*

Manufacturers' telephone numbers

Below is an alphabetical list of brand names for major products, including cars and car insurance, and the telephone numbers of their manufacturers. Use it to track down a specific model that you want to buy or for getting more information about a product.

Ace	630 990-6522
Acer	800 733-2237
Acura	800 862-2872
Admiral	800 688-9920
Advent	800 323-4815
Aiwa	800 289-2492
Allison	606 236-8298
Alphastar	203-359-8077
Altec Lansing	800 258-3288
Amana, Speed Queen	800 843-0304
American Sensors	800 387-4219
AmerTac	914 352-2400
Ametek	800 645-5427
Amway	800 544-7167
Apple	
computers, CD-ROM drives	800 538-9696
printers	800 767-2775
Ariens	800 678-5443
Asko	972 238-0794
AST	800 876-4278
AT&T	800 222-3111
Audi (cars)	800 822-2834
B.F. Goodrich, Michelin	800 847-3435
B.I.C.	800 348-6492
Bassett	941 676-6061
Behr	800 854-0133
Bell, BSI	800 456-2355
BellSouth	800 338-1694
Benjamin Moore	Contact local Benjamin Moore store
Betty Crocker	800 688-8782
Bianchi	510 264-1001
Bissell	800 237-7691
Black & Decker	800 231-9786
BMW (cars)	800 831-1117
Boca	561 241-8088
Bose	800 444-2673
Boston Acoustics	508 538-5000
Brainerd	716 586-0028
Braun	800 272-8611
Breadman	800 233-9054
Bridgestone	800 367-3872
Brita	800 442-7482
Brother	
fax machines & fax-modems	800 284-4329
printers	800 827-6843
Buick (cars)	800 521-7300
Bunn	800 637-8606
Cadillac (cars)	800 458-8006
Cambridge	800 367-4434
Canada	800 252-4334
Canon	
camcorders, cameras	800 828-4040
printers, copiers, fax machines & fax-modems	800 423-2366
Carrier	800 422-7743
Casablanca	888 227-2178
Cerwin Vega	805 584-9332
Chevrolet (cars)	800 222-1020
Chrysler (cars)	800 992-1997
Cobra	312 889-3087
Colonial Penn Franklin Insurance	800 335-2166
Compaq	800 345-1518
Cooper	800 854-6288
Costar	800 432-5599
Craftsman (Sears)	Contact local store
Creative Labs	800 998-1000
Cub Cadet	
mowers	330 273-4550
tractors & riding mowers	800 528-1009
Cuisinart	800 726-0190
Culligan	888 285-5442
CyberMax	800 443-9868
DCM	800 878-8463
Dell	800 879-3355
DeLonghi	800 322-3848
Denon	201 575-7810
Designer Series by Tappan	614 792-2153
Diamond	800 468-5846
Diamondback	805 484-4450
DirecTV	800 347-3288
Dixon	800 264-6075
Dodge	800 992-1997
Dunlop	800 548-4714
Dutch Boy	800 828-5669
Eagle	800 992-1997
Eagle Academy	800 441-3177
Echostar	800 333-3474
Ecko	847 678-8600
Economy Premier-Classic (Illinois)	800 323-6669
Ecowater	800 869-2837
Electrolux	800 243-9078
Emerson	
ceiling fans	800 237-6511
co detectors	201 884-5800
microwaves & VCRs	972 884-2350
Emerson	610 565-5600
Encon	817 927-5100
Englander	800 837-5337
Enzone	800 448-0535
Epson	800 463-7766
Estro	800 933-7876

Eureka	800 282-2886
Everpure	800 323-7873

Fantom	800 668-9600
Fasco	800 288-5588
Fedders	610 565-5600
Firestone	800 706-8473
First Alert	800 323-9005
First Years	800 533-6708
Fisher	
CD players, minisystems, receivers	800 421-5013
Fisher-Price	800 432-5437
Ford (cars)	800 392-3673
Friedrich	210 225-2000
Frigidaire	
dryers	614 792-2153
refrigerators	800 374-4432
air-conditioners, ranges	614 792-2153
washing machines, dishwashers	800 944-9044
Fuji	800 800-3854

Gaggia	201 939-2555
Gateway	800 846-2000
GE Saf-T-Gard	800 833-4933
GEICO General Insurance Co.	800 841-3000
Gem	516 273-2230
General	800 847-3349
General Accident-Penn General (Illinois)	800 888-0995
General Electric	
phones, VCRs	800 447-1700
air-conditioners, dishwashers, dryers, microwave ovens, ranges, refrigerators, washers	800 626-2000
TV sets	800 447-1700
General Electric	800 336-1900
Genie	800 654-3643
Geo	800 222-1020
Gerber	800 443-7237
Gerry	800 525-2472
Giant	800 874-4268
Gibson	614 792-2153
Giro	800 969-4476
Glacier Pure	617 568-1305
Glidden	800 221-4100
Global Village	800 736-4821
GMC	800 462-8782
Goldstar	800 243-0000
Goodyear	800 466-3932
GT	800-743-3248

Hamilton Beach, Proctor Silex	800 851-8900
Hampton Bay	Contact local Home Depot
Harbor Breeze	800 527-1292
Hayes	770 441-1617
Hewlett Packard	
computers	800 724-6631
fax machines & fax-modems, printers	800 752-0900
scanners	800 722-6538
Hitachi	800 448-2244
Home Water	800 547-3944
Honda (cars)	310 783-2000
Honda (mowers)	800 426-7701
Hoover	
carpet deep-cleaners	248 637-1382
vacuum cleaners	330 499-9499
Hotpoint	800 626-2000
Huffy	800 872-2453
Hunter	800 448-6837
Husqvarna	800 487-5962
Hyundai (cars)	800 633-5151

IBM	800 426-7235, ext. 4340
Infiniti (cars)	800 662-6200
Infinity	800 553-3332
Iomega	800 697-8833
Isuzu (cars)	310 699-0500

J.C. Penney	Contact local store
Jaguar (cars)	800 544-4767
Jeep (cars)	800 992-1997
Jenn Air	800 688-1100
John Deere	800 537-8233
JVC	800 252-5722

Kelly-Springfield	800 592-3267
Kenmore (Sears)	Contact local store
Kent	800 245-3123
Kenwood	800 536-9663
Kidco	847 970-9100
KinderGard	800 255-2634, ext. 222
Kinetico	800 944-9283
King Koil	800 888-6070
Kirby	800 494-8586
KitchenAid	
blenders, food processors	800 541-6390
dishwashers, dryers, ranges, refrigerators, washers	800 422-1230
Kodak	
cameras	800 242-2424
scanners	800 235-6325
Konica	800 285-6422
Krups	800 526-5377
Kubota	
mowers	310 370-3370
tractors & riding mowers	888 458-2682, ext. 900

Lasko	800 394-3267
Lawn Chief	800 800-7310
Lawn-Boy	800 348-2424
Leviton's	800 367-5424
Lexmark	800 358-5835
Lexus (cars)	800 872-5398
Lifesaver	800 654-7665
Lincoln (cars)	800 392-3673
Logitech	800 231-7717
Lucent Technology	800 222-3111

Macurco	303 781-4062
MAG	800 827-3998

Magic Chef
  dryers, ranges, washers,
    dishwashers....800 688-1120
  microwave ovens....800-753-0276
Magna....800 551-0032
Magnavox
  TVs....800 531-0039
  VCRs....423 475-8869
Marantz....630 307-3100
Maytag....800 688-9900
Mazda (cars)....800 222-5500
Melitta....800 451-1694
Mercedes-Benz (cars)....800 222-0100
Merchants Insurance Co.
  of N.H. (New York)....800 462-1077
Mercury (cars)....800 392-3673
Mercury Insurance Co.....800 579-3467
Microtek....800 654-4160
Miele....800 694-4868
Miller & Kreisel....310 204-2854
Minolta....201 825-4000
Mitsubishi....800 332-2119
Mitsubishi (cars)....800 222-0037
Mongoose....800 257-0662
Montgomery Ward....Contact local store
Motorola
  computers....800 759-1107
  pagers....800 548-9954
  phones....800 331-6456
MTD....800 800-7310
Mr. Coffee....800 672-6333
Muratec....972 364-3350
Murray
  bikes, mowers....800 251-8007
  tractors & riding mowers....800 224-8940
Mustek....714 247-1300

Nanao....800 800-5202
NEC
  CD-ROM drivers, monitors,
    computers....800 632-4636
  printers....800 388-8888
  pagers....800 421-2141
NHT....800 648-9993
Nighthawk....800 880-6788
Nikon....800 645-6687
Nilfisk....800 645-3475
Nissan (cars)....800 647-7261
Nokia....800 296-6542
NordicWare....800 328-4310
North Pacific Preferred
  (Washington)....800 888-0995
North States....612 541-9101

Ohio Casualty-West American
  (New Jersey)....800 843-6446
Okidata....800 654-3282
Oldsmobile (cars)....800 442-6537
Olympus....800 221-3000
Omni....800 937-6664
Onkyo....201 825-7950
Optimus....Contact local Radio Shack
Oreck....800 989-3535
Oster....800 597-5978
Osterizer....800 528-7713

Pacific....800 666-8813
Packard Bell....800 733-5858
Panasonic....800 222-4213
  computer back-up systems....800 742-8086
  printers....800 742-8086
  fax machines, phones, TV sets,
    vacuum cleaners,
    air-conditioners, microwave
    ovens, VCRs....800 222-4213
Paradigm....905 632-0180
Pentax....800 877-0155
Phase Technology....904 777-0700
Philips....800 531-0039
Pillsbury....800 858-3277
Pinnacle
  N.Y.....516 576-9052
  out of N.Y.....800 346-2863
Pinnacle....516 576-9052
Pioneer....800 746-6337
Pirelli....800 327-2442
Pittsburgh....800 441-9695
Plymouth (cars)....800 992-1997
Polaroid....800 343-5000
Polk Audio....800 377-7655
Pollenex....800 767-6020
Pontiac (cars)....800 762-2737
Porsche (cars)....800 767-7243
Power Computing....800 999-7279
Pratt & Lambert....800 289-7728
Primestar....800 774-6378
Pro-Action....800 288-4280
Prudential Property & Casualty....800 346-3778
PTI....800 515-0074
PUR....800 665-9787

Quasar....800 222-4213

Radio Shack....800 843-7422
Rainbow....810 643-7222
Rainsoft....800 860-7638
Raleigh....800 222-5527
RCA
  TV sets....800 447-1700
  VCRs....800 336-1900
Regal
  breadmakers....800 998-8809
  coffee makers....414 626-2121
  food processors....800 313-8807
Regina....800 847-8336
Restonic....800 898-6075
Reveal....800 326-2222
Ricoh....800 225-1899
Rinse 'N Vac/Carpet Magic,
  Rug Doctor....800 784-3628
Roadmaster
  kids' bikes....800 626-2811
  mountain bikes....618 393-2991
Rollerblade....800 232-7655

Roper 800 447-6737
Ross 800 338-7677
Royal 800 321-1134
Royce Union 800 888-2453
Ryobi 800 345-8746

S-Tech 800 203-7987
Saab (cars) 800 955-9007
Sabre 800 533-1377
Safe Plus 800 561-7946
Safety 1st 800 723-3065
Safety Source (Mericon) 800 327-3534
Samsung
  cameras 800 762-7746
  monitors, fax machines, TV sets, VCRs, microwave ovens 800 767-4675
Sanyo
  East 201 843-5100
  West 818 998-7322
  Central 630 775-0505
Sanyo
  West 818 998-7322
  Central 630-775-0505
  East 201 641-2333
Sanyo 818 998-7322
Saturn (cars) 800 553-6000
Schwinn 303 473-9609
Seagate 800 626-6637
Sears .... Contact local store
Serta 630 285-9300
Seymour 800 457-9881
Shaklee 800 742-5533
Sharp 800 237-4277
Sherwin-Williams 800 474-3794
Sherwood 800 962-3203
Shop Vac 717 321-7056
Sico (Quebec only) 800 463-7426
Signet 905 474-9129
Simmons 800 746-6667
Simplicity 800 987-5296
Singer
  vacuum cleaners 800 845-5020
  water filters 800 877-7762
Snapper 800 762-7737
Sony 800 222-7669
  computer back-up systems 800 226-9433
  computers 800 476-6972
Southwestern 800 255-8480
Specialized 408 779-6229
Speed Queen 800 843-0304
Storm 888 438-3279
Subaru (cars) 800 782-2783
Sunbeam (check)
  food processors 800 597-5978
  blenders 800 528-7713
Supra 800 727-8772
Suzuki (cars) 714 996-7040
Swatch 800 879-2824
Symphonic 201 288-2063
SyQuest 800 245-2278

Tappan
  ranges 800 374-4432
  microwaves 800 537-5530
Technics
  CD players, receivers 201 348-9090
  speakers 800 222-4213
Teledyne 800 525-2774
Texas Instrument 800 848-3927
Therapedic 908 561-6000
Toro 800 348-2424
Toshiba 800 631-3811
  computers 800 334-3445
Toyota 800 331-4331
Travelers Indemnity (Florida) 800 832-6842
  (All States except Mass. & N.J.)
Trek 800 369-8735
Troy-Bilt 800 437-8686
Tru-Test 800 642-7392

U.S. Robotics 800 342-5877
Umax 800 562-0311
Uniden 800 297-1023
USAA 800 282-2060
USSB 800 204-8772

Variflex 800 327-0821
Verlo .... 800 229-8957, ext. 213
ViewSonic 800 888-8583
Visioneer 800 787-7007
Vivitar .... 800 421-2381, ext. 444;
  Calif. 800 352-7481
Volkswagen (cars) 800 822-8987
Volvo (cars) 800 458-1552

Wal-Mart 800 925-6278
Waring 800 492-7464
West Bend
  breadmakers, food processors 800 367-0111
  coffee makers 414 334-6949
Whirlpool 800 253-1301
White 800 949-4483
White-Westinghouse
  dishwashers, dryers, washers 800 944-9044
  vacuum cleaners 309 823-5778
  air-conditioners, ranges 614 792-2153
Windmere 800 582-0179
Windsor 800 444-7654

Xerox 800 832-6979

Yamaha 800 492-6242
Yard Machine 800 800-7310
Yard-Man 800 800-7310
Yashica 800 526-0266
Yokohama 800-366-8473

Zenith 847 391-8752
Zoom 800 631-3116

8-year index to the last full report in CONSUMER REPORTS

This index indicates when the last full report on a given subject was published in CONSUMER REPORTS. It goes back as far as 1990. Note: Beginning with Volume 61 (January 1996), CONSUMER REPORTS stopped using continuous pagination throughout each volume year. From January 1996 forward, each issue begins on page 1. **Bold type** indicates Ratings reports or brand-name discussions; *italic type* indicates corrections, followups, or Updates. **Facts by Fax:** Some reports are available by fax or mail from our Facts by Fax 24-hour service. To order a report, note the fax number at the left of the entry and call 800 896-7788 from a touch-tone phone. (No code or * means a report is not available by fax.) You can use MasterCard or Visa. Each report is $7.75.

STATEMENT OF OWNERSHIP, MANAGEMENT, AND CIRCULATION
(Required by 39 U.S.C. 3685)

1. Publication Title: CONSUMER REPORTS. 2. Publication No: 0010-7174. 3. Filing Date: September 16, 1997. 4. Issue Frequency: Monthly, except two issues in December. 5. No. of Issues Published Annually: 13. 6. Annual Subscription Price: $24.00. 7. Complete Mailing Address of Known Office of Publication: 101 Truman Avenue, Yonkers, New York 10703-1057. 8. Complete Mailing Address of Headquarters or General Business Office of Publisher: 101 Truman Avenue, Yonkers, New York 10703-1057. 9. Full Names and Complete Mailing Addresses of Publisher, Editor, and Managing Editor. Publisher: Consumers Union of United States, Inc., 101 Truman Avenue, Yonkers, New York 10703-1057. President: Rhoda H. Karpatkin; Editor: Julia Kagan; Executive Editor: Eileen Denver. 10. Owner: (If the publication is published by a nonprofit organization, its name and address must be stated.) Full Name: Consumers Union of United States, Inc., a nonprofit organization. Complete Mailing Address: 101 Truman Avenue, Yonkers, New York 10703-1057. 11. Known Bondholders, Mortgagees, and Other Security Holders Owning or Holding 1 Percent or More of Total Amount of Bonds, Mortgages, or Other Securities. If none, so state: None. 12. For Completion by Nonprofit Organizations Authorized to Mail at Special Rates: The purpose, function, and nonprofit status of this organization and the exempt status for Federal Income tax purposes has not changed during preceding 12 months.

15. Extent and Nature of Circulation:

	Average no. copies each issue during past 12 mo.	Actual no. copies of single issue published nearest to filing date
A. Total no. of copies (net press run)	5,141,597	5,236,791
B. Paid and/or requested circulation		
1. Sales through dealers, carriers, street vendors, counter sales (not mailed)	132,445	113,130
2. Paid or requested mail subscriptions (include advertisers'proof copies/exchange copies)	4,774,298	4,892,475
C. Total paid and/or requested circulation (sum of 15b(1) and 15b(2))	4,905,743	5,005,605
D. Free distribution by mail (samples, complimentary, and other free)	8,225	3,923
E. Free distribution outside the mail	16,810	24,708
F. Total Free distribution	25,035	28,631
G. Total distribution (sum of 15 and 15f)	4,930,777	5,034,236
H. Copies not distributed		
1. Office use, leftovers, spoiled	8,542	5,385
2. Return from news agents	202,278	197,170
I. TOTAL (sum of 15g, 15h(1) and 15h(2) shown in A)	5,141,597	5,236,791
J. Percent paid and/or requested circulation	99.49%	99.43%

17. I certify that the statements made by me above are correct and complete.
Louis J. Milani, Senior Director, Strategic Marketing and Business Affairs

Buying Guide index

This index covers all the reports, brand-name Ratings' charts, and repair histories in this year's Buying Guide. To find the last full report published in CONSUMER REPORTS, see the eight-year guide that starts on page 346.

Consumer Reports test of light bulbs, 1943

Consumer Reports

Makes you one tough customer! Take it along when you shop.

☑ **YES! Send me a sample issue and my free 1998 Buying Guide.** If I choose to subscribe, I'll pay just $24 and get 11 more issues (12 in all). And the 1999 Buying Guide (when published) as a bonus!

NAME

ADDRESS APT

CITY STATE ZIP

YOUR GUARANTEE

If you choose not to subscribe, return the invoice marked "cancel" and owe nothing. The free Buying Guide and sample issue are yours to keep. Please allow 4-8 weeks for delivery of your sample issue and free guide. This rate is for the U.S only, all other countries please add $6.

NO POSTAGE
NECESSARY
IF MAILED
IN THE
UNITED STATES

BUSINESS REPLY MAIL

FIRST-CLASS MAIL PERMIT NO 1243 BOULDER CO

POSTAGE WILL BE PAID BY ADDRESSEE

Consumer Reports

SUBSCRIPTION DEPARTMENT
PO BOX 51166
BOULDER CO 80323-1166

NO POSTAGE
NECESSARY
IF MAILED
IN THE
UNITED STATES

BUSINESS REPLY MAIL

FIRST-CLASS MAIL PERMIT NO 1243 BOULDER CO

POSTAGE WILL BE PAID BY ADDRESSEE

Consumer Reports

SUBSCRIPTION DEPARTMENT
PO BOX 51166
BOULDER CO 80323-1166